Lecture Notes in Computer Science 9307

Commenced Publication in 1973
Founding and Former Series Editors:
Gerhard Goos, Juris Hartmanis, and Jan van Leeuwen

AF895954

Editorial Board

David Hutchison
Lancaster University, Lancaster, UK
Takeo Kanade
Carnegie Mellon University, Pittsburgh, PA, USA
Josef Kittler
University of Surrey, Guildford, UK
Jon M. Kleinberg
Cornell University, Ithaca, NY, USA
Friedemann Mattern
ETH Zurich, Zürich, Switzerland
John C. Mitchell
Stanford University, Stanford, CA, USA
Moni Naor
Weizmann Institute of Science, Rehovot, Israel
C. Pandu Rangan
Indian Institute of Technology, Madras, India
Bernhard Steffen
TU Dortmund University, Dortmund, Germany
Demetri Terzopoulos
University of California, Los Angeles, CA, USA
Doug Tygar
University of California, Berkeley, CA, USA
Gerhard Weikum
Max Planck Institute for Informatics, Saarbrücken, Germany

More information about this series at http://www.springer.com/series/7409

Gráinne Conole · Tomaž Klobučar
Christoph Rensing · Johannes Konert
Élise Lavoué (Eds.)

Design for Teaching and Learning in a Networked World

10th European Conference
on Technology Enhanced Learning, EC-TEL 2015
Toledo, Spain, September 15–18, 2015
Proceedings

Springer

Editors
Gráinne Conole
University of Bath Spa
Bath
UK

Tomaž Klobučar
Jožef Stefan Institute
Ljubljana
Slovenia

Christoph Rensing
Technische Universität Darmstadt
Darmstadt
Germany

Johannes Konert
Technische Universität Darmstadt
Darmstadt
Germany

Élise Lavoué
IAE Lyon
Université Jean Moulin Lyon 3
Lyon
France

ISSN 0302-9743 ISSN 1611-3349 (electronic)
Lecture Notes in Computer Science
ISBN 978-3-319-24257-6 ISBN 978-3-319-24258-3 (eBook)
DOI 10.1007/978-3-319-24258-3

Library of Congress Control Number: 2015948158

LNCS Sublibrary: SL3 – Information Systems and Applications, incl. Internet/Web, and HCI

Springer Cham Heidelberg New York Dordrecht London
© Springer International Publishing Switzerland 2015
This work is subject to copyright. All rights are reserved by the Publisher, whether the whole or part of the material is concerned, specifically the rights of translation, reprinting, reuse of illustrations, recitation, broadcasting, reproduction on microfilms or in any other physical way, and transmission or information storage and retrieval, electronic adaptation, computer software, or by similar or dissimilar methodology now known or hereafter developed.
The use of general descriptive names, registered names, trademarks, service marks, etc. in this publication does not imply, even in the absence of a specific statement, that such names are exempt from the relevant protective laws and regulations and therefore free for general use.
The publisher, the authors and the editors are safe to assume that the advice and information in this book are believed to be true and accurate at the date of publication. Neither the publisher nor the authors or the editors give a warranty, express or implied, with respect to the material contained herein or for any errors or omissions that may have been made.

Printed on acid-free paper

Springer International Publishing AG Switzerland is part of Springer Science+Business Media
(www.springer.com)

Preface

The tenth anniversary edition of the European Conference on Technology Enhanced Learning (EC-TEL) was held in Toledo (Spain) during September 15–18, 2015. This volume collects all peer-reviewed contributions that were included in the exciting program of this year's conference.

In the tenth year of its existence EC-TEL is becoming the major interdisciplinary venue for the community of technology-enhanced learning researchers in Europe and worldwide. Furthermore EC-TEL is a unique opportunity for researchers, practitioners, educational developers, and policy makers to address current challenges and advances in the field. Since 2006, EC-TEL has provided a reference point for relevant state-of-the-art research in TEL; first in Crete (Greece, also in 2007), and then in Maastricht (The Netherlands, 2008), Nice (France, 2009), Barcelona (Spain, 2010), Palermo (Italy, 2011), Saarbrücken (Germany, 2012), Paphos (Cyprus, 2013), and Graz (Austria, 2014).

The theme of EC-TEL 2015 was "Design for Teaching and Learning in a Networked World." Developments in information and communication technology, for example new communication patterns like in social applications, mobile devices, and ubiquitous network access, together with social and economical changes, have led to a networked world. The increasing networking on different scales from global to local is having a profound effect on learning and teaching. It makes new forms of collaborative and personalized learning experiences reality. Learners shift between formal, non-formal, and informal learning. They come together in different social settings and communities. Teachers' roles are also subject to change. The pressing need to shape learning arrangements in such a way that they exploit the potentials and meet the requirements of a networked world, was discussed during EC-TEL 2015.

Drawing on the core TEL disciplines of computer science, education, psychology, cognitive science, and social science, research contributions presented at EC-TEL 2015 addressed topics such as blended learning, self-regulated and self-directed learning, reflective learning, intelligent learning systems, learning communities, learning design, learning analytics, learning assessment, personalization and adaptation, serious games, social media, Massive Open Online Courses (MOOCs), and schools of the future.

This 2015 edition was again extremely competitive, given the high number of submissions generated. Out of around 200 initial abstract submissions, a total of 176 valid paper submissions were received. Of these, 128 were full papers. All submissions were assigned to at least three members of the Program Committee (PC) for review. One of the reviewers had the role of leading reviewer and initiated a discussion in case of conflicting reviews. All reviews as well as the discussions were checked and discussed within the team of PC chairs, and additional reviews or meta-reviews were elicited if necessary. Finally, 27 submissions were selected as full papers (resulting in an acceptance rate for full papers of 21 %). Additionally, 19 papers were presented as short papers, 9 as demonstrations, and 23 as posters. Table 1 shows the detailed statistics.

Table 1. Acceptance Rate in Different Submission Categories

		Published as			
Submitted as		Full Paper	Short Paper	Poster Paper	Demo Paper
Full Paper	128	27	14	13	1
Short Paper	26		5	6	
Poster Paper	10			3	
Demo Paper	12			1	8
Sum	176	27	19	23	9

The dedicated work of all the PC members as well as the additional reviewers must be acknowledged. Only with their help was it possible to deal with the high number of submissions and still keep all deadlines as originally planned.

Keynote presentations completed this competitive scientific program. Lisa Maria Blaschke from Carl von Ossietzky University of Oldenburg showed how self-determined learning or heutagogy had been applied across all learning communities and discussed how that approach could be used in practice. Mark Brown from Dublin City University helped the EC-TEL 2015 participants critically reflect on the digital future, and think more deeply about the opportunities, challenges, and threats facing the networked world in such uncertain times, while Juan Pelegrin, a representative of the EC, presented the Commission's perspective on the topic "technology enhanced learning."

Demonstrations and posters had a pronounced role in the conference program. A plenary session was organized as a "TEL demo shootout" in which the demonstrations were presented to arouse the audience's curiosity and highlight the unique aspects. Later on, all demos were exhibited "in action" giving the participants the possibility for "hands-on," sparking discussions between researchers, practitioners, and educational developers in order to base their voting for the best demo on this. A plenary session was dedicated to the exhibition of posters to foster discussions on on-going works and on the research issues we are facing. Besides, representatives from industry presented and discussed their vision of the field in the industry track.

The TEL community also proposed and organized a number of stimulating workshops as part of the conference. In all, 8 workshops and one tutorial were selected from the proposals and were organized. Some of them continue a series of well-established workshops, namely the workshops on motivational and affective aspects in TEL or on awareness and reflection in TEL. Others, like smart city learning, were first held in 2015. In addition, new topics, such as wearable enhanced learning, were considered. A doctoral consortium was organized concurrently with the workshops. It provided an opportunity for PhD students to discuss their work with experienced TEL researchers.

We would like to thank the many contributors without whom the conference would not have been possible. These include foremost the authors, the PC members, and reviewers, and the conference chairs, who all contributed to the program. We would also like to thank an enthusiastic and dedicated local organization team who made EC-TEL a smooth and memorable experience. The conference was partially supported by the European Association of Technology-Enhanced Learning (EATEL), the Carlos III University of Madrid (UC3M), Springer, and EasyChair.

September 2015

Gráinne Conole
Tomaž Klobučar
Johannes Konert
Élise Lavoué
Christoph Rensing

Organization

Executive Committee

General Chair

Christoph Rensing	Technische Universität Darmstadt, Germany

Program Chairs

Gráinne Conole	University of Bath Spa, UK
Tomaž Klobučar	Jožef Stefan Institute, Slovenia

Demo and Poster Chairs

Johannes Konert	Technische Universität Darmstadt, Germany
Élise Lavoué	Université Jean Moulin Lyon 3, France

Workshop Chair

Isa Jahnke	Umeå University, Sweden

Industry Chairs

Michael Amigot	IBL Studios, USA
Carmen Padron	Atos, Spain

Doctoral Consortium Chairs

Ulrike Lucke	Universität Potsdam, Germany
Katherine Maillet	Institut Mines-Télécom, Télécom Ecole de Management, France

Dissemination Chairs

Carlos Alario-Hoyos	Universidad Carlos III de Madrid, Spain
Pedro J. Muñoz-Merino	Universidad Carlos III de Madrid, Spain

Local Organization Chair

Carlos Delgado Kloos	Universidad Carlos III de Madrid, Spain

Program Committee

Marie-Helene Abel
Mohammad Al-Smadi
Carlos Alario-Hoyos
Liaqat Ali
Luis Anido Rifon
Tanja Arh
Inmaculada Arnedillo-Sánchez
Juan I. Asensio-Pérez
Antonio Balderas
Merja Bauters
Adriana Berlanga
Jason Bernard
Katrin Borcea-Pfitzmann
Yolaine Bourda
Andreas Breiter
Peter Brusilovsky
Manuel Caeiro Rodríguez
Lorenzo Cantoni
Manuel Castro
Mohamed Amine Chatti
Agnieszka Chrzaszcz
Miguel Ángel Conde
Gráinne Conole
John Cook
Audrey Cooke
Raquel M. Crespo García
Ulrike Cress
Alexandra Cristea
Mihai Dascalu
Paul De Bra
Carlos Delgado Kloos
Stavros Demetriadis
Christian Depover
Michael Derntl
Philippe Dessus
Darina Dicheva
Stefan Dietze
Yannis Dimitriadis
Vania Dimitrova
Juan Manuel Dodero
Peter Dolog
Hendrik Drachsler
Benedict Du Boulay
Erik Duval
Martin Ebner
Iria Estévez-Ayres
Baltasar Fernandez-Manjon
Alejandro Fernández
Carmen Fernández-Panadero
Christine Ferraris
Beatriz Florian-Gaviria
Muriel Garreta Domingo
Dragan Gasevic
Sebastien George
Denis Gillet
Fabrizio Giorgini
Carlo Giovannella
Christian Glahn
Sabine Graf
Monique Grandbastien
Andrina Granić
David Griffiths
Begona Gros
Franka Grünewald
Christian Gütl
Joerg Haake
Iassen Halatchliyski
Andreas Harrer
Ángel Hernández-García
Davinia Hernández-Leo
Knut Hinkelmann
Teresa Holocher-Ertl
Ulrich Hoppe
Sharon Hsiao
Hazra Imran
Seiji Isotani
Isa Jahnke
Marco Kalz
Nikos Karacapilidis
Micky Kerr
Michael Kickmeier-Rust
Andrea Kienle
Barbara Kieslinger
Ralf Klamma
Styliani Kleanthous Loizou
Joris Klerkx

Tomaž Klobučar
Johannes Konert
Vitomir Kovanovic
Milos Kravcik
Mart Laanpere
Lydia Lau
Élise Lavoué
Effie Lai-Chong Law
Danielle H. Lee
Derick Leony
Tobias Ley
Andreas Lingnau
Martin Llamas-Nistal
Ulrike Lucke
Rose Luckin
George Magoulas
Katherine Maillet
Nils Malzahn
Jean-Charles Marty
M. Antonia Martínez-Carreras
Martin Memmel
Agathe Merceron
Riichiro Mizoguchi
Yishay Mor
Pablo Moreno-Ger
Pedro J. Muñoz Merino
Rob Nadolski
Carmen Luisa Padron Napoles
Viktoria Pammer
Lucia Pannese
Pantelis Papadopoulos
Abelardo Pardo
Kai Pata
Zinayida Petrushyna
Niels Pinkwart
Elvira Popescu
Michael Prilla
Mar Pérez-Sanagustín
Eric.Ras Ras
Christoph Rensing
Luz Stella Robles Pedrozo
Adolfo Ruiz-Calleja
Demetrios Sampson
Andreas Schmidt
Ulrik Schroeder
Stylianos Sergis
Mike Sharples
Bernd Simon
Peter Sloep
Sergey Sosnovsky
Marcus Specht
Slavi Stoyanov
Kairit Tammets
Stefano Tardini
Deborah Tatar
Pierre Tchounikine
Stefaan Ternier
Vladimir Tomberg
Richard Tortorella
Christoph Trattner
Stefan Trausan-Matu
Sara Vannini
Terje Väljataga
Jo Wake
Wim Westera
Fridolin Wild
Martin Wolpers
Panagiotis Zervas
Sabrina Ziebarth

Additional Reviewers

Muhammad Anwar
Antonio Ascolese
Oliver Blunk
Irene-Angelica Chounta
Ahmed Mohammed Fahmy Yousef
Marion R. Gruber
Julio Guerra
Srecko Joksimovic
Alexander Kiy
Jeffrey Kurcz

Vlatko Lukarov
Christina Matschke
Jelena Nakic
Manuel Palomo-Duarte
Lucia Larise Stavarache
Hendrik Thüs
Chirayu Wongchokprasitti

Contents

Full Papers

Demo Papers

Full Papers

Weather-it Missions: A Social Network Analysis Perspective of an Online Citizen Inquiry Community

Maria Aristeidou(✉), Eileen Scanlon, and Mike Sharples

Institute of Educational Technology, The Open University, Milton Keynes, UK
{Maria.Aristeidou,Eileen.Scanlon,Mike.Sharples}@open.ac.uk

Abstract. Citizen inquiry is an innovative informal science learning approach, which engages members of the general public in scientific investigations sparked by their personal experience of everyday science, and to which other members can contribute. This paper aims to describe the network of interactions and contributions of Weather-it, an online Citizen Inquiry community accommodated by the nQuire-it platform, which involves people in creating and maintaining their own weather missions (investigations). The interaction patterns within Weather-it are mainly explored through social network analysis of community members and missions. The results indicate the quiet and active members within the community, their splitting into sub-communities, and their contribution and data collection methods and preferences. These results provide insight into the behaviour of people in such public engagement projects.

Keywords: Citizen inquiry · Engagement with science · Online community · Weather investigations · Social interactions · Social network analysis

1 Introduction

The term 'Citizen Science' describes the research collaborations between scientists and the public with the latter being volunteer non-experts. Inquiry-based Learning constitutes a powerful learning and teaching approach for gaining knowledge about the natural and social world [1]. Citizen Inquiry is an innovative method of informal science learning that aims to enable the engagement of citizens in online scientific investigations [2]. It combines aspects from Citizen Science and Inquiry-based Learning, such as knowledge sharing and peer review (Citizen Science) and experimentation, discovery, critique and reflection (Inquiry-based Learning). Citizen Inquiry involves people in planning and implementing their own investigations, sparked by their personal experience of everyday science, to which other people can contribute. This ownership over the investigation and its practices may lead to greater and active involvement and may add to the enhancement of competence, performance and recognition [3] and finally lead to subjects reaching higher levels of engagement [4].

However, while a number of existing studies explore the motivations around public engagement in projects that involve citizens with scientific investigation (e.g. [5]) and its impact in specific science fields (e.g. [6]), no current study explores the network of interaction and contributions between the project members. The aim of this study is to

© Springer International Publishing Switzerland 2015
G. Conole et al. (Eds.): EC-TEL 2015, LNCS 9307, pp. 3–16, 2015.
DOI: 10.1007/978-3-319-24258-3_1

explore the patterns in interactions between the Weather-it members, a community of people conducting weather investigations. The key question is what is the nature of interactions in an online community of investigation where citizens create and maintain their own projects to which other members can contribute? Social network analysis will be used as the primary method of analysis in order to gain insight into the relations of the community members with other members and the recourses.

2 Weather-It

Weather-it is a Citizen Inquiry project which aims to explore the creation of an active and sustainable community for citizens around the world to engage in online investigations. The members of the Weather-it community are people, experts and non-experts, interested in weather.

For the enrolment of members, invitations were released in different types of community. Some examples are the Royal Meteorological Society (RMetS) and the Tornado and Storm Research Organisation (TORRO) which have supported the project and helped in employing some weather experts. For the recruitment of less expert weather lovers, announcements were added to social networks (e.g. Facebook, Twitter) and other communities interested in weather (e.g. Flyer, OU modules), education (e.g. teachers forum) or Citizen Science (e.g. iSpot).

2.1 NQuire Toolkit

The Weather-it community is accommodated by the nQuire toolkit which consists of the online Citizen Inquiry platform nQuire-it and the Sense-it Android app. The nQuire toolkit has been designed as part of the project nQuire: Young Citizen Inquiry [7] and scaffolds the needs of Citizen Inquiry by assisting citizens in conducting their own science investigations, enhancing the social investigation aspect and promoting scientific thinking and exploration of the world.

The Sense-it Android app (available from the Play Store) activates the existing sensors of Android smartphones and tablets (e.g., light, humidity, pressure, and temperature sensors). It allows users to select sensors for measurements and then visualize, store and download the sensor data log files onto their mobile devices. Sense-it also creates profiles that can be connected to Citizen Inquiry investigations hosted at the nQuire-it platform, which uploads measurements to the platform automatically.

The nQuire-it platform (Fig. 1) offers three types of investigation (missions), with different methods of data collection, for the members to make their research more interesting, and a forum for further discussion. The three types of missions are Sense-it, Spot-it and Win-it: Sense-it missions are connected to the Sense-it Android application; Spot-it missions use uploaded pictures for the data collection; and Win-it missions have research questions which require text as an answer. Any member of nQuire-it can create a new mission for others to join by filling out a form with details of the mission and uploading a cover image. Creating a Sense-it mission involves also specifying the sensors to be used and how the data will be processed and displayed.

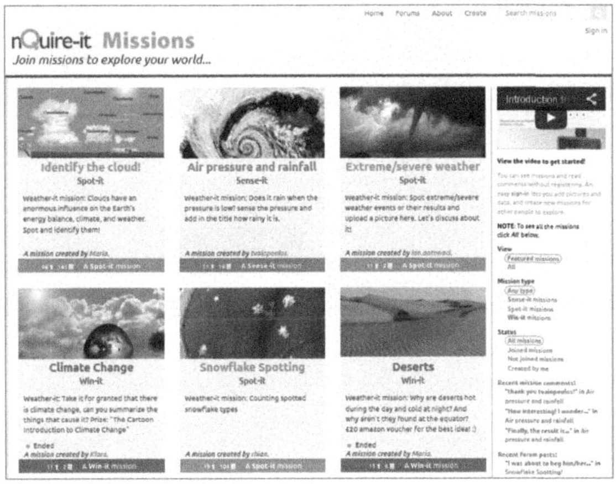

Fig. 1. The nQuire-it platform – www.nquire-it.org

2.2 Weather-it Activity

As Citizen Inquiry has the potential to encourage informal learning, the presence of both experts and non-experts in the community promotes the collaboration and knowledge sharing. Consequently, a member can discuss and exchange knowledge and methods, collaborate with weather experts to improve their investigation, or help non-experts.

The weather-missions can be weather questions which members have in their everyday life, a phenomenon they want to investigate, or something related to climate. Some examples from the Weather-it missions are:

- Record the sunlight (Sense-it mission): The members use the Sense-it Android app. to record and compare the sunlight daily, in different European countries at the same time.
- Identify the cloud (Spot-it mission): The members take pictures of clouds and upload them in order to identify the type of the cloud in collaboration with other members in the community.
- Earth vs Mars (Win-it mission): A member asks a challenging question aiming to research the climate differences between Earth and Mars. The investigator sets and adjusts the fields that the participants have to complete (methods, data, resources, etc.), and the timeline of the research (proposal, voting and outcome stage). The most voted answer wins a prize.

The participants, of all levels of weather expertise, can create or join weather missions and invite their network to join too. When becoming members of a mission, they can add their comments to the mission, or to specific data (i.e. pictures, sensor readings) (Fig. 2), and vote for their favourite data and response. In addition to the mission activities, they can create forum topics related to weather discussion, further discussion on the missions and off-topic threads for chat.

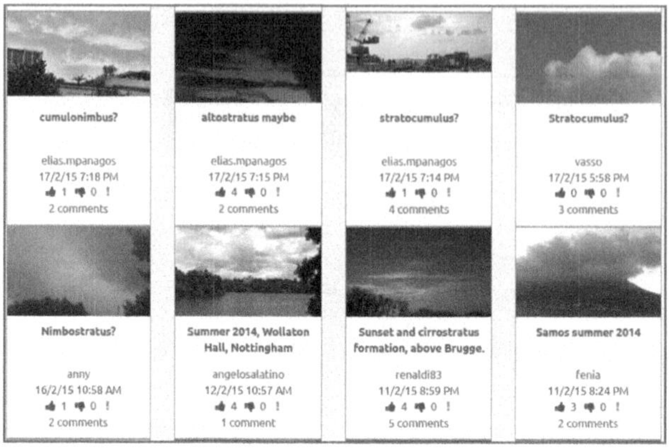

Fig. 2. Comments on the "Identify the Cloud" mission pictures

3 Methods

For the exploration of the Weather-it interactions a social network analysis (SNA) approach was taken. SNA can be used in the context of learning to explore and promote collaborative links between the learners and the resources, in order to help them develop their capabilities [8]. The analysis of the structure of social networks of informal learning networks, such as educational blogs, has also been featured in the past [9]. SNA should help appreciate the structure of the Weather-it community, the participation of members (who are active and peripheral participants), and the detection of sub-communities, to understand the patterns of interactions between the members and the missions, and answer questions like who contributed to whose data. Some of the findings are then supported and qualitatively described via data logs.

SNA conceptualizes individuals or resources as nodes, which will be connected by ties if a link exists between two nodes [10]. The SNA methodology has been applied to the interactions of the Weather-it community:

- Part I: The members are represented as nodes in graphs demonstrating who-contributed-to-whom. A directed tie is present between two nodes if one member contributed to the data of another member. The contribution may be (a) membership in missions, (b) data to missions, (c) comments to missions or posts, (d) liking posts, and (e) posting to the forum. Figure 3 (left) shows an example of this; Member A contributed three times to Member B, Member B twice to Member C and Member C once to Member A. The size of the nodes corresponds to their degree centrality (the number of their ties) and it means that the bigger the node, the more contributions the member received and sent. The ties are also weighted (thickened) according to the number of contributions from the one member to the other.
- Part II: The missions are represented as nodes in a graph demonstrating co-joined missions. An undirected tie is present between two nodes if one member has

joined both missions. Figure 3 (right) shows members A, B and C joining Missions 1, 2 and 3.

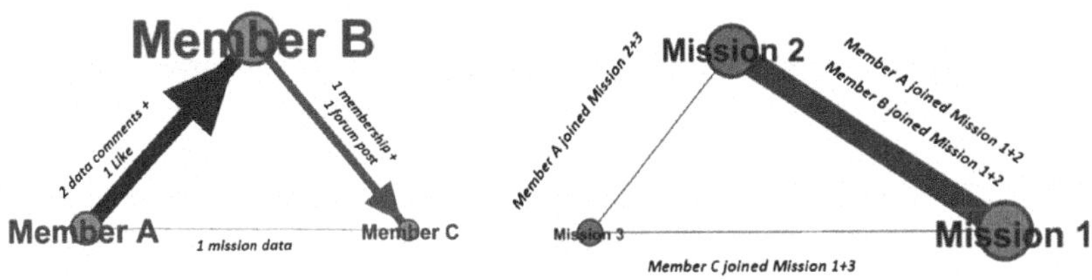

Fig. 3. Who-contributed-to-whom example (Left), Co-joined missions by members (right)

3.1 Preparing the Data

Although Weather-it missions continue to be available on the nQuire-it platform, in order to explore the interactions within the community, data from 14 weeks (23/11/2014–1/3/2015) were exported from the nQuire-it database. For the use of these data, the members of the community have given their consent for observation during that specific time interval. Prior to the analysis of the data, the names members used on the platform were changed to ones inspired by cloud and wind types (e.g. Cumulus, Zephyros). The final number of the contributions from the community members, including the two moderators, can be found in the table below (Table 1).

Table 1. Weather-it contributions

Weather-it registrations	Missions	Mission memberships	Data creation	Comments	Forum posts
101	24	206	422	441	188

The participants who registered for Weather-it but did not register with the nQuire-it platform (23) are excluded from the SNA as well as the members who did not join any mission or forum topic (15), as they are not able to create a tie in the network. Among the contributors there were some users who did not register with Weather-it and thus there was no access to their user ID and no consent to use their data; those were also excluded from the network. As a result, for part I, data from 63 members were included for constructing the whole network graph for who-contributed-to-whom. For further analysis of the interactions, and the community and hub detection and description, the contributions towards the moderators of the community (Maria and Mike) were excluded, in order to spot the hubs created by the members. Thus, for the *sub-communities network graph* 50 members were included.

For constructing the network graphs of specific type of contributions (missions, data, and forum posts) moderators were included in order to capture the contributions of members towards them. Thus, there are 40 members for the *who-contributed-data-to-whose-mission*, 36 for the *who-commented-to-whose-data*, and 29 for the *who-posted-to-whose-forum-post*.

For the part II and the co-joined missions, memberships from 57 members (moderators included) were added to the network. The lists of missions each member has joined were then rearranged to make pairs of co-joined missions, similarly to the method followed for co-studied massive open online course subjects [11] and the terms co-occurrence network [12]. The undirected ties that link two missions show that a member joined both of these missions. Duplicates were allowed in order to produce a weighted graph (showing the importance of the link between the missions), however, in some cases the members were "leaving" the mission and then re-joining; these kinds of duplicate were excluded from the data.

3.2 Importing to Gephi

The data were then imported into the Gephi visualization tool in a spreadsheet, creating a directed network for part I and undirected for part II. The network for part I consists of 63 nodes (members) and 421 ties. The network graph which indicates the whole network for who-contributed-to-whom is shown in Fig. 4 and it is obvious that the central person in the community is the moderator (Maria), with the most of the contributions directed towards her. The sub-communities network graph consists of 50 nodes and 338 ties; the missing nodes (13) were contributions from members only towards the moderators. The modularity algorithm was then used in order to detect communities [13] of members and their hubs. Further networks exclusively for the data creation, the comments and the forum posts were also produced, including 39 nodes and 63 ties, 41 nodes and 184 ties, and 28 nodes and 66 ties, respectively. These are all weighed networks in order to indicate the contribution preferences within the community. Basic social network analysis metrics were also used, such as centrality degree, betweenness centrality, and weighted degree to give insight for the members who are in direct contact to others, lie in the middle of other members, and are the most active people within the community, respectively [10].

The network for part II comprised 24 nodes (missions) and 186 ties. The number of the Weather-it missions is 13 but as the members were also allowed to take part in other missions available on the nQuire-it platform, the final number reached 24 missions. In part II the membership interconnection is being explored, measuring the average frequency and the standard deviation of the frequency of members joining missions and then spotting the dominant and peripheral missions within the weighted degree graph of co-joined missions. Finally, the modularity algorithm is used to detect groups of missions based on their "type of mission" attribute (Sense-it, Spot-it, Win-it). Taking into consideration the mission memberships helps in understanding whether the members of the community were only interested in weather investigation or they were open to any kind of investigation, their preferences towards the types of missions (and thus the data collection method), and their motivations for joining and staying in the community.

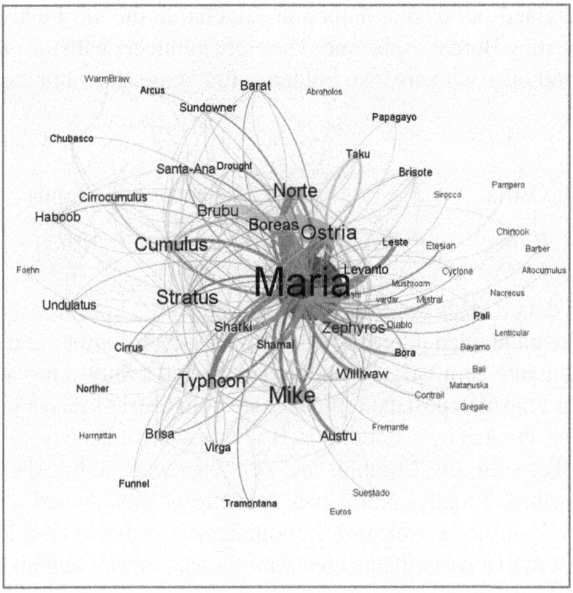

Fig. 4. Visualization of the whole network of *who-contributed-to-whom* in Weather-it. The nodes represent members, the ties the contributions, and the thickness of a tie corresponds to the volume of the contributions.

4 Results Part I

This section describes the results of part I *who-contributed-to-whom*. The graphs in this section represent Weather-it members and their ties according to their contributions to other members. The results in this section are divided into three main parts, the whole network, the sub-communities and the contribution by type.

4.1 Whole Network

Visualising the community, it is easy to identify the popular and the peripheral members of Weather-it. From the graph in Fig. 4 we can see that one of the Weather-it moderators, Maria, is notably the most important member in the community. Besides Maria and the second moderator, Mike, some other members (Ostria, Stratus, Cumulus, Norte, Typhoon, Boreas and Brubu) also seem to be high in the degree centrality ranking and thus ‘where the action is’ [10]. The rest of members have about the same level of importance overall at a lower degree of centrality, and finally there are thirteen members having a single tie – and the least importance. The moderators will be excluded in the following interpretation of the network. In the betweenness centrality and the weighted-in degree Ostria seems to come to the first place and becomes the most central member in the community and the member with the most received contributions. However, the results of the weighted-out degree helped in calculating the most active person of the community, indicating Boreas as the one. The eight members with the greatest weighted degree (both in and out), who are also bolder in Fig. 4 are shown in the Table 2.

Table 2. Members with greatest weighted degree values in Weather-it

1. Ostria	3. Norte	5. Zephyros	7. Stratus
2. Boreas	4. Typhoon	6. Cumulus	8. Brubu

From the log data it is shown that Ostria had created a Spot-it mission "Snowflake Spotting" and she maintained it, receiving many data contributions and providing feedback to her participants. Similarly, Typhoon had created a Spot-it mission in relation to "Sunsets". Boreas tended to post data (pictures) to both Ostria's mission and to "Identify the cloud" mission, created by a moderator. Brubu is a fan of Boreas' pictures and voted for almost all of them. Stratus, Cumulus and Zephyros were adding data and comments to all of the missions. Finally, Norte had created and maintained a Win-it mission "Rainfall duration", and at the same time he commented to almost all of Boreas' pictures. Whereas the most active participants create missions, contribute with data, comments and even votes, nine out of ten members with the smallest weighted degree value had joined a mission each, but had not contributed any further to it. The tenth member created a forum topic upon joining.

4.2 Sub-communities

Detecting sub-communities in the Weather-it contribution network effectively draws sub-communities of members that collaborated more often with each other. Gephi has detected five communities and they are represented in Fig. 5 in different colours. The graph (Fig. 5) shows the in-degree centrality and thus recognises the received contributions and indicates the "hubs" of the sub-communities. The modularity algorithm result is 0.2, suggesting no dense connections within the sub-communities and more connections with the other sub-communities. Thus, some of the members belong in more than one community and as a result their ties are coloured in different ways. For this analysis, the groups have not been given more meaningful labels, as the clusters were derived directly from the SNA data. Further investigation of the log files for contributions within the sub-communities showed that:

- Purple: The two members, Chubasco and WarmBraw, had only joined and contributed to a single mission, the "Deserts" Win-it mission, which included a prize for the winner.
- Green: The members who belong to the green sub-community (Zephyros, Levanto, etc.) were among the first Weather-it members and thus developed further ties with each other. Also, some of them may have stopped being active and did not get the chance to collaborate with newer community members.
- Red: Sundowner, Barat and Arcus have mainly contributed to the "Identify the Cloud" Spot-it mission and tended to collaborate with each other.

- Yellow: This sub-community consists of people whose base was the "Snowflake Spotting" Spot-it mission. Ostria, the creator of the mission, seems to be the hub of this group with the greater in-degree centrality value in the graph.
- Blue: The most of the members belong to this sub-community. Typhoon, Norte, Santa-Ana, Cumulus and Stratus have the greatest number of received contribution and thus the size of their nodes is the biggest constituting the hubs of this group. Typhoon had many contributions to her Spot-it mission "Sunsets" and Norte has also received many contributions to his "Rainfall duration" Win-it mission. Cumulus and Stratus have also created missions, the "Climate Change" Win-it mission and the "Extreme/Severe Weather" Spot-it mission respectively, but with fewer contributions. These four missions, in contrast to others (e.g. Snowflake Spotting) attracted a wide range of members. Santa-Ana has contributed interesting pictures to the "Identify the Cloud" Spot-it mission, becoming the focus of comments from a large number of members.

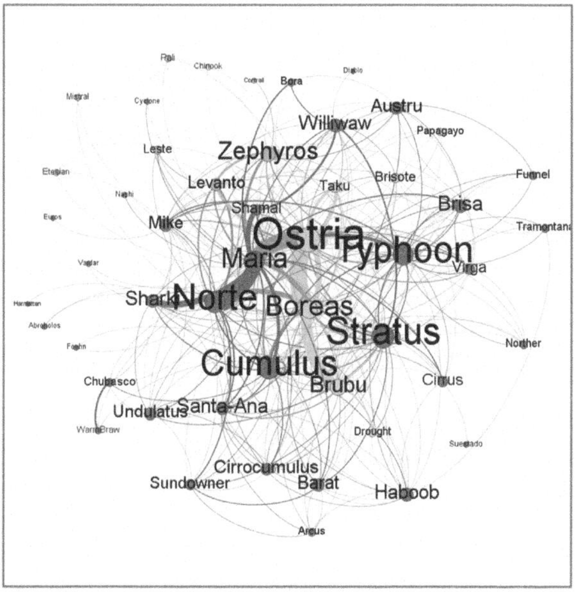

Fig. 5. Sub-communities in different colours detected in Weather-it. The sizes of the nodes (member names) indicate the hubs within the sub-communities (Color figure online).

On the whole, the creation of sub-communities may be related to the time of registration and the membership duration, the motivation for joining the community, the preference towards some mission topics or interesting data, or the wide range of contributions one may have. Analysis of interview data, currently underway, may provide further insight into motivations and preferences of participants.

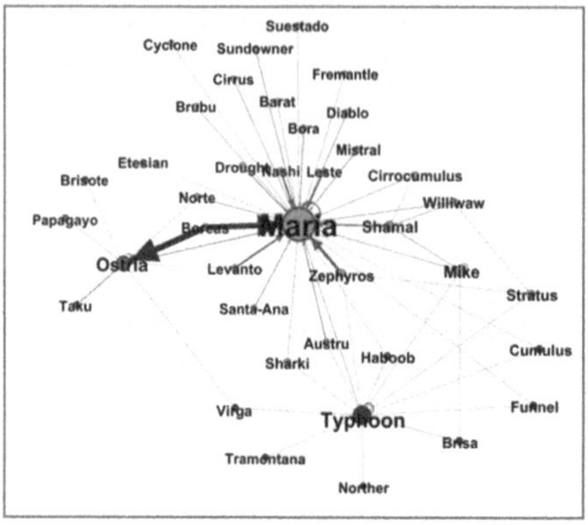

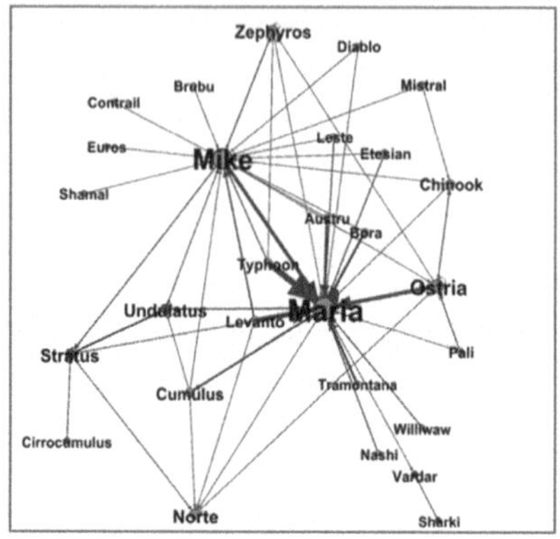

Fig. 6. Network graph: *Who-contributed-to-whose-mission (left).* (Color figure online).

Fig. 7. Network graph: *Who-contributed-to-whose-forum-post (right)*

4.3 Data Creation, Comments and Forum Posts

The data creation graph (Fig. 6) shows the weighted ties between the data contributors and the mission creators, separated in groups of different colours, that the modularity algorithm has detected. The green one, which is the largest one, has the moderator as its central member, as she has created the largest number of missions and thus most of the data have been created for those missions. The hub of the red group is the member Ostria, who managed to attract to her mission "Snowflake Spotting" members who also contributed to the moderator's missions (Norte, Boreas, Levanto) but also members who were not engaged in the missions created by the moderator (Papagayo, Brisote, Taku, Virga). Typhoon from the blue group, in the same way as Ostria, has attracted members who were only interested in contributing data to her mission "Sunsets" (Tramontana, Norther).

Comparing the graphs in Figs. 6, 7 and 8, we can say from their size that the Weather-it members interacted more through mission and data comments rather than forum posts. Only fifteen forum threads were created by the Weather-it members and there were not many contributions towards them. The most frequent post by the forum contributors was to the "Introducing myself" thread created by a moderator (Mike). In general, the most successful forum topics were related to off-topic discussion rather than weather and missions discussion.

The comments are the most popular way for the Weather-it members to contribute, indicated by the size of the graph in Fig. 8. The comments were directed either to a mission (a mission creator) or a data item (a data creator) and thus, the more missions/data one has contributed the bigger the chance of receiving a comment. The top contributors are the members Ostria, Boreas, Zephyros and Norte. An exception in this rule is the member Santa-Ana who had not added many data items but her few contributions were interesting enough (e.g. "Waterspout, Java Sea") to gather many comments and spark discussion around them.

From the above, we can draw some conclusions regarding the preference of members in relation to the type of contribution. Few members made use of the forum for their

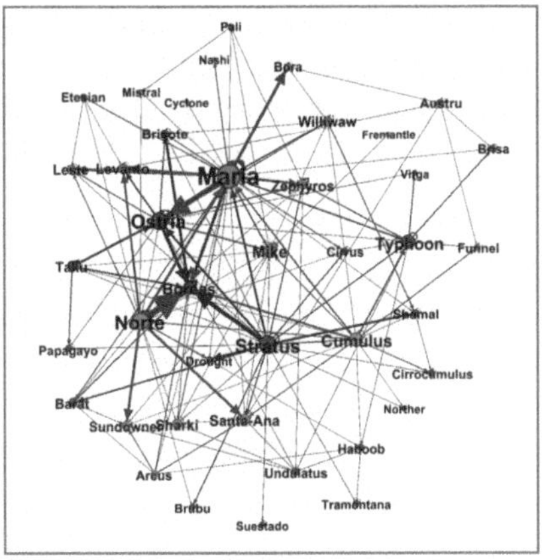

Fig. 8. Network graph: *who-contributed-to-whose-data (comments)*

interaction with other participants. Also, the data logs show that those who used the forum mainly contributed off-topic chat, rather than discussing the investigations. The preferred way for the members to contribute is by giving feedback and responses to missions and their data items. However, there are some exceptions (e.g. Boreas) who preferred to contribute data rather than commenting and discussing on other data.

5 Results Part II

This section describes the results of part II co-joined missions. The graphs in this section represent Weather-it missions and their undirected ties show co-membership between missions. The results in this section are divided into two main parts, the discussion around co-joined missions and the groups created according to the type of every mission.

5.1 Missions

Members in Weather-it joined a minimum of 1 mission and a maximum of 17 missions, with an average of three missions (mean = 3.6) and a high distribution (SD = 3.4) as the frequency of members joining a single mission was 19 and for joining 17 missions was one. The mission with the largest number of memberships was the "Identify the cloud" Spot-it mission, with 38 memberships from Weather-it people. The second most popular mission is "Record the sunlight" Sense-it mission with 27 Weather-it members. The third place is shared by three missions and 16 members each: "Snowflake spotting" and "Sunsets" Spot-it missions, and "Earth Vs Mars" Win-it mission.

Figure 9 shows the interconnection between the co-joined missions, with the largest memberships also being the most weighted. The least connected missions, which are also shown to be peripheral in the graph are "Frost", a new Win-it mission, and four non-Weather-it missions joined by Weather-it members (Computer loudness test, Noise map, reflective perspective, how loud can you scream?). The "Bee inspired" Win-it mission, although it is a non-Weather-it mission, seems to be well interconnected with the Weather-it missions and preferred by the members. However, the Google Analytics page-view reveals that the largest number of pages that visitors looked at on the nQuire-it site is for the Spot-it missions "Identify the cloud", "Snowflake spotting" and "Sunset" with 2525, 1001 and 435 views, respectively.

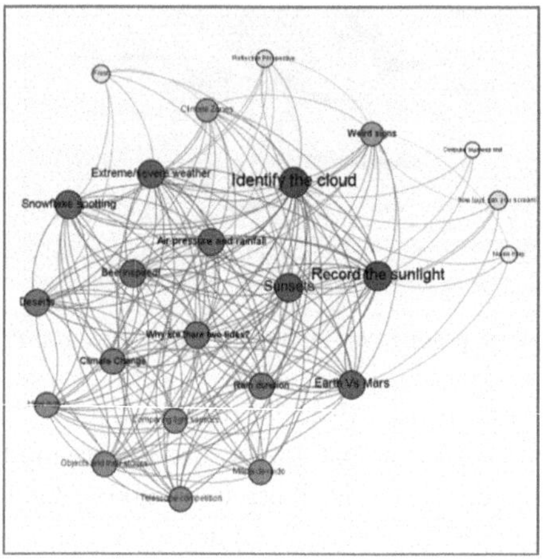

Fig. 9. Co-joined missions by Weather-it members

Figure 10 shows the missions which tend to be chosen together, separated in Sense-it (blue), Spot-it (green) and Win-it (red) mission types. The graph suggests that none of the mission types is dominant as they cover almost equal percentages: Win-it 37.5 %, Sense-it 33.3 %, and Spot-it 29.2 %. Moreover, the modularity algorithm equals to 0.08, indicating weaker ties within the mission types and stronger ties with other mission types.

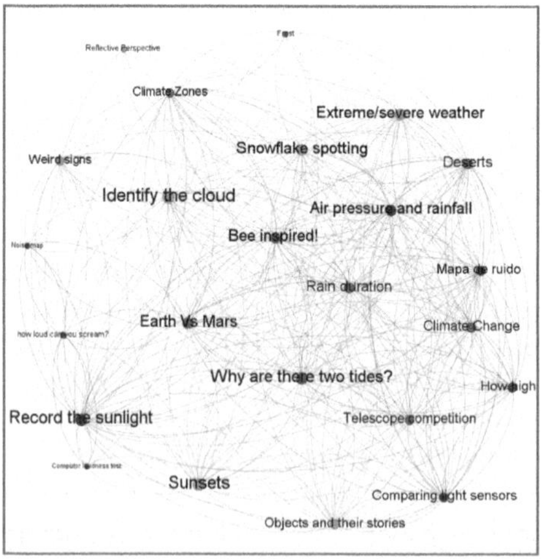

Fig. 10. Co-joined missions, colour-coded according to the mission type (Color figure online).

We can see that the Weather-it members may be interested in a single Weather-it mission and this might also be the reason they have joined the community, but we can also see members who are interested in general in investigation and they join not only weather missions, but also other missions available on nQuire-it platform. The three Spot-it missions that have the greatest page-views from Google Analytics, may also indicate that this kind of mission attracts many visitors to nQuire-it platform. However, a Sense-it mission which required daily participation for a month possesses the second spot within the Weather-it preferences. Finally, the overlap between the missions of different types shows that the Weather-it members are interested in joining missions of any type of data collection.

6 Conclusions and Further Work

This paper has looked at the visualised patterns of interactions of the online Citizen Inquiry community Weather-it. This preliminary analysis has been made with the social network analysis method and helped identify the structure of the community and the interactions between the members and the missions. The results of this research could indicate the types of activities a member of such a public engagement project is interested in. The contribution behaviour of Weather-it members varied according mainly to their investigation preferences. Members may be interested in any available mission, in Weather-it missions, in a specific type of mission (Sense-it, Spot-it, Win-it) and in a particular mission. Although we can recognise the most popular missions, there is an interconnection between the mission memberships and type of missions, which does not allow us to draw a pattern for co-joining missions and considering a specific type of mission as dominant.

The sub-communities within Weather-it grow mainly around the members who have created missions or contributed many data rendering them the community hubs. The creation of those sub-communities depends not only on the contribution preferences but also on the time of registration. Moreover, some members had more active contribution than others, creating missions or/and offering data to those missions, while some others contenting oneself in providing feedback and comments. Additionally, some contributions by some members are focused on missions or data by a single member - and in most cases that is the moderator. A last group of members that remained silent during the project is also spotted on the graphs, providing information on what attracted them initially to the community.

However, the results of this study raise more questions, such as the relationship between weighted degree and time, as the members with the greatest weighted degree values seem to have joined the community during the first six weeks. Dynamic visualization of interactions between the members and the missions should be formed in future work, in order to study the evolution of the community over time, track individual engagement, the drop outs, the new users, and the changes in the sub-communities and the mission memberships. Alongside the activity in terms of numbers and sizes, the visualisation of words should provide insight to the vocabulary of the community and initiate a further qualitative analysis on the engagement of members with weather investigations and its learning outcome.

References

1. de Jong, T.: Technological advances in inquiry learning. Science **312**(5773), 532–533 (2006)
2. Aristeidou, M., Scanlon, E., Sharples, M.: A design-based study of Citizen Inquiry for geology. In: Katherine, M., Tomaž, K. (eds.) Proceeding of the Doctoral Consortium at the European Conference on Technology Enhanced Learning co-located with the EC-TEL 2013 conference, pp. 7–13. CEUR (2013)
3. Jordan, R., Crall, A., Gray, S., Phillips, T., Mellor, D.: Citizen Science as a Distinct Field of Inquiry. BioScience **65**, 208–211 (2015)
4. Nov, O., Arazy, O., Anderson, D.: Technology-mediated citizen science participation: a motivational model. In: Proceedings of the AAAI International Conference on Weblogs and Social Media (ICWSM 2011), pp. 249–256 (2011)
5. Raddick, M.J., Bracey, G., Gay, P.L., Lintott, C.J., Murray, P., Schawinski, K., Szalay, A.S., Vandenberg, J.: Galaxy zoo: exploring the motivations of citizen science volunteers. Astron. Educ. Rev. **9**(1), 101–103 (2010)
6. Cooper, C.B., Shirk, J., Zuckerberg, B.: The invisible prevalence of citizen science in global research: migratory birds and climate change. PloS ONE **9**(9), e106508 (2014)
7. Herodotou, C., Villasclaras-Fernández, E., Sharples, M.: Scaffolding citizen inquiry science learning through the nQuire toolkit. In: Proceedings of EARLI SIG 20: Computer Supported Inquiry Learning, pp. 9–11. Malmö, Sweden (2014)
8. Haythornthwaite, C., de Laat, M.: Social networks and learning networks: using social network perspectives to understand social learning. In: 7th International Conference on Networked Learning. Aalborg, Denmark (2010)
9. Pham, M.C., Derntl, M., Cao, Y., Klamma, R.: Learning analytics for learning blogospheres. In: Popescu, E., Li, Q., Klamma, R., Leung, H., Specht, M. (eds.) ICWL 2012. LNCS, vol. 7558, pp. 258–267. Springer, Heidelberg (2012)
10. Wasserman, S., Faust, K.: Social Network Analysis: Methods and Applications. Cambridge University Press, Cambridge (1994)
11. Jordan, K.: Exploring co-studied Massive Open Online Course Subjects via social network analysis. Int. J. Emerg. Technol. Learn. **9**(8), 38–41 (2014)
12. Rabbany, R., Elatia, S., Takaffoli, M., Zaïane, O.R.: Collaborative learning of students in online discussion forums: A social network analysis perspective. In: Peña-Ayala, A. (ed.) Educational Data Mining, Studies in Computational Intelligence. Studies in Computational Intelligence, vol. 524, pp. 441–466. Springer International Publishing, Berlin (2014)
13. Blondel, V.D., Guillaume, J.-L., Lambiotte, R., Lefebvre, E.: Fast unfolding of communities in large networks. J. Stat. Mech. Theor. Exp. **10**, P10008 (2008)

Developing Mathematical Thinking with Scratch

An Experiment with 6th Grade Students

Luis Alberto Calao[1], J. Moreno-León[2](✉), Heidy Ester Correa[1], and Gregorio Robles[3]

[1] Institución Educativa Candelaria Hacienda de Lorica, Santa Cruz de Lorica, Colombia
inge484@yahoo.es

[2] Programamos.es, Sevilla, Spain
jesus.moreno@programamos.es

[3] Universidad Rey Juan Carlos, Madrid, Spain
grex@gsyc.urjc.es

Abstract. One of the latest trends in the educational landscape is the introduction of computer programming in the K-12 classroom to develop computational thinking in students. As computational thinking is not a skill exclusively related to computer science, it is assumed – but not yet scientifically proven – that the problem solving process may be generalized and transferred to a wide variety of problems. This paper presents a research designed to test whether the use of coding in Maths classes could have a positive impact on learning outcomes of students in their mathematical skills. Therefore, the questions we want to investigate in this paper are if the use of programming in Maths classes improves (a) modeling process and reality phenomena, (b) reasoning, (c) problem formulation and problem solving, and (d) comparison and execution of procedures and algorithms. We have therefore designed a quantitative, quasi-experimental experiment with 42 participating 6th grade (11 and 12 years old) students. Results show that there is a statistically significant increase in the understanding of mathematical processes in the experimental group, which received training in Scratch.

Keywords: Computational thinking · Maths · Learning · Coding · Scratch

1 Introduction

One of the latest trends in the educational landscape is the introduction of computer programming in the K-12 classroom to develop computational thinking (CT) in students, a skill defined by Jeannette Wing as one that "involves solving problems, designing systems, and understanding human behaviour, by drawing on the concepts fundamental to computer science" [22]. Although CT is not a skill exclusively related to computer science [4,20], research shows that programming is a very good mechanism for the development of this competence [12].

© Springer International Publishing Switzerland 2015
G. Conole et al. (Eds.): EC-TEL 2015, LNCS 9307, pp. 17–27, 2015.
DOI: 10.1007/978-3-319-24258-3_2

Thus, governments around the world are making computer programming part of their national curriculum. For instance, nine countries in Europe have already included coding into their schools: Bulgaria, Cyprus, Denmark, Estonia, Greece, Ireland, Poland, Portugal and the UK (England) [19].

One of the pillars of CT is, according to the operational definition developed by the Computer Science Teachers Association and the International Society for Technology in Education [3], "generalizing and transferring this problem solving process to a wide variety of problems". Hence, the general research question of this paper is how far CT affects other school subjects. In particular, this study was designed to test whether the use of coding in math classes could have a positive impact on learning outcomes of students in relation to their mathematical skills. Therefore, the specific questions we want to give an answer to in this research paper are following:

1. *Modeling*: Does the use of programming in math classes improve the modeling of processes and reality phenomena?
2. *Reasoning*: Does the use of programming in math classes improve reasoning?
3. *Problem solving*: Does the use of programming in math classes improve problem formulation and problem solving?
4. *Exercising*: Does the use of programming in math classes improve the comparison and execution of procedures and algorithms?

The structure of this paper is as follows: A brief overview of the mathematical skills of Colombian students is presented, and some research studies that have investigated relationships between coding with Scratch, the programming learning environment used in this experiment, in schools and learning are outlined in Sect. 2. Then, in Sect. 3 our work methodology is briefly described. Section 4 presents the results we have obtained from applying our methodology on a small group of Colombian students in the mathematics class. Finally, Sect. 5 contains the conclusions of our research, and some ideas and suggestions for future work are discussed.

2 Background

2.1 Colombian Students and Maths

The results in international tests show that there is still much room for improvement regarding the mathematical skills of Colombian students. In PISA 2012 [13] (Programme for International Student Assessment), which assessed the competencies of 15 year old students in reading, mathematics and science (with a focus on mathematics) in 65 countries and economies, Colombian students scored 376 points in mathematics on average, compared to an average of 494 points in OECD (Organisation for Economic Co-operation and Development) countries. Therefore, Colombia ranked 61st in mathematical competencies.

According to OECD report *Does math make you anxious?* [14], mathematics can "provoke worry, stress and even feelings of powerlessness in some students, and this anxiety towards mathematics is shown to be strongly related to mathematics performance." In order to measure that anxiety, PISA 2012 included questions regarding how students feel when they anticipate having to perform mathematical tasks, when they anticipate their performance in mathematics class, and while they are attempting to solve mathematics problems. The responses revealed that countries where students report higher levels of anxiety were also those where students perform poorer in mathematics. Thus, Colombia was one of the countries with higher levels of anxiety towards maths by students [13].

2.2 Code to Learn with Scratch

The educational use of programming is not new. Back in the 1960s Seymour Papert developed the Logo programming language aiming to allow children to use computers to create games, composing music or painting recursive drawings [15]. However, after a few years of success, programming disappeared from the K12 educational landscape because of the problems that students and teachers faced trying to learn the language syntax, among other reasons [16].

Nevertheless, in the last years new visual programming languages, such as Alice, Kodu and especially Scratch [18], have reawakened the interest of the educational community in coding, not as an end in itself, but as a tool to develop other skills and to improve learning outcomes and motivation in students, as Mitchel Resnick, creator of Scratch, argues in *Learn to code, code to learn* [17].

Regarding the usefulness of programming with Scratch as a tool to improve student learning, there is research literature that has a very promising outlook, as coding has been successfully utilized in subjects like mathematics, science, arts, writing or English as a second language, among others. Focusing on mathematics, Lewis and Shah [11] detect correlation between programming quizzes and math tests grades, Ke [8] explains that students showed significantly more positive attitude towards this discipline after the study, while Zavala, Gallardo and García-Ruiz [23] observe improvements in the identification and comparison of numbers, although no gain in relation to the spatial location was detected. However, most of the studies reviewed did not follow basic recommendations to develop research in education [2], and therefore, there is a need to carry out empirical studies using control groups and providing quantitative data to prove the potential of computer programming with Scratch as an educational tool to improve academic outcomes.

Furthermore, there are research studies that analyze the development of problem solving skills while learning to program with Scratch. Most of the articles reviewed confirm that students developed their problem solving skills after the investigation [1,5,9,10,21], while no significant differences were detected in one of the studies [6].

3 Methodology

3.1 Design

This research is a quantitative, quasi-experimental study, which includes a pre-post test design with both experimental and control groups. In this type of research, according to Hernandez, Fernandez and Baptista [7], an independent variable is deliberately manipulated in order to observe its effect and relation to one or more dependent variables through measurements of the subjects before and after treatment application.

3.2 Population

The population that was part of this experiment is composed 42 students of 6th grade of the Candelaria Hacienda school located in the municipality of Lorica, Department of Córdoba of Colombia. This institution is an official primary and secondary school. The sample is intentional and not probabilistic, and it is comprised of 24 students from 6th-1 group, taken as experimental group, and 18 students from 6th-2 group, as control group.

3.3 Data Collection

As an instrument for collecting data, a rubric was elaborated to evaluate students performance and skills in the mathematical processes involved in this investigation: modeling, formulation and problem solving, reasoning and exercising. This rubric was prepared taking into account the conceptual approaches set by the Ministry of National Education of Colombia in relation to the guidelines and basic competence standards in mathematics.

The rubric consists of a set of criteria that evaluates the development of the student in each of the four skills studied in this research. Depending on this criteria, the students gets an evaluation that may be *excellent*, *good*, *satisfactory* and *deficient*.

For instance, students with an excellent performance level in each skill should be able to:

- *Modeling*: The student properly solves all the problems related to the modeling process, in which the detection of variables and relationships among them that establish a mathematical model is required, as well as detecting patterns that are repeated in daily, scientific and mathematical situations, and reconstruct them mentally.
- *Reasoning*: The student properly uses the reasoning process to resolve all situation problems it faces, sensing regularities and relationships, making predictions and guesses, or justifying arguments and reasoning.
- *Problem solving*: The student easily solves problems in situations which require deployment strategies to interpret the statements given, to find results and to verify these results.

- *Exercising*: The student runs easily algorithmic procedures, realizing the concepts on which they rest and recognizing when you can apply a given technical or mathematical operation.

For the application of the rubric two standard test questionnaires were elaborated, one for the pre-test and one for the post-test, which were simultaneously applied to both the control group and the experimental group. Each questionnaire consisted of 16 questions equally distributed among the four skills to evaluate. A copy, both in Spanish and in English, of the rubric and the two questionnaires can be obtained from the replication package of this paper[1].

3.4 Areas of Intervention

The initial stage of the experimental intervention, the experimental group begins with several informal activities on sequences of processes, and then an introduction to the concepts of algorithm and programming is given. In a second stage, students begin to learn to use the Scratch graphical programming environment, conducting educational activities. These activities are initially aimed at basic interactions with the program and then focused on the use of animated dialogues.

In a third stage the use of loops, conditionals and variables is trained. Finally, in a fourth stage, the students test their creativity by programming their own games and simulations making use of images, sounds and movements.

The intervention on the experimental group took place along 3 months. Meanwhile the control group continued the classes using the same kind of methodology and activities they had been using up until that moment.

3.5 Data Analysis

For the data collection, as mentioned earlier, both a pre-test, developed before the intervention, and a post-test, performed after the intervention, were applied to both the control and experimental groups. In each of these tests, a rubric prepared from the conceptual definition of each of the mathematical processes that students are expected to develop in sixth grade of primary education in Colombia are used.

In addition of the overall average of the processes evaluated, the results of the tests offer information regarding the four mathematical processes assessed in this research. A t-test analysis for independent samples is performed comparing the results of the means obtained by the experimental group and the control group in the pre-test and post-test. Similarly, a t-test for related samples is applied to compare the control and experimental groups separately.

[1] http://gsyc.urjc.es/~grex/repro/2015-ectel.

4 Findings

Figure 1 shows the mean and standard deviation of the tests by the control and experimental groups before the intervention. As shown in the figure, the results of the pre-tests are very similar in both groups, which is congruent with the fact that the groups are formed by students of similar characteristics.

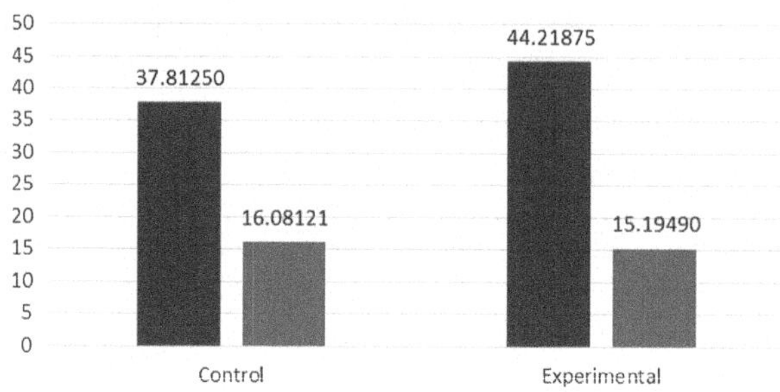

Fig. 1. Pre-test. Mean and deviation for control (left) and experimental (right) groups.

Figure 2 shows the mean and standard deviation of the tests by the control and experimental groups after the intervention. As shown in the figures, there is a remarkable difference in the results of the post-tests, as the mean of the results of the experimental group is 41.56 points above the one of the control group.

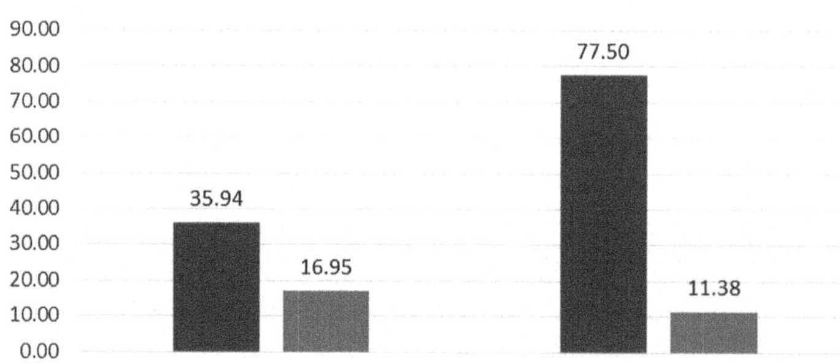

Fig. 2. Post-test. Mean and deviation for control (left) and experimental (right) groups.

Figure 3 offers a comparison of the results obtained for each of the four skills under study for the control and experimental groups.

If the results of each mathematical process before the intervention are compared, we can see that both the mean and the standard deviation are uniform, presenting small differences in the modeling, reasoning and exercising, and only showing a difference of more than 10 points in terms of problem solving where the experimental group shows a significant better performance than the control group.

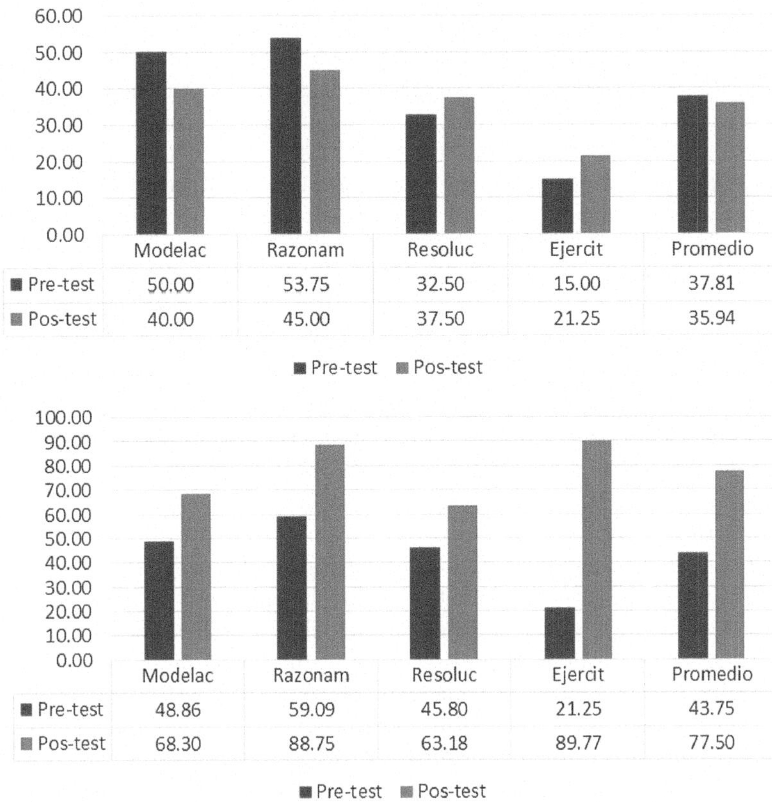

Fig. 3. Comparison. Means obtained for the control (upper) and experimental (lower) groups by mathematical process. *Modelac* stands for *modeling*, *Razonam* for *reasoning*, *Resoluc* for *problem solving*, *Ejercit* for *exercising* and *Promedio* for *average*.

If the results of each mathematical process after the intervention are compared, we can see that there is a significant difference in all the processes in favour to the experimental group. Especially noteworthy are the results of the *exercising* process, with a difference of over 68 points.

While no significant differences are observed in the results of the control group, a uniform gain is shown in the results of the experimental group, where the grades are significantly better in the post-test for all processes, and there is an average increase more than 33.5 points.

It is remarkable that the control group has obtained a lower mean value in the post-test than in the pre-test. While the difference is not significant, it however means that students have not progressed in these skills in the three months of the study. As this students have been attending their regular math classes as usual, this result may hint that (at least some parts of) the math curriculum in schools does not help in developing those skills.

The questions that have been included in the pre and post-test questionnaires are closely connected to the use of mathematics in real-life scenarios, and can be considered as applying mathematics to usual situations. From our results, it seems that math learning at schools is more focused on the internals of mathematics, rather than on acquiring skills to use math-based knowledge. For this type of skill development, our experiment has shown that the use of programming is of great value with a significant increase of the results obtained by learners.

If we look more in detail at the four skills under study, we see that modeling and reasoning are those skills that are more developed with the *traditional* way of learning math. However with *problem solving* and especially with *exercising* there is much room for improvement. From our experiment we have observed that the *exercising* skill in students is particularly increased with the introduction of programming. The mean value for this skill for the experimental group is even the highest among all skills. This finding shows that introducing programming offers students more insight in the comparison and execution of algorithms and procedures than in *traditional* classes, which sounds meaningful as the nature of programming is very related to those activities. In the case of *problem solving*, although the gain in the experimental group is significantly higher then the one for the control group, our results show that the growth is moderate. Further research should be devoted to find out how to further improve this skill, and if programming can be helpful in achieving this goal.

A t-test was performed to measure the average level of mathematical processes in the control and experimental groups in order to assess whether the results are similar or if they have significant differences. The null hypothesis states that there are no significant differences in the sample means.

First, data in Table 1 show that there are no significant differences in the results means of the control group and the experimental group in the pre-test, as the p-value (0.195) is greater than 0.05. However, there are statistically sig-

Table 1. T-test of independent samples in the pre-test and post-test

		Levene test	T-test for equal mean						
		F	Sig	t	Sig. (bilat)	Diff. means	Typ. error	95 % conf. interval	
								Inferior	Superior
Pre-test	Equal var. assumed	0.052	0.821	-1.319	0.195	-6.406	4.857	-16.223	3.410
	Equal var. not as.			-1.308	0.199	-6.406	4.898	-16.343	3.531
Post-test	Equal var. assumed	3.155	.084	-9.246	>0.001	-41.563	4.495	-50.663	-32.462
	Equal var. not as			-8.893	>0.001	-41.563	4.674	-51.125	-32.000

Table 2. Test of related samples. Control and experimental groups.

	Related differences					t	gl	Sig (bilateral)
	Mean	SD	Typical error	95 % confidence interval				
				Inferior	Superior			
Control group	1.875	11.250	2.652	-3.719	7.469	0.707	17	0.489
Exp. group	-33.750	14.315	3.0519	-40.097	-27.403	-11.05	21	>0.001

nificant differences in the results of both groups in the post-test, as the p-value (>0.001) is less than 0.05.

Second, we have applied the t-test to the related samples to study the differences between the pre-test and post-test. Table 2 shows that no statistically significant changes are observed in the control group between the pre-test and post-test , as the p-value (0.489) is grater than 0.05. However in the experimental group there were significant differences between the pre-test post-test, as the p-value (>0.001) is less than 0.05.

5 Conclusions and Further Research

The goal of this research was to analyze the effect of the development of computational thinking through the use of the Scratch visual programming environment in the development of mathematical skills in sixth graders of elementary education, for which a comparison was made between two groups of similar characteristics of the same grade, designating one as control group and the other as experimental group. The latter was the one who received intervention, which consisted in Scratch programming training for three months. Statistical tests were applied to both control and experimental groups before and after the intervention.

The results show that there is a statistically significant gain in the understanding of mathematical knowledge in the experimental group, which received training in Scratch. This therefore leads to the conclusion that the development of computational thinking using the Scratch visual programming environment allows students of primary education to improve their performance in terms of mathematical processes of modeling, reasoning, problem solving and exercising, while, in parallel it also facilitates the generation of a motivating learning environments.

Among the studied skills, we have found that the exercising skill (i.e., the comparison and execution of procedures and algorithms) is the one that is less developed in *traditional* math classes, but is the one that is especially strengthened by programming. Our findings show that modeling and reasoning skills benefit as well significantly from programming. Finally, the problem solving skill also increases, but is the one that has more room for improvement. Future research should focus on how programming may enhance the problem solving skill; some possible solutions could be to address this skill by designing specific programming tasks or by introducing specific methodologies to learn programming.

As a future line of research, we note that during the intervention process we observed that some learners faced some issues in reading and writing when working with lively dialogues. However, students were highly motivated to improve their skills and overcome the difficulties in order to create good Scratch projects. This suggests a possible investigation into how the use of the Scratch visual programming environment can have a positive impact on the development of reading and writing skills.

At this moment the authors are performing a study with more than 40 teachers from three different countries, Spain, Argentina and Ecuador, involving more than 500 students. In this investigation educators from different grades are using computer programming with Scratch to teach several kind of subjects, such as mathematics, literature, English as a second language or social studies, among others. Thus, the results of the research may allow us to measure to what extent the development of computational thinking can have a beneficial impact on the academic outcomes of learners in different disciplines.

Acknowledgments. The work of Jesús Moreno-León and Gregorio Robles has been funded in part under project "eMadrid - Investigación y Desarrollo de tecnologías para el e-learning en la Comunidad de Madrid" (S2013/ICE-2715) funded by the Region of Madrid. The work of Gregorio Robles has been funded in part by the Spanish Government under project SobreSale (TIN2011- 28110).

References

1. Brown, Q., Mongan, W., Kusic, D., Garbarine, E., Fromm, E., Fontecchio, A.: Computer aided instruction as a vehicle for problem solving: Scratch programming environment in the middle years classroom (2013). Accessed on September 22
2. Cohen, L., Manion, L., Morrison, K.: Research Methods in Education. Routledge, 2 ParkSquare, MiltonPark, Abingdon, Oxon OX14 4RN (2007)
3. CSTA, ISTE: Computational thinking, teachers resources. Technical report, CSTA and ISTE (2011). http://www.csta.acm.org/Curriculum/sub/CurrFiles/472.11CTTeacherResources_2ed-SP-vF.pdf
4. Denning, P.J.: The profession of it beyond computational thinking. Commun. ACM **52**(6), 28–30 (2009)
5. Giordano, D., Maiorana, F.: Use of cutting edge educational tools for an initial programming course. In: Global Engineering Education Conference (EDUCON), 2014 IEEE. pp. 556–563. IEEE (2014)
6. Gülbahar, Y., Kalelioğlu, F.: The effects of teaching programming via Scratch on problem solving skills: a discussion from learners perspective. Inform. Educ. Int. J. **13**(1), 33–50 (2014)
7. Hernández Sampieri, R., Fernández Collado, C., Baptista Lucio, P.: Metodología de la Investigación, 5th edn. McGraw-Hill, Mexico (2010)

8. Ke, F.: An implementation of design-based learning through creating educational computer games: a case study on mathematics learning during design and computing. Comput. & Educ. **73**, 26–39 (2014)
9. Lai, A.F., Yang, S.M.: The learning effect of visualized programming learning on 6th graders' problem solving and logical reasoning abilities. In: 2011 International Conference on Electrical and Control Engineering (ICECE), pp. 6940–6944. IEEE (2011)
10. Lai, C.S., Lai, M.H.: Using computer programming to enhance science learning for 5th graders in Taipei. In: 2012 International Symposium on Computer, Consumer and Control (IS3C), pp. 146–148. IEEE (2012)
11. Lewis, C.M., Shah, N.: Building upon and enriching grade four mathematics standards with programming curriculum. In: Proceedings of the 43rd ACM Technical Symposium on Computer Science Education. pp. 57–62. ACM (2012)
12. Lye, S.Y., Koh, J.H.L.: Review on teaching and learning of computational thinking through programming: what is next for K-12? Comput. Hum. Behav. **41**, 51–61 (2014)
13. OECD: Pisa 2012 results: What students know and can do student performance in mathematics, reading and science (volume i, revised edition, February 2014). Technical report, OECD (2014). http://www.content/book/9789264208780-en
14. OECD: Does math make you anxious? Technical report, OECD (2015). http://www.content/workingpaper/5js6b2579tnx-en
15. Papert, S., Solomon, C.: Twenty things to do with a computer. In: Soloway, E., Spohrer, J.C. (eds.) Studying the Novice Programmer. Lawrence Erlbaum Associates Inc., Hillsdale (1971)
16. Resnick, M.: Point of view: reviving papert's dream. Educ. Technol. **52**(4), 42 (2012)
17. Resnick, M.: Learn to code, code to learn. How programming prepares kids for more than math. EdSurge 8 (2013)
18. Resnick, M., Maloney, J., Monroy-Hernández, A., Rusk, N., Eastmond, E., Brennan, K., Millner, A., Rosenbaum, E., Silver, J., Silverman, B., et al.: Scratch: programming for all. Commun. ACM **52**(11), 60–67 (2009)
19. Schoolnet, E.: Computing our future. computer programming and coding priorities, school curricula and initiatives across europe. Technical report European Schoolnet (2014). http://www.eun.org/publications/detail?publicationID=481
20. Settle, A., Perkovic, L.: Computational thinking across the curriculum: a conceptual framework. Technical, report college of Computing and Digital Media Technical report(2010)
21. Wang, H.Y., Huang, I., Hwang, G.J.: Effects of an integrated Scratch and project-based learning approach on the learning achievements of gifted students in computer courses. In: 2014 IIAI 3rd International Conference on Advanced Applied Informatics (IIAIAAI), pp. 382–387. IEEE (2014)
22. Wing, J.M.: Computational thinking. Commun. ACM **49**(3), 33–35 (2006)
23. Zavala, L.A., Gallardo, S.C.H., García-Ruíz, M.Á.: Designing interactive activities within Scratch 2.0 for improving abilities to identify numerical sequences. In: Proceedings of the 12th International Conference on Interaction Design and Children. pp. 423–426. ACM (2013)

Facilitate Sharing of Training Experience by Exploring Behavior Discovery in Trainees Traces

Olivier Champalle[1,2(✉)], Karim Sehaba[1,3], and Alain Mille[1,2]

[1] Université de Lyon, CNRS,
Lyon, France
{olivier.champalle,karim.sehaba,alain.mille}@liris.cnrs.fr
http://www.liris.cnrs.fr
[2] Université Lyon 1, LIRIS, UMR5205,
F-69622 Villeurbanne, France
[3] Université Lyon 2, LIRIS, UMR5205,
F-69676 Lyon, France

Abstract. In this article, we propose a set of models and a prototype to capitalize and share knowledge of expert tutors using training simulators. This is a particularly important issue in contexts with strong stakes such as training of operators of nuclear power plants, where operators' accreditation strongly depends on skills of tutors and tolerate no errors. In such a context, observation, analysis and debriefing of interactions of trainees' operators are complex activities especially for the young tutors who do not have the expertise of confirmed tutors. Based on digital traces, our approach consists in providing a visual synthesis of trainees' activities by using the knowledge of experts. Such a synthesis, showing the relationships between low-level traces and high-level behaviors, enables tutors to enhance their understanding and better analyse the activity in order to prepare the debriefing. Our approach has been implemented in a prototype, called D3KODE, which was evaluated according to a comparative protocol conducted with a team of tutors from EDF Group (Electricity Of France). The result demonstrated that the visual synthesis and the higher informations provided by D3KODE helped the intructors to confirm/validate more easily realizations and no-realizations of educational objectives trainees and facilitated the exchanges between tutors and trainees.

Keywords: Knowledge sharing · Digital traces · Vocational training · Full scope simulator

1 Introduction

Sharing knowledge and experience between users (experts, tutors and/or learners) is a well studied topic in TEL system (Technology Enhanced Learning) [1–5]. *Indeed, sharing experiences can facilitate knowledge transfer between users,*

© Springer International Publishing Switzerland 2015
G. Conole et al. (Eds.): EC-TEL 2015, LNCS 9307, pp. 28–41, 2015.
DOI: 10.1007/978-3-319-24258-3_3

improve team performance and enhance communication and collaboration [6]. However, most research in this area focuses on helping learners to learn from experience of other learners. Assisting tutors in their task with the support of others tutors' knowledge is far less studied. Research on tutors' knowledge mainly addresses the design of learning analysis indicators. Such indicators are either closely linked to a system [7], fixed and immutable [4,5] or rely on a strong re-engineering process [1,8]. The knowledge to design and manage learning analysis indicators is important to share, but does not cover all what is necessary to manage a complex learning process. If they provide a partial view of the activity, they do not allow to explain the genesis of learners actions: explaining this genesis requires to be able to observe the activity in order to produce rich traces, allowing to understand the learning process by a precise time based analysis. Furthermore, current knowledge based approaches are mainly applied to e-learning. They have to be adapted to be applied in a context of vocational training with simulators.

At a general level, capitalization of tacit and explicit knowledge [9] is a paramount and remains a complex task to achieve for all companies organizations [10]. In this article, we focus on capitalization and sharing of expert knowledge in order to assist tutors during simulator training. More specifically, we address the case of full scale simulators (FSS) designed to train operators for maintaining and controlling Nuclear Power Plant (NPP) [11]. In such a context, training operators and delivering them certificates and accreditations strongly depends on the skills of tutors and requires a "no error" approach. Actually, observation, analysis and debriefing of individual and collective interactions of trainees are considered as very complex activities [12]. To assist tutors in their tasks, the NPP FSS uses several tools to follow, record and replay the captured parameters of the simulator and the observed actions of the operators. These tools are complex and specific and it is challenging fo new tutors to use them properly in a short time.

To overcome these difficulties, we propose to study how to use digital traces of a simulation scenario in order to provide a visual synthesis of the activity enriched with higher level analysis pieces of information that experts can infer on the basis on their experience and theoretical knowledge. Such a process enables tutors to synthetize their understanding and to trace their activity analysis to prepare debriefing. These higher level analysis traces are able not only to present what knowledge was necessary for the analysis, but also what were the patterns of trainees actions explaining such or such analysis. Our approach has been implemented in a prototype, called D3KODE which was evaluated according to a comparative protocol conducted with a team of tutors from EDF Group (Electricity Of France). The experiment showed that the visual synthesis and the higher level analysis traces provided by D3KODE helped the intructors to confirm/validate more easily realizations and no-realizations of the trainees. Moreover, this explicit knowledge facilitated the exchanges between tutors and trainees.

This work is part of a research project conducted in partnership with UFPI (Training Unit Production Engineering) of EDF group (Electricité De France)[1]. The main activity of UFPI (over 700 tutors, 3 million hours of training per year) is to provide professional training courses for staff working in the domains of power generation (nuclear, fossil-fired, hydraulic).

The paper is organized as follows: Section 2 describes the application context of our work concerning the training of operators of nuclear power plants of the UFPI. Section 3 presents the related works. Section 4 presents our approach for observation and analysis of trainees activities with new models and a tool implementing them. Section 5 presents the evaluation of our approach and its results. The last section is devoted to a conclusion and perspectives.

2 Context and Problem Statement

During the simulation session (Fig. 1), the trainees have to realize a *transitory*. A transitory represents the set of actions that the simulator has to process to move from an initial physical state e_0 at the moment t_0 to a final end state e_n at t_n.

To do this, trainees drive the simulator through expected actions according to so called "Pedagogical Objectives". These objectives are classified in more abstract "Pedagogical Objectives Families". Among these objectives we can cite: "Understanding state of the system", "Professional gestures", "Surveillance", "Communication", etc. These objectives correspond to the knowledge level and skills that are necessary to insure safety of the plant. During the simulation session, the tutor runs the simulation scenario, observes the trainees behaviour, controls the simulator on the basis of the actions performed by trainees and fills an observation balance sheet to prepare and conduct the debriefing step. An observation balance sheet contains a set of expected "Pedagogical Objectives" that trainees should be able to satisfy (see for example the Annexe G of [13]).

To assist tutors in their tasks, the NPP FSS offers several tools to follow, record and replay the parameters of the simulator and the actions of the trainees. These tools have some limitations:

- The data stored in the logs describes very low level events. In such a context, understanding and following the activity require a strong expertise that new tutors don't have;
- The amount of data collected during a simulation is so big that it is very difficult to analyse them manually to extract high level information synthetizing the behaviour of trainees;
- The synchronization of numerous and different types of data (video, sound, logs,...), is difficult and expensive. Moreover, the data are stored in different places, and do not share the same time representation.

To overcome these difficulties, we propose to:

[1] Electricity Of France.

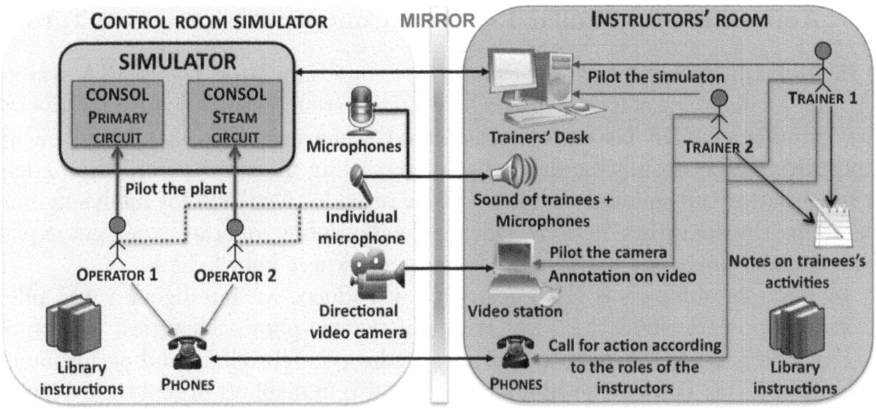

Fig. 1. Description of the *simulation environment.*

- Assist tutors in observation and analysis of activity by:
  - Providing a visual synthesis of the activity with the expected observations of the trainees (realized or not realized);
  - Allowing navigation through different abstraction levels to facilitate the analysis of the activity;
  - Allowing tutors to add dynamically their own expert observations during the phases of observation and analysis.
- Strengthen the debriefing by:
  - Providing trainees a visual synthesis of their activities in a reflexive way;
  - Providing tutors factual information to exchange with the trainees.
- Favour sharing of observation and analysis knowledge between tutors by:
  - Allowing tutors to exchange on their practices;
  - Allowing new tutors to reuse the knowledge of confirmed tutors.

To develop actual tools for tutors according to our proposals, we consider a deeper and more explicit exploitation of simulation data. In the following section, we presents a state of the art on related works based on exploitation of digital information.

3 Related Works

Exploiting digital traces of trainees' activity is a spread practice in the computerized dedicated environments for training. We consider as "digital traces" all numerical data produced during a complex activity needing to achieve various tasks through a computarized environment. These traces are built from human-system interactions and/or from system-system interactions.

We conducted a two steps state of the art: at first we have compared approaches close to our context and corresponding research proposals; in a second step, we focused our study in the general field of knowledge engineering to study existing approaches for capitalizing knowledge from observation and activity analysis.

3.1 Approaches on Similar Research Context: Assistance to Tutors

In the domain of Nuclear Power Plant Full-Scope Simulator, the SEPIA system [14], an artificial intelligence based training system, was designed for operators training of EDF Group on pre-defined scenarios. SEPIA is based on an expert-system encapsulating driving rules according to expert tutors knowledge. In batch, after the simulation time, SEPIA provides feedback for analysing and correcting the operators' actions. During the debriefing, operators can get explanations concerning any registered parameters (expert knowledge).

In Aircraft simulation (IIPDSS), [15] introduces an intelligent tutor pilot decision support system that uses traces of trainee-pilot's activities. The trace information is used to help tutor during simulation, debriefing, and performance evaluation tasks. During the simulation, the system displays in real time a list of messages to help tutors for understanding and guiding the trainee. For evaluation purpose, the system collects and displays various evaluation criteria applicable to a particular simulated mission. At the end of the simulation, the system provides a complete trace of the divergent actions of the trainee, associated with the corresponding data of the aircraft simulation environment. The system provides also a summary of the skills demonstrating trainee's difficulties.

The PPTS project (Pedagogical Platoon Training System) [16] assists tutors to observe and analyse the tactical behaviour of a platoon network of four LECLERC tank simulators. PPTS integrates an ITS which reproduces the expertise of tutors in order to exploit and analyse the digital traces of the simulation to highlight the three skills levels expected from each crew: technical, tactical and strategic skills. Each analysis level is constructed on the basis of lower level of analysis or observation. At the end of the simulation, the PPTS generates a summary on the skills of the crew. This summary is used as support by tutors in the debriefing phase.

Previously cited works use digital traces of activity to support diagnosis and analysis of trainees activity but miss important properties. First, the proposed tools for these approaches are closed systems. Second, their implementation is generally heavy (ITS, expert system) and requires a long and difficult collaboration with experts. A third limitation lies in the "static" status of the knowledge representation used by these systems. Indeed, once these systems are built, it is not possible for the tutors to create and share their own observation and analysis knowledge. It is also not possible to define the levels of expected skills.

These systems being very specific, with severe limitations due to their contexts, we studied more general approaches developed in the knowledge engineering community.

3.2 Knowledge Engineering and Capitalization Based on Trace

Reference [17] proposes the analysis tool Tatiana (Trace Analysis Tool for Interaction Analysts) which implements the concept of *replayable* in order to assist the analysis of heterogeneous data (videos, logs, ...). A replayable is a generic analytic artefact that models and capitalizes an analysis methodology through a user trace observation. A replayable can be visualized, replayed, enriched, transformed to produce a new replayable and synchronized with other like artefacts.

Reference [1] uses UTL (Usage Tracking Language) a meta-language dedicated to the modeling of indicators from raw data. This language is used for designing the tutors' observation needs in TEL system. Tutors can create and reuse their own indicators on the basis of a strong re-ingineering process.

The system ABSTRACT (Analysis of Behaviour and Situation for menTal Representation Assessment and Cognitive acTivitiy modeling) [18] is used to analyse human activity through a path of transformations starting at a low level of observation (primary trace). Transformations are based on SPARQL rules and can be reused in different contexts. Abstract provided the possibility to visualize traces and their transformations.

The TBS-IM (Trace Based System Indicators Moodle) [7] allows the creation of individual and collective indicators for educational activities on the learning platform Moodle. TBS-IM supports the user in the elaboration of indicators using successive abstraction steps for their construction. These indicators calculations are managed for the purpose of reuse.

These approaches are similar to our research objective. They are all based on the principle of using and reusing of transformation steps for abstracting a low level trace to build higher levels of knowledge. They demonstrate some differences and limitations: in [17], there is nothing to assist the tutors in the creation of the transformations rules; [1] as [7] proposed to facilitate the generation and the re-use of indicators but do not allow to view the activity on different levels of abstraction; ABSTRACT [18] does not allow transformation with several rules.

These approaches do not fit all the searched properties but Tatiana [17] and ABSTRACT [18] are the most flexible, facilitating explicit analysis and knowledge sharing regardless of a domain or an e-learning framework. Both approaches are based on the concept of modelled trace and transformation rules as proposed by the SILEX[2] team [19]. Our approach is based on these concepts too.

4 Contributions

A Modelled Trace, noted *M-Trace*, is a set of observed elements associated with the trace model itself. We call *observed element*, noted *obsel* any structured information generated from the observation of user activity on digital environment [18]. In our research context, the observed activity is a training simulation on a NPP FSS of EDF. The collected obsels comes from users interactions (trainees and tutors) with the FSS, and from the simulation of the NPP process itself. Formally, each observed element has a *type*, a *label* and a *time stamp* in the M-Trace. According to his type an obsel can have a set of attributes/values, which characterizes it. An obsel can potentially be in relation with other obsels of the same M-Trace through some *relation type* defined in the Trace Model. The Trace Model defines the types of observed elements (i.e. the attributes that

[2] http://liris.cnrs.fr/silex.

characterize them) and the types of relationships they can have between them. A Modelled Trace is then a structure of data (obsels and relations) explicitly associated with its trace model. Modelled Traces are managed with a Trace-Based Management System (TBMS) [19]. The TBMS manages a base of M-Traces (storage, rights management, index...) and their transformations. Transformations on M-Traces are operations as applying filters, rewriting and aggregating elements, etc. for interpreting and abstracting some M-Trace (source) in an other M-Trace (transformed trace). In turn, any transformed trace can be the source of an other transformation.

4.1 Visual Synthesis of the Activity

As stated before, the data collected during a simulation session are difficult to analyse. We distinguish four different levels of M-traces:

- Raw level (Primary M-Trace) (A) which represent obsels built directly from data provided by the simulator;
- Level "Pedagogical Objectives" (C), which represents the first level of expected obsels that trainees have to realize and tutors to check;
- Level "Pedagogical Objectives Families" (E). This higher M-Trace shows obsels that describe "pedagogical objectives family" (realized or not) as expressions of the expected trainees' capacities.
- Level "General Pedagogical Objectives" (G), reflects the necessary fundamental knowledge common to all trainee's role in Nuclear Power Plant: Operator, Supervisor, Safety personnal, etc.

These different levels of M-traces are obtained by applying rule-based transformations.

These rules make explicit the observation knowledge of tutors-experts. As shown in Fig. 2, each obsel belonging to a trace of level n is connected to its origin obsel(s) in the trace of level $n-1$. The obsels of the Primary M-Trace are connected with the data collected by the simulator. Such connections allow tutors to explore, analyse the trainees' activities with a top-down investigation. It is an efficient way to understand the reasons, either individual or collective, of failure. Consequently, this is a useful support for preparing and conducting the session's debriefing with trainees.

On the other hand, it would be possible to help new tutors to improve their skills by supporting the observation process of the trainees, through a free navigation in the traces transformation graph. For example, if the tutors want to understand why the obsel "Professional Gestures" of the M-Trace of Pedagogical Objectives Family (E on the Fig. 2) is KO[3], they have just to navigate through their different origin obsels of the M-Trace of Pedagogical Objectives. According to the Rule 12, the obsel "Professional Gestures" is OK only if all of these four origin obsels are OK. Tutors can clearly see that the obsel "Professional

[3] KO means that the operator did not validate this objective.

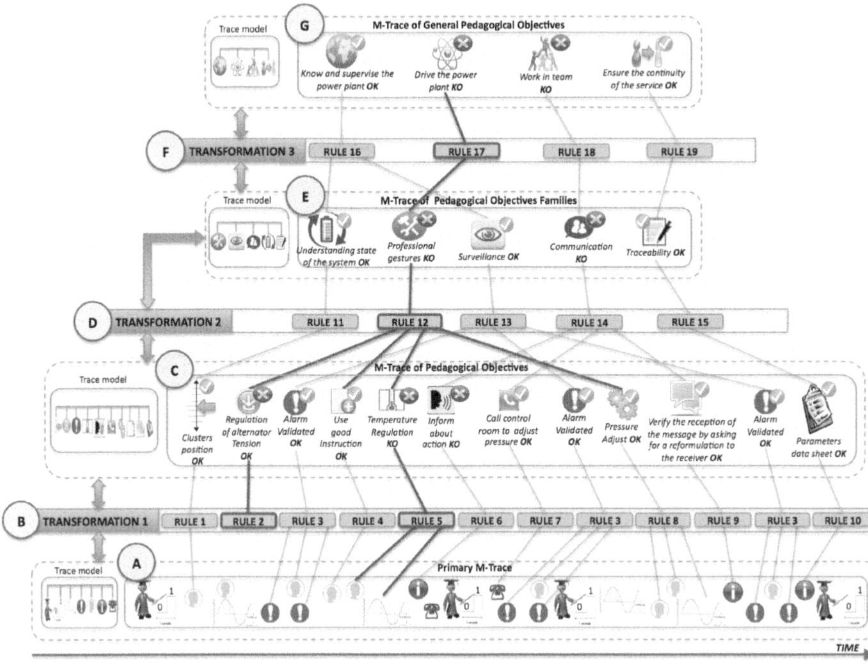

Fig. 2. Principle of analysis by transformation and visualization of trace.

Gestures" is KO because of two obsels of the M-Trace of Pedagogical Objectives (C on the Fig. 2). One of this obsel wasn't realized and the other wasn't correctly realized. For this last one tutors can continue to explore the origins of the action directly in the Primary M-Trace.

4.2 Generic Trace Model

Whatever the level of M-Trace, its model and the used simulator , we believe that a simulation M-Trace must get a specific identifier to be locatable and usable over time. This "identity card" of the M-Trace would be particularly useful for providing context during large-scale statistical research and/or analysis on a set of M-Trace corpus, and particularly to feed experience feedback, described in the Trace-Based framework presented in [20]. Through experience feedback, tutors try to understand good or bad practices on several simulations in order to improve contents of the future training sessions.

As described in the class diagram of Fig. 3, all the M-Traces of our model have an ID, a beginning and an end date, a level of M-Trace (Primary, Pedagogical Objectives,...), a type of simulator, a type of training (Initial or Retraining), a category (Summative, Formative), with the scenario of simulation and the training program (Op Reactor, Op Turbine,...). In our context, the obsels are built from direct and automatic observations of users' interactions (trainees and

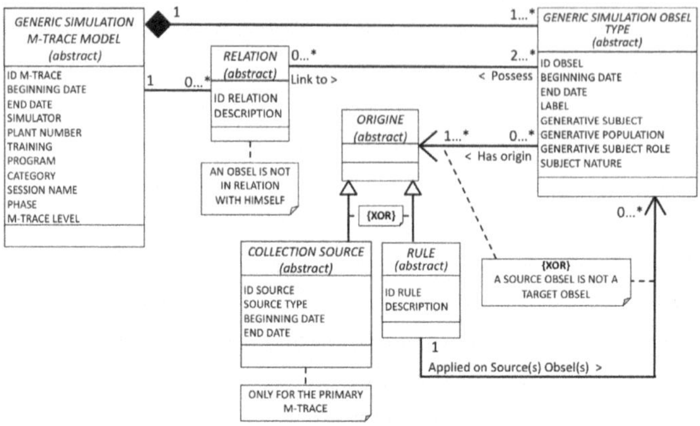

Fig. 3. Generic trace model.

tutors) with the FSS, and the message of the NPP simulation process (Primary M-Trace) or from transformations (M-Trace of Pedagogical Objectives, M-Trace of Pedagogical Objectives Family and M-Trace of General Pedagogical Objectives). Therefore, each obsel type has common attributes: an ID, a begin and an end date, a label, the ID of the Generative subject (Person, Group, Simulator), a SubjectNature (evaluated or not), the RoleSubject (Op Reactor, Op Turbine, Supervisor, etc.) and a realization attribute (OK or KO). This model can be designed for each M-Trace model as needed.

4.3 Transformation Model

Transformation allows generating a target trace of level n from a source trace of level $n - 1$. Each Transformation is composed of a set of rules which have a part *Condition* and a part *Construction* (Fig. 4). The condition part expresses constraints on the elements (obsel type, relationship type, values of attribute, etc.) of the M-Trace(s) source(s).

The construction part allows defining the obsel and the relationships of the new target M-Trace if all the constraints of the condition part are satisfied. For each part of a rule (condition and construction), it's possible to use specific operators as arithmetic, boolean and/or comparison in order to express constraints on the attribute values of sources obsels (condition) or make calculations to initialize the values of the attributes of the obsel target (construction).

4.4 D3KODE

D3KODE[4] as "Define, Discover, and Disseminate Knowledge from Observation to Develop Expertise" is a Web application, which stores and transforms traces according to the organization and the models presented in previous sections.

[4] http://liris.cnrs.fr/d3kode.

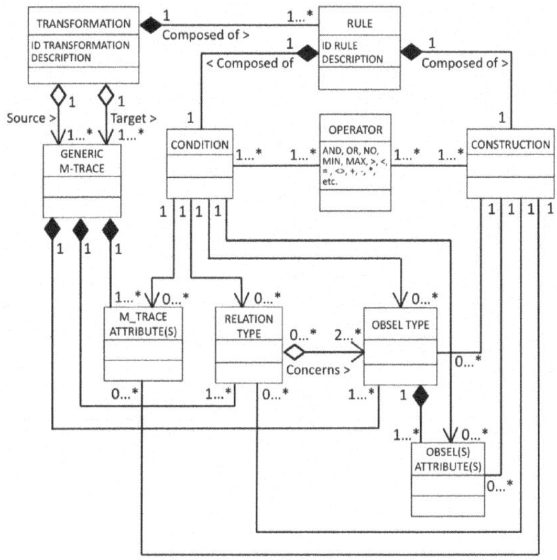

Fig. 4. Transformation model.

D3KODE also allows the user to interactively visualize the various trace levels. Tutors can explore the different abstraction levels for investigation and/or education purpose in order to target gaps and difficulties of each trainee.

Storage of M-Traces, transformation models and rules is based on a TBMS using the kTBS (kernel for Trace Base System) approach. The kTBS[5] is a kernel for a Trace-Based Management System architecture [19] developed by the SILEX team. Data of such a TBMS are encoded in RDF[6] (Resource Description Framework). Transformation rules are written in SPARQL1.1[7]. D3KODE is multi-user and multi-language.

Our proposals are summarized in Fig. 5.

5 Evaluation

In order to evaluate the properties of our approach we have defined an evaluation protocol based on a qualitative comparative method [21]. It consists in comparing the observation, analysis and debriefing of the trainees' activities with and without D3KODE. This evaluation was driven on a summative scenario on a FSS of an NPP of EDF Group. It mobilized 8 people : 2 confirmed tutors to drive the simulation and observe trainees, 4 trainees to drive the simulator (2 for each simulation) and 2 experts to observe the simulations and to judge the help brought by D3KODE. The trace models and transformation rules of the

[5] http://liris.cnrs.fr/sbt-dev/ktbs/.
[6] http://www.w3.org/RDF/.
[7] http://www.w3.org/TR/sparql11-query/.

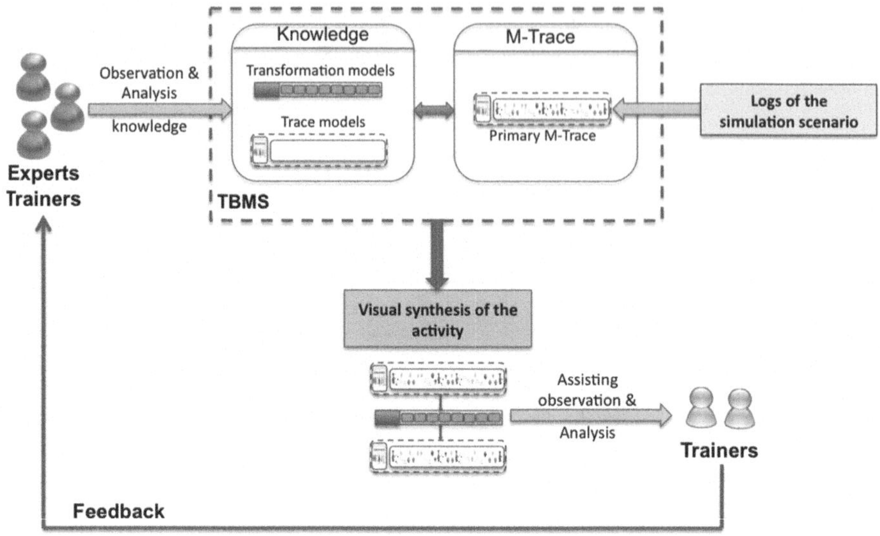

Fig. 5. Synthesis of the proposal.

scenario were modelled by an expert tutor who did not attend the evaluation step. A specific protocol was built to capture the knowledge of the expert, with interviews, videos and validation tests with D3KODE. This protocol ensures the correct evaluation of the sharing of knowledge between tutors.

5.1 Simulation with D3KODE

The first simulation lasted 1 hour and 14mn and generated 3591 obsels which were built into D3KODE. The tutors have observed 2 No Realizations (NR) tracked in the simulation logs and was observed also by D3KODE. During the analysis, the traces displayed by D3KODE were faithful to the simulation. Nevertheless, this visualization did not bring complementary information to tutors. However, tutors considered valuable and useful a quick access to information such as begin and end dates, obsel's labels, rule's descriptions, etc. This easy access facilitated the analysis and exchanges between tutors. The observation, in D3KODE, of the 2 NR was a significant contribution for the tutors. No Realization (NR) are indeed what is traditionally harder to be confirmed.

During the debriefing, D3KODE was used by tutors as a visual aid to re-trace the chronology of observation and exchange with the trainees. During this phase D3KODE has also helped to highlight a NR which was "missed" by the tutors.

5.2 Traditional Simulation

The second simulation lasted 1 hr and 13 mn. According to the evaluation protocol, D3KODE wasn't used for analysis and debriefing. During this simulation, the tutor observed 3 No Realizations (NR) tracked in the simulation logs. The analysis and debriefing phase of the operators took place in the same way that the simulation 1.

5.3 Global Analysis of the Results

The analysis of the results allowed us to collect several remarks on the contribution of D3KODE. First of all, the tutors were particularly interested in the visual synthesis of the activity on several levels. It should allow them, in the phase of analysis, to compare and verify the manual observations done during the session, in order to be sure that nothing has been missed and so to raise all ambiguities. In this way our proposal concerning the revealing of observable KO was very relevant.

This evaluation also confirmed that the approach of D3KODE, based on rules and transformations in order to share knowledge of observation and of analysis, was understood and validated by all tutors. They have also validated the interest of our approach for the creation of additional specific observations, beside the expected actions of the senario, to attend their analysis and decision on the conduct of trainees. D3KODE could, for example, be used for post-analysis and calculations that tutors cannot do in real time and/or during the analysis step.

For the debriefing step, the main contribution of D3KODE lies in the factual data presented through the visual synthesis of the activity. This functionality is considered by the tutors as a good mean to encourage self-analysis for the trainees and highlights what could be next improvements.

Globally, the evaluation of D3KODE in ecological condition demonstrated that the tutors considered the contribution of D3KODE as relevant to enrich and support their activity. D3KODE could strengthen the current tools of the follow-up and the analysis of the trainees' activities mainly *a posteriori*.

At a wider scale, D3KODE would be of a particular interest to analyse large volumes of traces of simulation to discover recurring errors of the trainees and to integrate them to the experience feedback and to design more adapted trainings. It is important to point out that, if tutors consider D3KODE as potentially beneficial, they pointed out that the use of D3KODE would introduce a change in their practices.

6 Conclusion

This article addresses the problem of observing and analysing trainees' behaviour on Nuclear Power Plant Full-Scope Simulator. This work, conducted in partnership with the UFPI of EDF Group, is applied in the context of training and maintaining the knowledge and skills of NPP control room staff. The objective of our work is to propose models and tools to support tutors tasks of capitalizing and sharing their observation experience and their analysis knowledge. The general result is improving observation, analysis and debriefing of trainees' activities during formative/summative assessment.

The approach we proposed is to transform the raw traces, based on data collected from the simulator, in order to extract high level information on the activities of trainees. For this we have proposed a dedicated trace model and transformation models. In order to guarantee the navigation between various levels of M-Trace, each obsel is connected to its origin.

We have developed a prototype, called D3KODE, which supports sharing of tutors' observation knowledge, and which stores, processes and visualizes the traces. This prototype implements the various models we have created. To validate our approach, we have conducted an evaluation based on a comparative method. This evaluation was conducted with a team of tutors from UFPI of EDF Group in an ecological context. The result of the evaluation demonstrated that our approach was favourably welcomed by the tutors and could be actually relevant to enrich their activity.

Our future work will address the second objective of the project: exploitation of traces for experience feedback to refine the needs and optimize training programs for fitting new needs and technologies.

Acknowledgements. This research work is financed by the ANRT and the UFPI of EDF Group. The authors thank all the tutors of the UFPI for their help.

References

1. Ngoc, D.P.T., Iksal, S., Choquet, C., Klinger, E.: Utl-cl: a declarative calculation language proposal for a learning tracks analysis process. In: Ninth IEEE International Conference on Advanced Learning Technologies, ICALT 2009, pp. 681–685 (2009)
2. Wan, A., Sadiq, S., Li, X.: On improving learning outcomes through sharing of learning experiences. In: 2010 IEEE 10th International Conference on Advanced Learning Technologies (ICALT), pp. 461–463 (2010)
3. Konert, J., Gobel, S., Richter, K., Bruder, R.: Knowledge sharing in the classroom: a social network approach for diagnostic assessment and learning together. In: 2011 11th IEEE International Conference on Advanced Learning Technologies (ICALT), pp. 350–354 (2011)
4. May, M., George, S., Prévot, P.: Travis to enhance online tutoring and learning activities: real time visualization of students tracking data. Int. J. Interact. Technol. Smart Educ. **8**, 52–69 (2011)
5. Popescu, E., Cioiu, D.: Instructor support for monitoring and visualizing students' activity in a social learning environment. In: ICALT 2012 - International Conference on Advanced Learning Technologies and Technology-Enhanced Learning, Rome (2012)
6. Sehaba, K.: Sharing experiences between learners with different profiles: adaptation of interaction traces. In: 2012 IEEE 12th International Conference on Advanced Learning Technologies (ICALT), pp. 488–492 (2012)
7. Djouad, T., Mille, A., Reffay, C., Benmohammed, M.: A new approach based on modelled traces to compute collaborative and individual indicators human interaction. In: ICALT 2010, 10th IEEE International Conference on Advanced Learning Technologies, pp. 53–54, Sousse, 5–7 July 2010

8. Zendagui, B.: How to support the specification of observation needs by instructional designers: a learning-scenario-centered approach. In: Cress, U., Dimitrova, V., Specht, M. (eds.) EC-TEL 2009. LNCS, vol. 5794, pp. 738–743. Springer, Heidelberg (2009)
9. Nonaka, I.: A dynamic theory of organizational knowledge creation. Organ. Sci. **5**, 14–37 (1994)
10. Wang, S., Noe, R.A.: Knowledge sharing: a review and directions for future research. Hum. Res. Manag. Rev. **20**, 115–131 (2010)
11. Theureau, J.: Nuclear reactor control room simulators: human factors research and development. Cogn. Technol. Work **2**, 97–105 (2000). doi:10.1007/s101110050031
12. Blanc, K.L.L., Boring, R.L., Gertman, D.I.: Review of methods related to assessing human performance in nuclear power plant control room simulations. In: Proceedings of the Seventh American Nuclear Society International Topical Meeting on Nuclear Plant Instrumentation, Control and Human-Machine Interface Technologies NPIC and HMIT, Las Vegas, pp. 411–422 (2010)
13. IAEA: use of control room simulators for training of nuclear power plant personnel. Report 36017984, International Atomic Energy Agency, Vienna (2004)
14. Dunand, R., Dravers, F., Guillermard, J.: Sepia : un système d'enseignement par intelligence artificielle pour les opérateurs d'edf. Revue Générale Nucléaire **3**, 254–257 (1989)
15. Bass, E.J.: Architecture for an intelligent instructor pilot decision support system. In: IEEE International Conference on Systems, Man, and Cybernetics. vol. 1, pp. 891–896, San Diego (1998)
16. Joab, M., Auzende, O., Futtersack, M., Bonnet, B., Le Leydour, P.: Computer aided evaluation of trainee skills on a simulator network. In: Cerri, S.A., Gouardéres, G., Paraguaçu, F. (eds.) ITS 2002. LNCS, vol. 2363, p. 521. Springer, Heidelberg (2002)
17. Dyke, G., Lund, K., Girardot, J.: Tatiana: an environment to support the CSCL analysis process. In: Proceedings of the 8th International Conference on Computer Supported Collaborative Learning, CSCL 2009, vol. 1, pp. 58–67, Rhodes, 8–13 June 2009
18. Georgeon, O., Mille, A., Bellet, T., Mathern, B., Ritter, F.: Supporting activity modelling from activity traces. Expert Syst. **29**(3), 261–275 (2011)
19. Settouti, L.S., Prie, Y., Marty, J.C., Mille, A.: A trace-based system for technology-enhanced learning systems personalisation. In: The 9th IEEE International Conference on Advanced Learning Technologies (2009)
20. Champalle, O., Sehaba, K., Mille, A.: Capitalize and share observation and analysis knowledge to assist trainers in professional training with simulation case of training and skills maintain of nuclear power plant control room staff. In: Helfert, M. (ed.) CSEDU 2013–5th International Conference on Computer Supported Education, pp. 627–632 (2013)
21. Per, R., Martin, H.: Guidelines for conducting and reporting case study research in software engineering. Empir. Softw. Eng. **14**, 131–164 (2009)

Using Educational Analytics to Improve Test Performance

Owen Corrigan[1(✉)], Alan F. Smeaton[1], Mark Glynn[2], and Sinéad Smyth[3]

[1] Insight Centre for Data Analytics, Dublin City University, Glasnevin, Dublin 9, Ireland
owen.corrigan@insight-centre.org, Alan.Smeaton@DCU.ie

[2] Teaching Enhancement Unit, Dublin City University, Glasnevin, Dublin 9, Ireland

[3] School of Nursing and Human Sciences, Dublin City University, Glasnevin, Dublin 9, Ireland

Abstract. Learning analytics are being used in many educational applications in order to help students and Faculty. In our work we use *predictive* analytics, using student behaviour to predict the likely performance of end of semester final grades with a system we call PredictED. The main contribution of our approach is that our intervention automatically emailed students on a regular basis, with our prediction for the outcome of their exam performance. We targeted first year, first semester University students who often struggle with making the transition into University life where they are given much more responsibility for things like attending class, completing assignments, etc. The form of student behaviour that we used is students' levels and types of engagement with the University's Virtual Learning Environment (VLE), Moodle. We mined the Moodle access log files for a range of parameters based on temporal as well as content access, and use machine learning techniques to predict likely pass/fail, on a weekly basis throughout the semester using logs and outcomes from previous years as training material. We chose ten first-year modules with reasonably high failure rates, large enrolments and stability of module content across the years to implement an early warning system on. From these modules 1,558 students were registered for one of these modules. They were offered the chance to opt into receiving weekly email alerts warning them about their likely outcome. Of these 75 % or 1,181 students opted into this service. Pre-intervention there were no differences between participants and non-participants on a number of measures related to previous academic record. However, post-intervention the first-attempt final grade performance yielded nearly 3 % improvement (58.4 % to 61.2 %) on average for those who opted in. This tells us that providing weekly guidance and personalised feedback to vulnerable first year students, automatically generated from monitoring of their online behaviour, has a significant positive effect on their exam performance.

Keywords: Learning analytics · Mining educational data · Predictive analytics · Machine learning

© Springer International Publishing Switzerland 2015
G. Conole et al. (Eds.): EC-TEL 2015, LNCS 9307, pp. 42–55, 2015.
DOI: 10.1007/978-3-319-24258-3_4

1 Introduction

Automated, weekly, personalised emails to students is an excellent adjunct to support from the Lecturer, tutors, lab supervisors or other student supports, but even with these in place, it is inevitable that some students will *slip through the cracks* because of the sheer numbers of students on some modules. As a motivating example, consider a lecturer who teaches a first year engineering module with +200 students. The lecturer may not have the time to deal with individual students, or be able to identify who needs help most urgently. If we automatically identify which students are struggling based on the characteristics of their online behaviour, then we could contact them directly and provide them with the resources they need to succeed. If we provide continuous feedback then they can monitor their own progress. The earlier we can intervene with students, the better.

In our University, students take written exams after taking a module, which is a 12-week course in a subject (e.g. Introduction to Law). Each module that we work with is at least partially graded based on a final end-of-semester written examination percentage mark.

We took data generated from students' online behaviour, and useed it to improve their learning experience and specifically, their performance in end-of-semester written examinations. We used log data from the University's online virtual learning environment, Moodle. We then combined this with past exam performance to build a predictor which accurately classifies whether a student in the current cohort of students is likely to pass or fail the module. Section 3 describes how this classifier was built.

This classifier leverages online behaviour and examination outcomes from past students, in order to inform current students as to how they are progressing. We target University students in their first semester when they are most vulnerable and often feel lost or overwhelmed by what is for most, a sudden change to University life. We use past, and present, log data to predict likely outcomes on a weekly basis and naturally the accuracy of our predictions is likely to get more accurate as the module progresses. As a form of alerting, students receive emails each week that advises them to study more, that they really need to study more, or that they seem to be doing OK, whatever is appropriate. Section 4 describes how the details of this intervention worked in practice.

For nine of the ten modules for which we ran the alerting service, examination consisted of a composite of continuous assessment and an end of semester exam. One subject was entirely exam based. Section 5 describes how we evaluated this experimentally and the results that we obtained.

The next section lists some related work in this area and describes how this related work compares to ours.

2 Related Work

There are several examples of using students' online behaviour to either monitor student performance or predict their performance in exams. The Open University ran a project to identify "at-risk" students in order to improve retention [9] and this complements our work in several ways. Similarly to our project, they used predictive modelling with inputs being engagement with VLE resources, assessment performance, previous exam performance and demographics of the students. However in their study they found that demographics play a less important role than VLE engagement. They also found that the best approach is to analyse data on a module-by-module fashion instead of across all modules, the same approach as we have taken.

The size of the Open University study is impressive, with 7,000 students targeted across three modules, whereas our study targeted 1,200 students across 11 modules. Their prediction target was similar to ours as they predicted failures in a module at regular intervals during semester, specifically, every time there was an exam. In contrast, our interval was weekly and our approach differs from theirs in several ways. They deal with a much wider variety of students, many working part full-time while doing modules, whereas ours were a more homogeneous set of students. However the main difference between approaches is that the Open University work predicted the set of students most in need of help, and left it up to the module organiser to intervene. In our work we alerted all students on the module directly, to inform them of their progress and likely outcome.

An influential early paper by Romero, Ventura and Garcia [8] describes a four-step framework for analysing VLE data. These steps are: collect data, process data, perform data mining/machine learning steps and deploy results. It also describes how data mining and machine learning methods can be applied to the data. That paper inspired the Purdue Signals project [1] which takes a variety of factors such as points on the module to date (which are assigned by the module instructor), time spent on a particular task and past performance in other exams. It then uses this to predict what a students score will be. The Purdue Signals project uses a different mechanism to deliver predictions compared to our work, although both are targeting the student. In the Purdue Signals system, students can see how well they are doing via a web application showing if they are classified as "green", "orange" or "red" for a given module. Another differentiating aspect is that our work uses the VLE data in a different way, updating the predictions automatically every week.

In a paper by Calvo-Flores et al. [2], the authors also predicted user exam performance based on VLE log data. Their aim was to find students who are in need of learning reinforcement. This work established that features derived from the access logs were enough to predict success with a high degree of confidence. Some of the features that they use are ratio of resources viewed and total resource views. In their case they tested it on a module with over 240 students and had a prediction accuracy of above 80 %. Our paper uses some of these same features, but we retrain our model for each week, allowing us to recalculate predictions on a weekly basis, which make our insights more actionable.

In [3] the authors performed a statistical analysis on the access logs of a VLE for three modules. They examined many features extracted from these access logs, checking if they were correlated with the final exam mark the students achieved. These features included VLE activity, unique page views, number of log ins, whether they were on or off campus, the coverage of resources the students accessed, and the effect of accessing Moodle on different days of the week. This work was useful in establishing which features would be useful to extract from the logs.

Similarly, in [4] work by Cocea and Weibelzah on feature extraction was an influence on ours. The features used in this study include number of pages accessed, time spent reading pages and student performance on mid-semester tests. Even though they were using a VLE targeted at one particular module, the features used were similar to ours. However their objective was different, with their goal being to estimate learners' levels of motivations.

In the next section we describe the raw data we used, how we processed it to extract features and train a series of machine learning classifiers, and then applied it to live student behaviour logs in order to alert students directly.

3 Data Analysis

3.1 Periodicity of VLE Logs

The basis for student behaviour that we used to feed our performance predictions was students' online interaction with the VLE, Moodle. By default, Moodle records every instance of a student accessing a Moodle page of any kind and records the page, date and time, the student identifier, and the IP address of the device used to access. In order to predict performance we need to be able to train on past student performance where the outcome is known and hence we need to work with modules where every year the log files follow the same patterns of access. Each module, by its very nature, will have different access frequency patterns which are influenced by scheduling of lectures, lab sessions, group sessions, mid-semester tests, assessment deadlines and final exams. Plotting the overall student activity for each module by simply counting the number of student accesses allows us to determine visually if the module displays an annual periodicity. This is useful for us in determining the set of modules for which there is enough training material from past years which can be used. For instance, if a module drastically changed in content or in delivery within the last year or two because a new lecturer took over and removed class tests, this would show up in the activity levels and would mean that because the training material has changed, that module would not be suitable as a basis for making weekly predictions. Other changes which do not affect scheduling of the module, such as adding additional content or modifying an exam, would not show up in these access or usage as much. We will compensate for this later by building a classifier and cross-validating the results of the classifier's prediction accuracy. If the prediction accuracy results are poor, perhaps because the course has changed so much that our models are not useful, then we would not use that model.

Figures 1 and 2 show the aggregate activity levels for all students over the past five years and each demonstrates a regular annual periodicity meaning that

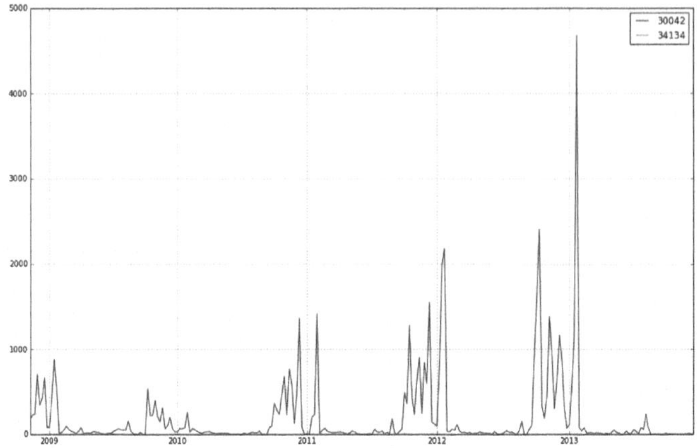

Fig. 1. Activity levels for module CA103 (Computer Systems Hardware)

student accesses from previous years, coupled with the performance of those students in those previous years, provides suitable training material for classifying this year's cohort of students.

3.2 Data Preparation

We initially receive Moodle logs in a format which contains the user id, module, timestamp, IP address and the Moodle resource being accessed. To this we add the result that each student obtained in the written end-of-semester exam,

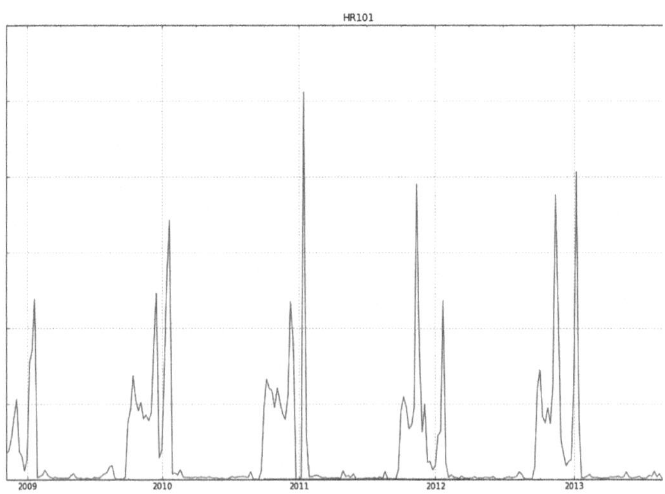

Fig. 2. Activity levels for module HR101 (Psychology in Organisations)

which constitutes the largest part of how the overall grade for the module is computed. However we then have to transform this raw data by extracting a set of features associated with each student and module which, in particular, focuses on temporal information associated with the logs.

3.3 Feature Extraction

We processed the Moodle logs by extracting a variety of features for each students' access to each module, in each year. One of the benefits of the support vector machine (SVM) [7] we used to build the classifiers, as described later, is that not all of these features have to be actually useful in terms of discriminating different forms of student outcome for the module. That means we can be open-minded about how we represent students' online behaviour and if a feature is not discriminative, the SVM learns this from the training material, i.e. from student data from previous years. We extracted the following three features from the logs

- A simple count of how many logs each student accessed.
- The average time that the logs were accessed.
- The ratio of clicks on weekends vs. weekdays.
- The ratio of on campus to off campus accesses. This was determined using the IP address.

We needed to take into account the fact that we would be downloading the logs as a constant stream. We updated the predictions once a week with the new data obtained. When training we added an additional column to the log data, which was the academic week number that the log took place. We then divided the log data into 12 separate columns, depending on which week it took place in and filtering out any accesses which took place after week 12. In the next section we will discuss how this was used in classification.

Corresponding to each student and set of features, we extract a student result. This was a simple binary variable, either a pass or a fail.

3.4 Classification

Once the features were extracted for past deliveries of modules, we built a set of classifiers, one for each week of semester and right up to the week of the final examination, which predict the student's likely pass/fail in the end-of-semester final grade. In most of the University's modules the examination pass rate is between 70 % and 95 % and so an issue with the data is that because passes are a lot more common than fails we need to re-sample the data so that the prediction result is not biased towards the most common case. Another issue is that there can be a lot of features and not a huge amount of students and so we have to be wary of over-fitting and choose modules which have large numbers of students.

To determine the accuracy of our predictions we used the Receiver Operator Characteristic Area Under Curve (ROC AUC) relevance measure [5]. We used this because it is more resilient to imbalanced classes than other measures, such as simple accuracy. An ROC AUC score greater than 0.5 is better than random. In evaluating the usefulness of different feature combinations we use cross-validation and because the number of samples can be small we use 5-fold validation which reduces the variability of the obtained prediction accuracy score.

Using the SciKit-Learn library [6] an SVM for classification was created. It was initialized with the following settings.

- A 'C' value of 0.1 was found to work well;
- A linear kernal was chosen;
- Probability estimates were enabled so that the ROC score could be generated. These also allowed us to rank the students in order of our predictions as to their likelihood of pass/fail for the module;
- The class weights were set to be inversely proportional to the class frequencies. This helped address the over-fitting problem.

Training the classifier involves

- Fitting the classifier with 80 % of the historic log data. The features are the from the features listed above. The target variable is whether the student passed the module that year.
- Testing the remaining 20 % of the historic log data and generating a prediction and a confidence score.
- Comparing these confidence scores with the known target variable to calculate the AUC ROC score
- Repeating this process with a different 20 % test set and taking the average to give a more accurate score.

We then trained 12 separate classifiers, one for each week of semester. This involved repeating the above proceedure 12 times. The classifier for the first week only contained the first week of data. The second including the first two weeks of data (to represent the situation in the second week), and so on. Each week 4 new features are added to the total number of features, so that by the end of week 12 we were making predictions based on 48 features in total.

To determine how effective a the set of 12 classifiers are over the semester, and to gauge at which point during the semester it is reliable enough for us to begin sending alerts, we calculate this measure for classifiers built for each of the 12 weeks of access log data that we have extracted features for. The features are then scaled using the standard score, and the transformation is saved so that it can be applied to the live data later.

As a rough heuristic, if the resulting ROC AUC value is at or below 0.5, we judge that the classifier is not performing better than random. Once this line is above 0.5 consistently, we regard the classifier as working. In our case, the best modules typically have a value between 0.6 to 0.7 for the weeks following week 3 or 4 of our 12-week teaching semester. This helps us to determine what week to start sending the predictions to students, and also to compare the performance of different classification algorithms on the same data. For examples, see Figs. 3 and 4. For the SS103 module, we decided that the ROC AUC score was consistently above 0.5 from week 3 onwards, so we started the email interventions then. For the MS136 module, the predictions were better earlier on, and so we started sending thise predictions to students in week 2.

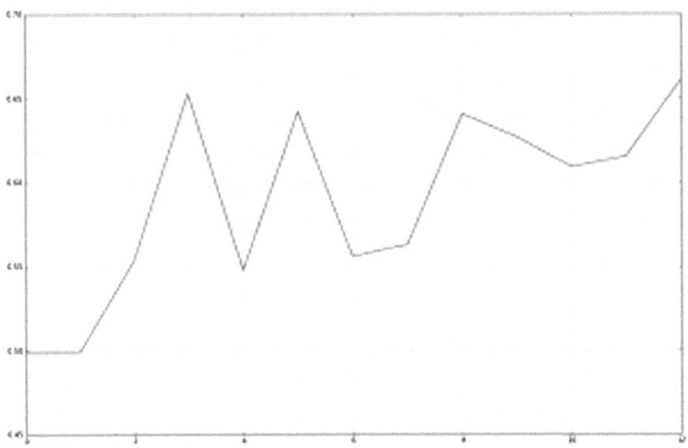

Fig. 3. Prediction accuracy for SS103 (Physiology for Health Sciences) by week

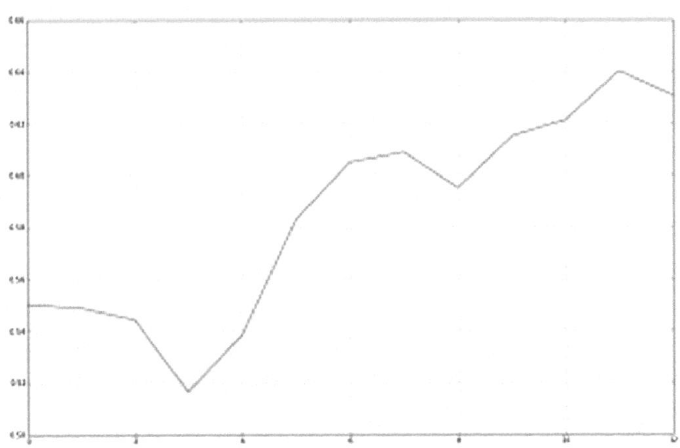

Fig. 4. Prediction accuracy for MS136 by week (Mathematics for Economics and Business)

3.5 Selecting Modules

We ran this procedure of assessing the suitability of modules across all of the larger modules given to first year students in Semester one in the university and then filtered them based on a number of criteria. The first is that there must be a minimum amount of students in a module, which we chose, to be 80 in order to have enough student instances so as to make the classification worthwhile. We also wanted to have the weekly alerts delivered to the largest number of students. Secondly, since the method of predicting pass/fail will work poorly if the module has a high pass rate and thus a classification bias, we chose modules which had a pass rate of less than 90 % for the examination component. Thirdly, we could only work with modules where the Moodle logs display periodicity as described in Sect. 3.1 above. Finally, when we plot the ROC AUC values for those modules remaining, only those which have a consistent value above random for a number of weeks were kept for the study. This left us with 10 modules outlined in Table 1 and a total of 1,558 eligible student registrations once repeat students, those under 18 years of age and visiting students from other Universities were eliminated. One limitation of this process is that we cannot run this on a new module, as we require data for at least a year to create our models.

To summarise, processing the data takes place in three steps as shown on the diagram below in Fig. 5. The first involves simply getting the activity levels of the modules and filtering modules them down based on criteria discussed earlier. The second step involves extracting features and producing classifiers on previous data. The final stage involves making predictions on current log data, and emailing the results to students as an intervention.

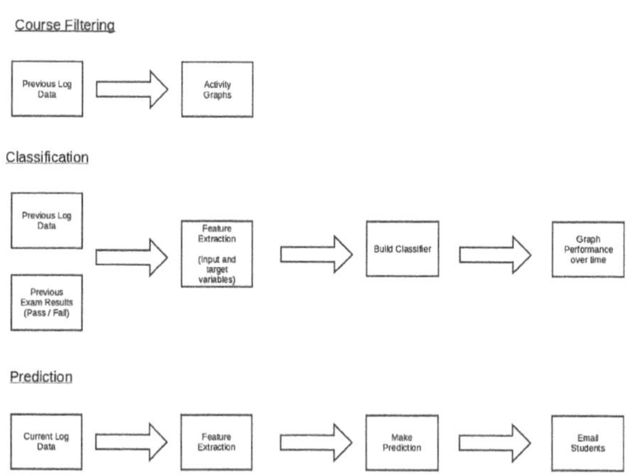

Fig. 5. Summary of data processing steps

4 Student Interventions

For each of the 10 modules in Table 1 and for each week after our predictions reach a usable accuracy, our classifier outputs a pass/fail prediction for each student taking the module, plus a confidence value for each. We used the output from this to rank students from least likely to fail to most likely to fail and we also have a tipping point or threshold pointing to the likely overall pass rate for the module. We now examine how we can use this information to feed back directly to students and to do this we tested two separate strategies.

For students in some of the modules we sent weekly emails based on our prediction of whether they would pass or fail. For each of these two groups we divided each into two more groups resulting in four groups — "bad" and "poor" for those predicted to fail, "good", and "great" for those predicted to pass. The rationale behind this is that the best way to divide the groups may be based what we think will happen with their results. Each group is sent a weekly email with "bad" for instance receiving an email saying how students need to work harder, while those in the "great" group told they are working well on the module. Each email contains pointers to resources the student can use, such as contact details for student support services and for their lecturer.

For students on each of the other set of modules, they were broken into 10 equally sized groups based on the overall prediction ranking and the emails informed each student of what percentile group among the class they fall into. The bottom 50 % of students are given a more encouraging email than the top 50 %, the idea being that students get an idea of how they are doing relative to their peers in the class. This might encourage some competition among students, incentivising them to and hopefully they would see the results of working harder sooner in the feedback loop.

Each week this process is repeated with the most recent log data downloaded from the Moodle log files. Predictions are generated for each module in the manner described above. For each week of semester, each student was sent a new email. All this was done with approval from the University's Research Ethics Committee, the University's Data Protection Officer, student services support, and the Module Co-ordinator's of the 10 modules. In addition, students were presented with a plain language statement of what their data was being used for and presented them with the choice to opt-in or opt-out of receiving the weekly alerts.

In the next section we will analyse the impact that receiving weekly prediction alerts had on student performance.

5 Results

We first examined the relationship between the scores that students obtained in their Leaving Certificate exams, equivalent to SAT tests in the United States, and whether they opted-into or out of the alerting service. For both conditions we plot both the University admission points (known as CAO points) that the student obtained in the Leaving Certificate, which is the sum of a students top six subjects (maximum 625). We also plot their grades in the exam in mathematics as that subject is regarded as a strong indicator of academic ability. We can see from Fig. 6 that there is little difference between those who opted-in to the alerting and those who opted out. This indicates no difference in the entry profiles of participants vs. non-participants overall and therefore there is no spurious relationship between the academic ability of the student and whether they opted-in to PredictED or not. This allowed us to gauge the impact the system had on students. However this opt-in method may have other issues, such as motivation differences, compared to a truly randomised group.

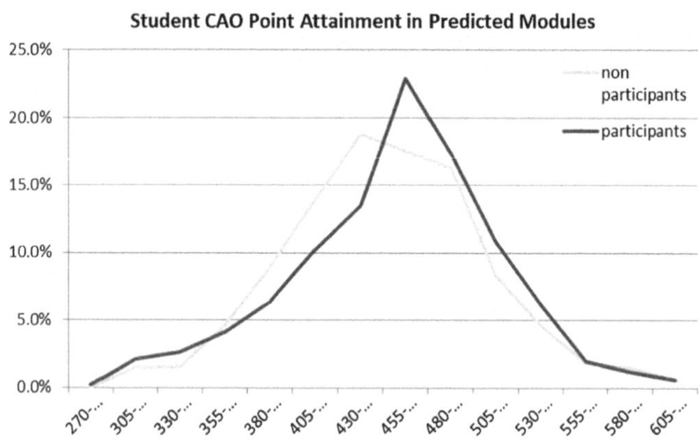

(a) CAO Points at University entry

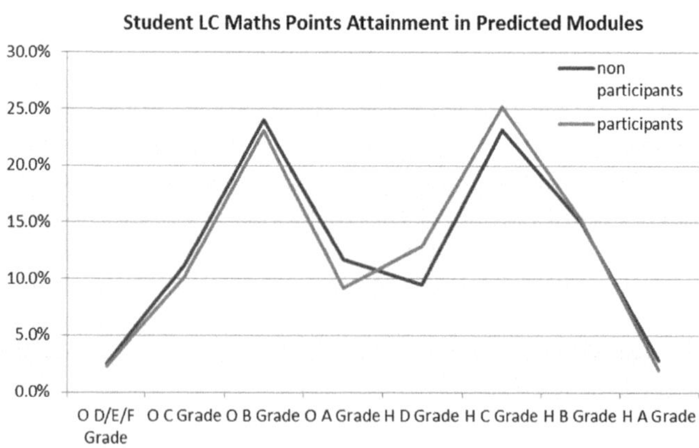

(b) LC Mathematics at University entry activity

Fig. 6. CAO points and leaving certificate mathematics results for student participants and non-participants

We also examined the relationship between the predictions that we made, and the actual results that the students ended up achieving overall. We did this by generating a binary pass or fail prediction for each student every week throughout the semester. Once the exams were over and the results available, we compared the predictions against the actual results that students achieved. We then counted the number of true positives, false positives, true negatives and false negatives and calculated the F1-score from this matrix for each week. The F1-score was used due to the highly imbalanced classes present in this results matrix and the F1-score results can be seen in Fig. 7. We can see from this figure that the F1-score remains consistently high, especially over the latter weeks of the semester.

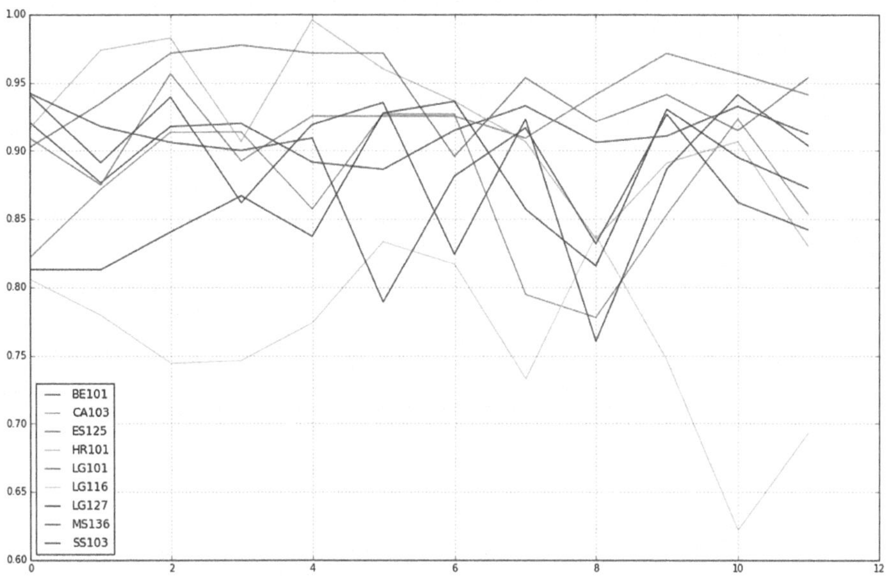

Fig. 7. F1 scores by week. Each coloured line represents a different module

The most important result that we obtained was when we looked at the difference between those who opted-in to receiving emails each week, compared to those who didn't opted-out. Table 1 shows this comparison and the last row indicates that for those who opt-in they can expect to see an average increase of +2.67 % in their actual exam marks, all other things being equal. The final column of Table 1 shows the impact of PredictED on a per-module basis with ✓✓ indicating significantly higher performance for participants (students) and ✓ indicating higher performance. This table shows that for 3 modules, BE101, HR101 and MS136, there was a significant improvement in students' exam performance while for 5 other modules there was improved performance. Only 47 students (of a possible 67) registered to take part in PredictED as part of ES125.

This low number of registrations for the module as a whole was unexpected but we decided to continue and make the weekly alerts available nonetheless. The average decrease of 0.5 % in exam performance can be discounted based on the low N for this group. One area for future research would be on what the impact of the text of the emails had on the students.

Table 1. Performance in end-of-module examination showing number of eligible students for module (Regs), and comparing average non-participants' exam mark (Non) vs. participants' average exam mark (Part.) and significance of difference between these (Signif.)

Code	Module title	Regs	Non	Part.	Signif.
BE101	Intro. to Cell Biology &Biochemistry	284	58.9 %	62.1 %	✓✓
CA103	Computer Systems Hardware	122	70.3 %	71.3 %	✓
CA168	Digital World	78	63.8 %	65.3 %	✓
ES125	Social and Personal Development with Communication Skills	47	67.0 %	66.5 %	-
HR101	Psychology in Organisations	152	59.4 %	63.3 %	✓✓
LG101	Introduction to Law	172	53.3 %	54.9 %	✓
LG116	Introduction to Politics	154	45.7 %	44.9 %	-
LG127	Business Law	288	60.6 %	61.8 %	✓
MS136	Mathematics for Economics &Business	157	60.8 %	69.4 %	✓✓
SS103	Physiology for Health Sciences	104	55.3 %	57.0 %	✓
Across all modules (weighted by participation)			**58.58 %**	**61.25 %**	✓✓

6 Conclusions

In this paper we described a method of predicting students outcomes in a first year University module or subject based on feature extraction from VLE access patterns, and the impact of feeding these predictions directly back to students on a weekly basis during semester. Our mechanism to deliver this information was to email students directly with a tailored message based on their predicted outcome for the module. A new message was sent every week to approximately 1,200 students who opted into this service, so that they could see how they are performing relative to the rest of their class. We developed a new method for constructing these predictions every week. We also demonstrated a method for evaluating which modules were best suited to this analysis.

The impact of these predictions on student performance in the end-of-semester written examinations was an average absolute increase of +2.67 % weighted by participation across the modules with 3 of 10 modules recording a significant increase and 8 of 10 modules recording increased performance. This demonstrates that we can use automated techniques to keep students informed of their progress on modules where there are a large number of students, and that when this is done then it will help students to progress.

Acknowledgements. This research was supported by Science Foundation Ireland under grant number SFI/12/RC/2289, and by Dublin City University. The authors wish to thank Aisling McKenna for her help with the statistical analysis of some of the results.

References

1. Arnold, K.E., Pistilli, M.D.: Course signals at purdue: using learning analytics to increase student success. In: Proceedings of the 2nd International Conference on Learning Analytics and Knowledge, LAK 2012, p. 267. ACM Press, New York, April 2012
2. Calvo-Flores, M.D., Galindo, E.G., Jiménez, M.C.P., Pérez, O.: Predicting students' marks from moodle logs using neural network models. In: Proceedings of the IV International Conference on Multimedia and Information and Communication Technologies in Education (M-ICTEE 2006), vol. 1, pp. 586–590 (2006)
3. Casey, K., Gibson, J.P.: (m)Oodles of data: mining moodle to understand student behaviour. In: O'Riordan, F., Toolan, F., Hernandez, R., Smyth, R., Becker, B., Casey, K., Lillis, D., McGing, G., Mulhall, M., O'Sullivan, K. (eds.) Proceedings of the 10th International Conference on Engaging Pedagogy (ICEP 2010), pp, pp. 61–71. Griffith College Dublin, Maynooth, Ireland (2010)
4. Cocea, M., Weibelzahl, S.: Can log files analysis estimate learners' level of motivation? In: LWA 2006, Lernen Wissen und Adaptivit. Lernen-Wissensentdeckung - Adaptivität, March 2006
5. Hanley, J.A., McNeil, B.J.: The meaning and use of the area under a receiver operating characteristic (ROC) curve. Radiol. **143**(1), 29–36 (1982)
6. Pedregosa, F., Varoquaux, G., Gramfort, A., Michel, V., Thirion, B., Grisel, O., Blondel, M., Prettenhofer, P., Weiss, R., Dubourg, V., Vanderplas, J., Passos, A., Cournapeau, D., Brucher, M., Perrot, M., Duchesnay, E.: Scikit-learn: machine learning in python. J. Mach. Learn. Res. **12**, 2825–2830 (2011)
7. Platt, J., et al.: Fast training of support vector machines using sequential minimal optimization. In: Advances in kernel methods: support vector learning, MIT Press, vol. 3, pp. 185–208 (1999)
8. Romero, C., Ventura, S., García, E.: Data mining in course management systems: moodle case study and tutorial. Comput. Edu. **51**(1), 368–384 (2008)
9. Wolff, A., Zdrahal, Z., Nikolov, A., Pantucek, M.: Improving retention: predicting at-risk students by analysing clicking behaviour in a virtual learning environment. In: Proceedings of the Third International Conference on Learning Analytics and Knowledge, LAK 2013, p. 145. ACM Press, New York, April 2013

Evaluation of Expert-Based Q-Matrices Predictive Quality in Matrix Factorization Models

Guillaume Durand[1(✉)], Nabil Belacel[1], and Cyril Goutte[2]

[1] National Research Council Canada,
Information and Communications Technologies, Moncton, Canada
{guillaume.durand,nabil.belacel}@nrc-cnrc.gc.ca
http://www.nrc-cnrc.gc.ca/index.html
[2] National Research Council Canada,
Information and Communications Technologies, Ottawa, Canada
cyril.goutte@nrc-cnrc.gc.ca

Abstract. Matrix factorization techniques are widely used to build collaborative filtering recommender systems. These recommenders aim at discovering latent variables or attributes that are supposed to explain and ultimately predict the interest of users. In cognitive modeling, skills and competencies are considered as key latent attributes to understand and assess student learning. For this purpose, Tatsuoka introduced the concept of Q-matrix to represent the mapping between skills and test items. In this paper we evaluate how predictive expert-created Q-matrices can be when used as a decomposition factor in a matrix factorization recommender. To this end, we developed an evaluation method using cross validation and the weighted least squares algorithm that measures the predictive accuracy of Q-matrices. Results show that expert-made Q-matrices can be reasonably accurate at predicting users success in specific circumstances that are discussed at the end of this paper.

Keywords: Cognitive models · Matrix factorization · Recommender systems · Competency-based learning

1 Introduction

Nowadays, recommender systems are extensively used. Technologies, usage and application domains including learning and education keep going further, bigger and wider. Recommenders are usually classified into two categories [10] depending on the approach they implement; content filtering or collaborative filtering. Content filtering requires the creation of user profiles to provide them with matching products. A lot of domain specific information is required. Collaborative filtering overcomes this difficulty by providing recommendations based on past actions of the users, finding similarities between them and extrapolating to future behaviors. Among collaborative filtering methods, latent factor models

© Springer International Publishing Switzerland 2015
G. Conole et al. (Eds.): EC-TEL 2015, LNCS 9307, pp. 56–69, 2015.
DOI: 10.1007/978-3-319-24258-3_5

are probably the most well known since they were popularized during the Netflix Prize. A latent factor model aims at discovering latent traits characterizing both users and their resources usage, in order to make predictions. Matrix factorization is a common technology used to perform latent traits modeling. A matrix factorization approximates a matrix R by the product of two smaller matrices Q and S, i.e., $R \approx QS = \hat{R}$. The link between latent traits modeling and cognitive diagnostic modeling, appeared obvious to many [6,19,20] since skills or competencies are latent attributes allowing to understand, assess [19,21,28] and to some extent predict [11,12,18,20] student success. The overlap between cognitive diagnostic modeling goes even further since matrix representations have been used for decades with Tatsuoka's [21] Rule-Space model and the introduction of the Q-matrix, a matrix representing the mapping between test items and skills. In this context, a matrix factorization recommender would predict the success or failure on unperformed items. Starting from a matrix R containing the results of students to items, a basic matrix factorization would produce a Q-matrix mapping test items to latent skills, and a matrix S containing the mapping between students and skills. Many researchers have recently tried to automatically generate [19,20] or improve [6,27] Q-matrices using matrix factorization methods. While the quality of the reconstruction of R is duly measured by comparing R to $\hat{R}$, the quality of the generated Q-matrix is difficult to evaluate. For instance, it is not unusual to generate a Q-matrix leading to a perfect R reconstruction but as good as chance in terms of predictive accuracy. In order to address this problem, we propose the method presented below (Sect. 3), that aims at specifically evaluating the predictive quality of a Q-matrix. We applied this method to several expert-made datasets (Sect. 4) and present our experimental results in Sect. 5.

2 Q-Matrix and Matrix Factorization

The Rule-Space model [21,24,25] was introduced in the eighties to statistically classify students items responses into a set of ideal response patterns associated to different cognitive skills. One of the major assumptions of Rule-Space is that students only need to master specific skills in order to successfully complete test items. Rule-Space aims at performing fine granularity diagnostic assessments. In its first phase, Rule-Space consists in identifying skills called attributes to create ideal response patterns. A second phase relies on statistical classification using item response analysis to map student answers to ideal response patterns. There were initially no real process specified by Rule-Space to design and develop the cognitive diagnostic assessments required by its first phase. However, Gierl et al. [7] in their tutorial proposed four sequential steps. In the first step, the (k) cognitive attributes are identified and their hierarchical relationships specified by cognitive experts. In a second step, an incidence matrix is built by considering the potential pool of items [3] representing all $(2^k - 1)$ combinations of attributes an item could evaluate. The incidence matrix also called Q-matrix is then reduced according to the attribute hierarchy. As reduction example, let's consider the skill "addition of natural numbers" as a prerequisite to the skill "addition of integers". If an item in the Q-matrix is designed to evaluate only "addition of integers", this item would be removed in the refinement process because it is deemed impossible to evaluate "addition of integers" without evaluating "addition of natural numbers". The third step consists in constructing the test items based on the reduced Q-matrix. Finally, in the fourth step, ideal item response vectors are created based on the reduced Q-matrix (Fig. 1). These ideal item response vectors are then used in the statistical pattern classification of student responses, the second phase of Rule-Space.

$$
Q = \begin{array}{c} \\ Item1 \\ Item2 \\ Item3 \\ Item4 \end{array}
\begin{array}{c} \begin{array}{cccc} Skill1 & Skill2 & Skill3 & Skill4 \end{array} \\
\begin{pmatrix} 1 & 0 & 0 & 0 \\ 0 & 1 & 0 & 0 \\ 0 & 0 & 1 & 0 \\ 0 & 0 & 0 & 1 \end{pmatrix} \end{array}
$$

Fig. 1. Example of a reduced Q-matrix with one skill per item.

To some extent, Q-matrix extraction could be seen as a Rule-Space reverse engineering exercise. The objective is to discover the Q-matrix from real response patterns having most of the time no information regarding the ideal response pattern and a very limited knowledge of the possible skills involved in the items.

The analysis starts from the result matrix R and approximates it as a product of Q-matrix and student matrix S:

$$R \approx Q \times S. \tag{1}$$

The estimates of Q and S minimize the reconstruction error $\| \hat{R} - R \|$ between R and its estimate $\hat{R} = Q \times S$. As explained by Desmarais and Naceur [6] this factorization correspond to a specific interpretation of the Q-matrix called *compensatory*. A compensatory Q-matrix assumes that each skill adds to the item success. Other interpretations include the *conjunctive* Q-matrix, which assumes that *all* skills in an item row are necessary for success, and the *disjunctive* Q-matrix, which assumes that knowledge of *any* skill in the row yields success. The conjunctive Q-matrix is widely used [1,6], and as noted by Desmarais et al. [5], it may be solved by applying the standard factorization to the Boolean negation of the result matrix $\neg R$ as:

$$\neg R \approx Q \times \neg S \tag{2}$$

The matrix factorization framework can therefore be applied to model conjunctive as well as compensatory Q-matrices making our method for evaluating and validating a Q-matrix relevant over a wider range of assumptions.

Algorithm 1. Q-matrix cross validation evaluation algorithm.

Data:
R: Result Matrix
Q: Q-matrix to evaluate
N: Number of cross validation folds
Result: Performance: The estimator Root Mean Square Error
$Performance \longleftarrow 0$
$Mask \longleftarrow$Mask of size R randomly populated by integers 1..N
for $Mask_i \in Mask$ **do**
  $Weight \longleftarrow$ matrix of size R populated by 1
  $Weight(Mask == i) \longleftarrow 0$
  $S \longleftarrow \text{wsolve}(R, Q, Weight)$
  $\hat{R} \longleftarrow Q \times S$
  $Performance \longleftarrow Performance + performance(R, \hat{R}, 1 - Weight)$
$Performance \longleftarrow Performance/N$

3 Q-Matrix Evaluation Method and Validation

The evaluation considers both conjunctive and compensatory factorization models (Eqs. 1–2). Assuming R (or $\neg R$) and Q known, we evaluate how well Q would predict missing values through a classical 10-fold cross validation algorithm detailed in *Algorithm 1.*

To obtain S we defined the function *wsolve* that uses a least squares method provided by the function Matlab *mldivide* ($S = Q \setminus R$) that solves the system or linear equations $Q \times x = R$. The function *wsolve* extends the function *mldivide* by taking into account a weight matrix that is a boolean matrix of the size of R having 0 where missing values are injected by the cross validation masks ($Mask_i$). *Wsolve* is an implementation of the *weighted least squares* method[1]. Instead of using directly the $Weight$ matrix, we calculate $w = \sqrt{Weight}$ and solve column by column k system $(w_k . \times Q) \times s_k = (w_k . \times r_k)$ with *mldivide*. Thus equations containing missing values are not used in the solving of the system.

Matlab offers many alternatives to weighted least squares like using the function *fminsearch* [26] implementing the Nelder-Mead optimization method over a cost function. The Nelder-Mead [14] algorithm is based on the simplex method for finding a local minimum. Using Nelder-Mead proved to be particularly inefficient in our case because of the slow convergence rate. An improvement over the simplex approach would have been to consider a simple or a conjugate gradient algorithm. However, gradients approach would not have been as fast as our analytic approach. Most results detailed in the following sections were obtained almost instantly on an average office laptop.

To validate our evaluation method, we used simulated data by defining a Q-matrix as shown in Fig. 2 and a matrix S detailing learners abilities.

[1] Weighted least squares method:http://en.wikipedia.org/wiki/Least_squares#Weighted_least_squares.

$$
Q = \begin{array}{c} \\ Item1 \\ Item2 \\ Item3 \\ Item4 \\ Item5 \\ Item6 \\ Item7 \\ Item8 \\ Item9 \\ Item10 \\ Item11 \\ Item12 \\ Item13 \\ Item14 \\ Item15 \end{array}
\begin{array}{c} \begin{array}{cccc} Skill1 & Skill2 & Skill3 & Skill4 \end{array} \\
\left(\begin{array}{cccc}
1 & 0 & 0 & 0 \\
0 & 1 & 0 & 0 \\
0 & 0 & 1 & 0 \\
0 & 0 & 0 & 1 \\
1 & 1 & 0 & 0 \\
1 & 0 & 1 & 0 \\
0 & 1 & 1 & 0 \\
1 & 1 & 1 & 0 \\
1 & 0 & 0 & 1 \\
0 & 1 & 0 & 1 \\
1 & 1 & 0 & 1 \\
0 & 0 & 1 & 1 \\
1 & 0 & 1 & 1 \\
0 & 1 & 1 & 1 \\
1 & 1 & 1 & 1
\end{array} \right) \end{array}
$$

Fig. 2. Q-matrix containing all the possible items ($2^4 - 1$) with 4 skills.

The student matrix S encodes the skills that each student has acquired. Students may have acquired anything between 0 and K of these skills, so the mapping is always "1-N" (with N possibly 0).

Assuming binary values, the simplest student matrix encoding all combinations of skills is presented in Fig. 3.

$$
S = \begin{array}{c} \\ Skill1 \\ Skill2 \\ Skill3 \\ Skill4 \end{array}
\begin{array}{c} \begin{array}{cccccccccccccccc} A & B & C & D & E & F & G & H & I & J & K & L & M & N & O & P \end{array} \\
\left(\begin{array}{cccccccccccccccc}
0 & 1 & 0 & 1 & 0 & 1 & 0 & 1 & 0 & 1 & 0 & 1 & 0 & 1 & 0 & 1 \\
0 & 0 & 1 & 1 & 0 & 0 & 1 & 1 & 0 & 0 & 1 & 1 & 0 & 0 & 1 & 1 \\
0 & 0 & 0 & 0 & 1 & 1 & 1 & 1 & 0 & 0 & 0 & 0 & 1 & 1 & 1 & 1 \\
0 & 0 & 0 & 0 & 0 & 0 & 0 & 0 & 1 & 1 & 1 & 1 & 1 & 1 & 1 & 1
\end{array} \right) \end{array}
$$

Fig. 3. Student matrix with all the possible student-skills mapping.

There are several ways of combining the information in the Q-matrix and student matrix, depending on how we combine the item line in Q and the student column in S:

1. Conjunctive: The student needs to have all the skills in the item to succeed.
2. Compensatory: The more required skills the student has, the more likely she is to succeed.
3. Disjunctive: The student succeeds if he has any of the skills necessary for the item. However, *"disjunctive models are closely related to compensatory models, in which lacking certain attributes can be compensated for by possessing other attributes"* [30].

While disjunctive approaches didn't appear relevant to us since we didn't find in the literature examples of disjunctive Q-matrix generations and because of its link with the compensatory case, we limited the validation of the evaluation method to the compensatory and conjunctive approaches creating the R matrices illustrated by Fig. 4. The compensatory matrix R_a has non-binary values and cells contain the probability of success. This matrix was calculated so that a student mastering one skill out of the two required is predicted to have 50 % chances of success. As R matrices in cognitive modeling are usually binary matrices, matrix R_b has been obtained by applying a threshold of .5 on R_a, converting values above this threshold to one and inferior values to 0.

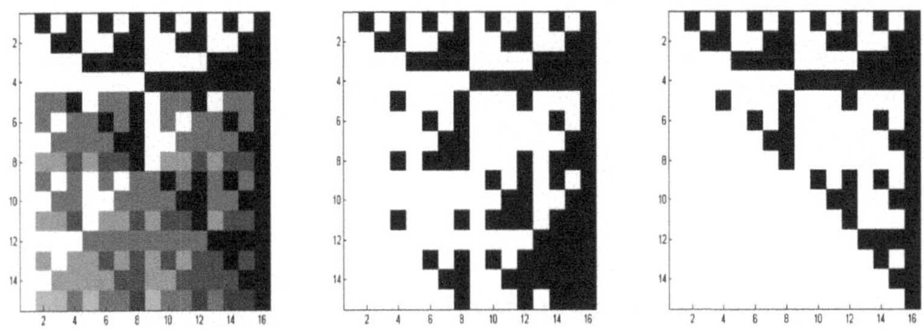

(a) Compensatory R_a (b) Comp. $R_b T > .5$ (c) Conjunctive R_c

Fig. 4. Graphical representation of the result matrices. From white to black, values in the cells go from 0 to 1.

Table 1. Average RMSE as computed by the evaluation method.

Data set	R_a	R_b	R_c
RMSE (Compensatory)	.2838	.3400	.4563
RMSE (Conjunctive)	.2838	.5218	**.1055**

We ran the evaluation algorithm one hundred time and obtained the averaged results in Table 1. While $\hat{R}_a$ was not rounded prior to calculate the RMSE (Root Mean Square Error), we calculated an optimal threshold and rounded $\hat{R}_b$ and $\hat{R}_c$ to calculate each fold RMSE. In the case of R_a, both conjunctive and compensatory models provide results of similar quality making difficult to discriminate from a conjunctive or a compensatory matrix. Compared to R_b, errors obtained by R_a on the compensatory model suggests that the calculus of the optimum threshold tends to increase the error. Finally, errors obtained by R_b and R_c show a big difference in the predictive quality between compensatory and conjunctive factorization validating the capacity of the evaluation method to discriminate properly between conjunctive and compensatory matrices in this simulated dataset. This is particularly significant in the case of the conjunctive matrix R_c that provides almost perfect predictions in a conjunctive factorization.

Table 2. R reconstruction coverage measure in percentages.

Data set	R_a	R_b	R_c
Av. best coverage (Compensatory)	85.90	94.89	90.04
Av. best coverage (Conjunctive)	85.90	91.53	**99.69**

In Table 2 we calculate the percentage of similarity between each cells of R and $\hat{R}$. Usage of weighted least square computations algorithm leads almost every-time to a perfect retrieval of R_c with the conjunctive model. Compared to the RMSE calculation, coverage does not only measure the accuracy of predicting the missing values. It is also a measure of the model stability since non missing values can differ in $\hat{R}$. Conjunctive matrix recovery is particularly stable with the conjunctive model.

4 Datasets

We considered four different datasets in our study. Some of them are available through the Cognitive Diagnosis Modeling (CDM)[2] package freely available with the statistical toolkit R. The selection process was guided by our will to experiment on real datasets with Q-matrices designed by cognitive modeling experts. Therefore we discarded from our selection process datasets with questionable Q-matrices origin and simulated sets. Each dataset is composed of a result matrix containing performances of the students to the same set or items and a Q-matrix associated with the same set of items to a list of skills. There is no missing data either on the R or Q matrices and both of them in each set are binary matrices.

The first dataset is a very well known cognitive model designed by Tatsuoka [22,23] involving 2144 middle school students answering 20 items (see Table 3) on fraction algebra. Eight skills were identified to answer correctly those items as follow [30]:

1. Convert a whole number to a fraction,
2. Separate a whole number from a fraction,
3. Simplify before subtracting,
4. Find a common denominator,
5. Borrow from whole number part,
6. Column borrow to subtract the second numerator from the first,
7. Subtract numerators,
8. Reduce answers to simplest form.

As all the required skills need to be present to answer properly each item, this dataset is intrinsically conjunctive [6]. The next datasets are all related to this first one.

[2] CDM: http://cran.r-project.org/web/packages/CDM/index.html.

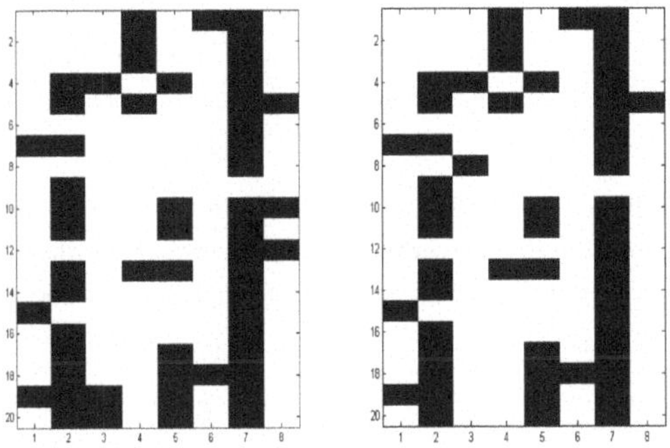

(a) Tatsuoka (20x8) (b) Desmarais (20x8)

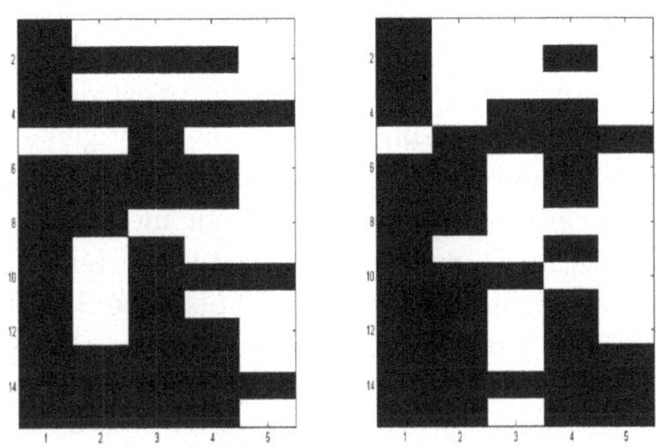

(c) Delatorre A (15x5) (d) Delatorre B (15x5)

Fig. 5. Graphical representation of the Q-matrices used in our evaluation. Black cells are populated in the Q-matrix by ones while white cells are associated with zeros.

Table 3. Items of Tatsuoka's fraction subtraction dataset [4].

1. $\frac{5}{3} - \frac{3}{4}$	11. $4 \times \frac{1}{3} - 2 \times \frac{4}{3}$
2. $\frac{3}{4} - \frac{3}{8}$	12. $1 \times \frac{1}{8} - \frac{1}{8}$
3. $\frac{5}{6} - \frac{1}{9}$	13. $3 \times \frac{3}{8} - 2 \times \frac{5}{6}$
4. $3 \times \frac{1}{2} - 2 \times \frac{3}{2}$	14. $3 \times \frac{4}{5} - 3 \times \frac{2}{5}$
5. $4 \times \frac{3}{5} - 3 \times \frac{4}{10}$	15. $2 - \frac{1}{3}$
6. $\frac{6}{7} - \frac{4}{7}$	16. $4 \times \frac{5}{7} - 1 \times \frac{4}{7}$
7. $3 - 2 \times \frac{1}{5}$	17. $7 \times \frac{3}{5} - \frac{4}{5}$
8. $\frac{2}{3} - \frac{2}{3}$	18. $4 \times \frac{1}{10} - 2 \times \frac{8}{10}$
9. $3 \times \frac{7}{8} - 2$	19. $4 - 1 \times \frac{4}{3}$
10. $4 \times \frac{4}{12} - 2 \times \frac{7}{12}$	20. $4 \times \frac{1}{3} - 1 \times \frac{5}{3}$

Table 4. Skills of Q-matrices A and B.

Skills in Q-matrix A	Skills in Q-matrix B
1. performing basic fraction subtraction operation,	1. performing basic fraction subtraction operation,
2. simplifying/reducing,	2. simplifying/reducing,
3. separating whole number from fraction,	3. converting whole number to fraction,
4. borrowing one from whole number to fraction,	4. converting mixed number to fraction,
5. converting whole number to fraction	5. column borrowing in subtraction

The second dataset proposed an "improved" version of initial Tatsuoka's Q-matrix. This refined Q-matrix was automatically discovered by a matrix factorization method proposed by Desmarais and Naceur [6]. This new Q-matrix contains the same number of skills but the mapping of skills 3 (Simplify before subtracting) and 8 (Reduce answer to simplest form) is slightly different as illustrated by Fig. 5b. Though this Q-matrix was not fully generated by an expert, it was evaluated and compared to the original Q-matrix on a previous paper [6] making it a good candidate to validate or not our method.

De la Torre [28,29] used as well two datasets derived from the initial Tatsuoka's 536 students by 20 items dataset. This time, the R matrix was modified as a subset of 536 students by 15 items and two smaller Q-matrices (A and B) containing only 5 skills were introduced. The 15 items was composed of items 2, 4, 6, 7, 9, 10, 11, 12, 14, 15, 16, 17, 18, 19 and 20 following the numbering of Table 3.

Each Q-matrices A and B were designed according to a specific solving strategies [13,29] (Table 4).

5 Experimental Results

The evaluation algorithm was executed one hundred times on all the datasets and the average RMSE as well as the Mean Absolute Error (MAE) were calculated on normalized $\hat{R}$. The normalization consisted in converting to 0 negative values and values above one to one prior to calculate the error at each iteration of the cross validation.

Results obtained (see Table 5) shows better results with conjunctive factorization model for all of the datasets. The cognitive models tested were designed to be conjunctive and the evaluation method was able to discriminate properly. The second result is regarding the automatically improved Q-matrix (b) that proves to be significantly more predictive with our method than the original Q-matrix (a) both with the compensatory and the conjunctive models. The results for matrix b obtained with our 10-fold non-stratified cross validation tend to support the results Desmarais and Naceur [6] obtained with their item stratified method. They calculated the MAE for the Tatsuoka's dataset with the original Q-matrix (a) ($MAE_{conj.} \approx .175, MAE_{comp.} \approx .190$) and their improved

Q-matrix (b) ($MAE_{conj.} \approx .155, MAE_{comp.} \approx .155$) and obtained lower errors but leading to the same conclusion.

Q-matrices (c) results are comparable to results obtained by Q-matrix (b) and slightly better than Q-matrix (a). This might advocate for a predominant strategy A over the alternative strategy B since Q-matrix (d) results are not as good as the previous ones. The cognitive strategies involved in the solving of the items and implemented in Q-matrices (c) and (d) might not be split in such exclusive way. It would be interesting to validate this assumption by attempting to split R by student strategies and reevaluate how Q-matrices (c) and (d) would perform.

The evaluation of simulated data has shown that the proposed method was almost perfect in the full conjunctive. With real data we can see that the error measured is more important. We assume that the difference observed is basically coming from several factors. The first factor is the Q-matrix quality and definitely the purpose of our work. Depending on the solving strategies identified by the expert, different Q-matrices can be proposed and their goodness of fit is variable as shown in the obtained results.

The second factor comes from the nature of education that may differ from other matrix factorization application domains. One major assumption of Rule-Space, we mentioned at the beginning of this paper, is that items should require only the students mastery of specific skills to be successfully completed. However, in practice students not having the skills can also succeed (by guessing the answer) and student having the required skills may also fail (slip into an error). As the linear model induced by matrix factorization is deterministic, it does not take into account those parameters contrary to other probabilistic cognitive diagnostic models like DINA [8]. Q-matrices (c) and (d) were studied in [29] with DINA, a model having guess and slip parameters, but the authors were interested in the capacity of DINA to fit the dataset. Intuitively, one would expect that Q-matrices misconceptions should produce a smaller residual error that would be compensated by the probabilistic parameters (guess and slip parameters for DINA) making difficult to discriminate the influence of the Q-matrix compared to the estimated parameters in the model goodness of fit. Adding parameters to a predictive model make the evaluation of the Q-matrix more difficult since the expert misconceptions can be more easily compensated. Some researchers were able to observe and study more in detail this phenomenon.

Table 5. Results obtained by the Q-matrix evaluation method on expert-made Q-matrices.

Dataset	(a) Tatsuoka	(b) Desmarais	(c) Delatorre A	(d) Delatorre B
RMSE (Compensatory)	.4270	.4064	.4251	.4911
RMSE (Conjunctive)	.4051	**.3810**	.3969	.4374
MAE (Compensatory)	.2737	.2537	.2633	.3417
MAE (Conjunctive)	.2531	**.2353**	.2321	.2893

6 Related Work

Rupp and Templin [16] evaluated the impact of ill-defined Q-matrices on the DINA [8] model using a simulation dataset. Considering 4 attributes, and subsequently 15 items, they generated 10000 respondents answer using a normal distribution of skill patterns. They defined Q-Matrix misspecification conditions by eliminating blocks of items (adding or removing skills for specific items) and representing incorrect dependency relationships (adding or removing skills when specific skills are present or missing). Under the effect of misconceptions, and depending on the category of misconceptions, the estimated guess and slip values became larger than the initial ones while the respondent misclassifications (learner skillset wrongly inferred) correlational measures (Kappa, Lambda, etc.) didnt necessary lead to significantly different results from the calculated value using the original Q-matrix.

Jimmy de la Torre [27] proposed an empirical method to validate a Q-matrix for DINA [8] as well. De la Torre observed from his δ-method and like Rupp and Tremplin [16] that small guess and slip parameters are sufficient but not necessary conditions to establish model-data fit. Therefore, he defined an optimization function that maximizes the difference of probabilities of correct response between examinees who have all the required attributes and those who do not. This difference of probability characterizes a discrimination index called δ that changes according to the item q-vector. A bigger δ would characterize a better q-vector and ultimately a better Q-matrix. De la Torre method proved to be successful at discriminating both simulated and real q-vectors. However the δ-method requires as input estimates of the guess and slip parameters that are variables from one item to the other.

Desmarais and Naceur [6] proposed a stratified cross validation mechanism to evaluate and compare improvement in Q-matrices in a matrix factorization model as presented in this paper. Instead of randomly injecting missing values as proposed in our evaluation method they calculated in turn expected results to each item given the outcomes obtained on the 19 others (Fig. 5a). For each iteration, S is calculated based on a 19 items Q-matrix. Then $\hat{R}$ is computed with the full Q-matrix and missing values in $\hat{R}$ compared to R are replaced by the "geometric mean of the average item difficulty and the examinee ability over the 19 given items". Therefore the error calculated add or withdraw to the Q-matrix goodness of fit the error coming from the heuristic to replace the missing values in $\hat{R}$. The error calculated may rather measure the heuristic than the Q-matrix goodness of fit in case where a lot of missing data would occur for the tested item.

7 Conclusion

We proposed in this paper to evaluate the predictive quality of expert-created Q-matrices in the context of matrix factorization recommender systems. The presented method has proven to be an efficient way to evaluate the predictive quality of conjunctive cognitive models. On the validation datasets, the model was able to fit the data in the case of a conjunctive R-matrix associated to the conjunctive factorization and experimental results supported results obtained by prior research studies [6]. As mentioned [2], matrix factorization models lead to prediction errors that are comparable to other cognitive diagnostic models. We were able to evaluate Tatsuoka's original dataset (a) with the item response theory model used by PSLC Datashop [9] and obtained for an unstratified 10-fold cross validation an rmse of 0.3751. The weighted least squares algorithm handles missing values without replacing them. This feature is particularly interesting for incomplete dataset. PSLC Datashop [9] offers numerous dataset with missing data and we were capable with very limited modifications to apply our method and to compare our results with the results obtained by the platform. Considering the dataset DS 605 [15,17] and the Q-matrices (aka Knowledge Component Models in Datashop) "KTracedSkills" and "Rules" we obtained an rmse of 0.3471 (compensatory) and 0.3249 (conjunctive) for "KTracedSkills" and 0.2675 (compensatory) and 0.2183 (conjunctive) for "Rules". Results obtained are consistent with the unstratified cross validation rmse of 0.304451 ("KTraced-Skill") and 0.186956 ("Rules") computed by Datashop. Those results comfort the potential of the proposed method to be used in practical cases where learners do not perform the same items, or progress at different paces. In this case, uncompleted items should not necessarily prevent the Q-matrix to be tested and iteratively improved in parallel with the testing activity. Beyond the exercise of evaluating expert-based Q-matrices, this evaluation method could allow practitioners to quickly evaluate cognitive models they design without requiring more sophisticated cognitive diagnostic models using multiple parameters and their sometimes heavy associated knowledge. This could prove to be particularly useful in technology enhanced learning environment to design competency-based learning functionalities that may be more accurate.

Acknowledgments. This work is part of the National Research Council Canada program Learning and Performance Support Systems (LPSS), which addresses training, development and performance support in all industry sectors, including education, oil and gas, policing, military and medical devices.

References

1. Barnes, T.: The Q-matrix method: Mining student response data for knowledge. In: AAAI Educational Data Mining workshop. p. 39 (2005)
2. Beheshti, B., Desmarais, M.C.: Predictive performance of prevailing approaches to skills assessment techniques: Insights from real vs. synthetic data sets (2014)
3. Birenbaum, M., Kelly, A.E., Tatsuoka, K.K.: Diagnosing Knowledge States in Algebra Using the Rule Space Model. ETS research report, Educational Testing Service, Educational Testing Service Princeton, NJ (1992)
4. DeCarlo, L.T.: On the analysis of fraction subtraction data: the DINA model, classification, latent class sizes, and the Q-matrix. Appl. Psychol. Meas. **35**(1), 8–26 (2011)

5. Desmarais, M.C., Beheshti, B., Naceur, R.: Item to skills mapping: deriving a conjunctive Q-matrix from data. In: Cerri, S.A., Clancey, W.J., Papadourakis, G., Panourgia, K. (eds.) ITS 2012. LNCS, vol. 7315, pp. 454–463. Springer, Heidelberg (2012)
6. Desmarais, M.C., Naceur, R.: A matrix factorization method for mapping items to skills and for enhancing expert-based Q-Matrices. In: Lane, H.C., Yacef, K., Mostow, J., Pavlik, P. (eds.) AIED 2013. LNCS, vol. 7926, pp. 441–450. Springer, Heidelberg (2013)
7. Gierl, M.J., Leighton, J.P., Hunka, S.M.: Exploring the logic of Tatsuoka's rule-space model for test development and analysis. Educ. Meas. Issues Pract. **19**(3), 34–44 (2000). http://dx.doi.org/10.1111/j.1745-3992.2000.tb00036.x
8. Junker, B.W., Sijtsma, K.: Cognitive assessment models with few assumptions, and connections with nonparametric item response theory. Appl. Psychol. Meas. **25**(3), 258–272 (2001). http://apm.sagepub.com/content/25/3/258.abstract
9. Koedinger, K.R., Baker, R.S.J.D., Cunningham, K., Skogsholm, A., Leber, B., Stamper, J., Ventura, S., Pechenizkiy, M., Baker, R.S.J.D.: A data repository for the EDM community: The PSLC DataShop. In: Romero, C. (ed.) Handbook of Educational Data Mining, pp. 43–56. CRC Press, Boca Raton (2010)
10. Koren, Y., Bell, R., Volinsky, C.: Matrix factorization techniques for recommender systems. Computer **42**(8), 30–37 (2009). http://dx.doi.org/10.1109/MC.2009.263
11. Lan, A., Studer, C., Baraniuk, R.: Quantized matrix completion for personalized learning. In: 7th International Conference on Educational Data Mining, pp. 280–283 (2014)
12. Liu, J., Xu, G., Ying, Z.: Data-driven learning of Q-matrix. Appl. Psychol. Meas. **36**(7), 548–564 (2012)
13. Mislevy, R.J.: Test theory reconceived. J. Educ. Meas. **33**(4), 379–416 (1996). http://dx.doi.org/10.1111/j.1745-3984.1996.tb00498.x
14. Nelder, J.A., Mead, R.: A simplex method for functional minimization. Comput. J. **7**, 308–313 (1965)
15. Ritter, S., Anderson, J., Koedinger, K., Corbett, A.: Cognitive tutor: applied research in mathematics education. Psychon. Bull. Rev. **14**(2), 249–255 (2007). http://dx.doi.org/10.3758/BF03194060
16. Rupp, A.A., Templin, J.: The effects of q-matrix misspecification on parameter estimates and classification accuracy in the dina model. Educ. Psychol. Meas. **68**(1), 78–96 (2008). http://epm.sagepub.com/content/68/1/78.abstract
17. Stamper, J., Ritter, S.: Cog model discovery experiment fall 2011. dataset 605 in datashop (2013). https://pslcdatashop.web.cmu.edu/datasetinfo?datasetid=605. Accessed
18. Stamper, J.C., Koedinger, K.R.: Human-machine student model discovery and improvement using DataShop. In: Biswas, G., Bull, S., Kay, J., Mitrovic, A. (eds.) AIED 2011. LNCS, vol. 6738, pp. 353–360. Springer, Heidelberg (2011)
19. Su, Y.L., Choi, K.M., Lee, W.C., Choi, T., McAninch, M.: Hierarchical cognitive diagnostic analysis for TIMSS] 2003 mathematics. Technical report 35, Center for Advanced Studies in Measurement and Assessment (CASMA), University of Iowa (2013)
20. Sun, Y., Ye, S., Inoue, S., Sun, Y.: Alternating recursive method for Q-matrix learning. In: 7th International Conference on Educational Data Mining, pp. 14–20 (2014)
21. Tatsuoka, K.K.: Rule space: an approach for dealing with misconceptions based on item response theory. J. Educ. Meas. **20**(4), 345–354 (1983)

22. Tatsuoka, K.K.: Analysis of errors in fraction addition and subtraction problems. Final report, Computer-based Education Research Laboratory, University of Illinois at Urbana-Champaign (1984)
23. Tatsuoka, K.K.: Toward an integration of item-response theory and cognitive error diagnosis. In: Frederiksen, N., et al. (eds.) Diagnostic monitoring of skill and knowledge acquisition, pp. 453–488. Lawrence Erlbaum Associates, Hillsdale, NJ (1990)
24. Tatsuoka, K.K.: Item Construction and Psychometric Models Appropriate for Constructed Responses. ETS research report, Educational Testing Service, Educational Testing Service Princeton, NJ (1991)
25. Tatsuoka, K.K.: Architecture of knowledge structures and cognitive diagnosis: a statistical pattern recognition and classification approach. In: Nichols, P.D., Chipman, S.F., Brennan, R. (eds.) Cognitively Diagnostic Assessment, pp. 327–359. Lawrence Erlbaum Associates, Hillsdale (1995)
26. The MathWorks, I.: Matlab 7, function reference. In: Matlab 7. Natick, Massachusetts (2008)
27. de la Torre, J.: An empirically based method of q-matrix validation for the dina model: development and applications. J. Educ. Meas. **45**(4), 343–362 (2008). http://dx.doi.org/10.1111/j.1745-3984.2008.00069.x
28. de la Torre, J.: DINA model and parameter estimation: a didactic. J. Educ. Behav. Stat. **34**(1), 115–130 (2009)
29. de la Torre, J., Douglas, J.: Model evaluation and multiple strategies in cognitive diagnosis: an analysis of fraction subtraction data. Psychometrika **73**(4), 595–624 (2008)
30. de la Torre, J., Douglas, J.A.: Higher-order latent trait models for cognitive diagnosis. Psychometrika **69**(3), 333–353 (2004)

Moving Through MOOCS: Pedagogy, Learning Design and Patterns of Engagement

Rebecca Ferguson[1(✉)], Doug Clow[1], Russell Beale[2], Alison J. Cooper[2], Neil Morris[3], Siân Bayne[4], and Amy Woodgate[4]

[1] The Open University, Milton Keynes, UK
Rebecca.Ferguson@open.ac.uk
[2] University of Birmingham, Birmingham, UK
[3] University of Leeds, Leeds, UK
[4] University of Edinburgh, Edinburgh, UK

Abstract. Massive open online courses (MOOCs) are part of the lifelong learning experience of people worldwide. Many of these learners participate fully. However, the high levels of dropout on most of these courses are a cause for concern. Previous studies have suggested that there are patterns of engagement within MOOCs that vary according to the pedagogy employed. The current paper builds on this work and examines MOOCs from different providers that have been offered on the FutureLearn platform. A cluster analysis of these MOOCs shows that engagement patterns are related to pedagogy and course duration. Learners did not work through a three-week MOOC in the same ways that learners work through the first three weeks of an eight-week MOOC.

Keywords: Learning analytics · Learner engagement patterns · Learning design · Moocs · Pedagogy

1 Introduction

The overarching label 'massive open online course' sets out some of the common features of this approach to learning and teaching: size, philosophy, mode of delivery and structure. The generic title does not specify the pedagogy, the theory of learning and teaching, which underpins MOOCs. Nor does it specify the types of learning design – the ways in which courses are planned, sequenced and managed – that work well with this model [4].

The first MOOCs [2] employed a connectivist approach, linking people and information on the basis that 'the connections that enable us to learn more are more important than our current state of knowing' [13]. Connectivist MOOCs were followed by xMOOCs, which typically employ a pedagogy based on content delivery [10].

The FutureLearn MOOC platform takes a different approach, and employs a social constructivist pedagogy that is based on the Conversational Framework [9, 11]. This is a theory of learning effectively through conversations with yourself and others [12]. In order to do this successfully, learners need access to both a shared representation of the

© Springer International Publishing Switzerland 2015
G. Conole et al. (Eds.): EC-TEL 2015, LNCS 9307, pp. 70–84, 2015.
DOI: 10.1007/978-3-319-24258-3_6

subject matter and tools that support reflection, comment and responses. These were incorporated into the design of the FutureLearn platform.

Despite these differences, MOOC providers all share a concern about dropout rates. Almost without exception, there is a large disparity between numbers registering and numbers completing a MOOC [6]. There are positive explanations for this discrepancy and many of those who leave early have gained what they wanted from the course and do not regard themselves as dropouts [1, 3]. Nevertheless, the open nature of MOOCs is not just about making more resources available to more people; it is also about extending opportunities.

An overview of this issue is provided by Jordan [5], and her website offers an opportunity to explore the data in more depth [6]. At the time of writing, 'MOOC Completion Rates: The Data' includes information about more than 180 MOOCs. Only two of these have reported a retention rate of over 40 %, and most have a completion rate of less than 13 %. A possible explanation is that this variation is due to differences in pedagogy and learning design.

Section 2 of this paper looks at past research to investigate patterns of engagement, including a cluster analysis of Coursera MOOCs that identified four engagement patterns, and subsequent work on Open University FutureLearn MOOCs, which showed that patterns of engagement are affected by pedagogy. Sections 3 and 4 introduce the method used to expand this study, using data from four universities. Section 5 reports the first research phase, indicating that learning design influences learner engagement. Section 6 covers the second research phase, which identifies elements of design that affect patterns of engagement, and Sect. 7 deals with the third phase, which identifies patterns of engagement in MOOCs with different learning designs. Sections 8 and 9 discuss these findings and set out the implications for research and practice.

2 Using Analytics to Investigate Engagement

Learning analytics are concerned with the use of trace data relating to learners and their contexts, for purposes of understanding and optimising learning and the environments in which it occurs [14]. They therefore provide ways of investigating patterns of engagement on MOOCs and, potentially, highlighting pedagogic approaches and learning designs that prove successful in retaining learners.

Kop and her colleagues have published several studies of connectivist MOOCS, including an analysis of patterns of engagement on PLENK2010 [8]. Their work pointed to two patterns of engagement, the *Visible Contributors* and the *Consumers*.

Kizilcec and his colleagues classified engagement on three MOOCs on the Coursera platform ('the Coursera study') [7] in terms of video lectures and assessments, and identified four patterns of engagement:

- *Sampling*: learners explored some course videos.
- *Auditing*: learners watched most videos, but completed assessments rarely, if at all
- *Disengaging*: learners reduced their engagement over time.
- *Completing*: learners completed most assessments

They noted that 'MOOC designers can apply this simple and scalable categorization to target interventions and develop adaptive course features'.

2.1 Engagement on Social Constructivist MOOCs

In order to explore whether these patterns could indeed be used by MOOC designers on any platform, a study of four MOOCs run by The Open University on the FutureLearn platform ('the OU study') [4] aimed to replicate the method employed on the Coursera study [7]. Learners' activity in each week was assigned to one of four categories: *on track* if they submitted assessment in the week it was set, *behind* if they completed an assessment after the week in which it was set, *auditing* if they engaged with content but not with the assessment, and *out* if they did not participate in a course week. Once engagement profiles had been created for learners, the *k*-means clustering algorithm was used to partition learners into a small number of groups. This produced two clusters that resembled the *Completing* and *Sampling* groups from the Coursera study, but neither an *Auditing* nor a *Disengaging* group [4, 7].

The original methodology prioritized engagement with content and assessment. However, the FutureLearn MOOCs laid stress on the social construction of knowledge, including discussion alongside each content step. The OU study therefore went on to create engagement profiles for learners that reflected engagement with content, with assessment and with discussion [4]. The method used to do this was employed in the current study, and is described in Sect. 4.1.

This generated seven clusters. *Samplers* visited a course briefly. *Strong Starters* left after the first week's assessment. *Returners* completed assessments in the first two weeks, then left. *Mid-way Dropouts* completed 3–4 assessments before leaving. The *Nearly There* cluster completed most assessments but left early. *Late Completers* completed most assessments but were either late in submitting these or missed some. *Keen Completers* engaged actively throughout. Typically, learners posted an average of around one comment for each week of engagement with the course [4].

MOOCs in the OU study were mainly eight-week courses with an assessment point at or near the end of each week. OU MOOC2 ran for a shorter period of time, and here the *Midway Dropouts* cluster was replaced by another cluster that fell between the *Samplers* and the *Strong Starters*. OU MOOC3, on the other hand, ran for eight weeks, but only included three assessments. In this case, the *Returners* and the *Midway Dropouts* were replaced with a cluster of *Samplers Who Comment*, and by a much smaller cluster of those whose engagement was concentrated on the final week.

The OU study showed that patterns of engagement are influenced by differences in pedagogy and course duration. This was an important point in terms of practice. If engagement patterns on different MOOCs are essentially similar once variations in pedagogy have been taken into account, then reducing course duration should reduce dropout. If MOOC learners find it difficult to complete assessment after the first week of a course, MOOCs could be structured to take this into account. However, if duration influences engagement patterns, then these approaches are less likely to succeed.

The research reported in this paper builds on the Coursera study and the OU study and investigates patterns of learner engagement on FutureLearn MOOCs from four universities. Each of these MOOCs has a different and carefully considered learning design, containing many elements. In this study, we have focused on two of these – length of course and distribution of assessment – as these can be easily identified within sets of activity data. The study asks whether the engagement patterns identified on the four Open University MOOCs are found on MOOCs delivered on the same pattern by different universities, and whether engagement patterns are influenced by changes in learning design.

3 FutureLearn Multi-University Dataset

To investigate these questions, we used data supplied by FutureLearn, a company owned by The Open University that has developed a social-constructivist platform for delivering free online courses, which currently has over 1.5 million registered learners. Course weeks are divided into steps. Except for assessments, each of these is associated with a free-flowing discussion. 'Typically, the discussion associated with any step on a FutureLearn MOOC will attract hundreds or thousands of contributions, with 'Like' and 'Follow' options providing ways of navigating these' [4].

Each partner institution has access to its own course data. Here, we focus on five MOOCs from four institutions. Together, these five sets of data include information about the activity of all 32,942 learners who engaged actively with these courses.

3.1 MOOCs in the Cross-University Dataset

LongMOOC1 was an eight-week course from the OU, including assessment in each week, focused on the hard sciences. It is included here because it was the MOOC for which the eight OU study cluster descriptions were first developed. The dataset includes activity data from 5,069 learners who were active on this MOOC.

LongMOOC2 was a seven-week course from the University of Edinburgh, including assessment each week, focused on the hard sciences. It was included to test whether the clusters generated by the OU study could be replicated on courses at other institutions. In all, 10,136 learners were active on this MOOC.

TalkMOOC3 was a six-week politics course from the University of Edinburgh. This was included because it had a distinctive learning design and pedagogy. The course provided a period of structured discussion, enabling participants to develop an informed position on an issue, so the course included no assessment. The dataset includes activity data from 6,141 learners who were active on this MOOC.

ShortMOOC4 was a three-week course from the University of Birmingham with a focus on the life/medical sciences. This was included because it was a short course, offering a broad introduction to concepts that could be explored in more depth in subsequent courses. In all, 6,839 learners were active on this MOOC.

ShortMOOC5 was a three-week course from the University of Leeds with a focus on the life/medical sciences. This was included alongside ShortMOOC 4 to test whether three-week courses showed consistent patterns of engagement. The dataset includes activity data from 4,756 learners who were active on this MOOC.

4 Clustering

4.1 Replicating the Method

The current study began by replicating the method used in the OU study. We made use of anonymised individual-level activity data. The data processing that took place before we received the data meant they were partially aggregated, and so we had access to the data and time of a learner's first visit to a content step, but we did not have access to the date and time of any subsequent visits. Graphical inspection of these data did not reveal any major differences that could be attributed to this process.

Although there is no compulsion to keep to the course schedule, an overview of data showed that activity followed a weekly cycle, spiking after the weekly course email was sent out on a Monday [4]. This weekly pattern meant that this study could follow previous studies and divide the data into weekly segments.

For each course week, we assigned learners an activity score of 1 if they viewed content, 2 if they posted a comment, 4 if they submitted their assessment in a subsequent week, and 8 if they submitted it early or on time. Individuals' activity scores were summed in order to give an activity score for each week. For example, if a learner visited content, commented and submitted on time in weeks 1–5 visited content and did the assessment late in week 6, visited content in week 7 and did not participate in week 8, their engagement profile would be [11, 11, 11, 11, 11, 5, 1, 0].

Possible weekly activity scores:

1 = Visited content only
2 = Posted comment but visited no new content
3 = Visited content and posted comment
4 = Submitted the assessment late
5 = Visited content and submitted assessment late
6 = Posted late assessment, saw no new content
7 = Visited content, posted, late assessment
8 = Submitted assessment early /on time
9 = Visited content, assessment early /on time
10 = Posted, assessment early /on time, no new content
11 = Visited, posted, assessment early /on time

Using these engagement profiles, we applied the *k*-means clustering algorithm to split the learners into a small number of groups. To cluster engagement patterns, we used the L_1 norm as the basis for one-dimensional k-means clustering, thus minimising the sum of the differences between individual patterns in each cluster. As *k*-means has random aspects, we repeated the clustering 100 times, selecting the solution with the highest likelihood.

Based on the number of weeks in a course, we used the *k*-means algorithm to extract clusters directly from the profiles, as a 3-, 6-, 7- or 8-dimensional vector for each learner, in order to allow for the possibility of clustering by time of activity.

A feature of *k*-means clustering is that it will always generate *k* clusters. We trialed the use of values for *k* ranging from 3 to 8, and compared the silhouette widths, in order to identify the best-fit value. This provided a graphical representation of how well each object lay within its cluster. We also used a scree plot to visualize the total within-groups sum of squares – an indication of how closely the clusters group together, and used 'kinks' in the slope to suggest the best choice of *k*.

4.2 The Three Phases of the Study

In **Phase One** of the study, we looked in detail at the clusters for which $k = 7$ provided the best fit. This value for *k* had also proved to be the best fit in the OU study. The Phase One dataset therefore included LongMOOC1 and LongMOOC2 and used the cluster descriptions that had been developed during the OU study. **Phase Two** used the sets of data for TalkMOOC3, ShortMOOC4 and ShortMOOC5 and explored why a value of 7 for *k* was not a good fit in these cases. **Phase Three** of the analysis used the most suitable value for *k* for TalkMOOC3, ShortMOOC4 and ShortMOOC5. Table 1 shows the values of *k* used for each phase of the study.

Table 1. Values for *k* used in the phases of this study.

MOOC	Phase 1: best-fit value for *k* aligned with OU study	Phase 2: testing $k = 7$ where this was not the best fit	Phase 3: Most suitable value for *k* in each set of data
LongMOOC1	7	-	-
LongMOOC2	7	-	-
TalkMOOC3	-	7	3
ShortMOOC4	-	7	4
ShortMOOC5	-	7	5

5 Analysis of Clusters: Phase One

LongMOOC1 and LongMOOC2 were both courses in the hard sciences, running for 7 or 8 weeks on a platform that linked discussion with comment throughout. In both cases, as on the OU study, seven clusters was the best fit for the data.

This section therefore describes the seven clusters outlined in the OU study, noting where LongMOOC2 differs from the data considered in that study. Where no differences are noted, the description holds true for the four MOOCs in the OU study (which included LongMOOC1) and for LongMOOC2. Typical engagement profiles are based on the average weekly activity scores in LongMOOC1.

Cluster I: Samplers is the largest cluster of learners (37 %–56 %). Its members, on average, visit about eight steps, with around one in ten visiting just one step. It includes a large number of latecomers – around a fifth of the people in this cluster were not active during Week 1. A few members of the cluster complete the Week 1 assessment, but do not go on to do so in subsequent weeks. No more than 18 % of cluster members post a comment and typically less than 15 %. A typical engagement profile for this cluster is: [1, 0, 0, 0, 0, 0, 0, 0].

Cluster II: Strong Starters is a smaller cluster, accounting for 8 %–14 % of the entire cohort. All members of this cluster submit the assessment in Week 1 but there is then a sharp drop-off in activity and members of the cluster typically do not complete another assessment. On average, over a third post a comment, with cluster members posting fewer than four comments each. On LongMOOC2, only 17 % of the cluster posted a comment and, overall, learners in all clusters on this course posted less frequently than on the OU MOOCs. This may be because the OU courses had no requirements for entry, other than an interest in the subject, while LongMOOC2 required 'a basic level of mathematical skills, at the level of a final-year school pupil'. This could have meant that it was more difficult to contribute to the discussion on this MOOC. A typical engagement profile for this cluster is: [9, 1, 0, 0, 0, 0, 0, 0].

Cluster III: Returners, 6 %–8 % of the cohort, all complete the assessment in Week 2, although up to 10 % may have missed it out in Week 1. On average, they visit fewer than half the steps on the course – for example, the mean number visited by this group on LongMOOC2 was 42 of 110 steps. After submitting their Week 2 assessment, members of this cluster usually leave. Overall, they post less than one comment each. A typical engagement profile for this cluster is: [9, 9, 0, 0, 0, 0, 0, 0].

Cluster IV: Midway Dropouts is typically a small cluster, making up just 4 %–6 % of the overall cohort. Learners in this cluster visit about half the course steps and submit assessment in three or four weeks then leave the course halfway through its run. In the OU study, just under half this cluster posted a comment. In LongMOOC2, this cohort posted less than on the OU study and only 29 % of this cluster contributed a comment. A typical engagement profile for this cluster is: [9, 9, 9, 4, 1, 1, 0, 0].

Cluster V: Nearly There is a variable cluster in percentage terms (5 %–19 %), and accounts for just 3 % of the LongMOOC2 cohort. These learners engage for longer than those in the clusters described above, submitting work in half or more of the course weeks and visiting around 80 % of the steps. They leave without completing the entire course and few, if any, submit work in the final week. A typical engagement profile for this cluster is: [11, 11, 9, 11, 9, 9, 8, 0].

Cluster VI: Late Completers Both this cluster and the following cluster are similar to the *Completing* cluster identified in the *Coursera* study. *Late Completers* make up 6 %–8 % of the cohort. They view most steps on the course. Each week, more than 94 % of the cluster completes the assessment. They submit the final assessment and most others, but either do so late or miss at least one of them. Less than half of them post a comment. A typical engagement profile for this cluster is: [5, 5, 5, 5, 5, 9, 9, 9].

Cluster VII: Keen Completers, 7 %–23 % of the cohort, can be regarded as model students. They visit more than 90 % of the course steps, submit all work on time and engage throughout. Typically, at least two-thirds of them comment at least once, posting about twice a week. Even on LongMOOC2, where engagement with comments was lower than on the courses included in the OU study, 58 % of this cluster posted a comment. A typical engagement profile for this cluster is: [11, 11, 9, 9, 11, 11, 9, 9].

6 Analysis of Clusters: Phase Two

In the case of TalkMOOC3, ShortMOOC4 and ShortMOOC5, seven clusters did not prove to be the best fit for the data, and so these MOOCS did not form part of the Phase One dataset. However, the k-means approach enabled us to segment the data to investigate why seven was not an appropriate value for k in these cases.

6.1 TalkMOOC3: Seven Clusters

In the case of TalkMOOC3, $k = 7$ did not generate clusters that were clearly equivalent to those found on other MOOCs. This was because TalkMOOC3 differed from others in that did not include any assessment. This affected the activity scores that could be obtained in any one week. As the description of possible weekly activity scores outlined above shows, weekly activity scores on most MOOCs considered here could range from 0–11. However, on TalkMOOC3 the range was between 0 (no activity) and 3 (viewed content and posted comment). This limited range effectively increased the importance of comments at the expense of content. Splitting this dataset into seven therefore produced seven clusters that were heavily dependent on small variations in posting behaviour and, of course, not at all influenced by assessment.

6.2 ShortMOOC4 and ShortMOOC5: Seven Clusters

ShortMOOC4 and ShortMOOC5 included assessment, but differed from other MOOCs studied in that they were much shorter: both ran for just three weeks.

When these two courses were segmented into seven, the resulting clusters included five that were the same as those found in Phase One. These clusters met the criteria described above for *Samplers*, *Strong Starters*, *Nearly There*, *Late Completers* and *Keen Completers*.

Three clusters were not found in these two MOOCs. *Returners* (learners who drop out in week 2 of an eight-week course) and *Midway Dropouts* (learners who drop out halfway through the course) were not represented, presumably because, on a three-week course, these clusters would be very similar to *Nearly There* (learners who drop out in the penultimate week). These two MOOCs also included no cluster of *Late Completers*, presumably because there were only three opportunities for late submission, rather than eight.

Other clusters were found on these MOOCs. Two, the *Saggers* and the *Improvers*, were found on both. *Surgers* and *Weak Starters* were found on only one MOOC.

Cluster a: Surgers concentrate their effort after the first week of a three-week course. On average, they visit more than two-thirds of the steps, engaging to some extent with each week. They do little in Week 1 other than submit their assessment late, engage more in Week 2, but still submit their assessment late (working on it in Week 3), and engage but do not submit in Week 3. On average, they post one or two comments. A typical engagement profile for this cluster is: [4, 6, 2].

Cluster b: Improvers fall behind in Week 1, submitting their first assessment late. They engage more in Week 2 and by Week 3 they are on schedule and submit their assessment on time. They view the majority of steps on the course and typically post more than one comment. A typical engagement profile for this cluster is: [5, 6, 9].

Cluster c: Saggers was only found in ShortMOOC4. The members of this cluster start strongly. They submit on time in the first week, they visit most steps on the course and they post an average of just over one comment a week. They engage less than Keen Completers, submitting late in Week 2, then engaging more in Week 3 and submitting their final assessment on time. Their engagement profile is: [10, 5, 8].

Cluster d: Weak Starters only appears in ShortMOOC5, engaging for longer than *Samplers* and less actively than *Strong Starters*. They engage in Week 1 and some submit the assessment. In Week 2 there is a low level of engagement, and few return in Week 3. On average, members of this cluster post one comment. A typical engagement profile for this cluster is: [4, 1, 0].

7 Analysis of Clusters: Phase Three

In the third and final phase of the study, we looked at the best-fit number of clusters for TalkMOOC3 ($k = 3$), for ShortMOOC4 ($k = 4$) and for ShortMOOC5 ($k = 5$).

7.1 TalkMOOC3: Three Clusters

As noted above, the lack of assessment on TalkMOOC3 meant that weekly activity scores ranged only from 0–3.

In this case, the method of assigning activity scores described above meant that higher scores were given to those who commented (2) and those who commented and viewed content (3). In the other MOOCs examined here, commenting had a less significant effect because it could only contribute 1 to a possible activity score of 11.

As discussions were linked with content, an activity score of 2 was rare because it was only possible for learners who did not engage with the current week's activities, but did return to a previous week to comment. The effective options for a weekly activity score were therefore 0, 1 or 3.

Cluster 1/3: Quiet is the largest cluster, containing around two-thirds of the cohort. On average, members of this cluster visit a quarter of the course steps. None of them contribute a comment during the first week of the course, and only 7 % post at any point. This cluster contains many late arrivals. Over a third arrive after Week 1, and over 9 %

only engage with the second half of the course. A typical engagement profile for this cluster is [1, 0, 0, 0, 0, 0].

Cluster 2/3: Week 1 Contributors Although number and frequency of comments are among the defining elements of many of the MOOC clusters identified in this study, it is only TalkMOOC3 that contains clusters in which every member comments at least once. In this cluster, which makes up 19 % of the cohort, every member posts a comment during the first week of the course, although half of them do not comment again. On average, this cluster visits 38 % of the course steps. A typical engagement profile for this cluster is [3, 1, 1, 0, 0, 0].

Cluster 3/3: Consistent Engagers makes up 11 % of the cohort. They have a mean activity score at least slightly above 1 in each week of the course, indicating that they engage throughout. On average, they visit 82 % of the course steps. All of them contribute at least one comment during the course, 95 % of them contribute more than three comments and 7 % contribute more than 100 comments each. A typical engagement profile for this cluster is [3, 3, 3, 3, 1, 1].

7.2 ShortMOOC4: Four Clusters

Cluster 1/4: Very Weak Starters is the largest group on this MOOC, accounting for 35 % of the cohort. Its profile is closest to that of the *Weak Starters* who were found in ShortMOOC5 when it was split into seven clusters. Overall, the *Very Weak Starters* show low levels of engagement, visiting 20 % of steps on average, commenting less than once per learner, and no individual achieves an activity score higher than 5 in Week 1 of the course. This indicates that none of these learners finishes their assessment on time in Week 1, although 18 % of the group completes this assessment late. A fifth of the cluster do not engage at all during the first week of the course. The engagement profile for this cluster is: [2, 1, 0].

Cluster 2/1: Strong Starters (Truncated) can be regarded as a version of the *Strong Starters* cluster described above. This is one of the smaller clusters, accounting in this case for 17 % of the entire cohort. Members of this cluster submit the assessment in Week 1, although 6 % submit late. There is then a drop-off in activity and members of the cluster typically do not complete another assessment. In the case of ShortMOOC4, almost half the group posts a comment and, overall, cluster members post just over one comment each. The engagement profile for this cluster is very similar to the beginning of the *Strong Starters*' profile: [10, 1, 0].

Cluster 3/4: Returners (Truncated) can be regarded as a version of the *Returners* cluster described above. These learners all complete the assessment in Week 2, although a few (17) miss it out in Week 1. On average, this cluster visits 81 % of the steps. This is a higher percentage than that visited by the *Returners* described above but, because this was a short course, it only represents 36 steps. After submitting their Week 2 assessment, members of this cluster engage in very little activity. On an eight-week course, their activity after Week 2 is spread thinly across the final six weeks. On this three-week course, all additional activity is concentrated in Week 3, which gives them a slightly higher average activity score in Week 3, as the engagement profile shows. The amount of people commenting was high across this MOOC (47 %) and was also high in this cluster, with half the group posting at least one comment. The engagement profile for this cluster is very similar to the beginning of the *Returners*' profile: [9, 9, 2].

Cluster 4/4: Keen Completers (Truncated) can be regarded as a version of the *Keen Completers* cluster described above. The description of the group is the same in both cases but the engagement profile shows that, overall, members of this group were less keen, because their average activity score in any week was never higher than 9. A typical engagement profile for this cluster is: [9, 9, 9].

7.3 ShortMOOC5: Five Clusters

Cluster l/5: Samplers (Truncated) can be regarded as a version of the *Keen Completers* cluster described above. The description of the group is the same in both cases. Once again, a large number of people do not participate during Week 1, with more than 25 % not registering any activity during that time. The typical engagement profile for this cluster is [1, 0, 0], but it should be noted that many learners did not participate in Week 1 although they visited in Weeks 2 or 3.

Cluster 2/5: Strong Starters (Truncated) is another instance of the *Strong Starters (Truncated)* cluster described in the analysis of ShortMOOC4. A small cluster, in which everyone submits the Week 1 assessment, but there is then a sharp decline in engagement. Engagement profile: [9, 1, 0].

Cluster 3/5: Returners (Truncated) is another instance of the *Returners (Truncated)* cluster described in the analysis of ShortMOOC4. These learners all complete the assessment in Week 2, although a few (20) miss it out in Week 1. In this case, average activity levels rise slightly in Week 2. This is not clear from the typical engagement profile of 8, 8, 2, but can be seen when the average engagement score for each week is shown to one decimal place: 7.8, 8.1, 1.6.

Cluster 4/5: Improvers is another instance of the *Improvers* cluster that was found when the three-week MOOCs were segmented into seven clusters. Activity in this cluster rises each week, and the final assessment is typically submitted on time. The engagement profile remains: [5, 6, 9].

Cluster 5/5: Keen Completers (Truncated) is another instance of the cluster found in ShortMOOC4. Engagement remains steady throughout the three weeks, with an average activity score of 9 or 10.

8 Discussion

This study investigated whether the engagement patterns identified in the OU study [4] were only found on MOOCs developed by The Open University, or whether they were also apparent in MOOCs from other universities. It also investigated whether engagement patterns are influenced by changes in learning design – in this case assessment and course length. This is an important issue, because the original, and highly cited, study of Coursera MOOCs suggested that MOOC designers would be able to apply the four patterns they had identified 'to target interventions and develop adaptive course features' [7]. The OU study [4] showed that MOOC designers should not do this without taking variations in pedagogy into account. The current study shows that they should also take account of design variations.

The seven clusters identified in the OU study: *Samplers*, *Strong Starters*, *Returners*, *Midway Dropouts*, *Nearly There*, *Late Completers* and *Keen Completers* were found here on MOOCs that employed similar assessment patterns to those from the OU and that also ran for seven or eight week. The same set of clusters was not found on three-week MOOCs, or on a MOOC that did not include assessment.

In the case of TalkMOOC3, the omission of assessment from the course can be seen not only as a shift in learning design, but also as a change in the underlying pedagogy. The original Coursera study clustered learners on the basis of their engagement with two key pedagogic elements: content and assessment. The OU study found that a different set of engagement patterns was seen when the key pedagogic elements were discussion, content and assessment. In the case of ShortMOOC4, the key pedagogic elements were discussion and content, and so a new set of clusters emerged.

These variations related to pedagogy highlight that the results of a cluster analysis are dependent on the variables that are selected as significant by researchers. A *k*-means analysis will produce *k* clusters for any value of *k*, but these will only be meaningful if priority is given to elements of the data that are significant in the context.

In the case of ShortMOOC4, where engagement with discussion was a key element of the course, the cluster descriptions set out here can be only partial. This is because the activity data included information about how many comments individuals posted, and when they posted them. However, there were no data available about ways in which people engaged with the discussion by reading or liking comments. Adding these elements in future studies would make it easier to identify and characterise engagement patterns in this type of course.

ShortMOOC4 and ShortMOOC5 both employed similar learning designs in that both ran for just three weeks. In the case of ShortMOOC5, this aspect of the learning design was, in part, intended to encourage completion by making the *Disengagement* identified in the Coursera study more difficult to achieve.

To some extent, this was the case. ShortMOOC4 included learners who displayed truncated versions of the engagement patterns of *Strong Starters*, *Returners* and *Keen Completers*. ShortMOOC5 included truncated forms of the engagement patterns of *Samplers*, *Strong Starters*, *Returners* and *Keen Completers*.

However, in both cases the *Late Completers* cluster was missing. In addition, there was a subtle shift in the engagement pattern of the *Keen Completers*. The overall activity levels of learners in this cluster were lower each week than they were on eight-week courses. On average, *Keen Completers* on the eight-week MOOCs engaged fully in most weeks, posting comments, visiting content and completing assessment on time. In the three-week MOOCs, the average *Keen Completer (Truncated)* did not do all those things in any week.

The clusters also suggest that participants in three-week MOOC tended to concentrate their activity in one or two weeks, and these did not necessarily include the first week. *Strong Starters* and *Weak Starters* concentrated on Week 1, but a notable feature of the *Sampler* cluster was the high percentage (on all the MOOCs examined here and in the OU study) that did not engage in the first week.

ShortMOOC5 included an *Improvers* cluster, which was seen for $k = 5$ and $k = 7$. The *Improvers* increased their activity over time. In Weeks 1 and 2 their average activity scores indicate that most of them submitted their assessment late, while they completed their Week 3 assessment on time. This suggests that they completed all the course assessment in Weeks 2 and/or 3.

When ShortMOOC4 and ShortMOOC5 were segmented into seven, both contained a *Surgers* cluster. In this case, cluster members typically did not engage during Week 1, submitted their Week 1 assessment late, engaged more in Week 2 but again submitted their assessment late, then did not submit their Week 3 assessment. Activity here is concentrated at the end of the course.

The study also included a cluster of *Saggers*, found on ShortMOOC4 when it was segmented into seven, who engaged more in Week3 and Week 1 than in Week 2.

It seems clear that many learners do not approach a three-week course in the same way as an eight-week course. There are limited opportunities to get far ahead of, or behind, the cohort, and so it is possible to dip in at different points without losing the sense of working on the course as part of a cohort.

Although these courses remained open to learners after their end-dates, and most FutureLearn assessment does not have to be submitted by a set date, none of the typical engagement profiles ends with a Fig. 4, which would have indicated that a significant engagement pattern involved completing the course after its end date.

9 Conclusion

This study has extended the findings of the OU study using new sets of data. The recommendations of that study can therefore be restated with more confidence – with the added proviso that they only apply in the case of seven- to eight-week MOOCs that support engagement with content, assessment and discussion.

The OU study suggested strategies for intervention and improvement:

- providing previews of course material
- setting up discussion steps for latecomers
- encouraging late arrivals to register for another course or for a later presentation
- providing bridges between course weeks, stressing links between those weeks [4].

In the case of course length, there are many good pedagogic reasons for creating short courses. However, educators should not assume that shortening the length of a course will necessarily increase learner engagement and course completion. This study indicates that may not be the case because the patterns of engagement shift.

In the case of pedagogy, it is clear from the Coursera study, the OU study and this study that changes to the basic pedagogic elements of a course are associated with shifts in patterns of engagement. The analysis of TalkMOOC3 gives some indication of the patterns of engagement on a course focused on content and discussion, but a lack of data limited that analysis and thus its implications are unclear.

As shifts in pedagogic approach can change the elements of a course that can be regarded as key, it is important that any future analysis of patterns of engagement is based on the elements that are most important to the pedagogy of the course under examination. Where the focus is heavily on discussion elements, it is necessary to have access to data about the reading and liking of contributions, as well as when and by whom they were written.

It is clear that changes to some elements of learning design can change learners' patterns of engagement with a MOOC. Future work should therefore investigate other elements of learning design in order to identify which of these are associated with desirable patterns of engagement.

Our understanding of patterns of engagement in MOOCs is developing rapidly. It initially seemed clear that these patterns held steady across MOOCs; we now know that those patterns are influenced by both learning design and pedagogy. Cutting a MOOC short in order to promote engagement originally seemed to a promising plan, but this study shows that such an approach is not a panacea. These insights can help us to produce learning designs that will support desirable patterns of engagement.

Acknowledgments. We thank FutureLearn, The Open University, the University of Birmingham, the University of Edinburgh and the University of Leeds for allowing us access to the data used in this study. We also thank the FutureLearn Academic Network for establishing connections between researchers with an interest in this area.

References

1. Clow, D.: MOOCs and the funnel of participation. In: Learning Analytics and Knowledge 2013 (LAK 13), pp. 185–189. ACM, New York (2013)
2. Downes, S.: Connectivism and connective knowledge (2012). http://www.downes.ca/files/books/Connective_Knowledge-19May2012.pdf
3. Downes, S.: Like reading a newspaper (2014). http://halfanhour.blogspot.co.uk/2014/03/like-reading-newspaper.html
4. Ferguson, R., Clow, D.: Examining engagement: analysing learner subpopulations in massive open online courses (MOOCs). In: Learning Analytics and Knowledge 2015 (LAK 15), pp. 51–58. ACM, New York (2015)
5. Jordan, K.: Initial trends in enrolment and completion of massive open online courses. IRRODL **15**(1), 133–160 (2014)
6. Jordan, K.: MOOC completion rates: the data. http://www.katyjordan.com/MOOCproject.html
7. Kizilcec, R., Piech, C., Schneider, E.: Deconstructing disengagement: analyzing learner subpopulations in massive open online courses. In: Learning Analytics and Knowledge 2013 (LAK 13), pp. 170–179. ACM, New York (2013)
8. Kop, R., Fournier, H., Sui Fai, J.M.: A pedagogy of abundance or a pedagogy to support human beings? Participant support on massive open online courses. IRRODL **12**(7), 74–93 (2011)

9. Laurillard, D.: Rethinking University Teaching: A Conversational Framework for the Effective Use of Learning Technologies. RoutledgeFalmer, New York (2002)
10. Littlejohn, A.: Understanding Massive Open Online Courses. CEMCA, New Delhi (2013)
11. Pask, G.: Conversation Theory: Applications in Education and Epistemology. Elsevier, New York (1976)
12. Ferguson, R., Sharples, M.: Innovative pedagogy at massive scale: teaching and learning in MOOCs. In: de Freitas, S., Rensing, C., Ley, T., Muñoz-Merino, P.J. (eds.) EC-TEL 2014. LNCS, vol. 8719, pp. 98–111. Springer, Heidelberg (2014)
13. Siemens, G.: Connectivism: a learning theory for the digital age (2004). http://www.elearnspace.org/Articles/connectivism.htm
14. SoLAR: Open learning analytics: an integrated & modularized platform (2011). White Paper, http://solaresearch.org/OpenLearningAnalytics.pdf

In-App Reflection Guidance for Workplace Learning

Angela Fessl[1(✉)], Gudrun Wesiak[1], Verónica Rivera-Pelayo[2], Sandra Feyertag[1], and Viktoria Pammer[3]

[1] Know-Center, Inffeldgasse 13, 8010 Graz, Austria
{afessl,gwesiak,sfeyertag}@know-center.at
[2] FZI Research Center of Information Technology, Haid-und-Neu-Str. 10-14, 76131 Karlsruhe, Germany
rivera@fzi.de
[3] Knowledge Technologies Institute, TU Graz, 8010 Graz, Austria
viktoria.pammer@tugraz.at

Abstract. In-app reflection guidance for workplace learning means motivating and guiding users to reflect on their working and learning, based on users' activities captured by the app. In this paper, we present a generic concept for such in-app reflection guidance for workplace learning, its implementation in three different applications, and its evaluation in three different settings (one setting per app). From this experience, we draw the following lessons learned: First, the implemented in-app reflection guidance components are perceived as useful tools for reflective learning and their usefulness increases with higher usage rates. Second, smart technological support is sufficient to trigger reflection, however with different implemented components also reflective learning takes place on different stages. A sophisticated, unobtrusive integration in the working environment is not trivial at all. Automatically created prompts need a sensible timing in order to be perceived as useful and must not disrupt the current working processes.

Keywords: Workplace learning · Reflective learning · Reflection guidance · Reflective note analysis

1 Introduction

Reflective learning can be seen as the conscious re-evaluation of past situations or experiences with the goal to learn from them and to use the gained outcomes to guide future behaviour. This is in-line with the definition of Boud et al. [3], who define reflective learning as *"those intellectual and affective activities in which individuals engage to explore their experiences in order to lead to new understandings and appreciations"*. In the area of workplace learning, reflection has been identified as a core process, with the goal to get new insights, derive better practices, and finally to improve the own work [3,25]. Because reflective learning is a cognitive process based on intrinsic and extrinsic motivation of the

© Springer International Publishing Switzerland 2015
G. Conole et al. (Eds.): EC-TEL 2015, LNCS 9307, pp. 85–99, 2015.
DOI: 10.1007/978-3-319-24258-3_7

individual, it cannot be directly enforced, but techniques like prompting [5,6,12] can foster reflection while using applications at work.

This work reports an in-app reflection guidance concept, that conceptualises reflection guidance as adaptive components. We see this concept as a promising instructional strategy, as these components aim at triggering reflective learning. At the workplace, such components should draw the workers' attention to their own thoughts and experiences, and motivate them to understand and reflect on their daily working tasks. To illustrate how the concept can be instantiated in work-related settings, we implemented different components of the concept in three applications, adopting various approaches to support reflective learning. The three studies cover mood tracking in a call centre [9,22], game-based learning in a hospital [8], and activity tracking in an IT company [16].

In this paper, we investigate the usefulness of the implemented reflection guidance components as well as the stage or depth of reflection (first, second and third stage [20]) achieved by the users. By analysing the results we aim at answering the following research questions: (i) How were the implemented reflection guidance components perceived with regard to their usefulness at work? (ii) To what extent (at which stage) does reflective learning occur?

2 Related Work

Technologically supported scaffolding types to trigger reflective learning are of major interest in the area of self-regulated learning and extensively investigated within learning management systems. In such settings, prompts are used very often to organise, retrieve, monitor or evaluate knowledge as well as to reflect on student's learning [2,12,13,31].

Davis [5] distinguishes between *self-monitoring prompts* and *activity prompts*. The first encourage students to reflect on their own learning by asking "Thinking ahead" or "Checking our understanding" questions. The second motivate students to reflect on their progress in the activity and specifically about whether they have devoted attention to each aspect of their project. In both cases different types of sentence starters are used. Furthermore, Ifenthaler et al. [12] follow the categorisation of prompts from Davis [6] and refer to *generic* and *direct* prompts. While the generic prompts only ask learners to stop and reflect about their current problem solving activities, the directed prompts also provide them with an expert model of reflective thinking in the problem solving process. In our work we follow Verpoorten et al. [29], who created the term *reflection amplifier*, which is a *"deliberate and well-considered prompting approach, which offers learners a structured opportunity to examine and evaluate their own learning"*. In work-related settings, there is little research on usage of prompts. Prilla [19] discusses the usage of prompts with regard to collaborative reflective learning at work. His prompting approach tries to motivate people to use his reflection tool and the socio-technical nature of communities or face-to-face meetings. Rivera et al. [23] investigate the notions of active (e.g. notifications) and passive (e.g.

visualisations) triggering in work-related settings. Another approach for reflection at work is the voice-enabled reflection app REFLECT [15], which supports scaffolding by community-based questions.

The work of Thillmann [27] puts the focus not only on what to prompt, but also when to prompt. Providing prompts before as well as during the learning process shows that presenting a prompt at the right time had a positive effect on the learning outcome. In this connection, the current user context plays an important role. First of all, by including the current context in the decision of when to present a prompt, the stress caused by interruptions can be reduced as presented for mobile devices in [11,18]. Secondly, using automatically or manually gathered context information for reflection (e.g. by giving a hint of what has happened during a working day or week) supports the re-evaluation of past experiences and therefore the reflection process itself.

Other tools and techniques to technologically trigger reflective learning are diaries, reflective journals and e-portfolios, which are predominantly used in formal educational settings [4,7,10,17]. Diaries are personal notes not meant to be shared, hence most studies focus on the effect diary writing has on learning e.g. [26]. In contrast, the term "journal" is mostly used to describe diaries that are intended for sharing. They are used in different training settings (e.g. athletes) [30] and sometimes also in work-related settings, e.g. with nurses [28]. E-Portfolios are mostly defined as a collection of information and (physical) artefacts, gathered for specific purposes by a user over time [1], in educational [7] as well as work related settings [10]. All these tools and techniques have in common that they are very time-consuming in being kept and maintained.

From literature we know that prompting approaches are very successful in formal learning environments, however only very little research has been conducted in work-related settings. Investigating and evaluating prompts in learning environments can benefit from the fact that the learning activities and tasks of the learners are known beforehand and the prompts can easily be adapted according to these activities. In contrast, in a work-related setting the tasks are not always known beforehand or only vaguely known. Therefore, it is very challenging to provide meaningful prompts in a working environment. Secondly, because a learner uses the learning environment actively while learning, the prompts can be displayed according to the current learning task. In a working environment the time to present prompts is not as obvious as in learning environments. Third, most workplaces are very stressful and work-intensive. Therefore, it has to be very well considered, if and how time consuming approaches like diaries can be applied in work-related settings.

3 Components of the Reflection Guidance Concept

Schön [25] defines *reflection-in-action* as reflection which takes place while doing own work, whereas *reflection-on-action* refers to analysing reactions to any situation and exploring the reasons and consequences afterwards. Consequently, the design components are divided in these two main categories:

3.1 Reflection-in-Action Components

"Reflection-in-action" components present motivational triggers to provide a more accurate guidance of the reflective process and should make people aware of any significant changes or unusual behaviour. These components are automatically presented to the user when starting to use an application or during the usage of an application. We define two types of reflection-in-action components:

Reflection Interventions: Reflection interventions are prompts that aim at motivating users to utilise an application in general. This type of prompts are similar to the *activity prompts* by Davis [5], which have the goal to facilitate the completion of specific aspects of given activities. Reflection interventions pop up when opening the application for the first time of the day or at the end of a day. They occur during a working day, if the application was not used for a longer time or if a new event (e.g. beginning of a meeting) is starting. All these prompts ask for input regarding the user's activities.

Reflection Amplifiers: Regarding the *reflection amplifiers*, we follow Verpoorten et al. [29] seeing them as deliberate and well-considered prompting approach for initiating reflection. This is also in line with Davis [5], whose so-called *self-monitoring prompts* provide questions to foster planning and reflection. At work, reflection amplifiers support planning and reflection by making users aware of deviations from standard behaviour, unusual working patterns or other significant situations on an individual or collaborative level. Furthermore, they motivate users to reflect about such situations and to insert their thoughts directly into a corresponding application.

3.2 Reflection-on-Action Components

"Reflection-on-action" components are features that can motivate users to reflect about the gathered data after having used the application, e.g. at the end of a working day. These components consist of reports as well as reflection diaries or reflection journals. "Reflection-on-action" components encompass:

Reports: Reports provide an automatically created summary of past experiences or events captured during work. Depending on the purpose of the application, such reports present working tasks or activities including unusual situations worth being reflected on. The aim is to provide guidance for reflection based on the available data and in relation to different time periods (e.g. hourly, daily, weekly reports). Re-evaluating or comparing them with own or others' working behaviours can lead to the detection of behavioural patterns, insights about one's own working behaviour and finally result in learning outcomes.

Reflection Diary: The reflection diary is used to store insights, thoughts, artefacts, or learning outcomes in a structured way. Using this diary consequently (e.g. at the end of each shift) in a reflective learning application can result in an important collection of learning outcomes. Re-evaluating these entries again can trigger reflective learning and in the end lead to the detection of significant working patterns or meaningful insights to guide future behaviour at work.

3.3 Intertwined Component

Contextualisation: In order to be able to return to experiences, which is a relevant step for reflection as suggested by Boud et al. [3], it is important to track the context either automatically or manually during the application usage. Automatically tracked context can gather all interactions with an application and consists therefore of vast amounts of data. In contrast, manually inserted context can be a self-defined word, a short phrase or the selection of pre-defined context types adapted to the current working environment; it is just a hint, which represents what is currently going on during work. This contextualisation can support reflective learning twofold: first directly when entering context information the user has to think about it. Secondly, displaying the available context information when revisiting the captured data later on (e.g. at the end of a day) supports the user to better remember the respective working situation.

4 Methodology

The applications and the implemented reflection guidance components were evaluated within user studies conducted in real work settings. All evaluations followed a similar approach using the tools listed in Table 1. Objective usage rates were captured via users' log-data and written text entries were collected within the apps. Demographic data was gathered in the pre-questionnaire, whereas the post-questionnaires contained questions on how supportive the apps were with respect to reflective learning (app-specific reflection questions) and how useful participants perceived the reflection guidance components. In the post-questionnaire, the items were presented as 5 pt. rating scales ranging from 1 - "I strongly disagree" to 5 - "I strongly agree". For the app-specific reflection questions we used an existing item pool of 43 questions (see [14], p. 38), which cover a wide variety of features reflection apps may provide. Out of this, an adequate subset of items was selected for each evaluation (see Table 2).

The conducted interviews and the workshop provided deeper information about the applications and the implemented reflection guidance components. For the analysis of the written content with regard to the achieved stages (first, second and third) of reflection, a qualitative analysis schema [20] was used. The first stage encompasses descriptions of experiences and emotions. The second stage includes the interpretation and justification of actions and working on solutions. The third stage consists of insights, learning and conclusions from reflection. All notes were independently analysed and categorised by three researchers.

5 Applications and Their Evaluations

In this paper, we focus on the usefulness of the reflection guidance components. More details regarding the applications and their support for reflective learning can be found in [8,9,16,21,22].

Table 1. Used evaluation tools

Tool	Application	Stage	Content
log data	all	at the end	interactions with the application, quiz results
pre-questionnaire	all	at the beginning	consent form, demographic data
post-questionnaire	all	at the end	feedback about the applications and the guidance components, questions about reflective learning
interviews	all	at the end	deeper feedback about the applications and the guidance components
workshop	Quiz	at the end	group discussion about the evaluation and the quiz

5.1 MoodMap App and Its Evaluation in a Call Centre

The MoodMap App [9,22] (MMA) is a web application that maps mood on a coloured map along the two dimensions of Russell's Circumplex Model of Affect: valence (feeling good - feeling bad) and arousal (high energy - low energy) [24]. In the MMA, the contextualisation component is implemented in a mandatory way. For each inserted mood, a pre-defined context has to be chosen (e.g. "after a call", "after a coaching session", "after a break" or "other") and a note has to be added. To support the note taking, a reflection amplifier question like *"What are you currently thinking?"* or *"What influences your current mood?"* is presented. The purpose of this mandatory contextualisation is to 'force' the user to think about the current inserted mood and add the user's thoughts into the application. Reports summarising the mood development of a day and a reflection diary were also available.

Setting: Four teams out of two call centres of a large telecommunication company in Great Britain participated in this evaluation (see [21], p. 52). Such call centres can handle an average of 27.000 calls from all over the UK every day, working in a range of functions from directory enquiries to residential and business broadband. Each team consists of call takers, coaches and managers. The call takers are responsible for taking the calls and solving any issues directly with the customers. The coaches support and coach the call takers for their work, while the managers ensure that the call takers are performing against their targets, review their performance and supervise the training sessions.

Learning: Mood self-tracking and reflection on own as well as the team's mood can lead to insights of how mood influences the work with regard to work performance and collaboration within a team.

Procedure: The evaluation lasted four weeks. The MoodMap App was introduced by the responsible project manager of the telecommunication company.

All participants (call takers, coaches and managers) were asked to integrate the MMA in their daily working routines. Their task was to state their moods, choose a mandatory context and add a note during all days of the evaluation period. They were also asked to reflect about their inserted moods and notes individually. The coaches and managers were additionally instructed to use the team visualisations in order to reflect about the mood development of their teams and take actions if necessary.

Participants: From the 33 participants who used the application and filled out the post-questionnaire, 2 gave interviews, and 24 shared their demographics. Of these, 14 are male, 10 female, 67 % were aged between 20 and 29, 26 % between 30 and 39, 8 % between 40 and 49.

5.2 The Medical Quiz and Its Evaluation at a Stroke Unit

The Medical Quiz [8] (MQ) is a web-based quiz especially developed for nurses working at a Stroke Unit in German hospitals. The quiz consists of four different quiz types presenting randomised content-based questions out of a question pool. The content-based questions are enriched with reflective questions - an integrated form of reflection amplifiers. Depending on the quiz type the reflective questions are posed at the beginning, during or at the end of the quiz. The reflective questions at the beginning address the current knowledge status (extracted from previous quiz attempts) and the user's play frequency. The in-between questions put the players' focus on the content-based questions, while the questions at the end of the quiz ask explicitly for gained insights or new knowledge with regard to the currently played quiz. Both draw a connection to real working experiences.

Setting: The Medical Quiz was introduced to the nurses participating in a qualification program for stroke nurses, which takes place once a year in a German hospital (see [21], p.137). All participants were nurses working in different German hospitals and were in education to become a nurse for a Stroke Unit. The qualification program lasted for 5 months. In one week of each month the participants came together for the training at the organising hospital.

Learning: The goal of the quiz is not only to provide an easy to use possibility to refresh existing knowledge or to gain new knowledge, but also to connect theoretical knowledge with working practices and to reflect about it.

Procedure: In the first week of the qualification program, the Medical Quiz was introduced to the participants by the evaluation responsible of the organising clinic. They were asked to play the quizzes consequently, on the one hand for memorising and strengthening their newly gained knowledge and on the other hand for reflecting about the content of the quiz and for drawing connections between the new knowledge and their daily work practices with the help of the integrated reflective questions. In the fourth week of the program, the post-questionnaire was handed out. In addition, a half-day workshop and interviews were conducted to collect deeper insights from the participants with regard to the quiz and its reflection support.

Participants: 18 nurses (16 female, 2 male) participated in this evaluation and 3 gave interviews; 66 % were aged from 20–29 and 33 % between 30 and 59.

5.3 KnowSelf and Its Evaluation in an IT Company

KnowSelf [16] (KS) is an application that automatically records working activities on a personal computer by capturing resources and applications used during work. Manual project and task recording, as well as manually inserted notes and comments complete the data captured by the application. The application visualisations expose, in particular, the frequency of application and resource switching, the time spent in numerous applications and the time spent on different activities. In this application, time-triggered reflection interventions and event-triggered reflection amplifiers are implemented. The time-triggered prompts are shown on a specific day at a specific time which remind the user of reflecting by offering feedback on various topics regarding the user's behaviour. The event-triggered amplifiers are generated when a significant change has been detected (e.g. when the number of switches is higher than usual or after long periods of idle time). Additionally a reflection diary is implemented, where all notes, thoughts or insights after reflection can be stored.

Learning: KnowSelf is designed to support individual reflective learning regarding time management and self-organisation of knowledge workers.

Setting: The evaluation took place in a consulting company that consults, sells, and personalises Customer Relationship Management (CRM) Software to help analyse and optimise the marketing, sales and service processes of their customer companies (small and medium enterprises). The employees have many meetings with customers at the customers' site and their daily work is heavily focused on customers' needs. This requires a high level of flexibility and the development of individual best practices. Consulting and sales thus involve a high degree of reflection regarding interactions with the customers.

Procedure: In a kick-off meeting at the company, the application was presented and explained to the participants by the evaluation responsible of the company (see [21], p. 25). They were asked to install KnowSelf on their business PCs and to use the app over a period of six weeks as well as to reflect on the collected data on a daily basis. During the six weeks, they received a weekly email including a reminder to reflect on the captured data, enter observations and to fill in a short online questionnaire to provide feedback.

Participants: 10 employees (3 females, 7 males) participated in the evaluation and 7 gave interviews; 10 % were younger than 19 years, 40 % each were aged from 20–29 and from 30–39 and 10 % were aged from 40–49.

6 Results

6.1 Usage Data

The MMA study had 33 participants; the Medical Quiz study 18 and the KnowSelf study 10 participants. During the evaluation period, the average number of interactions of the participants with the MMA was M = 42.67 (SD = 72.7), ranging from 1 to 338 interactions. KnowSelf was used on average for M = 38.5 min (SD = 23.8) by each participant, with a maximum of 53.72 and a minimum of 7.76 min. The participants of the Medical Quiz answered on average M = 461.9 (SD = 341.0) questions, with a maximum of 1358 and a minimum of 25 questions. Thus, participants used the apps frequently enough in order to test and evaluate the implemented reflection guidance components.

6.2 Reflective Learning

The post-questionnaires of the three studies contained seven app-specific reflection questions (see Table 2) for the MMA and the Medical Quiz and five questions for the KnowSelf. Mean ratings range from 3.25 (SD = .92) for the MMA over 3.28 (SD = .66) for the KnowSelf to 3.51 (SD = .42) for the Medical Quiz. The ratings indicate that all apps can slightly support reflective learning. Relating the objective usage data to these ratings, reveals positive correlations between the extent of app usage and how users perceive the apps' support for reflective learning. More exactly, for the Medical Quiz the Pearson coefficient reveals a significant correlation of r = .612 (p = .015), for the KnowSelf r = .850 (p = .015), whereas the correlation for the MMA (r = .226) is not significant.

6.3 Usage and Usefulness of Reflection Guidance Components

The implemented reflection guidance components were adopted as follows:

Contextualisation in the MMA was evaluated by means of three questions asking how helpful the contextualisation of mood points was for associating the inserted mood to certain situations (Q1), for recalling past experiences (Q2) and if the chosen activities (e.g. a call) helped to better reflect about a past situation (Q3). With mean ratings of Q1: M = 3.39 (SD=0.86), Q2: M = 3.21 (SD = 0.74) and Q3: M = 3.24 (SD = 0.94) the participants perceived the contextualisation as slightly positive. The analysis of the context information shows that 31 % of the moods were inserted "after a call", 6 % "after a break", 2 % after "a coaching session" and 61 % in "other", not pre-defined contexts.

Reflection interventions, in form of time-triggered prompts were implemented in KnowSelf and evaluated with two explicit questions in the post-questionnaire. Users rated the reflection intervention reminding them to use KnowSelf in general (e.g. by looking at the switching frequency between resources or writing diary entries) with M = 3.22 (SD = 1.09) whereas the reminder of project recording was perceived slightly negative M = 2.75 (SD = 1.28).

Table 2. Application specific reflection questions

Questions	Apps
[The app] helped me to collect information relevant to reconstructing experiences from work	MMA, KS
[The app] helped me to reflect on experiences from work	MMA
[The app] helped me to collect information that could help me decide when to reflect	MMA
[The app] helped me to reconstruct a work experience	MMA, MQ
[The app] helped me by capturing my reflection outcomes	MMA, KS
[The app] helped me by making reflection outcomes available for later use	MMA, MQ
[The app] helped me by capturing information for evaluation of learning/reflection	MQ
[The app] helped me by reminding me to reflect	MQ, KS
[The app] helped me by providing information relevant for the decision to reflect	MQ
[The app] helped me by providing accurate information about my work	MQ, KS
[The app] guided me in capturing information about my work experiences	MMA
[The app] guided me in deciding whether/when to reflect	MQ
[The app] provided relevant content for reflection	KS

Reflection amplifiers were implemented in all three apps. For the MMA, the amplifier in form of a prompt to add a note to the mood-context resulted in 475 notes inserted by the participants. The perceived usefulness of the prompts was not explicitly evaluated. In the Medical Quiz, we integrated reflection amplifiers by presenting reflection questions at the beginning, during and after a quiz play. Out of 1205 reflective questions, 603 (52 %) were answered in a meaningful way, which indicates that the quiz players have thought about the posed question and that reflective learning could be triggered. Looking at the time the questions were posed, results indicate that users preferred questions at the beginning of the quiz (59.3 % responses) over those at the end (51.5 %) and were most reluctant to deal with questions while playing the quiz (42.4 % answered). In KnowSelf, the usefulness of the event-triggered reflection amplifiers was explicitly raised. Participants rated the notifications about most used resources as rather helpful (M = 3.30, SD = 1.25), whereas the notifications about unusual amounts of idle time (M = 2.57, SD = 0.79) and notifications about specific amounts of switches (M = 2.30, SD = 1.34) were not perceived as very helpful.

In KnowSelf, the participants documented their experiences, insights and comments regarding the application in the **Reflection Diary**. Six participants were willing to share their explicit data and altogether 103 statements were inserted in the diary (the content is discussed in the next section). In contrast, the MMA provided **reports** including a **reflection diary** but these were not used by the participants. In the quiz there was no diary implemented.

6.4 Content Analysis of the Inserted Notes

The final coding of the analysed and categorised notes of the MMA and KnowSelf contains all those notes which were assigned in agreement after discussing deviating assignments. Altogether the MMA participants attached 475 non empty notes to 548 inserted moods. Out of these, 283 could be identified as individual reflective items. 95 % of the reflective notes were assigned to the first stage, which includes descriptions of experiences or emotions. The remaining 5 % belong to the second stage which refers to interpretations and justifications of actions and working on solutions. From the 103 statements inserted in KnowSelf, 33 statements were classified as non-reflective and for 11 entries there was no inter-coder agreement. The remaining 59 statements were classified as individual reflection items. Most of the notes, namely 47 %, were assigned to the second stage of reflection, 22 % to the first stage, and 27 % to third stage. For the latter, the diary entries included insights, learning outcomes, or conclusions drawn from reflecting. The coding schema could not be applied to the inserted answers of the reflective questions in the quiz, because in this case parts of the questions were formulated as closed questions which allowed a simple yes or no as answer.

7 Discussion

In the following, we discuss the reported results from the three conducted evaluations together with the findings obtained from the interviews and the workshop.

General Insights. The evaluation of the reflection guidance components implemented in three different applications revealed that the components were perceived as useful and that reflective learning has taken place. Results from two evaluations (Medical Quiz and KnowSelf) show a positive correlation between the extent of app usage and how users perceive the apps' support for reflective learning. This indicates that participants who used the apps more often, also dealt more intensively with their captured working activities or the quiz questions, and consequently also reflected more about it.

Usage and Usefulness of the Components. In the MMA evaluation, the participants confirmed that the contextualisation of each mood point helped to better reconstruct past working experiences. Although the predefined contextualisation possibilities had been defined together with managers and users of the call centre and were based on the main call takers' activities, they did not cover all the situations in which participants used the MMA. The "other" option was often chosen, which led to the assumption, that participants used the app not only in typical recurring work situation, but also in other work-related situations e.g. after dealing with a problem or successful event, start/end of day. Thus, contexts should be adaptable to individual preferences. This way, the contextualisation will encompass all relevant situations, but still be quick and easy to use.

By integrating reflective questions at the beginning, during and at the end of the quiz, we were able to show that asking the right questions at the right moment can trigger reflective learning. Altogether over 50 % of the 1205 posed reflective questions were answered in a meaningful way. The willingness to reflect on the reflection questions was given more with the questions presented at the beginning and at the end of the quiz. Interviews and workshop discussions revealed that the in-between reflection questions were perceived as more disruptive for the learning process. The results from the quiz are also in-line with the KnowSelf evaluation. Here, the participants perceived the notifications sometimes as disruptive because they popped up at times when they were working intensively on a task and were therefore seen as additional source of work fragmentation. On the other hand, the general reminder to reflect about the data in the app and the notification about the most used resources were positively evaluated. Taken together, the users did not profit from the prompts as much as we have expected it, especially when interventions disrupted the natural work-flow. In other words, reflective guidance does foster reflective learning, but the time of interventions is crucial with respect to acceptance. If timing is 'messed up', users will not accept the reflective learning guidance components, and consequently not learn (but rather spend their energy on being annoyed at the interruption).

Stages of Reflection. The analysis of the notes indicates that the participants reflected. The MMA evaluation showed that reflection took place mainly on the first and second stage of reflection, while the notes of the KnowSelf include all stages of reflection. Taking a closer look at the MMA notes, they deal with work experiences, encompass mostly emotional-based notes including own emotions, emotions of others (e.g. customers) and some notes regarding interpretation and justification of actions. This shows that the participants become aware of their own and others' mood and also reflected about them, which was the main purpose of the MMA. Most of the notes in the KnowSelf evaluation were related to the second stage of reflection. The participants did not only describe their experiences, but they were mostly explaining their experiences and suggested solutions to observed problems. Also more than a quarter of the reflective entries documented insights gained and conclusions drawn from personal experiences. These findings confirm that the participants gained new insights and a better understanding of their work experiences. These could then be used as a basis for changes in behaviour and thus sustainable improve related work processes, as e.g. time management. From the interviews conducted in all three evaluations, we also learned that a great part of the reflection process takes place in informal face-to-face communications. Thus, it is not possible to conclude from the captured notes, on which stages reflection was actually triggered by the guidance components. Especially with respect to the third stage, it seems reasonable that insights, learning and conclusions from reflection rather develop in personal discussions with colleagues than while using an app.

8 Conclusion

In this paper, we introduced an in-app reflection guidance concept to facilitate technology-supported reflective learning at work. Reflection-in-action and reflection-on-action components have been implemented in three different applications. Due to the fact that the apps were very heterogeneous, chances are high that reflection guidance can be successfully added to any app designed to support reflective learning. Generally, we observed that the users' perception of the apps' support for reflective learning positively correlates with the extent of app usage whereas the achieved reflection stage varied among the different settings. The correct timing of reflection interventions and reflection amplifiers is a crucial issue in order to avoid disturbing interruptions of the ongoing work process. This is not trivial at all, as identifying interruptibility is an ongoing research challenge. Therefore we suggest as good practice from software design to "simply" give users control over the way they are notified and when this notification should take place.

Acknowledgement. The project "MIRROR - Reflective learning at work" is funded under the FP7 of the European Commission (project number 257617). The Know-Center is funded within the Austrian COMET Program - Competence Centers for Excellent Technologies - under the auspices of the Austrian Federal Ministry of Transport, Innovation and Technology, the Austrian Federal Ministry of Economy, Family and Youth and by the State of Styria. COMET is managed by the Austrian Research Promotion Agency FFG. The authors thank Marina Bratic for her work with regard to the KnowSelf evaluation.

References

1. Alexiou, A., Paraskeva, F.: Enhancing self-regulated learning skills through the implementation of an e-portfolio tool. Procedia - Soc. Behav. Sci. **2**, 3048–3054 (2010)
2. Bannert, M., Reimann, P.: Supporting self-regulated hypermedia learning through prompts. Instr. Sci. **40**(1), 193–211 (2012)
3. Boud, D., Keogh, R., Walker, D.: Promoting reflection in learning: a model. In: Boud, D., Keogh, R., Walker, D. (eds.) Reflection: Turning Experience into Learning, pp. 18–40. Routledge Falmer, New York (1985)
4. Daudelin, M.W.: Learning from experience through reflection. Organ. Dyn. **24**(3), 36–48 (1996)
5. Davis, E.A.: Scaffolding students' knowledge integration: prompts for reflection in KIE. Int. J. Sci. Educ. **22**(8), 819–837 (2000)
6. Davis, E.A.: Prompting middle school science students for productive reflection: generic and directed prompts. J. Learn. Sci. **12**(1), 91–142 (2003)
7. Elango, S., Jutti, R.C., Lee, L.K.: Portfolio as a learning tool: students' perspective. Ann. Acad. Med. Singap. **34**(8), 511–514 (2005)
8. Fessl, A., Bratic, M., Pammer, V.: Continuous learning with a quiz for stroke nurses. Int. J. Technol. Enhanced Learn. **6**(3), 265–275 (2014)

9. Fessl, A., Rivera-Pelayo, V., Pammer, V., Braun, S.: Mood tracking in virtual meetings. In: Ravenscroft, A., Lindstaedt, S., Kloos, C.D., Hernández-Leo, D. (eds.) EC-TEL 2012. LNCS, vol. 7563, pp. 377–382. Springer, Heidelberg (2012)
10. Greaves, D.J., Gupta, S.K.: Portfolios can assist reflective practice and guide learning. Curr. Anaesth. Critic. Care **14**, 173–177 (2003)
11. Ho, J., Intille, S.S.: Using context-aware computing to reduce the perceived burden of interruptions from mobile devices. In: Proceedings of the SIGCHI Conference on Human Factors in Computing Systems, pp. 909–918. CHI 2005. ACM, New York, NY, USA (2005). http://doi.acm.org/10.1145/1054972.1055100
12. Ifenthaler, D.: Determining the effectiveness of prompts for self-regulated learning in problem-solving scenarios. Educ. Technol. Soc. **15**(1), 38–52 (2012)
13. King, A.: Facilitating elaborative learning through guided student-generated questioning. Educ. Psychol. **27**(1), 111–126 (1992)
14. Knipfer, K., Wessel, D., DeLeeuw, K.: D1.5 Specification of Evaluation Methodology and Research Tooling, June 2012. http://www.mirror-project.eu/research-results/downloads/finish/5/67
15. Kunzmann, C., Schmidt, A., Attwell, G., Chan, E., Heinemann-Grüder, M., Hughes, J., Lan, W., Vratny, A., Heberle, A.: REFLECT: community-driven scaffolding for voice-enabled reflection on the go. In: 3rd Workshop on Awareness and Reflection in Technology-Enhanced Learning, CEUR Workshop Proceedings (2013)
16. Pammer, V., Bratic, M.: Surprise, surprise: activity log based time analytics for time management. In: CHI'2013, 27 April - 2 May 2013, Paris, France (2013)
17. Park, S., Lim, J.: Promoting reflective thinking process in designing e-portfolios. In: Proceedings of Society for Information Technology & Teacher Education International Conference 2007, pp. 164–168 (2007)
18. Pejovic, V., Musolesi, M.: InterruptMe: designing intelligent prompting mechanisms for pervasive applications. In: Proceedings of the 2014 ACM International Joint Conference on Pervasive and Ubiquitous Computing. UbiComp 2014, pp. 897–908. ACM, New York, NY, USA (2014)
19. Prilla, M.: Collaborative reflection support at work: A socio-technical design task. In: Proceedings of European Conference on Information Systems (ECIS) (2014)
20. Prilla, M., Renner, B.: Supporting collaborative reflection at work: a comparative case analysis. In: Proceedings of ACM Conference on Group Work (GROUP 2014). ACM (2014)
21. Renner, B., Wesiak, G.: D10.3 Summative Evaluation of MIRROR Appsphere usage and effectiveness at test beds (2014). http://www.mirror-project.eu/research-results/deliverables/286-d103-summative-evaluation-of-mirror-appsphere-usage-and-effectiveness-at-test-beds
22. Rivera-Pelayo, V.: Design and Application of Quantified Self Approaches for Reflective Learning in the Workplace. Ph.D. thesis, Karlsruhe Institute of Technology, February 2015
23. Rivera-Pelayo, V., Zacharias, V., Müller, L., Braun, S.: Applying Quantified Self approaches to support reflective learning. In: Proceedings of the 2nd International Conference on Learning Analytics and Knowledge. LAK 2012, pp. 111–114. ACM, New York, NY, USA (2012). http://doi.acm.org/10.1145/2330601.2330631
24. Russell, J.A.: A circumplex model of affect. J. Pers. Soc. Psychol. **39**, 1161–1178 (1980)
25. Schön, D.A.: The Reflective Practitioner: How Professionals Think In Action, 1st edn. Basic Books, New York (1984)

26. Tang, C.: Reflective diaries as a means of facilitating and assessing reflection. Paper presented to the Pacific Rim Conference on Higher Education Planning and Assessment, Hilo, Hawaii, 3–7 June 2000
27. Thillmann, H., Kuensting, J., Wirth, J., Leutner, D.: Is it merely a question of "what" to prompt or also "when" to prompt? Z. Pädagogische Psychol. **23**(2), 105–115 (2009)
28. Thorpe, K.: Reflective learning journals: from concept to practice. Reflective Pract. **5**(3), 327–343 (2004)
29. Verpoorten, D., Westera, W., Specht, M.: Reflection amplifiers in online courses: a classification framework. J. Interact. Learn. Res. **21**(4), 654–666 (2010). Please check and confirm the edit made in Reference [29]
30. Walker, S.E.: Journal writing as a teaching technique to promote reflection. J. Athletic Training **41**(2), 216–221 (2006)
31. Xun, G., Land, S.: A conceptual framework for scaffolding iii-structured problem-solving processes using question prompts and peer interactions. Educ. Technol. Res. Dev. **52**(2), 5–22 (2004)

Training Workers for Improving Performance in Crowdsourcing Microtasks

Ujwal Gadiraju[1(✉)], Besnik Fetahu[1], and Ricardo Kawase[2]

[1] L3S Research Center, Leibniz Universität Hannover, 30167 Hannover, Germany
{gadiraju,fetahu}@L3S.de

[2] Mobile.de, Marktplatz 1, Europarc Dreilinden, 14532 Kleinmachnow, Germany
rkawase@team.mobile.de

Abstract. With the advent and growing use of crowdsourcing labor markets for a variety of applications, optimizing the quality of results produced is of prime importance. The quality of the results produced is typically a function of the performance of crowd workers. In this paper, we investigate the notion of treating crowd workers as '*learners*' in a novel learning environment. This learning context is characterized by a short-lived learning phase and immediate application of learned concepts. We draw motivation from the desire of crowd workers to perform well in order to maintain a good reputation, while attaining monetary rewards successfully. Thus, we delve into training workers in specific microtasks of different types. We exploit (i) *implicit training*, where workers are provided training when they provide erraneous responses to questions with priorly known answers, and (ii) *explicit training*, where workers are required to go through a training phase before they attempt to work on the task itself. We evaluated our approach in 4 different types of microtasks with a total of 1200 workers, who were subjected to either one of the proposed training strategies or baseline case of *no training*. The results show that workers who undergo training depict an improvement in performance upto 5 %, and a reduction in the task completion time upto 41 %. Additionally, crowd training led to the elimination of malicious workers and a costs-benefit gain upto nearly 15 %.

Keywords: Crowdsourcing · Workers · Training · Learning · Microtask · Performance

1 Introduction

In the recent years, crowdsourcing has become a convenient instrument for solving a multitude of problems that require human input. The methodology of crowdsourcing encompasses the 'outsourcing' of work to the crowd, where each crowd worker performs a small part of a task, commonly known as a 'microtask'. By accumulating the responses from workers through such 'microtasks', requesters solve different problems.

© Springer International Publishing Switzerland 2015
G. Conole et al. (Eds.): EC-TEL 2015, LNCS 9307, pp. 100–114, 2015.
DOI: 10.1007/978-3-319-24258-3_8

Crowdsourcing has been employed in many areas; to assemble dictionaries[1], to map the outer space[2], to aid in disaster relief [20], or in a most recent case, to support the search of a missing flight[3]. Wikipedia is a remarkable example of crowdsourcing that is well known to internet users. Millions of people contribute with small pieces of information to build a complete knowledge base. Lately, researchers in several fields are extensively employing crowdsourcing to collect human annotated data, build ground truths, to evaluate and validate results.

In this paper, our main goal is to tackle the aforementioned challenges that result in sub-optimal performance from crowd workers, and evaluate the best means to improve workers performance. Here we recognize the crowd worker as a learner, who is placed in an atypical learning set up that differs from traditional learning environments. First, there is no background information on the knowledge, skills or competences of the workers. Second, given the nature of the microtasks (short and less time-consuming), workers face an 'on-the-fly' learning situation. It is comparable to '*Experiential learning*' (the process of learning through experience, or learning by doing), where workers acquire experience during the execution of the task. It is also comparable to '*Microlearning*', which deals with small learning units and short-term learning activities. However, in many cases of microtasks, workers have no time to apply their gained experience. In some cases, workers who are performing badly throughout a task are not allowed to continue, while in other cases, workers are not aware of their performance. Thirdly, workers are highly motivated to perform tasks accurately, in order to receive the monetary reward. Finally, in this set up workers learn through training in a non-collaborative environment.

Taking into consideration this very particular learning setup, in this paper, we evaluate two different learning strategies that support the crowd workers to achieve high-quality performance, namely *implicit training* and *explicit training*.

Definition 1. Implicit Training. Workers are prompted with training information according to the microtask at hand, when they provide erroneous responses to questions with priorly known answers.

Definition 2. Explicit Training. Workers are required to complete a training session where they are prompted with training information according to the microtask at hand and asked to complete sample microtasks, before they begin responding to the questions within the task.

We deployed 12 crowdsourced tasks, spanning a total of 800 crowd workers who were subjected to one of these training strategies, and 400 workers who were not provided with any training at all. The main contributions of our research are listed below.

---

[1] http://www.wired.co.uk/news/archive/2011-01/13/the-oxford-english-wiktionary.

[2] http://edition.cnn.com/2014/08/17/tech/nasa-earth-images-help-needed/.

[3] http://tinyurl.com/kl3mmme.

1. We provide an analysis on the learning behavior of crowd workers.
2. We identify the best training strategy for crowdsourcing microtasks that optimize the quality of results produced.
3. We compare the qualitative affects of training on different types of microtasks.
4. We show that training workers can reduce the time required for task completion, deter the participation of malicious workers and improve the overall result quality.

In addition to these tangible contributions, we believe that we are delineating a new learning process that has not been investigated thoroughly or tackled, opening space for future research in the field. The main characteristics of this learning set up is that it is short term, on-the-fly, and typically for single use.

2 Related Literature

In this section, we review literature related to our work. First we motivate the direction of our work in this paper. Next, we present a discussion that is mainly centered around training crowd workers in virtual environments, and compares approaches that tackle a similar problem in a crowdsourcing setup.

In the crowdsourcing paradigm, motivation plays a big role in getting the crowd engaged. A sense of participation and community, reputation and altruism are general incentives that lead people to participate and contribute in crowdsourced initiatives. However, monetary incentive is a significant factor that motivates crowd workers to engage, especially in online setups. Our recent research work shows that monetary reward is in fact, the major incentive for crowd workers to perform these microtasks [4], and finding the right balance between *effort* required to solve a task and reward is a common problem faced by task administrators[4].

Much has been done towards improving crowdsourcing methodologies, in terms of increasing workers motivation and the quality of results [7,14], improving throughput [9], and reduction of task abuse [5]. In all these cases, the common goal was to optimize the outcomes of the crowdsourcing initiatives in terms of quantity and quality.

In the pursuit of monetary rewards, workers commonly perform tasks for which they do not possess the right competence or skills. Nevertheless, these workers in many cases ignore these limitations and still attempt to perform a given microtask. In some cases, as established in our recent work, *ineligible workers* intentionally ignore restrictive instructions [5], and in other cases, the workers are not aware of their lack of competence. Poor responses can also be a result of the lack of experience of workers or familiarity with microtasks and crowdsourcing platforms. As a consequence, workers provide sub-optimal input, and final outcomes may not be fully reliable. This leads to a waste of time and resources by both parties involved.

[4] A person who deploys a microtask in order to gather responses from the crowd. Also called a 'requester'.

Ensuring Quality of Crowdsourced Results. Many prior works have focused on improving worker accuracy and the quality of the responses produced by crowd workers [7,13]. A common approach to ensure the reliability of answers is by collecting multiple judgements from the crowd, such that the correct answer is determined via simple majority voting [16]. In our previous work, we have proposed tackling the challenge of improving the quality of crowdsourced results by preventing the participation of spammers and malicious workers on one hand [5], while improving microtask desgin on the other hand [12]. In contrast to such exisiting approaches, we propose training crowd workers within the specific microtask enviroment in order to improve their performance and the overall quality of the results produced. We experimentally investigate this approach on various types of microtasks.

Characterizing Crowds and Microtasks. In the work done by Lin et al. [11], authors tackled the problem of improving the accuracy of answers given by the crowd workers on open-ended questions (e.g. *find the mobile number of a CEO*). By modeling the workers and the microtasks as a generative probabilistic model, they inferred correct answers, hence reducing the number of answers needed in contrast to typical majority voting schemes. In a similar setting, Karger et al. [8] proposed an optimization model with given constraints such as the reliability and monetary cost of a task. The main goal of this approach was to achieve an acceptable reliability of a task with a given budget constraint. Welinder et al. [17] additionally introduced the notions of difficulty of a task and the skill-set of workers. By doing so, they grouped workers that have a certain skill-set and hence produce more reliable answers corresponding to the task difficulty. Whitehill et al. [18] proposed an approach that goes one step further and automatically infers labels for a given microtask, outperforming the majority voting mechanism. The difference between the aforementioned works and our work in this paper are twofold. We consider a variety of tasks that go beyond multiple choice questions, and through training the workers we show that we can improve the reliability of answers provided by the crowd. Hence, previous approaches that can be used to improve existing baselines such as *majority voting*, are rather complementary to our approach.

Crowd Training - *Workers* as *Learners*. One of the first works on teaching crowds by Goldman and Kearns [6], define the *teaching dimension*. It deliberates on the minimum number of examples needed to teach a given concept. The teaching problem is a binary classification problem, where a given hypothesis for teaching is accepted or rejected with respect to a given concept. The difference when compared to our *explicit* and *implicit* crowd training, is that we engage the crowd workers through guidelines, hints and tips that go beyond mere instructions (for example providing details on how to find the middle-name of an actor). With such training, we find that crowd workers can succesfully complete tasks at faster rates. This is all the more important, since typically crowdsourced microtasks [4] go well beyond the scope of binary answers.

In [1], the authors analyzed the task performance and the learning outcomes on a real-world classroom setup. They showed an improvement in the task performance of students subjected to appropriate learning conditions. Conversely, crowdsourcing has been used to improve the learning process in classrooms [2,19]. The main usage is primarly for obtaining feedback on the learning material and other classroom work. In our setup we train the workers to use appropriate tools and strategies to solve the tasks under evaluation adequately. Le et al. [10] investigated the effect of training questions distribution on the performance of crowd workers. They studied the relevance categorization task, and showed that a uniform distribution of training within a task produces optimal peaks in worker performance. In another closely related previous work by Singla et al. [15], the authors propose *teaching with partial feedback* for binary classification problems. The approach is iterative and at each iteration a learner is required to guess the label of an example. The learning process is influenced by showing the true label of the example. While we adopt a similar training process, we additionally investigate the effect of training on various types of microtasks.

3 Approach

In this section, we describe the methodology that we have adopted to gather data and design tasks of different types. We aim to investigate the following research questions:

- **RQ#1:** Can *training* workers on carrying out particular microtasks successfully lead to an improvement in their task performance?
- **RQ#2:** What kind of *training* results in an improvement in the quality of the results produced?
- **RQ#3:** How do *training processes* qualitatively affect different types of microtasks in crowdsourcing systems?

3.1 Methodology

We consider different microtask types according to the microtask taxonomy presented in our previous work [4]. The top-level microtask types in the proposed taxonomy are : *Information Finding*, *Verification and Validation*, *Interpretation and Analysis*, *Content Creation*, *Surveys*, and *Content Access*. Due to the fact that tasks of the type *Surveys* are subjective and questions in surveys predominantly reflect opinions, we do not consider crowd training for such microtasks. Similarly, *Content Access* tasks typically require workers to merely consume certain content, and we do not consider this type of microtask for training either.

We deploy the following tasks, to gather data representing the different types of microtasks that we aim to investigate.

- Finding the middle-names of famous people (Information Finding-**IF**)
- Spam detection (Verification and Validation-**VV**)
- Sentiment Analysis (Interpretation and Analysis-**IA**)
- Image transcription (Content Creation-**CC**)

3.2 Tasks Design and Particulars

We consider three different setups for each of the four types of tasks: implicit training (**IT**), explicit training (**ET**) and no-training (**NT**). We use a premier crowdsourcing platform, CrowdFlower[5], to deploy the 12 microtasks. We gather responses from 100 independent crowd workers in each case. On average, we offer a monetary incentive of 5 USD cents for each worker that successfully completes a task. In each task, the order of the questions are randomized for different workers, to avoid any bias possibly introduced due to specific order of the questions. In addition, clear instructions are provided to the workers for each task, in order to avoid bias due to the misinterpretation of the tasks. Lengths of the different tasks were designed such that the required completion times are similar, in order to make sound comparisons.

3.3 Training Crowd Workers

In our work, we aim to investigate the affect of *Implicit* and *Explicit Training* on the performance of crowd workers with respect to different types of microtasks.

Information Finding. In case of the *IF* tasks, workers are asked to find the middle-names of famous people. There are 20 units in each task. For the *implicit training*, on committing errors workers are trained with the workflow of finding accurate middle-names by leveraging proper search mechanisms as shown in Fig. 1. For the task with *explicit training*, workers are provided with similar training on 5 units before they begin working on the actual task.

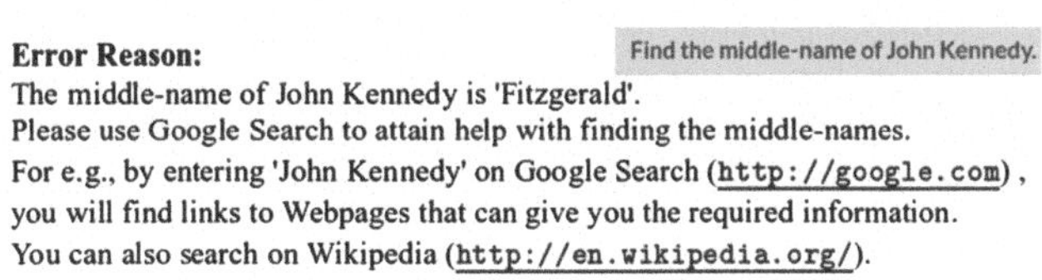

Fig. 1. Training in the IF task of finding middle-names (the question is inset here).

Verification and Validation. In case of the *VV* tasks, workers are asked to detect the spam SMS from a set of 5 SMS texts in each of 30 units, as shown in the Fig. 2. Workers are trained in the *implicit* and *explicit* training tasks with examples that emulate the following: 'fake advertisements or meaningless offers are good candidates of being spam messages'.

[5] http://www.crowdflower.com/.

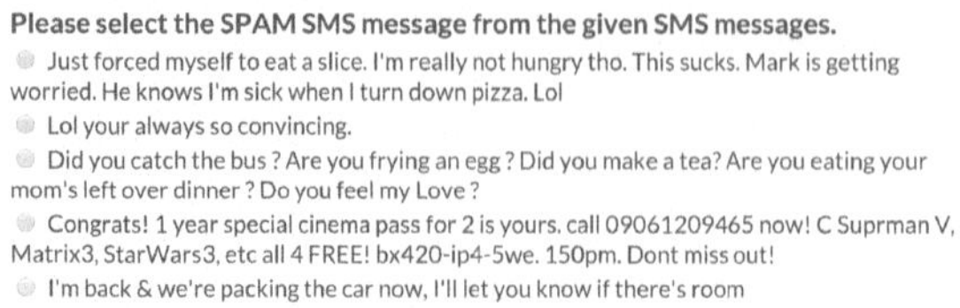

Fig. 2. Example unit in the spam detection (VV) task.

Interpretation and Analysis. In the *IA* tasks, workers are asked to assess the sentiment expressed within tweets (`Positive`, `Negative` or `Neutral`). These tasks also consist of 30 units, such as the example portrayed in Fig. 3.

Workers are provided training in the tasks with *implicit* and *explicit* training to identify tweets with each of the 3 sentiments. For example, an excerpt from the training is: "In order to determine the underlying sentiments of a tweet, adjectives and adverbs play a key role (as expressed in this tweet through the term, '`awesome`')."

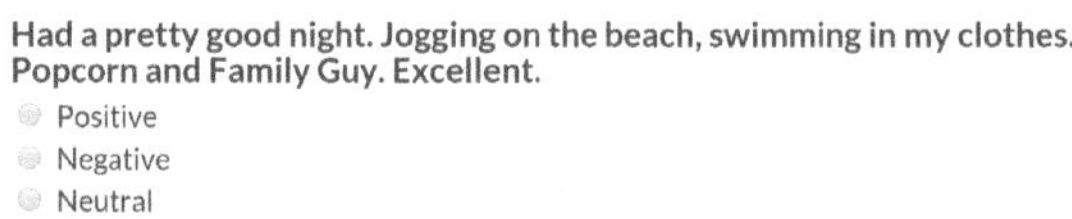

Fig. 3. Example unit in the sentiment analysis (IA) task.

Content Creation. Finally, in case of the *CC* tasks, workers are asked to transcribe CAPTCHAs[6] in 30 units within the tasks as shown in Fig. 4. As a part of the training, workers are provided with tips on recognizing subtle differences between letters to perform accurately. An example excerpt is the following: 'NOTE that the second letter is '`g`'. While it may seem similar to a '`q`', the '`g`'s have a small curve at the bottom, while the '`q`'s have an underscore at the bottom'.

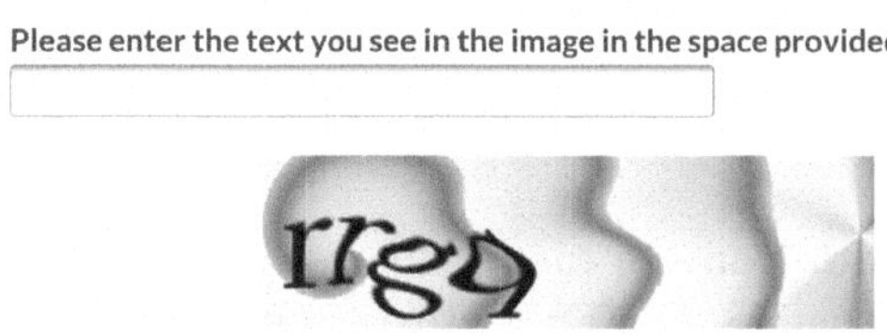

Fig. 4. Example unit in the image transcription (CC) task.

12 tasks were deployed as described above, with varying microtask type and training setups. Responses from workers were thereby collected in order to study the implications of training crowd workers.

[6] http://www.captcha.net/.

4 Data Analysis

In this section, we first present details regarding the geographical distribution of crowd workers that provided responses to the different types of microtasks. Then we disuss the effect of training on various aspects.

Note that, we detect *malicious workers* based on the approach described in [5], and discard the responses from these workers in our analysis, unless stated otherwise. Malicious workers are those workers who provide ill-fitting or arbitrary responses in order to complete a given task quickly and attain the monetary compensation.

We analyzed the geographical distribution of workers who participated in each of the 12 tasks deployed. Note that we did not enforce any restrictions in the participation of workers. In case of the *Information Finding* tasks we found that over 50 % of the workers were from India, followed by nearly 25 % workers from Turkey. Interestingly, we note that 53 % of workers in case of the *Verification and Validation* tasks were from Spain, while another 24 % are from Italy. For the *Interpretation and Analysis* tasks, we observed that a majority of workers (around 37 %) were from Bosnia and Herzegovina, followed closely by workers from Turkey (over 31 %). Finally, in case of the *Content Creation* tasks, we found that around 40 % of the workers were from the Philipines and 30 % of the workers were from Great Britain. We believe that these differences in the geographical distribution of the workers is primarily due to the difference in the timings at which the tasks were deployed.

4.1 Impact of Training on the Accuracy of Workers

In order to assess the impact of training on the accuracy of workers, across the different types of tasks, we analyze the responses gathered from the 12 tasks as mentioned in Sect. 3. Figure 5 presents our findings. In Fig. 5(a), we see that in the case of an Information Finding task, training helps to improve the accuracy of workers. However, there is very little difference between the increase in accuracy achieved due to *implicit* and *explicit training*. On average we find that IT and ET improve the accuracy of workers by over 2 % in the IF task.

Interestingly, we find that training did not result in an improvement in the accuracy of workers in case of the Verification and Validation task ((Fig. 5(b)). We note that workers achieve an accuracy of around 82 % without any training. When implicit training is provided the accuracy of workers deteriorates to 65 %. In case of explicit training, the accuracy of workers reduces to nearly 77 %. We believe that this is due to the ease of the VV task we have considered (detection of a spam SMS), as confirmed by the average unit completion time for this particular task when compared to other tasks in the absence of training (see Fig. 6b).

In the case of either an IA task (Fig. 5(c)) or a CC task (Fig. 5(d)), we note that training improves the accuracy of workers by around 3 % and 5 % on average respectively. We observe a trend where, explicit training results in the biggest improvement in the accuracy of workers, followed by implicit training. Based on

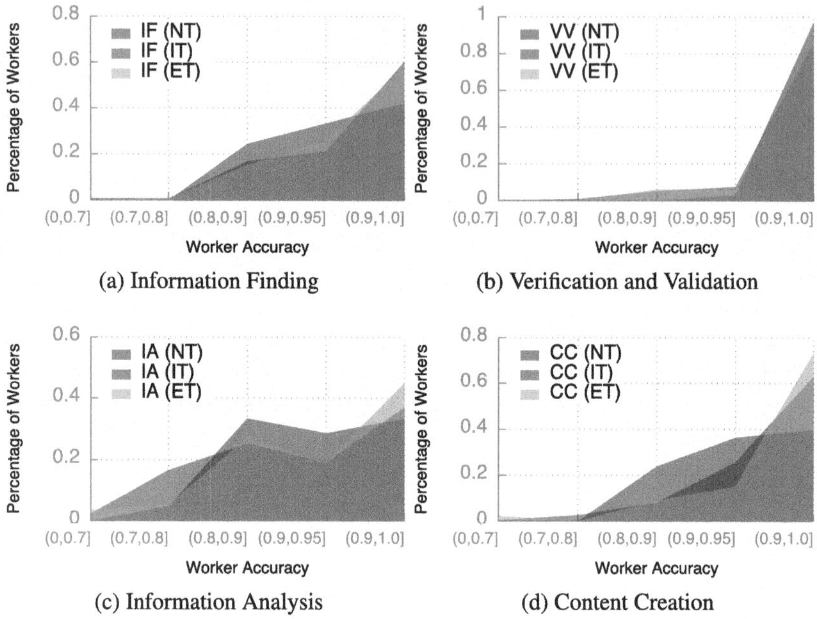

Fig. 5. Accuracy of workers in different training scenarios (*no training* (**NT**), *implicit training* (**IT**), and *explicit training* (**ET**)) for (a) IF, (b) VV, (c) IA, and (d) CC types of microtasks.

our experimental findings, we observe that training workers either implicity or explicity improves their performance across all types of microtasks.

4.2 Impact of Training on Distribution of Elite Workers

As defined in our previous work [5], *elite workers* are those crowd workers that provide perfect responses to all questions within a task. We additionally analyze the affect of training workers through the distribution of *elite workers*. Figure 6a presents our findings. We observe that in the IF, IA and CC tasks, training increases the number of elite workers. In these cases, explicit training brings about the biggest increase in the percentage of elite workers, followed by implicit training. Interestingly, in case of the VV task, we observe that training decreases the number of elite workers.

4.3 Impact of Training on Unit Completion Time of Workers

We analyze the average time that the workers take to complete a single unit in each of the different tasks, and within different training settings. We present our findings in the Fig. 6b. We find that the biggest impact of training is observed in case of the *Information Finding* task. In this task workers were trained with directions on finding middle-names in an efficient manner. We observe that such

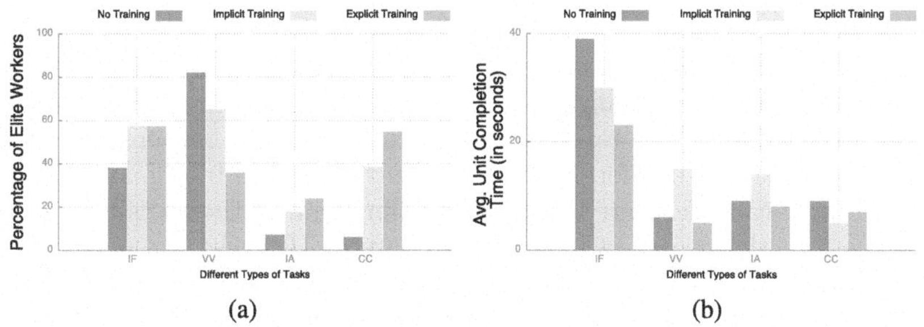

Fig. 6. Effect of training on (a) the distribution of elite workers, and (b) the average unit completion time of workers in different types of tasks.

training given implicitly reduces the average *Unit Completion Time* (UCT) by 23 %, and explicit training reduces the average UCT by 41 %. We observe a similar trend where training decreases the average UCT of workers in case of the other task types. Interestingly, we note that implicit training increases the UCT of workers in case of the IA task.

4.4 Impact of Training on Malicious Workers and Its Implication on Costs-Benefit Ratio of the Responses

We additionally analyze the effect of training crowd workers with respect to the number of malicious workers attracted to a task, and present our findings in Table 1. We observe a general trend where the training process results in a decrease in the number of malicious workers. In case of the **IF** tasks, we note that implicit training (IF-IT) reduces the fraction of malicious workers from 10 % to 5 % and explicit training reduces this further to only 1.5 %. We observe a similar trend with respect to implicit and explicit training for the tasks of type **IA** and **CC**. In case of the **VV** task, we note that while implicit training (VV-IT) seems to increase the fraction of malcious workers, explicit training reduces this by a big margin. Overall, we find that explicit training dissuades the participation of malicious workers to a large extent.

Table 1. Effect of different types of training on the fraction of malicious workers in varying types of microtasks.

Microtask type	No training (NT)	Implicit training (IT)	Explicit training (ET)
IF	10 %	5 %	1.5 %
VV	2 %	3.2 %	0.6 %
IA	37 %	25.7 %	22.4 %
CC	12.9 %	9.9 %	4.2 %

The effect of training, resulting in the decrease of malicious workers has important implications on the monetary compensation that task requesters have to provide. Note that the financial rewards that malicious workers attain on task completion contribute to a wastage of resources, since their responses cannot be used by a requester. Therefore, with the reduction in the fraction of malicious workers in a given task, there is a corresponding gain in the costs-benefit ratio with respect to the responses gathered. In case of **IF** tasks, we note that ET improves the costs-benefit ratio by 8.5 % and IT improves the costs-benefit ratio by 5 %. Similarly, we note an increase in the costs-benefit ratio by 1.4 % in case of **VV** tasks, 14.6 % in case of **IA** tasks, and 8.5 % in case of **CC** tasks through explicit training of crowd workers.

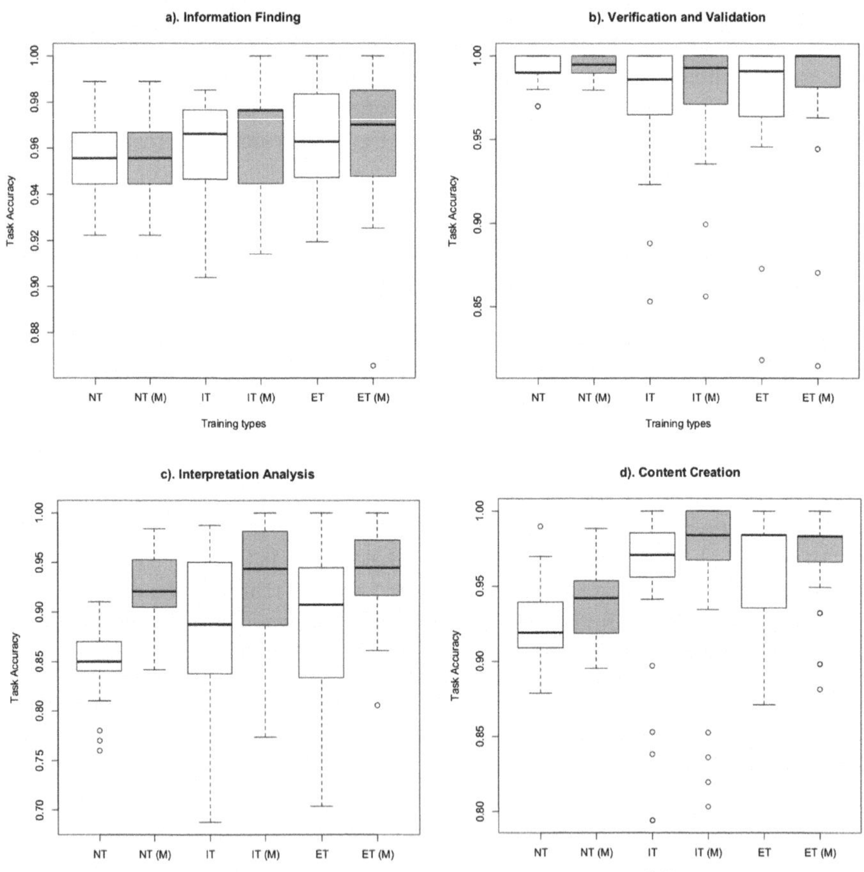

Fig. 7. Overall accuracy of tasks in different training settings in the presence and absence of malicious workers. '(M)' indicates the absence of malicious workers.

4.5 Overall Accuracy of Tasks in Different Training Settings

We finally investigate the overall accuracy that is achieved in tasks of different types under the varying training setups. The box-plots in Fig. 7 depict our findings. We observe that the overall task accuracy improves when the crowd workers are trained either implicitly or explicitly. In case of the VV tasks, we note that there is no significant improvement due to the training. As discussed earlier, we believe that this is due to the relative ease of the particular *Spam Detection* task that was considered. We clearly observe that the detection and removal of malicious workers improves the overall task accuracy across different task types, when compared to their contrasting counterparts.

5 Discussion

Through our analysis of the different types of microtasks we investigated in varying crowd training settings, we can conclude that training workers improves the accuracy of the workers, thereby enhancing the overall quality of the results produced. An important implication of *implicit* and *explicit training* of crowd workers is that tasks can be completed at faster rates. We observe that this trend holds good across all the task types considered, in case of explicit training of crowd workers. Depending on the type of the task, this can help task administrators reduce costs with respect to time to a great extent. For example, when crowd workers learn to complete a relatively complex task in the easiest and most adequate manner, they not only find it easier to complete the task successfully, but they also take lesser time to complete the task at hand.

We highlight that training workers on a particular task goes beyond providing comprehensive instructions. In the explicit training process, workers are required to complete a certain number of units while implementing suggested mechanisms. In the implicit training process, workers are prompted with the training suggestions each time they commit an error. Through our results, we show that these aspects help a worker learn the ideal way to complete a particular microtask successfully. Note that in our work we do not evaluate the quality of the training itself that is provided. We believe that the training process is dependent on the task, and there may be multiple training options for a given task. In the future, we will investigate the research question regarding different training types, durations and their effect on the performance of crowd workers for specific microstasks.

Due to the existing reputation systems in crowdsourcing platforms (such as the *trust-score* in CrowdFlower, we believe that many crowd workers are highly motivated to perform accurately in order to maintain a good reputation or *trust-score*. Previous works have shown that honest workers are also prone to providing inaccurate responses due to their inattentiveness, boredom [5], or in some cases poor instructions and task design [14]. By training the crowd workers, we can help the honest workers in creating and maintaing a good reputation. We observe that the number of *elite workers*, i.e., workers with a 100 % task accuracy, increases across different types of tasks due to implicit and/or explicit training.

Interestingly, we note that the training processes discourage malicious workers. It has been established by prior works that malicious workers are mostly attracted to tasks which can be easily completed in short periods of time [3]. From our findings presented in the previous section, we infer that the training processes, both implicit and explicit disrupt a malicious worker from achieving his goal to game the microtask quickly. Such reduction in the fraction of malicious workers, results in a gain in the costs-benifit ratio with respect to the workers responses. In this way, requesters can increase the quantity of useful responses obtained from workers for the costs incurred.

Finally, we address the issue of overheads due to training. Intuitively, the overheads arise primarily due to the training process in terms of time and costs (i.e., monetary compensation). However, we have already established the fact that training crowd workers can actually shorten the time required for task completion. We believe that depending on the crowdsourcing platform being used, the monetary compensation for the additional training processes is either negligible, or worth the minor additional investment.

Although we present the geographical distribution of the workers in our microtasks, we refrain from drawing conclusions with respect to the correlation between specific countries and the types of task. This is due to the fact that the geographical distributions may be skewed by factors such as the time of the day at which the microtasks were deployed on the platform, and the absence of a controlled environment for worker participation. In this regard, more experiments under specific settings are necessary, which is beyond the scope of this work.

6 Conclusions and Future Work

In this paper, we have carried out a comprehensive investigation on the effects of training processes on the performance of workers, in different types of microtasks. We have considered all the applicable types of top-level microtask types according to the taxonomy proposed in our previous work [4].

We delve into two different types of crowd training setups; *implicit* and *explicit* training. Here, we treat crowd workers as *learners* in an atypical learning environment that is characterized by a short learning phase and immediately preceeds the application of learned concepts. Workers learn independently and exploit the training in order to complete the microtasks more efficiently.

Through our experimental results, we have identified that training workers on the specific tasks at hand during their participation in the microtasks, can lead to substantial improvements in their performance (**#RQ1**). In addition, we study the effect of particular kinds of training (implicit/explicit) to assess the optimal kind of training process, in comparison to the cases of 'no-training'. We found that explicit training yields the biggest improvements in the individual performance of workers as well as the overall quality of the results produced (**#RQ2**). Next, we studied how implicit and explicit training effect tasks of different types. We note a trend where explicit training results in the highest improvements across different types of microtasks, followed by implicit training (**#RQ3**). Finally, we studied the effect of training on several aspects such as elite workers (who complete tasks with a 100 % accuracy), malicious workers (who attempt to game tasks to avail the monetary compensation easily and quickly), the task completion time, and the overall accuracy of the tasks. We find evidence of a positive impact in all these cases. Training enables workers to complete tasks in shorter time spans, deters malicious workers, and improves the overall task accuracy.

As a part of imminent future work, we plan to model, quantify, and investigate the ideal 'amount of training' that results in high performance gains. We also plan to experiment with varying task lengths, to identify the optimal lengths that render tasks suitable for crowd training. In addition, we intend to investigate other modes of training processes such as a combination of implicit and explicit training.

Acknowledgements. This work has been carried out partially in the context of the DURAARK project, funded by the European Commission within the 7th Framework Programme (Grant Agreement no: 600908).

References

1. Do-Lenh, S., Jermann, P., Cuendet, S., Zufferey, G., Dillenbourg, P.: Task performance vs. learning outcomes: a study of a tangible user interface in the classroom. In: Wolpers, M., Kirschner, P.A., Scheffel, M., Lindstaedt, S., Dimitrova, V. (eds.) EC-TEL 2010. LNCS, vol. 6383, pp. 78–92. Springer, Heidelberg (2010)
2. Dow, S., Gerber, E., Wong, A.: A pilot study of using crowds in the classroom. In: 2013 ACM SIGCHI Conference on Human Factors in Computing Systems, CHI 2013, pp. 227–236, Paris, France, 27 April - 2 May 2013 (2013)
3. Eickhoff, C., de Vries, A.P.: Increasing cheat robustness of crowdsourcing tasks. Inf. Retr. **16**(2), 121–137 (2013)
4. Gadiraju, U., Kawase, R., Dietze, S.: A taxonomy of microtasks on the web. In: 25th ACM Conference on Hypertext and Social Media, HT 2014, pp. 218–223, Santiago, Chile, 1–4 September 2014 (2014)
5. Gadiraju, U., Kawase, R., Dietze, S., Demartini, G.: Understanding malicious behavior in crowdsourcing platforms: The case of online surveys. In: Proceedings of CHI Conference on Human Factors in Computing Systems, CHI 2015 (2015)
6. Goldman, S.A., Kearns, M.J.: On the complexity of teaching. In: Proceedings of the Fourth Annual Workshop on Computational Learning Theory, COLT 1991, pp. 303–314. Morgan Kaufmann Publishers Inc., San Francisco (1991)
7. Ipeirotis, P.G., Provost, F., Wang, J.: Quality management on amazon mechanical turk. In: Proceedings of the ACM SIGKDD Workshop on Human Computation, pp. 64–67. ACM (2010)
8. D.R. Karger, S. Oh, and D. Shah. Iterative learning for reliable crowdsourcing systems. In: Advances in Neural Information Processing Systems 24: 25th Annual Conference on Neural Information Processing Systems 2011. Proceedings of a meeting held 12–14 December 2011, Granada, Spain, pp. 1953–1961 (2011)

9. Kobren, A., Tan, C.H., Ipeirotis, P.G., Gabrilovich, E.: Getting more for less: optimized crowdsourcing with dynamic tasks and goals. In: Proceedings of the 24th International Conference on World Wide Web, WWW 2015, Florence, Italy, 18–22 May, 2015, pp. 592–602 (2015)
10. Le, J., Edmonds, A., Hester, V., Biewald, L.: Ensuring quality in crowdsourced search relevance evaluation: the effects of training question distribution. In: SIGIR 2010 Workshop on Crowdsourcing for Search Evaluation, pp. 21–26 (2010)
11. Lin, C.H., Mausam, M., Weld, D.S.: Crowdsourcing control: moving beyond multiple choice. In: Proceedings of the Twenty-Eighth Conference on Uncertainty in Artificial Intelligence, Catalina Island, CA, USA, 14–18 August, 2012, pp. 491–500 (2012)
12. Marshall, C.C., Shipman, F.M.: Experiences surveying the crowd: reflections on methods, participation, and reliability. In: Proceedings of the 5th Annual ACM Web Science Conference, pp. 234–243. ACM (2013)
13. Oleson, D., Sorokin, A., Laughlin, G.P., Hester, V., Le, J., Biewald, L.: Programmatic gold: targeted and scalable quality assurance in crowdsourcing. In: Human computation, vol. 11, issue no. 11 (2011)
14. Rogstadius, J., Kostakos, V., Kittur, A., Smus, B., Laredo, J., Vukovic, M.: An assessment of intrinsic and extrinsic motivation on task performance in crowdsourcing markets. In: ICWSM (2011)
15. Singla, A., Bogunovic, I., Bartók, G., Karbasi, A., Krause, A.: On actively teaching the crowd to classify. In: NIPS Workshop on Data Driven Education (2013)
16. Vuurens, J., de Vries, A.P., Eickhoff, C.: How much spam can you take? an analysis of crowdsourcing results to increase accuracy. In: Proceedings of ACM SIGIR Workshop on Crowdsourcing for Information Retrieval (CIR 2011) (2011)
17. Welinder, P., Branson, S., Belongie, S., Perona, P.: The multidimensional wisdom of crowds. In: Advances in Neural Information Processing Systems 23: 24th Annual Conference on Neural Information Processing Systems 2010. Proceedings of a meeting held 6–9 December 2010, Vancouver, Canada, pp. 2424–2432 (2010)
18. Whitehill, J., Ruvolo, P., Wu, T., Bergsma, J., Movellan, J.R.: Whose vote should count more: optimal integration of labels from labelers of unknown expertise. In: Advances in Neural Information Processing Systems 22: 23rd Annual Conference on Neural Information Processing Systems 2009. Proceedings of a meeting held 7–10 December 2009, Vancouver, Canada, pp. 2035–2043 (2009)
19. Xu, A., Rao, H., Dow, S.P., Bailey, B.P.: A classroom study of using crowd feedback in the iterative design process. In: Proceedings of the 18th ACM Conference on Computer Supported Cooperative Work & Social Computing, CSCW 2015, Vancouver, Canada, 14–18 March 2015, pp. 1637–1648 (2015)
20. Zook, M., Graham, M., Shelton, T., Gorman, S.: Volunteered geographic information and crowdsourcing disaster relief: a case study of the haitian earthquake. World Med. Health Policy **2**(2), 7–33 (2010)

Engaging Teaching Professionals in Design for Online Learning

Marianne Georgsen(✉)

School of Continuing Education, VIA University College, Aarhus, Denmark
mage@via.dk

Abstract. Teaching and learning in higher education institutions have for some time now been seen to integrate on line activities, materials and student interaction into otherwise campus based programmes. Traditional teaching is often both classroom-based, teacher centred as well as with an emphasis on content delivery. Transformation of existing teaching practice, however, is often a daunting task for teaching professionals, and one which calls for an organizational approach. To support teaching staff in such transformation, a methodology for learning design has been developed and implemented into the organisation of a school for continuing education. Despite support from e-learning experts in the design process, most projects undertaken by teaching staff were modest in degree of innovation, and existing practices were reinforced rather than transformed. The workshops and design methodology have now become part of a so called organizational framework for learning design in order to provide a stronger incentive and better support for transformation of practice.

Keywords: Learning design · Organizational design frame · Workshop methodology · CoED · Further education

1 Introduction

Teaching and learning in higher education institutions have for some time seen the need to integrate on line activities, materials and student interaction into otherwise campus based programmes. This is done to accommodate requests from students and other stakeholders mainly in continuing education, such as employers. Students' everyday use of on line media and subsequent increased request for flexibility regarding access to materials and time spent on study activities have been strong motivators for institutions to rethink their general approach to teaching and learning. Traditional teaching is often both classroom-based, teacher centred as well as with an emphasis on content delivery. Transformation of existing teaching practice into more student centred learning with meaningful use of on line activities is often a daunting task for teaching professionals, and one which calls for an organizational approach. This paper presents findings from an organizational development project aiming at three goals: Expanding the pedagogic repertoire of the teaching staff; increasing the use of ICT in teaching and learning; and building capacity towards on line and blended learning in the organisation. The main challenges for the school were to expand its portfolio of educational modules and to

© Springer International Publishing Switzerland 2015
G. Conole et al. (Eds.): EC-TEL 2015, LNCS 9307, pp. 115–126, 2015.
DOI: 10.1007/978-3-319-24258-3_9

build capacity for transforming parts of the existing teaching practices. In short, the project encountered a number of issues concerning the motivation of the teaching staff some of whom faced the project with a demand for justification for the changes in teaching and learning mode. Also a fear of becoming redundant (partly due to lack of skills, but also due to changes in the role of the teacher) was found to concern the staff. In order to address these fairly common concerns a project was launched where teaching staff were invited to participate in a number of learning design workshops. The chosen method (the Collaborative e-Learning Design Method or CoED [1, 2]) for the learning design activities is user driven, involves the participants, is led by experts, and puts the teacher/tutor in the role of the expert when it comes to the content, the characteristics of the modules, and the students or target group. Learning design is here to be understood as a methodology which enables teachers or designers to make more informed decisions in designing learning activities and interventions, which are pedagogically informed and make effective use of appropriate resources and technologies. A key principle of learning design is making the design process more explicit and shareable. Learning design as an area of research and development combines gathering empirical evidence to understand the design process and the development of a range of learning design resources, tools and activities [3, 11].

Findings from the project have confirmed that a method for learning design which gives structure to the design process and helps participants to visualise their designs and make them explicit and shareable, is very helpful for teaching professionals with no or minimal experience in on line or blended learning. However, we also found that there is a need to stimulate the imagination of the participants, both in relation to planning of teaching and learning and in relation to the role technology can play. Although this was part of the methodology it turned out to be a bigger problem than anticipated. Furthermore, we found that many of the participants in the design workshops were unsure about the organizational and managerial priorities in relation to development of on line and blended learning, and this turned out to be perhaps the biggest issue for the project. Participants expressed a need to know more precisely in which direction management wanted to take the teaching and learning culture. They also wanted to be assured that the new designs would 'fit' the organisation in terms of the general teaching style, the technological infrastructure and support system, and the marketing of modules towards potential students, companies and organisations. This led to a stronger focus on the organizational framework within which the design activities took place. A result of this, a so called organizational design frame has been developed which will serve as a guide in the future. The design framework, which will be described in more detail below, describes three levels of policy, resources and procedures in the organisation:

- The strategic level, which presents the design frame defined by the organisation and the goals connected to it
- The tactical level, which describes the organizational support for e-learning design, capacity building, IT-support, managerial support and interest, etc.
- The operational level, which describes the teaching and learning philosophy and clearly outlines the freedom to act for the teaching professionals.

In the following paragraph, the general conditions of further education in Denmark are presented in order to outline the case of this paper. This is followed by a more detailed description of the development project initiated to support the transformation of the teaching and learning culture into more blended and on line learning, followed by a short description of the data from the project. The learning design method is described and discussed in the following section, followed by an account of the findings from the project. This serves as background for the presentation of the first version of the organizational design frame and our expectations for future use of this.

2 The Case of Further Education in Denmark and via University College

The work of teaching staff is influenced by decisions, strategies, policies and other conditions, many of whom are outside the primary control of the teaching professional herself. In Denmark, further and in particular continuing education is mainly offered by public educational institutions which are given accreditation to run diploma programmes and courses. It is required by law to demand tuition fees, which is contrary to most other educational programmes, which are free to attend. The tuition fee may lead to a regarding the employer or the student as customers, and can sometimes inhibit the desire to experiment with e.g. course designs. Very often, schools of continuing education are regarded as business units within their institutions, and as such they are expected to turn out a profit from their activities, unlike e.g. bachelor or master programmes.

For diploma programmes, applicants must fulfil specific entry requirements such as previous education, working experience, etc. Continuing education can be both full time and part time. Till recently, public employers have been entitled to some compensation from the government when an employee enrols in an accredited diploma programme where teaching takes place within normal working hours. This has made it affordable for workplaces to give priority to education, both for the employer and the employee, who would often keep his or her regular salary while attending the programme. This has recently changed, and it is expected that the need for more flexible and more on line programmes will grow in the near future. In the private sector, this is already the case, as many employees do not get time off to attend continuing education. In overview, one might say that in the realm of further and continuing education, the teaching and learning culture is framed by the following:

- The majority of programmes are part time and caters for participants who are in jobs, often full time jobs. To get away from the daily work, participants have traditionally preferred fixed times of studying away from the work place
- The extent and duration of the course or program. In short courses it is important that the use of IT does not take up unnecessary time or requires too much attention
- Participants in further education and workplace learning usually identify with the teachers they meet, rather than with the teaching organisation itself. This means that the teachers, in addition to being professional teaching and content experts, also need to have sufficient IT-proficiency to assist learners with the most urgent IT-problems they may encounter

- Mandatory tuition fees (contrary to most other education, which in Denmark is free)
- The need for user-oriented design is bigger in further education, as the groups of participants, the contents, the ways of teaching and studying often vary greatly across different courses
- The need for user-orientation means that the organisation should hold capacity to design and support a variety of solutions/designs for learning support.

This project took place in the school of continuing education in VIA University College, Denmark [4]. VIA is Denmark's largest university of applied sciences with more than 18,000 students and app. 2000 employees. The institution is based in the Western part of the country, and has 8 campuses and teaching facilities at 25 different addresses in the region. The school of continuing education offers programmes at diploma level, higher adult education, vocational training and courses and conferences. Programmes are offered within a wide range of topics and study programmes, mainly within the public sector (health; teaching and education; social welfare; public administration; management) but increasingly also within the private sector (project management; management and administration; innovation and entrepreneurship).

The specific challenges for VIA in this regard are twofold. In 2012, a survey based evaluation of general and teaching specific IT-skills was carried out in VIA. The survey covered all teaching staff across the institution. This led to a stronger focus on skills development in this area in the school, most specifically regarding use of IT in teaching. Furthermore, the expected changes in the demand for further and continuing education caused management to aim for development in the pedagogical repertoire of the teaching staff as well as an expansion of the range of teaching and learning methods applied in the programmes. In particular, more use of blended and on line learning was desired, both in existing and in new modules and programmes. In order to support this development, a strategic project was established and a specialist consultant was hired to help design and run the project.

3 Design of On Line and Blended Learning – The Project

In 2013, a project was launched with the following aims:

- To expand the repertoire for use of IT in teaching and learning in the organisation
- To identify needs for organizational support for teaching staff who engage in on line and blended teaching and learning
- To develop criteria for high quality use of IT in teaching in the school of continuing education, including on line and blended modules
- To further develop and implement a model for agile learning design with a high degree of user involvement.

The main activity in the project was a number of learning design workshop with teaching staff, focusing on the design or redesign of modules and programmes. The expectation was that based on the designs made in the workshops, a number of good practice-examples would appear, and that these cases or examples would fit into an on line resource site to be established in the organisation. Other elements in the project were an evaluation of the use of the standard LMS in the school, and establishment of a review board for the project to ensure feedback on the methodology and results of the project. The project met with the review board twice a year, and discussed progress, problems and perspectives of the work undertaken. Board members were experts in different areas relevant to the project (innovation; e-learning; teaching and learning; organizational development) and proved to be a great source of inspiration for the project lead.

The main questions in the research carried out in relation to the development project are:

1. In which way can skills development in relation to use of IT in teaching be integrated into the work practices of teaching staff?
2. What are the best conditions for developing high quality, contextually based and learner centred on line and blended learning?

In the project, teaching staff was invited to join a series of three design workshops where they would design or redesign specific course modules together with their teaching colleagues. The general idea with the workshops was to combine skills development with the design activities. The workshops were facilitated by experts, and the participants worked with authentic cases of their own choice and preferably supported by their heads of education. The aim was to complete a process of *analysis*, *idea generation*, *design*, *construction*, *test* and *implementation* during the course of the workshops.

In VIA in general, teaching and learning is supported by a learning management system (LMS), which is designed to fit the needs of the vast majority of the bachelor programmes in VIA. This system is designed and supported by a centralised IT-unit, and all students and teachers have a personal account and email account to the system. It is mainly used for distribution of information, displaying teaching schedules and materials, for assignments, and for communication between teachers and students. In all of VIA's 50+ study programmes the system looks the same, has the same functionality and user interface, and as such can be labelled a 'standard system'. This is a common situation in many educational institutions, and has the advantages of stability, professional support/help desk, and good integration with other standard tools in the institution. In the field of further education, however, the conditions are different in a number of ways from those in bachelor or master programs (as described above). This has led to a rather minimal use of the LMS in the school of continuing education, and one of the challenges in the project was to motivate teaching staff to look at the LMS in a new light, and see the additional options and extra functionality, which had not previously been used.

3.1 Methods and Data

In this study, I look mainly at question 2 above: What are the best conditions for developing high quality, contextually based and learner centred on line and blended learning? I have looked at a number of specific issues, among these are: The experiences of the participants in the learning design workshops; the role of IT in existing learning designs; the degree to which staff go beyond the standard IT tools and systems provided by the organisation (LMS + additional tools for e.g. communication); and the way in which participation in the project has been balanced with daily tasks by the staff. For the purpose of studying the case of 'project on line and blended learning', collection of data has been carried out during the course of the project. I have three main sources of data:

- Interviews with participants in the first round of workshops, carried out in June 2014
- Documents from design workshops (sketches, design documents, etc.)
- State-of-the art evaluation of course sites in LMS (90 course sites have been analysed in May 2014).

During the course of the project, a log was also maintained to document activities. This was done with very brief account of actions, mainly in an attempt to keep track of the development of a number of simultaneously running series of design workshops.

Interviews were conducted as part of a midway evaluation of the workshop methodology, all participants from the spring were interviewed and interviews were recorded and later transcribed (9 interviews in total). Documents from the design workshop are mainly large posters, which have been photographed, but also stored for later study. Other documents from the workshops are lists of problems identified; the most highly valued characteristics of teaching; module overviews; module designs; mock ups of LMS design; and other results of the processes in the workshops. A report on the development of each learning design has also been put together, thus documenting the final design propositions. Finally, the evaluation of the course sites was carried out as document analysis. From a total of app. 500 sites, 70 course sites were randomly selected to represent the 'average' use of the LMS. In addition, a smaller number of innovative teachers and avid IT-users were identified, and one site from each of these was also analysed, thus making a total of 90 course sites. The analysis of the course sites were guided by three questions:

- How are the standard templates used? Are they used fully, and to what extent do teachers add extra functionality?
- Are other digital services in use, and how do these connect with the use of the course site?
- What types of digital learning material are in use, and to what extent are digital materials found?

The study of the LMS shows that there are clear differences between the two groups of sites which were analysed. The advanced LMS-use involves more external tools and resources as well as a wider range of different types of digital materials. The large group of randomly selected sites showed very little variety, which could be seen as an indication that the template works as a strongly regulating instrument for teaching staff. For many of the participants in the workshops, the use of the LMS is core in their experience with using IT in teaching and learning and shapes their expectations and imagination about the potential and role IT can play. Even so, it came as a surprise that the majority of designs produced in the workshops were far from transformative. The participants generally preferred solutions which were close to the original format of the course or module they were redesigning.

4 Collaborative e-Learning Design Method (CoED)

As mentioned in the introduction, the project made use of the CoED method as the main inspiration for its learning design-workshops. In this section I will describe the method and the experiences we got from using it. As a general description of what a method for learning design is, one can say that it should provide at least two things: It serves to formalise the procedures of design, and it helps externalise the design thinking by shaping solutions and ideas into concrete artefacts, e.g. drawings, lists, diagrams, etc. This can also said to be true for the CoED method and the way it has been adjusted and used here.

The CoED method provides guidelines for how to conduct design oriented workshops to help practitioners and designers in designing (online) learning courses, modules or other educational activities. In this way it is similar to other LD-methods such as Participatory Pattern Workshops [5] and the Carpe Diem Workshop Planner [6, 7]. The point of departure in the CoED method is the preferences and objectives of the teaching practitioners and their pivotal role in the design process. Thus, a very important part of the CoED method is the negotiation and collaboration on establishing a shared pedagogical vision among practitioners. CoED can be viewed as what Conole terms "mediating design artefacts" like 'toolkits' (a structured resource that can be used to plan, scope and cost an activity [8]. The method divides the design process into three phases and uses specific tools and techniques in each phase. It draws on existing techniques which are often employed within iterative design processes such as card sorting and rapid prototyping; however, it entails some novel elements. Firstly, it seeks to address the gap between theoretical models of learning and actual learning designs. It does so by promoting negotiation and reflection among teachers by leading them to identify core pedagogical values, and focusing on embedding these in the actual design. Secondly, it specifically supports a collaborative approach to the design processes where teams of participants (ideally with different disciplinary backgrounds) co-develop learning designs. Thirdly, an accompanying web based software tool makes it easy to re-design the cards used as part of the method. This makes the method both scalable and applicable in different contexts.

The CoED method facilitates the design process by following five overarching principles, and furthermore by splitting the early design process into three phases. The five principles in the CoED method:

- Facilitates conversations about e-learning design
- Structures conversations about e-learning design
- Produces design specifications and/or actual designs rapidly
- Involves e-learning experts, domain specialists and future users of the e-learning design
- Involves at least two people in the design process.

The principles are relatively straightforward and act as guidelines for the overarching purpose of the CoED method: To support structured dialogues and concrete design activities among a diverse group of participants (more than two), and ideally with participants from different domains. Following principle number four, the design process ideally involves learning experts, domain specialists and future users of the learning design.

4.1 Experiences with CoED

In this particular project, some minor adjustments were made to the original CoED-concept. The groups of participants were not always as collaborative as could be wished for. This was the result of the way participants for the LD-workshops were selected in the organisation. We emphasised that participation should be group based and that participants should bring to the workshops a specific module or programme to work with. However, some participants joined together with colleagues, but wanted to work on individual projects. Others worked on the project of a colleague, which reduced their sense of ownership to both the process and the result. After the midway evaluation, the importance of both collaborative projects and managerial support were emphasised prior to finding participants for the second round of workshops. The workshop facilitators had the role of e-learning experts and at the same time as facilitators of the process. The participating teachers were the content/domain specialists and also the learning experts. The participant had various backgrounds and domain knowledge; some were from the health sciences, some from education and teaching, and others from social welfare-programmes. This meant that in some workshops there was very little knowledge about IT and much knowledge about learning and teaching. In others, participants very experienced IT-users and unexperienced teachers or planners of teaching. This meant that the role of the facilitators were slightly different in each workshop, and that presentations could never be fully reused, but had to be adjusted - often spontaneously during the course of the workshop. Also the involvement of future users was not possible in the sense that students did not participate in the workshops. To always keep in mind the perspective of the learner became the shared responsibility of all participants.

In addition to the five principles, the design process is split into three phases:

- Focus the e-learning design process (presentation).
- Identify overarching values and design principles (card sorting and selection through a process of prioritising).
- Specify design (card sorting and design).

The presentation in phase 1 was given by the facilitator, and as mentioned above it was accommodated to the needs and interests of the particular group of participants in each workshop. Before moving to phase 2, participants were asked to outline the case they would be working with in the workshops – at this point the first sketch was produced. This was followed by phase 2, in which participants would have a structured discussion about the core values in their teaching and learning design (structured by a card sorting tool, see Fig. 1 for an example). This is followed by further analysis of the case, identifying strengths in the current design and ideas for the future design. At this point participants produced a list of their ‘problems and wishes’ which became part of the design documents. In phase 3, participants moved on to specifying the design (this would most often take place at workshop 2). As a request from many of the participants, we added at this point a session of inspirational examples which fitted into the projects in the particular workshop. Some of the things we demonstrated were various types of video based materials for flipped classroom teaching; use of discussion forums in blended designs; collaborative writing tools; wikis; etc. We were challenged to maintain focus on the construction of new designs, rather than turning the workshops into a course-like activity (which, by the way, several of the participants requested).

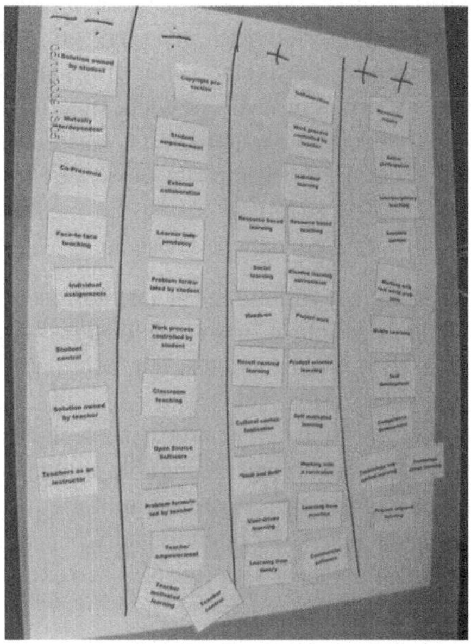

Fig. 1. Picture from card sorting-process. The goal was to identify no more than three characteristics of teaching and learning which the participants could agree on to be of core value to their design.

The process of specifying the design was supported by both a template for sketching the flow of the module (describing both learning outcomes, roles of the students, activities, materials used and produced, ways in which the work is organized, etc.), and by lists of terms to be used in specifying the design. The terms would both serve as inspiration for the participants and as a way of developing a shared vocabulary. The duration of the three phases would vary greatly, depending on a number of things. Some of the factors which would determine the production of the final design were:

- The urgency of the case – when the new design is needed
- The scale of the design – it turned out that rather than redesign the actual module, some participants preferred to work on details within the existing design such as presentation materials or even content
- The ownership to the case – some groups were appointed to the LD-workshops by educational managers and asked to work on projects formulated by others than themselves. This resulted in circular motion where participants several times returned to the justification for the case rather than move into the phase of specifying a design

- The participants' knowledge of IT and their powers of imagination in relation to the use of tools they have little or no experience with.

In general, the sum of experiences with the CoED method in this project shows that within short time, practitioners often manage to create relatively detailed preliminary designs (prototypes), while also negotiating a shared pedagogical vision for such a design. Moreover, the CoED method provides practitioners with a space for discussing their values, design concrete learning activities, and representing these in a very flexible, yet structured manner. Therefore, the method introduces an adaptable and scalable design concept that allows for different levels of detail in terms of the resulting design, while maintaining a strong focus on the negotiation of shared pedagogical core values among a potentially diverse group of participants. However, some critical issues were also found, which may relate specifically to using the method in the organizational context of the school of continuing education. These are:

- The task of providing sufficient technological inspiration in the workshops turned out to be critical to the production of innovative designs. A number of the designs produced were only slightly revised versions of the original designs (much like what Puentedura refers to as 'substitution' [9]
- The invitation to collaborate on the design process, which is a core instrument in the method, was not welcomed by everyone. A possible explanation can be found in the way teaching tasks are organized in most continuing education divisions, where teaching staff is highly specialised and often the only person or one in a few people within specific knowledge domains. They often plan and execute their teaching alone, and many enjoy this dimension of the job
- Ownership to the design case, the problem and the solutions represented in the design suggestion, is crucial to the commitment of the participants. However, many of our participants expressed concern or insecurity about how management would value and support radically new designs
- The IT-infrastructure and the access to tools and technologies, support, help in solving specific problems, etc., are of major importance to many participants, but not to all. The degree to which staff relies on tested and secure designs and solutions varies a great deal (or in other words, their willingness to take risks in the teaching situation)
- To know and trust in the greater organizational project is of importance to many participants, however, not to all. In the realm of further and continuing education, demands and conditions change regularly; however, the demand for high quality teaching from domain experts is a constant factor. Staff will refer to this in both their private and shared thoughts about the decision to go on line or use more blended learning. This stresses the importance of clear communication and actions from management to support the project.

5 Organizational Design Framework

Based on the experience from the workshops, the interview data, and feedback from the review board it became clear that the issue of managerial clarity in relation to the project was key to some of the challenges we were facing. With inspiration from Christensen et al. [10] we have addressed this through the formulation of a so-called organizational design framework which will guide the future development of the teaching and learning culture. The design framework describes policy, resources and procedures at three levels, namely at the *strategic*, the *tactical* and the *operational* level. The three levels are interrelated and describe three dimensions of the overall decision-making process when it comes to facilitating a change or transformation in the teaching and learning culture. As illustrated in Fig. 2, the strategic level is the basis in the model and as such key to successful dealing with the other levels. The strategic level will deal with the justification of the project, whereas the tactical level describes what needs to be in place to carry out the strategy. This level deals with resources and capacity in the organisation, as well as policies, values in teaching and learning, standards of quality, managerial support, etc. The tactical level also makes explicit how the effort of teaching staff within this area is given priority. The operational level describes how to proceed in order to achieve what is described at levels 1 and 2, what methods to use, what is regarded good practice, etc. Furthermore, it describes the teaching and learning philosophy and clearly outlines the freedom to act for the teaching professionals within the design framework. The workshop methodology described in this paper is an example of such an operational guide. Recently, representatives for the teaching staff and educational management in the school of continuing education have described core values in teaching and learning, a document which will also influence decisions made at the operational level.

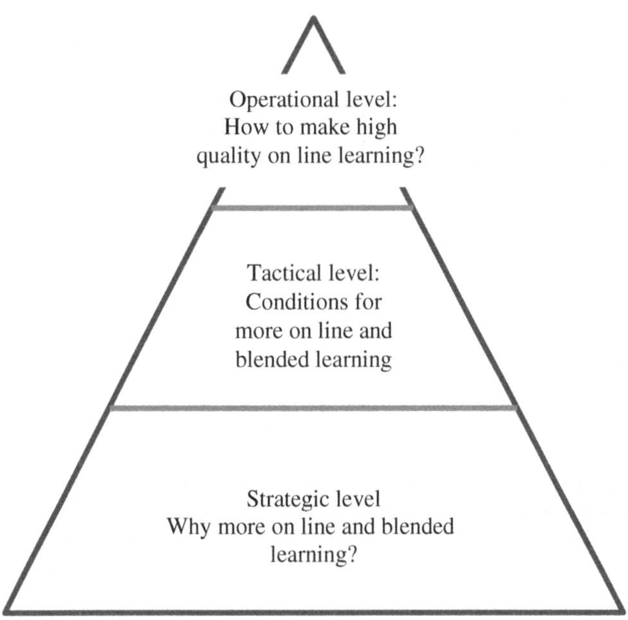

Fig. 2. Three levels in the organizational design framework in hierarchical order

6 Conclusion

An increased organizational focus has several benefits for the parties concerned:

- Teaching staff get the support, incentives and guidance for the development work. The relevance of their choices and their effort becomes clear to them.
- Students get a clear picture of what to expect in terms of teaching and learning culture, and also of what is expected from them as active learners.
- Management' claims for specific development in the teaching and learning practice can be legitimately put forward with reference to the strategies and policies.
- The work of individual members of staff becomes part of a guided, collective effort.

However, the design framework will not make much difference in itself. As also pointed out by Salmon [12], higher education institutions still struggle with the task of fulfilling the promises of IT in teaching and learning. Based on the findings and experience from the blended learning-project, it is clear that such a tool for communication, planning and carrying out transformation of teaching practices will strengthen the effort to combine high quality teaching and domain expertise in on line and blended learning modules.

References

1. Nyvang, T., Georgsen, M.: Collaborative e-Learning Design Method (CoED). e-Learning Lab Publication Series, no. 12, p. 25. Aalborg University, Denmark (2007)
2. Ryberg, T., Buus, L., Nyvang, T., Georgsen, M., Davidsen, J.: Introducing the collaborative e-learning design method (CoED). In: Mor, Y., Craft, B., Maina, M. (eds.) Art and Science of Learning Design. Sense Publishers, Rotterdam (2015)
3. Conole, G.: Designing for Learning in an Open World. Springer, New York (2013)
4. VIA University College: http://www.viauc.com/about/Pages/about-us.aspx
5. Mor, Y., Warburton, S., Winters, N.: Participatory pattern workshops: a methodology for open learning design inquiry. Res. Learn. Technol. **20**(0) (2012). doi:10.3402/rlt.v20i0.19197
6. The learning design grid. http://www.ld-grid.org/resources/methods-and-methodologies/carpe-diem
7. Salmon, G., Wright, P.: Transforming future teaching through 'Carpe Diem' learning design. Educ. Sci. **4**, 52–63 (2014)
8. Conole, G.: Describing learning activities; Tools and resources to guide practice. In: Beetham, H., Sharpe, R. (eds.) Rethinking Pedagogy for a Digital Age: Designing and Delivering e-Learning, pp. 81–91. Routledge, New York (2007)
9. Puentedura, R.R.: As we may teach: educational technology, from theory into practice (2009). http://www.hippasus.com/rrpweblog/archives/000025.html
10. Christensen, O., Christiansen, R.B., Gynther, K., Helms, N.H., Schlüntz, D.: Can We Learn from Others? International Experience with e-Learning and Blended Learning in Vocational Education and Teacher Training. University College Zealand, Sorø (2014). (in Danish)
11. Goodyear, P., Dimitriadis, Y.: In medias res: reframing design for learning. Res. Learn. Technol. Suppl. **21**, 19909 (2013). doi:10.3402/rlt.v21i0.19909
12. Salmon, G.: Flying not flapping: a strategic framework for e-learning and pedagogical innovation in higher education institutions. ALT-J **13**(3), 201–218 (2005)

Beyond Delivery Modes and Apps: A Case Study on Mobile Blended Learning in Higher Education

Christian Glahn[1(✉)], Marion R. Gruber[2], and Olga Tartakovski[3]

[1] Blended Learning Center, HTW Chur, Chur, Switzerland
christian.glahn@htwchur.ch
[2] Faculty of Arts and Social Sciences, University of Zurich, Zurich, Switzerland
marion.gruber@phil.uzh.ch
[3] IPMZ, University of Zurich, Zurich, Switzerland
o.tartakovski@ipmz.uzh.ch

Abstract. Mobile learning has received an increasing attention by the TEL community since 2010. While much research is available on the effectiveness of individual apps and educational approaches and despite that many higher education institutions introduced special mobile learning apps, relatively little is known about the rationale of scaling up mobile learning in higher education institutions. It reports on a case study, in which a mobile app solution has been integrated into a lecture at a major Swiss university. The study analyses the student's use of mobile media and the use of a smart-phone app in a mobile blended learning setting. The results indicate that today's students live in a multi device environment and are likely to use mobile apps in new contexts and settings if this is supported by an app. They also show that mobiles will not replace other delivery modes or technologies. Instead, the findings indicate that students used the mobile learning solution for extending and enriching their learning environment. Therefore, this study suggests that mobile learning needs to blend into rich learning environments, in which they co-exist with paper books, classroom experiences, laptops, and tablets. The insights define new requirements for both, mobile apps and virtual learning environments, in order to meet the future challenges of TEL in higher education.

Keywords: Blended learning · Case-study · Device ecologies · Device usage · Educational design · Evaluation · Higher education · Mobile learning · Seamless learning

1 Introduction

Scaling up technology enhanced learning in traditional higher education requires much didactical and technical reasoning. This is even more the case when new technologies are integrated into an already technology enhanced environment. Educational technologists working with mobile learning solutions find themselves often in a situation to work with both, enthusiasts who will follow a new technological trend for the technologies sake and the pragmatists who reasonably argue that the existing technology is

© Springer International Publishing Switzerland 2015
G. Conole et al. (Eds.): EC-TEL 2015, LNCS 9307, pp. 127–140, 2015.
DOI: 10.1007/978-3-319-24258-3_10

satisfying their and their students' educational demand. The study underlying this paper started from integrating a mobile solution into a university course that is already setup following a blended learning approach in order to better understand the requirements, attitudes, and practices of lecturers and students towards using mobile technologies.

This paper reports on the initial findings of using a mobile micro-learning solution in a blended learning lecture in a major university in Switzerland during the fall semester 2014. The underpinning case study addressed the framing, attitudes, and practices of using mobile learning in a blended university lecture. While a lot has been written on mobile learning tools, architectures and educational designs, scaling up mobile learning into higher education practice needs to take a broader perspective beyond usability and attractiveness. Yet, very limited research is available on the technological framing in which mobile learning solutions should be used, while at the same time many higher education institutions are rolling out mobile apps. Typically, generic market studies such as [1] are used as reference, but it has been reported that the reality within an organization can divert significantly from the general market [2].

Scaling up mobile learning also requires well-understood educational concepts. Wong and Looi [3] introduced the educational design concept "seamless learning". Seamless learning is anchored in mobile learning because contextualizing learning is a distinct aspect addressed by mobile learning research [4]. Seamless learning abstracts approaches and practices for bridging and linking learning experiences across contexts, among which is bridging or linking learning across space and time. While these two characteristics are genuine to flexible learning and have been inherited by blended learning, it has been claimed that special approaches using mobile technologies can expand the existing notion [5, 6].

The present research grounds on the concept of "mobile blended learning". This concept refers to educational designs that include mobile devices for special learning activities in combination with other learning educational approaches and technologies. Compared to common use of "blended learning" [7–9] the added "mobile" highlights that learning activities differ for each technology used in the learning scenario. Therefore, it goes beyond device related content adaptation and "responsive design".

Unlike seamless learning, mobile blended learning refers to educational designs without considering learning contexts other than the device dimension. The smaller focus of mobile blended learning allows addressing questions on contextual implications of technologies and instructional designs that help to develop a better understanding for the interplay of educational experiences and technological affordances in seamless learning.

2 Question for Research

The present case study responds to the need of contemporary higher education institutions to introduce technological innovation in education while many technological and conceptual uncertainties exist. At the same time new approaches in TEL are unlikely to remain isolated. Instead, they are used in combination with established tools and concepts. This raises concerns about the usefulness of extending educational toolkits.

Therefore, it is required to address the technological and educational benefit of integrating mobile learning into the mainstream practice. Consequently, the present study tackles the following question in order to provide a baseline for scaling up mobile blended learning in higher education.

What benefits does mobile technology contribute to an already technology enhanced learning environment?

In order to answer the primary research question, two subordinate questions were isolated. Through these questions this study seeks to integrate the techno-social perspective as well as the educational technology perspective.

The first question addresses the technological ecosystem and the related practices of university students by asking: what technologies are available and practices are common to students in higher education? Answering this question provides insights on the technological status quo that allows relating to broader oriented market studies. The resulting information also allows estimating potential areas for investment in infrastructure, tools, or practice development.

The second question focuses on the mobile technology-related affordances for contextualizing learning in a higher education setting by asking: are there intrinsic context-related affordances that allow to bridge learning activities into uncommon contexts? This question addresses a design problem for operationalizing seamless learning as well as for contextualization. The problem is to what extent "context" has to be explicitly considered in an educational design and to what extent it is already inherent to the tooling. This aspect influences the perception of lecturers and instructional designers regarding the complexity of integrating seamless learning.

Given the scope of the present study it is impossible to provide comprehensive generalisable answers. The responses to these questions might not be directly transferable to other organizational and national contexts or to different tool arrangements. However, by addressing these questions this study connects the organizational and the educational-design dimensions; and thus contributes to the development of a better understanding of the baselines for using mobile technologies as parts of broader technology-enhanced learning environments in higher education.

3 Method

The case study has been conducted as part of an introductory lecture on media studies and communication science at a major Swiss university. The lecture is mandatory during the first term of the related bachelor program and is repeated annually. Consequently, the lecture's curriculum and learning resources have been standardized, while professors of the institute rotate the responsibility for holding the lecture every academic year. One or more teaching assistants support the professor. The lecture has already implemented a voluntary online component using the university's learning management system. The teaching assistants primarily maintain the lecture's online component. The existing online learning material consists of references to reading material, the lecture slides, a discussion forum for subject matter related questions, a discussion forum for organizational questions, and a question pool that is used for self-assessment throughout the duration of the lecture as well as for the final exam.

The lecture has been extended by the mobile micro learning [10, 11] app "Mobler Cards" [12] in order to evaluate the feasibility of providing mobile learning support in this introductory lecture. The solution builds on the existing self-assessment resources. Providing more timely learning opportunities to the students and to estimate their adoption of such an added service has motivated this extension of the lecture using a mobile tool.

3.1 Mobile App Integration into the Blended Learning Setting

Mobler Cards is a smart phone app that implements a flashcard learning inspired micro learning approach. Micro learning is defined as the arrangement of minimal and complete learning activities [10]. A learning activity is complete if it consists of a task affordance, a learner action, and a feedback that is provided to the learner in response to the action. A learning activity is considered minimal if it cannot be further separated into smaller complete learning activities. Mobler Cards uses test items as micro learning activities and repeatedly presents them to a learner (Fig. 1). Test items are particularly suitable for micro learning because they consist of a question (task affordance), require a learner response to the question (learner action), and define rules for assessing the learner response for providing feedback.

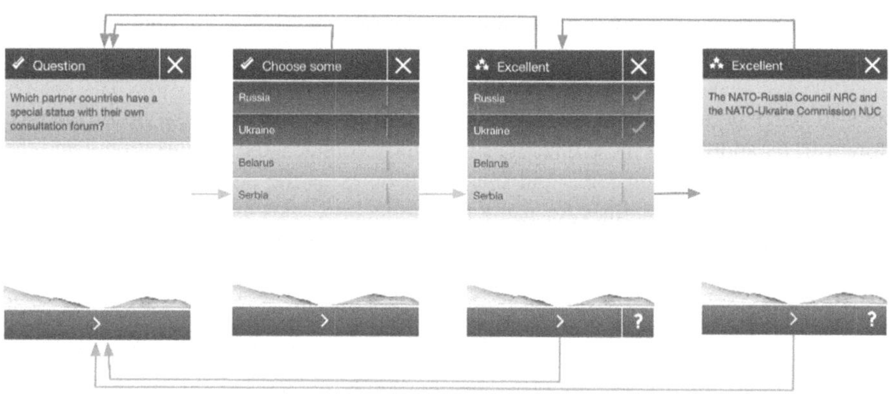

Fig. 1. The Mobler Cards' micro learning loop with screen captures

Mobler Cards is designed for easy integration into online learning environments and for the repurposing of existing learning resources. For this purpose, the app relies on three REST services for connecting to learning management systems: a content broker, a learning record store (LRS), and a learner profile.

The content broker service selects app suitable learning material for the learners' settings. It uses the learning management access control to determine, which content is available on the learners' personal devices. This way content can be personalized according to the learners' courses, to their learning path, to their performance, or to the timing in a course. Timing was the only parameter for parameterizing the content broker during the present case study.

The LRS provides a unified way for storing traces of learning experiences. The LRS used by Mobler Cards is defined by the Experience API (XAPI) specification [13]. The LRS is at the core for orchestration and information functions of the Mobler Cards app [14].

Finally, Mobler Cards uses a learner profile service. This service informs the app on a student's preferences and the courses, into which the student is enrolled.

All services are present for the learning management system as well as for the app itself. This way the app decouples student interaction with the service synchronization. This is a prerequisite for the fully offline function of Mobler Cards. The app can connect to LMSes by following the principles of the ADL Training and Learning Architecture (ADL TLA) model [15]. This enables a bi-directional integration of the Mobler Cards app into the learning environment. The integration architecture is illustrated in Fig. 2.

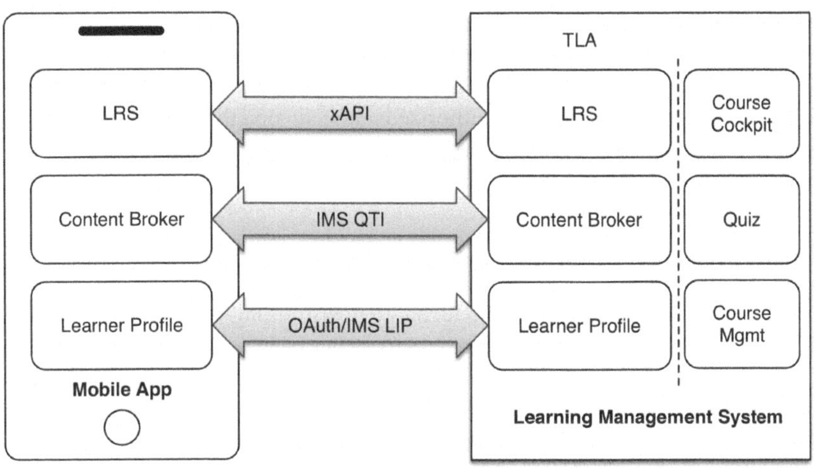

Fig. 2. Architecture for the Mobler Cards-LMS integration

3.2 Instructional Design of the Mobile Blended Learning Settings

The lecture has been conducted as a weekly face-to-face lecture with 13 sessions throughout the fall semester 2014. As an introductory lecture, the lecturer presented an overview of the theories and concepts of the subject with minor student interaction during the face-to-face sessions. At the end of the semester a final written exam tested the students' knowledge on these topics. The exam took place 3 weeks after the last face-to-face session.

Each session briefly repeated the key points and theories of the preceding session and provided the students the opportunity to request clarification on difficult aspects. Given the size of the lecture, students often do not raise questions or indicate their challenges in understanding certain concepts. To overcome this barrier the lecture included special online quizzes that were made available to the students each week. The quiz results were used as an indication on the concepts that were well understood and those that were challenging for the students. A quiz consists of 5–8 test items. Similar but not the same questions were used for the examination. After the last session the quizzes were extended with additional questions in order to support the students' exam preparation. In total 125 test-items were presented in the quizzes. The number of attempts per quiz was not limited.

The Mobler Cards app used the same test-items as the weekly quizzes. After each session during the term new questions were included into the app. Therefore, the number of items that were presented to the students grew towards the end of the term. Finally, for exam preparation all additional questions were also added to the question pool. Each attempt to answer a question was stored in the LRS at the LMS and provided the input for the course cockpit. In the course cockpit the course facilitators are able to see the average student performance for each test-item. Additionally, the cockpit provides an overview on the student activity with respect to the app. For organizational reasons the app was promoted with a one-week delay after the online quizzes.

Both, the Mobler Cards app and the conventional online quizzes were voluntary for the students and had no influence on the students' grades. Compared to other practices, the test-items were entirely teacher authorized and managed the same way, both, online and mobile. This way the students were assured that all questions reflect the topics that are relevant for the lecture's exam.

3.3 Data-Collection and Analysis

To answer the question regarding the technological framing as well as to identify the qualitative aspects of using Mobler Cards a survey has been conducted after the lecture's final exam. All students of the lecture were invited to participate in the survey.

The survey includes items regarding mobile device adoption and usage, regarding the usage context of Mobler Cards in a mobile blended learning setting, as well as items regarding the perceived usability of the app. The items covering the device adoption and usage were taken from a market study [1] as well as from a prior study on mobile device adoption in a professional education context [2]. The items on the contextual device use were taken from the same survey and adapted to match the concrete scenario of the case study. The items on the perceived usability are based on commonly used usability evaluation sheets [16, 17]. The items consist of nominal scales, Likert scales and open questions for qualitative feedback. The survey was implemented as an online questionnaire using the EvaSys system [18], which is the source for the reported descriptive survey results. The usability scales in the survey were only displayed to those participants who used the app.

In addition to the data from the survey quantitative data provided by the app and the learning management system has been used to triangulate the intrinsic contextual factors of the technology used in this setting. Mobler Cards automatically records each attempt answering a question in the LRS. The entries in the LRS include references to the test-item, the time of the attempt, the duration of the attempt, and the score for the answer.

The duration of the attempt is defined by the time from accessing answer perspective of the test-item for the first time until the answer is submitted to receive the feedback. The score is defined as 0 for wrong answers, 0.5 for partially correct answers, and 1 for correct answers.

The LRS of the learning management system integrates the attempts for all students into a single activity stream for the entire course in the XAPI JSON format. This activity contains only Mobler Cards records. In a second step the activity stream is anonymized for a descriptive comparison with the online quizzes.

To measure the participation in the online quizzes and the app, the ratio between the active students and the total number has been calculated. This calculation has been chosen because no data on the weekly participation in the face-to-face sessions could be collected for that lecture.

4 Results

410 students participated to the lecture that provided the framing for this case study. From the student records 300 students were identified as female and 109 as male. At the end of the term 125 students (30 %) used Mobler Cards at some point during the semester. Among these students were 38 students (9 %) who used the app at least on 5 different days throughout the semester. In the following this group is referred as "frequent learners". The seemingly limited uptake of the app might be related to different launch dates for the mobile app and the online quizzes.

During the semester on average 201 students (49 %) voluntarily completed each online quiz before the next session and on average 225 students (55 %) completed each online quiz during exam preparation.

In total the students responded 13298 times to the test items using the mobile app, while the students who used the app frequently account for 65.3 % of the responses. On average each test item has been answered 108 times ($\partial = 59.9$) by 47.2 students ($\partial = 15.8$) using the mobile device and answered each test items on average 2.2 times ($\partial = 0.5$). The frequent learners have responded on average 228.6 times ($\partial = 142.0$) to the test items.

All participating students used the app in 547 sessions with on average 24.3 responses ($\partial = 33.5$). Among the students the number of sessions greatly varies between 1 and 21 sessions, while on the average student used the app in 4.4 sessions ($\partial = 4.2$). For the frequent learners the average number of session was 9.6 ($\partial = 4.11$). During the sessions the students responded on average to 24.3 test-items ($\partial = 33.5$). Compared to the frequent learning group there is little difference with respect to the amount of responses given per session ($\mu = 23.9$, $\partial = 28.5$).

The sessions were not equally distributed throughout the semester. The data shows that the students were more active at the beginning of the semester and towards the exam (Figs. 3 and 4). For the frequently learning students a more continuous participation has been detected. Although in this group the activity reaches a low between week 8 and 11 (Fig. 3), these students account for almost all responses during this period. This shows that these students used the app more continuously.

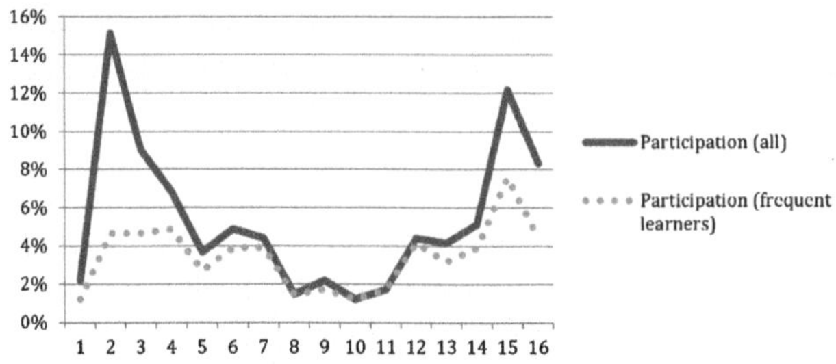

Fig. 3. Weekly Mobler Cards usage during the semester and exam preparation

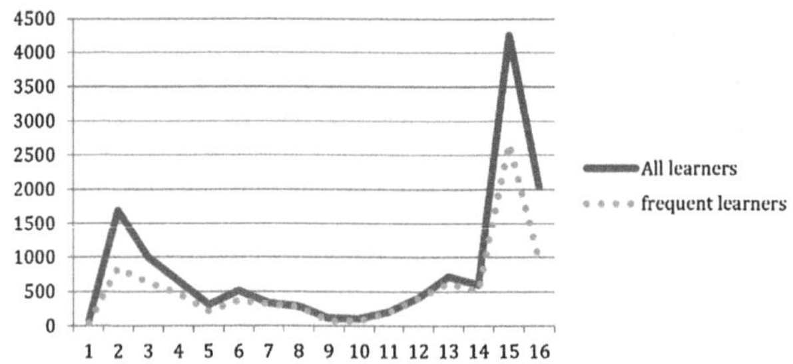

Fig. 4. Weekly number of test item responses in Mobler Cards

While in absolute terms the online quizzes were used more intensively than the mobile app (72194 test items answered), the average online test item has been answered 1.4 times during the lecture phase ($\partial = 0.2$) and 1.7 times during exam preparation ($\partial = 0.1$) in this mode. The participation and the number of responses were declining the later a topic has been taught during the semester. This trend is observable during the lecturing phase as well as during the exam preparation. These trends are depicted in Figs. 5 and 6. The data also shows that the students were using the online quizzes more intensively during the exam preparation phase than during the rest of the semester.

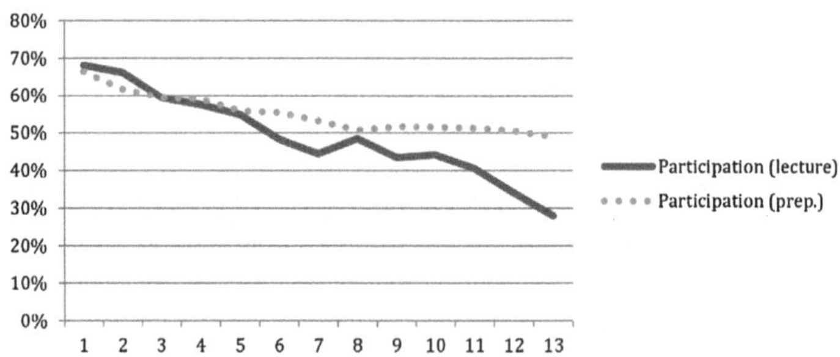

Fig. 5. Participation to the online quizzes during the lecture and the exam period

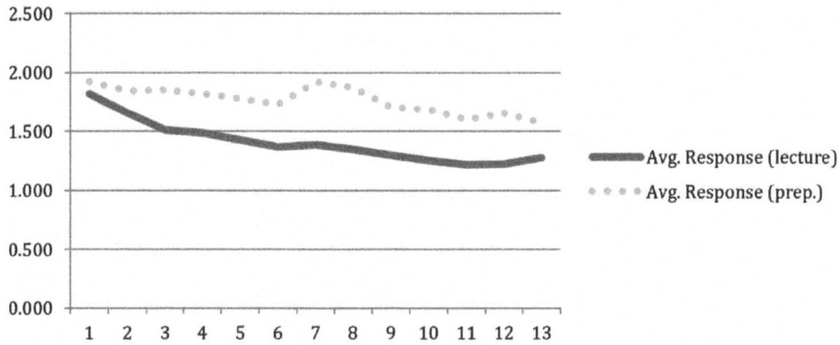

Fig. 6. Responses to test-items in the online quizzes during the lecture and the exam period

At the end of the case study 50 students (12 %) completed the online survey after their exam. Considering that the online survey has been conducted already during the semester break a 12 % response rate is considered a success.

4.1 Device Adoption and Use

The first section of the survey dealt with student's ownership und usage of mobile devices. Participants were interviewed on which smart phones they have, where and how often they use smart phones as well as what services they apply frequently. Finally, they were asked about other frequently used mobile devices.

All students who participated in the survey report to own smart phones with a dominant share of iPhones of 72 %. Respectively, they report to use the following mobile operating systems: Apple iOS 72 %, Android 26 %, and Windows 2 %. Almost all respondents use their smart phones every day at home (98 %), on the way (92 %) and at the university (92 %). Slightly less smart phones are used in leisure time (86 %) and at work (69 %).

Smart phones are not the only mobile devices owned by students. Also notebooks (92 %) and tablets (48 %) are used frequently. The majority of the students (64 %) responded that they use frequently 3 or more mobile devices at the time and 34 % use 2 devices together.

The answers to the question about frequently used services indicate that the respondents do not use their smart phones as gaming devices often. Only 18 % of respondents play every day on their smart phones, but just as many do not play at all, 24 % play less frequently than monthly, 22 % monthly and 18 % weekly.

As Fig. 7 shows the most popular everyday used services and apps on student's smart phones are: texting (94 %), online search (74 %), social networking (72 %), online services such as blogs and news (62 %), e-mail (61.2 %), and photos (52 %). Other services are used less frequently: camera (50 % weekly), navigation (52 % weekly), telephony (52 % weekly) and videos (44 % weekly). Responses to the open-ended question about the 5 most important apps used on mobile phones correspond to the distribution of responses represented in Fig. 7. The students mentioned 54 apps they use frequently on their smart phones. The most popular app is WhatsApp followed by navigation apps (such as maps and public transportation apps), news apps, Facebook and e-mail. Gaming apps were mentioned only three times, which underlines the limited relevance of gaming for this audience.

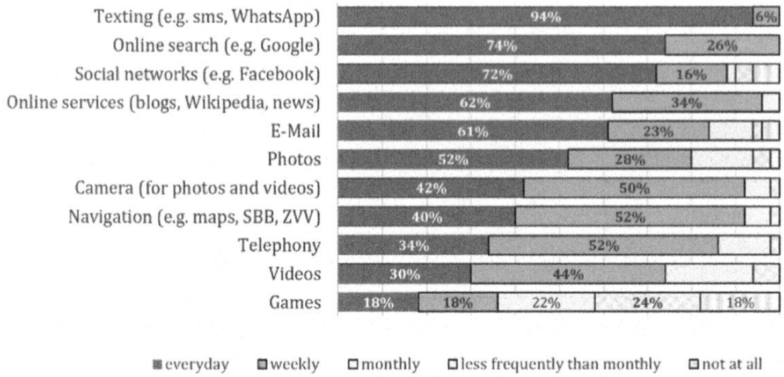

Fig. 7. Responses to the question: "how frequently do you use the following services on your smart phone?"

4.2 Device Usage for Learning

The second part of the survey focused on students' usage of the Mobler Cards app during the lecture. Students' feedback as well as their opinion about the further development of the app and its integration in other courses was of particular importance for the study.

12 students stated that they learned with the app regularly, 16 occasionally and 9 used the app only once. The remaining 13 participants have not used the app at all: 6 of them pointed problems with installation and the authentication. 3 students solved the quizzes using LMS. 4 students have not specified any reason.

Students have preferred to learn at home (weekly 38.9 % and monthly 22.2 %) and on the way (weekly 36.1 % and monthly 25 %). When working (not at all 84.4 %), in leisure time (not at all 75 %) and at the university (not at all 66.7 %) they hardly used the app (Fig. 8). This data has been also confirmed by the data from the activity stream.

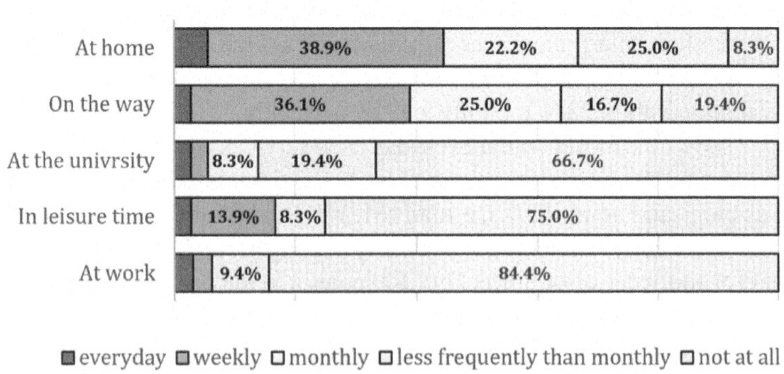

Fig. 8. Responses to the question: "where and how often have you used the mobile app?"

4.3 App Usability

The rating of the app concerning technical implementation, usability and its integration in the lecture was very positive. While all of survey respondents, who used the app (n = 37) had positive experience with app installation and the majority of them with operation (91.9 %), the usability of the app was rated a little bit less positive: the user interface was easy to understand for 77.8 % of these participants, attractive for 59.9 % and functional for 85.7 %.

Especially good rating achieved didactic integration of the app in the lecture. All respondents agreed that the app is a useful addition to the course. 91.8 % of students mention that Mobler Cards is useful for learning. 97.1 % stated that the app did not create unnecessary workload for learning. 91.9 % considered the app as a useful addition to LMS quizzes ($\mu = 5.5$, $\partial = 0.7$) and complementary to the online quizzes ($\mu = 5.1$, $\partial = 1.3$). However, the respondents disagreed with the replacement of the conventional LMS quizzes by the mobile app ($\mu = 3.4$, $\partial = 1.9$).

Most students would continue to use the app voluntarily; few 5.6 % would only use the app if it would be a compulsory part of the lecture ($\mu = 1.5$, $\partial = 1.1$). A better integration of the app in the lecture would not necessarily lead to a more frequently app usage at large: only 55.8 % of students claim that they would learn with the app more frequently.

The opinions are diverse concerning the motivational aspect of the app: 57.1 % of students stated that the app helps them to learn more regularly and 51.3 % are motivated to learn more intensively. 91.6 % of students would recommend learning with the app to their fellow students.

Table 1. Responses to the open question: "what do you like about the mobile app?"

Response	n
Context aspects	
Learn at any time and at any place	7
Learn in the short time, e.g. on your way	6
Optimal for learning with mobile phone	3
Ease of use	2
Didactic aspects	
Useful addition to the lecture	3
Questions weren't divided into sections/many questions	3
Possibility for exercise, repeat, and verification	3
Simple but good questions/well formulated sentences	2
Learning statistics	1

All students are of the same opinion about the future of the Mobler Cards app: it should be offered in the future, but it should be developed further and adapted to their needs (97.3 %). Furthermore, 86.5 % of respondents would appreciate the app integration into other courses.

Particularly pleasing is the fact that many students have expressed their feedback and suggestions for app improvements. Students justified their positive attitude towards the app by noting that they can learn with the app at any time, at any place and within a short time on their way. Also the students emphasized didactic aspects in their feedback (Table 1).

Improvement suggestions focused primarily on didactic aspects. 11 out of 26 students find that the division of available test items in lecture topics is very important. Also students would like to be able to choose whether they answer all available test items or only test items of a particular topic. Furthermore, they would like to highlight or store such test items in a separate folder in order to have a possibility to repeat them later.

5 Conclusions and Further Research

The presented case study focused on the integration of a mobile learning solution into a blended learning curriculum in a university lecture. The solution was a mobile micro learning app that repurposed the lecture's test-items for more "casual" learning activities. The lecture served as a pilot in order to develop a better understanding on the practical conditions and constraints of expanding the technological support. Two questions were addressed by this research through a mixed method approach involving a survey and learning activity records.

The first question asked for the technologies that are available to the students and what are common practices of using them. The results of this case study indicate that already more than two-thirds of the responding students are commonly working in a multi-device environment with 3 or more devices. Although smart phones are available to all respondents, they were by no means the technology of choice for all learning activities. Furthermore, the findings indicate that smart phones are tools to support communication, collaboration and orientation, while gaming was not very relevant to the respondents. These results are in line with earlier findings, which suggest that they draw a realistic picture of the lecture's audience. This baseline enables lecturers and professors to realistically estimate the impact of mobile technologies on their students. Most important here is that concerns regarding the digital divide are today closer related to platforms rather than to the access to technology as such. An insight that tool developers and instructional designers must consider as well. However, the present data only provides a narrow image of the situation in higher education. Particularly, large-scale studies and course evaluations should therefore consider including additional items to expand the understanding of the students' technological framing.

The second question addressed the intrinsic context-related affordances of mobile learning tools for bridging learning activities into uncommon contexts. The survey results indicate that the students were using the app primarily at home or while commuting. Some students reported that they used the mobile solution during leisure time such as being out with friends. The use on the campus was not relevant to them. It was no surprise that the app wasn't used in the workplace because the majority of freshmen at the university are entering directly after school. These results indicate that the students were using the app for expanding their learning time into contexts that were previously unavailable to them. The usage data from the frequent learners suggests that this can help students to balance their workload towards the exam preparation. The effects can be only related to the technology-intrinsic affordances because the educational design of the lecture as well as the learning resources did not suggest, promote, or encourage particular uses. This finding is relevant because it indicates that predefined application settings and the limitation to specific environments, such as the university campus, might be too limited to match the students' learning needs. The difference between technology-intrinsic and educational design affordances has not been considered by previous research. Especially, for the emerging field of seamless learning separating these dimensions is important for isolating the causes of the observed effects.

These findings allow a preliminary answer to the overarching research question on the benefits of mobile technology for already technology-enhanced learning environments. The results show that contemporary students are already living embedded in a technological ecosystem and that they are willing to use different tools to make more efficient use of their study time. Therefore, integrating mobile tools into a blended learning curriculum does not imply to fully replace existing approaches, methods, or tools. Instead, mobile technologies can enrich and balance the overall learning experience in a multi device environment. The related educational design challenge is to define practices and tools that enable such enrichment in a multi-device environment by creating the traits that enable students and lecturers to reach out to and bridge between contexts that were previously unavailable for studying. Consequently and within its limitations, this case study suggests that design decisions regarding technology-enhanced learning should be rather guided by the interplay of the different devices used by the audiences than by unifying the experience across devices.

Acknowledgements. The research presented in this paper was partially supported by the IIL funds of the Faculty of Arts and Social Sciences at the University of Zurich. The authors thank Prof. Frank Esser and Nicole Ernst for supporting this study in their lecture.

References

1. Google Inc.: Our mobile planet. http://think.withgoogle.com/mobileplanet/en
2. Glahn, C.: Mobile learning in security and defense: foundations, technologies, approaches and challenges. Report; Center for security studies. ETH Zürich, Zürich, Switzerland (2013). https://lo-f.at/glahn/2015/03/30/REPORT_MLearning_v14%20-%20final%20-%20with %20CC%20%281%29.pdf
3. Wong, L.-H., Looi, C.-K.: What seams do we remove in mobile-assisted seamless learning? A critical review of the literature. Comput. Educ. **57**(4), 2364–2381 (2011)
4. Börner, D., Glahn, C., Stoyanov, S., Kalz, M., Specht, M.: Expert concept mapping study on mobile learning. Campus-Wide Inf. Syst. **27**(4), 240–253 (2010)

5. Kukulska-Hulme, A., Sharples, M., Milrad, M., Arnedillo-Sánchez, I., Vavoula, G.: The genesis and development of mobile learning in Europe. In: Parsons, D. (ed.) Combining e-Learning and m-Learning: New Applications of Blended Educational Resources, pp. 151–177. Information Science Reference, Hershey (2011)
6. Traxler, J.: Defining mobile learning. In: Isaías, P., Borg, C., Kommers, P., Bonanno, P. (eds.) Proceedings of IADIS International Conference on Mobile Learning 2005, pp. 261–266. IADIS, Malta (2005)
7. Graham, C.R., Woodfield, W., Harrison, J.B.: A framework for institutional adoption and implementation of blended learning in higher education. Internet High. Educ. **18**(7), 4–14 (2013)
8. López-Pérez, M.V., Pérez-López, M.C., Rodríguez-Ariza, L.: Blended learning in higher education: Students' perceptions and their relation to outcomes. Comput. Educ. **56**(3), 818–826 (2011)
9. Ziebarth, S., UH, H.: Moodle4SPOC: a resource-intensive blended learning course. In: de Freitas, S., Rensing, C., Ley, T., Muñoz-Merino, P.J. (eds.) EC-TEL 2014. LNCS, vol. 8719, pp. 359–372. Springer, Heidelberg (2014)
10. Glahn, C., Hug, T., Gassler, G.: Embedded e-learning. New. Educ. Rev. **1**, 243–254 (2005)
11. Gassler, G., Glahn, C., Hug, T.: Integrated micro learning – an outline of the basic method and first results. In: Auer, M., Auer, U. (Eds.) International Conference Villach/Austria "Interactive computer aided learning" ICL 2004. The future of Learning (2004)
12. Mitsopoulou, E., Glahn, C.: Interoperability issues and solutions for integrating mobile micro learning with learning management systems. In: Proceedings of the Microlearning 7.0 Conference, Krems, Austria, 25–26 September 2013
13. ADL Initiative: Experience API (2015). https://github.com/adlnet/xAPI-Spec/blob/master/xAPI.md
14. Glahn, C.: Using the ADL experience API for mobile learning, sensing, informing, encouraging, orchestrating. In: Proceedings of the 7th International Conference on Next Generation Mobile Apps, Services and Technologies (NGMAST). IEEE Computer Society (2013)
15. ADL Initiative: Training and learning architecture (TLA) (2013). http://www.adlnet.gov/tla
16. Bangor, A., Kortum, P., Miller, J.: Determining what individual SUS scores mean: adding an adjective rating scale. J. Usability Stud. **4**(3), 114–123 (2009)
17. Brooke, J.: SUS: a "quick and dirty" usability scale. In: Jordan, P.W., Thomas, B., Weerdmeester, B.A., McClelland, A.L. (eds.) Usability Evaluation in Industry, pp. 189–194. Taylor & Francis, London (1996)
18. Electric Paper Evaluations systeme GmbH: EvaSys. https://www.evasys.de/uebersicht-evasys-suite.html

SafeChild: An Intelligent Virtual Reality Environment for Training Pedestrian Safety Skills

Yecheng Gu, Sergey Sosnovsky(✉), and Carsten Ullrich

German Research Center for Artificial Intelligence (DFKI), Stuhlsatzenhausweg 3, 66123 Saarbrücken, Germany
{yecheng.gu,sergey.sosnovsky,carsten.ullrich}@dfki.de

Abstract. Training children safe behavior in traffic situations is both important and challenging. One of the problems is children's limited perceptual-motor abilities and associated difficulties with important cognitive skills required to be safe pedestrians. Existing traffic education programs focus more on theoretical knowledge, while training practical skills in the real world is dangerous, expensive and hard to organize. This paper presents a promising alternative – an intelligent virtual reality training environment that allows children to practice their pedestrian skills. It describes the interface and architecture of the system, as well as the skill model of the pedestrian safety domain. The results of the conducted pilot study show that children of the target age group rarely have problems with applying (and acquiring) "basic" pedestrian skills in the developed virtual environment. However, when applying and learning "advanced" skills, they require additional support.

Keywords: Virtual reality · Student modeling · Intelligent tutoring system · Pedestrian safety

1 Introduction

Child pedestrians, especially aged 5 to 9, are endangered traffic participants [1]. According to statistics, just in 2013 in Germany, they were involved in over 3.000 traffic accidents [2]. In USA, more than 11.000 of pedestrian injuries in 2011 happened to children under 14 [3], and the numbers worldwide are also alarming [4]. There are many reasons for children to be especially endangered in traffic. They are hard to see, physically fragile, and their perceptual-motor abilities are still limited [4]. Mentally, children not only lack the knowledge about traffic safety, but also have difficulties with the cognitive skills that are required to be safe pedestrians [1, 5]. On the bright side, several studies indicate that children's behavior on roads can improve significantly through individualized practical street side training [6]. However, a number of requirements must be met for organizing such training. This includes particular weather and traffic conditions as well as sufficient personnel to guide the training and ensure the safety of the children. Yet, even when the

© Springer International Publishing Switzerland 2015
G. Conole et al. (Eds.): EC-TEL 2015, LNCS 9307, pp. 141–154, 2015.
DOI: 10.1007/978-3-319-24258-3_11

requirements can be met, roadside training remains unpredictable and hard to control [5]. Therefore it is very challenging for educational institutions (such as schools and kindergartens) to provide a sufficient amount of practical traffic safety training.

One promising way to tackle these problems is to employ Virtual Reality (VR) and conduct training in virtual road environments that are not only realistic and immersive, but also safe and controllable. With the increase in computing and graphical power of home PCs and the recent emergence of immersive displays and natural, gesture-based input devices on the consumer market, VR can be even brought into private households, which enables parents and children to train whenever they want.

In this paper, we present the SafeChild platform that combines a rich and open-ended virtual city environment with the functionality of Intelligent Tutoring Systems (ITS) to provide children with guided and assisted training in a wide range of training scenarios. We describe the architecture and the interface of the system, the designed domain model of pedestrian safety skills and the set of exercises training these skills. Further, we present a user study evaluating the feasibility of the system, discuss its results and outline plans for future work.

2 Related Work

A number of previous studies have investigated the use of Virtual Reality (VR) as a tool for practical child pedestrian training. In a study by McComas et al., children from 4th to 6th grade attending urban and suburban schools went through a VR intervention that was intended to teach several pedestrian safety skills [7]. The results showed that children were able to significantly improve within the VR application but only the children from suburban schools were able to transfer the improvement into the real world. Another study by Thomsen et al. focused on the skill of finding appropriate gaps in traffic to cross a road with children aged 7, 9 and 11 [8]. The outcome of the study indicated that, after VR training, children were able to cross faster, determine crossing times better and missed fewer opportunities to cross. Further studies that confirm the potential of VR as a tool for training child pedestrians include those conducted by Congiu et al. [9] and Schwebel et al. [10, 11]. Oron-Gilad et al. employed VR as a research tool to understand child-pedestrian's deficits of hazard perception abilities [5]. They showed that children are less sensitive to potential hazards and that the ability to detect such hazards increases with age.

In the above-mentioned studies, VR was used primarily as a tool for human teachers and researchers. Developed VR applications focused on providing a realistic representation of real world scenarios but lacked diagnostics and tutoring capabilities to guide or assist children through training. Furthermore, these systems were limited in terms of interaction possibilities and training scenarios.

In other domains, the advantages of combining VR environments with Intelligent Tutoring Systems (ITS) have been addressed both conceptually [12] and practically. Successful implementations include STEVE – a system for training Navy personnel to use complex machines [13], HERA – a system for training operations at high-risk sites [14], PEGASE – a system used for training collaborative procedures on aircraft carriers and for firefighters intervening high-risk areas [15], etc.

Based on the early success of VR as a tool for training child pedestrians and the promising work in other domains on combining VR and ITSs, we have developed the SafeChild training system. In this system, a diverse and flexible VR environment works together with an ITS component to improve the aforementioned limitations of current VR child pedestrian training. While the VR environment provides a wide range of different training scenarios, the ITS analyzes and interprets learners' behavior to detect individual errors and deficiencies in higher-level cognitive skills, which enables automated generation of individualized instructions in the training VR environment.

3 Child Pedestrian Safety Skills

Any ITS requires a Domain Model that describes the knowledge to be taught. For the domain of child pedestrian safety, there are several behavior rules that children need to know and corresponding skills that they need to master in order to become safe pedestrians. In the reminder of this paper, we concentrate on the skills involved in different variations of the road-crossing scenario, which is at the core of any child pedestrian safety training.

Although described with slight variations and different granularity, there is an agreement on a number of core behavior rules with varying degree of difficulty for young children. Van der Molen et al. have analyzed the task of road crossing and decomposed safe execution of this task into 26 sub-tasks [16]. Further, Thomson et al. [17] defined three high-level skills that are mandatory: (I) making judgments about safety of a crossing place; (II) identifying traffic that could pose a threat and (III) integrating information from different aspects of the traffic situation. These high-level skills require a number of underlying abilities that are especially challenging for young children since their cognitive apparatus is still developing [5]. For instance for (I), it is essential to detect potential threats that might not be physically present at the moment. In experiments described in [18], it has been shown that children aged 5 to 7 exclusively rely on visible presence of cars to determine whether a certain place is dangerous to cross. Factors such as obstacles obscuring the view are not recognized as threat by them. For (II), an important skill is to pay selective attention to those parts of traffic that are relevant for one's safety. Hill et al. showed that children aged 4–9 have difficulty paying attention to relevant information and ignoring irrelevant one [19]. Last but not least, for (III), it is important to be able to observe the road from a global perspective, which is also more difficult for young children [20].

We have conducted a cognitive analysis of this domain informed by the existing literature on pedestrian traffics safety and in consultation with traffics safety experts. As a result, we have identified two groups of skills: the "basic skills", which are less demanding cognitively and should be easier for children to apply and master, and the "advanced skills" that involve meta-cognitive processes, more complex planning and decision making procedures and maintaining the awareness of others. For SafeChild, the hierarchical organization of skills becomes an additional source of information to elaborate student modeling (by propagation) and adaptation strategies (e.g., by task sequencing). The complete hierarchy of skills is shown in Fig. 1.

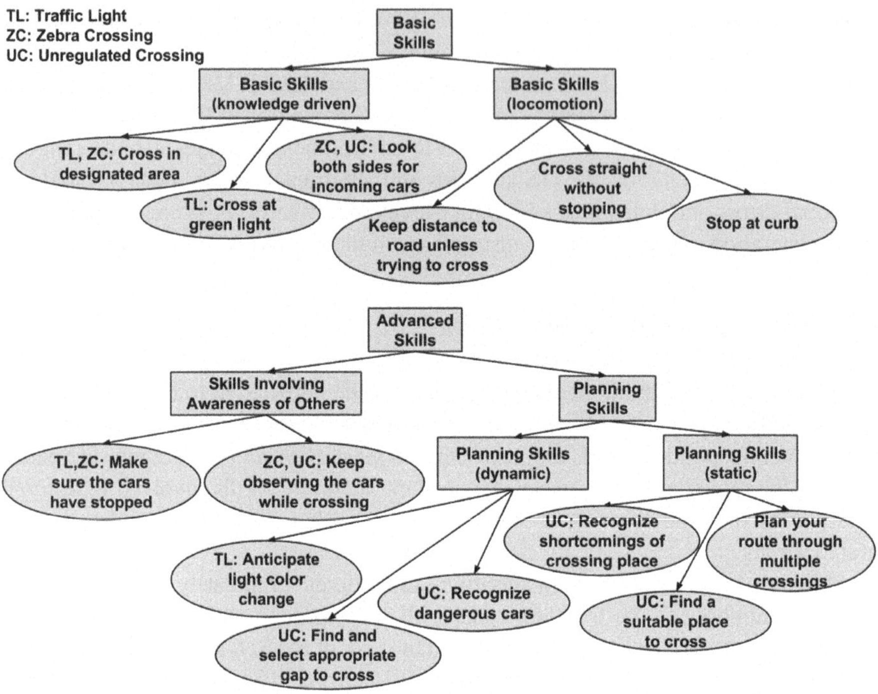

Fig. 1. Skills in SafeChild. Zebra crossings are common pedestrian walks consisting of light and dark stripes. Unregulated crossings describes crossings that do not have designated crossing places for pedestrians.

We plan to subject this model to further investigation and examine its robustness toward experimental data. Open research questions include: at which age a certain skill can be trained, whether particular skills should be further decomposed (or combined) and how well improvements of individual skills in VR translates to improvements in the real world.

4 SafeChild System

The SafeChild system has been designed to support assessment and training of the identified pedestrian safety skills. In general, SafeChild consists of three major components: a VR city environment providing the training area, a flexible interface to interact with this environment and an ITS that monitors learner's behavior, detects correct and incorrect applications of target skills, maintains the detailed representation of learner's pedestrian abilities and supervises the training process.

The VR city environment consists of realistic urban architecture and a traffic simulation developed with the Unity3D game engine. It is freely explorable by the user who can engage in typical pedestrian activities such as crossing the road under different conditions. Several simulation parameters can be adjusted, including car speed, traffic density and walking speed of the user.

The flexible interface supports different display configurations and input devices. The basic setup consists of a standard monitor as the display and a standard keyboard as the input device. This is still the most common setup for home computers nowadays and, since one of the goals for SafeChild is to provide child pedestrian training in private households, the support of this setup is necessary. However, one can assume that interfaces enabling children to practice in a more natural and immersive way would lead to higher engagement, easier control and better transfer of skills. Therefore, SafeChild has been designed to support a wide range of different input and output devices including multi-monitor setups, Head-Mounted-Displays (HMDs), Gamepads and gesture trackers. Although research on the usability and applicability of such immersive interfaces is still in an early stage, first promising results have been already achieved by combining the Oculus Rift as a display and a combination of Myo armband and Leap Motion hand tracker as input devices [21].

The overall architecture of SafeChild is presented on Fig. 2. It consists of the four typical ITS components [22]: the Domain Model presented in Sect. 3, the Student Model representing child's current states of learning, the Pedagogical Model that defines how to teach the child and the Interface Model that serves road-crossing exercises (described in Sect. 4.1). In SafeChild, the Interface Model can be interpreted as the combination of the VR city environment and the flexible interface. The Interface Model is connected to the other ITS components via a designated Instructor Agent described in Sect. 4.2.

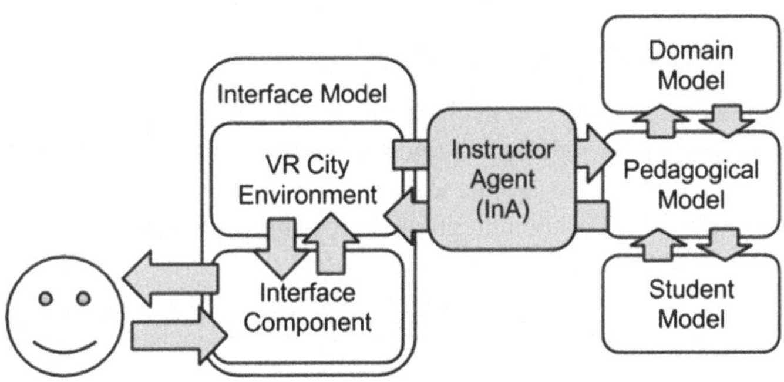

Fig. 2. SafeChild architecture

4.1 Road-Crossing Exercises

In order to help children train skills described in Sect. 3, SafeChild provides a set of ten road-crossing exercises. Each exercise requires the learner to cross the road under different conditions and, consequently, involves a unique sequence of skills. Figure 3 shows examples of two exercises with the corresponding skills.

The complete set of exercises consists of three tasks related to using traffic light; three tasks related to using zebra crossing, three tasks related to unregulated crossings and one combination exercise. For traffic light and zebra crossing, the learner starts once directly in front of the designated crossing area; once, within a small distance, but with

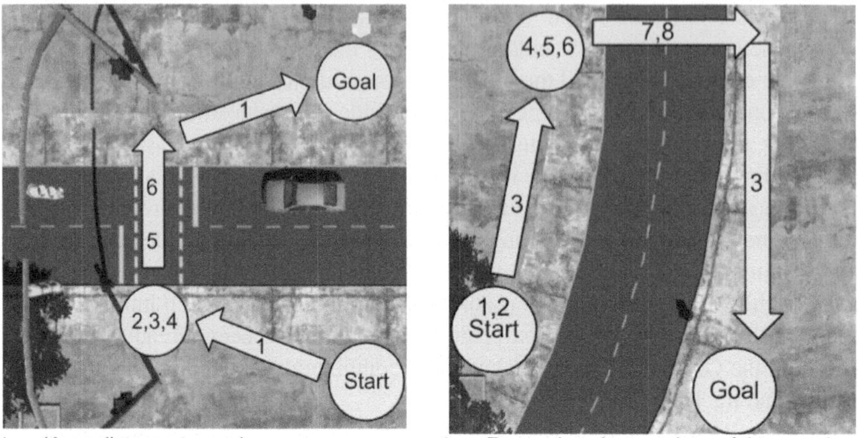

1. Keep distance to road
2. Stop at curb
3. Cross at green light
4. Make sure the cars have stopped
5. Cross in designated area
6. Cross straight without stopping

1. Recognize shortcomings of the crossing place (road curvature)
2. Find a suitable place to cross
3. Keep distance to road
4. Stop at curb
5. Look both sides for incoming cars
6. Recognize dangerous cars
7. Cross straight without stopping
8. Keep observing cars while crossing

Fig. 3. Traffic light and unregulated crossing exercise and corresponding sequences of skills

the traffic light/zebra crossing still in sight; and once, further away, where a turn in the virtual city environment is required to find the designated place to cross. In all cases, the final goal is directly visible and the learner is supposed to utilize the available regulated crossing to reach it. For the unregulated crossings tasks, the user starts once on a sidewalk next to a straight road without obstacles; once, with a parking truck as an obstacle; and once, close to a road curve obstructing the field of vision. The task is to recognize shortcomings of the crossing place if they are present and cross the road safely. In the final exercise the learner can plan own route to the goal and is given the opportunity to either cross the road once with an unregulated crossing or to cross twice using traffic light and zebra crossing; the expected behavior is to prefer the combination of traffic light and zebra crossings over the unregulated crossing.

The left part of Fig. 4 shows a screenshot of an exercise execution process, with the yellow arrow designating the goal. The top-right part of the figure shows the feedback screen generated by SafeChild if the learner fails to achieve the goal (is hit a by a car). The top-bottom part shows the feedback produced after reaching the goal.

4.2 Interaction Agent

The Instruction Agent (InA) has two main tasks. First, it observes exercise performance in real-time and determines at any point during training, which skills are required and whether they are being carried out correctly. In the pedestrian safety domain, correct behavior is dependent on dynamic objects such as cars and traffic lights and requires time-dependent

Fig. 4. Road crossing task from user perspective and GUI overlays for getting hit by a car and reaching the goal.

decision making such as finding the correct time window to cross a road. In order to meet these requirements, a novel method has been developed based on Behavior Trees (BT) [23]. Each exercise is represented by a BT that hierarchically organizes all behaviors required to perform this exercise. One or several skills described in Chap. 3 can be associated with a behavior. During exercise performance, the state of the BT is updated in real time and indicates for each behavior whether it is currently needed or has already been completed (successfully or not). Depending on the state of the BT, different information about the city environment needs to be enquired in order to carry out the update. However, not all information can be directly retrieved from the raw data of the simulation. For many pedestrian safety skills, it is important that the learner is aware of task-related information within the environment. Therefore, a Short-term Memory Model (SMM) is maintained as well during exercise execution. This model contains information about which objects were visible to the user and at which state the objects had at that time.

The second main task of InA is to carry out in the city environment adaptive instructional interventions produced by the Pedagogical Module. For this purpose, InA includes an Adaptation Controller that is able to change simulation parameters, to manipulate objects in the VR and generate instruction and feedback in the city environment. A complete update cycle that is performed in every frame is shown in Fig. 5 and consists of 4 steps. Due to the update mechanisms of a BT, this can be achieved in an efficient manner and is, therefore, suited for real-time environments.

1. The current field of view of the learner based on her/his current position and orientation within the simulation is analyzed to update the SMM;
2. Additional information from the simulation is processed together with the Memory Model to update BT;
3. The state of the BT passed to the Pedagogical Model and analyzed to decide whether direct intervention or a student model update is required;
4. Necessary interventions are implemented in the city simulation through the Adaptation Controller and Student Model updates are performed.

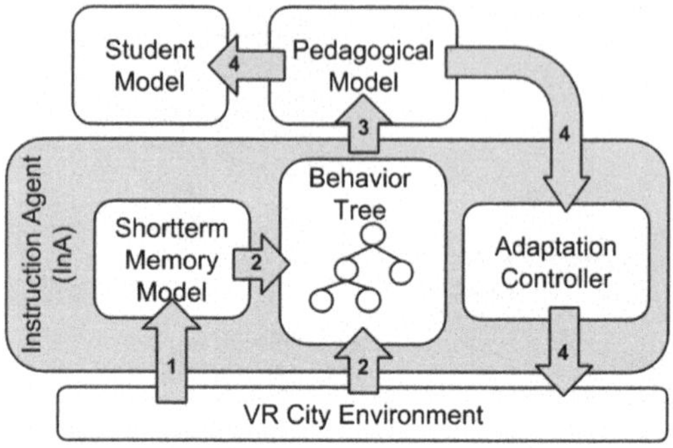

Fig. 5. Instruction agent (InA) update cycle

In Fig. 6, the (simplified) behavior tree is shown next to instructions for the following situation. The learner has seen the goal on the other side of the road (which means a crossing is required), but has not yet explored the environment. Thus, a number of nodes within the BT are in the "Running" state, including "Cross" and "Find Place to Cross". Based on this information, SafeChild can provide the learner with instruction directly adapted to his/her specific situation. Once the learner turns his/her head in the virtual environment and detects the traffic light, several steps execute. First, the SMM is updated with the information about a safe place to cross the road. Next, the BT is updated and the behavior "Find a place to cross" switches to the "Success" state and causes the behavior "Go to a Place to Cross" to switch to the "Running" state. As a consequence, the new instructions are presented. Besides generating instructions in the form of direct guidance, a number of additional functionalities can be integrated based on the given information. For instance, the skill "Keep distance from road" is assigned to the behavior "Find a place to cross" and "Go to place to cross". Thus the system keeps track of the distance of the learner to the road in this situation and would notice an error and display a warning if it fell below a threshold.

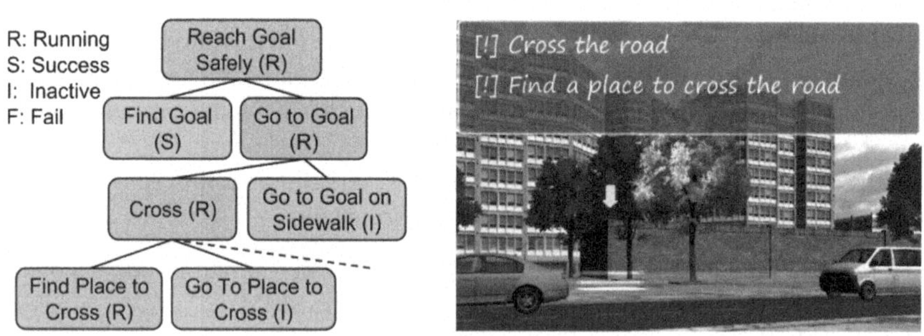

Fig. 6. BT state and instructions (1)

5 Experiment

The experiment described in this section was conducted as a first evaluation of SafeChild and focused on the investigation of the two basic research questions:

1. Is the training provided by SafeChild positively accepted by children?
2. Do children perform better on basic skills than advanced skills in SafeChild?

5.1 Experiment Design

The experiment was designed for German-speaking children from 6 to 9 years old to match the critical age group (see Sect. 1). 5 year olds have been excluded, because (1) we believed that the controls would be too hard for them to use; (2) they are rarely exposed to traffic situations when alone, since they do not go to school yet. The participants were supposed to conduct the experiment at home, under the supervision of their parents. SafeChild was provided to the volunteers as a Web-application or a download. The application itself contained detailed information and instructions for parents and children. Parents were involved for several reasons. As they hold the main responsibility for traffic safety education of their child, by supervising the study, they could detect her or his individual weaknesses and misconceptions and work on them after the study. Parents could help children with the controls and the questionnaires (but were asked to avoid helping with completion of the exercises), and provide us with valuable feedback on the SafeChild approach and implementation. Last but not least, they could choose the most convenient time to conduct the study.

The application for the pilot study was a customized version of the SafeChild platform. Once started, it guided the participant through the three steps of the experiment: (1) A pre-questionnaire, (2) a set of road crossing tasks within the SafeChild city environment and (3) a post-questionnaire. The application logged experiment data to the central webserver. This data included questionnaire answers as well as replay-able log files for each road-crossing task.

5.2 Pre- and Post-questionnaires

The pre-questionnaire consisted of seven questions; it focuses on children's demographic data (age, gender) and prior experience with traffic safety education and video gaming. The post-questionnaire also continued seven questions asking about the just completed road-crossing tasks and the overall SafeChild experience. This included children's general attitude toward the approach, their opinions on whether they could learn something in such an environment, and whether the environment was realistic. Further children were asked if they got tired during the experiment, and whether or not the controls and the tasks were too hard or too easy. The last two questions asked parents whether they helped their child and how. They were also given the opportunity to provide comments on the general approach.

5.3 Road Crossing Tasks

All ten exercises described in Sect. 4.1 and a familiarization task at the beginning had to be completed. The simulation parameters used for the road-crossing task were chosen to match the real-world conditions: car speed was around 50 km/h (the upper speed limit in German cities) and the walking speed of the child was set to 1.2 m/s (a common speed for 6 year olds [24]). For the "unregulated crossing" tasks, the frequency of incoming cars was high in the beginning and decreased over time to create larger gaps. Since the study was designed to be conducted by parents with their children in their own home, the standard interface configuration consisting of one monitor and keyboard was used. The controls were based on 6 keys for forward and backward movement, turning left or right and turning the head left or right. Head turning were included as separate action to allow the participant to look to both sides while crossing the road. The ITS functionalities were not activated for the study as our goal was to obtain baseline performance data and validate the overall approach.

6 Discussion of the Results

6.1 Questionnaire Analysis

A total of 10 participants took part in the study. The results of the pre-questionnaire including demographics are presented in the Table 1 (part A), while the results of the post-questionnaire containing feedback on the system are shown in Table 1 (part B).

The feedback about the current version of the SafeChild indicates, that most children liked the overall experience, and, even more important, most of them believed that they could improve their pedestrian skills through such training. Children also considered the traffic simulation realistic. However, controls via keyboard are a problem for many children. Thus, either a better introduction of controls or other interaction methods, such as gamepads, should be considered. Half of the children considered the exercises to be too easy, although none of them was able to demonstrate all required skills and three of them failed on more than a half of the advanced skills. An explanation could be that when these children were able to complete most of the tasks, they assumed that they performed correctly even when exhibiting unsafe pedestrian behavior. Also half of the children said that they did tire while participating. This result matches with the observation of the tasks performances where children sometimes needed more than 6 min to finish an exercise. As a comparison, adults are able to finish the entire sequence of exercises a little under 5 min. The problems with the controls also may be a factor here. Finally, seven parents reported that they helped their child a little, but limited the help to the controls and not completing the tasks. In summary, it can be concluded for the first research question (Is the kind training provided by SafeChild well accepted by children in general?) that the system goes into the right direction, but an improvement of controls is much-needed. Further, differences in perceived difficulty and need for adult help in many cases indicate that the ITS could improve user experience by adjusting exercises and providing adaptive assistance.

Table 1. Questionnaire summary

A: Pre-questionnaire		B: Post questionnaire	
Total number of participants: 10			
Question	Number	Question	Number
Male	6	Liked the system in general	8
Female	4	Thought he/she could improve	9
Age 6	4	Thought the graphics were real.	9
Age 7	3	Thought controls were easy	4
Age 8	0	Did get tired	5
Age 9	3	Found exercises too easy	5
Traffic ed. school/kindergarten	7	Parents did help	7
Traffic ed. parents	9		
Video game experience	7		

6.2 Performance on Traffic Tasks

Any traffic task implemented in SafeChild can have only two outcomes: if a child crosses the street and reaches the goal, it is a success; if a child is hit by a virtual car, it is a failure. Out of 96 completed tasks, 82 constituted successful attempts and 14 – car hits. However, even when the goal is reached, it does not mean that the child has exhibited correct (safe) behavior and successfully demonstrated all the pedestrian skills involved in the task. In fact only 15 times were tasks solved without a single failed skill. It is important to understand, that due to the fact the SafeChild problem-solving environment is highly dynamic with random-generated elements, children can get lucky and complete a task without applying some necessary skills. However failing skills on a regular basis will eventually result in a car hit, which is rather similar to real-life traffic situations. In order to investigate the second research question (*Do children perform better in basic skills compared to advanced skills in SafeChild?*), we have computed the average basic skill performance and average advanced skill performance for each learner. Then we could compare their means using the paired t-test. The test shows that on average a learner performs significantly better on basic skills ($M = .93$; $SD = .04$) than on advanced skills ($M = .53$; $SD = .17$), $t(9) = 8.11$, $p \ll .001$, $d = 2.56$. Both the p-value and the Cohen's d indicate a very strong difference between the two variables. This, essentially, confirms that difficulties in advanced pedestrian skills reported in traffic education literature [5] are reflected SafeChild. As a consequence, the ITS in SafeChild should especially focus on the improvement of such skills.

Despite the very small sample size, a first analysis with regard to learning in SafeChild was conducted. Basically, the only instructional support that the system gave was the immediate knowledge-of-result feedback at the end of a task completion. A failure to apply a particular skill, which leads to a car hit, triggered an error message. This allowed a child to self-reflect on what s/he had done wrong and, next time, exhibit a safer behavior. Having this in mind, we analyzed the logs of 14 incorrect task attempts and identified the skills responsible for each failure. In some cases a combination of skills was causing an incorrect attempt (e.g. "*find an appropriate gap to cross*" and "*keep observing traffic while crossing*"); and in some cases, it was hard to decide, which of the two skills is responsible (e.g. "*recognize shortcomings of crossing place*" and "*find a suitable place to cross*"). In such situations, both skills were treated as a probable cause. After each such case, we looked if there was another opportunity for a child to reflect on her/his error and apply the skill correctly. We found seven such occurrences: three, when the causing skills were basic and four, when they were advanced. Remarkably, in all three "basic" cases, children have been able to correctly apply the failure-causing skills on the next iteration and never failed it again, including the new context of the combined traffic tasks. On the other side, all four cases of failed advanced skills were followed by more occurrences of the same erroneous behavior. This indicates that, even with minimum instructional support children could improve their incorrect traffic behavior, when they needed to acquire a basic skill and even transfer it to a novel context; but, without additional support, they could not master the advanced skills and exhibited the same dangerous behavior even after failing several traffic tasks and receiving several error flag messages.

6.3 Limitations of the Study

Despite the interesting results obtained during the study, there are a number of limitations that need to be considered when analyzing the results. First, the experiments were conducted in a home environment and the level of support provided by parents was not observable. Second, there was no sound in the simulation that could have warned children of incoming cars and third the interface and especially the keyboard based controls were difficult for many participants. Furthermore, the potential higher level of fatigue in later tasks could influence children's performance. Another important drawback of the experiment is the small number and high variability of subjects. It is important to underline, that 6-years-olds and 9-years-olds are very different categories of traffic safety learners. Not only do they possess very unequal amounts of real worlds traffic experience, but they also significantly differ in terms of development of cognitive and perceptual-motor abilities important for mastering pedestrian safety skills, controlling themselves in a VR and cognitive transfer. We have been able to observe it firsthand, as the data generated by 9-years old children and 6-years-old children vary substantially. For examples, according to Piaget [25], before the age of 7, children remain egocentric in their thinking, having problems perceiving the world from the viewpoint of others. In the future, SafeChild will explicitly account for age as one of core learner parameters.

Nonetheless, the study has been valuable overall and allowed us to pilot the approach, elicit the general attitude of the target population toward the system and validate important hypotheses that will influence the future design of SafeChild.

7 Conclusion and Future Work

This paper presents research on and with SafeChild, an intelligent Virtual Reality environment for training pedestrian safety skills. An analysis of the child pedestrian safety education domain was conducted to extract and classify skills that such a system should target and support. Further, the SafeChild system was presented with a foundation for a structural representation and a method for determining traffic safety skills for an individual learner. In order to evaluate the general feasibility of SafeChild and the classification of skills, a user study was conducted with 6–9 years old children using the SafeChild platform. The results of the study indicate SafeChild is well accepted in general but requires further improvement. Also, the results show that while having almost no problems with applying and acquiring basic traffic skills in SafeChild, children require additional tutoring support on applying and learning advanced pedestrian skills.

Our future work will continue along the two main directions. We will use the results of the described study to further develop (in consultation with domain experts) the pedagogical model of the SafeChild ITS that will especially address the advanced skills. We will continue our analysis of the pedestrian safety domain to refine a more structured representation taking into account types of relations between the skills and adding important conceptual knowledge elements. We also plan to conduct another user study of SafeChild using a more immersive VR setup and more convenient set of controls. This last goal might require development of a more elaborate mechanism for modeling learner perception and intention, as the flexibility of the interface would inescapably cause the input channel to become more noisy and low-level [26].

Acknowledgements. This research was conducted within SafeChild project funded by BMBF (grant 01IS12050) under the Software Campus program.

References

1. Whitebread, D., Neilson, K.: The contribution of visual search strategies to the development of pedestrian skills by 4-11 year-old children. Br. J. Educ. Psychol. **70**(4), 539–557 (2000)
2. Federal Statistical Office of Germany: Child pedestrian injury in traffic 2013. https://www.destatis.de/DE/Publikationen/Thematisch/TransportVerkehr/Verkehrsunfaelle/UnfaelleKinder5462405137004.pdf
3. National Highway Traffic Safety Administration: Traffic safety facts: 2011 data. http://www-nrd.nhtsa.dot.gov/Pubs/811767.pdf
4. Toroyan, T., Peden, M. (eds.): Youth and road safety. WHO, Geneva (2007)
5. Oron-Gilad, T., Meir, A., Tapiro, H., Borowsky, A.: Towards understanding child-pedestrian's deficits in perceiving hazards when crossing the road. Final Report (2011)
6. Schwebel, D.C., Davis, A.L., O'Neal, E.E: Child pedestrian injury: a review of behavioral risks and preventive strategies. Am. J. Lifestyle Med. **6**(4), 292–302 (2012)
7. McComas, J., MacKay, M., Pivik, J.: Effectiveness of virtual reality for teaching pedestrian safety. CyberPsychology Behav. **5**(3), 185–190 (2002)
8. Thomson, J.A., Tolmie, A.K., Foot, H.C., Whelan, K.M., Sarvary, P., Morrison, S.: Influence of virtual reality training on the roadside crossing judgments of child pedestrians. J. Exp. Psychol. Appl. **11**, 175–186 (2005)

9. Congiu, M., Whelan, M., Oxley, J., Charlton, J., D'Elia, A., Muir, C.: Child Pedestrian: Factors Associated with Ability to Cross Roads Safely and Development of Training Package. Monash University Accident Research Centre, Victoria (2008)
10. Schwebel, D.C., Gaines, J., Severson, J.: Validation of virtual reality as a tool to understand and prevent child pedestrian injury. Accid. Anal. Prev. **40**(4), 1394–1400 (2008)
11. Schwebel, D.C., McClure, L.A., Severson, J.: Usability and feasibility of an internet-based virtual pedestrian environment to teach children to cross streets safely. Virtual Reality **18**(1), 5–11 (2014)
12. Lane, H.C., Johnson, W.L.: Intelligent tutoring and pedagogical experience manipulation in virtual learning environments. In: The PSI Handbook of Virtual Environments for Training and Education, vol. 3 (2008)
13. Johnson, W.L., Rickel, J.: Steve: an animated pedagogical agent for procedural training in virtual environments. ACM SIGART Bull. **8**(1–4), 16–21 (1997)
14. Amokrane, K., Lourdeaux, D., Burkhardt, J.M.: HERA: learner tracking in a virtual environment. Int. J. Virtual Reality **7**(3), 23–30 (2008)
15. Buche, C., Bossard, C., Querrec, R., Chevaillier, P.: PEGASE: a generic and adaptable intelligent system for virtual reality learning environments. Int. J. Virtual Reality **9**(2), 73–85 (2010)
16. Van der Molen, H.H., Rothengatter, J.A., Vinjé, M.P.: Blueprint of an analysis of the pedestrian's task I. Accid. Anal. Prev. **13**(3), 175–191 (1981)
17. Thomson, J.A., Tolmie, A., Foot, H.C., McLaren, B.: Child development and the aims of road safety education. Road Safety Research Report No. 1. HMSO, London (1996)
18. Ampofo-Boateng, K., Thomson, J.A.: Children's perception of safety and danger on the road. Br. J. Psychol. **82**, 487–505 (1991)
19. Hill, R., Lewis, V., Dunbar, G.: Young children's concepts of danger. Br. J. Dev. Psychol. **18**, 103–120 (2000)
20. Underwood, J., Dillon, G., Farnsworth, B., Twiner, A.: Reading the road: the influence of age and sex on child pedestrians' perceptions of road risk. Br. J. Psychol. **98**, 93–110 (2007)
21. Orlosky, J., Weber, M., Gu, Y., Sonntag, D., Sosnovsky, S.: An interactive pedestrian environment simulator for cognitive monitoring and evaluation. In: 20th International Conference on Intelligent User Interfaces, pp. 57–60 (2015)
22. Corbett, A.T., Koedinger, K.R., Anderson, J.R.: Chapter 37 intelligent tutoring systems. In: Handbook of Human-Computer Interaction. Elsevier Science B.V., Amsterdam (1997)
23. Millington, I., Funge, J.: Behavior trees. In: Artificial Intelligence for Games, 2nd edn, pp. 334–370. Morgan Kaufmann Publishers Inc., San Francisco (2009)
24. David, K.S., Sullivan, M.: Expectations for walking speeds: standards for students in elementary schools. Pediatric Phys. Therapy **17**(2), 120–127 (2005)
25. Piaget, J.: The Origins of Intelligence in Children. International Universities Press, New York (1952)
26. Gu, Y., Sosnovsky, S.: Recognition of student intentions in a virtual reality training environment. In: 19th International Conference on Intelligent User Interfaces, pp. 69–72 (2014)

What Should I Do Next? Adaptive Sequencing in the Context of Open Social Student Modeling

Roya Hosseini[1](✉), I-Han Hsiao[2], Julio Guerra[3], and Peter Brusilovsky[3]

[1] Intelligent Systems Program, University of Pittsburgh, Pittsburgh, PA, USA
roh38@pitt.edu

[2] School of Computing, Informatics and Decision Systems Engineering, Arizona State University, Tempe, AZ, USA
sharon.hsiao@asu.edu

[3] School of Information Sciences, University of Pittsburgh, Pittsburgh, PA, USA
{jdg60,peterb}@pitt.edu

Abstract. One of the original goals of intelligent educational systems was to guide each student to the most appropriate educational content. In previous studies, we explored both knowledge-based and social guidance approaches and learned that each has a weak side. In the present work, we have explored the idea of combining social guidance with more traditional knowledge-based guidance systems in hopes of supporting more optimal content navigation. We propose a greedy sequencing approach aimed at maximizing each student's level of knowledge and implemented it in the context of an open social student modeling interface. We performed a classroom study to examine the impact of this combined guidance approach. The results of our classroom study show that a greedy guidance approach positively affected students' navigation, increased the speed of learning for strong students, and improved the overall performance of students, both within the system and through end-of-course assessments.

Keywords: Personalized guidance · Open social student modeling · Adaptive navigation support · E-learning · Java programming

1 Introduction

One of the original goals of intelligent educational systems was to guide each student to the most appropriate educational content. Starting with the first reported ITS system SCHOLAR [7], a range of knowledge-based guidance technologies have been reported. Different technologies in this group include instructional planning [1], course sequencing [3], course generation [14], and adaptive navigation support [2]. All these knowledge-based approaches were based on the same principles: by using a combination of domain models, course goals, and overlay student models, the sequencing engine decides which content is the most appropriate for an individual student at any given moment and delivers it to the student through the interface, which either directly brings the student to the

© Springer International Publishing Switzerland 2015
G. Conole et al. (Eds.): EC-TEL 2015, LNCS 9307, pp. 155–168, 2015.
DOI: 10.1007/978-3-319-24258-3_12

right content (as in sequencing), or delivers the content through suggested links (as in course generation and navigation support). Despite the known power of this technology, there are few practical applications, due to the large amount of effort required to build the domain models and analyze the content.

In our recent research, we discovered and evaluated a new approach to guide students to the "right" content, based on the ideas behind open social student modeling (OSSM) [10]. OSSM is a recent expansion of open student modeling (OSM), a popular approach that makes traditionally hidden student models available for students to explore [5,11,13]. OSM is known for its ability to increase student engagement, motivation, and knowledge reflection. The goal of OSSM is to integrate its cognitive aspects with social aspects by allowing students to explore each others' models or to view a cumulative model of the class [4]. In our studies, we explored several versions of a visual OSSM, based on comparative visualization of the student's own open knowledge model and the models of students with similar learning goals. While our original goal was to increase student engagement, which is a known value of social approaches, our studies have also demonstrated the navigational support power of OSSM. Our system was able to guide students to the most appropriate self-assessment problems [10] almost as efficiently as the knowledge-based guidance that we previously explored [9]. Since the main power of OSSM comes from the overall community of learners, it also requires considerably simpler domain and user models in order to reach maximum efficiency. However, our studies also revealed that the OSSM approach can make students more conservative in their work with content, which decreases the 'personalization' power of such 'social' guidance.

This paper explores the idea of combining social guidance with more traditional knowledge-based guidance in the hope of supporting more optimal content navigation. This idea was motivated by the success of hybrid approaches in recommender systems that demonstrated several efficient ways to combine content-based and collaborative filtering approaches [6]. We introduce a greedy sequencing approach for selecting learning activities that could maximize student's level of knowledge, and demonstrate the ways in which this approach could be implemented in the context of OSSM. We also present a classroom study that examines the added impact of this combined guidance approach.

The remainder of this paper presents the sequencing approach and its implementation in the OSSM interface and reports the results of the evaluation. We conclude with a discussion of the results and plans for future work.

2 Adaptive Sequencing in the Context of OSSM

In our study, adaptive guidance was implemented in the context of a specific OSSM interface called Mastery Grids. To explain the technology, we will start with a brief presentation of Mastery Grids, follow by explaining how the suggestions generated by the sequencing algorithm were added to the OSSM interface, and finally explain the details of our specific sequencing approach, which we call Greedy Sequencing.

2.1 Mastery Grids, an OSSM Interface

Mastery Grids is an OSSM interface that combines a visual open student model presentation with an interface to access online course materials. The design of Mastery Grids was informed by our earlier studies of OSSM [10], where we discovered that students achieve higher success rates and engage with non-mandatory content more frequently in the presence of OSSM. A classroom study confirmed these effects for the first version of Mastery Grids [12].

Figure 1 shows a screenshot of the Mastery Grids interface. The system organizes course content into topics, which are displayed as columns of the grid. The first row shows the current student's topic-by-topic knowledge progress by using shades of green in different densities; the darker the color, the higher the progress. The third row shows the aggregated progress of the rest of the students of the class in shades of orange. The second row presents a differential color that compares the current student's progress to the overall class progress. For example, in Fig. 1, the student shows a higher progress than the rest of the class in most of the topics where the cells in the second row are green, but the class has advanced farther in two of the topics (13th and 20th column) where the cells in the second row are orange. The student has the same progress as the class in the four topics shown in a light gray color (11th, 15th, 18th, and 19th column). By clicking in a cell, the student can access the content that falls inside the topic. For example, in Fig. 1, the student has clicked the topic *Classes*, and the system displays cells to access questions and examples related to this topic. Additionally, by clicking the button "Load the rest of learners", a grid shows an anonymized, ranked list of individual student models (Fig. 2).

2.2 Enhancing OSSM Interface with Sequencing

To implement adaptive sequencing in the context of the Mastery Grids interface, we used the top three content item recommendations generated by the adaptive sequencing approach and displayed their presence in the topic using red stars that appear on both recommended items and the topics that they contain. The size of the stars shows the position of the recommended items in the top-three list. Note that our approach to *sequencing* is consistent with the navigational support nature of the interface: it does not force students to go to the sequenced content, but simply informs the students and helps them to make their next navigational step. The resulting interface combines the social guidance of OSSM with the personal guidance that sequencing provides.

2.3 Greedy Sequencing

The intelligence behind the sequencing interface is provided by a sequencing algorithm that we call *greedy sequencing* (GS). This algorithm was specifically developed to compensate for the conforming nature of the OSSM on student navigation. The goal of GS is to guide students through learning materials by proactively recommending student activities that could *maximize* the chance to

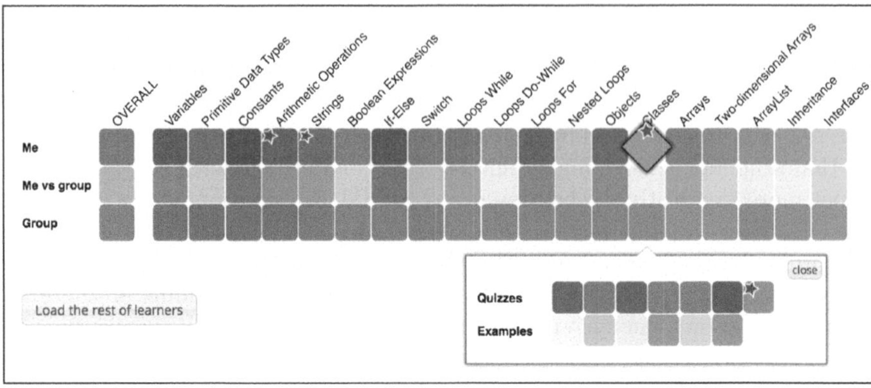

Fig. 1. The presentation of recommendations in the context of Mastery Grids' OSSM interface; a cell with a star symbol represents a recommended item

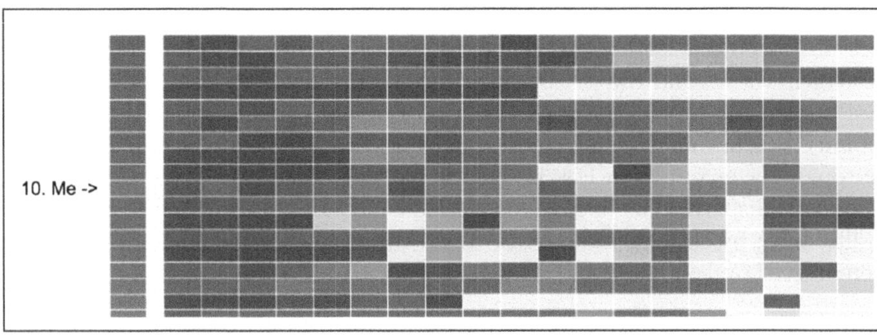

Fig. 2. List of peer models ordered by progress on topics in the course. The student with the highest progress appears at the top of the list. This list is anonymized and the current student can see herself in the position that she has obtained, according to her topic-based progress. In this case, the student, who is shown by the label "Me", is in position 10.

gain new knowledge while avoiding content that is too complex for the student to comprehend. As with other knowledge-based sequencing approaches, GS uses information about concepts associated with content: more specifically, it focuses on prerequisite and outcome concepts for each activity. Prerequisites are the concepts that students need to master before starting to work with a given activity. Outcomes are the concepts that are being learned in the process of work with the activity. In our work, all concepts associated with an activity were determined using our concept parser [8]. The parser indexes the activities with concepts of Java ontology[1]. The extracted concepts for each activity are then separated into prerequisites and outcomes. In the activity, we marked a

[1] http://www.sis.pitt.edu/~paws/ont/java.owl.

concept as a prerequisite if it has appeared in prior topics, and as an outcome if it is the first topic where the concept appears.

The GS algorithm ranks activities by balancing the knowledge level of each student in the prerequisite concepts with the knowledge that can be gained from the outcome concepts. The rank of an activity is calculated using (1) based on the student's level of knowledge in the prerequisite and outcome concepts of that activity:

$$R = \frac{n_p P + n_o O}{n_p + n_o} \tag{1}$$

$$P = \frac{\sum_i^{n_p} k_i w_i}{\sum_i^{n_p} w_i} \tag{2}$$

$$O = \frac{\sum_i^{n_o} (1 - k_i)\, w_i}{\sum_i^{n_o} w_i} \tag{3}$$

where n_p and n_o are the number of prerequisite and outcome concepts in the activity, respectively; P represents the amount of known prerequisites and is calculated as the weighted average of student's knowledge in the prerequisite concepts of the activity; and O represents the amount of unknown outcomes and is calculated as the weighted average of knowledge that is not learned in each of the outcome concepts. These two variables can be calculated using (2) and (3), respectively.

In (2) and (3), k_i is the student's level of knowledge of the concept i, has the minimum value of 0 (no knowledge) and asymptotically reaches 1 (maximum knowledge). The term $1-k_i$ in (3) is the amount of knowledge that is not learned in the outcome concept i. The w_i is the smoothed weight of the concept obtained by performing a *log* function on TF-IDF values of the concepts. The rank R of an activity lies in the interval $[0, 1]$ with 1 representing the highest rank.

3 Study Design

To explore the effect of GS on student navigation and performance, we ran a classroom study in an undergraduate course of Object-Oriented Programming & Data Structures offered by the Computer Science Engineering program of the Arizona State University in fall 2014. The course focused on data structures with Java. In this course, the Mastery Grids interface extended with GS was used to access supplementary course materials. A total of 143 students were enrolled in the course. The instructor informed the students about the learning materials that could be accessed using the Mastery Grids interface. The instructor encouraged students to explore this content, but indicated that the use of this system was not mandatory.

To investigate how students navigated both with and without the presence of the sequencing, we split the course into two parts. Part 1, from Aug. 21 to Sep. 25, used the Mastery Grids system with no sequencing. In part 2, from Sep. 26 to Oct. 21, sequencing was enabled. At the beginning of the course, students took a pretest to evaluate their initial knowledge of Java programming concepts. To measure the students' knowledge gain, a post-test was administered on Oct. 21. The pretest and post-test had the same set of questions and the score ranged from 0 to 21. At the end of the semester, we collected questionnaires that asked students to report their opinions on the sequencing used in the Mastery Grids system.

The course's learning materials included parameterized questions on the semantics of Java, administered by the QuizJET system [9], and annotated code examples, administered by the Webex system. The parameterized nature of semantics questions allowed students to attempt to answer the same question several times, each time with a different parameter. As a result, the correct answer is different across attempts on the same question. An annotated code example is a complete program that has an expert's annotation (comments and explanations) for some lines of code. Students could interactively explore these annotations by clicking on the annotated lines. The learning materials were organized into topics defined by the course instructor. Overall, the course contained 111 questions and 103 examples spread over 19 topics.

4 Evaluation

We collected student logs for the analysis period between the pretest and the post-test. The data consisted of students' attempts at topics and activities, as well as information that showed whether attempted topics and activities (questions or examples) were recommended by the system or not. We removed all sessions with a duration of less than 30 s from the data. Then, we excluded students that were not sufficiently active in the system by discarding the data of those who had fewer than 30 attempts on questions, i.e. about $\frac{1}{4}th$ of the available questions. In total, 86 students used the system during the analysis period. Out of this number, there were 21 students with no attempt to solve questions and 12 students with less than 30 attempts on questions. After discarding data from these less active students, we had data from 53 students for our analysis.

4.1 Navigational Pattern Analysis

While the OSSM interface demonstrated a good ability to move the students along the common path through the topic sequence in a timely fashion, the goal of the GS algorithm was to help the students in breaking out from the common path when it is personally beneficial and to have students not spend too much time on topics that they have already sufficiently mastered, while also making sure that knowledge from previous topics is adequately mastered. To see to what extent the GS encouraged non-sequential navigation, we classified students' moves from current to next activity into four groups (patterns):

- Within-Topic: moving between activities in the same topic
- Next-Topic: moving from an activity in a topic to the activity in the next topic (according to the sequence of topics in the course)
- Jump-Forward: jumping to an activity in a topic that is two or more steps further away from the current topic
- Jump-Backward: jumping to an activity in an earlier topic

The Within-Topic and Next-Topic groups represent sequential navigation, and the Jump-Forward and Jump-Backward groups represent non-sequential navigation.

Table 1 shows the frequency of each pattern in the three contexts: part 1 (with no sequencing) and part 2 (with sequencing) separating student navigation to *Not-recommended* (part 2-N) and *Recommended* activities (part 2-R). The relative frequencies of the four patterns in each context are shown in Fig. 3. The value in each cell is the probability (relative frequency) of the corresponding pattern in the corresponding context. A light blue color in the cell denotes a lower probability and a dark blue cell denotes a higher probability.

Table 1. Frequencies of the four topic-based navigational patterns in part 1 (with no sequencing), and part 2 (with sequencing). Part 2-N and Part 2-R represent activities in part 2 that were Not recommended and Recommended, respectively.

Pattern	Part 1	Part 2-N	Part 2-R
Within-Topic	1801	4569	451
Next-Topic	431	689	189
Jump-Forward	216	287	162
Jump-Backward	219	328	161
Total	2667	5873	963

According to this table, when students make navigation decisions without sequencing (Part 1) or ignore it entirely (Part 2-N), they mostly follow a sequential pattern, working Within-Topic until they feel that their knowledge is sufficient and then moving to Next-Topic. This shows that students tend to attempt most of the activities in the topic before moving to the next topic, even if it is not the best strategy to improve their overall knowledge. The OSSM does hint to the students when it's time for them to move, but its guidance is quite conservative, since it is defined by the class as a whole. On the other hand, when students follow GS recommendations, their "groupthink" stay on the current topic shortens considerably, as students move to the next topic more quickly and expand their non-sequential navigation. There is good evidence in our study that the GS promotes non-sequential navigation. However, we cannot conclude whether following the recommendations made by sequencing could benefit learning by more efficiently directing students to relevant activities. We examine this question in the next section.

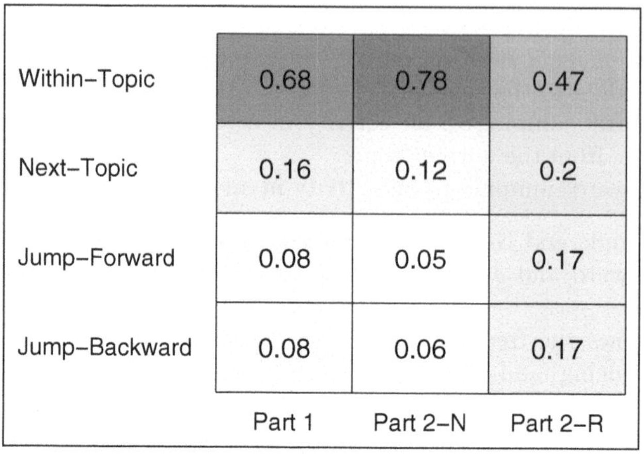

Fig. 3. Relative frequencies of four topic-based navigational patterns in part 1, not recommended items in part 2-N, and recommended items in part 2-R

4.2 The Value of GS: Amount of Learning and Speed

The mere presence of personalized guidance is not sufficient to provide an impact: what matters is whether the students choose to follow the guidance or to ignore it. We examined the added value of GS by comparing the *amount of learning* and *learning speed* of students who did not follow the guidance *(non-followers)* to the ones who did *(followers)*. To achieve this goal, we used normalized learning gain and learning speed as our evaluation measures. The normalized learning gain (*nGain*) is defined as the actual gain divided by the possible gain and is obtained using the score of the student on both the pretest and post-test. The speed of learning is defined as the ratio of normalized learning gain to the number of questions student attempted between the pretest and post-test ($nGain/n_q$). We multiplied this number by 100 to express it as a percentage (*%speed*). To separate *non-followers* from *followers*, we calculated the *following ratio* per student that represents the fraction of activity accesses made when following recommendations. This ratio considers attempts on questions made in the second part of the study, when sequencing was available.

Figure 4 shows the distribution of the *following ratio*. As we can see from the skewed distribution, most of the students have a ratio of 0.2 or less; namely, they had followed a recommendation in less than $\frac{1}{5}$th of their attempts. We selected $\frac{1}{5}$ as the cut-off for separating *non-followers* from *followers*. The *non-followers* group consists of 36 students with a following ratio of less than $\frac{1}{5}$ and the *followers* group contained 17 students with a *following ratio* of greater than or equal to $\frac{1}{5}$. There were 8 students in the *non-followers* group and 6 in the *followers* group who either had a missing pretest or post-test, or seemed not motivated to work seriously on the post-test, as they got a lower score on the post-test than they did on the pretest. We filtered out those students and finally had 28 and 11 students left in the *non-followers* and *followers*

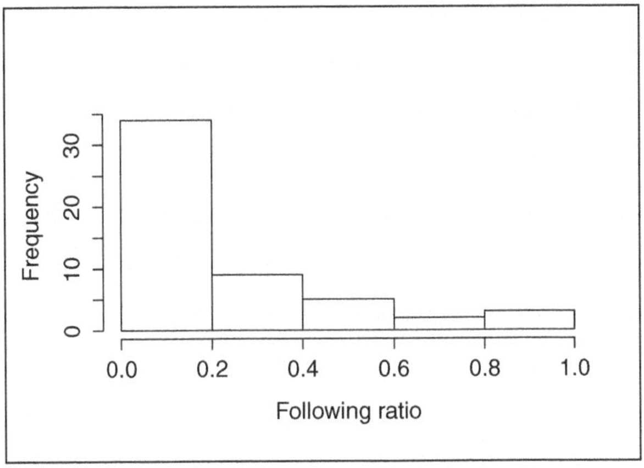

Fig. 4. Histogram of the following ratio of the students who participated in the study

group, respectively. We found that there were no significant differences between the groups, as far as the normalized learning gain. The speed of learning was higher among the *followers* ($M = 0.97\,\%, SD = 0.88\,\%$) than the *non-followers* ($M = 0.54\,\%, SD = 0.27\,\%$) but only reached borderline significance when compared to the *non-followers* group ($p = .083$ using a Welch t-test).

Since learning gain and learning speed might vary across students with different prior knowledge, we also separately compared *followers* and *non-followers* with low and high prior knowledge. If the pretest was less than the median of pretest scores, i.e. 11, a follower/non-follower was labeled as *low pretest*, otherwise it was labeled as *high pretest*. Table 2 provides a more detailed summary of these two parameters, as *followers* and *non-followers* within the low and high pretest score groups. The t-test was used in all of the comparisons, since parametric statistics assumptions were held.

We found that the mean of the normalized learning gain was not significantly different across *non-followers* and *followers* with low or high pretest scores, but that the speed was much higher for *followers* and reached a significant difference for students with high pretest scores. This implies that the GS may provide an efficient guidance that leads to a shorter learning path, at least for students with higher pretest scores. While this result seems promising, we have to account for other possible explanations given the design of our study. For example, since students were not randomly assigned to conditions, it is possible that the students who followed recommendations were more diligent students, so that their improved performance was due to a selection effect known as 'selection bias.' For this reason, the above analysis needs another evaluation, and we hope to address this concern in a future study.

Table 2. Mean±SD of evaluations measures for *non-followers* and *followers* separated by pretest group

	Low pretest (n=20)			High pretest (n=19)		
	Non-followers (n=14)	Followers (n=6)	p-value	Non-followers (n=14)	Followers (n=5)	p-value
ngain	0.51±0.28	0.42±0.19	.440	0.48±0.26	0.46±0.29	.870
%speed	0.55 %±0.34 %	0.97 %±0.88 %	.128	0.54 % ±0.27 %	1.02 %±0.70 %	.039*

Significance level * :< .05

4.3 The Impact of the GS on System and Class Performance

To see the effect of attempts suggested by sequencing on student performance, we fitted mixed models to predict the performance of the students in (1) attempts on self-assessment questions in the system (*in-system performance*), and (2) final exam taken at the end of the term (*out-of-system performance*). In all models, a random effect was included to account for unobserved variations between students. The models used the filtered data that had attempts from 53 active students (see Sect. 4).

To identify the influence of the GS on student *in-system performance*, we explored whether the student had a higher chance to answer the question correctly if it was suggested by GS. The variables of interest were (1) *correctness of attempt*, a binary variable that shows a correct or incorrect answer; and (2) *attempt type*, which shows whether an attempt was offered by sequencing or not. We fitted a logistic mixed effects model with *attempt type* as the fixed effect and *correctness of attempt* as the response variable. The collected data in part 1 (no sequencing) and part 2 (with sequencing) of the study consisted of a total of 5760 attempts on questions, from which 5275 were not offered by the GS and 485 were offered by the GS. The results indicated that the *attempt type* was a significant predictor of overall correctness ($\chi^2(1, 5760) = 14.17, p < .001$). The success was more frequent for questions recommended by the GS: the odds of having the correct answer when a question was offered by GS was 1.59 ($SE = 0.19$) times the odds of having the correct answer when a question was not offered by GS. This indicates that the GS guided students to questions at the proper difficulty.

To identify the influence of the GS on student *out-of-system performance*, we explored how the work in the system affected the score on the final exam, which ranges from 0 to 100. To address this question, we used the filtered data and separately counted the total number of attempts on activities both recommended by the GS and not recommended by the GS made by 40 students who had taken the final exam and used the system. We considered mixed models for predicting the score with a different set of predictors: (NQ), the total number of attempts on questions not recommended; (NQ_{GS}), the total number of attempts on questions recommended by the GS; (NA), the total number of attempts on activities (questions or examples) not recommended; and (NA_{GS}), the total number of attempts on activities (questions or examples) recommended by the GS. Table 3 reports a summary of the estimated effects for the two fitted models: A and B. An interesting finding was that in Model A, the total number of questions accessed by the recommendations of the GS (NQ_{GS}) was significantly related

Table 3. Summary of the model fits for predicting student scores on the final exam

Model A		Model B	
	$\beta \pm SE$		$\beta \pm SE$
$Intercept$	$68.50 \pm 6.24^{***}$	Intercept	$68.84 \pm 5.37^{***}$
NQ	0.11 ± 0.06	NA	$0.06 \pm 0.03^{*}$
NQ_{GS}	$0.69 \pm 0.30^{*}$	NA_{GS}	$0.56 \pm 0.24^{*}$

Significance level $^{*}:< .05;^{**}:< .01;^{***}:< .001$

to the student's final exam score. Attempting one question recommended by the GS was associated with an increase of 0.69 (or 0.69 %) in the final exam score ($SE = 0.30, p = .019$). Model B also showed significant support for both the total number of attempts on activities that were not recommended (NA) and activities that were recommended by the GS (NA_{GS}): attempting one activity recommended by the GS was associated with an increase of 0.56 (or 0.56 %) in the final grade ($SE = 0.24, p = .017$). At the same time, attempting one activity that was not offered was associated with a much lower increase of 0.06 in the final score ($SE = 0.03, p = .045$). In other words, working on both recommended and not recommended activities positively influenced the student's final exam score; however, the impact of activities that were recommended by GS was about 9 times greater than the activities that were not recommended.

5 Subjective Evaluation

At the end of the term, we administered a questionnaire that consisted of six questions about the recommendation features in the Mastery Grids system with answers in a 5-point Likert Scale (1:Strongly Disagree to 5:Strongly Agree). The questions are listed in Table 4 and the distribution of the answers is shown in Fig. 5(a). Out of 95 students who participated, we kept only the answers of 51 students who used the system at least once.

As the data shows, students seemed to agree that they like to receive recommendations ($Q1 : M = 4.10, SE = 0.11$) and that the use of red stars to represent recommendations was clear ($Q2 : M = 3.86, SE = 0.14$). They also

Table 4. Subjective evaluation questions

#	Question
1	In general, I would like the system to recommend me topics &content to focus on
2	It was clear to me that red stars were recommendations
3	Recommendations that I received this semester in Mastery Grids were useful for me
4	I could not understand why some topics and content areas were recommended to me
5	Recommendations distracted me from planning my work
6	It would be useful to see why some topics or content areas were recommended to me

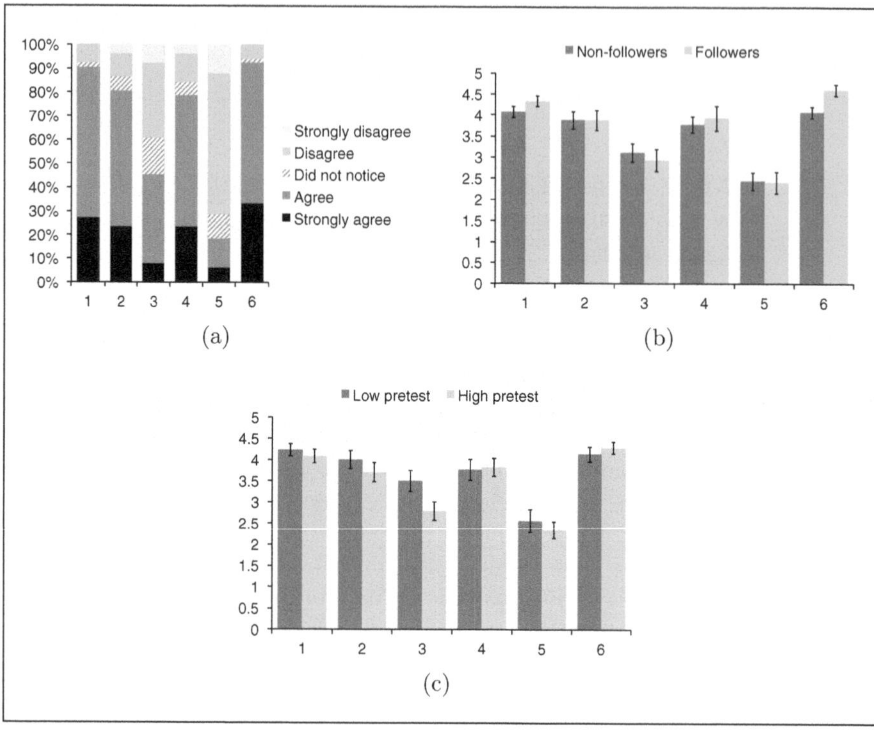

Fig. 5. (a) Distribution of answers by question, (b) Average score by question for followers and non-followers, (c) Average score by question for pretest groups

disagreed that recommendations were distracting ($Q5 : M = 2.41, SE = 0.15$). At the same time, it was less clear to them why some content was recommended ($Q4 : M = 3.82, SE = 0.15$), and they were interested to know the reasons why such recommendations were made ($Q6 : M = 4.20, SE = 0.11$). When we made a more detailed comparison between *followers* and *non-followers*, we noticed that *followers* ($M = 4.60, SE = 0.131, N = 15$) were even more curious than *non-followers* ($M = 4.07, SE = 0.135, N = 30$) to know why some topics or contents were recommended (see Fig. 5(b)). This difference was significant when using a Mann-Whitney test ($U = 133.5, p = .012$).

Furthermore, we found that while the average class opinion was somewhat neutral on the overall usefulness of the recommendations ($Q3 : M = 3.06, SE = 0.16$), students with low pretest scores gave significantly higher scores to the usefulness of the sequencing ($Q6 : M = 3.50, SE = 0.24, N = 22$) than students with high pretest scores ($Q6 : M = 2.79, SE = 0.22, N = 24$). This difference was also significant when using Mann-Whitney test ($U = 173.5, p = .037$) (see Fig. 5(c)). This is an indication that the GS guidance helped students with lower scores as well.

6 Discussion and Future Work

This paper investigated the added value of knowledge-based guidance in the context of open social student modeling (OSSM). We presented a greedy sequencing (GS) approach that attempted to maximize student knowledge and demonstrated how it was implemented through the use of Mastery Grids, an OSSM interface for accessing learning materials. The evaluation of this combined approach provided several interesting findings.

The proposed approach encouraged non-sequential navigation patterns that guided weaker students to not-mastered materials in previous lectures and advanced stronger students to master materials in future lectures. As a result, it increased the learning speed of stronger students, which led these students to more optimal content navigation. In addition, we observed that the amount of work with materials selected by a proposed approach was associated with achieving considerably higher scores on the final exam. Although this does not mean that the proposed approach caused a higher grade on the final exam in every case, it still shows promising perspectives that could be further explored in future studies.

In future studies, we hope to address the limitations present in this study. First, it was focused on the domain of Java programming. Although the proposed GS approach can be adapted to other domains, more research is required before the findings of this study could be generalized. Second, the subjects in our study were undergraduate students who already knew the basics of Java programming. This could, in fact, explain the reason why relatively few students followed the guidance in our study. We need to plan a future study in an introductory Java course, where sequencing assistance is likely to be more critical. Finally, the survey report demonstrated that the interface needs to be modified in order to encourage students to follow recommendations. We would also like to increase the transparency of the proposed approach by increasing student awareness of the reasons to recommend specific learning content.

References

1. Brecht, B., McCalla, G., Greer, J., Jones, M.: Planning the content of instruction. In: Proceedings of 4th International Conference on AI and Education, Amsterdam, pp. 24–26 (1989)
2. Brusilovsky, P.: Adaptive navigation support. In: Brusilovsky, P., Kobsa, A., Nejdl, W. (eds.) Adaptive Web 2007. LNCS, vol. 4321, pp. 263–290. Springer, Heidelberg (2007)
3. Brusilovsky, P.L.: A framework for intelligent knowledge sequencing and task sequencing. In: Frasson, C., McCalla, G.I., Gauthier, G. (eds.) ITS 1992. LNCS, vol. 608, pp. 499–506. Springer, Heidelberg (1992)
4. Bull, S., Britland, M.: Group interaction prompted by a simple assessed open learner model that can be optionally released to peers. In: Proceedings of Workshop on Personalisation in E-Learning Environments at Individual and Group Level (PING), User Modeling, vol. 2007 (2007)

5. Bull, S., Kay, J.: Student models that invite the learner in: the smili:() open learner modelling framework. Int. J. Artif. Intell. Educ. **17**(2), 89–120 (2007)
6. Burke, R.: Hybrid web recommender systems. In: Brusilovsky, P., Kobsa, A., Nejdl, W. (eds.) Adaptive Web 2007. LNCS, vol. 4321, pp. 377–408. Springer, Heidelberg (2007)
7. Carbonell, J.R.: AI in CAI: an artificial-intelligence approach to computer-assisted instruction. IEEE Trans. Man Mach. Syst. **11**(4), 190–202 (1970)
8. Hosseini, R., Brusilovsky, P.: Javaparser: A fine-grain concept indexing tool for java problems. In: The First Workshop on AI-Supported Education for Computer Science (AIEDCS 2013), pp. 60–63 (2013)
9. Hsiao, I.H., Sosnovsky, S., Brusilovsky, P.: Guiding students to the right questions: adaptive navigation support in an e-learning system for java programming. J. Comput. Assist. Learn. **26**(4), 270–283 (2010)
10. Hsiao, I.H., Bakalov, F., Brusilovsky, P., König-Ries, B.: Progressor: social navigation support through open social student modeling. New Rev. Hypermedia Multimed. **19**(2), 112–131 (2013)
11. Lindstaedt, S.N., Beham, G., Kump, B., Ley, T.: Getting to know your user – unobtrusive user model maintenance within work-integrated learning environments. In: Cress, U., Dimitrova, V., Specht, M. (eds.) EC-TEL 2009. LNCS, vol. 5794, pp. 73–87. Springer, Heidelberg (2009)
12. Loboda, T.D., Guerra, J., Hosseini, R., Brusilovsky, P.: Mastery grids: an open source social educational progress visualization. In: de Freitas, S., Rensing, C., Ley, T., Muñoz-Merino, P.J. (eds.) EC-TEL 2014. LNCS, vol. 8719, pp. 235–248. Springer, Heidelberg (2014)
13. Mitrovic, A., Martin, B.: Evaluating the effect of open student models on self-assessment. Int. J. Artif. Intell. Educ. **17**(2), 121–144 (2007)
14. Vassileva, J., Deters, R.: Dynamic courseware generation on the www. Br. J. Educ. Technol. **29**(1), 5–14 (1998)

Improving Automatic Affect Recognition on Low-Level Speech Features in Intelligent Tutoring Systems

Ruth Janning[(✉)], Carlotta Schatten, and Lars Schmidt-Thieme

Information Systems and Machine Learning Lab (ISMLL),
University of Hildesheim, Hildesheim, Germany
{janning,schatten,schmidt-thieme}@ismll.uni-hildesheim.de
http://www.ismll.uni-hildesheim.de

Abstract. Currently, a lot of research in the field of intelligent tutoring systems is concerned with recognising student's emotions and affects. The recognition is done by extracting features from information sources like speech, typing and mouse clicking behaviour or physiological sensors. According to the state-of-the-art support vector machines are the best performing classification models for those kinds of features. However, single classification models often do not deliver the best possible performance. Hence, we propose an approach for further improving the affect recognition performance, which is based on ideas from ensemble approaches and feature selection methods. The approach is proven by experiments on low-level speech features extracted from data which was collected in a study with German students solving mathematical tasks. In these experiments the proposed approach reached on average an affect recognition performance improvement of about 59 % in comparison to a single SVM.

Keywords: Affect recognition · Low-level speech features · Intelligent tutoring systems · Feature selection · Ensemble · Classification performance improvement

1 Introduction

Automatic emotion and affect recognition is a relatively young and very important research field in the area of adaptive intelligent tutoring systems (ITSs). Some research has been done to identify useful information sources and appropriate features able to describe student's emotions and affects. Those information sources can be speech input, written input, typing and mouse clicking behaviour or input from physiological sensors. Appropriate state-of-the-art methods for automatic affect recognition on those features are classification methods like support vector machine, k-Nearest-Neighbour, decision tree or ensembles of those (see e.g. [15,25]). The best performing state-of-the-art method in this field is, according to the literature, a support vector machine. Support vector machines are supervised machine learning methods which can be used for

© Springer International Publishing Switzerland 2015
G. Conole et al. (Eds.): EC-TEL 2015, LNCS 9307, pp. 169–182, 2015.
DOI: 10.1007/978-3-319-24258-3_13

classification tasks and deliver in many areas the best performance in comparison to other classification approaches. Single classification models however often do not deliver the best possible performance. An improvement can be reached by means of methods like feature selection or ensemble approaches. However, ensemble approaches with the same kind of models need as input different input feature vectors and feature selection alone is not reasonable if there is already just a small amount of features. In this paper we propose an approach which overcomes this obstacles by combining ideas from feature selection and ensemble approaches for improving automatic affect recognition. The proposed approach generates one uncorrelated input feature vector per extracted feature. Subsequently, it trains classifiers (whose outputs finally are fed into a second stage classifier) on a subset of the generated input feature vectors with best AIC value. We prove our approach by experiments on two different kinds of low-level speech features extracted from data which was collected in a study with German students solving fractional arithmetic tasks.

2 Related Work

For the purpose to recognise affect in speech one can distinct linguistics features, like n-grams and bag-of-words, and low-level features like prosodic features, disfluencies, e.g. speech pauses ([10,11]), (see e.g. [25]) or articulation features ([12]). If linguistics features are not extracted from written but from spoken input, a transcription or speech recognition process has to be applied to the speech input before affect recognition can be conducted. Linguistic features for affect and emotion recognition from conversational cues were presented and investigated e.g. in [15,16]. Low-level features are used in the literature for instance for expert identification, as in [13,18,27], for emotion and affect recognition as in [10–12,17] or for humour recognition as in [20]. The advantage of using low-level features like disfluencies is that instead of a full transcription or speech recognition approach only for instance a pause identification has to be applied before computing the features. That means that one does not inherit the error of the full speech recognition approach. Furthermore, these features are independent from the need that students use words related to affects. Another kind of features which is independent from the need that students use words related to affects are features gained from information about the actions of the students interacting with the system (see e.g. [14]) like features extracted from a log-file (see e.g. [2,19,24]). Also the keystroke dynamics features used in [6] belong to this kind of features. In [6] emotional states were identified by analysing the rhythm of the typing patterns of persons on a keyboard. A further possibility of gaining features is using the information from physiological sensors as for instance in [1]. However, bringing sensors into classrooms is time consuming and expensive and one has to cope with students' acceptance of the sensors. Because of the mentioned advantages and disadvantages of the described feature types in this paper we focus on low-level speech features.

Dependent on the kind of features used there are different possible methods for automatic affect recognition. Linguistics features from spoken input are gained by a preceding speech recognition process and can be processed by methods coming from the areas sentiment classification and opinion mining [22]. Especially methods from the field of opinion mining on microposts seem to be appropriate if linguistics features are considered. State-of-the-art methods in opinion mining on microposts use methods based on optimisation approaches (see e.g. [9]) and Naive Bayes (see e.g. [23]). The process of gaining disfluencies like pauses is different to the full speech recognition process. For extracting for instance pauses usually an energy threshold on the decibel scale is used as in [13] or an SVM is applied for pause classification on acoustic features as in [21]. The articulation features proposed in [12] are gained by an intermediate step of speech recognition. As mentioned above, appropriate state-of-the-art methods for automatic affect recognition on low-level speech features are classification methods like support vector machine, k-Nearest-Neighbour, decision tree or ensembles of those (see e.g. [15,25]). Ensemble methods like majority voting or stacking use multiple learning models to obtain a better prediction performance. Majority voting takes the majority decision of several single classification models as classification output. Stacking, or stacked generalisation respectively (explained and investigated for instance in [26]), learns to combine the classification decisions of several single classifiers by a further classifier which gets as input the outputs of the other classifiers.

3 Low-Level Speech Features

As mentioned above we use two different kinds of low-level speech features which are described in Sects. 3.1 and 3.2. These features are engineered to be applicable for perceived task difficulty recognition, as a special case of affect recognition, within adaptive ITSs. That means that we try to recognise by means of that features the personally perceived task difficulty (in terms of *over-challenged*, *under-challenged* and *appropriately challenged*) from the view of the student at any time while the learning session. The reason for the decision of engineering the proposed low-level speech features for perceived task difficulty recognition was the observation in the study described in Sect. 5.1 that the children often exhibited longer pauses of silence while thinking about the problem when they were *over-challenged* or produced fewer and shorter pauses while communicating when they were *appropriately challenged*. The recognised perceived task difficulty can then be used for giving hints, motivation or feedback to the students. That is, while a student is interacting with an ITS (which speaks to the student and prompts him/her to speak, like the iTalk2Learn system in [7]), after certain time portions the low-level speech features are extracted from speech recordings and depending on the recognised perceived task difficulty a personalised hint, motivation or feedback is created.

3.1 Articulation Features

The proposed *articulation features* where engineered on the basis of the articulation features in [12], which are related to tasks – i.e. extracted at the end of a task – for the purpose to support task sequencing. The features presented in the following are independent from the end of single tasks but can be used any time while the learning session. The *articulation features* are gained from an intermediate step of speech recognition which delivers information about lengths of vowels and consonants (obstruents or fricatives) and silence. This feature type is composed of 13 features:

f_0: $\frac{n_{sil_i}}{n_{sil_i}+n_{V_i}+n_{O_i}+n_{F_i}}$ (ratio between num. of silence tags and num. of all tags)

f_1: $\frac{\frac{\sum_u V_i^{(u)}}{n_{V_i}}}{\max_u(V_i^{(u)})}$ (ratio between avg. length of vowels and max. length of vowels)

f_2: $\frac{\frac{\sum_w O_i^{(w)}}{n_{O_i}}}{\max_w(O_i^{(w)})}$ (ratio avg. length of obstruents and max. length of obstruents)

f_3: $\frac{\frac{\sum_z F_i^{(z)}}{n_{F_i}}}{\max_z(F_i^{(z)})}$ (ratio avg. length of fricatives and max. length of fricatives)

f_4: $\frac{\frac{\sum_r sil_i^{(r)}}{n_{sil_i}}}{\max_r(sil_i^{(r)})}$ (ratio avg. length of silence tags and max. length of silence tags)

f_5: $\frac{\min_u(V_i^{(u)})}{\max_u(V_i^{(u)})}$ (ratio between min. length of vowels and max. length of vowels)

f_6: $\frac{\min_w(O_i^{(w)})}{\max_w(O_i^{(w)})}$ (ratio min. length of obstruents and max. length of obstruents)

f_7: $\frac{\min_z(F_i^{(z)})}{\max_z(F_i^{(z)})}$ (ratio min. length of fricatives and max. length of fricatives)

f_8: $\frac{\min_r(sil_i^{(r)})}{\max_r(sil_i^{(r)})}$ (ratio min. length of silence tags and max. length of silence tags)

f_9: $\frac{\min_u(V_i^{(u)})}{\frac{\sum_u V_i^{(u)}}{n_{V_i}}}$ (ratio between min. length of vowels and avg. length of vowels)

f_{10}: $\frac{\min_w(O_i^{(w)})}{\frac{\sum_w O_i^{(w)}}{n_{O_i}}}$ (ratio min. length of obstruents and avg. length of obstruents)

f_{11}: $\frac{\min_z(F_i^{(z)})}{\frac{\sum_z F_i^{(z)}}{n_{F_i}}}$ (ratio min. length of fricatives and avg. length of fricatives)

f_{12}: $\frac{\min_r(sil_i^{(r)})}{\frac{\sum_r sil_i^{(r)}}{n_{sil_i}}}$ (ratio min. length of silence tags and avg. length of silence tags)

where n_{sil_i}, n_{V_i}, n_{O_i} and n_{F_i} are the numbers of silence tags, vowels, obstruents and fricatives within the considered speech input i and $V_i{}^{(u)}$, $O_i{}^{(w)}$, $F_i{}^{(z)}$ and $sil_i{}^{(r)}$ are the lengths of the uth vowel, wth obstruent, zth fricative and rth silence tag. The input feature vector for a classification model applied to these features is $(f_0, \ldots, f_{12})$. The idea behind this kind of features is that depending on how challenged the student is, the student shortens or lengthens vowels and consonants.

3.2 Amplitude Features

The proposed *amplitude features* are based on the speech pause features presented in [10,11]. However, the features in [10,11] are also related to tasks – i.e. extracted at the end of a task. The features presented in the following in contrast are independent from the end of single tasks but can be used any time while the learning session. The *amplitude features* are taken from the raw speech data from which information about speech pauses is gained by means of an energy threshold on the decibel scale. The *amplitude features* consist of 7 features:

f_0: $\frac{s_i}{p_i}$ (ratio between speech and pauses)
f_1: $\frac{n_{p_i}}{n_{p_i}+n_{s_i}}$ (ratio between num. of pause segments and num. of all segments)
f_2: $\frac{n_{s_i}}{n_{p_i}+n_{s_i}}$ (ratio between num. of speech segments and num. of all segments)
f_3: $\frac{p_i}{(p_i+s_i)}$ (percentage of pauses of input speech data)
f_4: $\frac{\frac{\sum_x p_i^{(x)}}{n_{p_i}}}{\max_x(p_i^{(x)})}$ (ratio avg. length of pause segm. and max. length of pause segm.)
f_5: $\frac{\frac{\sum_y s_i^{(y)}}{n_{s_i}}}{\max_y(s_i^{(y)})}$ (ratio avg. length of speech segm. and max. length of speech segm.)
f_6: $\frac{n_{p_i}+n_{s_i}}{p_i+s_i}$ (ratio between number of all segments and number of seconds)

where s_i and p_i are the total lengths (in seconds) of pauses and speech within the considered speech input i, n_{s_i} and n_{p_i} are the numbers of pause segments and speech segments and $s_i^{(y)}$ and $p_i^{(x)}$ are the yth speech and xth pause segment. When these features are used as input for a classification model they are put into one feature vector $(f_0, \ldots, f_6)$. The idea behind this kind of features is that depending on how challenged the student feels, the student makes more or less and shorter or longer speech pauses.

4 Uncorrelation Ensemble Approach

As mentioned above we want to use methods from feature selection and ensemble models for our approach for improving the affect recognition performance. However, ensemble methods need more than one, i.e. several different, input feature vectors. Hence, the idea is to generate one new feature vector for each of the extracted features and these new feature vectors shall later on serve as input for the ensemble models. To reach that those feature vectors are likely different we create, based on ideas coming from feature selection methods, new feature vectors with uncorrelated features only. These uncorrelated feature vectors are gained in two steps: first we create the correlation matrix reporting about the correlations between each pair of extracted features. By means of this matrix we create for each single feature f_y a set

$$uncorr_y := \{f_y\} \cup \{f_x \mid f_x \text{ is uncorrelated to } f_y\} \quad (1)$$

containing f_y and all other features f_x not correlated to f_y. *Not correlated* means in this case that the correlation value $v_{x,y}$ of the pair (f_x, f_y) in the correlation

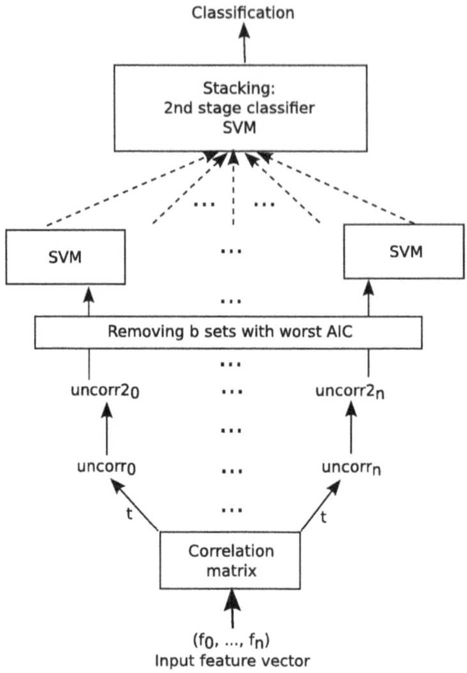

Fig. 1. Uncorrelation ensemble approach.

matrix is near to 0.0, or more explicitly, $|v_{x,y}|$ is smaller than some positive threshold t, i.e.

$$uncorr_y := \{f_y\} \cup \{f_x \mid t > |v_{x,y}|\} . \tag{2}$$

A set $uncorr_y$ contains all features uncorrelated to f_y but between the features within this set there could still be correlations. Consequently, we compute for each feature f_y a set

$$uncorr2_y := \{f_y, f_a, \ldots, f_k\} \tag{3}$$

where $f_y, f_a, \ldots, f_k$ all are uncorrelated. These sets $uncorr2_y$ are gained for each feature f_y by sequentially intersecting $uncorr_y$ with the sets belonging to the features within $uncorr_y$, or the intersection respectively (see Fig. 2). Although we aim at delivering as many input feature vectors as possible for the subsequent ensemble approach, we remove some of the $uncorr2_y$ sets before they are fed into the ensemble models. The reason is that there could be input feature vectors build by $uncorr2_y$ sets which lead to bad performing models. Hence, for each $uncorr2_y$ set we compute the Akaike information criterion (AIC) – indicating the quality of a model – after applying a logistic regression, and remove the b worst $uncorr2_y$ sets, i.e. those with the worst AIC values. The remaining $uncorr2_y$ sets are fed into a classifier each. In a final step we apply a stacking ensemble approach by feeding the outputs, i.e. the classification decisions, of the classifiers into a second stage classifier, which learns how to generate one common classification decision. The whole *uncorrelation ensemble* approach is shown in Fig. 1 and the input generation algorithm can be found in Fig. 2. The described *uncorrelation ensemble* approach possess two hyper parameters: (1) the threshold t for deciding about correlation or not, and (2) the number b of $uncorr2_y$ sets with bad AIC to remove. In our experiments we investigated different values for the threshold t and observed that the larger t the larger are the $uncorr_y$ and $uncorr2_y$ sets, the better becomes the average AIC value of the $uncorr2_y$ sets and the smaller becomes the number of unique $uncorr2_y$ sets. The $uncorr2_y$ sets should not be too small and there should not be too much not unique $uncorr2_y$ sets for achieving good results with the classifiers and the ensemble method. These observations result in the finding that estimating the best value for hyper parameter t is a trade-off between the size of the $uncorr2_y$ sets (and AIC) and the number of unique $uncorr2_y$ sets. The experiments reported in the next section show that the affect recognition performance of an SVM can be improved significantly with our proposed *uncorrelation ensemble* approach.

5 Experiments

We prove the proposed *uncorrelation ensemble* approach by experiments on the two above described kinds of features. The features were extracted from data gained by a study with German students solving mathematical tasks. The data is presented in the following Sect. 5.1. The experimental settings are described in section Sect. 5.2 and the results are discussed in Sects. 5.3 and 5.4.

5.1 Data

The data we used for our experiments were gained by conducting a study in which the speech and actions of ten 10 to 12 years old German students were recorded and their perceived task-difficulties were reported. The labelling of these data was done on the one hand concurrently by a human tutor and on the other hand retrospectively by a second reviewer. Divergences in the both labellings were clarified later on by discussions between the reviewers. During the study a paper sheet with fraction tasks was shown to the students and they were asked to paint – by means of a software for painting with a computer – their solution and prompted to explain aloud their observations and answers. The fraction tasks are subdivided into similar subtasks and cover exercises like assigning fractions to coloured parts of a circle or rectangle, reducing, adding or subtracting fractions and fraction equivalence. Originally, there are 10 tasks with 1 up to 10 subtasks but not each task was seen by each student. We made a screen recording to record the painting of the students and an acoustic recording to record the speech of the students. The screen recordings were used for the retrospective annotation. The acoustic speech recordings, consisting of 10 wav files with a length from 15 up to 20 min, were used to gain the amplitude and articulation features. The data collection resulted in 36 examples labelled with *over-challenged*

Input: feature vector $(f_0, \ldots, f_n)$, hyper parameters t, b
Output: *uncorr2sets* (set of $uncorr2_y$ sets)

compute correlation matrix $\mathbf{V}$ with values $v_{x,y}$ for each pair $f_x, f_y \in \{f_0, \ldots, f_n\}$;
for each feature f_y in the input feature vector $(f_0, \ldots, f_n)$ **do**
  $uncorr_y := \{f_y\} \cup \{f_x \in \{f_0, \ldots, f_{y-1}, f_{y+1} \ldots, f_n\} \mid t > |v_{x,y}|\}$;
endfor
for each feature f_y in the input feature vector $(f_0, \ldots, f_n)$ **do**
  $intersection := uncorr_y$;
  for x from n down to 0 **do**
    if $(f_x \neq f_y) \wedge (f_x \in intersection)$ **then do**
      $intersection := intersection \cap uncorr_x$;
    endif
  endfor
  $uncorr2_y := intersection$;
  compute AIC$(uncorr2_y)$;
endfor
$uncorr2sets := \{uncorr2_y | y = 0, \ldots, n\}$;
for i from b down to 1 **do**
  $uncorr2sets := uncorr2sets \setminus \{\arg\max_{uncorr2_y \in uncorr2sets}(\text{AIC}(uncorr2_y))\}$;
endfor
return *uncorr2sets*;

Fig. 2. Algorithm of the input computation for the uncorrelation ensemble approach.

(12 examples) or *appropriately challenged* (24 examples), respectively 48 examples (24 of class *appropriately challenged*, 24 of class *over-challenged*) after applying oversampling to the smaller set of examples of class *over-challenged* to eliminate the unbalance in the data.

5.2 Experimental Settings

In our experiments we used the state-of-the-art classifier support vector machine (SVM). An SVM ([3,5]) searches for a hyperplane which optimally – with maximal margin – separates the examples of different classes in the space of the example vectors. By means of the kernel trick and a kernel function also non-linear problems can be solved by an SVM. Originally, an SVM solves binary classification problems but can be extended to multi-class classification problems (see [4]). For the experiments we used the library LIBSVM ([4]) delivering an implementation of support vector machines. We conducted a 3-fold cross validation and we applied SVMs with an RBF-kernel and for each SVM used we conducted a grid search (according to [8]) on each fold to estimate the optimal values for the hyper parameters.

We report for all experiments two different error measures: (1) the classification test error and (2) the F-measure for both classes (*over-challenged*, *appropriately challenged*). The classification test error corresponds to the number of incorrectly classified examples of all examples within the test data. The F-measure is computed from two other measures, Precision (P) and Recall (R):

$$R = \frac{tp}{tp + fn}, \; P = \frac{tp}{tp + fp}, \; F - measure = 2 \cdot \frac{P \cdot R}{P + R}, \tag{4}$$

where tp (*true positives*) are examples of a class c which are correctly classified as belonging to class c, fn (*false negatives*) are examples of a class c incorrectly classified as not belonging to class c and fp (*false positives*) are examples of another class than c which are incorrectly classified as belonging to class c. Hence, Recall reports how many of all examples of a class c are correctly recognised as members of that class. Precision shows how many of the examples classified as belonging to class c actually belong to class c and *F-measure* is the harmonic mean of Recall and Precision.

5.3 Experiments on Articulation Features

The baseline for evaluating our proposed *uncorrelation ensemble* approach is a single SVM applied to one input feature vector containing all articulation features (see Table 1, left). The result of the single SVM is compared to the *uncorrelation ensemble* approach with different values for hyper parameter t. We tried out values between 0.2 and 0.5 for t. 0.1 would have been too small as it leads to empty $uncorr_y$ sets. For hyper parameter b was chosen the value delivering the best result. This value was identified by starting with all $uncorr2_y$ sets and then leaving out step by step the $uncorr2_y$ set with worst AIC value until only one $uncorr2_y$ set is left. The classification test errors and the F-measures of these experiments are reported in Table 1. The best classification performance delivers the *uncorrelation ensemble* approach with $t = 0.4$. This model, but also the other three *uncorrelation ensemble* models, outperforms the single SVM and delivers a significant classification performance improvement of 64 %.

Besides classification test error and F-measure we investigated also the behaviour of the minimal, maximal and average AIC value of the $uncorr2_y$ sets, the number of not unique $uncorr2_y$ sets (%) and the average size (number of elements) of $uncorr2_y$ sets (%) for different values of hyper parameter t for the articulation features (see Fig. 3). As one can see in Fig. 3, the AIC values decrease with growing t, while the number of not unique $uncorr2_y$ sets and the average size of $uncorr2_y$ sets increase. The best classification performance, i.e. the

Table 1. Classification test errors (%) and F-measures of a single SVM and of the *uncorrelation ensemble* approach (UncorrEns) with different values for hyper parameter t applied to the articulation features.

	SVM	UncorrEns ($t = 0.2$, $b = 2$ (15 %))	UncorrEns ($t = 0.3$, $b = 8$ (62 %))	UncorrEns ($t = 0.4$, $b = 11$ (85 %))	UncorrEns ($t = 0.5$, $b = 7$ (54 %))
Error (%)	22.92	14.58	14.58	**8.33**	16.67
F-measure	0.81, 0.72	0.87, 0.83	0.87, 0.83	**0.92, 0.91**	0.85, 0.81

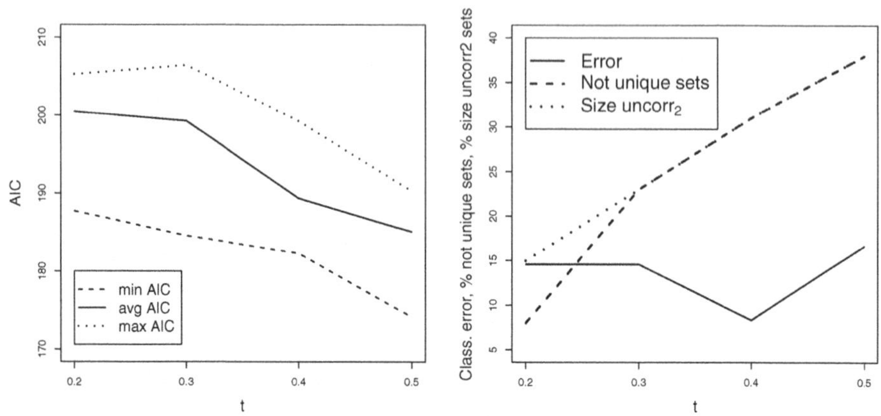

Fig. 3. Behaviour of AIC, classification test error (%), number of not unique $uncorr2_y$ sets (%) and the average size of $uncorr2_y$ sets (%) for different values of hyper parameter t for the articulation features.

smallest classification test error, lays somewhere in the middle. That means that finding the best value for t is a trade-off between average AIC value and the number of not unique $uncorr2_y$ sets. The reason is that larger $uncorr2_y$ sets and smaller AIC values are good, but an increasing number of not unique $uncorr2_y$ sets is contra productive. Furthermore, we compared applying a single SVM to applying our *uncorrelation ensemble* approach, on the one hand with a majority ensemble and on the other hand (as in the other experiments) with a stacking ensemble as second stage classifier, for different values of hyper parameter t as well as different values of hyper parameter b (or different numbers of $uncorr2_y$ sets respectively). Figure 4 shows that stacking ensemble performs always better than majority ensemble and for a number of more than 3 $uncorr2_y$ sets also always better than or equal to the single SVM. If b is chosen wisely, then the *uncorrelation ensemble* approach with stacking as second stage classifier is able to improve the classification performance significantly compared to the classification performance of a single SVM.

5.4 Experiments on Amplitude Features

For the amplitude features we compared the result of a single SVM to the *uncorrelation ensemble* approach with values between 0.3 and 0.7 for hyper parameter t (0.2 would have been already too small as it leads to empty $uncorr_y$ sets). The value for hyper parameter b delivering the best result was in each case 0, i.e. no $uncorr2_y$ sets were removed as removing did not improve the performance. The reason might be that the amplitude features consist of much less features than the articulation features (7 instead of 13), and that as a consequence the percentage of not unique $uncorr2_y$ sets is higher. That means that from the already small amount of 7 $uncorr2_y$ sets some are not unique and hence each unique $uncorr2_y$

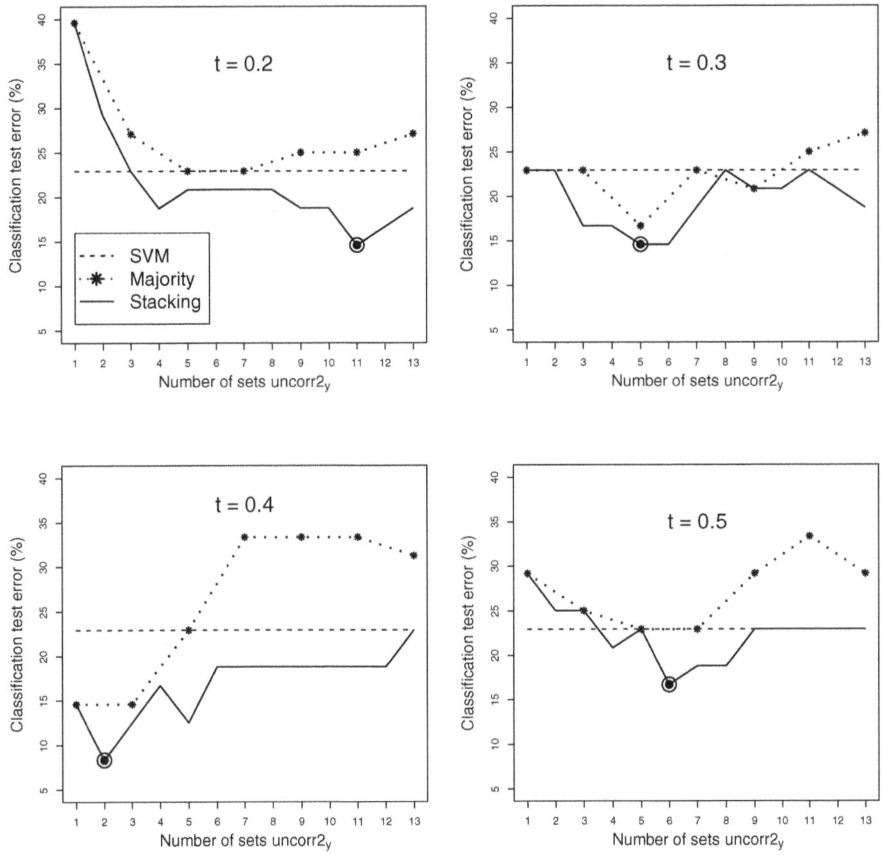

Fig. 4. Classification test error (%) of a single SVM (dashed straight horizontal line), majority (dotted line with stars, only for uneven number of $uncorr2_y$ sets) and stacking ensemble (not dashed line) mapped to the number of the remaining $uncorr2_y$ sets (after removing those with worst AIC) for $t = 0.2, 0.3, 0.4, 0.5$ applied to the articulation features. The circle indicates the minimal classification test error.

set is needed to deliver enough different input for the ensemble approach. The classification test errors and the F-measures of these experiments are reported in Table 2. The best classification performance delivers the *uncorrelation ensemble* approach with $t = 0.4$, 0.5 or 0.6. These three *uncorrelation ensemble* models outperform the single SVM and deliver a significant classification performance improvement of 53 %.

Also for the amplitude features we investigated the behaviour of the minimal, maximal and average AIC value of the $uncorr2_y$ sets, the number of not unique $uncorr2_y$ sets (%) and the average size of $uncorr2_y$ sets (%) for different values of hyper parameter t (see Fig. 5). As in Figs. 3 and 5 the AIC values decrease with growing t, while the number of not unique $uncorr2_y$ sets and the average size of $uncorr2_y$ sets increase and the best classification performance lays somewhere in

Table 2. Classification test errors (%) and F-measures of a single SVM and of the *uncorrelation ensemble* approach (UncorrEns) with different values for hyper parameter t applied to the amplitude features.

	SVM	UncorrEns (t = 0.3, $b = 0$)	UncorrEns (t = 0.4, $b = 0$)	UncorrEns (t = 0.5, $b = 0$)	UncorrEns (t = 0.6, $b = 0$)	UncorrEns (t = 0.7, $b = 0$)
Error (%)	31.25	31.25	**14.58**	**14.58**	**14.58**	35.42
F-measure	0.75, 0.59	0.76, 0.55	**0.87, 0.84**	**0.87, 0.84**	**0.87, 0.84**	0.71, 0.54

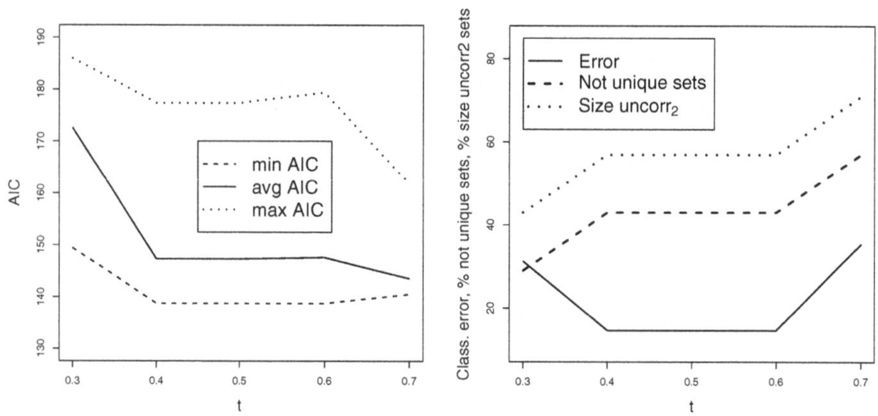

Fig. 5. Behaviour of AIC, classification test error (%), number of not unique $uncorr2_y$ sets (%) and the average size of $uncorr2_y$ sets (%) for different values of hyper parameter t for the amplitude features.

the middle. That means that also for the amplitude features holds that finding the best value for t is a trade-off between average AIC value and the number of not unique $uncorr2_y$ sets.

6 Conclusions

We have presented the *uncorrelation ensemble* approach for improving the automatic affect recognition in ITSs. The proposed approach uses principles from feature selection and ensemble approaches for performance improvement. Experiments on low-level speech features show that the *uncorrelation ensemble* approach is able to reach on average a classification performance improvement of about 59 % in comparison to applying a single SVM. Future work would be to integrate and test the proposed affect recognition approach in a real ITS.

Acknowledgements. The research leading to the results reported here has received funding from the European Union Seventh Framework Programme (FP7/2007 – 2013) under grant agreement no. 318051 – iTalk2Learn project (www.italk2learn.eu).

References

1. Arroyo, I., Woolf, B.P., Burelson, W., Muldner, K., Rai, D., Tai, M.: A multimedia adaptive tutoring system for mathematics that addresses cognition, metacognition and affect. Int. J. Artif. Intell. Edu. **24**, 387–426 (2014)
2. Baker, R.S.J.D., Gowda, S., Wixon, M., Kalka, J., Wagner, A., Salvi, A., Aleven, V., Kusbit, G., Ocumpaugh, J. and Rossi, L.: Towards sensor-free affect detection in cognitive tutor algebra. In: Proceedings of the 5th International Conference on Educational Data Mining (EDM 2012), pp. 126–133 (2012)
3. Boser, B.E., Guyon, I., Vapnik, V.: A training algorithm for optimal margin classifiers. In: Proceedings of the Fifth Annual Workshop on Computational Learning Theory, pp. 144–152. ACM Press (1992)
4. Chang, C.C., Lin, C.J.: LIBSVM: a library for support vector machines. ACM Trans. Intell. Syst. Technol. **2**(3), 1–27 (2011)
5. Cortes, C., Vapnik, V.: Support-vector network. Mach. Learn. **20**, 273–297 (1995)
6. Epp, C., Lippold, M., Mandryk, R.L.: Identifying emotional states using keystroke dynamics. In: Proceedings of the 2011 Annual Conference on Human Factors in Computing Systems (CHI 2011), pp. 715–724 (2011)
7. Grawemeyer, B., Gutierrez-Santos, S., Holmes, W., Mavrikis, M., Rummel, N., Mazziotti, C. Janning, R.: Talk, tutor, explore, learn: intelligent tutoring and exploration for robust learning. In: Proceedings of the 17th International Conference on Artificial Intelligence in Education (AIED) (2015)
8. Hsu, C.W., Chang, C.C., Lin, C.J.: A practical guide to support vector classification. Technical report, Department of Computer Science, National Taiwan University (2011). http://www.csie.ntu.edu.tw/cjlin/
9. Hu, X., Tang, L., Tang, J., Liu, H.: Exploiting social relations for sentiment analysis in microblogging. In: Proceedings of the Sixth ACM WSDM Conference (WSDM 2013) (2013)
10. Janning, R., Schatten, C., Schmidt-Thieme, L.: Multimodal affect recognition for adaptive intelligent tutoring systems. In: Extended Proceedings of the 7th International Conference on Educational Data Mining (EDM 2014), pp. 171–178 (2014)
11. Janning, R., Schatten, C., Schmidt-Thieme, L.: Feature analysis for affect recognition supporting task sequencing in adaptive intelligent tutoring systems. In: Proceedings of the European Conference on Technology Enhanced Learning (EC-TEL 2014), pp. 179–192 (2014)
12. Janning, R., Schatten, C., Schmidt-Thieme, L., Backfried, G.: An SVM plait for improving affect recognition in intelligent tutoring systems. In: Proceedings of the IEEE International Conference on Tools with Artificial Intelligence (ICTAI) (2014)
13. Luz, S.: Automatic identification of experts and performance prediction in the multimodal math data corpus through analysis of speech interaction. In: Second International Workshop on Multimodal Learning Analytics, Sydney Australia (2013)
14. Mavrikis, M.: Data-driven modelling of students interactions in an ILE. In: Proceedings of the International Conference on Educational Data Mining (EDM 2008), pp. 87–96 (2008)

15. D'Mello, S.K., Craig, S.D., Witherspoon, A., McDaniel, B., Graesser, A.: Automatic detection of learners affect from conversational cues. User Model User-Adap Inter. **18**, 45–80 (2008). doi:10.1007/s11257-007-9037-6
16. D'Mello, S.K., Graesser, A.: Language and discourse are powerful signals of student emotions during tutoring. IEEE Trans. Learn. Technol. **5**(4), 304–317 (2012)
17. Moore, J.D., Tian, L., Lai, C.: Word-level emotion recognition using high-level features. In: Gelbukh, A. (ed.) CICLing 2014, Part II. LNCS, vol. 8404, pp. 17–31. Springer, Heidelberg (2014)
18. Morency, L.P., Oviatt, S., Scherer, S., Weibel, N., Worsley, M.: ICMI 2013 grand challenge workshop on multimodal learning analytics. In: Proceedings of the 15th ACM on International Conference on Multimodal Interaction (ICMI 2013), pp. 373–378 (2013)
19. Pardos, Z.A., Baker, R.S.J.D., San Pedro, M., Gowda, S.M., Gowda, S.M.: Affective states and state tests: investigating how affect and engagement during the school year predict end-of-year learning outcomes. Inaugural issue J. Learn. Anal. **1**(1), 107–128 (2014)
20. Purandare, A., Litman, D.: Humor: prosody analysis and automatic recognition for F * R * I * E * N * D * S *. In: Proceedings of the 2006 Conference on Empirical Methods in Natural Language Processing (EMNLP 2006), pp. 208–215 (2006)
21. Qi, F., Bao, C., Liu, Y.: A novel two-step SVM classifier for voiced/unvoiced/silence classification of speech. In: International Symposium on Chinese Spoken Language Processing, pp. 77–80 (2004)
22. Sadegh, M., Ibrahim, R., Othman, Z.A.: Opinion mining and sentiment analysis: a survey. Int. J. Comput. Technol. **2**(3), 171–178 (2012)
23. Saif, H., He, Y., Alani, H.: Semantic sentiment analysis of Twitter. In: Cudré-Mauroux, P., Heflin, J., Sirin, E., Tudorache, T., Euzenat, J., Hauswirth, M., Parreira, J.X., Hendler, J., Schreiber, G., Bernstein, A., Blomqvist, E. (eds.) ISWC 2012, Part I. LNCS, vol. 7649, pp. 508–524. Springer, Heidelberg (2012)
24. San Pedro, M.O.C., Baker, R.S.J.D., Bowers, A., Heffernan, N.: Predicting college enrollment from student interaction with an intelligent tutoring system in middle school. In: Proceedings of the 6th International Conference on Educational Data Mining (EDM 2013), pp. 177–184 (2013)
25. Schuller, B., Batliner, A., Steidl, S., Seppi, D.: Recognising realistic emotions and affect in speech: state of the art and lessons learnt from the first challenge. Speech Commun. **53**, 1062–1087 (2011)
26. Ting, K.M., Witten, I.H.: Issues in stacked generalization. J. Artif. Intel. Res. **10**, 271–289 (1999)
27. Worsley, M., Blikstein, P.: What's an expert? using learning analytics to identify emergent markers of expertise through automated speech, sentiment and sketch analysis. In: Proceedings of the 4th International Conference on Educational Data Mining (EDM 2011), pp. 235–240 (2011)

Lessons Learned from Creating a Mobile Version of an Educational Board Game to Increase Situational Awareness

Roland Klemke[1(✉)], Shalini Kurapati[2], Heide Lukosch[2], and Marcus Specht[1]

[1] Welten Institute – Research Center for Learning, Teaching and Technology, Open University of the Netherlands, P.O. Box 2960, 6401 DL Heerlen, The Netherlands
{Roland.Klemke,Marcus.Specht}@ou.nl

[2] Faculty of Technology, Policy and Management, Delft University of Technology, P.O. Box 5015, 2600 GA Delft, The Netherlands
{S.Kurapati,H.K.Lukosch}@tudelft.nl

Abstract. This paper reports on an iterative design process for a serious game, which aims to raise situational awareness among different stakeholders in a logistics value chain by introducing multi-user role-playing games. It does so in several phases: After introducing the field of logistics as a problem domain for an educational challenge, it firstly describes the design of an educational board game for the field of disruption handling in logistics processes. Secondly, it describes how the board game can be realized in an open-source mobile serious games platform and identifies lessons learned based on advantages and issues found. Thirdly, it derives requirements for a re-design of the mobile game and finally draws conclusions.

Keywords: Mobile learning · Game-based learning · Multi-user games · Logistics · Multi-role game-design

1 Introduction

Decision-making in sociotechnical systems is complex and error-prone due to interdependencies of tasks, conflicting goals in distributed responsibilities and a lack of information among the various stakeholders involved in decision-making [1]. The active sharing of relevant situational information might help to improve shared situational awareness (SSA) among the stakeholders involved [2], which can lead to improved decision making processes within sociotechnical systems. Therefore, it is crucial to understand the role of communication among stakeholders [3].

The SALOMO[1] project aims to provide training solutions to create situational awareness [2] to cope with this situation and to highlight the importance of communication. As multi-stakeholder decision situations confronted with time restrictions and incomplete information such as emergencies have been recognised as a relevant field

[1] SALOMO: Situational Awareness for LOgistic Multimodal Operations.

© Springer International Publishing Switzerland 2015
G. Conole et al. (Eds.): EC-TEL 2015, LNCS 9307, pp. 183–196, 2015.
DOI: 10.1007/978-3-319-24258-3_14

for training [4–6], a multi-user board game has been designed, which emulates the decision process in the port environment. The goal of the game is to sensitize stakeholders in a value chain about communication and inter-dependencies. The game was conceived to achieve a set of key objectives [7]:

- Understanding the impact of increased shared situational awareness (SSA) on individual, group and system level performance
- Setting a foundation to identify measures to increase SSA
- Offering a frame of reference to assess SSA in the organization and network
- Serving as a training tool for disruption management

The game focuses on how to handle disruptions in the transportation network, and whether and when to communicate information relating to the disturbance to other players. Several roles are played in the game; the vessel planner, the yard planner, the control tower, the resource planner and the sales department. Thus, the paper-based version of the game requires no more and no less than five players.

To improve the scalability of the board game, we aim to provide a computerized version of the board game, simplifying the game distribution and execution by providing an automated execution environment for locally distributed players.

While most game-based learning approaches focus on skill development and motivational aspects (see e.g. the meta-review in [8]), little work is reported on the aspect of shared-situational awareness in multi-stakeholder decision training (decision training itself is however covered e.g. in [9, 10]). With this work, we aim to provide new insights to this field of research, illustrated by an example in logistics. The main contribution of this paper is to reflect on a design process that started with a board game, which was transferred into a computerized mobile game and was redesigned into a new version according to lessons learned. While we do not report on a comparative study performed to assess the performance of each version, we rather give insights into design and application experiences as well as limitations of each approach.

In the remainder of this paper we give background information about the problem situation in logistics followed by an introduction of situational awareness in multi-stakeholder decision situations. We introduce and discuss our board game design as training game to increase situational awareness in a logistics decision situation and report on experiences made with this game. We continue describing the transfer of this game to a mobile serious game platform, and describe experiences made with the mobile game. From these experiences we derive requirements and design features for the second version of the mobile game. Finally, we draw conclusions.

2 Problem Situation in Logistics

In an international port, like the Port of Rotterdam, thousands of containers are moved every day in and out through different channels in container terminals [11]. A container terminal is the point of interaction between the different parties involved in container transportation [12]. Containers need to be moved as fast as possible to meet the delivery time expectations of customers. Safety of the port and its operating personnel needs to be guaranteed at all times. To ensure the smooth operation of the port, different stakeholders, equipped with different responsibilities have to interoperate: *Control tower* ensures the overall smooth operation; *Resource planner* assigns the port personnel; *Yard planner* is responsible for the internal storage of containers in the port; *Vessel planner* is responsible to deliver containers to and from vessels; *Sales manager* is interested in customer satisfaction.

Unplanned and unanticipated events affecting the normal flow of goods and operations in supply and transport networks are termed as disruptions [13]. Disruptions have become common phenomena in port operations. The main categories are port accidents, port equipment failures, dangerous goods mishandling, port congestion, inadequacy of labour skills, hinterland inaccessibility, breach of security, and labour strikes [14]. Disruptions may cause severe ripple effects resulting in high costs and dire consequences on the wellbeing of the surrounding environment [15]. A machinery breakdown in the port may e.g. lead to a security risk, causing an area to be closed. This may delay the unloading of ships, which delays also their loading and planned departure, which also affects the trucks, etc. The operating individuals, mentioned above, need to take decisions to mitigate the disruptions together with external stakeholders. However, they are not always aware of these interdependencies and effects. Given the undesirable ripple effects of the disruptions in seaport operations, it can be deduced that the resilience of seaports, and their terminals, is essential for the resilience and robustness of transport networks as a whole.

As a first step to address this problem, this paper introduces a tabletop simulation game as an approach towards increasing situational awareness of planners and decision makers in seaport operations during disruption management to improve the resilience of seaport container terminals. In the following, we introduce how we conceptualize shared situational awareness and why it is so crucial in container transportation, before we illustrate how we translated this concept into a simulation board game.

3 Situational Awareness

Situational awareness (SA) is the broadly accepted definition describing the level of awareness that an individual has of a situation, an operator's dynamic understanding of 'what is going on', including the perception and comprehension of a situation and the prediction of its future state [16]. Much has been written about the construct, yet it remains profoundly contentious. Of the definitions and approaches available, Endsley's three level, information-processing-based model has received the most attention [16]. Due to the significant presence of teams in contemporary organizational systems, the construct of team SA is currently receiving increased attention from the human factors community [17]. Distributed teams comprise members interacting over time and space via technology-mediated communication [18]. Team performance itself comprises two components of behaviour, teamwork (team members working together) and task work (team members working individually). Shared situational awareness (SSA) is multidimensional, comprising individual team member SA, shared SA between team members and also the combined SA of the whole team, the so-called 'common picture'.

Add to this the various team processes involved (e.g. communication, coordination, collaboration, etc.) and the complexity of the construct quickly becomes apparent. Most attempts to understand team SA have centred on a 'shared understanding' of the same situation. Nofi, for example, defines team SA as: 'a shared awareness of a particular situation' [19] and Perla et al. suggest that 'when used in the sense of ''shared awareness of a situation'', shared SA implies that we all understand a given situation in the same way' [20]. In the following, we introduce a study in which we research in how far a simulation game session can support a group of players in developing SSA by providing different levels of communication and cooperation. The increased level of SSA should lead to improved resilience in container terminal operations.

4 Phase 1: Board Game Design

Simulation games can be defined as 'conscious endeavour to reproduce the central characteristics of a system in order to understand, experiment with and/or predict the behaviour of that system' [21]. It is a method in which human participants enact a specific role in a simulated environment [22]. In our case, we focus on the use of simulation games as a training tool, which is meant to improve communication between stakeholders, and to improve their SSA in seaport container terminals as an example of a complex system. For the conceptualization of our game, we follow a framework by Meijer [23], which is based on the work of Klabbers [24]. According to this, a simulation game is always designed with an objective (for learning purposes) or based on a research question (research purposes). The game consists of objectives, rules, roles, constraints, load and situation, which are defined by the game designer [23]. In our case the game follows predefined disruption processes within which players interact to take decisions. These decisions are scored and influence game parameters (such as performance, safety, and customer satisfaction).

Resilience is the ability for a system or organization to bounce back to normality when affected by a disruption [25]. For seaport container terminals, bouncing back to normal can be quantified in terms of the Key Performance Indicators (KPIs). The KPIs can be categorized as efficiency of operations and costs, safety, customer relationship, sustainability, strategic/competitive position in the market, profits and losses [26]. As the game only focuses on operations, the KPIs considered for the game are safety, efficiency of operations, and customer satisfaction. Based on literature and brainstorming sessions with professionals in the container terminal business, the challenges in disruption management in container terminal operations have been translated into contextualized game play. The development of the game took over 8 months, as it was an iterative process following design, evaluation and validation cycles.

The resulting disruption management game for intermodal transport operations in ports is a 5-player tabletop board game. The game is presented to the participants in the form of a game session (see Fig. 1). One game facilitator supports the game play. Every game session begins with a briefing lecture, introducing the concept and motivation, rules, set-up and scoring of the game (see Table 1). At the beginning, each player starts with a limited number of communication tokens.

Table 1. Input and Output elements in the disruption management game

Input/Output	Description in the game
Roles	Vessel planner, Yard planner, Resource planner, Control tower manager, Sales
Rules	• There are individual game boards for each participant as well as an overall game board for the container terminal system with KPIs, contain varying information and rules based on the level of the game play
	• The KPIs are all maximum at the start of the game, they deteriorate after every round, and can be increased by mitigation actions of participants
	• Participants have information cards as well as action cards, the former used for communication, the latter for performing mitigation actions
	• Communication can be (virtually) done via e-mail, phone and conference, with differing effectiveness and costs. Limited tokens have to be used to communicate, showing communication costs (time and resources)
	• The information cards contain disruption details. After a round of information sharing, participants have to perform mitigation actions
	• Mitigation cards vary for each round. They contain 3 choices from which participants need to choose one mitigation action card
	• Based on the actions of the participants the game master changes the scores of the KPIs after every round
Objectives	*Overall:* To maintain resilient transport operations
	Individual: To maintain individual performance indicators as well as the overall KPI of the terminal
Constraints	Information availability, time, resources to communicate
Load	Different disruption situations, different levels of escalation of disruptions, varying channels and cost of communication and information sharing
Situation	University classrooms; Logistics, supply chain and transportation companies; Professional and knowledge institutes
Participants	Academic researchers, students and professionals in the transportation, logistics and supply chain industry
Qualitative data	Observations from the game session by the game master, report of decisions after every round
Quantitative data	Post-game survey

Fig. 1. The board game in action

The game play begins after the briefing session. Each level of the game play has five rounds. Within each round, each participant receives individual information, which may be incomplete, irritating, or misleading. Each player can spend one of his/her communication tokens to share information with other players. Consequently he/she has to take decisions on follow-up activities, which influence individual scores and group scores.

After every round, the individual and group scores are explained, when the game facilitator reads out the effects of the decisions made by the players on the KPIs. At the end of each level, an overview of the situation based on the participants' decisions is presented. For evaluation purposes, the game play is observed thoroughly by the game facilitator, while the decisions and scores are recorded.

The game session concludes with a de-briefing session, where the game facilitator explains the principles of disruption management, the challenges faced by practitioners, the relationship of the game elements to the challenges, a review of the scores and the reasons for obtaining such scores, alternative strategies, comparison between scores of different play groups and the reasons for it. This session is mainly to provide a learning experience for the participants.

After the de-briefing session the game facilitator encourages the participants to provide feedback about the game and their experience, which is recorded. After the game session, the participants fill in an online survey on the usefulness of the game.

5 Experience with the Board Game

The data gathered from the game and the survey is analysed qualitatively to gather insights into disruption management for resilient intermodal port operations. Several game sessions were conducted based on the above design, played with 10 researchers, 15 experts, and 80 graduate students in supply chain, logistics and transportation. The most important result that emerged was the clear difference in the behavioural patterns of players at different game levels. Based on their awareness of the disruption scenario, roles and objectives of others, there was a difference regarding relevant information sharing for mitigating the disruption.

In level 1 of the game play, all the players had limited awareness of the disruption scenario, the effects of their decisions and their objective in the game. In level 2, players made good use of the available communication channels, as they understood where to send and receive information. Several discussions and negotiations were made among the players during level 3. Players teamed up to jointly mitigate the situation. Sometimes, players sacrificed their individual KPIs to boost the overall KPIs. Well-informed decisions were made in level 3.

The results from the mentioned sessions create a helpful learning experience in the field of disruption management and resilience of container terminal operations. While these positive results motivate us to continue, we also observed and collected a number of reasons motivating the transfer of the board game to a mobile version:

- As the board game requires a human game facilitator to control the complex game processes, the mobile version should use automated processes.
- This automatisation should also simplify the game's distribution and scalability.
- Game results should be traceable for the necessary debriefing phase. While in the board game only the human memory is available for debriefing, the mobile version should track all user interactions and decisions.
- The board game requires all players to be present in a single room. While this fosters a common game experience, it imposes an unrealistic situation, as in reality the different persons would be distributed across the port.

In the following, we illustrate how the board-game concept has been translated into a mobile multi-player game, taking into account above-mentioned reasoning.

6 Phase 2: Transfer of the Board Game into a Mobile Game

Based on the board game described above, we designed a version for mobile devices using ARLearn. ARLearn is a platform for the flexible, pattern-based design of mobile process-based learning games [27, 28] comprising an authoring interface, which allows binding content items and task structures to locations, events, and roles and to use game-logic and dependencies to structure the game process. The platform has been recently used for several pilot studies in the cultural heritage domain [29], in security-related fields [30], and in health care related emergency training [31].

Related approaches comprise the ARIS platform [32], which offers the possibility to author location-based mobile games. While ARIS has been successfully used in several application examples [33], it does not support multi-player/multi-role games. QuestInSitu is a mobile learning platform which mainly focuses on assessment [34] in location-based contexts. Robles et al. [35] describe an implementation of a team-enabled mobile gaming platform. The location-based task model allows for linear games, where a new task description follows the previous one.

In the mobile version of the board game, the game facilitator is replaced with the automated ARLearn game logic. The game design follows the board game process as described in the section 'Board game design and experience'. Figure 2 depicts one round in the game process. Each level consists of five rounds, which are synchronized after each decision. Each round gives access to a new situation description.

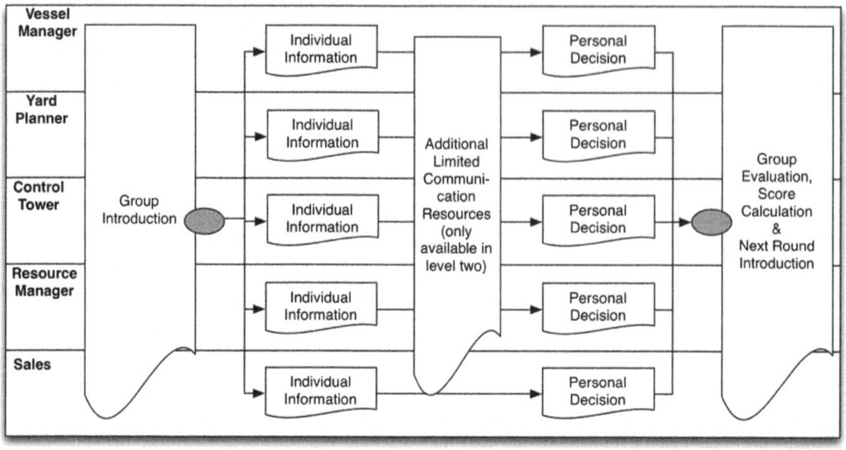

Fig. 2. One round of level one/level two with communication

While level one of the game isolates the different players completely, subsequent levels give access to limited communicative resources. This shall foster the players to exchange information creating awareness for other player's situation and the overall consequences of own decisions (Fig. 2). Figure 3 displays screenshots of the mobile SALOMO game showing communication messages and decision points. In this example, the player can choose between alternative actions, leading to different scores.

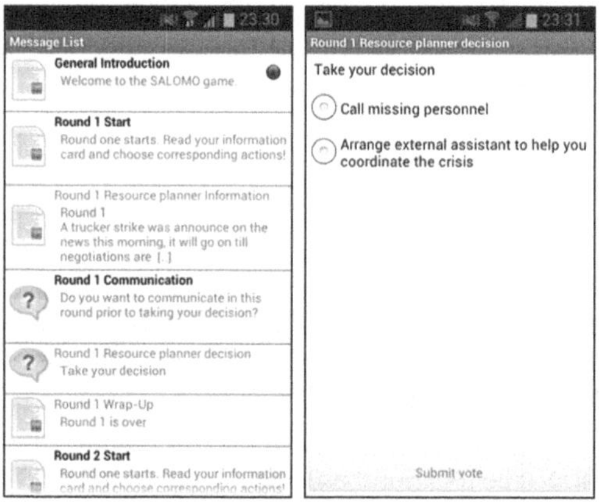

Fig. 3. Screenshots of the SALOMO game: message overview and decision point

7 Experiences with the Mobile Game

For the first version of the mobile game we collected feedback in internal playtests. Even though, we aimed to create the mobile version as close as possible to the board game, its playability differs in some aspects significantly from the board game:

- Five players can play the game in separate locations as their mobile devices are synchronised automatically via ARLearn. The ARLearn game engine automatically synchronizes the game state between the different players
- No human game facilitator is required, as the game engine automatically updates the game state, evaluates player decisions and distributes information. Game rules, processes, decisions and all other game resources are encoded as game design script in ARLearn.
- The mobile devices provide a realistic situation scenario, as the players use communication means similar to their daily activities as the game interaction is based on mobile devices: users receive messages and interact with question items. Multimedia dialogue sequences complement the message driven approach to provide more immersive situations.
- Players don't need to be in one location but can be mobile. All communication and synchronisation tasks are performed via the ARLearn platform

The ARLearn platform supports the automatic logging of all player interactions. Through a web-based front-end this data can be retrieved and used for a debriefing session. While the logging data is available, the debriefing itself is not (yet) automatized and has to be performed together with a trained expert. While these differences represent improvements with respect to the applicability of the game, our internal playtests also revealed some drawbacks of the mobile version.

Player dependence: the game process is synchronized across the players. After a player took his/her decision in one round he/she has to wait until the other players also finished the round before the game continues. While this mechanism is copied from the board game, it leads to frustration in the mobile game as the players are not necessarily around one table. Consequently, they cannot observe the game process of the other players while waiting nor can they communicate with the others (and e.g. putting social pressure on them to speed up), which is possible in the board game.

Missing motivation for communication: players get access to a limited number of communication features in levels higher than level one. However, we observerd that players rather aim to keep their communication tokens instead of spending them. While this effect can also be observed in the board game, it is stronger in the mobile game, probably increased by the following issue.

Missing feedback for effects of decisions & communications: while the board game keeps all players around one table and thus allows a lot of informal or non-verbal communications among players, the mobile players are cut off this communication channel. Consequently, they can hardly judge in how far a specific communication message leads to an improved decision at the receiving player.

No direct measurement of communication: one important aspect in the board game is, that players can observe other players' communicative behaviour and thus can adapt their own communicative behaviour. In the mobile version, players can only refer to that part of the communication that is directed towards them and thus miss a relevant part of ongoing communication.

Complexity of the role definitions: five players in five roles with different involvements in the game appear to be too complex for the mobile game. Again, putting the players around one table, enabling their direct communication, and supporting them with a game facilitator simplifies this problem. Players can better feel the role dependencies in this situation. As the isolated players of the mobile version do not get this kind of direct feedback, it is harder to understand conflicts between the different roles and importance of each role.

8 Phase 3: Re-designing the Mobile Game

Based on the experiences drawn with the previous version of the mobile game, we redesigned the game process to deliver an updated version, which keeps the advantages of the mobile game but aims to eliminate its current drawbacks. Consequently, we still want the game to be playable by distributed players in different roles without a human game facilitator. Also, we do not want to change the realistic messaging-approach. However, we clearly aim to address the observed drawbacks.

Gain player independence: To get rid of annoying waiting times, we aim to get rid of the majority of synchronisation points in the game process. Instead, we want to allow each player to follow her game process independently. The different players shall still play connected in the way that they can exchange messages, but they can follow their individual decision paths without having to wait.
Clearly motivate communication: Instead of relying on a limited number of communication means, we aim to reward effective communication by giving positive score for important messages shared on time and by giving negative score for unimportant or late messages. As messages represent shared received information the importance of a message can be specified at design time.
Give feedback for effects of decisions & communications: Players sharing messages should receive feedback stating, if the message was received on time (i.e., before the receiving player took a corresponding decision). Also, negative feedback (e.g. late arrival or unnecessary information) should be given to the player. The feedback should be given in form of acknowledge message and will be auto generated.
Direct measurement of communication: While players should not be able to sneak into other players' messages, they should be aware of the amount of ongoing communication. This feature, which is not available in real life, could help the players to adapt their own communication strategy to the group level.
Simplify role definitions: We plan to reduce the number of roles playing the mobile game to three by combining two of the previously defined roles (control tower and resource planner) into the new controller role and by omitting the vessel planner role. Control tower and resource planner have a strong overlap and can be combined. The vessel planner only participates in the game play in a limited way and can thus be ignored. This way, the roles are better balanced (about equal effort for each role).

Figure 4 displays one round of information, communication, and feedback in the redesigned game. The number of roles is reduced to three (*simplification of roles*). Each player receives information at slightly different points in time and needs to take an individual decision (*player independence*). Each player can also decide to inform other players about the information received and/or their decision taken. If their communication message arrives the other player in time and can influence their decision (see message from sales to yard planner as an example), they receive positive feedback (*motivation and feedback for communication*). If they communicate too late (see message from controller to yard planner as an example), they receive negative feedback (*feedback for communication*).

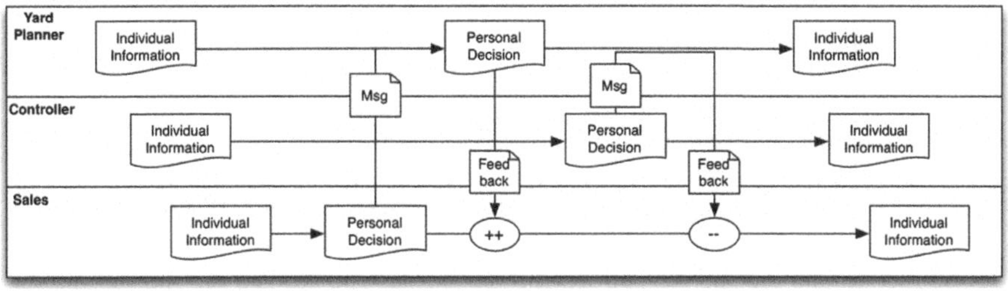

Fig. 4. One round of the redesigned mobile game

9 Conclusion

From disruption management processes observed at a large international port, we have designed a board game simulating these processes with a varying degree of communication means available to players. This board game has been successfully trialled with various user groups. Some difficulties of its game design are that it requires a skilled game facilitator to be available during game play, which leads to decreased scalability of the game. Furthermore, the board game requires all players to be within a single room, which is unrealistic for the stakeholders in a big port.

Consequently, we have chosen a multi-user, multi-role enabled mobile game environment (ARLearn), to create a computerized version of the game, which can be played by players in the different roles simultaneously. While the mobile version of the game could improve the identified weaknesses of the board game [36], we identified a number of new issues arising. These issues are mainly due to cutting off the informal communication among players by separating them.

The main contribution of this paper is to reflect on the design process, which transfers the board game into a mobile game, and to analyse the problems solved and the issues introduced during this process. Table 2 compares the transitions from the board game to the mobile game and the planned changes towards its second version along the dimensions execution, scalability, location independence, introduction & debriefing support, group experience, realism, player independence, motivation for communication, feedback, measurement of communication, and complexity of the roles.

We have learned, that transferring a board game to a mobile game by producing a close copy of the gameplay can lead to a completely new situation. The mobile game play comes along with changed communication behaviour and requires more explicit feedback mechanisms and stronger motivations to foster desired behaviour. We believe that our insights can be transferred to other fields of multi-stakeholder decision training

Table 2. Transitions from the board game to two versions of the mobile game

Dimension	Board game → Mobile game (v1)	Mobile game (v1) → (v2)
Execution of game process	Human game facilitator no longer needed; scores and progress automatized.	(No change wrt. to v1)
Scalability	Game scalability increased.	(No change wrt. to v1)
Location independence	Location independence and mobility introduced but leads to isolation.	Isolation effect reduced bye better motivation for communication.
Introduction support	In-game tutorial and explanations replace costly introduction process.	(No change wrt. to v1)
Debriefing support	Debriefing activity supported through automated data collection.	(No change wrt. to v1)
Group experience	Informal communication between players cut-off	Group experience to be increased by better communication and feedback mechanisms.
Realism	More realism through isolation and message style communication. Player dependence limits realism.	Player independence shall increase realism.
Player independence	Turn-based board game process leads to player frustration in mobile game.	Gain player independence by introducing asynchronous game phases.
Motivation for communication	Due to missing motivation players do not consume their communication tokens	Rewards for effective communication shall foster communication among players.
Feedback	Lack of informal communication leads to loss of awareness	Explicit feedback about communication, decisions, and timing to raise awareness
Communication measure	Adjusting own behaviour by observing other players is hardened in the mobile version due to isolation	Indicators for own communication behaviour in relation to others' aim to grasp the own position in the network of players
Complexity of roles	The number of roles is perceived as being to complex for effective game play.	Number of roles shall be condensed for more effective game play.

situations by clearly separating formal and informal communication aspects and respecting them systematically within the game-design.

The work described here represents a starting point for the sound design and implementation of multi-user decision training games for various training scenarios. While we have first results indicating that this kind of games is helpful and can provide effects [37] in other case studies, we are looking for ways to further formalise the design and implementation of multi-user decision training games [38]. Our research therefore follows two directions: firstly, the further development of our game scenarios and technical implementation focuses on enhancing the immersiveness of our games. Secondly, the further evaluation of training scenarios in various settings should deliver stronger evidence about their usefulness and about measurable effects.

Acknowledgements. The SALOMO project is funded by the Dutch Institute of Advanced Logistics (DINALOG).

References

1. De Bruijn, J.A., Heuvelhof, E.F.: Management in Networks: On Multi-actor Decision Making. Routledge, London (2008)
2. Kurapati, S., Kolfschoten, G., Verbraeck, A., Drachsler, H., Specht, M., Brazier, F.: A theoretical framework for shared situational awareness in sociotechnical systems. In: Proceedings of 2nd Workshop on Awareness and Reflection in TEL, pp. 47–53 (2012)
3. Salmon, P.M., Stanton, N.A., Walker, G.H., Jenkins, D.P., Mcmaster, R., Young, M.S.: What really is going on? Review of situation awareness models for individuals and teams. Theor. Issues Ergon. Sci. **9**(4), 297–323 (2008). doi:10.1080/14639220701561775
4. Crichton, M.T., Flin, R., Rattray, W.A.: Training decision makers–tactical decision games. J. Contingencies Crisis Manage. **8**(4), 208–217 (2000)
5. Dowell, J., Hoc, J.M.: Coordination in emergency operations and the tabletop training exercise. Le Travail Humain, pp. 85–102 (1995)
6. Klemke, R., Ternier, S., Kalz, M., Schmitz, B., Specht, M.: Multi-stakeholder decision training games with ARLearn. In: Proceedings of the Fourth International Conference on eLearning (eLearning 2013), pp. 26–27. Belgrade, Serbia, Sept 2013
7. Kurapati, S., Kolfschoten, G.L., Verbraeck, A., Corsi, T.M., Brazier, F.M.T.: Exploring shared situational awareness using serious games for supply chain disruptions. In: Proceedings of the 10th International ISCRAM Conference, Baden-Baden, Germany (2013)
8. Sitzmann, T.: A meta-analytic examination of the instructional effectiveness of computer-based simulation games. Personnel Psychol. **64**(2), 489–528 (2011)
9. Alessi, S.: Designing educational support in system-dynamics-based interactive learning environments. Simul. Gaming **31**(2), 178–196 (2000)
10. Kopainsky, B., Alessi, S.M., Pedercini, M., Davidsen, P.I.: Exploratory strategies for simulation-based learning about national development. In: 27th International Conference of the System Dynamics Society, Albuquerque, NM (2009)
11. Vis, I.F., De Koster, R.: Transshipment of containers at a container terminal: an overview. Eur. J. Oper. Res. **147**(1), 1–16 (2003)
12. Bandeira, D.L., Becker, J.L., Borenstein, D.: A DSS for integrated distribution of empty and full containers. Decis. Support Syst. **47**(4), 383–397 (2009)
13. Svensson, G.: A conceptual framework for the analysis of vulnerability in supply chains. Int. J. Phys. Distrib. Logistics Manage. **30**(9), 731–750 (2000)
14. Loh, H.S., Thai, V.V.: The role of ports in supply chain disruption management. In: Proceedings of the International Forum on Shipping, Ports and Airports, pp. 325–337, Hong Kong (2012)
15. Yliskyla-Peuralahti, J., Spies, M., Tapaninen, U.: Transport vulnerabilities and critical industries: experiences from a finnish stevedore strike. Int. J. Risk Assess. Manage. **15**(2/3), 222–240 (2011)
16. Endsley, M.R.: Towards a theory of situation awareness in dynamic systems. Hum. Factors **37**(1), 32–64 (1995)
17. Fiore, S.M., Salas, E., Cuevas, H.M., Bowers, C.A.: Distributed coordination space: toward a theory of distributed team process and performance. Theor. Issues Ergon. Sci. **4**(3–4), 340–364 (2003)
18. Ciolfi, L., Bannon, L.J.: Space, place and the design of technologically-enhanced physical environments. In: Turner, P., Davenport, E. (eds.) Spaces, Spatiality and Technology, pp. 217–232. Springer, Netherlands (2005)
19. Nofi, A.: Defining and Measuring Shared Situational Awareness. DARPA, Center for Naval Analyses Alexandria, VA (2000)

20. Perla, P.P., Markowitz, M., Nofi, A.A., Weuve, C., Loughran, J.: Gaming and Shared Situation Awareness. Center for Naval Analyses Alexandria, VA (2000)
21. Duke, R.D.: A paradigm for game design. Simul. Games **11**(3), 364–377 (1980)
22. Duke, R.D., Geurts, J.: Policy Games for Strategic Management, Rozenberg (2004)
23. Meijer, S.: The organisation of transactions: studying supply networks using gaming simulation. Ph.D. Thesis, Wageningen University, Netherlands (2009)
24. Klabbers, J.H.: The Magic Circle: Principles of Gaming & Simulation. Sense Publishers, Rotterdam (2009)
25. Chen, L., Miller-Hooks, E.: Resilience: an indicator of recovery capability in intermodal freight transport. Transp. Sci. **46**(1), 109–123 (2012)
26. Port of Rotterdam Authority: Change Your Perspective. Port of Rotterdam, Rotterdam, Netherlands (2012)
27. Ternier, S., Klemke, R., Kalz, M., Van Ulzen, P., Specht, M.: ARLearn: augmented reality meets augmented virtuality. J. Univ. Comput. Sci. Spec. Issue Technol. Learn. Across Phys. Virtual Spaces **18**(15), 2143–2164 (2012)
28. Kelle, S., Klemke, R., Specht, M.: Design patterns for learning games. Int. J. Technol. Enhanced Learn. **3**(6), 555–569 (2011)
29. Ternier, S., De Vries, F., Börner, D., Specht, M.: Mobile augmented reality with audio. In: InSuEdu 2012 Workshop, 10th International Conference on Software Engineering and Formal Methods, Thessaloniki, Greece (2012)
30. Gonsalves, A., Ternier, S., De Vries, F., Specht, M.: Serious games at the UNHCR with ARLearn, a toolkit for mobile and virtual reality applications. In: Specht, M., Sharples, M., Multisilta, J. (eds.) Proceedings of 11th World Conference on Mobile and Contextual Learning (mLearn 2012), pp. 244–247. Helsinki, Finland, 16–18 Oct 2012
31. Schmitz, B., Ternier, S., Kalz, M., Klemke, R., Specht, M.: Designing a mobile learning game to investigate the impact of role-playing on helping behaviour. In: 8th European Conference on Technology Enhanced Learning, Paphos, Cyprus (2013)
32. Gagnon, D.J.: ARIS: an Open Source Platform for developing Mobile Learning Experiences. University of Wisconsin at Madison, Madison (2010)
33. Holden, C.L., Sykes, J.M.: Leveraging mobile games for place-based language learning. Int. J. Game-Based Learn. (IJGBL) **1**(2), 1–18 (2011)
34. Santos, P., Pérez-Sanagustín, M., Hernández-Leo, D., Blat, J.: QuesTInSitu: from tests to routes for assessment in situ activities. Comput. Educ. **57**(4), 2517–2534 (2011)
35. Robles, G., Gonzales-Barahona, J.M., Fernandez-Gonzales, J.: Implementing gymkhanas with android smartphones: a multimedia m-learning game. In: Global Engineering Education Conference (EDUCON), 2011 IEEE, pp. 960–968. IEEE (2011)
36. Klemke, R., Kurapati, S., Lukosch, H., Specht, M.: Transferring an educational board game to a multi-user mobile learning game to increase shared situational awareness. Advanced Interaction Systems in Technology Enhanced Learning and Training (accepted). In: Proceedings of the 17th International Conference on Human-Computer Interaction (HCI International 2015), Los Angeles, CA, USA (2015)
37. Schmitz, B., Schuffelen, P., Kreijns, K., Klemke, R., Specht, M.: Putting yourself in someone else's shoes: the impact of a location-based, collaborative role-playing game on behaviour. Comput. Educ. **85**, 160–169 (2015)
38. Klemke, R., Ternier, S., Kalz, M., Schmitz, B., Specht, M.: Immersive multi-user decision training games with AR-learn. In: Rensing, C., de Freitas, S., Ley, T., Muñoz-Merino, P. (eds.) Open Learning and Teaching in Educational Communities. Proceedings of the 9th European Conference on Technology Enhanced Learning (EC-TEL). Lecture Notes in Computer Science 8719, pp. 207–220. Springer International Publishing, Graz, Austria (2014)

MOOC Video Interaction Patterns: What Do They Tell Us?

Nan Li[(✉)], Łukasz Kidziński, Patrick Jermann, and Pierre Dillenbourg

École polytechnique fédérale de Lausanne, Lausanne, Switzerland
{nan.li,lukasz.kidzinski,patrick.jermann,pierre.dillenbourg}@epfl.ch

Abstract. For MOOC learners, lecture video viewing is the central learning activity. This paper reports a large-scale analysis of in-video interactions. We categorize the video behaviors into patterns by employing a clustering methodology, based on the available types of interactions, namely, pausing, forward and backward seeking and speed changing. We focus on how learners view MOOC videos with these interaction patterns, especially on exploring the relationship between video interaction and perceived video difficulty, video revisiting behaviors and student performance. Our findings provide insights for improving the MOOC learning experiences.

Keywords: MOOC · Online education · Video analysis · Video interaction · Clustering analysis

1 Introduction

Online education, with the recent revolution of the Massive Open Online Courses (MOOCs), is beginning to show itself as a disruptive innovation. MOOCs, as their current forms, typically replicate traditional classroom pedagogy online, featuring with video lectures, quizzes, tutorials, discussion forums and wikis. As recent studies [2,12] show, video lecture viewing is the central activity in MOOC learning, but little research work has yet endeavored to analyze click-level video interactions. For MOOC instructors, it is of great importance to understand how the students interact with lectures videos as well as how they perceive them.

The availability of large-scale MOOC data has made deeper video interaction analysis possible. As thousands of students interact with the same set of videos, we can plausibly categorize video interactions into groups of similar patterns, hereafter referred to as **video interaction patterns**. These patterns describe how the students typically use MOOC videos to achieve their learning goals. This paper attempts to categorize MOOC video interaction patterns by employing a clustering-based methodology, based on the available types of interactions, namely, pausing, forward and backward seeking and speed changing. Our hypothesis is that students adapt their video interactions to the video difficulties, their personal capability and learning strategies. So our analysis in this paper is further extended to explore the potential associations between video

© Springer International Publishing Switzerland 2015
G. Conole et al. (Eds.): EC-TEL 2015, LNCS 9307, pp. 197–210, 2015.
DOI: 10.1007/978-3-319-24258-3_15

interaction patterns and the following aspects: (1) perceived video difficulty (2) video revisiting behaviors (3) students' performance.

In this paper we categorize the video interaction patterns, but more significant contributions lie in the application of these patterns to reveal the relationship between video interactions and other factors, in order to address educational and design issues in MOOC. We summarize our contributions below:

- Analyzed the associations between video interaction and subjective video difficulty, and found video interaction patterns reflect perceived video difficulty.
- Identified the video interaction patterns that are linked to higher probability of video revisiting.
- Investigated the differences in video interaction patterns between weak and strong students, finding the weak students pause significantly more, and mostly during the presentation of code examples.
- Provided data-driven insights on improving the MOOC video interface

2 Related Work

2.1 Video Interaction Analysis

Videos players typically offer a limited types of interactions, each of which is associated with a time span. The sequential execution of the actions entail the Markov model a popular approach for video analysis. In early research, such analyses mostly aimed at evaluating the quality of service issues [3,10,13]. Research that attempted to model video click behaviors came to light since Branch et al. found that video interaction behaviors, in terms of the time spent on each viewing mode (i.e. play, pause, fast-forward, fast-rewind) can be modeled with lognormal distributions [1]. They also proposed a first-order Markov chain model for modeling different types of actions. Later Syeda-Mahmood et al. studied subjective video browsing states with a Hidden Markov approach [14], with the goal of generating video previews that best represents interesting video segments. All of the above studies were conducted in the time when the control menu of video players were restricted to only continuous interactions, lacking discontinuous interactions that are common in today's video player controls, such as seeking forward/backward, which allow jumping between different time positions.

Research on clustering video interaction behaviors also started before the MOOC era. In the early 2000s, Mongy et al. [11] proposed a method to apply K-means clustering with the Kulbach-Leibler distance between the state-transition matrices, but little is discussed about the data collection, the validation of the results and the scalability of the approach.

2.2 MOOC Analysis

With the rapidly popularized MOOCs, researchers have now enormous data for learning student's behaviors. Research on MOOC video interactions are usually centered on analyzing lecture-to-lecture navigation strategies [5], predicting dropout [6,15] and in-video dropouts [7]. Among these work, only [7,15] contain click-level video analysis. [7] emphasizes on the video interaction peaks while ignoring other silent interactions such as speed changing. [15] analyzed the video interactions sequences with n-gram analysis, which aimed at predicting dropouts. As an intermediate result, the information processing index computed from the click sequences serve for identifying and interpreting different video behaviors. The main problem is that the analysis did not consider the duration of each action. Furthermore,the interpretations of the click events are mostly based on "common sense knowledge" with little empirical evidence.

Existing MOOC literature with clustering analysis mainly aim at categorizing MOOC students' engagement [8], where the authors adopted unsupervised K-means method based on the students' longitudinal online learning activities. As far as we are concerned, clustering video behaviors with click-level interactions remain gap in MOOC research.

3 Video Interaction Dataset

We analyze two undergraduate MOOCs offered in Cousera: "Reactive Programming (RP)" and "Digital Signal Processing (DSP)". The former covers advanced topics in programing and the latter is a foundation course in Electrical Engineering. Table 1 summarizes descriptive information of these two MOOCs. Both courses have similar presentation styles, i.e. the professors present the lecture with PowerPoint slides, with a digital pen as both pointer and annotator.

Table 1. Overview of the two MOOCs in our dataset.

Subject	Week	Videos	Length	Quiz	Active	Passed	Sessions	Events
RP	7	36	18:50	6	22,794	5,276	470,994	4,001,992
DSP	10	58	16:20	16	9,086	263	117,959	1,138,558

The RP course attracted much more active students (those who at least watched a video) than the DSP course. There were no mid-term or final exams in both courses. Instead, assessments of students were made with weekly quizzes. Students' grades were computed as the sum of their best quiz scores of all trials in each week. The RP course allowed an unlimited number of quiz submissions, while the DSP course permitted five submission per quiz at maximum. The differences in grading schemes perhaps led to higher pass rate in the RP course (23.15 %), compared to only 2.89 % in the DSP course.

3.1 Data Wrangling Pipeline

In our data wrangling process, we first reconstruct the watching histories of each user from the raw video interaction logs. For each unique video in our dataset, user-based watching histories are created by arranging the events in chronological order. Revisited and first-time video sessions are separated. The next step is to aggregate the events in each watching segments into video features, which will be explained in detail in Sect. 4.

The processed video events include pauses, seeks and speed changes. The number of events shown in Table 1 includes the video events in all video sessions. Coursera does not only generate pauses when a user clicks the pause button. Automatic pauses are generated when an in-video quiz pops up or when the video is played to the end. Such automatic pausing events are removed for the analysis in this paper. In addition, students usually watch the lecture videos in uncontrolled environments, so the pauses are found to last for a maximum of several days. We removed the pause events that have a duration of more than 10 min, which are rather "breaks" than "pauses". In addition, a seek event is created when the user clicks or scrubs the playhead to a new position on the time bar. When scrubbing interactions occur, the logging system automatically generates a number of intermediate seeking events. Following the approach in [15], the seek events that are within 1 s interval are grouped as a single seeking event.

4 Video Interaction Clustering

Our first goal is to cluster video sessions into categories that characterize the video interactions. We computed a set of video features for each interaction type to characterize both the frequency and time dimension of the interactions. The features used for clustering are listed in Table 2.

Table 2. Video features used for clustering

1. Number of pauses (NP)	5. Number of backward seeks (NB)
2. Median duration of pauses (MP)	6. Replayed video length (RL)
3. Number of forward seeks (NF)	7. Average video speed (AS)
4. Proportion of skipped video content (SR)	8. Effective video speed change (SC)

Most of the features in the list are self-explanatory, but we will explain some of them in details. A video session may contain pauses of different durations. We use median statistic for pauses because it is more robust compared to the mean and sum statistics for the highly skewed, long-tail distribution of the pause duration data. As for the video speed, Coursera video player offers 7 levels of speed ranging from 0.75 to 2.0 with a stepwise change of 0.25 and the video player inherits the video speed from the users' previous sessions. That is, a video may contain no speed changing events, even though it is played at a speed other than 1.0. The *average video speed* feature refers to the weighted arithmetic mean of the video speeds at all video seconds. Since the videos may start at different speeds, the *average speed* feature alone may not always tell if the changes have happened during the video session. In combination with this feature, we also use *effective video speed change*, which is the average amount of speed change during the video session. This feature is computed by subtracting the starting video speed from the *average video speed*. We don't use the frequency of speed change events because it is inflated, i.e. the speed always has to be changed in multiple steps of 0.25. The datasets contain a large number of video sessions with **in-video dropout**, i.e. the student left the video before they reached the end. Such behaviors are different from skipping with forward seeks, because the user never reached later part of the video. When we compute the *proportion of skipped video content*, we only consider the proportion that is skipped by forward seeks. While discarding the video sessions that do not reach the very end sounds over-correct, we group all the video sessions that did not reach the last 10 % into the "in-video dropout" category, and our unsupervised clustering will be performed only on the remaining "complete" video sessions.

4.1 Clustering Pipeline

The datasets contain a large number of video sessions with no video interaction events (e.g. 17 % for the RP). These video sessions are filtered out and clustering is performed on the remaining dataset of the two MOOCs independently with the 8 video features presented before. After preprocessing with PCA dimension reduction, we obtain 6 new uni-variance variables which account for 90 % of the original variance.

The goal of clustering is to obtain a minimal number of interpretable clusters explaining user behaviors. For clustering, we use Neural Gas, a neural network-based convex clustering algorithm which is a robustly converging alternative to the k-means. The Simple Structure Index (SSI) [4] is used as a criterion for selecting the optimal number of clusters, since this index is known to multiplicatively combine several elements which influence the interpretability of a partition solution. For the RP course, we vary the number of clusters from 3 to 15, and find that 9 clusters maximize the SSI value (0.356 in [0,1] scale), as compared to the minimum value of 0.1 with 5 clusters. We then partition 9 video interaction clusters for the dataset. Similarly, 9 clusters are obtained for the DSP dataset as well.

4.2 Video Interaction Patterns

The centers of the 9 clusters for the RP dataset are shown in Table 3, and the results for the DSP course are analogous. The full names for the abbreviated feature names can be found in Table 2. We label each cluster with an intuitive name according to the corresponding dominating features (marked as bold) in the table. For example, the *LongPause(LP)* video sessions have an average median duration of pauses (MP) of 284.96 s. Note that the average number of pauses (NP) for this cluster is small (1.71). So it actually represents video sessions with infrequent long pauses.

Table 3. Cluster centers for the RP dataset

Pattern	Proportion	NP	MP	NF	NB	SR	RL	AS	SC
Replay (RP)	3 %	4.73	62.58	5.86	12.84	0.05	**531.44**	1.10	−0.00
HighSpeed (HS)	10 %	1.17	23.19	1.18	0.95	0.10	27.14	**1.66**	−0.01
SpeedUp (SU)	3 %	1.38	27.16	1.66	1.04	0.09	25.13	1.53	**0.39**
SkimSkip (SS)	4 %	1.00	30.73	**21.70**	4.94	**0.75**	17.46	1.14	0.00
Inactive (IA)	38 %	1.93	39.05	0.71	1.28	0.03	36.65	1.05	−0.00
FrequentPause (FP)	4 %	**13.39**	40.58	2.87	5.13	0.05	109.37	1.08	−0.00
JumpSkip (JS)	13 %	0.45	11.62	**5.38**	1.10	**0.71**	9.40	1.06	0.00
LongPause (LP)	6$	1.71	**284.96**	1.34	1.26	0.08	44.62	1.07	0.00
SpeedDown (SD)	1 %	2.13	42.93	1.61	1.73	0.08	44.42	1.24	**−0.58**

While Table 3 only presents the centroids of the clusters, the distributions of these features are illustrated as boxplot in Fig. 1, in terms of standard scores (z-scores) of the variables. 50 percent of the data points are enclosed in the boxes. The upper and lower whiskers extend from the hinge to the highest or lowest value that is within 1.5 interquartile range of the hinge. Data beyond the end of the whiskers are considered as outliers and are not shown in the figure. The multidimensionality, continuity, skewed distribution, and inter-correlation natures of the features imply that clear separations are unlikely to be found based on the current feature sets, and this explains why the maximum SSI (0.356) of the partition solutions is relatively small. Nevertheless, the dominating features in each cluster are still prominent, as shown in Fig. 1.

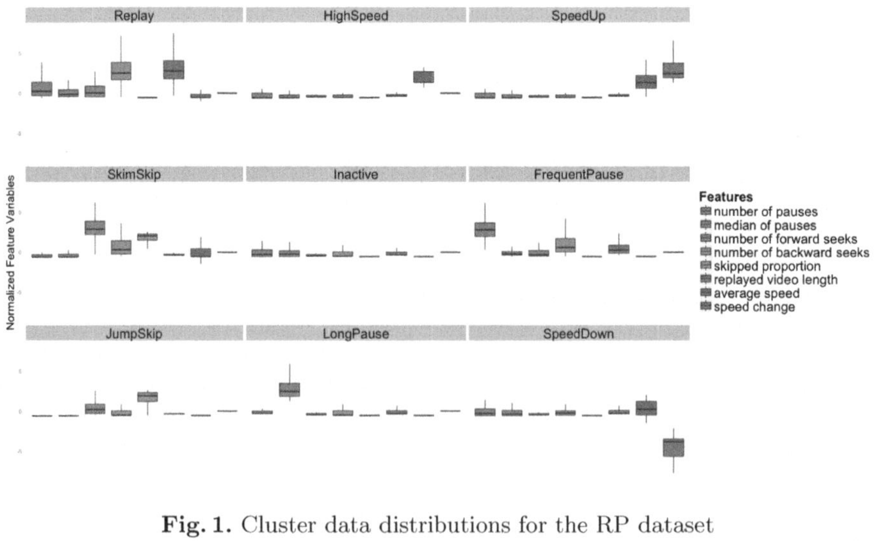

Fig. 1. Cluster data distributions for the RP dataset

In addition to the presented 9 patterns, we have (17 %) of the data removed before the clustering because they contain no video events. These sessions are labeled as *Passive (PS)*. It should be noted that most video sessions contain few video events, i.e. *PS*, *IA* and *HS* account for 65 % of the dataset, indicating a small number of video interactions satisfy the students' need for most of the time. On the other hand it also implies the adoption of rarer patterns may reflect certain changes in the students' learning state. We will discuss them in the upcoming sections.

5 Perceived Video Difficulty

Perceived video difficulty, i.e. how easy or difficult it is for a student to understand the content of a video, is a subjective measure of learning experiences. This measure reflects the students' cognitive states while watching lecture videos. We hypothesize that MOOC students may adapt their video interaction strategy to the video difficulty. Thus, our research question is: ***How do the different video interaction patterns reflect different levels of perceived video difficulty?***. In our recent work [9], we studied each type of interaction separately, but in this section we will examine the relationship between perceived video difficulty and video interaction patterns. The analysis may provide insights for MOOC practitioners to detect when a student may encounter difficulties.

5.1 Method

The perceived video difficulty is subjective and cannot be measured directly from video interactions, so we used in-video surveys placed at the end of each video during the enactment of the two courses to assess the subjective video difficulty. Only one question was asked: *How easy was it for you to understand the content of this video?* These surveys are posteriori evaluations that were typically answered by the learners right after they finished watching the video content, providing ground-truth knowledge of their situational perceived difficulty. The surveys were not graded, so the students participated voluntarily. The responses were then coded with integer values from 1 to 5 to represent the difficulty ratings from "Very Easy" to "Very Difficult". Students may watch the videos multiple times and leave more than 1 ratings for the same video. In the analysis of this section, we will only focus on the ratings of the first watching sessions. The response rate for the RP course is 49.1 % with an average difficulty of 2.699. For the DSP course, the rate is 32.8 % with an average difficulty of 2.594.

Since in our datasets the same users are measured multiple times, we used mixed-effect model by grouping the users as random effects to estimate the mean video difficulty. Mixed model are known to be robust to missing values and unbalanced groups, and Least-square means mimic the main-effects means but are adjusted for imbalanced group sizes.

5.2 Result

Mixed-model ANOVA shows significant effects of video interaction patterns on perceived video difficulty (RP: F(9,124964) = 313, p<0.0001; DSP: F(9, 17505) = 24, p<0.0001). We plot the Least-square mean difficulty with confidence interval in Fig. 2. The colored labels underneath the name of each pattern along the x-axis depict the number of video sessions with difficulty ratings and the total number of video sessions belonging to the corresponding pattern. The two numbers are separated with a slash sign "/".

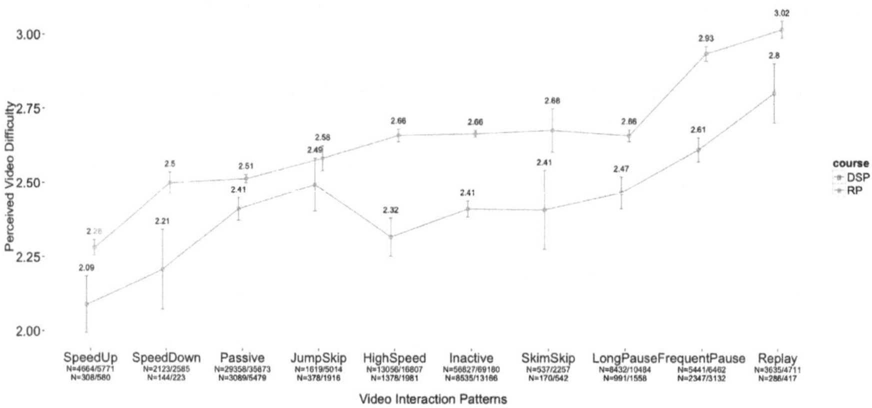

Fig. 2. Video interaction patterns and perceived video difficulty

Figure 2 shows that relative least-square mean differences in perceived video difficulty of different video interaction patterns are more or less consistent across two courses (with a systematic difference attributed to the course intrinsics), though the clusters are generated independently. Therefore, clusters generated from another course are likely to follow a similar trend.

The *Replay(RP)* and *FrequentPause(FP)* patterns reflect significantly higher video difficulty. They are employed as strategies to cope with difficult videos. Students may use the former to clarify doubts within the videos by rehearing the explanation, while the latter may be used when the explanations cannot be found within the video (requiring external resources) or the verbal/visual explanations are too fast to be processed (requiring buffer time)

The *SpeedUp(SU)* pattern reflects significantly lower video difficulty compared to the other patterns, indicating explicitly increasing the speed during video playback are commonly used by the students to adapt to easy videos. This way they can quickly grasp the gist of the video without skipping content. However, video sessions with *HighSpeed(HS)* pattern, i.e. the sessions that were started with high speeds inherited from previous sessions do not show significantly higher difficulty, compared to those with *Inactive(IA)* pattern. This suggests that the correlation effect of inherited speed on perceived video difficulty is weak, and may reflect personal preference rather than video difficulty.

Note that video sessions with large skipped content or with inherited higher speeds are not necessarily associated with easy videos. On the other hand, video sessions containing long pauses do not reflect significantly higher difficulty compared to *Passive* and *Inactive* patterns.

6 Video Revisiting Behaviors

Compared to traditional classroom lectures, MOOC videos are permanently preserved online, which makes revisiting certain videos a common practice. Students may revisit an older video for checking concepts while watching new videos or doing homework. Kim et al. find out [7] that first-watching sessions are more sequential while the revisiting sessions are more selective, i.e. the students selectively navigate the video into specific parts. We will inspect another perspective of video revisiting behaviors by asking ***With which first-time video interaction patterns are the videos more likely to be revisited?***. The analysis in this section may provide insights to MOOC designers for redesigning the user interface for improving the video revisiting experiences.

To start with, we first take a global overview of video revisiting behaviors on all the video sessions, including those "in-video dropout" video sessions, which are excluded for the analysis in this paper so far. We start by comparing the video sessions that are completely viewed and those containing "in-video dropout", because we found "in-video dropout" is strongly related to the occurrences of revisiting video sessions. As Table 4 shows, around one fifth of the completed videos (the "Completed" column) are revisited later. In comparison, videos that contain in-video dropout (the "Dropped-out" column) in the first-time watching sessions are significantly more likely to be revisited (73.7 % for the RP and 59.3 % for the DSP), according to the reported Chi-squared statistics. Note that in this paper all the Chi-squared tests hereafter are conducted with frequency of occurrences, though in the table we use percentage for presentation.

If we compare the video interaction patterns for complete video sessions only, then the result is as shown in Table 5. In each cell the percentage represents the observed probability of revisiting after the first view with the corresponding patterns. The expected probability for a video to be revisited for RP and DSP courses are 20.1 % and 23.5 % respectively, under the null hypothesis that video revisiting is independent of the interaction patterns. Chi-Squared tests show that the chances of revisiting significantly depend on the first-time video interaction patterns. Post-hoc residual analysis further reveals which cells contribute most to the Chi-Squared value. This is expressed by the adjusted standardized residuals, as shown below the percentage values in each cell. Significant positive residuals at $\alpha = 0.05$ (adjusted standardized residuals that are more than 2) are highlighted in bold. These highlighted cells indicate the frequency of occurrences for the corresponding patterns are significantly overly observed with respect to the expected frequency.

Table 4. Proportion of video revisiting for complete and in-video dropout sessions

	RP		DSP	
	Completed	Dropped-out	Completed	Dropped-out
Revisiting	20.6 %	73.7 %	23.5 %	59.3 %
No Revisiting	79.4 %	26.3 %	76.5 %	40.7 %
	$\chi^2(1{,}220875) = 55805.1$, $p < .0001$		$\chi^2(1{,}38825) = 5114.1$, $p < .0001$	

Table 5. Proportion of video revisiting for complete sessions

		RP	HS	SU	SS	IA	FP	JS	LP	SD	PS
RP	Revisiting	35.7 %	17.2 %	15.0 %	25.6 %	21.6 %	26.1 %	21.6 %	21.1 %	21.3 %	20.6 %
		25.9	−11.3	−10.5	**5.96**	**8.93**	**11.1**	1.86	1.31	0.99	−16.8
	No Revisiting	64.3 %	82.8 %	85.0 %	74.4 %	78.4 %	73.9 %	78.4 %	78.9 %	78.7 %	79.4 %
		−25.9	**11.3**	**10.5**	−5.96	−8.93	−11.1	−1.86	−1.31	−0.99	**16.8**
		$\chi^2(9{,}156517) = 1293.7$, $p < .0001$									
DSP	Revisiting	41.5 %	21.8 %	16.5 %	22.5 %	22.1 %	32.0 %	23.9 %	23.6 %	26.6 %	21.6 %
		7.8	−1.6	−3.57	−0.47	−4.49	**10.7**	0.32	0.1	0.95	−3.24
	No Revisiting	58.5 %	78.2 %	83.5 %	77.5 %	77.9 %	68.0 %	76.1 %	76.4 %	73.4 %	78.4
		−7.8	1.6	**3.57**	0.47	**4.49**	−10.7	−0.32	−0.1	−0.95	**3.24**
		$\chi^2(9{,}22717) = 197.7$, $p < .0001$									

For both courses, the videos with *JumpSkip(JS)*, *LongPause(LP)* and *SpeedDown(SD)* do not show significance in revisiting behaviors. Interestingly, we find that the videos viewed with *Replay (RP)* and *FrequentPause (FP)* are significantly more likely to be revisited, while less revisiting probabilities are found with the *SpeedUp (SU)* and *Passive(PS)*. In Sect. 5, *RP*, *FP* and *SU* are shown to reflect respectively the highest and lowest subjective difficulties. Therefore, we infer that the video difficulty may confound between the interaction patterns and the probability of video revisiting. However, as other patterns are weaker indicators of the perceived difficulty, the revisiting behaviors may in this case be confounded largely by other factors such as the course intrinsics. For example, the videos with *Inactive (IA)* pattern are significantly more likely to be revisited in the RP and less in the DSP. The potential reasons are hard to identify in this case. In this section we highlight the more general findings that videos with *RP* and *FP* patterns are more likely to be revisited, and more follow-ups of this finding will be discussed in Sect. 8.

7 Student Performance

Students in MOOCs often have diverse background and learning abilities. Depending on their levels, MOOC students may watch video lectures in different ways. For example, we may hypothesize that strong students selectively watch

MOOC videos while weak students spend more time with the learning materials. Our research question in this section is ***How do Strong and Weak students differ in lecture video viewing behaviors?*** The video interaction patterns provide us with a handy tool for diagnosing the students' video behaviors, so our analysis will be based on comparing the strategy of employing the patterns. The analysis would deepen our understanding of how students of different performances use MOOCs, thus proving insights for the instructors to design solutions for helping the weak students.

7.1 Method

The foremost challenge for the analysis in this section is to define *Strong* and *Weak* students. Considering MOOC is an open platform, students have different motives. A great proportion of the students drop out in the early or middle of the courses for various reasons. Even those who watch all the videos do not necessarily aim at obtaining a certificate or completing all the learning activities. This means the students who obtain 0 point in the final score are not necessarily weak in their learning abilities. As mentioned in Sect. 3, the two courses in our datasets do not have exams, and weekly quizzes are the only mean for assessing students. The quizzes for the RP course can be submitted unlimited times, and we have seen many students submitted more than 10 times for a quiz. The consequence is that 82 % of the passed students got certificates of distinction, which is a quite inflated percentage. In order to compare the students who are strong and weak in learning abilities, we take a subset of the data which includes only the students who completed all the assignments. Thus we can maximally believe the remaining students have a similar learning goal, which is to complete the courses. As shown in Table 1, in the DSP course, only 263 (less than 3 %) of the total students finished, and only 23 students got distinction results, whilst the RP course has a 23 % completion rate. In the analysis hereafter, we only analyse the RP students who submitted all of the 6 assignments. To simplify the analysis, the students who obtained 80 % of the total points in their *FIRST* submissions are defined as *Strong*. Otherwise, they are labeled as *Weak*. The subset contains 4555 (86.3 %) of the passed students, of which 35.3 % are *Strong* students. In addition, only the first-time watching patterns are analyzed.

7.2 Result

A video session has an expected probability of 37.6 % to come from *Strong* students under the null hypothesis that the employment of video interaction patterns is independent of students' performance (Table 6). Chi-square test shows that the adoptions of video interaction patterns are significantly different between strong and weak students. Post-hoc residual analysis reveals that strong students tend to interact less with the videos, so the frequency of *HighSpeed(HS)*, *SpeedUp(SU)*, *Passive(PS)* and *Inactive(IA)* sessions are significantly higher. On the other hand, weak students interact more with videos, they use significantly more *SkimSkip(SS)*, *JumpSkip (JS)*, *FrequentPause(FP)* and *LongPause(LP)*.

Table 6. Proportion of video interaction patterns based on students performance

	RP	HS	SU	SS	IA	FP	JS	LP	SD	PS
Strong	38.7 %	46.1 %	39.7 %	31.6 %	35.9 %	32.4 %	33.8 %	35.5 %	38.6 %	39.0 %
	−1.2	**17.3**	**2.1**	−4	−9	−6.6	−3.6	−3.2	0.7	**3.8**
Weak	61.3 %	53.9 %	60.3 %	68.4 %	64.1 %	67.6 %	66.2 %	64.5 %	61.4 %	61.0 %
	1.2	−17.3	−2.1	**4**	**9**	**6.6**	**3.6**	**3.2**	−0.7	−3.8
	$\chi^2(9{,}76094) = 406.3$, $p < .0001$									

Recall that both *FrequentPause(FP)* and *Replay(RP)* reflect the highest video difficulty. Interestingly, the usage of *Replay* pattern is not significantly different between the two student groups, suggesting that replaying behaviors may not discriminate students' performance.

We are more interested in deeply understanding two pausing patterns, since on one hand we observe significantly more video sessions of these patterns, on the other hand, the pauses provide MOOC designers with opportunities to augment the video with supporting information. We have discussed in Sect. 5 that pauses may occur when the presented information is overloaded so that the students require buffer time or external material to understand the content. Weak students are found to use both *FrequentPause(FP)* and *LongPause(LP)* significantly more often than strong students. In order to understand how the weak students adopt the two pausing patterns, we randomly selected 50 video sessions with *FrequentyPause(FP)* pattern and another 50 with *LongPause(LP)* pattern from the weak students' interaction logs and manually examine the situations under which the associated 698 pauses happened. We categorize the pauses by the occasions when the professor was explaining *example codes* (46.7 %), *programing grammar* (12.7 %), *demos* (4.8 %), *theories* (33.8 %) and *others* (2 %)(e.g. in summary). Fisher's exact test shows no significant differences in the categories of pauses in sessions between *FrequentPause(FP)* and *LongPause(LP)* patterns ($p = 0.47$). Nearly half of the pauses occur when example code snippets are shown in the video frame, and more than half of the pauses are related to the presentation of code (code, grammar and demo). This result indicates that the weak students may have significant problems in understanding the code compared to strong student. We need solutions to support the weak students in this regard.

8 Design Insights for MOOC Practitioners

Our analyses in this paper show that MOOC students follow different video interaction patterns while watching lecture videos. The strategy of adopting the patterns may vary for different videos, depending on the students' perceived video difficulty, their capability and whether or not a video is watched for the first time. The analyses of the video interaction patterns presented so far provide the following insights for improving the MOOC learning experiences.

1. Detect the Change of Video Interaction Patterns [Algorithm]. The MOOC platform should detect the changes of video interaction patterns for the students, because such changes may indicate variations in perceived video difficulty. If we detect the students are experiencing difficulty, then proper interventions, such as external materials can be suggested to provide a more personalized learning experience.

2. Provide Quick Access for Revisiting Videos [User Interface]. Since a video session with in-video dropout may have 60 % – 70 % chances to be revisited, it is advisable to provide the students with short-cut access to those videos. In addition, we find out that video sessions with interaction patterns that reflect higher difficulty, such as the *Replay(RP)* and *FrequentPause(FP)* are more likely to be revisited. A possible solution is to design a side bar which lists the videos that will be potentially revisited, so that the students can be aware of them and make easy re-access.

3. Make Use of the Pauses [Information Interaction]. Weak students tend to use more *FrequentPause(FP)* or *LongPause(LP)* to buffer the professors' explanation in the video into their mind. It is advisable to reduce the information overload in the lecture slides. However, this might be less feasible for programming courses, as often code blocks have to be presented. A possible solution is to make use of the time when the pauses occur. For example, when a student pauses at a particular video frame with code blocks, auxiliary information that helps the students to understand the code can be displayed as overlay.

9 Conclusions and Future Work

This paper shed light on the relationships between video interaction patterns and some important aspects in MOOC learning such as the perceived video difficulty, video revisiting behaviors and students' performance. Based on the findings, our research proposed design suggestions to improve MOOC learning experiences. Concrete implementations of these general suggestions as well as validations of their effectiveness are however left as future work. In this work we pursue generalization through statistical inferences rather than specificity, so the patterns were categorized based on in-video interaction features without considering the longitudinal nature of the course or the differences in video content. In addition, MOOC is a multi-faceted learning platform, lecture videos play an important role but do not explain the complete picture. Activities in the forum, quiz, students' motivations all may relate to the aspects we described in this paper. Future work may also incorporate these factors to gain a more comprehensive understanding about how students learn in MOOCs.

References

1. Branch, P., Egan, G., Tonkin, B.: Modeling interactive behaviour of a video based multimedia system. In: 1999 IEEE International Conference on Communications, ICC 1999, vol. 2, pp. 978–982. IEEE (1999)

2. Breslow, L., Pritchard, D.E., DeBoer, J., Stump, G.S., Ho, A.D., Seaton, D.: Studying learning in the worldwide classroom: research into edxs first mooc. Res. Pract. Assess. **8**, 13–25 (2013)
3. Dey-Sircar, J.K., Salehi, J.D., Kurose, J.F., Towsley, D.: Providing vcr capabilities in large-scale video servers. In: Proceedings of the Second ACM International Conference on Multimedia MULTIMEDIA 1994, pp. 25–32. ACM, New York (1994)
4. Dolnicar, S., Grabler, K., Mazanec, J.A., Woodside, A., Crouch, G., Oppermann, M., Sakai, M. et al.: A tale of three cities: perceptual charting for analysing destination images. CABI Publishing (1999)
5. Guo, P.J., Reinecke, K.: Demographic differences in how students navigate through moocs. In: Proceedings of the First ACM Conference on Learning @ Scale Conference L@S 2014, pp. 21–30. ACM, New York (2014)
6. Halawa, S., Greene, D., Mitchell, J.: Dropout prediction in moocs using learner activity features. In: Proceedings of the Second European MOOC Stakeholder Summit, pp. 58–65 (2014)
7. Kim, J., Guo, P.J., Seaton, D.T., Mitros, P., Gajos, K.Z., Miller, R.C.: Understanding in-video dropouts and interaction peaks inonline lecture videos. In: Proceedings of the First ACM Conference on Learning @ Scale Conference L@S 2014, pp. 31–40. ACM, New York (2014)
8. Kizilcec, R.F., Piech, C., Schneider, E.: Deconstructing disengagement: analyzing learner subpopulations in massive open online courses. In: Proceedings of the Third International Conference on Learning Analytics and Knowledge LAK 2013, pp. 170–179. ACM, New York (2013)
9. Li, N., Kidzinski, L., Jermann, P., Pierre, D.: How do in-video interactions reflect perceived video difficulty? In: Proceedings of the Third European MOOC Stakeholder Summit (to appear, 2015)
10. Li, V.O.K., Liao, W., Qiu, X., Wong, E.W.M.: Performance model of interactive video-on-demand systems. IEEE J. Sel. Areas Commun. **14**(6), 1099–1109 (1996)
11. Mongy, S., Djeraba, C., Simovici, D.A.: On clustering users' behaviors in video sessions. In: Stahlbock, R., Crone, S.F., Lessmann, S. (eds.) DMIN, pp. 99–103. CSREA Press (2007)
12. Seaton, D.T., Bergner, Y., Chuang, I., Mitros, P., Pritchard, D.E.: Who does what in a massive open online course? Commun. ACM **57**(4), 58–65 (2014)
13. Shenoy, P.J., Vin, H.M.: Efficient support for scan operations in video servers. In: Proceedings of the third ACM international conference on Multimedia, pp. 131–140. ACM (1995)
14. Syeda-Mahmood, T., Ponceleon, D.: Learning video browsing behavior and its application in the generation of video previews. In: Proceedings of the Ninth ACM International Conference on Multimedia MULTIMEDIA 2001, pp. 119–128. ACM, New York (2001)
15. Sinha, T., Jermann, P., Li, N., Dillenbourg, P.: Your click decides your fate: inferring information processing and attrition behavior from mooc video clickstream interactions. In: Proceedings of the 2014 Empirical Methods in Natural Language Processing Workshop on Modeling Large Scale Social Interaction in Massively Open Online Courses (2013)

Comparing Two CbKST Approaches for Adapting Learning Paths in Serious Games

Javier Melero(✉), Naïma El-Kechaï, and Jean-Marc Labat

LIP6, Université Pierre et Marie Curie, Paris, France
{javier.melero-gallardo,naima.el-kechai,
jean-marc.labat}@lip6.fr

Abstract. Competence-based Knowledge Space Theory (CbKST) is considered a well-fitting basis for adapting Serious Games (SGs). CbKST relies on the domain model associated to a given SG to infer the so-called *competence structure*. However, building such a model can be time-consuming and a tough task for experts. We propose another approach to overcome this issue by considering the Q-Matrix that contains the mapping between the SG activities and the addressed competences. We compare the two approaches, one based on the domain model and the other on the Q-Matrix, in three SGs. We apply both approaches to two SGs, while in a third one, we apply only the Q-Matrix approach since no domain model is available. The main findings when comparing both approaches refer to the issues derived from the generated *competence structures* and the definition of competences at a suitable granularity level. This exploratory work can provide meaningful insights when applying CbKST for adapting SGs.

Keywords: Serious games · Competence-based Knowledge Space Theory · Domain model · Adaptation

1 Introduction

Nowadays, Serious Games (SGs) have become a popular educational approach to motivate learners in many topics. Like other Technology-Enhanced Learning (TEL) environments, one significant challenge that deserves further research is the need to adapt SGs to the current state of the learner's competences. The main goal is to support the learner's progress and enhance learning. One approach to reach this goal is to perform a non-invasive real-time assessment of the learner's attributes (competences, skills, preferences, etc.) [1, 2]. In the field of SGs, adaptation is based on decisions that suggest activities (levels, quizzes, etc.) so that learners are neither unchallenged nor overwhelmed by the complexity of the contained tasks [3]. The idea is to keep learners in a state of flow [4], i.e. completely immersed in the gaming experience by maintaining a balance between the pleasure of playing and the challenge of acquiring knowledge and competences.

A meaningful approach to adapt learning paths in SGs is based on the Competence-based Knowledge Space Theory (CbKST) [5–8]. One of the main advantages of CbKST is that it provides a basis for structuring a domain of knowledge

© Springer International Publishing Switzerland 2015
G. Conole et al. (Eds.): EC-TEL 2015, LNCS 9307, pp. 211–224, 2015.
DOI: 10.1007/978-3-319-24258-3_16

and for representing the knowledge based on precedence relations [9–11]. Besides, in CbKST-based approaches, learners' assessment is performed by inferring the current state of their competences by tracking their actions during the game playing. The definition of a domain model associated to an SG is required to provide adaptation and to guarantee meaningful and coherent ways in which the educational material is presented to the learner [9]. However, one of the limitations in CbKST is that defining such models can be time-consuming and a tough task for experts, mainly because of the difficulties in defining dependencies between competences of a given domain [12]. In this paper, we propose another approach to obtain the implicit domain model that underlies the SG. More precisely, we propose to identify the different links between competences by considering the Q-Matrix [13] that contains the mapping between activities and their addressed competences. We define an activity as an atomic entity of an SG that contains tasks to be performed and that typically corresponds to a level within an SG.

This paper focuses on understanding the issues that occur when comparing the two approaches based on CbKST to generate the so-called *competence structures*: a top-down one, based on domain models defined by experts; and a bottom-up one, based on the Q-Matrix. The main aim is to analyse the weaknesses and strengths of both approaches for creating adaptive learning paths.

This paper is structured as follows. In Sect. 2, we present the main concepts of CbKST. In Sect. 3, we describe the two proposed approaches for building *competence structures*. In Sect. 4, we apply these approaches to three different SGs. In the Sect. 5, we describe the main findings by highlighting strengths and weaknesses of applying the two approaches based on CbKST to the three SGs. Finally, in Sect. 6, we conclude with a discussion on the work presented and we outline some future research directions.

2 Main Concepts of CbKST

Competence-based Knowledge Space Theory (CbKST) is an approach that allows the assessment of learners' competences and hence adaptation. CbKST relies on three main concepts: the *precedence relation*, the *competence states* (*states*, from now on) and the *competence structure.* Concretely, CbKST requires an assessment designer to develop a model of a given knowledge domain as a finite set of competences and *precedence relations* between them. A *precedence relation* $a \leq b$ indicates that competence 'a' is prerequisite to acquire competence 'b'. Considering *precedence relations*, *states* are the resulting meaningful combinations of single competences. A *competence structure* associated to a certain domain is obtained by deriving all the admissible *states* [9, 14]. Besides, a *competence structure* represents different learning paths, from the empty *state* (i.e. a state that does not have competences) to the *state* that contains all the competences of a domain [14]. Figure 1 shows an example of *precedence relations* between five competences 'C {a, b, c, d, e}' and the resulting *competence structure*. In this example, the set {a, c} cannot be a *state* since competence 'b' is also required to master competence 'c'.

CbKST is considered a suitable approach for creating adaptive SGs [5–8]. For example, in the projects 80Days [6] and ELEKTRA [8], adaptation based on CbKST

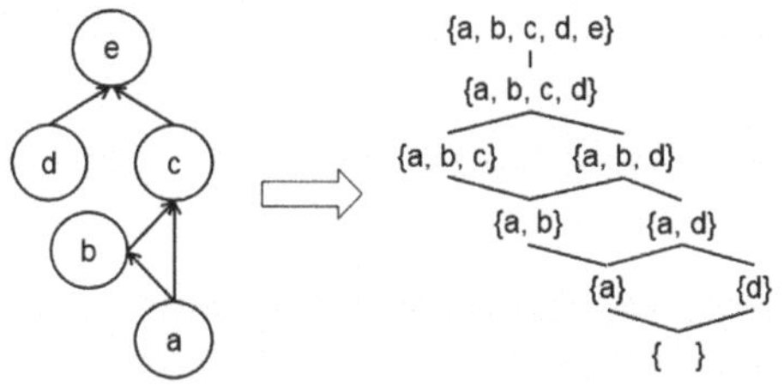

Fig. 1. Example of *precedence relations* (left graph) and *competence structure* (right graph)

has successfully been implemented as motivational and hinting support, and meta-cognitive feedback. However, defining dependencies and links between knowledge and/or competences of a given learning domain is the most demanding task [12]. In order to overcome these difficulties, we propose to use another approach to infer the implicit domain model that underlines the SG. More precisely, we propose to rely on the Q-Matrix [13], which is considered as a transfer model since it captures the domain structure [15].

The Q-Matrix represents the links between activities and competences. If we have A activities and C competences, then rows correspond to activities and columns to competences. Each element of the matrix $q_{i,j}$ is set to 1 if the activity 'i' involves the competence 'j'; 0 otherwise. For instance, if the activity 1 involves only competences c_2 and c_3, then $q_{1,2}$ and $q_{1,3}$ will be set to 1, and all other entries for that activity ($q_{1,\cdot}$) will be set to 0. When an activity involves multiple competences and when the low mastery of a single one is sufficient for failing this activity, the model is considered conjunctive [15, 16]. That means that all competences are necessary to succeed the activity.

3 Two Approaches for Generating Competence Structures of SGs

3.1 Top-Down Approach: Building the Competence Structure by Using the Domain Model

The first approach consists in building the *competence structure* of an SG considering the model defined by experts for a given learning domain. Before going further, we point out that the work presented in this paper is framed in the context of the Play Serious project [17]. The purpose of this project is to develop tools to facilitate the design and implementation of SGs. In the context of the project, three different links have been proposed to conceptualize domain models:

- A "Precedence" link between a competence 'a' and a competence 'b' indicates that it is advisable to work first on competence 'a' than on 'b'.
- A "Prerequisite" link between a competence 'a' and a competence 'b' indicates that it is mandatory to work first on competence 'a' than on 'b'.

- A "Composition" link represents a competence that is formed by a subset of other competences. In Fig. 2, competence 'a' is composed by competences 'b' and 'c'.

Considering these links, the following steps are applied to build the *competence structure*:

- First, "precedence" and "prerequisite" links can be directly mapped in CbKST. For "composition" we only consider the low-level competences because they define more precisely the tasks that can be performed in SG activities. In practice, we convert "composition" links compliant with CbKST as shown in Fig. 2. If a competence 'a' is composed of 'b' and 'c'. Then, a precedence link between 'a' and 'd' is transformed by two links: one with 'b' and 'd'; and the other with 'c' and 'd'.

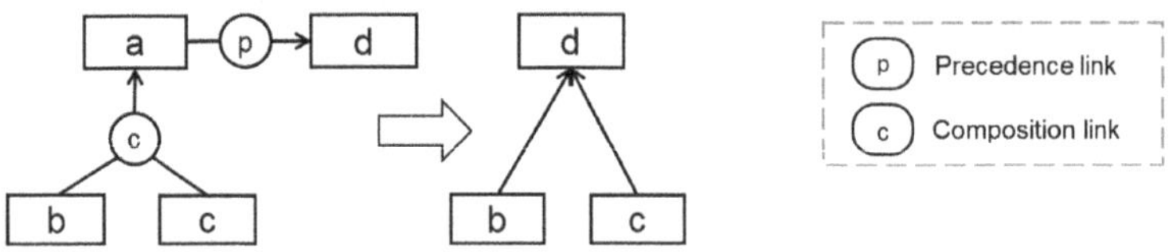

Fig. 2. Example of transformation of the domain model to *precedence relations*

- From the updated domain model, we derive all the admissible *states* by applying the traditional approach of CbKST.
- Finally, each activity of the SG is linked to an *state*. In other words, the set of competences worked on in an activity forms the so-called *state*.

3.2 Bottom-up Approach: Building the Competence Structure by Using the Q-Matrix

If an explicit domain model is not available (the whole model is too hard to define, there is no domain expert available to do it, etc.), we propose to rely on the Q-Matrix [13]. Therefore, it is necessary that the description of SG activities contains the information about their addressed competences. Thus, if the Q-Matrix is available, we proceed in two main steps:

- First, by looking at the Q-Matrix, we select the competences worked on in each activity of the SG to obtain the different *states*. In other words, from the Q-Matrix we can build the different *states* that correspond to the set of competences that are involved in each activity (see Fig. 3).
- Second, we create links between the *states* to build the competence structure. A link is created between two *states* if one *state* contains n competences, and the other *state* contains exactly the same n competences plus one more.

$$\begin{matrix} & \text{competences} & \\ \text{activities} & \begin{pmatrix} q_{1,1} & \cdots & q_{1,k} \\ \vdots & \ddots & \vdots \\ q_{i,} & \cdots & q_{i,k} \end{pmatrix} & \begin{matrix} \leftarrow CS_1 \\ \vdots \\ \leftarrow CS_i \end{matrix} \end{matrix}$$

Fig. 3. *States* obtained from the Q-Matrix

In the following section, we apply both top-down and bottom-up approaches to the first two SGs, while in the third one we only apply the bottom-up approach since no domain model is available.

4 Analysis of Applying the Two CbKST Approaches to Three SGs

4.1 Blockly: Maze

Blockly: Maze[1] is an SG in which learners have to practice programming fundamental concepts. The SG contains 10 activities in which learners have to play and interact with different blocks representing chunks of programming code. No information about the domain model nor the Q-Matrix are provided by the SG. However, as teachers of computer science, we analysed the actions that can be performed in the SG, and proposed a domain model by adapting the list of learning objectives for programming fundamentals proposed by [18]. Figure 4 depicts the proposed domain model.

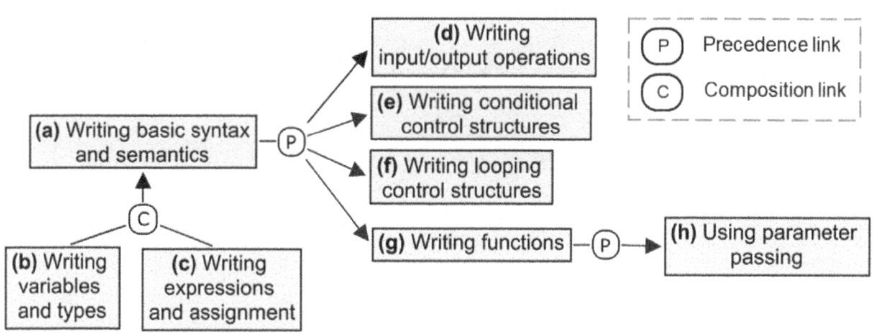

Fig. 4. Proposed domain model for *Blockly: Maze*

We also indexed each activity of *Blockly: Maze*. We linked the competences worked on in each activity by considering the actions that can be performed and the programming blocks involved (see Table 1).

[1] https://blockly-demo.appspot.com/static/apps/maze/index.html. (Last accessed 24 March 2015).

Table 1. Q-Matrix in *Blockly: Maze*

	[a]		[e]	[f]	Competence states
	[b]	[c]			
Level 1	0	1	0	0	[c]
Level 2	1	1	0	0	[b, c]
Level 3	1	1	0	1	[b, c, f]
Level 4	1	1	0	1	[b, c, f]
Level 5	1	1	0	1	[b, c, f]
Level 6	1	1	1	1	[b, c, e, f]
Level 7	1	1	1	1	[b, c, e, f]
Level 8	1	1	1	1	[b, c, e, f]
Level 9	1	1	1	1	[b, c, e, f]
Level 10	1	1	1	1	[b, c, e, f]

Therefore, we compared the resulting competence structures built by considering the domain model (Fig. 5, generated as explained in Sect. 3.1) and the Q-Matrix (Fig. 6). In order to graphically represent the obtained competence structures, we used the open source graph visualization tool called GraphViz (http://www.graphviz.org).

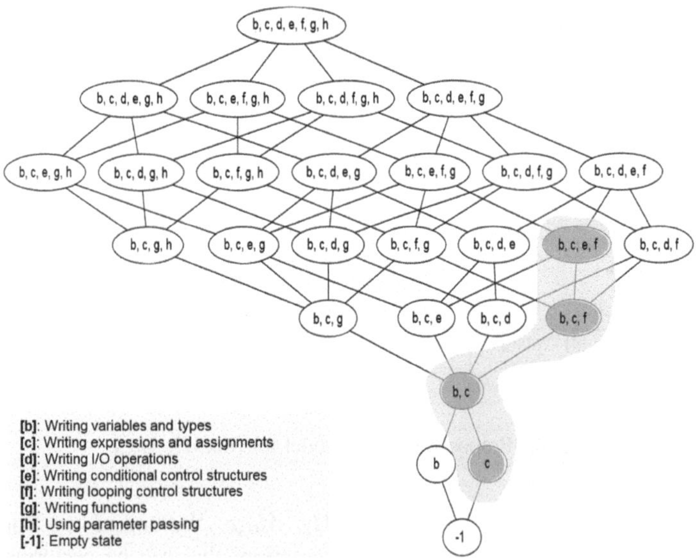

Fig. 5. *Competence structure* of *Blockly: Maze* based on the domain model

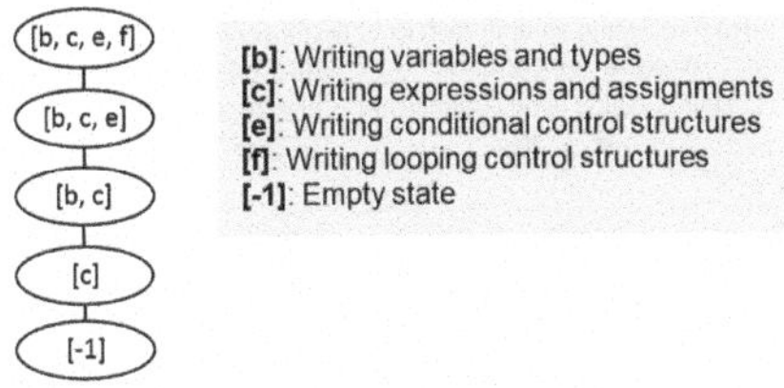

Fig. 6. *Competence structure* of *Blockly: Maze* based on the Q-Matrix

Before describing the next game, we can highlight the following observations when looking at the generated *competence structures*:

- Observation 1 (Ob1.1): In the top-down approach based on the domain model, the number of *states* that contain activities is very small (4 *states* - '[c]', '[b, c]', '[b, c, f]', '[b, c, e, f]' - out of 35; i.e. grey *states* in Fig. 4).
- Observation 2 (Ob1.2): In the bottom-up approach based on the Q-Matrix, the resulting *competence structure* is linear as could be expected.
- Observation 3 (Ob1.3): When comparing both approaches, we observe that the resulting *competence structure* built by considering the Q-Matrix is a subset of *states* in the *competences structure* built by the domain model (i.e. highlighted path in Fig. 4).

4.2 Les Cristaux d'Éhère

Les Cristaux d'Éhère[2] is an SG prototype that consists of 11 levels that are designed to teach concepts related to physics. The goal for each level is to reach the exit indicated by a teleport item. Learners must move an avatar and interact with certain objects to solve problems concerning concrete physics-related topics. A secondary education teacher, expert on physics, designed the domain model associated to the game (see Fig. 7).

Moreover, the same teacher also indexed the SG activities and the associated competences. Table 2 shows the resulting Q-Matrix.

As with the previous SG, we can generate the competence structures considering the information from the designed domain model (see Fig. 8) and the Q-Matrix (see Fig. 9).

Several aspects can be observed from both structures:

- Observation 1 (Ob2.1): In the top-down approach, based on the domain model defined by an expert, the number of *states* that contain activities is very small (7 *states* out of 266; i.e. grey *states* in the dotted circle in Fig. 8).

[2] http://seriousgames.lip6.fr/Cristaux_Ehere. (Last accessed 24 March 2015).

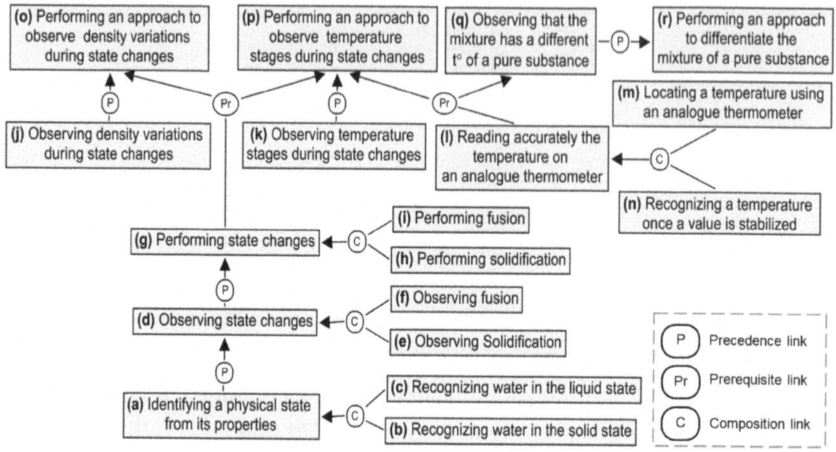

Fig. 7. Domain model for *Les Cristaux d'Éhère*

Table 2. Q-Matrix in *Les Cristaux d'Éhère*

SG activities	[a]		[d]		[g]		[p]	[l]		[r]	Competence state
	[c]	[b]	[e]	[f]	[i]	[h]		[m]	[n]		
Lv. 1	0	0	0	0	0	0	0	1	0	0	[m]
Lv. 2	0	1	0	0	0	0	0	1	0	1	[b, m, r]
Lv. 3	0	0	1	1	0	0	1	1	1	0	[e, f, p, m, n]
Lv. 4	0	1	0	1	0	0	0	1	1	0	[b, f, m, n]
Lv. 5	0	0	1	0	0	0	0	1	1	0	[e, m, n]
Lv. 6	0	1	0	0	1	0	0	1	0	0	[b, i, m]
Lv. 7	0	0	0	1	1	0	0	1	1	0	[f, i, m, n]
Lv. 8	1	0	1	0	0	1	0	0	0	0	[c, e, h]
Lv. 9	1	0	1	0	0	0	0	1	1	0	[c, e, m, n]
Lv. 10	0	0	0	0	0	0	0	1	1	0	[m, n]
Lv. 11	0	0	0	0	0	0	0	1	1	0	[m, n]

- Observation 2 (Ob2.2): The *competence structure* generated by the Q-Matrix is not well connected. Besides, the connected subset of *states* is a linear *competence structure*.
- Observation 3 (Ob2.3): When comparing both approaches, some *states* (grey squares in Fig. 8) built by the Q-Matrix do not match any *states* of the *competence structure* built by the domain model (e.g. *states* "[e, f, p, m, n]" associated to the activity "Lv. 3" does not exist in *the competence structure* generated by the domain model). This fact raises different questions: why do these inconsistencies appear between the two approaches? Is the domain model designed by the expert containing flaws? Or are these issues coming from the Q-Matrix?

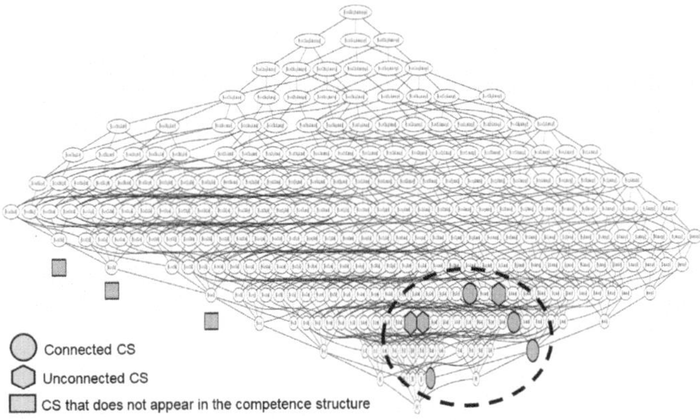

Fig. 8. *Competence structure* of *Les Cristaux d'Éhère* based on the domain model (Available at: http://javiermelero.es/Cristaux_ECTEL15.png)

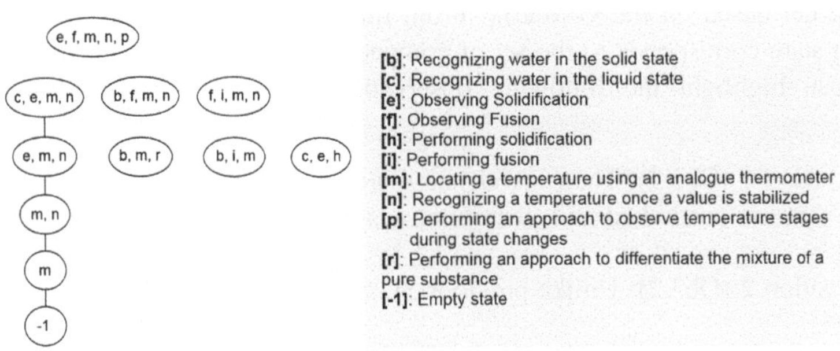

Fig. 9. *Competence structure* of *Les Cristaux d'Éhère* based on the Q-Matrix

- Observation 4 (Ob2.4): The set of *states* generated by the Q-Matrix seems addressing a specific well-defined part of the whole *competence structure* generated by the domain model (dotted circle in Fig. 8).

4.3 Refraction

Refraction[3] is a game that consists of 61 levels grouped into 7 worlds. The aim of this game is to consolidate the skills on addition and multiplication of fractions. Learners have to combine the available items in each level to connect a laser so that the learner can propose a solution for obtaining a required fraction. For this SG, a math secondary education teacher proposed a list of competences to work on (see Fig. 9 for the complete list of competences). She analysed the tasks performed in each SG activity and filled the Q-Matrix for *Refraction* (see Table 3 for a sample).

[3] http://games.cs.washington.edu/refraction/refraction.html. (Last accessed 24 March 2015).

Table 3. A sample of the Q-Matrix of *Refraction* (5th world)

World 5	[a]	[b]	[c]	[d]	[e]	[f]	[g]	[h]	[i]	[j]	[k]	[l]	States
Lv. 5.1	0	0	0	0	1	0	0	0	0	0	0	0	[e]
Lv. 5.2	0	0	0	0	1	0	0	0	0	0	0	0	[e]
Lv. 5.3	1	0	1	0	1	1	0	0	0	0	0	0	[a, c, e, f]
Lv. 5.4	0	0	0	0	1	0	0	0	0	0	0	0	[e]
Lv. 5.5	0	0	0	0	1	1	0	0	1	1	0	0	[e, f, i, j]
Lv. 5.6	0	0	0	0	1	1	0	0	1	1	1	0	[e, f, i, j, k]
Lv. 5.7	1	1	1	0	1	1	0	1	0	0	0	0	[a, b, c, e, f, h]
Lv. 5.8	1	1	0	0	1	1	0	0	1	1	0	0	[a, b, e, f, i, j]
Lv. 5.9	1	1	1	1	1	1	0	1	0	0	0	0	[a, b, c, d, e, f, h]
Lv. 5.10	1	1	1	0	1	1	0	0	1	1	1	0	[a, b, c, e, f, i, j, k]

(Complete Q-Matrix available at: http://javiermelero.es/Refraction_ECTEL15.pdf)

Figure 10 depicts the *competence structure* obtained by applying the second approach, i.e. based on the Q-Matrix. From this approach we obtained 23 different *states* (an state corresponds to the set of competences worked on in an SG activity).

We can highlight the following observations from the resulting *competence structure*:

- Observation 1 (Ob3.1): The *competence structure* is not well connected. There are *states* that are not linked and, therefore, adaptation could be unfeasible at certain stages.
- Observation 2 (Ob3.2): Unlike previous SGs, the connected subset of *states* is not linear.

Therefore, taking into consideration the obtained *competence structures* from the three SGs, we report in the next section the main findings when applying the proposed approaches.

5 Findings from Applying the Two CbKST Approaches

The main findings from the obtained *competence structures* are the following:

- The *competence structure* obtained from the domain model could be considered as an interesting approach to validate the design of SG activities. Indeed, comparing the *states* obtained from the Q-Matrices of *Blockly: Maze* and *Les Cristaux d'Éhère* with the domain models, we could validate if all the designed activities fit a given domain model (Ob1.3) or not (Ob2.3).
- The *competence structures* derived by the Q-Matrices are simpler than those generated by the domain models. When an SG contains few activities, the resulting *competence structure* tends to be a linear sequence of *states* such as in *Blockly: Maze* and *Les Cristaux d'Éhère* (Ob.1.2, Ob.2.2). However, when SGs contain a

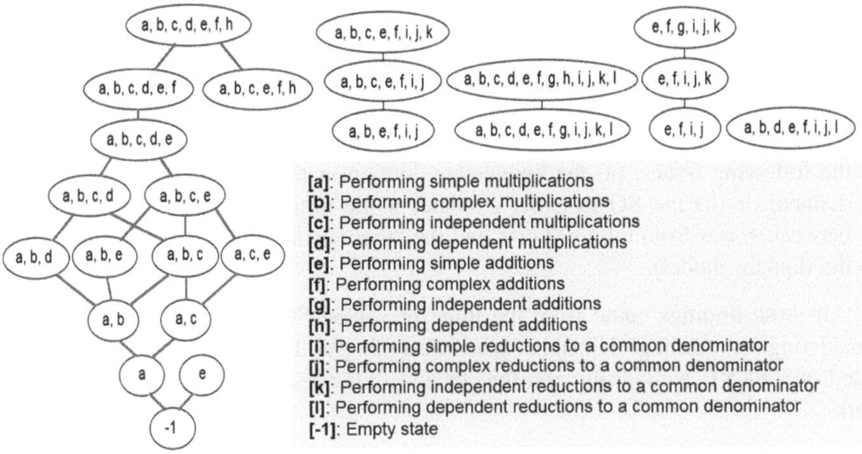

Fig. 10. Competence *structure* of *Refraction* based on the Q-Matrix

larger number of activities, the obtained *competence structure* can contain different learning paths (Ob.3.2), and adaptation can then be performed.

- *The competence structures* obtained by the top-down approach are more complete since they cover a larger scope than those derived by the bottom-up approach. On the contrary, the *competence structures* generated by the bottom-up approach are more tightly linked to the SG designs. Besides, a *competence structure* based on a domain model can be generated once and be applied to different games that target the same domain; while a *competence structure* based on the Q-Matrix has to be generated for every game.
- All the *states* of a *competence structure* built by the Q-Matrix contain activities since each *state* is built by the set of competences worked on in each SG activity. On the contrary, the *competence structures* built by the domain models may contain a large number of *states* that are not linked to activities (Ob1.1. Ob2.1). This could imply that more activities are required if designers of SGs aim that every *state* contains, at least, one activity. However, one cannot expect an SG to cover all the *states* for a given domain. Instead, an SG could be designed to only cover a particular subset of a domain model (Ob2.4).
- It is advisable that the competences have to be described at a suitable level of granularity. For instance, in *Les Cristaux d'Éhère,* low-level competences make the *competence structure* too large (see Fig. 8). This level is more suitable for assessment purposes, but adaptation may be more complex to perform.
- There could be gaps between *states* in the *competence structure* generated by the Q-Matrix. Based on CbKST a link between two *states* is possible if one state contains n competences and the other contains exactly the same n competences plus one. It is possible that from the Q-Matrix this condition is not met as in *Les Cristaux d'Éhère* (see Fig. 9) and *Refraction* (Fig. 10). In other words, there is no gradual progression in the design of the activities. This opens an interesting point of departure for investigating the gaps in the "practical" state space (resulting from

Q-Matrix). In this sense, the Q-Matrix approach can be used to reflect the designer's intention.
- Some *states* obtained by the Q-Matrix do not correspond to any of the *states* of the competence structure obtained by the domain model (Ob.2.3). Comparing the resulting *states* from the Q-Matrix with the domain model's could highlight some of the following issues: (a) the knowledge domain or the Q-Matrix may not be well defined, or (b) the SG designer excludes some notions that lead to a mismatch between *states* from the Q-Matrix and the "theoretical" state space (resulting from the domain model).

All these findings come from the three presented SGs but these could be worth considering as meaningful insights when designing and creating other adaptive SGs based on CbKST. New discussion threads and future research lines emerge from this work.

6 Discussion and Conclusions

In this work, we have considered two approaches for designing domain models. Both the top-down approach (based on explicit domain models) and the bottom-up approach (based on Q-Matrices) are complementary. Inferring the domain model by the Q-Matrix could facilitate the task of domain experts when dependences between competences are difficult to define. Besides, these two approaches have been also applied an evaluated in the third SG, *Les cristaux d'Éhère*, for providing adaptation (Melero et al. [19]). In particular, the authors describe and evaluate how three different strategies have been applied in *Les cristaux d'Éhère* by means of CbKST.

If CbKST is expected to be used as a framework for adapting learning paths, two main considerations have to be taken into account. On the one hand, when an SG relies on a domain model, activities should be designed so that they correspond to meaningful *states*; otherwise, some activities could be not related to any *state* of the resulting *competence structure*. On the other hand, if no explicit domain model is defined for an SG, it is advisable to design activities so that competences are worked on gradually. Otherwise, the *competence structures* that only rely on the Q-Matrix could contain gaps between *states* and, therefore, adaptation could not be feasible at certain stages. In this case, one solution may consist in creating well-connected *states*, for instance by generating as many new *states* as necessary to link the isolated competences.

As previously shown, the *competence structures* generated by domain models tend to be more complete than those built by Q-Matrices. However, the high number of obtained *states* could be a drawback if one aims to design activities for each single *state*. Solutions to this issue would imply: (a) to design SGs that only address a selected subset of *states* (a part of the whole *competence structure* built by the domain model); or (b) to find the most suitable level of granularity to describe the competences of the domain model.

Designing adaptive SGs that only rely on the Q-Matrix approach could require a thoughtful design of the activities. Designed activities should be varied in terms of worked competences in order to allow the possibility of creating a richer number of learning paths. Otherwise, the resulting *competence structures* tend to be fairly linear and adaptation would be less relevant.

We have seen that there can be some inconsistencies between a domain model proposed by experts compared to the Q-Matrix. In that sense, the *competence structure* built by the domain model could be considered a relevant tool at the design stage to create new activities that fill gaps in the learning paths and to check the SG for pedagogical flaws.

Future research lines include: (a) the consideration of domain models made by experts as a validation approach for the design of SG activities; (b) the comparison between scenarios made by teachers with learning paths generated by the *competence structure*.

Acknowledgements. This work was supported in part by the Region Ile de France and by the French Ministry for the Economy, Industry and Employment (FUI). We would like to thank them for their support in the "PlaySerious" project. The authors would like to thank John Wisdom and Bertrand Marne for their very helpful support.

References

1. Shute, V.J., Zapata-Rivera, D.: Adaptive educational systems. Adapt. Technol. Train. Educ. 7–27 (2012)
2. Bass, K.M., Glaser, R.: Developing Assessments to Inform Teaching and Learning. UCLA, Graduate School of Education and Information Studies, Los Angeles (2004)
3. Göbel, S., Wendel, V., Ritter, C., Steinmetz, R.: Personalized, adaptive digital educational games using narrative game-based learning objects. In: Zhang, X., Zhong, S., Pan, Z., Wong, K., Yun, R. (eds.) Edutainment 2010. LNCS, vol. 6249, pp. 438–445. Springer, Heidelberg (2010)
4. Csíkszentmihályi, M.: Flow : The Psychology of Optimal Experience. Harper Perennial, New York (1991)
5. Augustin, T., Hockemeyer, C., Kickmeier-Rust, M.D., Podbregar, P., Suck, R., Albert, D.: The simplified updating rule in the formalization of digital educational games. J. Comput. Sci. **4**, 293–303 (2013)
6. Kickmeier-Rust, M.D., Göbel, S., Albert, D.: 80Days: melding adaptive educational technology and adaptive and interactive storytelling in digital educational games. In: International Workshop on Story-Telling and Educational Games, Maastricht (2008)
7. Kopeinik, S., Nussbaumer, A., Bedek, M., Albert, D.: Using CbKST for learning path recommendation in game-based learning. In: 20th International Conference on Computers in Education, pp. 26–30 (2012)
8. Peirce, N., Conlan, O., Wade, V.: Adaptive educational games: providing non-invasive personalised learning experiences. In: Presented at the 2nd IEEE International Conference on Digital Games and Intelligent Toys Based Education (2008)
9. Heller, J., Mayer, B., Albert, D.: Competence-based knowledge structures for personalised learning. In: 1st International ELeGI Conference on Advanced Technology for Enhanced Learning, Vico Equense-Naples, Italy (2005)
10. Kickmeier-Rust, M.D., Albert, D.: Micro adaptivity: protecting immersion in didactically adaptive digital educational games. J. Comput. Assist. Learn. **7**, 95–105 (2010)

11. Korossy, K.: Modeling knowledge as competence and performance. In: Albert, D., Lukas, J. (eds.) Knowledge Spaces: Theories, Empirical Research, and Applications, pp. 103–132. Lawrence Erlbaum Associates, Inc., Mahwah (1999)
12. Falmagne, J.-C., Cosyn, E., Doignon, J.-P., Thiéry, N.: The assessment of knowledge, in theory and in practice. In: Missaoui, R., Schmidt, J. (eds.) Formal Concept Analysis. LNCS (LNAI), vol. 3874, pp. 61–79. Springer, Heidelberg (2006)
13. Tatsuoka, K.K.: Rule space: an approach for dealing with misconceptions based on item response theory. J. Educ. Meas. **20**, 345–354 (1983)
14. Reimann, P., Kickmeier-Rust, M., Albert, D.: Problem solving learning environments and assessment: a knowledge space theory approach. Comput. Educ. **64**, 183–193 (2013)
15. Pavlik Jr., P.I., Cen, H., Koedinger, K.R.: Learning factors transfer analysis: using learning curve analysis to automatically generate domain models. In: Proceedings of the 2nd International Conference on Educational Data Mining, pp. 121–130 (2009)
16. Desmarais, M.C., Baker, R.S.: A review of recent advances in learner and skill modeling in intelligent learning environments. User Modell. User-Adapted Interac. **22**, 9–38 (2011)
17. Play Serious Project. http://www.playserious.fr/
18. IEEE-CS and ACM Computing Curricula 2001: Computer Science. http://www.acm.org/education/curric_vols/cc2001.pdf
19. Melero, J., El-Kechaï, N., Labat, J.M.: What's next? Different strategies considering teachers' decisions for adapting learning paths in serious games. In: Proceedings of the 7th International Conference on Computer Supported Education, pp. 101–108 (2015)

Towards an Integrated Specialized Learning Application (ISLA) to Support High Functioning ASD Children in Mathematics Learning

Aydée Liza Mondragon(✉), Roger Nkambou, and Pierre Poirier

Université de Québec à Montréal (UQAM), Montreal, Canada
{Aydeelizamondragon, nkambou, pierre.g.poirier}@gmail.com

Abstract. Autism spectrum disorder (ASD) is a neurological disorder affecting the way in which the brain processes information. It can affect all aspects of a person's development. Autism is characterized by impairments in learning and communication, in the social interaction, imaginative ability as well as in repetitive and restricted patterns of behavior (Diagnostic and statistical manual of mental disorders: DSM-IV [12]). This research contributes to the advancement of intelligent tutoring systems by proposing a computational model in the field of specialized education in order to overcome the lack of individualized intervention, such as in the specialized education of individuals with autism. The affective intelligent tutoring system ISLA is an adaptive application evolving along with the learner's needs. ISLA is unique and its contribution entails the model of accompaniment to help autistic children manage their emotions by analyzing the learning trace and considering the student's current performance to respond accordingly to it during a mathematical learning situation such as addition.

Keywords: Autism · Affective intelligent tutoring systems · Specialized education · Personalized education · Model of accompaniment

1 Introduction

1.1 Motivation

The motivation and inspiration to pursue this research project comes from one's own experience as a parent of children with ASD. Despite the challenges that they face in their daily activities, they amazingly continue to persevere and demonstrate remarkable courage. Individuals with ASD usually display particular communication and social deficits (DSM-IV), but these characteristics cover a wide spectrum, with individual differences in terms of: age of onset, levels of functioning, challenges with social interactions, number and particular kinds of symptoms from mild to severe. In the educational system, the lack of one-on-one intervention as it pertains to the domain of specialized education related to autism pose a 'complex multi-factor' problem. Emotions and learning have been broadly recognized as challenging among individuals diagnosed with autism. The socio-cognitive and behavioral problems experienced by

© Springer International Publishing Switzerland 2015
G. Conole et al. (Eds.): EC-TEL 2015, LNCS 9307, pp. 225–239, 2015.
DOI: 10.1007/978-3-319-24258-3_17

individuals with ASD are considered to stem from the difficulty of understanding others' mental states [4, 14]. The lack of joint attention displayed by individuals with ASD is regarded as a necessary 'precursor' to a 'developmental building block' [32]. Thus generalization of gains is difficult to maintain for children in the spectrum [16]. Within the domain of intelligent tutoring systems, [3] points out that the companion agent has the potential of providing students of all ages with information that will help the student to become self-regulated, consequently become independent learners. Here, we present an affective intelligent tutoring system (ISLA) to overcome the problem of one-on-one intervention with the purpose of helping the ASD learner to calibrate his/her emotions to a mathematical learning situation such as addition. This paper is divided into five sections. The first section is the introduction. The second part is the problematic and the ASD. The third part is devoted to the specific architecture of ISLA presenting the domain model, along with the model of accompaniment, the learner, and the pedagogical model. The preliminary experiment and results are introduced in section four. Finally, the conclusion and the limitations are presented outlining the contribution of this research in the field of specialized education. The very question being addressed in this study is: *How do we develop a virtual companion capable of establishing the affective state of an autistic child to a mathematical situation such as adding and thereby responding effectively to it*? Two important questions are considered: (1) *What is the affective state and performance of the ASD student during a learning situation such as addition without the use of a pedagogical agent such as ISLA*? (2) *What is the affective state and performance of the ASD student during a learning situation such as addition with the use of a pedagogical agent such as ISLA*?

2 Problem Statement

2.1 What Is the Autism Spectrum Disorder (ASD)?

Studies reveal that individuals with learning disabilities pose a 'complex multi-factor' problem in the educational system, as most educational institutions do not have the necessary tools to provide extra time on learning-related tasks or cost-effective instructions tailored to each individual [35]. In fact, these studies suggest that individuals with learning disabilities (LD) who require extra resources comprise 13 % percent of all students in the USA (NCES 2009 [22]). The problem stems from the fact that in the educational system, one-on-one intervention is difficult to implement due to budgetary and human constraints. In the last decade, research carried out in the United States and Canada concerning the prevalence of ASD reveals an increasing trend in the occurrence of autism. For instance, according to the Center for Disease Control (CDC), a comparison of the incidence rates for 2008 in the United States suggests an increase in ASD prevalence of approximately 23 % compared with the 2006 estimates and 78 % compared with 2002. In Canada, the recent estimates (March 2014) by the [8] and the Developmental Disabilities Monitoring (DDM) suggest that 1 in every 68 children were born with an ASD. The dramatic increase in ASD prevalence rates has resulted in more attention and overseeing of ASD highlighting the necessity of implementing new effective interventions systems which are essential to the treatment of autism.

2.2 Specialized Education in Autism

Reference [11], have developed the 'Cognitive Assessment System' used in the understanding, assessment and diagnosis in the intervention of different educational problems like autism, reading disabilities, attention deficit disorder, etc. Most teaching and learning approaches to autism have a tendency to integrate a variety of educational and psycho educational programs from the disciplines of behaviorism and psychology [23]. The goal is to tackle three main aspects of intervention among children with autism. The first deals with communication and social interaction; the second with developmental and educational strategies. The last one deals with behavioral techniques to improve learning and behavior. Research in autism has proven that early intervention is fundamental to any child on the spectrum. Some forms of early intervention include physical and social therapy, Applied Behavioral Analysis (ABA), and speech-therapy. For instance, ABA approach and Verbal Behavior are drawn on the research and theories of [29]. Other approaches, to tackle the issue of social communication impairments faced by children with ASD, have been made by using virtual reality technologies [20]. In this research, we propose an affective intelligent tutoring system ISLA to detect and appropriately respond to the affective state of an ASD learner in a mathematical situation. With these concepts in mind, the question to ask is: *As human beings, do we all have metacognitive capabilities that enable us to adapt and respond to our environment?* The answer is that most metacognitive skills that we take for granted are poor or absent in children with autism.

2.3 Emotions and Autism

Through the use of functional neuro-imaging studies, several researchers are investigating the neural underpinnings of the theory of mind deficit associated with autism. The theory of mind has been broadly studied in individuals with and without ASD [4]. Theory of mind consists of being able to infer a full range of mental states such as beliefs, desires, intentions, imagination, and emotions that cause action as: 'one being able to reflect on the contents of one's own and other's mind' [15]. One must wonder about the relationship between emotion and learning among children with autism? The process of teaching autistic individuals is challenging. During intervention, one important challenge is due to the difficulty of anticipating and recognizing negative behaviors, consequently calibrating the child's affective state to effective intervention and learning. These deficiencies vary from child to child as these individuals may have profound cognitive deficiencies while others may have IQ scores that are equal to or higher than the typical person (DSM-IV). This diversity of profiles causes multiple challenges in terms of methodologies and teaching programs directed towards autistic children. This is the reason why we believe that modeling affect is the proper approach for ISLA to teach mathematics to children with autism.

2.4 Intelligent Tutoring Systems (ITS) and Affect Management

An ITS is a computer system designed with the objective of providing instant and customized instruction or feedback to learners. This is generally done without intervention from a human teacher, and with the intention of enabling learning in a meaningful effective way by using a variety of computing technologies [26], Many ITSs have been developed and are being used in different domains in formal education (i.e. Auto Tutor [15], ANDES [33], among others). Some ITSs exist for corporate and industry training, including SHERLOCK [19], all of which have demonstrated their capabilities and limitations. Researchers claim that if computers are to interact naturally with humans, they must also be able to recognize, affect and express social competencies [27]. The 'affective' approach within intelligent tutoring system has been validated as having a positive impact on the learner's intuition, and on his/her self-esteem, as it relates to problem solving tasks [9, 24]. Thus 'cognition', 'motivation' and 'emotional affect' are three components of learning [13]. In [2], they have demonstrated different sensors that can be used to detect emotions during a learning session such as the conductance bracelet sensor, facial expression sensor, pressure mouse sensor, and eye detection sensor, among others. Sensors are associated with specialized software able to assess an emotion or a set of emotions. Other examples of physiological sensors that have a direct correlation according to two dimensions valence (positive or negative emotion), and arousal (intensity of emotion) are the GSR sensor (Galvanic Skin Response), the RSP sensor (respiration), the BVP sensor (Blood Volume Pressure), from which heart rate (HR) data can be extracted. TEMP sensors allow the recording of temperature variation. One example of AITS is the Wayang tutor intended for middle school and high school level mathematical learning. In its use, Jake and Jane, two virtual agents play the role of affective learning companions in an attempt to emulate empathy and help keep high school children more engaged in the lesson. Its sensor platform has been tested with more than 1,000 students. It is composed of four physiological sensors such as mental state camera, skin conductance bracelet, pressure sensitive mouse, and pressure sensitive chair [2, 38].

2.5 Intelligent Tutoring Systems (ITS) and Cognitive Diagnosis (CD)

Within an ITS, the objective of CD is to accurately determine why the student made an error and where to focus the subsequent learning activity [30]. For instance, [34] suggests a mechanism to cognitive diagnoses dealing with 'behavioral' description, and adaptation used in AutoTutor [15], and Andes [33]. Reference [1] outlines the importance of the models' 'flexibility' and its cognitive 'fidelity'. In [3] they examined the effectiveness of pedagogical agents (PAs') with MetaTutor for the purpose of training students on self-regulated learning (SRL) processes to cognitive diagnosis through prompting and providing feedback that facilitated learning about the human circulatory system.

3 System Overview and Pedagogical Methodology

3.1 ISLA Architecture

As illustrated in Fig. 1, ISLA is an affective intelligent tutoring system capable of detecting the emotional state of an autistic child in a mathematical learning situation,

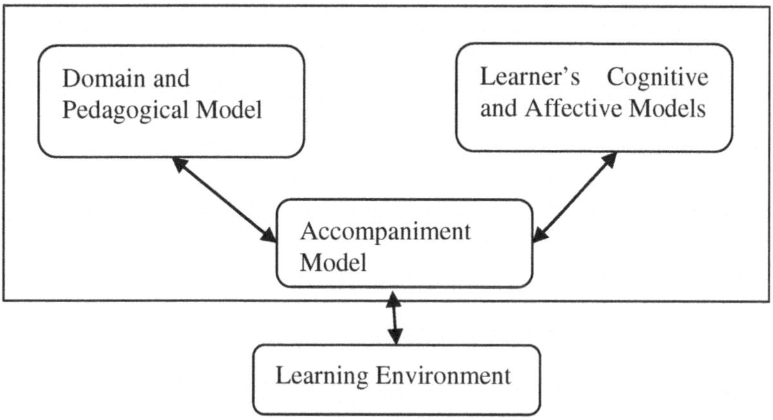

Fig. 1. The architecture of ISLA

thus when engaged in an addition task and subsequently responding to this emotional state by means of the use of a virtual pedagogical agent called 'Jessie'.

This is displayed in the user's interface and related to the accompaniment model. The interface will provide a three-dimensional view that allows personalizing the interaction of the three core models of ISLA. This is from the domain model point of view (by providing tools to manipulate domain objects), the accompaniment model point of view through Jessie (companion agent), and the learner model point of view using an open-learner modeling approach [7]. The open-learning model will promote 'reflection' and 'planning' in order to help the ASD student to 'mirror' his/her own learning. The accompaniment model of ISLA is drawn from the self-regulated learning theory highlighting the essential role that metacognition plays in self-regulation and learning [28]. ISLA is unique and its contribution entails the model of accompaniment to help autistic children manage their emotions. This is done by analyzing the learning trace and the student's current performance. ISLA is an adaptive application that evolves along with the learner's needs. Through the incorporation of aspects of the accompaniment model, ISLA both supports and integrates the domain and learner models. For example, ISLA makes use of a personalized individual plan, along with educational learning activities and teaching techniques employed by different actors to best meet the individual's learning needs. Next, each model of the application will be covered in detail.

3.2 The Domain Model of ISLA

The domain model of ISLA deals with the tutor expert plus the design and implementation of agent-based architecture of a Personalized Education System. The domain model of ISLA concerns the learning system related in teaching addition to children with autism. Competencies are at the heart of the domain model of ISLA. According to [30] a competency is defined as 'an integrated set of skills, knowledge, and attitudes that enables one to effectively perform the activities of a given occupation or function to the standards expected'. In this study, we have considered the competencies of: *analyze, utilize, correct, adapt, manage, explicit* and *modify* for the acquisition of several skills associated with knowledge in mathematics from different domains such as cognitive and affective among children with autism. Thus, ISLA is able to help the learner to develop these competencies at different levels: beginner, intermediate, and advance. For instance, at an intermediate level, if the learner made an error related to carrying and writing 1 s and 10 s, then he/she is expected to be able to analyze, utilize and correct his/her learning trace without prompting.

3.3 The Accompaniment Model of ISLA

What exactly is 'accompaniment'? In the context of music, the concept of 'accompaniment' describes: the composed music, arrangement, or improvised performance that is played to 'back up' the soloist in a 'supportive manner'. As illustrated in Fig. 2, in the context of ISLA, accompaniment makes use of an individualized intervention plan (IIP), along with educational learning activities and teaching techniques employed by different actors to best meet the individual's learning needs. The process of accompaniment for children presenting autism is controlled by ISLA and the specialized educator. The IIP is the framework for the model. Its integration into ISLA is essential because it provides guidance and key elements about the curriculum, the pedagogy, the behavior required from the autistic person, among others. Studies have revealed that recognizing the possible behaviors that may indicate an autistic child's affective states are essential for effective intervention for the child [27]. As observed in Fig. 2, the output from the process of accompaniment is associated with methodologies and teaching programs which turn into the output for the process of a specialized educational plan that best fits the student's needs.

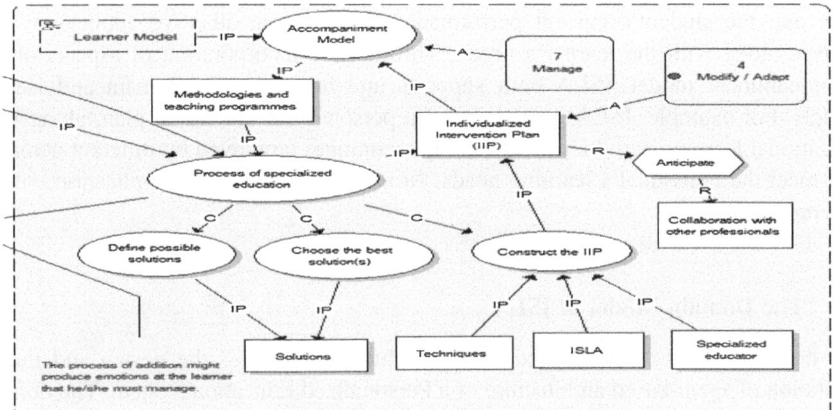

Fig. 2. The accompaniment model of ISLA

3.4 The Learner Model of ISLA

In this part of the project, the 'clinical profile of the learner' is personalized to the student and involves two important processes. The first process deals with the cognitive profile and the second one relates to the affective profile of the learner. Both processes are controlled by ISLA and the specialized educator. To start with, the accompaniment model is drawn from the self-regulated learning (SRL) theory [28]. SRL refers to our 'ability' to understand and control our learning environment and consists of three main components: cognition, metacognition, and motivation. Within the domain of specialized education, as it pertains to the teaching of autistic children, the affective impairments of individual within the spectrum have been recognized as having an important impact on intervention [17]. Autistic individuals displaying a normal or high IQ are considered as having high functioning autism, which is characterized by lower function in social and language skills, in contrast to visuospatial skills [21]. The technique used in ISLA to model the cognitive state of the learner is based on prior probability criteria that the concept of adding is known by the learner. In addition, the learner is capable of discriminating numbers up to 100. Thus, the specialized educator performs a baseline measure of performance through a quiz consisting of thirty additions grouped in four different levels of competencies for each participant. The criteria baseline is provided in the first part of the experiment and is described in Sect. 4. In ISLA, the computational model which detects the affective state of the autistic child relies on the framework of emotions proposed by [25] where happiness is positively-valenced, surprise, sadness, and neutral are non-valenced, and frustation and fear are negatively-valenced emotions. This affect recognition evaluation framework has been broadly validated among 'typical' students with intelligent tutors [26]. By contrast, research on the correlation of affect recognition through the use of sensor indicators and the affective states of individuals presenting autism is poor [10]. In this study, the affective model of the learner is based on state-of-the-art face reader technology sensors. As children on the spectrum display communicative (nonverbal and verbal) deficits (DSM-IV), it makes it difficult for observational methodologies. The affective profile selected in this study includes the affects of: (1) interest, (2) frustration, (3) anxiety, and (4) happiness because they are considered relevant in autism intervention practices [18].

3.5 The Pedagogical Model of ISLA

We have designed and implemented the pedagogical model of ISLA in terms of learning process of mathematics in the field of specialized education highlighting the important role of 'competencies' in the course of teaching addition to children with autism. The idea behind competencies is to help and support the autistic student to develop mathematical skills. Mastering learning requires that the tutoring system has some way of assessing the students' level of knowledge [5]. In this regard, we have considered the work of [6] who explains three important types of representations when learning mathematics: concrete, image and symbolic. The pedagogical model of ISLA entails a 'behavioral' approach to cognitive diagnoses in which tasks are assigned in a predetermined sequence.

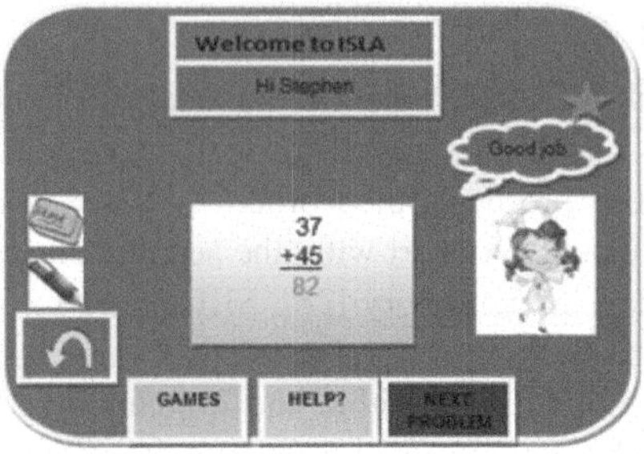

Fig. 3a. Correct answer

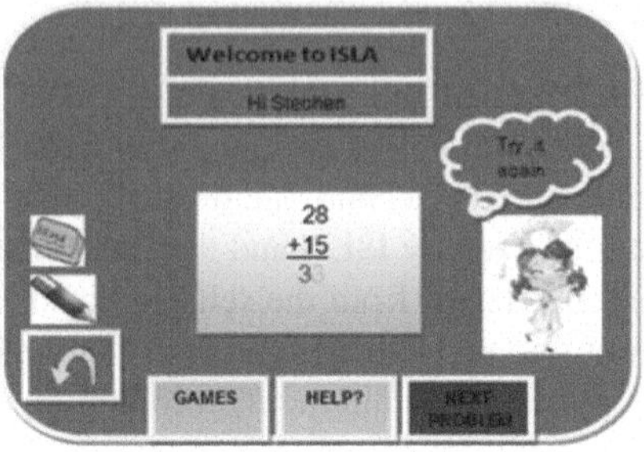

Fig. 3b. Incorrect answer

The learner must finish a task before moving to the next phase increasing the chance that the ASD student has mastered the prerequisites of a task. Error Analysis is performed to determine whether the objectives are met [31]. The error analysis is presented in Table 3 covered in Sect. 4. Different types of feedback are suggested to the student by the pedagogical agent Jessie. As observed in Fig. 3a, color-based flag feedback is used indicating the correctness of the answer. Second, a buggy message which is a specific text message related to the error made by the student can be provided. Third, a chain of hints is used if the student needs help. A 'hint' can be given if it is needed. In Fig. 3a, the idea is that when the learner provides the right answer, the pedagogical agent will reward him/her with social encouragement: 'Good job', 'Champion', 'you did it', etc. If the learner gets frustrated by the activity and reacts negatively towards the task, ISLA is able to anticipate and detect the learner's emotional state ahead of time, and thus shifts his/her attention to a ludic activity to diminish negative behavior. Once the learner's negative behavior has shifted to positive behavior, ISLA is able with 'hints' to provide by means of pedagogical scenarios the motivational needs to the student. To keep track of the cognitive state of the student, a window of the errors is made, along with any corrective action taken by the learner. This approach provides the appropriate feedback to answer the following questions: How many errors and what kind does the student make? How often does the learner succeed with or without prompting?

3.6 Affect Detection Cycle in ISLA

As illustrated in Fig. 4, in this research, the affective recognition cycle consists of four steps or phases and is triggered when the participant with autism interacts with (ISLA). His/her emotional states are measured and processed in real-time through the use of face reader state-of-the-art technology sensors illustrated in phase 2.

The captured affective states are measured and processed which in turn sends back the information as an input to the affect detection system (phase 3). In phase 4, the 'manager' associated with specialized software is able to gather and analyze a set of emotional signals from the autistic learner. It then returns it as a 'conditioned affective state', which becomes the input for ISLA to respond accordingly to it in order to help the ASD learner to calibrate his/her emotions in a mathematical learning situation.

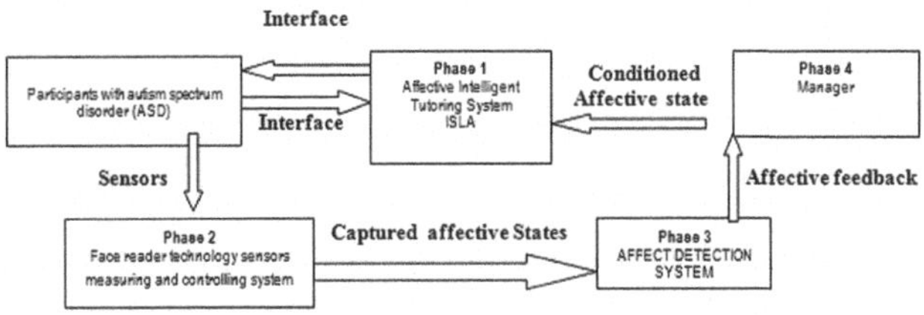

Fig. 4. Affect detection cycle in ISLA

4 The Methodology

The sample is limited to high functioning children in order to use a standardized training method. The participants recruited in this study come from private clinics specializing in autism, as well as centers for adaptation and specialized education related to autism located in Montreal, Canada. The research population consists of fifteen participants diagnosed with high functioning autism spectrum disorders (ASDs) boys and girls within the ages of 6 to 12 years old, with the consent of their parents under the supervision of a specialized educator. During a period of 1 h, in a one-on-one structured intervention in a mathematical learning situation such as addition, two important questions are considered: *(1) What is the affective state and performance of the ASD student in a learning situation such as adding* ***without the use of a pedagogical ag****ent such as ISLA? (2) What is the affective state and performance of the ASD student in a learning situation such as adding* ***with the use of a pedagogical agent*** *such as ISLA?*

The experimental process is comprised of two parts. The first part entails a training period in order to familiarize the ASD student with ISLA. The second part deals with validating the specialized learning application and the use of a pedagogical agent to provide effective help to the student during a mathematical operation such as adding, by establishing the affective state of an autistic child.

4.1 The Preliminary Experiment

The preliminary experiment in this study consisted of a Wizard of Oz experiment played by the specialized educator simulating the behavior of an affective intelligent tutoring system ISLA and its pedagogical agent called 'Jessie' in a mathematical learning activity such as addition. The pedagogical agent 'Jessie' illustrated in Figs. 3a and 3b is capable of managing the student's affective state with the purpose of anticipating negative behavior. This helps the autistic student to calibrate his/her emotions and consequently complete the mathematical task at hand. Though we aim to have fifteen students for the project, so far only three have been successful in fulfilling the criteria and their profiles are presented in Table 1. Prior to the one-on-one

Table 1. Participants profile

Participant code	Diagnosis	Age	Gender
#1	Autism disorder	12	Male
#2	Autism disorder	10	Male
#3	Asperger syndrome	5	Female

Table 2. Reward System

Reward code	Reward	Reward examples
S	Social	Bravo, good job, excellent
E	Edible	Snacks
L	Ludic activity	Games

intervention, a questionnaire of five questions was provided to the parent in order to predict the affective state of the child during the mathematical activity.

In this regard, two questions concerning the affective state dealing with positive or negative behaviors that the student might experience must be tested during the mathematical activity. The effects of interest, frustration, anxiety and happiness could be displayed. The list of rewards is presented in Table 2. The one-on-one intervention lasted for 1 h, at a time for 2 h and was divided into two parts.

4.2 Experiment: Without the Use of a Pedagogical Agent

In the first part of the experiment, the following question was addressed: *What is the affective state and performance of the ASD student in a learning situation such as adding* ***without the use of a pedagogical agent*** *such as ISLA?*

The specialized educator performed a baseline measure of performance for each participant. Consequently, in the first experiment a quiz was presented individually to each student consisting of thirty additions which he/she had to solve without the use of a pedagogical agent such as 'Jessie' played by the specialized educator.

The list of errors that the student might encounter performing the mathematical activity is presented in Table 3 [31]. The additions in the quiz were grouped in four different levels of competencies from 1 to 4 presented in Table 4. The duration of the quiz was for 15 min and a score between 91 %–100 % excluded the participant from the study.

Results and Discussions: The results of this preliminary study about the affective state and performance of the ASD student in a learning situation such as addition ***without the use of a pedagogical agent*** are presented in Table 5. As illustrated, one can see that the affect profile for participant #1 was 'Neutral' and the level of difficulty was '1',

Table 3. List of Error Analysis

Error #1	Difficulty with 1s and 10s tens in carrying and writing
Error #2	Difficulty with understanding regrouping
Error #3	Difficulty in discriminating H (100) D (Decimals), U (Units)
Error #4	Difficulty with carrying 10s and 100s

Table 4. Score criteria baseline

Level of competency	Score	Criteria
1) Beginner	>50 %	Recruited
2) Intermediate	>60 %	Recruited
3) Advanced	>85 %	Recruited
4) Mastered	<95 %	Excluded

consequently he performed with 100 % in the quiz that was given to him. The activity lasted 5 min. This is probably due to the fact that he already knows addition. The score of 100 % in the quiz at a mastered level excluded this participant from the study. By contrast, participant #2 performed poorly in the quiz with a '1' measure of accomplishment and a difficulty level of '4' experiencing the affects of frustration and anxiety. He played with his hair and complained by saying 'I hate math', 'This is hard for me'. The activity lasted 15 min and scored 50 % in the quiz at a beginner level. He was selected to participate in the second experiment of this study.

Table 5. Affective profile ASD participant without the use of a pedagogical agent

Participant	Affective profile	Difficulty	Accomplishment Scale	Score quiz
#1	Neutral	1 = Not difficult	5	100 %
#2	2,3	4 = Very difficult	1	50 %
#3	3	3 = Difficult	2	45 %

In addition to the results, participant #3 performed poorly in the quiz with a '2' measure of accomplishment and a difficulty level of '3' experiencing the affects of anxiety. Even though, the level of accomplishment was '2' greater than participant #2, she did not complete the quiz. She seemed very distracted and anxious. At different moments, she flapped her hands and asked for 'help'. The specialized educator had to interrupt the evaluation due to the negative behavior of the student. She scored 45 % on the quiz at a beginner level and was selected to participate in the second experiment of this study. The scores compiled indicated that the students with the exception of participant #1 did not succeed on the quiz. As illustrated in Table 5, the results of this preliminary experiment allowed us to determine that the affective state and performance of the ASD student in a mathematical situation without the use of a pedagogical agent to provide support and encourage motivation was negative for participants #2 and participant #3.

4.3 Experiment: With the Use of a Pedagogical Agent

In the second experiment of this study, the following question was addressed: *What is the affective state and performance of the ASD student in a learning situation such as adding* ***with the use of a pedagogical agent*** *such as ISLA?*

Consequently, a second quiz was presented individually to each student consisting of fifteen additions reflecting his/her level of competency. The student was asked to perform the task with the use of a pedagogical agent such as 'Jessie' played by the specialized educator to provide support who was hiding in another room.

It is essential to measure and keep track of the student performance and learning to validate the acquisition of the objectives. The list of errors performed by each participant is presented in Table 6. Therefore, having assessed the baseline for each student, the specialized educator was able to gather the level of competency for each participant.

Table 6. List of error analysis with the use of a pedagogical agent

Error	Description	Participants
#1	Difficulty with 1 % and 10 % in carrying and writing	2,3
#2	Difficulty with understanding regrouping	3
#3	Difficulty in discriminating H (100) D (decimals), U (Units)	2,3
#4	Difficulty with carrying 10 % and 100 %	2,3

Table 7. Participants rewards

Participants	Rewards
#2	Snacks, games, social
#3	Social, snacks

The list of rewards is presented in Table 7. Furthermore, a schedule was also implemented by using pictograms helping the student to follow the activity.

Results and Discussions: The results are presented in Table 8. One can see that participant #2 performed better in the second quiz with a '2' measure of accomplishment and a difficulty level of '3' displaying the affects of interest, frustration and happiness. He stands up and complained by saying 'I don't remember'. The activity lasted 20 min and he scored 65 % on the quiz. In addition to the results, participant #3 also performed better in the second quiz. Even though, she seemed anxious and played with her fingers, she asked for 'help' and was able to complete the task with a '3' experiencing the affects of interest, anxiety, and happiness. The activity lasted 25 min and she scored 60 % on the quiz. Both children required extra time to complete the task.

Table 8. Affective profile ASD participants with the use of a pedagogical agent

Participant	Affective profile	Difficulty	Accomplishment scale	Score quiz
#2	1, 2, 4	3 = Difficult	2	65 %
#3	1, 3, 4	3 = Difficult	3	60 %

During the intervention provided to each participant, they were prompted individually by Jessie played by the specialized educator to help the child to calibrate his/her emotions by providing real-time immediate visual feedback to diminish frustration and promote motivation so that the mathematical task can be accomplished.

Table 9. Participant scores

Participant	Score without the use of a pedagogical agent	Score with the use of a pedagogical agent
#1	100 %	Excluded
#2	50 %	65 %
#3	45 %	60 %

For example as Fig. 3a, when participants #2 provided the right answer, the pedagogical agent prompted him with social rewards such as 'good job'. By contrast, when participant #2 provided the incorrect answer (Fig. 3b), the pedagogical agent 'Jessie' prompted him with 'hints' by the means of pedagogical scenarios suggesting 'Error #1' dealing with difficulty in carrying and writing 1 s and 10 s. Jessie invited the learner to 'try again' to complete the task. Table 9 illustrates the scores of each participant during the two experiments (without and with the use of a pedagogical agent. The results indicated that the affective state and performance of the ASD student in a mathematical situation such as adding with the use of a pedagogical agent had a positive impact on the performance of participant #2 and participant #3. By comparing the two scores 50 % (*without* the use of pedagogical agent) and 65 % (*with* the use of pedagogical agent), participant #2 benefited from real-time feedback provided by the pedagogical agent Jessie. For participant #3, she scored 45 % in the first experiment (without the use of pedagogical agent), whereas in the second experiment (with the use of the agent) she was able to complete the task with a 60 % score.

5 Conclusion, Limitations and Future Work

We have presented the architecture of ISLA related to the domain of specialized education. ISLA is unique and its contribution entails the model of accompaniment to help ASD learners manage their emotions by analyzing the learning trace and current performance in a mathematical activity. The affective profiles indicators selected were interest, frustration, anxiety, and happiness because they are considered relevant in autism intervention practices. This research contributes to the advancement of intelligent tutoring systems by proposing a computational model in the field of specialized education to overcome the lack of individualized intervention. ISLA supports and integrates the domain and Learner models with the intention to deliver individualized instruction in real-time as 'effective' as one-on-one human instruction. As discussed in Sect. 4, the results of the preliminary experiment revealed that the performance of the ASD student in a mathematical situation such as adding with the use of a pedagogical agent to provide real-time support had a positive impact on the performance of these participants. Future work of this research will be dealing with a larger group of twelve participants with high functioning autism in which, one controlled group of six student will be interacting without the pedagogical agent Jessie, while the test group of six participants will be interacting with the pedagogical agent Jessie. A full development of ISLA is scheduled once the prototype has been validated.

References

1. Aleven, V., McLaren, B.M., Sewall, J., Koedinger, K.R.: The cognitive tutor authoring tools (CTAT): preliminary evaluation of efficiency gains. In: Ikeda, M., Ashley, K.D., Chan, T.-W. (eds.) ITS 2006. LNCS, vol. 4053, pp. 61–70. Springer, Heidelberg (2006)
2. Arroyo, I., Cooper, D.G. Burleson, W., Woolf, B.P., Muldner, K., Christopherson, R.: Emotion sensors go to school. In: Proceeding of AIED 2009, pp. 17–24, Brighton. IOS Press, Amsterdam (2009)
3. Azevedo, R.: Theoretical, methodological, and analytical challenges in the research of metacognition and self-regulation: a commentary. Metacognition Learn. **4**, 87–95 (2009)
4. Baron-Cohen, S., Leslie, A.M., Frith, U.: Does the autistic child have a theory of mind? Cognition **21**(1), 37–46 (1985)

5. Bloom, B.S.: The 2 sigma problem: the search for methods of group instruction as effective as one-to-one tutoring (1984)
6. Bruner, J.S.: On Knowing: Essays for the Left Hand. Harvard University Press, Cambridge (1966)
7. Bull, S., Kay, J.: Open learner models. In: Nkambou, R., Bourdeau, J., Mizoguchi, R. (eds.) Advances in Intelligent Tutoring Systems, pp. 318–338. Springer, Berlin (2010)
8. Centre for Disease Control (CDC): cdc.gov
9. Chalfoun, P., Frasson, C.: Optimal affective conditions for subconscious learning in a 3D intelligent tutoring system. In: Jacko, J.A. (ed.) HCI International 2009, Part IV. LNCS, vol. 5613, pp. 39–48. Springer, Heidelberg (2009)
10. Shalom, D.B., Mostofsky, S.H., Hazlett, R.L., Goldberg, M.C., Landa, R.J., Faran, Y., McLeod, D.R., Hoehn-Saric, R.: Normal physiological emotions but differences in expression of conscious feelings in children with high-functioning autism (2006)
11. Das, J.P., Naglieri, J.A., Kirby, J.R.: Assessment of Cognitive Processes. Developmental disabilities monitoring (ADDM) (1994)
12. Diagnostic and statistical manual of mental disorders: DSM-IV. American Psychiatric Association (2000)
13. D'Mello, S.K., Craig, S.D., Gholson, B.F.S., Picard, R.W.: Interacting effects sensors in an intelligent tutoring systems. In: Affective Interactions: The Computer in the Affective Loop Workshop (2005)
14. Frith U.: Interacting minds. Biological Basis Review (1999)
15. Graesser, A.C., Moreno, K., Marineau, J., Adcock, A., Olney, A., Person, N.: AutoTutor improves deep learning of computer literacy: is it the dialogue or the talking head? In: Proceedings of Artificial Intelligence in education, pp 47–54. IOS Press, Amsterdam (2003)
16. Green, J., et al.: Parent-mediated communication-focused treatment in children with autism (2010)
17. Seip, J.: Teaching the autistic and developmentally delayed: A guide for staff training and development (1996)
18. Dautenhahn, K., Werry, I.: Towards Interactive Robots in Autism Therapy. University of Hertfordshire (2004)
19. Lajoie, S.P., Lesgold, A.: Apprenticeship training in the workplace: computer coached practice environment as a new form of apprenticeship. Mach. Mediated Learn. **3**, 7–28 (1989)
20. Mitchell, P., Parsons, S., Leonard, A.: Using virtual technologies environments for teaching to adolescents with ASD (2007)
21. Mottron, L., Belleville, S.: A study of perceptual analysis in a high-level autistic subject with exceptional graphic abilities. Brain Cogn. **23**, 279–309 (1993)
22. National Center for Education Statistics (NCES)-2009-nces.ed.gov
23. National Research Council: Educating Children With Autism. National Academy Press, Washington, DC (2001)
24. Nkambou, R.: Towards affective intelligent tutoring system. In: ITS 2006 Workshop on Motivational and Affective Issues in ITS, Taiwan (2006)
25. Ekman, P., Saron, C.D., Senulis, J.A., Friesen, W.V.: Approach/withdrawal and cerebral asymmetry: Emotional expression and brain physiology. Int. J. Pers. Soc. Psychol. (1992)
26. Postka, J., Massey, L.D., Mutter, S.A.: Intelligent Tutoring Systems, Lessons Learned. Laurence Erlbaum, Hillsdale (1988)
27. Picard, R.W.: Future affective technology for autism and emotion communication. Philos. Transa. R. Soc. B Biol. Sci. **364**(1535), 3575–3584 (2009)
28. Schraw, G (1998), Promoting general metacognitive awareness, Instructional Science 26
29. Skinner, B.F.: Verbal Behaviour. Prentice Hall, New York (1957)

30. Tchetagni, J., Nkambou, R., Bourdeau, J.: A framework to specify a cognitive diagnosis component in ILES. J. Interact. Learn. Res. **17**(3), 269–293 (2006)
31. Tindal, G.A., Marston, D.B.: Classroom-Based Assessment. Merrill, Columbus (1990)
32. Tomasello, M.: Joint attention as social cognition. In: Moore, C., Dunham, P.J. (eds.) Joint Attention: Its Origin and Role in Development, pp. 103–130. Cambridge University Press, Cambridge (1995)
33. VanLehn, K., Lynch, C., Schulze, K., Shapiro, J.A., et al.: The andes physics tutoring system: lessons learned. Int. J. Artif. Intell. Educ. **15**(3), 678–685 (2005)
34. VanLehn, K.: The behaviour of tutoring systems. Int. J. Artif. Intell. Educ. **16**(3), 227–265 (2006)
35. Woolf, B., Arroyo L., Muldner, K., Burleson, W., Cooper, D., Dolan, R., Christopherson, R.: The effect of motivational learning companions on low high achieving students and students with learning disabilities. In: International Conference on Intelligent Tutoring Systems, Pittsburgh (2010)

Automatic Tagging of Learning Objects Based on Their Usage in Web Portals

Katja Niemann(✉)

Fraunhofer Institute for Applied Information Technology (FIT),
Schloss Birlinghoven, 53754 Sankt Augustin, Germany
katja.niemann@springer.com

Abstract. Data sets coming from the educational domain often suffer from sparsity. Hence, many learning objects are not accessible by the users as they are not able to find these objects using for example a text-based search. Furthermore, the lack of information makes it difficult or even impossible to recommend such hidden learning resources. In order to address the data sparsity problem, this paper presents a new way to enhance the objects' semantic representations. This is done by automatically assigning tags and classifications to learning objects offered by educational web portals. This way, we aim to increase the accessibility of the learning objects as well as to enable their recommendation. In contrast to popular tagging approaches that usually base the tagging of a learning object on its content or on the tags already assigned to it, the approach proposed in this paper is solely based on the objects' usage. Therefore, tags and classifications can be exchanged between the objects and also previously un-tagged objects that do not hold any textual content can be automatically assigned with tags and classifications.

Keywords: Automatic tagging · Data mining · Educational web portals · Findability · Information retrieval · Technology enhanced learning

1 Introduction

Many educational web portals allow users and domain experts to manually enrich the learning resources with social metadata like free-text tags or classifications from a controlled vocabulary. Additionally to ratings and detailed comments which are rarely used in educational web portals [1], these tags and classifications provide powerful knowledge that can be used to improve the quality of searching and recommendations [2,3]. Especially when dealing with multimedia objects that provide little or no textual context (e.g. photos or videos), tags and classifications provide meaningful descriptors of the objects [4].

Nevertheless, data sets coming from the domain of technology enhanced learning (TEL) often suffer from sparsity in respect to semantic and social metadata describing the learning objects [1]. This hinders the accessibility of the learning resources since users cannot easily find them. Additionally, the sparsity impedes the recommendation of suitable learning resources.

© Springer International Publishing Switzerland 2015
G. Conole et al. (Eds.): EC-TEL 2015, LNCS 9307, pp. 240–253, 2015.
DOI: 10.1007/978-3-319-24258-3_18

We envision two scenarios to address the data sparsity problem, i.e. tag recommendation and automatic tagging. Tag recommendation supports the users by recommending tags they might want to add to a learning object. This simplifies the tagging process for the users and, thus, motivates them to add more tags [5,6]. Furthermore, users tend to add different tags to objects to describe the same concept which makes it difficult to retrieve and compare the objects. For example, a user searching for *memorial* will not find learning objects tagged with *monument*. In fact, in the data sets used for the evaluation in this paper more than half of the tags are only added to one object. Using a tag recommender, the usage of the already existing tags can be increased. In contrast, automatic tagging describes the process of automatically assigning tags to objects without any user interaction. This process is usually based on the same algorithms as the tag recommendation, though, it can immediately enable better retrieval and recommendations if the quality of the tags is sufficient.

The approach presented in this paper focusses on automatic tagging. First, the similarity of all learning object pairs is calculated by comparing their usage contexts, i.e. their most significant co-occurrences. This approach was already successfully applied in [7,8] to support the recommendation process of learning objects and movies, respectively. Second, for each learning object, the tags and classifications of its similar objects are selected as candidate tags. Third, these candidates are weight according to the objects' similarity and the tags' and classifications' frequency in the data set. Finally, the most promising candidate tags are added as new tags to the respective learning objects.

The paper is structured as follows. Chapter 2 gives an overview of the research conducted in the area of tag recommendation and automatic tagging. Chapter 3 analyses the data sets coming from the educational web portals MACE and Learning Resource Exchange. Thereafter, Chapter 4 introduces the approach applied in this paper while Chapter 5 discusses the evaluation results in detail. Finally, Chapter 6 holds a conclusion and an outlook on future work.

2 Related Work

Tag recommendation and automatic tagging have been studied extensively in many domains in the last years, e.g. for web sites (i.e. web bookmarks) [9,10], scientific publications [11], pictures [4,12], and learning objects [2,13]. Here, the most popular approaches base on the data objects' content or on tag co-occurrences and are shortly discussed in the following paragraphs.

Content-based approaches analyse the objects' contents to select their most representing keywords as new tags. For example, Diaz-Aviles et al. [13] propose the usage of α-*TaggingLDA* that is based on the Latent Dirichlet Allocation probabilistic topic model to automatically extract suitable tags from the learning objects' contents. While this approach addresses the cold-start problem, it also requires the learning objects to hold a sufficient amount of textual content to enable the extraction of suitable tags. However, many learning objects do not hold any textual information but for example only pictures or videos [14].

Furthermore, the tagging of learning objects with terms that are contained in their textual content does not necessary increase the objects' retrieval. Song et al. [10] introduce a two-way Poisson mixture model in which the documents as well as their words and already assigned tags are represented by two bi-partite graphs which can be partitioned into clusters. This way, terms can be selected as candidate tags for objects that are not contained in these objects' contents but belong to semantically related objects. However, similarly to the first approach, it requires the objects to hold at least some content or semantic metadata to discover connections between the objects.

Another approach is the usage of tag co-occurrences. Here, tags that often co-occur, i.e. that are often assigned to the same objects, are assumed to hold a semantic relation. Therefore, for each object, the tags that are most related to the tags it already holds are selected as candidate tags. This approach has especially been exploited in the area of tag recommendation for photos which by nature do not hold textual content. Sigurbjörnsson et al. [4] use this approach to assist users in the photo annotation task using the example of flickr. Additionally, they use WordNet to assign categories (e.g. *location* or *person*) to the tags. They found that this approach is especially suited to recommend tags that refer to locations or artefacts but not to persons or events. Furthermore, tags that do not appear in WordNet have a low acceptance rate as well. Rae et al. [12] also use flickr to evaluate their approach that is based on tag co-occurrences. In contrast to the previous approach, they incorporate user-specific information in the tag recommendation process. Here, a user's contexts, e.g. her personal context (that holds the tags she assigned to photos) and her social context (that holds the tags assigned by friends), are incorporated to recommend personalised tags. While approaches based on tag co-occurrences do not require textual content they only work when a large quantity of supporting data is available [4]. Furthermore, they are not able to recommend tags for un-tagged objects.

In contrast, the approach presented in this paper solely analyses the usage of the learning objects to establish relations between them. These relations are then utilised to enable the exchange of tags between the objects. Thus, tags can also be added to un-tagged objects that do not hold any textual content. It is sufficient if a learning objects was used a few times (or even only once) as we have presented in [8]. In fact, the approach has shown to especially work well for rarely used learning objects.

3 Data Sets

3.1 MACE

The MACE (Metadata for Architectural Contents in Europe) project relates digital learning objects about architecture with each other across repository boundaries to enable a simplified discovery and access [15]. Users are able to search for learning objects and filter the results, e.g. according to their language, the original repository, and the classification terms they hold. Furthermore, the portal offers a social search based on tags.

While interacting with the MACE portal, users are monitored, i.e. their activities are recorded as CAM (Contextualised Attention Metadata [16]) instances. The event types that include the use of a learning object are accessing the metadata of a learning object in the MACE portal, accessing the learning object in its origin repository, as well as metadata provision activities, i.e. rating, tagging, and commenting. Each CAM instance comprises at least the event type, the identifier of the user who conducted the event, a timestamp, and the identifier of the involved resource. The CAM instances were collected in a period of three years from October 2009 to September 2012. The data set holds 117,907 events on 12,442 learning resources conducted by 630 registered users.

The MACE portal offers users and domain experts the possibility of editing parts of the metadata, e.g. by adding tags and classifications. The tags are free text and can be assigned to learning resources by logged-in users. The classifications are defined in a controlled vocabulary consisting of 2,884 terms and can only be set by domain experts. 78.69 % of the learning resources hold such additional semantic metadata. More specifically, 70.8 % hold tags, 14.83 % hold classifications, and 8.82 % hold both. Each tagged learning resource holds on average 6.59 tags and each classified learning resource holds on average 2.27 classifications.

Figure 1 shows an overview of the usage of the 13,291 distinct tags and classifications in MACE. As the tags are free text, about 73 % of the 13,291 distinct tags are only used once and only about 4 % of the tags are added to more than 10 objects. This shows the speciality of the tags which impedes the discovery of the objects they describe. Additionally, this tag distribution hinders the recommendation of learning objects as tags that are only used once cannot be used to compare the objects. The usage of the classifications is slightly more equally distributed with about 39 % of the classifications being only used once and about 77 % of the classifications being used at maximum 5 times.

Finally, logged-in users are able to rate the learning resources. In total, 429 learning resources were rated by 76 users, each of these learning resources was rated at least once and at maximum 4 times (on average 1.11 times), and each of the 76 users rated 1–91 learning resources (on average 6.52). These ratings will be used in this paper's experimentation chapter to evaluate the quality of the automatically added tags and their suitability to enhance recommendations.

3.2 Travel Well

The Travel well data set [17] was collected for the Travel well resources[1] on the Learning Resource Exchange (LRE) portal[2] that makes open educational resources available from more than 20 content providers in Europe and elsewhere. The learning resources exist in multiple languages and conform to a variety of national and local curricula. The registered users, mostly primary and secondary school teachers, come from a number of different European countries.

[1] http://lreforschools.eun.org/web/guest/travel-well.

[2] http://lreforschools.eun.org.

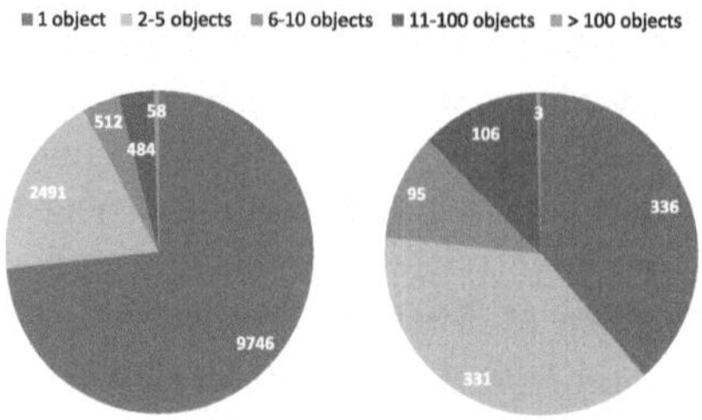

(a) no. of objects per tag (b) no. of objects per classification

Fig. 1. Tag and classification distribution in MACE

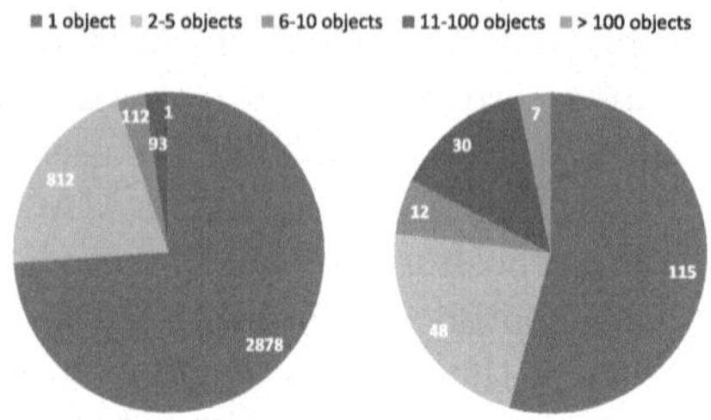

(a) no. of objects per tag (b) no. of objects per classification

Fig. 2. Tag and classification distribution in Travel well

The Travel well data set contains information about the rating and tagging events of 98 registered users collected over a period of six months (August 2008 - February 2009). In total, 14,248 user events were recorded on 1,924 resources. For each event, the date, user identifier, resource identifier, and the value of the tag, respectively of the rating is stored.

The learning resources can hold classification keywords from a controlled vocabulary and free text tags added by the users. Overall, 97.97 % of the learning resources hold tags or classifications, 95.53 % hold tags, 69.04 % hold classifications, and 66.6 % hold both. Here, each tagged resource was assigned with 6.5 tags on average and each classified resource holds on average 2.25 classifications.

Figure 2 presents an overview of the usage of the distinct tags and classifications in Travel well. 74 % of the 3,896 distinct tags are only used once and only about 2 % of the tags are added to more than 10 objects. Similarly, 54 % of the 212 distinct classifications are only used once. 17 % of the classifications were assigned to more than 10 learning objects, though.

Finally, 73 users rated 1,597 learning resources in which each learning resource was rated 1–10 times (on average 1.34 times) and each user rated 1–108 learning resources (on average 29.29).

4 Approach

In this chapter, we first describe the calculation of the usage context-based similarities between the learning objects. Thereafter, we show how these similarities can be used to automatically assign the learning objects with the tags and classifications that can be obtained from related objects.

4.1 Usage Context-Based Learning Object Similarity

We assume learning objects to hold a semantic relation if they are often used in the same usage contexts, i.e. together with the same co-occurrences. In this section, we first specify the term usage context and present the significance calculation for co-occurrences to then explain the calculation of the learning objects' usage context-based similarities.

Specification of the Term Usage Context. We focus on the notion of usage context that was inspired by the concept of word contexts successfully used in linguistics. Words stand in linear orders, e.g. in speech or in written texts. The context of a word can thus easily be defined by the words that occur before and after it. If two words have very similar contexts (e.g. words they often co-occur with in sentences), they are said to be paradigmatically related [18]. For example: In many contexts, the word *car* can be replaced by the word *vehicle*, i.e. they share similar usage contexts containing for example the terms *driver* and *highway*. Thus, paradigmatic relations lead us to semantic relations or, as Heyer et al. [19] states, context similarity correlates with content relatedness. We take up this insight and form our hypothesis that it holds true not only for words but also for other entities that a usage context-based similarity provides an indication for a content relatedness.

Similar to words used in sentences, data objects are used in user sessions. The definition of the term *user session* depends on the conditions. For example, a session can comprise all events conducted by a user between logging in and out of a portal. Thus, the usage context of an object is the result of the objects significantly often accessed before or after it in the same sessions. When comparing two data objects, they are assumed to be semantically related if their usage contexts' significantly overlap. Please note that two objects can have highly similar usage contexts, even if they were never used together.

Figure 3 shows two exemplary user sessions from two different users. Both users access a text documents describing the *Grand Palais* and a picture showing the *Centre Pompidou*, i.e. two buildings located in Paris. Thereafter, the first user accesses a video about *Renzo Piano* while the second user opens a text document having *Richard Rogers* as topic. This means that although the learning objects about *Renzo Piano* and *Richard Rogers* are not used together they are used in similar usage contexts, i.e. together with the learning objects about the *Grand Palais* and the *Centre Pompidou*. Hence, the learning objects about *Renzo Piano* and *Richard Rogers* are assumed to have a semantic relation. This is in fact true, as they denote those two architects who designed the *Centre Pompidou* together.

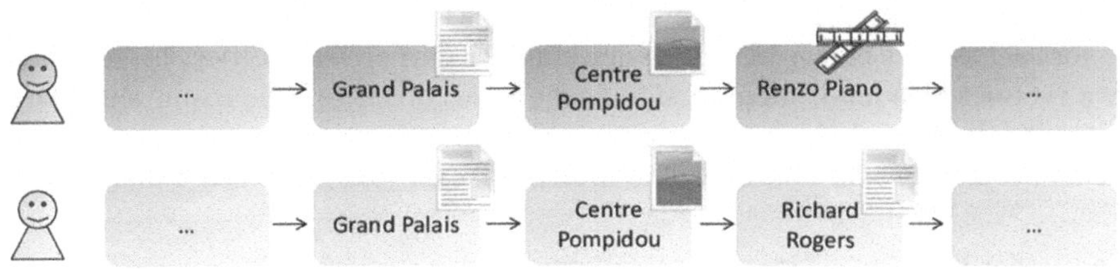

Fig. 3. Exemplary user sessions

This example shows how the knowledge of the users is implicitly given by their activities and can be exploited without asking them to explicitly share it.

Significance of Co-occurrences. We define two objects to be co-occurrences if they co-occur in at least one user session. However, not every co-occurrence is significant, rather most co-occurrences are coincidental. Basic association measures like Mutual Information (MI, see formula 1) calculate a significance score by comparing the observed frequency O of a co-occurrence with its expected frequency E. Such association measures often give close approximation to the more sophisticated association measures like the χ^2-test (that compares the expected and observed values for each cell in the contingency table) [20].

$$\mathrm{MI} = log_2 \frac{O}{E} \tag{1}$$

In previous experiments we compared the suitability of the association measures Mutual Information, log likelihood, the Yates' corrected χ^2-test, and a Poisson-based similarity for selecting the most representing co-occurrences [7,8]. It has shown that the usage of MI leads to the best results when dealing with data sets coming from the domain of TEL. This is due to the fact that these data sets predominantly hold rarely used items, i.e. items used only once or twice.

Object Representation. After the calculation of the co-occurrences' significance values, the most significant ones must be selected for each object. There are two ways to do so, i.e. by ranking or by using a threshold. Ranking means that the co-occurrences are sorted by their significance values and only the n most significant co-occurrences are selected. When using a threshold, only co-occurrences with a significance value higher than the threshold are selected. However, there is no standard scale of measurement to draw a clear distinction between significant and non-significant co-occurrences [21]. The previous experiments have shown that for learning objects it is best to use an object-specific threshold, i.e. the average significance of its co-occurrences. This way, each object is described by as many co-occurrences as possible (which is important in sparse data sets to establish relations to other objects by comparing their co-occurrences) while still filtering the truly coincidental co-occurrences.

Object Similarity Calculation. We calculate the usage context-based similarity for each object pair using the cosine similarity where each object is described by a vector which holds its most significant co-occurrences. The cosine similarity measures the angle between two vectors, thus, it takes the significance values of the co-occurrences into account and always takes a value between 0 and 1.

4.2 (Semi-)Automatic Tagging

We have shown that two learning objects that are used in similar usage contexts exhibit a semantic relationship [8]. However, while these usage context-based

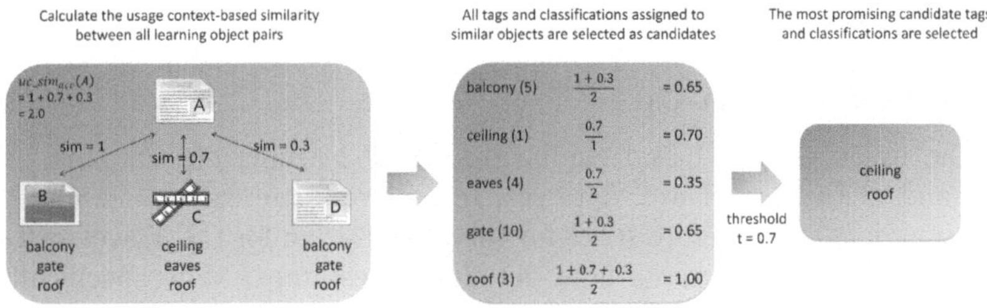

Fig. 4. Example

relations directly can be used to enhance recommender systems, they do not necessarily increase the retrieval of the learning resources in the users' searching processes. Therefore, we aim to enhance the learning objects' semantic metadata representations by automatically assigning tags and classifications based on the available usage context-based object relations.

The set of all learning objects is represented by $\mathcal{L}$. For each object $i \in \mathcal{L}$ the tags and classifications that are assigned to an object $j \in \mathcal{L}$ that hold a usage context-based similarity $uc\_sim(i, j)$ to object i that is greater than zero are selected as candidate tags. Thereafter, for each candidate tag t of object i, a weight $w(t, i)$ is calculated that states its adequacy to describe object i. In order to calculate the weight $w(t, i)$, the similarity values of all objects holding tag or classification t are accumulated and normalised. Here, the set of all objects holding t is denoted by $\mathcal{L}_t \subset \mathcal{L}$. The normalisation of the weight is conducted by dividing it by the maximum value it can reach, i.e. its frequency in the data set $|\mathcal{L}_t|$, or by the maximum value any tag or classification can reach for the given item i, i.e. $uc\_sim_{acc}(i)$, whatever is smaller, see Eqs. 2 and 3.

$$w(t,i) = \frac{\sum_{j \in \mathcal{L}_t} uc\_sim(i,j)}{min(uc\_sim_{acc}(i), |\mathcal{L}_t|)} \tag{2}$$

$$uc\_sim_{acc}(i) = \sum_{j \in \mathcal{L}} uc\_sim(i,j) \tag{3}$$

This approach is exemplary illustrated in Fig. 4. Object A does not hold any tags or classifications so far. However, it holds usage context-based relations to the objects B, C, and D that each hold three tags. Overall, these three objects are assigned with five distinct tags, i.e. *balcony*, *ceiling*, *eaves*, *gate*, and *roof*, that are, thus, possible candidate tags to be assigned to object A. The total number of learning objects each tag is assigned to is given in brackets, e.g. *balcony* is assigned to five objects in total. Using a threshold of 0.7, only the tags *ceiling* and *roof* are selected to be assigned to object A. The tag *roof* is assigned to all three similar learning objects and, thus, receives the highest possible weight. The tag *ceiling* is only used once in the whole data set, i.e. for object B. Since object A and object B have a sufficient similarity (i.e. 0.7 which equals the threshold), it is selected as well. The selection of a suitable threshold is an exploratory investigation, though, and further discussed in the evaluation section.

5 Evaluation

5.1 Experimental Set-Up

First, the usage context-based similarities of all learning object pairs in the MACE and in the Travel well data set, respectively, are calculated. Here, the user session definition is more strict for the MACE than for the Travel well data set because the MACE events hold detailed timestamps. More specifically, in MACE, a new user session is assumed to start whenever the user did not conduct any events in more than an hour. In Travel well, all events conducted by a user on one day are assumed to belong to one user session because the events in the Travel well data set only hold the date. After the calculation of the usage context-based similarities, the candidate tags and classifications are selected and their weights are computed as described in the previous chapter. Finally, the most promising tags and classifications, i.e. those with a weight that equals or exceeds the pre-defined threshold are selected and added to the respective objects. The selection of a suitable threshold is an exploratory investigation, thus, we vary the threshold t from 0.1 to 1.0 in the following experiments in which 1.0 is the highest weight a tag or classification can get.

In the following sections, we depict statistics showing how the automatic tagging enhances the learning objects' semantic metadata representations. Additionally, we evaluate the quality of the automatically added tags and classifications by using them to calculate rating predictions. Equation 4 shows how a predicted rating $\hat{r}(u,i)$ of user u on a learning object i is calculated with $P(u)$ being the profile of user u holding all ratings on other objects. The content-based similarity of two objects i and j is denoted by $con\_sim(i,j)$.

$$\hat{r}(u,i) = \frac{\sum_{j \in P(u), i \neq j} (con\_sim(i,j) * r(u,j))}{\sum_{j \in P(u), i \neq j} |con\_sim(i,j)|} \tag{4}$$

We perform a 5-fold cross evaluation to compare the performance of the content-based recommender system that only uses the tags and classifications assigned by the users and domain experts, respectively, with the performance of the same recommender system which additionally uses the automatically added tags or classifications or both. In order to do so, we calculate the predictive evaluation metric mean average error (MAE), see formula 5. The MAE measures the deviation of a predicted rating $\hat{r}(u,i)$ and the user's true rating $r(u,i)$ of object i for all users $u \in U$. Additionally, we calculate the coverage, i.e. the percentage of user-item pairs in the test set for which a rating can be predicted.

$$\text{MAE} = \frac{\sum_{u \in U} \sum_{i \in P(u)} |\hat{r}(u,i) - r(u,i)|}{\sum_{u \in U} |P(u)|} \tag{5}$$

5.2 Tags and Classifications per Object

In the MACE data set, 8,620 out of 12,442 learning objects hold on average 6.58 tags each. When applying the automatic tagging, the number of tagged learning objects raises by at least 8 % (9,309 tagged objects with t = 1.0) up to 25 % (10,783 tagged objects with t = 0.1). Additionally, the number of tags an object holds on average increases drastically. When setting the threshold t to its maximum, a tagged object holds on average 34.72 tags while with a lower threshold, the number of tags per object raises up to 680.06 (with t = 0.1). Furthermore, 1,806 MACE objects have been classified by domain experts, each holding on average 2.27 classifications. After the automatic tagging the number of classified objects increases by 19 % (2,144 classified objects with t = 1.0, each holding on average 2.72 classifications) up to 245 % (6,229 classified objects with t = 0.1, each holding on average 7.59 classifications).

In the Travel well data set, 1,839 out of 1,924 learning objects hold on average 6.09 tags each. When applying the automatic tagging, the number of tagged learning objects increases by at least 0.33 % (1,845 tagged objects with t = 1.0) up to 4.24 % (1,917 tagged objects with t = 0.1). The number of tags an object holds on average increases remarkably as well, i.e. when setting the threshold t to its maximum, a tagged object holds on average 21.28 tags while with a higher threshold, the number of tags per object increases up to 125.72 (with t = 0.1). Additionally, 1,376 objects hold classifications that were assigned by domain experts where each classified object holds on average 2.25 classifications. After the automatic tagging, the number of classified objects increases by 5.74 % (1,455 classified objects with t = 1.0, each holding on average 2.56 classifications) up to 32.27 % (1,820 classified objects with t = 0.1, each holding on average 8.76 classifications).

5.3 Rating Predictions

Figure 5 shows the mean average error (MAE) and the coverage (i.e. number of user-item pairs in the test set for which a rating can be predicted) of the content-based recommender systems for the MACE data set and varying thresholds. It can be seen that the coverage increases with a decreasing threshold. This is due to the fact that more tags and classifications can be assigned to the learning objects which leads to more content-based object relations. More specifically, the coverage increases by 3.34 % (t = 1.0) up to 48 % (t = 0.1) compared to the baseline when considering the newly added tags and classifications. The MAE increases up to 13.61 % (t = 0.2 using tags and classifications), though, which indicates that the quality of the automatically assigned tags and classifications decreases with the threshold. However, the MAE can even be improved compared to the baseline if the threshold is high enough. When using t = 1.0, the MAE decreases by 0.54 %. When comparing the tags and classifications it is remarkable that the automatically added classifications neither increase the MAE nor the coverage as much as the tags. This can be motivated by the fact that less classifications than tags are added. However, as the sole usage of classifications can decrease the MAE, it can be further assumed that the automatically added classifications are more qualitative than the added tags.

Figure 6 shows the MAE and the coverage of the content-based recommender system for the Travel well data set and varying thresholds. The trend of both

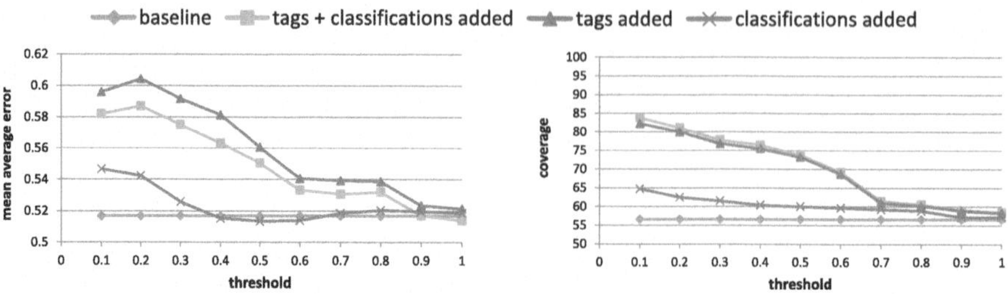

(a) Mean average error (MAE)

(b) Coverage

Fig. 5. MACE

measures is similar to those of the MACE data set. However, the effect is not as distinctive for the Travel well than for the MACE data set which is due to the fact that less tags and classifications were added to the Travel well objects. When considering the newly added tags and classifications, the MAE worsens for a threshold of 0.5 and lower (up to 0.83 % for t = 0.1) compared to the baseline and improves for a threshold of 0.6 or higher (up to -1.78 % for t = 0.7). The coverage increases by 6.35 % (t = 1.0) up to 20.45 % (t = 0.1 and 0.2). Similarly as for the MACE data set, the automatically added tags increase the coverage more than the classifications. In contrast, the usage of the automatically added classifications does not result in better results than the usage of the automatically added tags. However, the performance difference is rather low.

To conclude, the lower the threshold, the more tags and classification can automatically be assigned to the learning objects. We aim to only add tags and classifications of high quality, though, which seems to be the higher, the higher the threshold. Hence, we recommend the usage of the maximum threshold, i.e. t = 1.0. In the following section we analyse how the automatic tagging influences the usage of the distinct tags and classifications.

5.4 Tag and Classification Distribution

Figure 7 shows an overview of the usage of the distinct tags and classifications, respectively, in the MACE data set after the automatic tagging using the maximum threshold. The number of tags that were only assigned to one object halve through the automatic tagging process, i.e. from 73.33 % (9,746) to 37.1 % (4,930 tags) of all distinct 13,291 tags. In turn, the percentage of the tags that are used 2–100 times increases from 26.24 % (3,487) to 56.65 % (7,530). The percentage of tags that are assigned to more than 100 objects only increases from 0.44 % (58) to 6.25 % (831). This shows that indeed the rarely used tags are assigned more often to objects by the automatic tagging than the already frequently used ones.

The percentage of classifications that are only used once decreases from 38.59 % (336) to 19.06 % (166) in the MACE data set. The percentage of classifications used 2–5 times only increases slightly from 38 % (331) to 44.55 % (368). Finally, 36.62 % of the classifications are assigned to 10–100 objects after the automatic tagging while the number of classifications assigned to more than 100

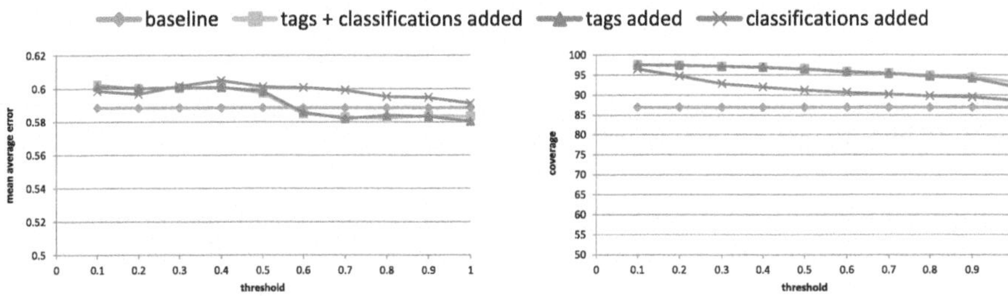

(a) Mean average error (MAE)

(b) Coverage

Fig. 6. Travel well

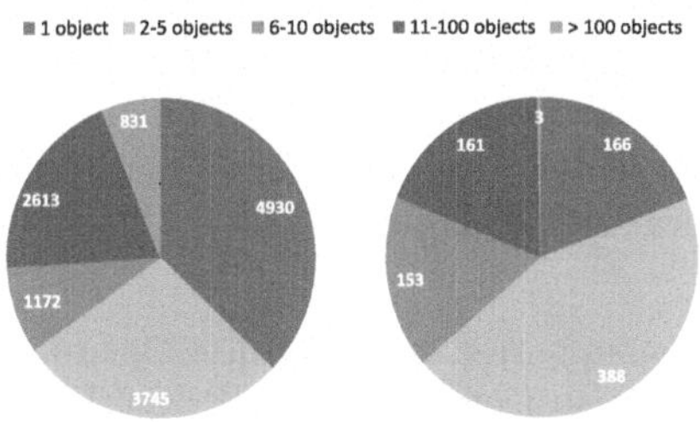

(a) no. of objects per tag

(b) no. of objects per classification

Fig. 7. Tag and classification distribution in MACE with t = 1.0

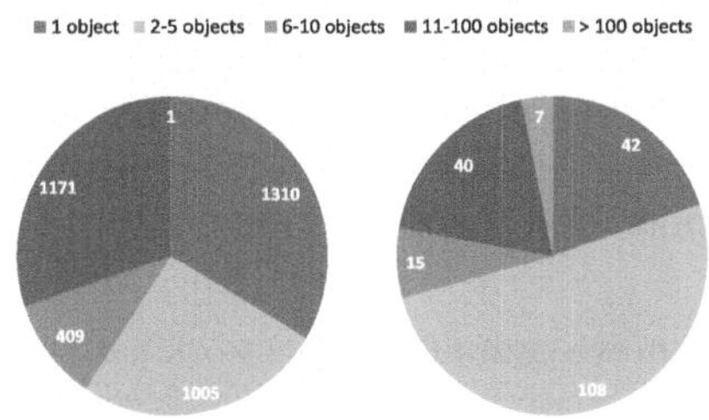

(a) no. of objects per tag

(b) no. of objects per classification

Fig. 8. Tag and classification distribution in Travel well with t = 1.0

objects stays the same. Hence, it can be assumed that especially rarely assigned classifications are spread.

The tags and classifications in Travel well behave similarly. Figure 8 shows an overview of the usage of the distinct tags and classifications, respectively, in the Travel well data set after the automatic tagging. The percentage of tags that are only assigned to one object decreases from 73.87 % (2,878) to 33.62 % (1.310). Similarly to the MACE data set, the percentage of tags that are used 2–100 times increases from 26.10 % (1,017) to 66.35 % (2,585). In contrast, the number of tags assigned to more than 100 learning objects stays the same.

About 50 % of all classifications in the Travel well data set are assigned to 2–5 learning objects after the automatic tagging. The percentage of classifications that are only assigned to one object decreases from 54.25 % (115) to 19.81 % (42).

6 Conclusion

We proposed a new way to automatically enhance the semantic metadata representations of learning objects offered by educational web portals to enhance their retrieval. This is done by exchanging tags and classifications between the objects based on the objects' usage context-based similarities. Thus, no content information about the objects is needed to detect similarities. We found that this way even learning objects that previously did not hold any tags or classifications can be automatically tagged and classified. Furthermore, we found that especially the rarely used tags and classifications are assigned to new objects.

We evaluated the quality of the newly added tags and classifications by using them in a content-based recommender system. It has been shown that the new information can increase the performance of the content-based recommender in terms of quality and quantity. Hence, we assume the new tags and classifications to possess a similar quality than the user-generated ones.

The results motivate us to further continue on this track. Therefore, we plan to conduct a more detailed study on the automatically assigned tags and classifications. Here, we are interested in the kind of tags and classifications (e.g. location or person) that are correctly or incorrectly exchanged between the objects. Furthermore, we plan to conduct an online evaluation in which the automatically added tags and classifications are made available in a web portal to directly support the users in retrieving the most suitable learning resources.

Acknowledgments. This work has been partly supported by the project Open Discovery Space project that is funded by the European Commission's CIP-ICT Policy Support Program (Project Number: 297229).

References

1. Verbert, K., Manouselis, N., Ochoa, X., Wolpers, M., Drachsler, H., Bosnic, I., Member, S., Duval, E.: Context-aware recommender systems for learning : a survey and future challenges. IEEE Trans. Learn. Technol. **5**(4), 318–335 (2012)
2. Lohmann, S., Thalmann, S., Harrer, A., Maier, R.: Learner-generated annotation of learning resources - lessons from experiments on tagging. In: Proceedings of the International Conference on Knowledge Management, I-KNOW 2008, pp. 304–312 (2008)
3. Sen, S., Vig, J., Riedl, J.: Tagommenders. In: Proceedings of the 18th International Conference on World Wide Web, WWW 2009, p. 671. ACM Press, New York (2009)
4. Sigurbjörnsson, B., van Zwol, R.: Flickr tag recommendation based on collective knowledge. In: Proceedings of the 17th International Conference on World Wide Web - WWW 2008, p. 327. ACM Press, New York (2008)
5. Rendle, S., Balby Marinho, L., Nanopoulos, A., Schmidt-Thieme, L.: Learning optimal ranking with tensor factorization for tag recommendation. In: Proceedings of the 15th ACM SIGKDD International Conference on Knowledge Discovery and Data Mining, KDD 2009, p. 727. ACM Press, New York (2009)
6. Song, Y., Zhang, L., Giles, C.L.: Automatic tag recommendation algorithms for social recommender systems. ACM Trans. Web **5**(1), 1–31 (2011)
7. Niemann, K., Wolpers, M.: A new collaborative filtering approach for increasing the aggregate diversity of recommender systems. In: Proceedings of the 19th ACM SIGKDD International Conference on Knowledge Discovery and Data Mining, KDD 2013, pp. 955–963. ACM Press, New York (2013)
8. Niemann, K., Wolpers, M.: Usage context-boosted filtering for recommender systems in TEL. In: Hernández-Leo, D., Ley, T., Klamma, R., Harrer, A. (eds.) EC-TEL 2013. LNCS, vol. 8095, pp. 246–259. Springer, Heidelberg (2013)

9. Heymann, P., Ramage, D., Garcia-Molina, H.: Social tag prediction. In: Proceedings of the 31st Annual International ACM SIGIR Conference on Research and Development in Information Retrieval, SIGIR 2008, p. 531. ACM Press, New York (2008)
10. Song, Y., Zhuang, Z., Li, H., Zhao, Q., Li, J., Lee, W.c., Giles, C.L.: Real-time automatic tag recommendation. In: Proceedings of the 31st Annual International ACM SIGIR Conference on Research and Development in Information Retrieval, SIGIR 2008, p. 515. ACM Press, New York (2008)
11. Jäschke, R., Marinho, L., Hotho, A., Schmidt-Thieme, L., Stumme, G.: Tag recommendations in folksonomies. In: Kok, J.N., Koronacki, J., Lopez de Mantaras, R., Matwin, S., Mladenič, D., Skowron, A. (eds.) PKDD 2007. LNCS (LNAI), vol. 4702, pp. 506–514. Springer, Heidelberg (2007)
12. Rae, A., Keynes, M.: Improving tag recommendation using social networks. In: Proceedings of the 9th International Conference on Recherche d'Information Assistée par Ordinateur, RIAO 2010, pp. 92–99 (2010)
13. Diaz-Aviles, E., Fisichella, M., Kawase, R., Nejdl, W., Stewart, A.: Unsupervised auto-tagging for learning object enrichment. In: Kloos, C.D., Gillet, D., Crespo García, R.M., Wild, F., Wolpers, M. (eds.) EC-TEL 2011. LNCS, vol. 6964, pp. 83–96. Springer, Heidelberg (2011)
14. Verbert, K., Drachsler, H., Manouselis, N., Wolpers, M., Vuorikar, R., Duval, E.: Dataset-driven research for improving recommender systems for learning. In: Proceedings of the 1st International Conference on Learning Analytics and Knowledge, LAK 2011, pp. 44–53. ACM Press, New York(2011)
15. Stefaner, M., Dalla Vecchia, E., Condotta, M., Wolpers, M., Specht, M., Apelt, S., Duval, E.: MACE – enriching architectural learning objects for experience multiplication. In: Duval, E., Klamma, R., Wolpers, M. (eds.) EC-TEL 2007. LNCS, vol. 4753, pp. 322–336. Springer, Heidelberg (2007)
16. Schmitz, H.C., Wolpers, M., Kirschenmann, U., Niemann, K.: Contextualized attention metadata. In: Roda, C. (ed.) Human Attention in Digital Environments, pp. 186–209. Cambridge University Press, Cambridge (2011)
17. Vuorikari, R., Massart, D.: dataTEL challenge: european schoolnet's Travel well dataset. In: Manouselis, N., Drachsler, H., Verbert, K., Santos, O.C. (eds.) Proceedings of the 1st Workshop on Recommender Systems for Technology Enhanced Learning, RecSysTEL 2010, pp. 2773–2998. Elsevier - Procedia Computer Science (2010)
18. Saussure, F.: Cours de Linguistique Générale [Course in General Linguistics]. Kluwer Academic, Dordrecht (1916)
19. Heyer, G., Quasthof, U., Wittig, T.: Text Mining: Wissensrohstoff Text. Konzepte, Algorithmen, Ergebnisse. W3L GmbH, Bochum (2006)
20. Evert, S.: The statistics of word cooccurrences: word pairs and collocations (Dissertation). Ph.D. thesis, University Stuttgart (2004)
21. Evert, S.: Corpora and collocations. In: Lüdeling, A., Kytö, M. (eds.) Corpus Linguistics. An International Handbook, pp. 1197–1211. Mouton de gruyter, Berlin (2008)

On Modeling Learning Communities

Zinayida Petrushyna(✉), Ralf Klamma, and Milos Kravcik

Advanced Community Information Systems Group, RWTH Aachen University, Ahornstrasse 55, 52056 Aachen, Germany
{petrushyna,klamma,kravcik}@dbis.rwth-aachen.de

Abstract. The aim to support learning communities by Web 2.0 technology leads to their investigation through the prism of learning theories. However, self-observation and self-modeling requires appropriate tools and skills. In this paper we focus on users of a forum platform and propose several tools that perform community detection, social network analysis, text mining, natural language processing, and clustering. The outcomes serve as inputs for community models that are automatically established using the *i** information modeling approach. Stakeholders can recognize issues in their communities by visual analytics of the models. Based on this, they can refine community learning processes and community environments by retrieving new community requirements from the models. The process of model establishment was evaluated by experts in *i** information modeling and the results show their acceptance of the proposed techniques. This solution enables also support of various well-known modeling approaches (like IMS Learning Design).

Keywords: Learning communities · Modeling forum communities · Communities of practice · *i** Modeling

1 Introduction

Incalculable actions of users represent a major problem of information system development process. In Web 2.0, behavior of stakeholders has a huge impact on digital media sustainability. It is a challenge to model collective influence of users and retrieve their requirements regarding social media. The problem is applicable to learning communities emerging in digital media environments. In the past, success of learning depended mostly on communities of learners [1] and their activities [2–4]. With too few learner interactions communities become static and knowledge inside the communities does not change a lot [5]. If learners find a solution to a discussed issue and no more issues exist, there are no more reasons that can encourage the learners to new actions.

Learning communities have been transferred into the digital world where they have to consider social media as a new actor in their environment as well as the digital media have to react to community requirements. In our particular case and due to the abstract nature of models, we operate among others with

© Springer International Publishing Switzerland 2015
G. Conole et al. (Eds.): EC-TEL 2015, LNCS 9307, pp. 254–267, 2015.
DOI: 10.1007/978-3-319-24258-3_19

actors of communities that have no physical or technological representation. Following this we create more precise models reflecting views of learning theories on communities. Therefore, our research question is *how to model learning communities that have used digital media connecting technology and learning theories.* In this paper we continue the work on language learning forums [6] and community models [7]. We detect communities, their evolution and cluster community members' behavior based on their structural properties calculated with social network analysis [8]. Furthermore, we analyze community-generated content to detect community goals, topics and sentiments using information retrieval and text mining techniques. The results serve as inputs for a modeling service [9] that automatically create learning community models as $i*$ models [10]. In the following we discuss the related work, after that we introduce the data in Sect. 3 and the methods we use for experiments in Sect. 4. Later we present the outcomes of the modeling service in Sect. 5 and the evaluation of models in Sect. 6. The paper is ends with discussions and future work.

2 Related Work

In Technology Enhanced Learning there are many approaches to model learners [11–13], collaborative learning [14–19] and communities [20–22]. The type of modeling differs: there are computational models [20], models based on specifications [15,17] and conceptual models [14,21,22].

[14] modeled effective collaborative learning teams and emphasized the need of participation in a group by all group members to reach best results in a learned topic. A model of the approach correlates with needs of learning theories as it highlights common understanding, shared goals, helping each other and benefiting from each other. Tools for collaborative learning were designed and developed using the model. Even though, it did not consider communities and affordance of learning technologies that help to define learning communities states and explain failures of learners in case their goals are not fulfilled.

Many approaches modeled real-world collaborations using well-known specifications. [17] collected user interactions and maintained only profiles continuously using RDF representation. Both [13,23] modeled users based on their activities and properties that appeared in social media such as Twitter or Facebook. [13] utilized generic user modeling formats like Grapple Core and enriched user profiles with named entities [24] extracted from user texts. They concentrated on user profiles only, while [23] payed special attention to the social life of users. Their perspective allowed to capture cases when a user was a part of one or many different communities and networks. Even though, they focused on activities of users but not artifacts users operated with, such as e-mails, posts, or comments that are useful to model communities of practice [1].

Also IMS Learning Design (LD)[1] allows to model users, their roles and activities. But [25] and later [26] criticized IMS LD inflexibility in collaboration support and support of learner interactions. There is no possibility to interact for

[1] IMS LD http://www.imsglobal.org/learningdesign/, Last access on 23.05.2014.

learners unless appropriate services were initiated by a learning designer. Furthermore, user roles are static thus it is hard to adapt a learning environment to support different types of learners during runtime. Due to such flaws modeling possibilities are limited for the need of modeling communities. The extension of IMS LD from [15] considers many relevant aspects for collaborative learning such as learner activities and groups of users, but since it uses Unified Modeling Language it can hardly model social and intentional setting [27]. Although the reviewed approaches miss to model communities, user models may include valuable information for enriching learning community models.

One of the few solutions that considered theoretical aspects of communities together with technologies to model communities is represented by [21] that was refined later in [22]. For modeling, they considered characteristics of individual users, relations between these users, and user knowledge in learning topics. The authors chose organizational psychology as a background for community modeling. They emphasized (1) relationships between individuals and their knowledge, (2) shared mental models that respect shared content and domain understanding, and (3) cognitive consensus that let community members find solutions collaboratively. [21] modeled the flow of knowledge between individuals but not between communities and individuals. The continuation of the work resulted in community knowledge sharing patterns [22] that considered different types of users and provided notifications that may explain community problems. Similarly, [20] regarded learning theories and generated advices for learners according to their communication activities, types of discussion messages, group interaction patterns and group cohesiveness. Nevertheless, a representation of communities using a modeling approach was out of the research scope.

Other existing works operated with communities of learners and their outcomes included learning community analysis that can refine community models. For example, [18] investigated communities of learners during their collaboration in chats and forums. Their framework resulted in content and collaboration analysis. Class activities captured in Moodle allowed to create activity-based learner models of students [12] that consisted of learning processes and acquired competences information. [11] as well modeled students and provided the information about their peers to invoke self-assessment and self-reflection processes. [28] described tools that analyzed and visualized student activities and their key skills. [29] detected scaffolding patterns analyzing forum threads. Outcomes of mentioned approaches can be used for creating, refining, and maintaining community models. Furthermore, tracking of mobile activities [30] or activities in development tools [31] and connection of these with learning processes can extend community models further. Or the models can be enriched by other indicators that are defined by learners themselves [32].

Presented approaches are quite promising, but they focus mainly on users and communities of learning environments in formal settings. Such a focus is relevant for community stakeholders to reflect community experience though it is not enough to explicitly model an influence of communities on the development process of digital media as well as community requirements. Just a few consider learning theories requirements that are important for learning community modeling. Our approach addresses these omissions.

3 Data Collection

Forums represent popular social software for learning communities. Learners can share their knowledge, ask questions, get feedback and suggestions. Most realized forums include basic functionalities like posting, quoting and creating a new thread. Some others classify users according to the amount of published posts.

3.1 Forum as a Learning Community

Forums let learners organize Communities of Practice (CoP) [1]. Forum environments afford learners to interact with each other through posting in threads. Due to these interactions the learners are engaged in collaborations that are based on trust of learners to each other. These interactions reflect the CoP mutual engagement dimension (D_1). The other joint enterprises dimension (D_2) echoes by participating in forum environments, following their rules and supporting the general idea or goal of a community. The shared repertoire dimension (D_3) is supported by forum communities since they are organized around particular topics interested to all community members.

Studies of forums in the learning context showed benefits for learners in academic performance [33,34] and benefits additionally to formal learning [35,36]. For example, [37] found that learners who participated more actively in a forum were more successful with academic achievements. There is the need of understanding student interactions as they can affect student knowledge evaluation and student motivation and help design learning environments efficiently [38].

3.2 Data

In this experiment we focus on language learning forums URCH[2]. Here usually users prepare for the English tests such as TOEFL, GMAT, or GRE. They discuss exercises of the tests, share essays, write and ask for feedback from other forum users. We analyze the URCH forums where users deal with learning for the tests while we leave off-topic forums out of consideration.

The data from the forum is collected using the Mediabase Forumwatcher and stored in the Mediabase [39]. The schema of the Mediabase emphasizes different actors such as Media, Agent, Process, Artifact and Network. Such a schema facilitates modeling of community environments emphasizing human and non-human actors.

We crawled learning forums from URCH covering a period of 10 years [6]. As a result we collected 429 K of posts that have been done by 21 K of users that

[2] URCH forums http://www.urch.com/forums/forum.php, Last access on 20.04.2014.

created 67 K threads. The longest depth of a thread is 318 messages while the average depth is 6 messages. Messages are written in English and can include up to 105 K characters, in average a message included 360 characters.

4 Methods

Before we introduce the methods, we explain our method selection supported by [39]. Since we focus on informal learning, the communities are formed without given boundaries. Therefore, for the analysis we need to turn to community detection and evolution algorithms since they allow to deal with complex calculations of numerous highly fluctuating communities. In our choice we rely on D_1, D_2 and D_3 of CoP. D_1 estimates collaborations, thus roles of community users depend on their collaborations that can be represented through relations to other learners (e.g. learner-to-learner interactions) and therefore require a social network analysis technique [8] to detect the roles. Except of collaborations, goals and sentiments have been shared between community users according to D_2 and D_3. To detect goals we appeal to Natural Language Processing techniques for tagging words with parts of speech and detecting particular syntactic patterns. Creating classifiers based on training sets and available vocabularies, we detect sets of sentiments that characterize communities. Moreover, data mining of community texts specifies community expertise (D_3) that can be represented by discussed topics and retrieved using Named Entity Recognition [24].

4.1 Community Detection and Evolution

Before detecting communities we need to define how to design networks where the communities are going to be find. Since we are interested in a learner-to-learner interactions we reconstruct them from the Mediabase using learner-to-resource interactions. Particularly, posts of learners define their belonging to a community since posts are devoted to a thread that connect all learners with each other.

Communities we consider are short-term and dynamic. Therefore we regard the time component in their analysis. Particularly, we divide the observed period into time intervals. Each interval is used to take snapshots of a forum network that include nodes and edges actual for the time interval. Communities, tightly connected groups, are detected in these snapshots using the Louvain algorithm [40]. After that we define a strategy for mapping communities in different time snapshots. With this strategy we can define evolution of communities, e.g. community states in two different snapshots.

The communities c_{i_j} and c_{i_k} in the snapshot s_i include non-overlapping sets in the time interval $interval_i$.

$$\forall j, k : c_{i_j} \cap c_{i_k} = \emptyset, \text{ where } \left\{c_{i_k}, c_{i_j}\right\} \in s_i,\ c_{i_k}(U) \subseteq U_i \text{ and } c_{i_j}(U) \subseteq U_i \text{ and } \\ k \neq j, \text{ where } U_i \text{ is a set of all users in the snapshot } s_i$$

All users from communities c_{i_j} and c_{i_k} are in the set of users U_i. The snapshots s_i, s_r are defined by time intervals $interval_i \neq interval_r, r = i + 1$. Community users of these snapshots c_{i_j} and c_{r_k} may belong to sets of users in both snapshots

$$c_{i_j}(U) \subseteq U_i, c_{r_k}(U) \subseteq U_r$$
$$c_{i_j} \in s_i \ , c_{r_k} \in s_r$$
$$\exists j \exists k : c_{i_j}(U) \cap c_{r_k}(U) \subseteq U_i \cap U_r \neq \emptyset$$

The algorithms maps communities if the communities appear in consecutive snapshots and the modified Jaccard similarity [41] of the communities meets the given threshold.

$$Sim(c_{i_j}(U), c_{r_k}(U)) = max(\frac{c_{i_j}(U) \cap c_{r_k}(U)}{c_{i_j}(U)}, \frac{c_{r_k}(U) \cap c_{i_j}(U)}{c_{r_k}(U)}) >= threshold$$
$$threshold \in \{0, 1\}$$

If communities exist only in one snapshot, they are left unmapped. This strategy allows finding evolving communities where the number of users increase or decrease. Other community evolution events as split or merge are not captured.

4.2 Community Analysis

Forum posts consists of language items such as texts that are results of mental processes [42]. Therefore, investigating content of users' texts reveals reified user knowledge, goals, and emotional attitude to a discussed topic. Such an analysis responds to the requirements from CoP to consider *joint enterprises* and *shared repertoire* dimensions.

For investigating positive and negative texts and discovering texts indicating cognitive work we utilize Linguistic Inquiry and Word Count (LIWC) vocabulary [43]. Based on it we create training sets with 150 K sentences that help us to define emotional posts or posts denoting cognitive work from 1,700K posts.

Further analysis of texts is based on extraction of named entities, arguments of information units, and mapping them with entities from Linked Open Data Cloud[3]. We choose Open Calais[4] as it concentrates on extracting relevant concepts from social media. It outputs machine-readable RDF (Resource Description Framework) files with all the information about requested texts. We store RDF files in the RDF repository Sesame[5].

The way how people acquire knowledge and perform tasks depends on their goals [44]. Intents, parts of goals, are important to understand *joint enterprises* of learning communities. We detect more than 132 K intent phrases in the URCH forum [6]. In average each fourth post includes an intent.

Patterns of community users are extracted by firstly generating community networks where forum users are nodes and their collaborations are edges, i.e., users in a forum thread organize a complete graph. Later measures like inverse connectiveness (C) and betweenness (B) [8] are computed. Using k-means clustering algorithm we find groups of users with similar measures. The most relevant are

---

[3] Linked Open Data cloud http://lod-cloud.net, Last access on 07.05.2014.

[4] The home page of Open Calais http://www.opencalais.com/, Last access on 06.10.2014.

[5] Java framework for processing and handling RDF data http://rdf4j.org/, Last access on 20.02.2015.

betweenness and less relevant is closeness centralities. Found groups are questioners ($C \approx 2$, $B > 3$)that used to ask a lot of questions, answering persons ($C \approx 3$, $B > 4$) that used to answer questions, newbies ($C \approx 1$, B$\approx$ 0) that are new in communities, usual users ($C \approx 1.5$, B$\approx$ 0) that participate ordinary in forums both asking and answering questions and conversationalists ($C \approx 4$, B$\approx$ 0) that prefer to participate in discussions much more than others.

4.3 Community Modeling

We use *i** modeling approach that highlights dependencies between actors and is appropriate to model social and intentional settings [27]. *i** stands for distributed intentionality that spreads on social networks of autonomous actors [45]. It allows to emphasize different individuals that are relevant for learning communities, dependencies between community learners, community learners and communities, people-based actors and technology-based actors. Furthermore, *i** depicts dependencies of various types such as goal, softgoal, task and resource dependencies. [46] modeled a community using the *i** modeling approach but learning processes were not in the focus of the work.

In our recent work [9] we presented the i*-REST services that allow to create i* models automatically. We use the services to generate *i** models after community analysis is performed. The services create models in iStarML format, the extension of XML, store them and visualize as SVG files.

5 Results

We model communities that are mapped (Sect. 4.1), analyzed (Sect. 4.2) and have at least three members. As a result, we operate with 132 communities.

Figure 1 shows a community with 44 users. We use ids of users instead of their names to avoid privacy issues. The community includes twenty two *questioners*, five *newbies* and sixteen *usual users* in the community. Therefore, based on the distribution of roles we can assume that the model represents a question-answer community where threads consist from questions and answers and no further discussions [7]. Some of the users have goal dependencies on the *Community* actor. These goal dependencies specify intents that users have and want to achieve with the help of their community. Examples of these goals are *how to solve ans*, *want to resolve problem*, *wanted to solve question* and others. These consist of detected parts of sentences that can better explain learner goals. Other dependencies are trivial like the *Community post* in the *Forum*. The *Threads keep a Forum alive*. The *Named Entities*, detected topics, *appear* in the content of the *Threads* because *talks about* or *use* them.

Figure 2 shows a set of intentional phrases of one user. It is an example of additional information that appear as a tooltip in a SVG representation of a community model. Users of models can retrieve not only intents but as well titles of *Threads* and topics of threads (*NE* actor) to clarify topics of communities and their expertise. Further tooltips provide information (1) about user characteristics, (2) about average values of all characteristics for the *Community* actor that

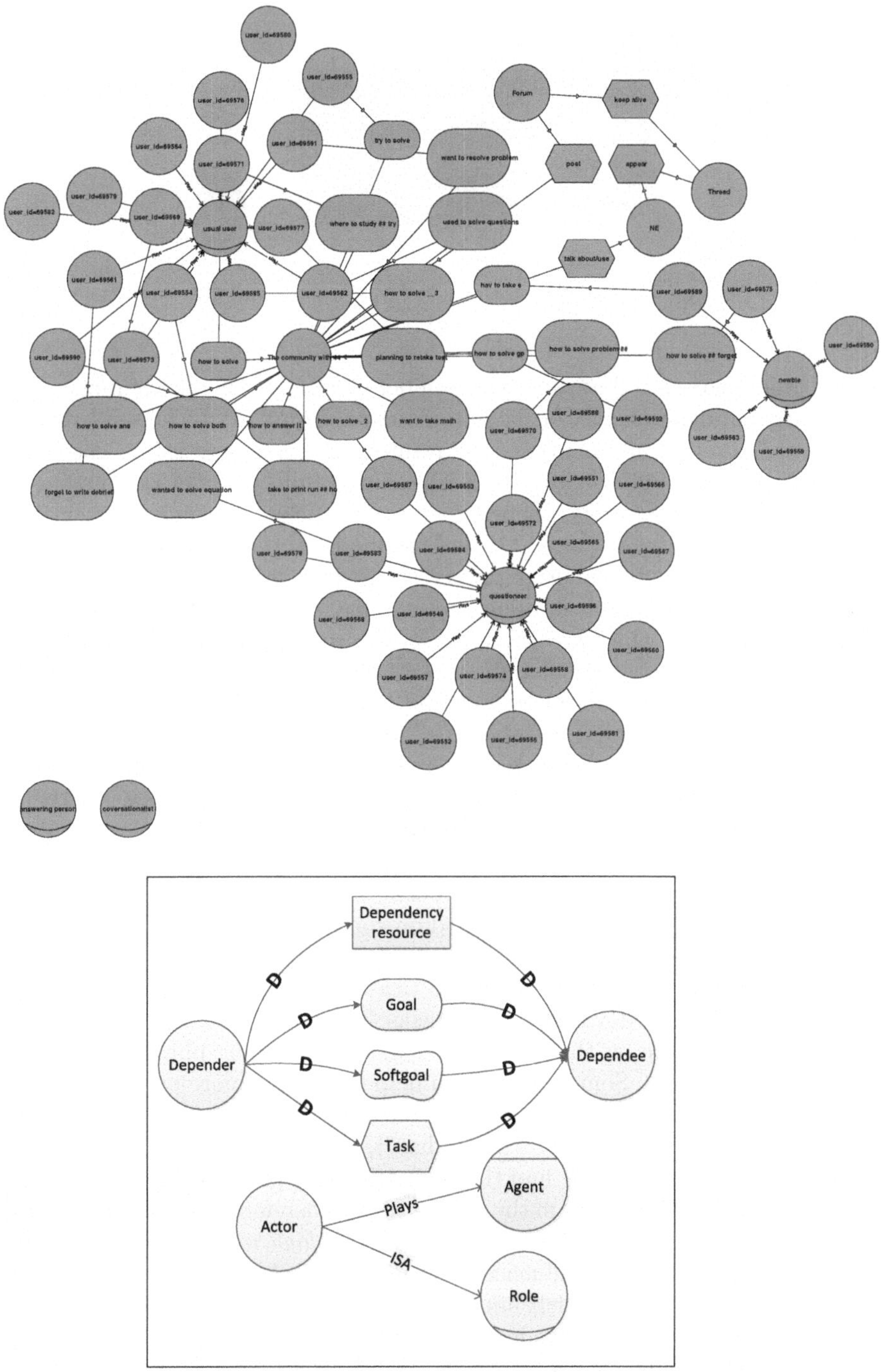

Fig. 1. A model of the community with 44 users

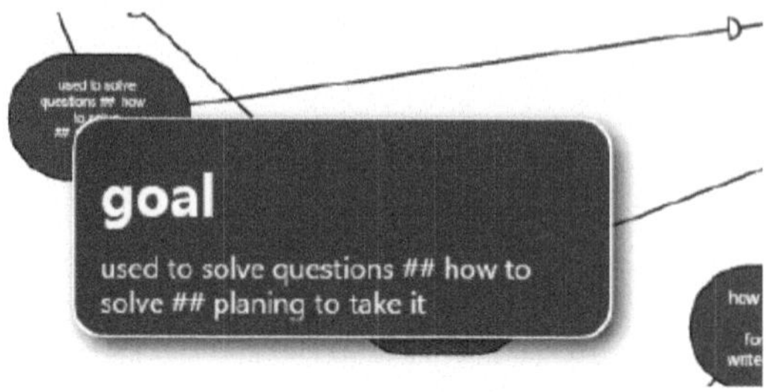

Fig. 2. Intents of one of users from the community

include other statistical data such as a number of users, (3) about characteristics of the roles that define ranges of characteristics according to which users are affiliated with the role. Emotional analysis resulted in characteristics for each user and community. The information that is retrieved from a model can further be used to classify communities, define experts, recommend learning partners and communities [39]. Figures 1 and 2 depict the model of the same community but colors of model elements and other properties used for visualization are different.

Figure 3 presents models of a community that has two states, i.e. an initial and an evolved state, which are defined according to our strategy. The models are automatically generated but the representation on Fig. 3 was done manually to facilitate the comparison. One model represents the state of the community between December, 1 and December, 10, 2004. The other shows the community between December, 08 and December, 17, 2004. We choose such short time frames since interests of community users are devoted to short-term tasks therefore we assume that community lives are short as well.

We can get some trivial statistical data such as the number of posts, the number of users and the number of adjacent nodes[6] from the community models. *High* and *low influence users* are defined based on connectiveness and betweenness of users [8].

We also include word clouds of thread titles for both communities. For both communities topics are devoted to math tasks. The phrases we discovered during the intent analysis are on the bottom of Fig. 3. All learning phrases define the desire of users to learn. Some phrases can help to identify more precise information about goals by investigating sentences where learning phrases appear, e.g., *how to answer* (what?), *need to learn* (what?), (what?) *take to solve* (what?).

Comparing two models we find that the number of posts and users decreases so the user activity diminishes in the second state. Therefore, the number of adjacent nodes is decreasing as well as the number of *high influence users* though some of them may have less influence and thus become *low influence users*. Trivial statistical data of the models and information discovered by applying social network analysis reveal changes in community activities that can be caused by

[6] It clarifies how central the communities are.

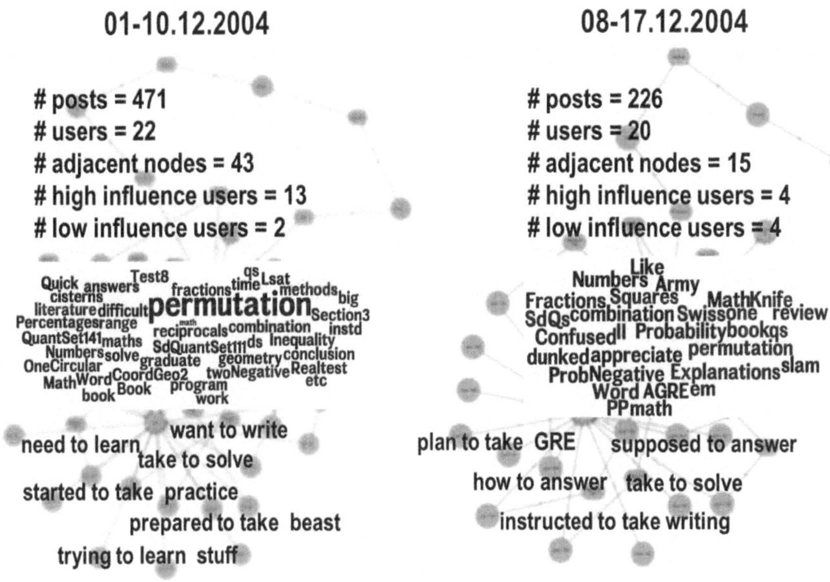

Fig. 3. Example of 2 models of an evolving community

disinterest of community members in community topic. The depicted community can not be found later in time since their users are not connected tightly enough. Therefore, we state that the community became dead after two previously described states.

6 Evaluation of Models

Since the evaluation of technology results has been partly done for [6], we concentrate on the evaluation of technologies used for models. It was conducted within the seventh i^* workshop[7] in Thessaloniki [47]. Twenty one experts in i* modeling answered a survey that aims, among other things, to evaluate techniques that are used to support community needs. The inter-rater reliability or agreement between authors is not reliable according to the Krippendorff's alpha (0.0056) [48] that may lie on the number of experts. Anyway, we find that the majority found social network analysis (15/21) and intent analysis (19/21) *relevant or more or less relevant* for the i^* model generation. Six of participants found *social network analysis* and two found *goal mining* less relevant. The rates for *community detection & evolution* are distributed between *relevant* (5/21), *more or less relevant* (6/21) and *average* (3/21) rates. Most participants agreed that *named entity recognition* technique is *more or less relevant* (11/21).

Another question of the survey estimates if *community stakeholders* - teachers, instructors, community managers of learning communities - *can follow changes*

[7] i^* workshop in 2014 http://istar14.wordpress.com/, Last access on 8.10.2014.

in communities and recognize problems and conflicts just by following i models.* Most of experts divided into those who agreed with the statement (9/21) and those who more or less agreed (9/21) with the statement. Some experts commented that *i** models can be *abstract* and *not straightforward.* Therefore, *training is required* before community stakeholders can use models for analyzing their communities.

Results of the evaluation show the acceptance of the used techniques between i* modeling experts. Moreover the evaluation indicates that *i** models are promising for community stakeholders' usage, though some limitations addressed in the next section need to be considered.

7 Discussions and Future Work

In this paper we introduce an approach for learning community modeling. The general idea of the approach is to describe influence of learning communities on digital media and vice versa. The solution supports learning community stakeholders in estimating situations of communities and their requirements. The models are designed respecting CoP dimensions [1] and classical models [7]. Analyses of interactions of community members, community texts and intents are performed reacting on the dimensions. The results are used for automatic establishment of community models. The modelling of learning communities can be exploited for various purposes, including reflection of their current statuses, prediction of future development, recommendation of adjustments and actions, adaptation of shared environment, comparison of different CoPs or of one in various moments, simulation of CoP development.

Nevertheless, the current work includes various shortcomings. First of all, the readability of models has to be refined. Since i* modeling approach is complex, their visual representation need to be improved so that models become as clear as social network graphs. Moreover, the conducted evaluation estimated only the usage of technologies and models from the view of modeling experts. In the future we need to evaluate models in real settings with stakeholders, focusing on support the models provide to them. The approach presents only a part of information we know about communities and their members. Deeper analysis of texts and user activities as well as communities can contribute positively to the community modeling. Furthermore, models have to be adopted for different types of community stakeholders to emphasize important information depending on the type. Using the expertise of our group in near-real time collaborative modeling, the environment can be extended in the future to enable changing positions of actors, adding new actors and their dependencies, as well as working collaboratively on models using browsers [49,50]. Such an extension will refine the modeling process.

Acknowledgments. The work of Zinayida Petrushyna was supported by NRW State within the B-IT Research School and RWTH Aachen University. This work was partially funded within the FP7 ICT Work Programme of the European Community: *Learning Layers - Scaling up Technologies for Informal Learning in SME Clusters* (http://www.learning-layers.eu, grant no: 318209).

References

1. Wenger, E.: Communities of Practice: Learning, Meaning, and Identity. Cambridge University Press, Cambridge (1998)
2. Vygotsky, L.: Mind in Society: The Development of Higher Psychological Processes. Harvard University Press, Cambridge (1978)
3. Engeström, Y.: Learning by Expanding. Orienta-Konsultit Oy, Cambridge (1987)
4. Iandoli, L., Zollo, G.: Organizational Cognition and Learning: Building Systems for the Learning Organization. Information Science Pub, Hershey (2008)
5. Roberts, J.: Limits to communities of practice. J. Manage. Stud. **43**(3), 623–639 (2006)
6. Krenge, J.A., Petrushyna, Z., Kravcik, M., Klamma, R.: Identification of learning goals in forum-based communities. In: Proceedings of the 11th ICALT, pp. 307–309 (2011)
7. Petrushyna, Z., Klamma, R., Kravcik, M.: Designing during use: modeling of communities of practice. In: Proceedings of 4th IEEE DEST, pp. 612–617 (2010)
8. Wasserman, S., Faust, K.: Social Network Analysis: Methods and Applications. Cambridge University Press, Cambridge (1994)
9. Petrushyna, Z., Ruppert, A., Klamma, R., Renzel, D., Jarke, M.: i*-REST: lightweight i* modeling with RESTful web services. In: Proceedings of the 7th International i* Workshop at the 26th CAiSE (2014)
10. Yu, E.S.K.: Towards modelling and reasoning support for early-phase requirements engineering. In: Proceedings of the 3rd RE, pp. 226–235 (1997)
11. Brusilovsky, P., Hsiao, I.-H., Folajimi, Y.: QuizMap: open social student modeling and adaptive navigation support with treemaps. In: Kloos, C.D., Gillet, D., Crespo García, R.M., Wild, F., Wolpers, M. (eds.) EC-TEL 2011. LNCS, vol. 6964, pp. 71–82. Springer, Heidelberg (2011)
12. Florian, B., Glahn, C., Drachsler, H., Specht, M., Fabregat Gesa, R.: Activity-based learner-models for learner monitoring and recommendations in moodle. In: Kloos, C.D., Gillet, D., Crespo García, R.M., Wild, F., Wolpers, M. (eds.) EC-TEL 2011. LNCS, vol. 6964, pp. 111–124. Springer, Heidelberg (2011)
13. Abel, F., Celik, I., Hauff, C., Hollink, L., Houben, G.J.: U-Sem: semantic enrichment, user modeling and mining of usage data on the social web. In: Proceedings of USEWOD2011 at the 20th WWW Conference (2011)
14. Soller, A.: Supporting social interaction in an intelligent collaborative learning system. IJAIED **12**, 40–62 (2001)
15. Nodenot, T., Marquesuzaá, C., Laforcade, P., Sallaberry, C.: Model based engineering of learning situations for adaptive web based educational systems. In: Proceedings of the 13th WWW Conference, pp. 94–103 (2004)
16. Rebedea, T., Dascalu, M., Trausan-Matu, S., Banica, D., Gartner, A., Chiru, C., Mihaila, D.: Overview and preliminary results of using PolyCAFe for collaboration analysis and feedback generation. In: Wolpers, M., Kirschner, P.A., Scheffel, M., Lindstaedt, S., Dimitrova, V. (eds.) EC-TEL 2010. LNCS, vol. 6383, pp. 420–425. Springer, Heidelberg (2010)
17. Settouti, L., Guin, N., Luengo, V., Mille, A.: Adaptable and reusable query patterns for trace-based learner modelling. In: Kloos, C.D., Gillet, D., Crespo García, R.M., Wild, F., Wolpers, M. (eds.) EC-TEL 2011. LNCS, vol. 6964, pp. 384–397. Springer, Heidelberg (2011)

18. Nistor, N., Dascalu, M., Trausan-Matu, S., Mihaila, D., Baltes, B., Smeaton, G.: Virtual communities of practice in academia: automated analysis of collaboration based on the social knowledge-building model. In: Hernández-Leo, D., Ley, T., Klamma, R., Harrer, A. (eds.) EC-TEL 2013. LNCS, vol. 8095, pp. 623–624. Springer, Heidelberg (2013)
19. Trausan-Matu, S., Dascalu, M., Rebedea, T.: PolyCAFe–automatic support for the polyphonic analysis of CSCL chats. Int. J. Comput. Support. Collab. Learn. **9**(2), 127–156 (2014)
20. Suh, H.J., Lee, S.W.: Collaborative learning agent for promoting group interaction. ETRI **28**(4), 461–474 (2006)
21. Kleanthous, S., Dimitrova, V.: Semantic enhanced approach for modelling cognitive relationships in virtual communities. In: Proceedings of SociUM Workshop held at the 11th International Conference on UM (2007)
22. Kleanthous, S., Dimitrova, V.: Analyzing community knowledge sharing behavior. In: De Bra, P., Kobsa, A., Chin, D. (eds.) UMAP 2010. LNCS, vol. 6075, pp. 231–242. Springer, Heidelberg (2010)
23. Karam, R., Fraternali, P., Bozzon, A., Galli, L.: Modeling end-users as contributors in human computation applications. In: Abelló, A., Bellatreche, L., Benatallah, B. (eds.) MEDI 2012. LNCS, vol. 7602, pp. 3–15. Springer, Heidelberg (2012)
24. Grishman, R., Sundheim, B.: Message understanding conference-6: a brief history. In: Proceedings of GOLING, pp. 466–471 (1996)
25. Paramythis, A.: Adaptive support for collaborative learning with ims learning design: are we there yet. In: Proceedings of the Workshop on Adaptive Collaboration Support, held at the 5th International Conference on AH, pp. 17–29 (2008)
26. Derntl, M., Neumann, S., Oberhuemer, P.: Lost in Interaction in IMS learning design runtime environments. Edu. Technol. Soc. **17**(3), 332–342 (2014)
27. Mylopoulos, J.: Information modeling in the time of the revolution. Inf. Syst. **23**(3–4), 127–155 (1998)
28. Harrer, A., Pfahler, K., de Groot, R., Abdu, R.: Research on collaborative planning and reflection – methods and tools in the metafora project. In: Hernández-Leo, D., Ley, T., Klamma, R., Harrer, A. (eds.) EC-TEL 2013. LNCS, vol. 8095, pp. 139–150. Springer, Heidelberg (2013)
29. Tammets, K., Laanpere, M., Ley, T., Pata, K.: Identifying problem-based scaffolding patterns in an online forum for construction professionals. In: Hernández-Leo, D., Ley, T., Klamma, R., Harrer, A. (eds.) EC-TEL 2013. LNCS, vol. 8095, pp. 526–531. Springer, Heidelberg (2013)
30. Tabuenca, B., Kalz, M., Specht, M.: Lifelong learning hub: a seamless tracking tool for mobile learning. In: de Freitas, S., Rensing, C., Ley, T., Muñoz-Merino, P.J. (eds.) EC-TEL 2014. LNCS, vol. 8719, pp. 534–537. Springer, Heidelberg (2014)
31. Karkalas, S., Gutierrez-Santos, S.: Eclipse student (in)activity detection tool. In: de Freitas, S., Rensing, C., Ley, T., Muñoz-Merino, P.J. (eds.) EC-TEL 2014. LNCS, vol. 8719, pp. 572–573. Springer, Heidelberg (2014)
32. Ruipérez-Valiente, J.A., Muñoz-Merino, P.J., Kloos, C.D.: A demonstration of ALAS-KA: a learning analytics tool for the khan academy platform. In: de Freitas, S., Rensing, C., Ley, T., Muñoz-Merino, P.J. (eds.) EC-TEL 2014. LNCS, vol. 8719, pp. 518–521. Springer, Heidelberg (2014)
33. Davies, J., Graff, M.: Performance in e-learning: online participation and student grades. Br. J. Edu. Technol. **36**(4), 657–663 (2005)
34. Morris, L.V., Finnegan, C., Wu, S.S.: Tracking student behavior, persistence, and achievement in online courses. Internet High. Edu. **8**(3), 221–231 (2005)

35. Deslauriers, L., Schelew, E., Wieman, C.: Improved learning in a large-enrollment physics class. Sci. **332**(6031), 862–864 (2011)
36. Palmer, S., Holt, D., Bray, S.: Does the discussion help? the impact of a formally assessed online discussion on final student results. Br. J. Edu. Technol. **39**(5), 847–858 (2008)
37. Carceller, C., Dawson, S., Lockyer, L.: Improving academic outcomes: does participating in online discussion forums payoff? Int. J. Technol. Enhanced Learn. **5**(2), 117–132 (2013)
38. Anderson, A., Huttenlocher, D., Kleinberg, J., Leskovec, J.: Engaging with massive online courses. In: Proceedings of the 23rd WWW Conference, pp. 687–698 (2014)
39. Klamma, R.: Community learning analytics – challenges and opportunities. In: Wang, J.-F., Lau, R. (eds.) ICWL 2013. LNCS, vol. 8167, pp. 284–293. Springer, Heidelberg (2013)
40. Blondel, V.D., Guillaume, J.L., Lambiotte, R., Lefebvre, E.: Fast unfolding of communities in large networks. J. Stat. Mech. **10**, P10008 (2008)
41. Gliwa, B., Saganowski, S., Zygmunt, A., Bródka, P., Kazienko, P., Kozlak, J.: Identification of group changes in blogosphere. In: Proceedings of ASONAM, pp. 1201–1206 (2012)
42. Ferguson, R., Wei, Z., He, Y., Buckingham Shum, S.: An evaluation of learning analytics to identify exploratory dialogue in online discussions. In: Proceedings of the 3rd LAK Conference, pp. 85–93 (2013)
43. Pennebaker, J.W., Chung, C.K., Ireland, M., Gonzales, A., Booth, R.J.: The Development and Psychometric Properties of LIWC2007 (2007)
44. Zukier, H.: The paradigmatic and narrative modes in goal-guided inference. In: Handbook of motivation and cognition: Foundations of social behavior, pp. 465–502. Guilford Press, New York (1986)
45. Yu, E.S.: Social modeling and *i**. In: Borgida, A.T., Chaudhri, V.K., Giorgini, P., Yu, E.S. (eds.) Conceptual Modeling: Foundations and Applications. LNCS, vol. 5600, pp. 99–121. Springer, Heidelberg (2009)
46. Ferreira, T.L., da Silva, A.R.: Foster an implicit community based on a newsletter tracking system. In: Meersman, R., Panetto, H., Dillon, T., Rinderle-Ma, S., Dadam, P., Zhou, X., Pearson, S., Ferscha, A., Bergamaschi, S., Cruz, I.F. (eds.) OTM 2012, Part I. LNCS, vol. 7565, pp. 398–415. Springer, Heidelberg (2012)
47. Dalpiaz, F., Horkoff, J., eds.: Proceedings of the 7th International i* Workshop at the 26th CAiSE, vol. 1157, CEUR (2014)
48. Krippendorff, K.: Estimating the reliability, systematic error, and random error of interval data. Edu. Psychol. Meas. **30**(1), 61–70 (1970)
49. Derntl, M., Nicolaescu, P., Terkik, B., Klamma, R.: SynC-LD: synchronous collaborative IMS learning design authoring on the web. In: Hernández-Leo, D., Ley, T., Klamma, R., Harrer, A. (eds.) EC-TEL 2013. LNCS, vol. 8095, pp. 540–543. Springer, Heidelberg (2013)
50. Nicolaescu, P., Derntl, M., Klamma, R.: Browser-based collaborative modeling in near real-time. In: Proceedings of the 9th IEEE Collaboratecom 2013, pp. 335–344 (2013)

Studying Teacher Orchestration Load in Technology-Enhanced Classrooms
A Mixed-Method Approach and Case Study

Luis P. Prieto(✉), Kshitij Sharma, and Pierre Dillenbourg

CHILI Lab, École Polytechnique Fédérale de Lausanne, Lausanne, Switzerland
{luis.prieto,kshitij.sharma,pierre.dillenbourg}@epfl.ch

Abstract. Teacher orchestration of technology-enhanced learning (TEL) processes plays a major role in students' outcomes, especially in face-to-face classrooms. However, few studies look into the fine-grained details of how such orchestration unfolds, the challenges and cognitive overload that using technologies at a classroom level pose for teachers. This paper proposes a mixed-method approach to the study of orchestration cognitive load, combining physio-behavioural (eye-tracking) and subjective measurements (questionnaires, stimulated recall interviews). We illustrate the approach by applying it to study the orchestration of two technology-enhanced geometry lessons, by a secondary school teacher. The results of our mixed-method analyses highlight the difficulty of classroom-level (as opposed to individual- or group-level) interactions, especially in modelling students' progress and understanding. Such insights can be useful in the design of new classroom technologies, and to focus researchers' attention on critical orchestration episodes during their evaluation.

Keywords: Orchestration load · Eye-tracking · Stimulated recall · Cognitive load · Classroom studies

1 Introduction

Teacher facilitation of the learning process plays a crucial role in students' learning outcomes, especially in co-located settings (see, e.g., [14,19]). TEL researchers have recognized this importance, and the unique challenges that practitioners face when applying technological innovations to their everyday practice, under the term 'orchestration' [22], often defined as "the process of productively coordinating supportive interventions across multiple learning activities occurring at multiple social levels" [11].

Although the term 'orchestration' has rapidly gained traction within the TEL research community, its current use is rather varied, even confusing (e.g., [22] identifies up to eight different aspects TEL researchers refer to when talking about orchestration). Taking the metaphor of orchestration as "classroom-level", or "third circle" usability (individual and small-group usability being

© Springer International Publishing Switzerland 2015
G. Conole et al. (Eds.): EC-TEL 2015, LNCS 9307, pp. 268–281, 2015.
DOI: 10.1007/978-3-319-24258-3_20

the first two [12]), we find that classroom-level technology usability studies are still in its infancy, undoubtedly due to the technical and logistic difficulties of doing research about such a complex activity, within the multiple constraints of authentic classroom conditions [25].

Current studies on the orchestration of novel educational technologies are normally based on ad-hoc quantitative measurements of efficiency (e.g., [1]), or on the combination of keen researcher observation and subjective questioning of the actors (e.g., [17]), majoritarily looking at whole sessions as the unit of analysis (i.e., "did the lesson work well?"). More recently, there have also been attempts to do finer-grained quantitative analyses of orchestration, using mobile eye-tracking [23,24]. However, we are still far from the current state on individual usability studies (e.g., website usability), in which the researcher can rely on an array of qualitative and quantitative methods to study the (admittedly, simpler) user tasks of interest, both from behavioral/physiological, and subjective perspectives. Paraphrasing Bob Bailey in his account of early usability studies in the 1970s, most classroom orchestration studies are "focused simply on determining if three or four participants were able to complete the tasks" [3].

This paper proposes *a novel approach to study instances of technology-enhanced, face-to-face orchestration, combining multiple methods for data gathering and analysis.* Our ultimate goal with this approach is to gain a deeper understanding of the orchestration process at different granularity levels, with the aim of obtaining insights to guide the design (and aid in the evaluation) of new classroom technologies that can overcome the unique challenges of orchestrating such classrooms.

After a section describing related work on orchestration studies, orchestration load and cognitive load as an important factor in it, we present our mixed-methods approach to the study of orchestration instances. The approach is illustrated through its application on a case study that recently took place in a school in Switzerland, in which a teacher conducted two 80 min lessons on geometry (with different groups of students) using laptops and other common classroom technologies. We conclude the paper with a discussion of the main implications of our results and future research lines derivating from this work.

2 Related Work

2.1 Orchestration and Usability at the Classroom Level

The complex challenges of classroom management are by no means a new topic in educational literature. The classroom has always been recognized as a highly-demanding public space with its own history, where multiple activities take place simultaneously, with high immediacy and unpredictability [13]. Once digital technologies started being integrated in the classroom, it became clear that technology not always provided solutions to these pressures, also adding a new layer of complexity to them. In TEL, this notion of managing multiple activities at different social levels using multiple technological tools, often in a formal education setting, has become known as'orchestration' [11,22,25].

Dillenbourg and colleagues, from a technology designer perspective, have put forward the notion of 'designing for orchestration', drawing the parallelism with the notions of usability for individuals (long studied by human-computer interaction) and for small groups (focus of computer-supported collaborative work/learning). Thus, classroom technologies should be designed to cope with the pressures and constraints of whole-classroom usage [12]. In this line, several authors have started putting forward guidelines for the design of classroom technologies, drawing from their experience testing technologies in authentic educational settings [8, 10, 17]: the establishment of mutual and class-wide awareness mechanisms, providing teachers with means of controlling the flow of activities and improvisedly adapting it, or dividing activities into sequences of phases, are some of the most commonly appearing ones.

These insights and guidelines are invariably derived from keen observation and reflection of the researcher team after trying out a certain technology or set of technologies for a few times in authentic classroom conditions. While this kind of expert advice is certainly very useful when designing new technologies for use in the classroom, as TEL researchers we still lack a systematic way of studying the process of orchestration in any technology-enhanced classroom, beyond reflecting (or asking the teacher) about 'how the session went'. As usability pioneers Gould and Lewis stated, usable computer systems require (1) an early and continual focus on users; (2) iterative design and testing; and (3) empirical measurement of usage [15]. The first two are already a part of how many TEL researchers approach technological innovation in the classroom. The third one is made very difficult by the simultaneity and immediacy of face-to-face classroom activities. If we want to produce technologies that are usable while performing such multi-dimensional task, gathering empirical evidence of how the process unfolds, not only at the temporal scale of a 60 min session, but also in more fine-grained critical episodes of minutes or even seconds will prove unvaluable (what Newell denominates the 'rational' and 'cognitive' bands of action [18]).

2.2 Orchestration Load, Cognitive Load and Its Measurement

One prominent notion appearing frequently in recent TEL literature is 'orchestration load', that is, "the effort necessary for the teacher – and other actors – to conduct learning activities" at the class-wide level [8]. Currently, orchestration load is still a fuzzy and abstract concept, but we can safely assert that it has a physical component (e.g., moving around the class, handing out worksheets to students) and a cognitive side as well (remembering the content to be explained, modelling students' learning progress, deciding how to adapt the lesson plan). In a TEL classroom, the cognitive part of orchestration is a more interesting focus of study. Fortunately, cognitive load (related to the executive control of working memory, and the limited capacity of human cognitive processing capacity [20]) has been widely studied in psychology and human-computer interaction.

Measuring Cognitive Load. We can find in the literature multiple methods to estimate cognitive load of a task, including subjective (e.g., questionnaires) and objective ones (e.g., dual-task performance), as well as direct (e.g., brain imaging) or indirect measurements (e.g., heart-rate monitoring) [5]. However, most of these measurements have been utilized in relatively simple, single-user tasks – not multi-dimensional and highly social ones, such as the orchestration of a classroom.

Indeed, the aforementioned characteristics of face-to-face classroom management tasks (simultaneity, immediacy, etc.) greatly restrict the variety of techniques that can be used to measure the orchestration cognitive load. For instance, subjective questionnaires can be used, but require continuous interruptions during the lesson, or relying on the subject's memory of a very long period (although this could be mitigated by using 'stimulated recall' interviews where the teacher is shown videos from the lesson). Reliable brain imaging is currently impractical given the mobility of classroom facilitation, and dual-task performance measures would be too obstrusive as they would add another task to an already multi-task situation [21]. Physiological measures of cognitive load, such as pupillary response and other measurements detectable by eye-tracking are normally taken in carefully-controled lightning conditions (a luxury we often do not have in a classroom), and might be confounded by certain visual features of the setting (e.g., a wide spread of students in the visual field of the teacher might make average saccade speed higher). However, in previous works, we have shown the feasibility of using the triangulation across different measurements using mobile eye-tracking to record teacher orchestration *in situ*, approximating relative cognitive load within a session [23,24].

Multi-method Approaches. As we can see, there is no single method which can be reliably used to estimate the cognitive load of orchestration, at different temporal granularities, within the constraints of a classroom setting. An alternative is to take a pragmatic stance and use a mixed-methods approach [7], in which different qualitative and quantitative data gathering and analysis techniques (including both behavioral/physiological and subjective information) are triangulated to understand how the orchestration process (and its cognitive load) unfolds, from the second-to-second actions to the overall result of an hour-long session.

To the best of our knowledge, no other mixed-method approaches exist to systematically study the phenomenon of classroom orchestration. However, this sort of multi-method approaches are not unhead-of in areas related to cognitive load studies: [9] combined dual-task and subjective measurements of cognitive load to separate different cognitive load components in the context of multimedia learning tasks; [4] combined stimulated recall interviews and measurements of cognitive load to obtain a more comprehensive view of the effects of an ICT tool in learning. In the area of eye-tracking studies, [6] used four different eye-tracking measurements to distinguish cognitive load in a learning task supported by artifical intelligence.

3 Multi-method Approach to Study Teacher Orchestration

Against this backdrop, it can be seen that "empirically measuring" the multi-layered, time-constrained orchestration process is not an easy task, and probably cannot be accomplished using a single method or technique. Our aim thus is to propose a combination of methods that can be used consistently to track and better understand the unfolding and critical episodes of the orchestration of a lesson (typically spanning from 40 min to 2 h) and, if possible, to make meaningful comparisons among different sessions (as long as many of the sessions' elements, like the teacher, the kind of classroom, or the general activity structure, remain unchanged). Furthermore, our method intends to be feasible to use within relatively short research cycles and limited manpower (as iterativity is a common requirement of most current technology design/research approaches), by focusing the researchers' attention on the most critical orchestration episodes.

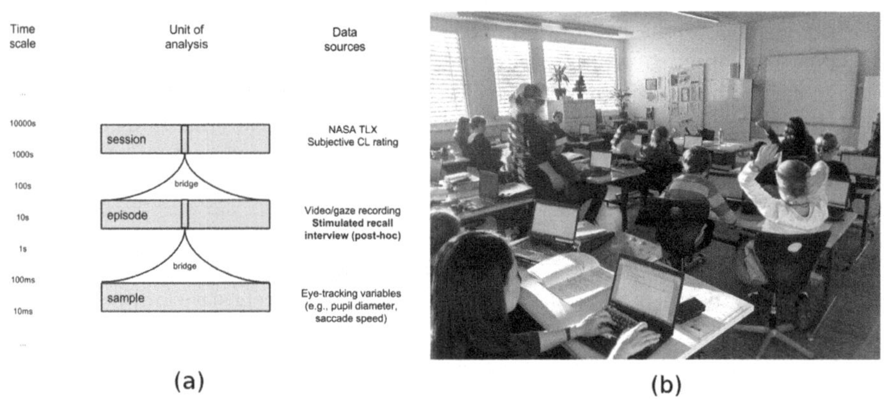

Fig. 1. (a) Units of analysis and data sources used in the proposed mixed-method approach. (b) Classroom disposition during one of the case study sessions.

Since we try to understand the orchestration process at different granularity levels, we have selected different data gathering techniques, best suited for each temporal scale and applicable within classroom constraints (see Fig. 1a): session-level subjective ratings of cognitive load (including both quantitative questionnaires such as NASA's TLX [16] and open-ended questions), first-person video/gaze recordings that can be analyzed by researchers, as well as used in stimulated recall interviews with the teacher (for the 10 s episode level). Finally, fine-grained physiological measures from the in-situ usage of a mobile eye-tracker provide information at the milliseconds scale. It is also important to note that, in order to understand how the teacher actions at these different scales relate to each other, analyzing the data at each scale has to be complemented with analysis processes that implement "bridges" among scales, aggregating smaller units of analysis to build meaning at higher-level ones [2]. The data analysis process is as follows:

1. *From Samples to Episodes (Eye-tracking).* Four eye-tracking measurements which have been related with cognitive load (pupil diameter mean, pupil diameter standard deviation, number of long fixations and average saccade speed, see [6]) are calculated throughout the session. Each of these four measurements is aggregated into 10 s episodes (thus bridging from sample- to episode-level), and the median value of these aggregated measurements for each session is calculated. By performing a median cut (i.e., for each 10 s episode, how many of the four measurements are over the session's median), a "load index" ranging from 0 to 4 is calculated, indicating the likelihood that a certain 10 s episode represented a higher load than the session average (see [23,24] for a more detailed explanation of this process).
2. *Subjective Episode Analysis (Stimulated Recall).* From this collection of 10 s episodes (and their associated load index based on eye-tracking measures), a subset is selected from consistently high- or low-load periods during the session, and 10 s video snippets of the subjective camera view of the teacher are generated for each selected episode. These videos are then used in a post-hoc stimulated recall interview with the teacher, in which the teacher is asked to rate subjectively each snippet using a standard 9-level mental effort scale, using a think-aloud protocol to express the rationale behind each rating. The numerical ratings are used to triangulate the load index obtained using eye-tracking, and the think-aloud output goes through qualitative analysis for triangulation and interpretation at larger granularity levels.
3. *Objective Episode Analysis (Video Coding).* All the extreme load index episodes (ELEs, i.e., those 10 s episodes with values 0 or 4) are then video coded by the researcher team[1], along three main dimensions characterizing orchestration (as per [11]'s definition of orchestration): the *activity* being performed by the teacher (e.g., explanation, monitoring), the *social plane* of the interaction (e.g., class-wide, with individual students) and the *main focus of the teacher's gaze* (a student laptop, students' faces, etc.). The video code counts are then aggregated for the whole session (thus bridging from the episode- to the session-level), and statistical tests (Pearson's chi-squared) are used to determine which coding dimensions and which video codes contribute most significantly to the differences between high- and low-load episodes, and using these codes to create distinct profiles for each.
4. *Session-level Analysis.* Finally, the session-level subjective ratings provided by the teacher (both quantitative scales and qualitative open responses) are triangulated with the qualitative data coming from the stimulated recall interview, to understand the overall perception of (cognitive) orchestration load at

[1] We restrict ourselves to the extreme load episodes as a way to keep the needed manpower under control (in a hour-long session the number of extreme load episodes to code tends to be around 100, while the total number of episodes can be close to 1000), and to focus the attention on the most critical orchestration episodes, contrasting them with the 'least critical' ones [23].

the session-level. These ratings can also be used to make comparisons among different sessions (e.g., which of two sessions was more difficult, and why). These inter-session comparisons can also be triangulated by comparing the medians used for the load index cut in step 1 above (after normalization by the first-episode values to cancel out physiological or ambiental differences among different sessions).

4 Case Study: Orchestrating a Technology-Enhanced Geometry Class

To illustrate our mixed-methods approach to study teacher orchestration, we provide an account of how it was applied in a small case study in secondary education. This study is part of a larger design-based effort to understand and enhance orchestration in classrooms using augmented paper interfaces. Within this larger project, however, the present study was intended as a test-drive of the approach, and to gather evidence about orchestration processes in the teacher's *usual* technology-enhanced practice. Hence, the goal of the study is not to prove or disprove that the technology worked better than an alternative – rather, it is to provide a deep comprehension of what was the teacher/classroom's baseline of technology usage. Further details, raw datasets and analytical code to generate the results of this study are publicly available online[2].

4.1 Context of the Study

The study comprised two secondary education geometry sessions that took place in an international school near Lausanne (Switzerland). The two sessions followed the same general structure, and were run by the same teacher (a practitioner with more than 15 years of teaching experience), with two different cohorts of students, of 22 and 23 students respectively (aged 11–12 years old). During the 80 min sessions, the teacher guided the students in individual and dyad work about geometrical figures and tessellations, using laptops and specialized geometry software (Geometer's Sketchpad[3]), interspersed with small periods of explanation/lecturing. Students thus were mostly working at their own laptops, following a paper worksheet that guided them through different exercises using the geometry software, attending to occasional explanations by the teacher, and asking questions when some exercise or concept was unclear. To support her orchestration of the lesson, the teacher was using a projector connected to her computer (see Fig. 1b), and the school's usual software for classroom management (NetSupport School[4]). During the two sessions, data was gathered from multiple data sources, and later analyzed as described in Sect. 3.

[2] https://github.com/chili-epfl/ectel2015-orchestration-school.
[3] http://www.keycurriculum.com/.
[4] http://www.netsupportschool.com/.

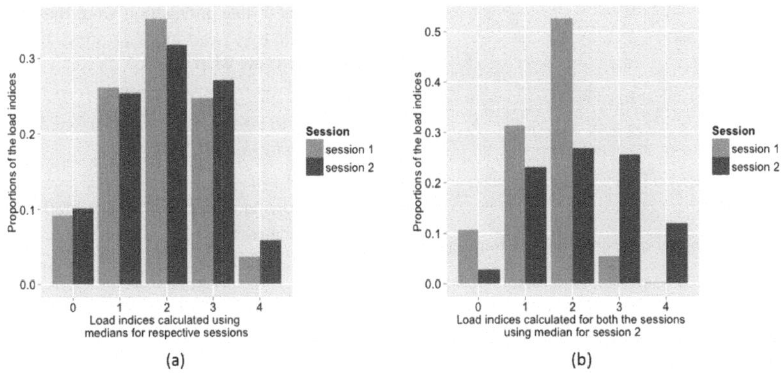

Fig. 2. Proportions of load indices calculated from eye-tracking measures. (a) Load indices calculated using each session's respective median. (b) Load indices calculated using session 2's median applied over both sessions; in this case load indices of session 1 are clearly skewed towards lower values, suggesting that session 2 was more difficult to orchestrate.

4.2 Results

From Samples to Episodes. Using the eye-tracking data from the sessions, we calculated the four eye-tracking metrics related to cognitive load (from [6]), and aggregated them (through averaging or counting) into 10 s episodes, using a rolling window with 5 s slide, thus obtaining the "load index" for each episode (i.e., likelihood that an episode is higher cognitive load than others in the session, from 0–4). As we can see in Fig. 2a, in both sessions the distribution of load indices is approximately gaussian (which is to be expected, given the way such index is calculated with respect to the session median for each eye-tracking metric).

Subjective Episode Analysis. From the 10 s episodes generated in the previous step, 20 were selected from sustained high-/low-load periods. The subjective video feed from the teacher's eyetracker for each of these episodes was extracted, and the teacher was asked to rate her mental effort (from 1–9) in each one and provide a rationale for each value, in a post-hoc stimulated recall interview.

We then triangulated the teacher's subjective ratings with the load indices computed from the eye-tracking data. We found that the teacher's ratings were significantly lower for the low load episodes than those for the high load episodes ($F[1, 18] = 4.89$, $p = .04$, see Fig. 3a), even if the correlation between such subjective ratings and the eye-tracking load indices was far from perfect.

A qualitative coding of the think-aloud protocol followed during the interview (see Fig. 3b) shows that in the higher-load episodes (both subjective and based on eye-tracking) teacher often mentions attempts to model students' understanding, or the need to take a decision about what would be the best immediate course of action. On the other hand, in lower-load episodes (from subjective rating and eye-tracking index), the individual explanations after a student error (what we could term 'repairs'), and the technical details or problems in using the technological

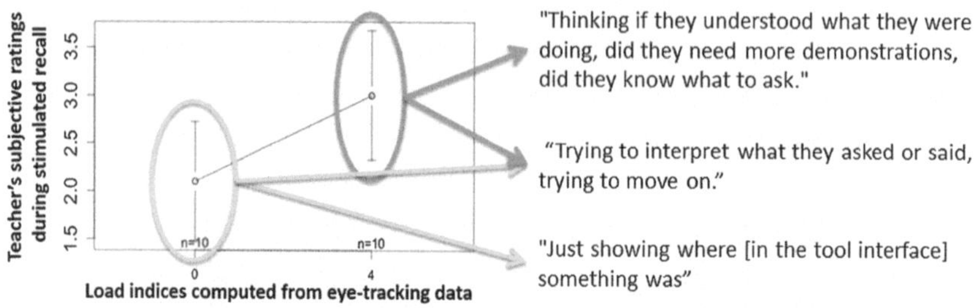

Fig. 3. Comparison of subjective load ratings and eye-tracking load index (means and confidence intervals), from a sample of 20 low (0) and high (4) episodes *(left)*. Examples of teacher quotes when explaining the rationale for the subjective ratings *(right)*.

tools appear more often. Interestingly, the need to make the lesson progress according to plan (i.e., be within the time/curriculum constraints) appears very often in high-load moments, but also appears in low-load ones (maybe indicating a background concern at all times, even in the lower-load moments)

Objective Episode Analysis. We manually coded the videos of all the ELEs (10 s episodes with an eye-tracking load index of 0 or 4), along the dimensions of teacher activity, social plane of the interaction and main focus of gaze. By aggregating the code counts for each of these dimensions in a session we can bridge from the episode-level analysis to have an idea of what kind of episodes are often high or low load (see Table 1). We can find several *common trends* in the orchestration load episode profiles of the two sessions:

- The high-load episodes are characterised by the teacher giving explanations/lecturing (EXP) and asking questions (QUE) (χ^2 [DoF = 5] = 131.14, $p < .001$); the social plane being whole-class (CLS) (χ^2 [DoF = 1] = 90.89, $p < .001$); and the main focus of the teacher being the faces of the students (FAC) (χ^2 [DoF = 3] = 161.95, $p < .001$).
- On the other hand, low-load episodes in both sessions are characterised by the teacher doing 'repairs' (REP – i.e., solving a question or misunderstanding of a student) more often (χ^2 [DoF = 5] = 131.14, $p < .001$); the social plane being individual/small-group (GRP) (χ^2 [DoF = 1] = 90.89, $p < .001$); and the main focus of the teacher being the activity paper sheets of the students (PAP) (χ^2 [DoF = 3] = 161.95, $p < .001$).

By looking at the video codes, however, we can also detect a few *differences between the two sessions* (see Table 1). Compared to the first session, in the second session we can see the appearance of a new category of episodes (disciplinary remarks, DISC), in the high-load episodes. Also, we can observe that the significance of differences in several of the video codes is increased for the second session: the predominance of repairs in low-load episodes, higher appearance of focus on paper worksheets in low-load episodes as well as the relative absence of focus on the students' laptops on high-load episodes.

Table 1. Video code counts of extreme (high and low) load episodes, for each dimension of coding. In parentheses, the standard Chi-squared residuals (absolute residual values larger than 1.96 are considered significant, marked with an '*'). Differences in significance between the two sessions are highlighted **in bold**

Session/	Activity						Social plane		Main focus of gaze			
Load	DISC	EXP	MON	QUE	REP	TDT	CLS	GRP	FAC	LAP	PAP	TCOMP
1 – Low	0	1 *	14	0 *	61	2	13 *	25 *	1 *	40	25	12
	(NA)	(-2.15)	(0.49)	(-2.94)	(1.81)	(-0.11)	(-2.75)	(2.03)	(-4.01)	(1.17)	(1.63)	(1.13)
1 – High	0	8 *	3	12 *	6 *	1	65 *	5 *	24 *	6	0 *	0
	(NA)	(3.47)	(-0.79)	(4.74)	(-2.92)	(0.18)	(4.44)	(-3.27)	(6.47)	(-1.89)	(-2.63)	(-1.82)
2 – Low	0	2 *	9	0 *	**66** *	10	15 *	36 *	0 *	48	**28** *	11
	(-1.41)	(-2.98)	(0.12)	(-2.57)	**(2.40)**	(0.71)	(-3.24)	(2.58)	(-4.60)	(1.77)	**(2.18)**	(0.32)
2 – High	**3** *	14 *	4	10 *	8 *	2	72 *	8 *	32 *	**8** *	0 *	4
	(1.98)	(4.20)	(-0.17)	(3.02)	(-3.38)	(-1.01)	(4.44)	(-3.64)	(6.48)	**(-2.49)**	(-3.06)	(-0.46)

Session-Level Analysis. Moving onto the overall session-level cognitive load analysis (and the eventual comparison between the two sessions), we can take a look at the subjective ratings provided by the teacher at the end of each session. In both cases the teacher assessed the overall load as involving 'some mental effort' (6 out of 9 in the standard subjective mental effort scale [5]). The teacher, however, considered the second session as slightly more difficult to manage (6 vs. 5 out of 9). This perception can be expanded by looking at the teacher's responses to the TLX questionnaire [16] about the sessions workload: In both cases responses were quite similar (overall workload scores of 53.3 and 56.3 out of 100 for sessions 1 and 2, respectively). However, by looking at the scores and weighting of the different workload components (mental, temporal or physical demands, performance, effort and frustration), we see that in session 2 the value and weighting of the 'frustration' component were much higher (value=5, weight=4 in session 2, vs. value=2.5, weight=1 in session 2), which also accounts for the larger part of the increase in overall perceived workload.

The qualitative (open) responses about self-perceived high-load episodes were also quite similar in both sessions, referring to worries about student progress ("when students could not follow the directions and were confused as what to do next"). However, we can find that only in the second session the teacher referred to the aforementioned disciplinary concerns ("when students try to log off while demonstrating"), which may help explain the higher frustration component of that session.

To triangulate this perception with more objective data, we can also look at the eye-tracking measures. If we apply the median values of the four eye-tracking measures of interest[5] of session 2 to the data in session 1, we can obtain a quantitative approximation to the relative difficulty between the two sessions. As we can see in Fig. 2b, in this case the distribution of load indices for session 1

[5] After normalization by the first 10 s episode of each session, to account for variability in the data due to the different time of the day or wakefulness of the teacher in the concerned days.

is skewed towards the lower end (thus indicating that fewer episodes in session 1 were as high a load as the high-load episodes in session 2, χ^2 [DoF = 4] = 344.29, $p < .001$). This again supports the idea that session 2 was (overall) higher load than session 1.

5 Discussion

The results of the different analysis methods outlined above provide us with a very detailed view of how the orchestration of these secondary school geometry lessons took place, from triangulated empirical evidence (both behavioral and subjective). The two sessions shared similar profiles in terms of high- and low-load episodes: high load episodes tended to be explanations or questioning (or the occasional disciplinary remark) in the class-wide plane, very often looking at the faces of students (in an attempt to assess their progress and understanging). On the other hand, low-load episodes tended to be individual or small-group repairs, with the teacher often focusing on the students paper worksheets or laptops. These similarities across sessions are to be expected given the fact that only the cohorts were different between the lessons, and the rest of the elements (teacher, classroom layout, technologies and subject matter) remained essentially the same.

Our triangulated data sources also helped us find orchestration load differences between these very similar sessions: both the subjective session-level data and eye-tracking metrics confirm a higher difficulty of session 2. The presence of more accentuated differences in the profiles of high- and low-load episodes seems to be a hallmark of sessions that are more difficult to manage. In this particular case, it looks like the presence of more disciplinary remarks and concerns by the teacher was one of the main drivers of this increase in orchestration load (especially, of its frustration component).

These results largely confirm several trends already observed in our previous work using mobile eye-trackers to follow orchestration load [23,24]: the higher load that class-level interactions pose for teachers, or the fact that assessing student progress across the classroom is also a high-load activity (often represented by looking at the students' faces, in the absence of other glanceable information), or the fact that more marked statistical differences in the high-/low-load episode profiles seem to be correlated with more difficult sessions (as in [23]'s comparison between a novice and an expert teacher). It is interesting to note that these common trends are preserved even across very different educational settings and technologies (small master-level classrooms with laptops, primary school tabletop classrooms, or mid-sized secondary school classrooms). Compared with this previous work to understand classroom orchestration in deeper detail, the method proposed here allows for better explanatory power by adding subjective data about the orchestration load, and also allows for meaningful comparisons among different sessions (at the expense of extra work by the research team).

An issue that might be surprising is the fact that most of the findings about the orchestration load do not seem very related to the technological support in the classroom. This can be partly explained by the fact that the teacher was using her usual set of technologies and setup (thus, in a sense, the technology was 'invisible' to her). However, this may not be the case if we were to compare technology-enhanced and traditional versions of same a lesson, or two different technologies applied to the same lesson. Also, we should consider that the technology might be playing a more subtle role in the orchestration load: the relatively low appearance of the teacher computer as the gaze of focus (where she could in theory access each student's screen through the classroom management software) seem to indicate that the teacher did not see great value in the way such monitoring was implemented[6], and preferred to roam physically around the classroom. Looking beyond what looks like a perfectly reasonable implementation of orchestration support features, into how it is used in actual classrooms, is one of our main aims when proposing the present mixed-method approach.

6 Implications and Future Work

After showing the current lack of methods to study in detail the cognitive load that facilitating a technology-enhanced classroom poses for teachers, we have proposed a mixed-method approach to such studies. The illustrative case study presented here shows how our approach enables the detection of common orchestration load trends across sessions and settings, but also how it detects and provides probable explanations for differences between two sessions' orchestration (which, let us remember, is very contextual and non-repeatable by nature).

The orchestration load trends detected by using our approach are largely compatible with much of the existing advice about designing technology for classroom orchestration. However, even if the insights derived from the application of this approach are not (yet) revolutionary, they provide empirical evidence to help technology designers *prioritize* which orchestration problems to work on first. In this concrete case, the results of our case study support the importance of research efforts in learning analytics and classroom-level visualizations, which are important not only in online environments, but also in face-to-face classrooms.

Naturally, the concrete results of this case study are hardly generalizable beyond the teacher, classroom technologies and activities described here. However, as more and more studies using these methods are performed, we expect to see several general trends about orchestration load emerge (indeed, some of these trends can already be seen throughout our previous and present work). In order to help other researchers to start performing such studies, and to enable the open discussion and improvement of these methods (e.g., more sophisticated methods of inferring cognitive load from eye-tracking data, the addition of other physiological measures), we have made the datasets and analytical code public.

[6] Teacher could see either a mosaic with the miniature version of all screens where little could be made out, or a single student's screen – which often provides an incomplete view unless the teacher actually walked there to talk with the student.

Also, we should note that these methods could be applied, not only to evaluate technological innovations in the classroom, but also pedagogical ones, from the point of view of the orchestration load they impose on the teacher (a factor often ignored by learning scientists).

Our own immediate future work includes the introduction of novel technologies in the classroom setting described here, and the observation of its effects on teacher orchestration load, as a way to help us in the design and evaluation of classroom technologies. Also, further validation and evolution of the mixed-method approach will be performed, by manipulating the conditions of similar classroom sessions (e.g., the number of facilitators) to provide some kind of"ground truth" to validate the selected physiological measurements (or the addition of new ones).

Acknowledgment. This research was supported by a Marie Curie Fellowship within the 7th European Community Framework Programme (MIOCTI, FP7–PEOPLE–2012–IEF project no. 327384). Special thanks to Wendy Farden and the International School of Lausanne for their collaboration.

References

1. Alavi, H.S., Dillenbourg, P.: An ambient awareness tool for supporting supervised collaborative problem solving. IEEE Trans. Learn. Technol. **5**(3), 264–274 (2012)
2. Anderson, J.R.: Spanning seven orders of magnitude: a challenge for cognitive modeling. Cogn. Sci. **26**(1), 85–112 (2002)
3. Bailey, B.: Usability testing: an early history. http://webusability.com/usability-testing-a-early-history/. Accessed on 17 March 2015
4. Beers, P.J., Boshuizen, H.P., Kirschner, P.A., Gijselaers, W., Westendorp, J.: Cognitive load measurements and stimulated recall interviews for studying the effects of information and communications technology. Edu. Technol. Res. Develop. **56**(3), 309–328 (2008)
5. Brunken, R., Plass, J.L., Leutner, D.: Direct measurement of cognitive load in multimedia learning. Edu. Psychol. **38**(1), 53–61 (2003)
6. Buettner, R.: Cognitive workload of humans using artificial intelligence systems: towards objective measurement applying eye-tracking technology. In: Timm, I.J., Thimm, M. (eds.) KI 2013. LNCS, vol. 8077, pp. 37–48. Springer, Heidelberg (2013)
7. Creswell, J.W.: Research Design: Qualitative, Quantitative, and Mixed Methods Approaches. Sage publications, Thousand Oaks (2013)
8. Cuendet, S., Bonnard, Q., Do-Lenh, S., Dillenbourg, P.: Designing augmented reality for the classroom. Comput. Edu. **68**, 557–569 (2013)
9. DeLeeuw, K.E., Mayer, R.E.: A comparison of three measures of cognitive load: evidence for separable measures of intrinsic, extraneous, and germane load. J. Edu. Psychol. **100**(1), 223 (2008)
10. Dillenbourg, P.: Design for classroom orchestration. Comput. Edu. **69**, 485–492 (2013)
11. Dillenbourg, P., Järvelä, S., Fischer, F.: The evolution of research on computer-supported collaborative learning. In: Balacheff, N., Ludvigsen, S., de Jong, T., Lazonder, A., Barnes, S. (eds.) TEL, pp. 3–19. Springer, The Netherlands (2009)

12. Dillenbourg, P., Zufferey, G., Alavi, H., Jermann, P., Do-Lenh, S., Bonnard, Q., Cuendet, S., Kaplan, F.: Classroom orchestration: the third circle of usability. In: Proceedings of CSCL 2011, vol. 1, pp. 510–517 (2011)
13. Doyle, W.: Ecological approaches to classroom management. In: Evertson, C.M., Weinstein, C.S. (eds.) Handbook of Classroom Management: Research, Practice, and Contemporary Issues , pp. 97–125 (2006)
14. Gómez, F., Nussbaum, M., Weitz, J.F., Lopez, X., Mena, J., Torres, A.: Co-located single display collaborative learning for early childhood education. Int. J. Comput. Support. Collab. Learn. **8**(2), 225–244 (2013)
15. Gould, J.D., Lewis, C.: Designing for usability: key principles and what designers think. Commun. ACM **28**(3), 300–311 (1985)
16. Hart, S.G., Staveland, L.E.: Development of NASA-TLX (task load index): results of empirical and theoretical research. Adv. Psychol. **52**, 139–183 (1988)
17. Kharrufa, A., Martinez-Maldonado, R., Kay, J., Olivier, P.: Extending tabletop application design to the classroom. In: Proceedings of the 2013 ACM International Conference on Interactive Tabletops and Surfaces, pp. 115–124. ACM (2013)
18. Newell, A.: Unified Theories of Cognition. Harvard University Press, Cambridge (1994)
19. Onrubia, J., Engel, A.: The role of teacher assistance on the effects of a macro-script in collaborative writing tasks. Int. J. Comput. Support. Collab. Learn. **7**(1), 161–186 (2012)
20. Paas, F., Renkl, A., Sweller, J.: Cognitive load theory: instructional implications of the interaction between information structures and cognitive architecture. Instr. Sci. **32**(1), 1–8 (2004)
21. Paas, F., Tuovinen, J.E., Tabbers, H., Van Gerven, P.W.: Cognitive load measurement as a means to advance cognitive load theory. Edu. Psychol. **38**(1), 63–71 (2003)
22. Prieto, L.P., Dlab, M.H., Gutiérrez, I., Abdulwahed, M., Balid, W.: Orchestrating technology enhanced learning: a literature review and a conceptual framework. Int. J. Technol. Enhanced Learn. **3**(6), 583–598 (2011)
23. Prieto, L.P., Sharma, K., Wen, Y., Dillenbourg, P.: The burden of facilitating collaboration: towards estimation of teacher orchestration load using eye-tracking measures. In: Proceedings of the 11th International Conference on Computer-Supported Collaborative Learning, Vol. I, pp. 212–219 (2015)
24. Prieto, L.P., Wen, Y., Caballero, D., Sharma, K., Dillenbourg, P.: Studying teacher cognitive load in multi-tabletop classrooms using mobile eye-tracking. In: Proceedings of the Ninth ACM International Conference on Interactive Tabletops and Surfaces, pp. 339–344. ACM (2014)
25. Roschelle, J., Dimitriadis, Y., Hoppe, U.: Classroom orchestration: synthesis. Comput. Edu. **69**, 523–526 (2013)

Coflection – Combining Mutual Support and Facilitation in Technology Enhanced Learning

Michael Prilla[1(✉)] and Carmen Wolf[2]

[1] Ruhr University of Bochum, Bochum, Germany
michael.prilla@rub.de
[2] Karlsruhe Institute of Technology, Karlsruhe, Germany
carmen.wolf@kit.edu

Abstract. Coaching and reflection are established methods for learning from experiences and peer support at work. They support people with different means: While coaching is a rather formal, planned, structured and systematic process, reflection is rather informal, spontaneous and emergent. Despite these differences, coaching and reflection may complement each other. This helps to overcome barriers of the respective other method and closes a gap between formal-systematic and informal-self-organized approaches of learning at work. In this paper we ask how this complement can be supported by tools and describe an intertwined concept of reflection and coaching called "coflection". We identify challenges associated with this concept, we present a prototype and we explain how the concept may solve problems at work by using real-world scenarios. The paper contributes to TEL by providing a concept that enables transitions between formal and informal learning.

Keywords: Reflection · Coaching · Coflection

1 Introduction

In modern workplaces with changing conditions and high requirements methods of mutually facilitating learning from experiences such as learning from others and peer support are important aspects of workplace learning [1, 2]: Peers are used to and efficient in supporting each other in coping with problems or successful task completion, dealing with changes and developing new practices. Similar observations have been made for workers facilitating the learning of clients [3].

Concerning self-directed learning, in which workers support each other (that is, in which they facilitate each others' learning), there are challenges to be overcome in many workplaces. First, in many workplaces there is little or no active (tool) support for non-formal and self-directed learning, which is often supposed to happen in social interaction [1, 4]. Second, even if methods for informal learning are used, they are often not well connected and cover (only) specific learning, group processes and purposes. It is then up to humans knowledgeable about these methods to choose and apply them in practice. Third, there is a need to integrate methods and tools into everyday work.

© Springer International Publishing Switzerland 2015
G. Conole et al. (Eds.): EC-TEL 2015, LNCS 9307, pp. 282–296, 2015.
DOI: 10.1007/978-3-319-24258-3_21

For example, people need to find the time required for (synchronous) coaching sessions and to continuously reflect despite other pressuring tasks [5].

Two recently discussed means for learning from each other and peer support are **coaching and reflection**. Coaching can be defined as a process in which experts (coaches) lead a client from a problem setting to possible solutions and change. This is accomplished by fostering self-directed learning through asking the right questions [6]. Reflection is a process in which one or more individuals engage in re-assessing experiences in order to turn these experience into learning [7, 8]. There are differences (e.g., formality in coaching vs. flexibility in reflection) and similarities (e.g., learning from experiences) between these methods. In this paper we argue that these two methods can complement each other and that there is potential in combining coaching and reflection at work. We then describe how tools can support this combination and how this closes gaps in existing support for peer groups helping each other at work.

Our work is in line with existing work on supporting group learning and learning at work. For example, Dillenbourg et al. [9] have argued that rather than discussing whether formal or informal processes and guided or free communication provide best support for complex learning situation we should be open for transitions between these means to support learning. Likewise Eraut [10] describes a combination of mutual consultation, mentoring and informal relationships to be beneficial for people to actively engage in thinking and talking about their knowledge at work. Adding to this work in this paper we describe how concrete methods and tools for learning can be combined, and how tool support for such a combination can be provided.

2 Technology Enhanced Coaching and Reflection

Coaching and reflection differ in certain aspects, but share the same intention, learning matter and triggers for learning. Below we summarize existing work on support for coaching and reflection and analyse differences and synergies between them.

2.1 Supporting (Peer) Coaching

Coaching can be defined as structured communication process in which a coach assists a client to identify his or her set of goals to improve professional performance and personal satisfaction. This is accomplished by fostering the ongoing self-directed learning and personal growth through asking the right questions [6]. It is a systematic, solution-focused support of solving problems and improving self-reflection, as well as facilitating persons or groups in aware self-transformation and self-development [11]. Coaching often follows a sequence of problem analysis, identification of goals and solution finding[1] (see Fig. 1), and is organized in multiple sessions.

Besides the most common type of coaching, in which a (professional) coach supports a client, there are also social types of coaching. Among those, **peer coaching** "[...] refers to a specific form of coaching carried out among colleagues. The members

[1] Sometimes this is done in different order, e.g. in the GROW-model by [12].

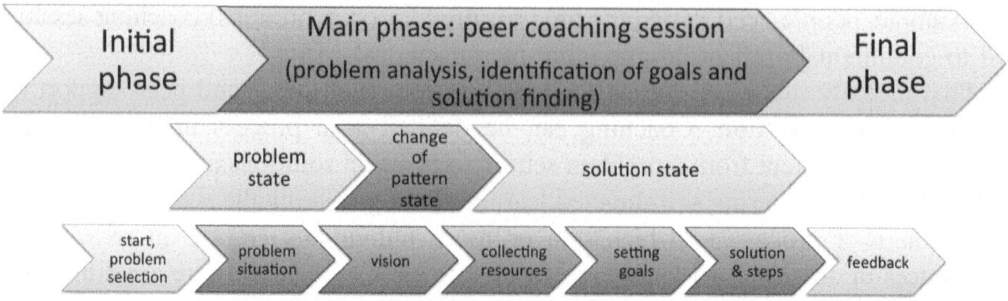

Fig. 1. Peer coaching process based on typical coaching processes (top) and desired self-directed learning steps (middle), broken down into steps conducted by peers (bottom).

of the group take turns in adopting the role of coach and thus provide coaching to each other. All members are responsible for the coaching process." [13]. While preserving the structure and purpose of coaching (see Fig. 1) there is no need for a professional coach in peer coaching. There are three roles taken by the participants:

- the **client** or **coachee** brings in the problem to be solved,
- the **moderator** or **peer coaching facilitator** (e.g., a trained employee, no need for a professional coach) takes over a coach-like role and leads the process and
- a group of **advisors** gives advice and feedback to the client.

Referring to tools supporting coaching we use the term "Technology Enhanced Coaching" (TEC), which is not as common as synonyms like E-Coaching, Online Coaching and Virtual Coaching. As TEC is still a young discipline there are only a few technology approaches for supporting coaching, among which we may differentiate between coaching **mediated by** the use of certain technology such as media also available for other purposes (e.g., coaching via video conference) and technology **specifically created for or tailored to** coaching (e.g., supporting certain interventions), thus actively supporting the coaching processes and improving it [14].

2.2 Supporting (Collaborative) Reflection

Reflection is a process of returning to past experiences, re-assessing them in the light of current experiences and knowledge and deriving consequences for future behaviour from this assessment [7]. While most research on reflection regards it as an individual, thus cognitive process, there is also a social side of reflection [15]. However, this has only recently been taken up in research on tool support [16–18].

Collaborative reflection differs from individual reflection in that it needs communication among actors reflecting together to exchange experiences, perspectives, ideas and other thoughts. Such processes are cyclic (see Fig. 2): Reflection can usually not be finished in one session but is spread across many (sometimes short) sessions of reflection – the reflection participants decide whether and how to go on with reflecting and what to take away from it [16]. These processes enable a group to reflect together and to create results that transcend individual reflection results, as they enable learning from each other and crafting knowledge from shared experiences [15, 19].

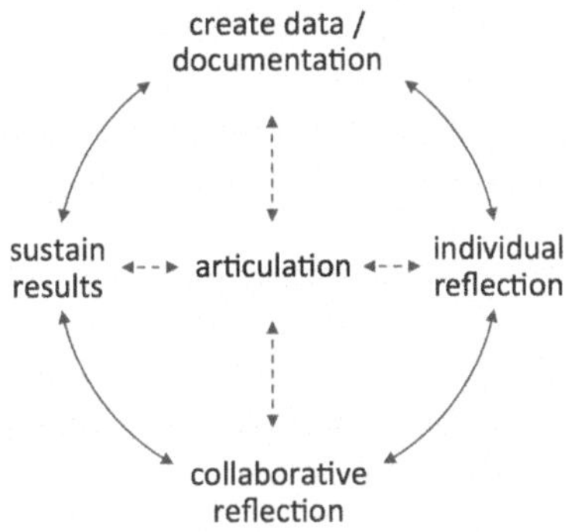

Fig. 2. Model of collaborative reflection by [23].

In collaborative reflection participants do not follow a script but share experiences, comment on them and draw conclusions when they find the time to do so. This makes collaborative reflection a flexible process. Involving many people, this process also becomes complex to conduct, as the many different actors need to be coordinated [20], and as synchronous reflection sessions need time and space. Tools for collaborative reflection need to support this communication, make it available to possible collaborators (asynchronously), structure it and sustain content exchange over time [5, 21]. While reflection in face-to-face settings such as meeting is desirable, it often limits the amount of people who can take part in reflection (lowering the likelihood of similar experiences present in a session) and it causes effort to bring together people for a reflection session. Asynchronous exchange and commenting have been found supportive for collaborative reflection at work [22].

Among the scarce approaches of collaborative reflection support, Fleck and Fitzpatrick [23] show how a series of pictures can represent daily activities and trigger reflection in a group, Scott [21] shows how learning portfolios can support collaborative reflection in education and Prilla et al. [22] present a tool in which users can write down, share and reflect on experiences. While these approaches show how collaborative reflection can be initiated and supported, they do not provide solutions for challenges such structuring reflective communication to diminish the complexity of collaborative reflection [20] or providing guidance and moderation as in face-to-face collaborative reflection sessions [19, 24]. As an example for solution proposals in this area Davis [24] suggests **prompts** to guide reflection participants to reflective actions, e.g. by providing questions leading to meaningful contributions [22].

2.3 Peer Coaching and Collaborative Reflection: Synergies and Comparison

Coaching and reflection share similar purposes, as both are means to better understand practices and work experiences, to learn from them and to improve in future work. Both rely on experiences being shared with other, both have been found to be valuable additions to ordinary learning at work, and both coaching and reflection are usually triggered by problems and other situations in which people experienced discrepancies from their expectations (including positive discrepancies). Despite these similarities there are many differences such as the formality of the learning process, the model of cooperation and the mode of learning, which are shown in Table 1.

Major differences can be found in the organisation of the process. Coaching provides a clear role division between the learner (client) and the coach (or moderator)[2], while in collaborative reflection all participants may provide experiences, perspectives and ideas. Therefore, coaching requires at least certain training on the role of a coach, while there is no such need in reflection. Coaching sessions usually follow a certain process (see Fig. 1) and guided communication, including different tools and methods the coach may use to guide clients in the process of understanding. On the contrary, even if moderation of reflection session is recommended to support the coordination of participants [19], structuring collaborative reflection is widely left to participants [20]. Roughly we may thus state that coaching is a more systematic, structured and formal process, while reflection is an emergent, discursive, collective and informal process of crafting knowledge together. This resembles discussions on scaffolding and scripting in learning, in which there are advocates for both ends [9].

Coaching and reflection in groups differ in labour division, goals and implementation of the process. Peer coaching is a concept of **cooperative** work, in which participants take different roles and tasks in the coaching process (e.g., supporting the client or being coached) that help to reach the (common) goal of succeeding in the coaching session. For reflection in groups there is no role division and therefore participants **collaborate** (see [25] for a commonly used distinction of cooperative and collaborative processes), meaning that they share the same goal (learning about practices). Therefore, in line with work on media choice [26], coaching processes often rely on synchronous sessions, in which coach(es) and client(s) meet face-to-face or virtually, and as described above, reflection support is often asynchronous [22].

While the differences discussed above separate coaching and reflection from each other they also show the **potential of combining coaching and reflection** to complement each other. In particular, coaching and reflection support can **connect formal and informal processes of learning from work experiences**. Such a combination could help to overcome challenges in both methods, for example the need of co-availability of coach(es) and client(s). Reflection could be used for the many situations in which a coach (or facilitator) is not available or there is no time for a (peer) coaching session, and coaching could be used in processes in which the creation of outcomes needs a more focused approach. Iterating between reflection and coaching may then help to reify both processes. Eraut [1] describes this "balance between support provided by people on the spot (…) and support from a designated mentor or manager" as an ideal combination for practicing and getting closer to expertise.

The potential of combining coaching and reflection is especially present for social ways of coaching and reflection: transitions between peer coaching and collaborative reflection are much smoother than for other combinations: Roles are not as clearly defined and separated in peer coaching as in one-on-one coaching sessions, and the

---

[2] Despite this role division no hierarchy must be involved in coaching.

Table 1. Differences between concepts (and their implementation) of coaching and reflection.

	Coaching	Reflection
Learning goal	Understanding practice and learning for the future	
Learning matter	Experiences, practices	
Trigger(s)	Problem situation, discrepancy to expectations	
Learning approach	(Rather) Formal, guided	Informal, emergent
Roles in the process	Coach, client (coachee)	Reflection participants (equal)
Interventions in the process	Many tools and interventions for different steps in the process	Questions, moderation of group reflection
Labour division model	Cooperation: Coach provides structure (process expert), client digs into issues (content expert)	Collaboration: All participants engage in reflection on same context
Goal for session	Common goal: Positive outcomes from coaching, capacity to act (but different individual goals)	Shared goal: Learning about same/similar issue(s)
Barriers	Time and personnel (coaches) needed[a]	Time to step back, continuity, integration into daily work
Implementation (technical support)	Synchronous (partly asynchronous, e.g. preparation)	Asynchronous (partly synchronous, e.g. meetings)
Training	Required (role taking)	Not required

[a]Except for self-coaching

degrees of formality in peer coaching and collaborative reflection converge: participants have a higher degree of flexibility and process steering in peer coaching, and a reflection group needs to be guided in order to diminish the complexity caused by many participants reflecting together. Therefore, enabling transitions between (peer) coaching and (collaborative) reflection provides potential to help groups of people working together to flexibly apply the support they need in learning about their work.

3 Motivation: The Need for Combining Coaching and Reflection

Below we illustrate the need for and potential of combining coaching and reflection by using two examples from real world cases.

The first example is taken from work with a German hospital, in which (assistant) physicians were supported in learning about conversation with residents of their patients [22]. Talking to relatives often puts young physicians in a stressful situation [27], as they have to convey (bad) news in an emotionally loaded situation. To learn how to conduct these conversations professionally without being stressed needs experiences with such situations, which cannot be acquired only by training [28].

Therefore we created a tool supporting physicians in writing down experiences, sharing them with each other and reflecting on them together by exchanging comments on shared experiences [22]. This worked well for sharing and reflecting on experiences, and participants adopted the tool well for this, but the usage of the tool dropped over time. Asked about this participants told us that while they saw value in exchanging experiences, they felt they needed more systematic support and guidance to derive insights from these experiences for their future work. Using the content they created in the tool in coaching would have been a solution, but neither a coach nor technical support was available.

The second example is taken from a project with European professional employment services (PES), in which employees from a PES organisation were supported in dealing with constant change [29]. As part of strategic shift staff was required to more intensively work together with employers and to motivate clients to take chances of a job even if it is not a perfect fit for them. This turned out to be difficult, as very few members of staff have experiences with these new tasks. There are fixed times allocated to interacting with employers and clients and there is not much time for training. Therefore, there is a need to learn during work from initial experiences and too build good practices. (Peer) coaching was considered to be supportive in these situations and as a continuous offering to staff, but was found not to be feasible: Given number of staff to be coached too many coaches would have been required and there not enough time for synchronous peer coaching groups. To enable exchange and learning from each other outside face-to-face sessions we provided staff with an asynchronous platform for experience exchange and reflective discussions.

The examples above describe a common problem we also found in other cases, which is caused by mutually exclusive needs and constraints such as forming peer groups to understand practices while being bound to fixed time slots, and freely exchanging experiences while needing support in systematically deriving insights from them. In both cases, offering one type of support for learning from experiences led to a lack of support in certain situations. This led us to the *concept of coflection*, which flexibly combines coaching and reflection processes.

4 Coflection: Combining Coaching and Reflection

Based on our theoretical and empirical work as outlined above we created the concept of **Coflection**[3] and its prototypical implementation.

[3] The term "coflection" is used by others to describe a "meta-thinking process by means of which people, together, bend on each other's thoughts and actions in a conscious way" [30] or "to capture the socially critical nature of the interactions among teachers within professional learning" [31]. However, we use this term as explained above, as it literally stands for our aim to closely intertwine coaching and reflection.

4.1 Combining Coaching and Reflection: Two Conceptual Levels

The coflection concept combines coaching and reflection support on three levels. First, it includes the ability to **combine coaching and reflection on a process level**, meaning that a coaching process can directly follow a reflection process and vice versa. Second, the concepts includes **processes composed from elements of coaching and reflection**, meaning that support for reflection can be used in coaching and vice versa. On a third and meta level coaching and reflection may reinforce each other, but this level is out of scope for this paper.

Concerning the first level, tools should be able to support both (collaborative) reflection and (peer) coaching processes to enable users to choose a method suitable for each problem and time. This requires content created during a peer coaching session to be available for follow-up reflection and vice versa. Users may then start collaborative reflection, in which they share experiences and comment on them until they reach a situation in which there is a need for more intensive clarification of the process. They may then negotiate a time to meet as a peer coaching group and use the content created during their reflection to start the coaching process. After that they can use outcomes from coaching for further reflection on the experiences that triggered the peer coaching session. While this level is most obvious from our analysis, it already provides support for different situations (synchronous and guided with coaching, asynchronous and flexible in reflection) to people. In addition, it enables learning from experiences when there is not time or group of (peer) coaches available and allow for more intensive learning sessions when this is the case. To our knowledge and despite its potential this level had not been implemented in tools so far.

Concerning the second level, tools may no more include a distinction between coaching and reflection but offer support in which elements of both processes are closely intertwined. This might include (but is not limited to):

- **Using prompts in coaching sessions**, which ask participants bound to the role of a peer coach or advisor (thus not allowed to provide own experiences) to share similar experiences with the coachee. This may help to create solutions by comparing similar experiences and deriving insights that help beyond single problems.
- **Structuring (collaborative) reflection processes along typical phases from coaching processes**, for example giving participants a timeframe to create comments to clarify the problem in shared experiences and then switching to a phase in which participants are asked to provide solution proposals. This may structure the otherwise flexible reflection process and guide people to create results from it.
- **Switching between situations in which users have special roles (coaching) to situations in which they are equal participants of the process (reflection).** This offers guidance and support created by (peer) coaches when necessary and provides flexibility and exchange otherwise (Fig. 4).

The implementation of the second coflection level will offer synchronous peer coaching sessions, which are enhanced by the ability to share experiences, and prompts asking participants to comment on experiences (adding reflection features to coaching). It will also allow users to reflect collaboratively and take on roles from coaching in order to structure the support they can give each other. A tool may then either contain

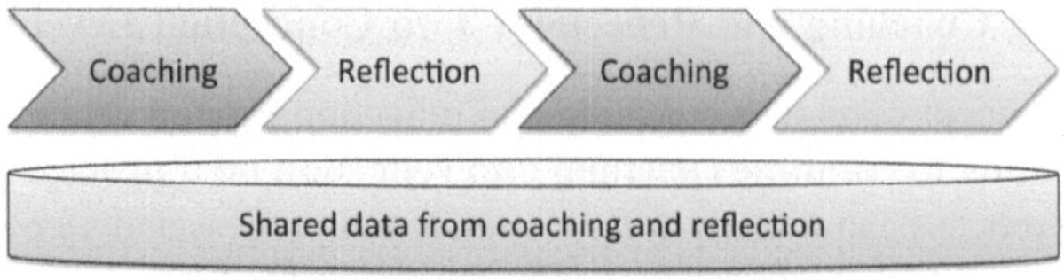

Fig. 3. Combined coaching and reflection on a process level

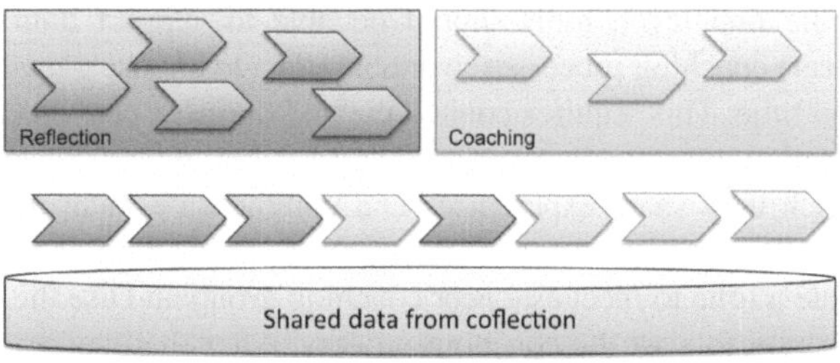

Fig. 4. Processes composed from elements of coaching and reflection

pre-defined coflection setups (procedures) or allow users to configure their own process. The user no more needs to differentiate between coaching and reflection but uses a process that fits the constraints and culture of the workplace best.

On a third level, which will not be described in detail, coaching may support people in developing skills to reflect together (coaching to support reflection) and collaborative reflection can be used by peers to learn from peer coaching session. This forms a meta-level of reinforcing reflection by coaching and the other way round.

4.2 A Prototype for Coflection Support: Coaching and Reflection in a Community of Practice

To investigate the feasibility and effects of combining coaching and reflection in practice the coflection concept was integrated into a community of practice platform (see [32] and Fig. 5). The platform was built to support practitioners in employment services in dealing with legal, economic and ethical changes in their work.

Figure 5 exemplifies how reflection is supported in the community platform: Besides common features used in other community platforms as well (e.g., the forum structure shown on the left side, tags available for contributions etc.) the platform provides the user with reflection prompts (see no. 1 on the right side of Fig. 5), which stimulate collaborative reflection (e.g. “Have you ever been in a similar situation” as a stimulus for sharing and comparing similar experiences in Fig. 5).

In addition to reflection features the platform provides a (peer) coaching room, which is being developed at the time of writing this paper. It is designed to be a separate area in the platform, enabling synchronous exchange between peer coaching group members. Features include taking and switching roles as well as guidance in the

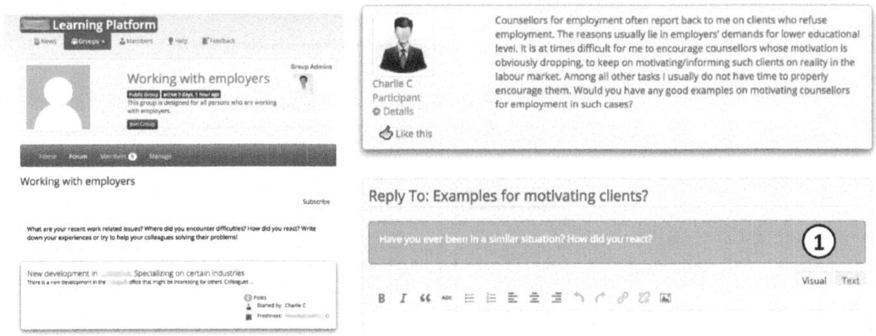

Fig. 5. Prototype for coflection in a community of practice platform.

peer coaching process, including the time left for phases and what to do in the current and next phases. Content from threads created in collaborative reflection as shown in Fig. 5 can be transferred (linked) to the peer coaching room, and content created in the peer coaching room can be exported to a thread in the collaborative reflection area. Figure 6 shows the design of the peer coaching room.

The platform will be used to investigate the feasibility and effect of coflection support in practice. At the time of writing it is rolled out for smaller user groups in European professional employment service agencies. It will initially focus on the first conceptual level of coflection, but will be extended to support the second level in further development. For example, the supportive material in the peer coaching room will be complemented with explicit reflection prompts as shown in Fig. 5 to foster reflection between and in coaching sessions.

4.3 Envisioning Coflection in Practice: Supporting the Examples

Applying the concept of coflection to the scenarios described above shows that the concept provides a flexible approach that creates value for peer-to-peer support and learning at work. Taking the first example coflection could be a supportive element to go deeper into certain problem situations by making use of peer coaching methods. In this case, physicians using a coflection tool could decide to initiate a coaching session after reflection and discuss situations in which it was especially hard to talk to the relatives. This can help them to find out what made it hard and what could be done to improve this situation, providing the guidance and systematic approach the physicians asked for in our work with them. Using the outcomes of peer coaching in further reflection could then connect peer coaching activities and collaborative reflection into a cycle of mutual support for finding out about and improving challenges at work.

In the second example our approach would be the solution to have a mixture between asynchronous and synchronous exchange between peers. Rather than having trouble in organising peer coaching session frequently PES practitioners could use asynchronous collaborative reflection between coaching sessions to support the problem solving process. Using coflection support would provide them merely with the

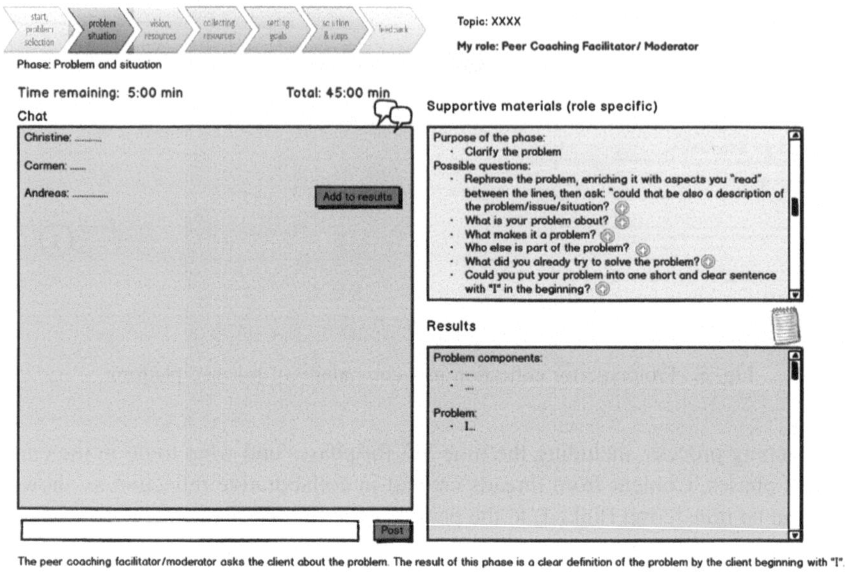

Fig. 6. Prototype for the peer coaching room.

choice of whether to meet synchronously or to exchange content asynchronously. This could increase support for the person searching a solution and support learning how to do peer coaching, which can then be used in the interaction with clients.

5 Challenges for Coflection: Socio-Technical Support Needed

During our work on the concept and prototype of coflection we identified certain challenges that need to be overcome in order to offer coflection to learners in organisations. It is a commonality to all of these challenges that they cannot be met solely by technology, but need to be aligned with individual and social activities.

5.1 Facilitation and Scaffolding Support: Balancing Structure and Freedom

Concerning **facilitation and scaffolding support** there is a gap that needs to be overcome: As described activities in (peer) coaching are usually carried out by different roles. This needs awareness and structure for activities needed in certain phases. In reflection a facilitator or tool may prompt users with questions that make reflection more likely, but there is no pre-structured process when this needs to happen. This raises at least two requirements for the provision of scaffolding support: For coflection on level 1 there is a need for users to switch between pre-structured and open processes when switching from coaching to reflection support and vice versa. This has to be communicated to the user. "Process change bumps" as described by [3], which provide awareness and offer distinct change actions between processes, may help to facilitate this switching. Second, on level 2 of our coflection concept there is a need to find a balance between structure and freedom in scaffolding that enables different degrees of blending coaching and reflection support (cf. [33]). Keeping in mind that such support may be provided by human facilitators *or* features in a tool, there is a need to recognize the type of process learners are engaged in order to adapt the scaffolding feature or to propose means for structuring the process to a human facilitator.

5.2 Transitions Between Coaching and Reflection: Time, Groups and Content

Another challenge can be found in creating transitions between the temporal and groups structures of coaching and reflection. First, there is a need to create **transitions between synchronous (coaching) and asynchronous (reflection) activities**. Second, there is a need to **combine (smaller) peer coaching groups and the (wider) audience in a reflection community**. Allowing users of coflection tools to smoothly switch between synchronous and asynchronous activities as described by [34] is key to overcome this challenge. The transition between a large community and the small coaching (peer) group, which has been described by Stahl [35] as a challenge, needs to enable user to keep a group identity while interacting with a wider audience.

Both of these needs are closely connected to the challenge of **making available and pre-processing the content** created in coaching or reflection for the respective other method. This needs activities of pre- and post-processing content and making it available for later usage that are known as **"gardening"** in other contexts of learning and collaboration [36]. We assume that automatic content processing such as creating transcripts and summaries of discussions cannot account for these actions alone, but need to be (at least) complemented by humans taking over the role of a gardener.

5.3 Designing Coflection Processes: Pre-structuring and Meta-Design

A major challenge in implementing coflection in practice is the **design of coflection processes**, that is, how much reflection to include in coaching and vice versa. There are different ways of providing coflection support to users, including pre-defined processes that provide some of the enhancements described in Sect. 4.1 or leaving the choice to the user. The former would need context detection and recognition in order to provide a process that suits the needs to the learning process intended by the users. The latter is a case of meta-design [37], in which systems are designed in a way that users can design processes and interaction. For coflection this would mean to enable users in combining coaching and reflection flexibly and on the fly if they encounter a need for (further or different) support. Successful combinations of these features may then be used by others as well.

5.4 The Need for Socio-Technical Solutions

As can be seen from the challenges described above they afford socio-technical solutions that combine processes of interaction and organisation with technical support. Further work will be dedicated to exploring how these challenges can be met in practice and how to successfully implement coflection in practice. Besides these challenges the question remains whether and how to prepare users for the application of coflection in practice. For reflection there is hardly any need of training [22], but the roles and process structure integral to peer coaching make training necessary. As coflection combines both methods and adds complexity by leaving the choice of which method to apply when to its users we assume that it therefore needs additional support and training. This will be subject to further investigation.

6 Conclusion

In this paper we have presented an approach of combining coaching and reflection, showing how these methods might complement each other in a concept we named "coflection". We consider coflection to bridge the gap between informal and formal, structured and unstructured, facilitator-driven and self-regulated as well as synchronous and asynchronous support for learning at work.

Our work contributes to the body of work in the TEL community by combining reflective learning, which has been a topic of interest in TEL for a long time, and coaching, which is a well-established method in practice, into an integrated concept. To the knowledge of the authors there is no such concept, and there is no work available that deals with coaching and reflection support in the same tool(s). We especially contribute to the EC-TEL 2015 theme of "Design for Teaching and Learning in a networked World" by providing a new approach of supporting learners to learn with each other and to help each other in networked learning, which builds on established methods and enhances them with tool support. We are aware of the fact that our concept and tools are work in progress, and we discussed challenges we expect to face for the implementation of coflection in daily practice. Overcoming these challenges will be the focus of our future work.

Acknowledgements. EmployID (http://employid.eu) "Scalable & cost-effective facilitation of professional identity transformation in public employment services" is a research project supported by the European Commission in the 7th Framework Program (project no. 619619). We would like to thank all colleagues and associated partners in the project for their cooperation and our fruitful discussions.

References

1. Eraut, M.: Informal learning in the workplace. Stud. Continuing Educ. **26**, 247–273 (2004)
2. Schein, E.H.: Helping: How to Offer, Give, and Receive Help. Berrett-Koehler Publishers, San Francisco (2009)

3. Giesbrecht, T., Schenk, B., Schwabe, G.: Learning with facilitation affordances: the case of citizens' advice services. In: Proceedings of the Twenty Second European Conference on Information Systems (ECIS 2014) (2014)
4. Littlejohn, A., Milligan, C., Margaryan, A.: Charting collective knowledge: supporting self-regulated learning in the workplace. J. Workplace Learn. **24**, 226–238 (2012)
5. Prilla, M., Pammer, V., Krogstie, B.: Fostering collaborative redesign of work practice: challenges for tools supporting reflection at work. In: Proceedings of the European Conference on Computer Supported Cooperative Work (ECSCW 2013) (2013)
6. Grant, A.M., Stober, D.R.: Introduction. In: Stober, D.R., Grant, A.M. (eds.). Evidence Based Coaching Handbook. Putting Best Practices To Work For Your Clients. New Hersey, Wiley. pp. 1-19 (2006)
7. Boud, D.: Reflection: Turning Experience into Learning. Kogan Page, London (1985)
8. Schön, D.A.: The Reflective Practitioner. Basic Books, New York (1983)
9. Dillenbourg, P., Järvelä, S., Fischer, F.: The evolution of research on computer-supported collaborative learning. Technology-Enhanced Learning, pp. 3–19. Springer, Berlin (2009)
10. Eraut, M.: Non-formal learning and tacit knowledge in professional work. Br. J. Educ. Psychol. **70**, 113–136 (2000)
11. Greif, S.: Coaching und ergebnisorientierte Selbstreflexion: Theorie, Forschung und Praxis des Einzel-und Gruppencoachings. Hogrefe Verlag, Oxford (2008)
12. Whitmore, J.: Coaching for Performance: Growing Human Potential and Purpose: The Principles and Practice of Coaching and Leadership. Nicholas Brealey Publishing, London (2009)
13. Ajdukovic, M., Cajvert, L., Judy, M., Knopf, W., Kuhn, H., Madai, K., Voogd, M.: ECVision. A European Glossary of Supervision and Coaching (2014)
14. Anthony, K., Nagel, D.-A.: A brave new world: coaching online. Coaching Today (2012)
15. Hoyrup, S.: Reflection as a core process in organisational learning. J. Workplace Learn. **16**, 442–454 (2004)
16. Krogstie, B., Prilla, M., Pammer, V.: Understanding and supporting reflective learning processes in the workplace: the RL@Work model. In: Proceedings of the Eighth European Conference on Technology Enhanced Learning (EC-TEL-2013) (2013)
17. Baumer, E.P., Khovanskaya, V., Matthews, M., Reynolds, L., Sosik, V.S., Gay, G.K.: Reviewing reflection: on the use of reflection in interactive system design. In: Proceedings of DIS 2014 (2014)
18. Marcu, G., Dey, A.K., Kiesler, S.: Designing for collaborative reflection. In: Proceedings of PervasiveHealth 2014 (2014)
19. Daudelin, M.W.: Learning from experience through reflection. Organ. Dyn. **24**, 36–48 (1996)
20. Cressey, P., Boud, D., Docherty, P.: Productive reflection at work. In: Boud, D., Cressey, P., Docherty, P. (eds.) Productive Reflection at Work: Learning for Changing Organizations, pp. 11–26. Routledge, New York (2006)
21. Scott, S.G.: Enhancing reflection skills through learning portfolios: an empirical test. J. Manag. Educ. **34**, 430–457 (2010)
22. Prilla, M., Degeling, M., Herrmann, T.: Collaborative reflection at work: supporting informal learning at a healthcare workplace. In: Proceedings of the ACM International Conference on Supporting Group Work (GROUP 2012), pp. 55–64 (2012)
23. Fleck, R., Fitzpatrick, G.: Reflecting on reflection: framing a design landscape. In: Proceedings of the 22nd Conference of the Computer-Human Interaction Special Interest Group of Australia on Computer-Human Interaction, pp. 216–223. ACM, Brisbane, Australia (2010)

24. Davis, E.A.: Scaffolding students' knowledge integration: prompts for reflection in KIE. Int. J. Sci. Educ. **22**, 819–837 (2000)
25. Roschelle, J., Teasley, S.: The construction of shared knowledge in collaborative problem solving. In: O'Malley, C. (ed.) Computer Supported Collaborative Learning, pp. 69–97. Springer, Heidelberg (1995)
26. Dennis, A.R., Valacich, J.S.: Rethinking media richness: towards a theory of media synchronicity. In: HICSS-32. Proceedings of the 32nd Annual Hawaii International Conference on System Sciences, pp. 10–19 (1999)
27. Maynard, D.W.: Bad News, Good News: Conversational Order in Everyday Talk and Clinical Settings. University of Chicago Press, Chicago (2003)
28. Delvaux, N., Merckaert, I., Marchal, S., Libert, Y., Conradt, S., Boniver, J., Etienne, A.-M., Fontaine, O., Janne, P., Klastersky, J., Mélot, C., Reynaert, C., Scalliet, P., Slachmuylder, J.-L., Razavi, D.: Physicians' communication with a cancer patient and a relative. Cancer **103**, 2397–2411 (2005)
29. Bimrose, J., Brown, A., Holocher-Ertl, T., Kieslinger, B., Kunzmann, C., Prilla, M., Schmidt, A.P., Wolf, C.: The role of facilitation in technology-enhanced learning for public employment services. Int. J. Adv. Corp. Learn. (iJAC) **7**(3), 56 (2014)
30. Valero, P.: Deliberative mathematics education for social democratization in Latin America. ZDM Math. Educ. **31**, 20–26 (1999)
31. Crockett, M.D., Buckley, L.A.: The role of coflection in equity-centered mathematics professional development practices. Equity Excellence Educ. **42**, 169–182 (2009)
32. Prilla, M., Blunk, O.: Reflective TEL: augmenting learning tools with reflection support. In: Proceedings of the Tenth European Conference on Technology Enhanced Learning. Springer, Berlin (2015)
33. Dillenbourg, P.: Over-scripting CSCL: the risks of blending collaborative learning with instructional design. In: Kirschner, P. (ed.) Three Worlds of CSCL: Can We Support CSCL, pp. 61–91. Open Universiteit Nederland, Heerlen (2002)
34. Hrastinski, S.: Asynchronous and synchronous e-learning. Educause Q. **31**, 51–55 (2008)
35. Stahl, G.: Theories of cognition in CSCW. In: ECSCW 2011: Proceedings of the 12th European Conference on Computer Supported Cooperative Work, 24–28 September 2011, Aarhus Denmark, pp. 193–212 (2011)
36. May, G.L., Short, D.: Gardening in cyberspace: a metaphor to enhance online teaching and learning. J. Manag. Educ. **27**, 673–693 (2003)
37. Fischer, G., Herrmann, T.: Socio-technical systems: a meta-design perspective. Int. J. Sociotechnol. Knowl. Dev. **3**, 1–33 (2011)

Towards Reading Session-Based Indicators in Educational Reading Analytics

Madjid Sadallah[1,2(✉)], Benoît Encelle[3], Azze-Eddine Maredj[2], and Yannick Prié[4]

[1] Computer Science Department, University of Bejaia, 06000 Bejaia, Algeria
[2] Research Center on Scientific and Technical Information CERIST, Algiers, Algeria
{msadallah,amaredj}@cerist.dz
[3] LIRIS, UMR 5205 CNRS, Université de Lyon 1, 69622 Lyon, France
bencelle@liris.cnrs.fr
[4] LINA - UMR 6241 CNRS, Université de Nantes, Nantes, France
yannick.prie@univ-nantes.fr

Abstract. It is a challenging task to identify eLearning courses parts that have to be revised to best suit learners' requirements. Reading being one of the most salient learning activities, one way of doing so is to study how learners consume courses. We intend to support course authors (e.g. teachers) during courses revision by providing them with reading indicators. We use the concept of reading session to denote a learner's active reading period, and we provide several associated reading indicators. In our server-side approach, reading sessions and indicators are calculated using web server logs. We evaluate the relevance of our proposals using logs from a major French eLearning platform. Results are promising: calculated reading sessions are theoretically more precise than other best applicable approaches, and course authors consider suggested indicators to be appropriate to courses revision. Using reading sessions and associated indicators could facilitate authors' work of course reengineering.

Keywords: Reading analytics · Reading monitoring · Reading indicators · Reading sessions · Web log mining

1 Introduction

More and more educational documents have been made available online by thousands of authors, and are being accessed by millions of learners each day, be it for rapid consultation or through active reading. Authors of online educational material can obtain automated feedback on how learners proceed through it. Such information may help them to get hints on users' learning experiences, spot reading issues or infer what knowledge is exactly gained from courses. This can help them make informed decisions on how their documents should be improved, from local clarifications to deeper restructurations. Our general interest is related with helping authors do the maintenance and evolution of eLearning documents. Educational settings are cyclic in nature and authors can

© Springer International Publishing Switzerland 2015
G. Conole et al. (Eds.): EC-TEL 2015, LNCS 9307, pp. 297–310, 2015.
DOI: 10.1007/978-3-319-24258-3_22

take benefit of each cycle to evolve their courses to maximize their learning efficiency (by being more precise, more comprehensible, more adapted to learners' needs, etc.). We investigate the use of learners' reading logs to support authors during these adaptation/improvement stages. To achieve this goal, we advocate "usage-based document reengineering" [1], a process defined as a kind of reengineering that changes document content and structures based on the analysis of readers' usages as recorded in logs.

In this paper, we focus on building indicators of learners' reading behaviors for authors to understand how their courses are used. We build on related work concerning reading-based indicators and session identification (Sect. 2). Using consumption logs of several courses provided by a major French eLearning platform (Sect. 3), we present our algorithm for computing *reading sessions* (Sect. 4) that denote active learners reading periods as well as categories of reading indicators constructed from reading sessions (Sect. 5). We evaluate the quality of our algorithm by comparing the results with other methods, and we estimate the usefulness of our indicators through a survey (Sect. 6).

2 Related Work

Monitoring Reading. Reading is a fundamental activity and the basis of learning. Different actions and interactions between the learner and the reading material are at the core of reading. Studies have shown that capturing and interpreting this data are an effective means to reflect and predict, with good precision, the users' reading usages and behavior [2,3]. Crawler-gathered data originated from either the server side data, the client side data or from both the sources, are often used. In education, a high level interpretation of this data is performed by assessing various computed metrics called indicators. These can range from simple measures and usage statistics like number of visits or visits per web page [4] to more advanced indicators like inferring students' attitudes that affect learning [5] and predicting students' knowledge [6].

Solely relying on request-based information to study reading has a major drawback that requesting a page is not necessarily equivalent to reading everything that is presented on it [2]. The use of time between requests is shown to be an effective and unobtrusive way to improve the derived assumptions without interfering with user behavior and environment [7]. However, a difficulty arises from the fact that time generally cannot be directly obtained from the events stream since web logs only contain actions timestamps with no explicit markers of their ends. Hence, each action duration must be estimated as the time difference between its occurrence and the subsequent one. Such a method could be imprecise since inactivity periods may be contained within the assessed duration. A recent study demonstrates that the adoption of a particular estimation strategy can have a significant impact on the fit of analytical models of learners' performance and their interpretation [8]. The precision of indicators highly depends on the correct estimation of action durations.

Sessions-Based Indicators. A body of work targeted the estimation of action durations using web log analysis (see [8] for an extensive background on time-on-task estimation methods). Any adopted method aims to identify active and inactive periods from a user trail. The set of the actions performed by one user in a sustained and continuous activity is often referred to as a "session". A session can be seen as *a delimited and sustained set of pages visited by the same user within the duration of one particular visit to a particular website.*

The session-based indicators encode the navigation behavior of users over time [9], a valuable aspect that advocates their use to analyze reading efficiently beyond the course and page levels perspectives. Appropriately selecting these indicators have shown to provide good insightfulness in understanding learners activity. Learning sessions (defined in [10] as a set of sessions) duration and length were used to estimate the success and difficulty of the learning task [11]. Analysis of number of visits per session is studied in [12]. Navigation properties within them are studied in [13] and many navigation patterns were extracted to help evaluate and interpret online course activities [14] and to give insight into dependencies between page requests [15]. However, apart from such general session descriptive metrics common in web-based navigation, session-based reading indicators are not explicitly addressed. There is even no common definition of the "session" concept in eLearning.

Sessions Identification. In eLearning, some authors use specific approaches for session identification like estimating the needed time for reading using an average reading time (in words per minute) [16] or learners self-reports on the time spent [17]. However, methods originated from the field of Web usage mining are often used. This field aims to reveal the knowledge hidden in navigation logs [18] and defines two main classes of approaches for session identification: time-oriented and navigation-oriented. The first is based on the limitation of total session time or page-stay time. In the first case, the total duration of a session is limited by a predefined timeout delimiter (threshold), generally 30 min [19], and if the duration of accumulated page view-times exceed that cut-off, the session is classified as having ended. A threshold can also be defined for any page (generally 10 min): a session is terminated on a given page if the difference between its access time and the next accessed page is greater than the threshold. A new session is assumed to start with this next accessed page. The navigation-oriented approach uses web topology as a graph and assumes that nodes are web pages and hyperlinks are directed edges connecting these nodes [20]. If a web page is not connected with the previously visited page in a session, then it is considered as contained within a different session. The methods using time-based thresholds are the most commonly used in eLearning and are recommended in [10], without providing precise threshold values. As no generalized model exists for estimating a threshold in a given situation [21], authors rely on their data corpus and context characteristics to define thresholds values: 30 min [22], 60 min [23] or even 7 hours [24].

Sessions Identification Issues in eLearning. The time-based approach for identifying sessions best suits the needs of our study context; moreover, the navigation-based method cannot be used given that connections may exist between all course webpages. However, we identified two main drawbacks of using a unique time threshold value (for pages or for sessions): (1) *eLearning activities are diverse*: reading, searching, commenting, doing assessments, etc. Depending on the underlying difficulty, some activities are easier to perform and hence take much less time than others. The existing solutions however do not make distinction of the different learning tasks. (2) *Activity context may change*, a context being related to the learning activity (e.g. time needed to make an assessment depends on the questions difficulties, navigating within a learning portal may be more time demanding than a news one). Hence, each website (course) being unique should have its own session time threshold [18]. As educational websites may have a complex structures and content, different difficulty levels for reading and understanding are induced to their pages (introductory parts may be easier to read and understand than more complex ones). Consequently, each part/page of the same course webpages is different (with regard with its inner-complexity) and thus requires a dedicated reading time. The efficient detection of sessions requires to take into account both the activity that is carried out and the context on which it is performed.

3 Study Objectives, Data Source and Corpus Description

This paper is concerned with solely reading activity and proposes to define for each course webpage the most suitable time needed by learner to achieve its reading. This time is used to specialize the concept of session in reading and to draw specific indicators beyond the aforementioned general ones. The detected learners' sessions of reading will allow not only to give more precision and expressiveness to existing reading indicators (e.g. durations, visits and revisits) but also to enrich reading analysis toolkit with specific session-based indicators.

Our proposals are implemented and evaluated using data from the major French e-learning platform *OpenClassrooms*[1]. Course authors are generally domain-experts, some of them are academic teachers and instructors. Our corpus data is constituted from web logs on 842 courses (mainly in computing and information technologies) over a 75 days period. Courses are organized as the nesting of *parts* (corresponding to chapters, sub-chapters, sections, etc.), each part being contained in a dedicated webpage. Logfiles contain information about website visitor activity and are automatically created by the web server. Common cleaning and preprocessing steps are performed to obtain for each record a *timestamp* (datetime of the request) along with the *request identifier*, the *user* (empty if anonymous), the *server-side session*, the *course* and the *course part*.

Statistics about the corpus are presented in Table 1 (left) along different facets: number of requests, number of course parts, total number of distinct

[1] With more than 850 courses and 1 million members, OpenClassrooms totalizes about 2.5 million unique visitors every month. See http://www.openclassrooms.com/.

Table 1. Statistics for (Left) all the 842 courses and (Right) the 4 selected courses

	Median	Mean	SD
Parts	17	28	35
Actions	8 922	45 681	197 549
Sessions	2 055	6 283	22 536
Users	199	476	1 252

	Screensaver	XML	Node.js	Java
Parts	11	107	36	164
Actions	4 380	10 284	61 387	1 099 295
Sessions	678	486	6 377	140 508
Users	80	34	611	4 582

web-sessions and number of distinct authenticated readers. As the standard deviation (SD) values indicate, there's evidence of distribution inequality of these variables within the different courses. We selected a subset of 4 courses for our experiments as follows: 2 courses with the nearest values to respectively the median (`Screensaver`) and the mean (`Nodejs`), the most popular course (`Java`) and an atypical one (`XML`). Their respective properties are given in Table 1 (right).

4 Reading Sessions

To study reading in eLearning, we use the concept of "*reading session*" to denote the period during which a reading activity takes place. It refers to a set of consecutive reading actions from a learner that can be considered continuous (apart from small interruptions, e.g. for reading email). This means that a learner who actually spends one-hour time on a course will carry out a one-hour reading session. Similarly, this concept was used in former studies to characterize reading, for instance on Wikipedia [25]. We manage to identify reading sessions using course part (i.e. page) reading-time thresholds which are computed based on actual time spent by learners on parts. Since part thresholds are used to delimit reading sessions, we define a threshold as the maximum time needed for reading the corresponding part. Our method is composed of five consecutive steps, with the first two ones (*user identification* and *actions duration estimation*) as preprocessing steps. In the remainder of this paper, we will use *action* as a shortcut for *reading action*. The synthetic algorithm is given in Listing 1.

User Identification. Most modern web servers use the session concept to maintain persistent communication with their clients. For instance, they can associate a unique identifier to each client process accessing the server during all the client visit. In our proposal, we use this data as a means to identify unique users. If the user identification is available, we reconstruct for each user his set of requests. If we lack this information or if we suppose that the identification is not required, we assume that each web session is connected to a dedicated anonymous user, each anonymous user being different from the others.

Actions Duration Estimation. Because the explicit end time of users' actions (an action being between two consecutive requests of the same user) is not captured by server-based logging systems, actions duration are not directly available. As a consequence, we use the time order in requests from a given user to assign user's actions end times and durations. For each sequence of actions of a given

Algorithm 1. Synthetic algorithm for reading session computation

```
// 1. Computing end timecodes and durations
foreach User in Data do
    foreach (Action,NextAction) of User do
        Action.End = NextAction.Begin
        Action.Duration = Action.End − Action.Begin
// 2. Computing parts thresholds
foreach Part in Data do
    PartData = Actions from Data, observed on Part
    Part.Threshold = Max(Peirce(PartData.durations))
// 3. Computing reading sessions per user
foreach User in Data do
    FirstAction = first Action of User
    FisrtAction.RS = 1
    foreach (Action,NextAction) of User do
        if Action.duration <= Part.Threshold then NextAction.RS =
        Action.RS;
        else NextAction.RS = Action.RS + 1;
```

user, the begin time of each of his request is considered as the end time of his previous action to compute the assumed duration of the action.

Part-threshold Values. Server-based monitoring can lead to very large durations, up to days, for parts that can be read in a couple of minutes. This is because a user may access a course part then change his activity momentously, for a long time or definitively. Moreover, some actions may be very short and hence not correspond to actual reading actions. To minimize the impact of these actions on the threshold calculation, we solely use "normal actions", excluding duration-excessive and duration-insignificant actions. This is performed by applying Peirce's criterion, a method that eliminates the presence of several suspicious data values (outliers) [26]. The maximum value of the remaining subset is then taken as the part reading threshold.

Dealing with unknown Durations. Unknown durations occur for the last action since no other request can be used to define its end time. In order not to affect the corpus, and rather than skipping these actions, we assign them with the threshold values of the read parts.

Delimiting Reading Sessions. Using the reading thresholds, actions of each user are grouped into reading sessions. A reading session is assumed finished when the time spent for reading a part is greater than the time threshold of that part.

Example. Figure 1 presents data about the first three reading sessions of a randomly chosen reader of the `Node.js` course. The data include the count of the read parts, the cumulative total of the unique read parts (compared to the 36 parts of the course), the ordered list of the read parts along with the graphical representation of the list, and finally the total duration of the session.

User	Reading session	Parts count	Total read parts	Path	Path graph	Duration
175	1	7	07/36	3;4;5;6;10;34;36		2m
	2	8	10/36	2;3;4;5;6;7;8;10		15m 2s
	3	4	13/36	10;11;12;13		6m 56s

Fig. 1. `Node.js` course: data about the reading sessions of a user

5 Reading Session-Based Indicators

We have defined several reading indicators based on reading sessions, organized in four categories. Each category is supplemented with higher level reading indications, computed from its indicators, to denote important detected reading facts and possible issues. The whole set consists of 27 indicators and 21 reading indications[2]. These indicators make use of subsets or the whole of the reading sessions, they can be related to one or many courses and to one or many users. In the following, we present these categories with some indicators as illustrations.

5.1 Category 1: General Facts About Course Reading

The distribution of the reading sessions over several dimensions can highlight many facts about learners' readings and provide basic hints for readings characterization within reading sessions. For instance, *Reading session duration* can serve as an indication of success and difficulty of the learning task (i.e. reading and understanding) [11]. Figure 2 presents three indicators on the four courses.

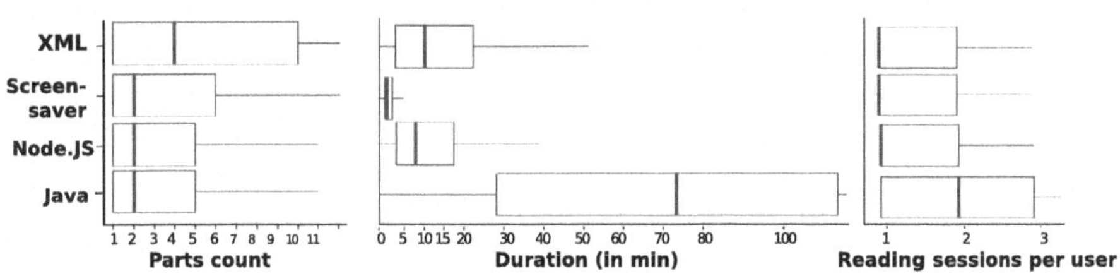

Fig. 2. Boxplots of three global indicators for the four courses, based respectively on reading sessions: number of parts, duration and number per user

5.2 Category 2: Reading Paths and Transitions

The reading path of a user is the sequence of parts that have been within his reading sessions. We analyse the most *Redundant/representative paths* and their *Deviation from the author expected one*. This allows to estimate *Global and per reading session progression ratio* and to detect *Paths covering the entire course*. Navigation properties were found to be correlated with learning task success [27]. For instance, the user path and its deviation from the optimal one are used to

[2] The full set of indicators is briefly described at http://bit.ly/reading-indicators.

predict a possible user disorientation [28]. A user transition between two course parts allows reporting a relation between them. We have studied for each part the *Identities of the provenance and destination parts* and the *Linearity* of these transitions. This may help to point out needed restructuration of the course.

Figure 1 contains the reading path of a randomly chosen reader of the `Node.js` course. The traversal is mainly linear with some jumps especially in the first reading session. Some of the skipped parts have been read later in the following reading sessions (e.g.: parts 2 and 7). The linearity of the reading within the `XML` course is illustrated in Fig. 3 (left), together with provenance and destination for one specific part (right).

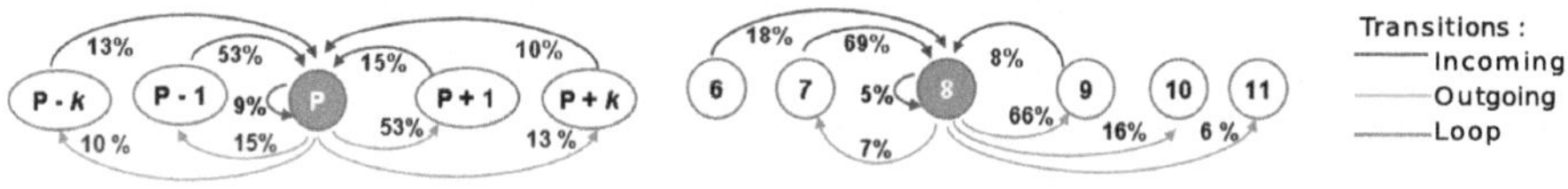

Fig. 3. Transitions ratios in `XML` reading: (Left) from and to a typical part, and (right) from and to *Part 8* ratios.

5.3 Category 3: Rereading

Revisitation is a common browsing behavior and one of the most used strategies in reading for learning. It can indicate reading facts like potential users disorientation [29], parts popularity and detecting relationship between parts. We differentiate rereads that occur on the same reading session (*Within-session rereads*) from those that are performed on different reading sessions (*Between-session rereads*). Reading the same content many times is a potential indicator that readers are struggling with it. Between-session rereads may indicate that the reader needs a reminder of the earlier read parts (e.g.to understand new concepts presented later or to replace himself within the course context). Figure 4 presents the rereading data of the `Node.js` course. Ratio for the two reread types are presented on the left: parts 3 and 13 have an important within-session rereads ratio that may indicate their difficulty. Distribution of these rereads are presented on the right: rereads are mainly done within the same reading sessions, which may reflect potential difficulties in reading the course.

5.4 Category 4: Reading Session Interruption

Analyzing reading session interruptions allows determining the parts where reading stops definitively (*Final stop parts*) or with later resume (*Reading session break parts*). Resuming may take place on the same part (*Self resume*) or on the next one (*next resume*), cases which can be seen as normal. Resuming may also take place on distant forward or backward parts (*Back resume* and *Forward resume*) which may indicate the need for a more detailed analysis. Figure 5 illustrates these cases for the `Java` course. 82 % of interruptions are final and concern

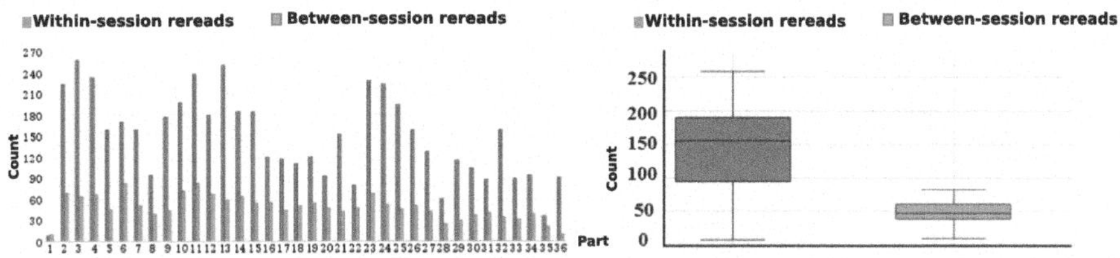

Fig. 4. Reread in `Node.js` course: (Left) Reread distribution on the first 20 parts (Right) Boxplot of the two reread types

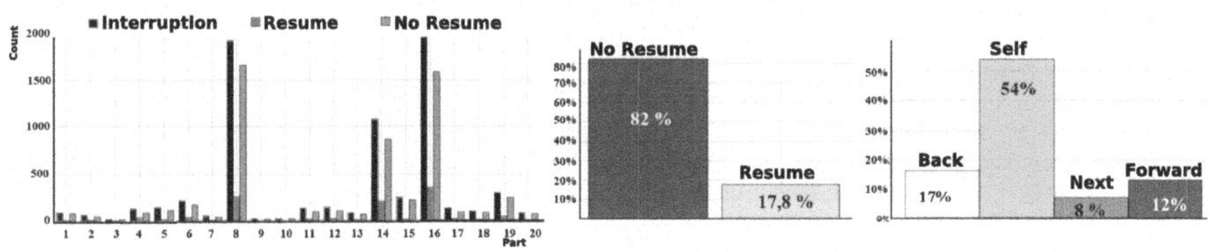

Fig. 5. Reading interruptions and resumes in `Java` course: (left) distribution on the course parts; (center) ratios of different types of interruption; (right) ratios of different types of resume

parts 8 and 16. Resumes are often done on the same interruption parts and in some cases are back or forward. A deeper analysis may indicate whether there is an issue in the course structuring since resuming on the next part has the less important value or whether it is a normal reading pattern for this course.

6 Evaluation and Discussion

6.1 Reading Session Calculation

Quality of the Reconstruction. As no effective measurement can assess the compliance of the reconstructed sessions with the actual ones, the reconstruction quality is often measured using the empirical observed Power Law distribution proposed in [30,31]. This law states that most visits to a website are concentrated on a small number of pages. Evaluating this can be performed by a linear regression on the logarithm of the number of the distinct read parts and the logarithm of the total number of reading sessions. The quality measure is given by the regression correlation coefficient R^2 and the standard error *err*. The closer R^2 coefficient is to one and the *err* near to zero, the better the session identification result. Results for our method applied on the four courses are shown on Fig. 6 as well as results using our method and the two other time-based methods with two threshold values: 10 min for pages and 30 min for sessions are shown on Table 2. They confirm our method capabilities in our context of study since it gives good fit results with an acceptable accuracy given by the error values.

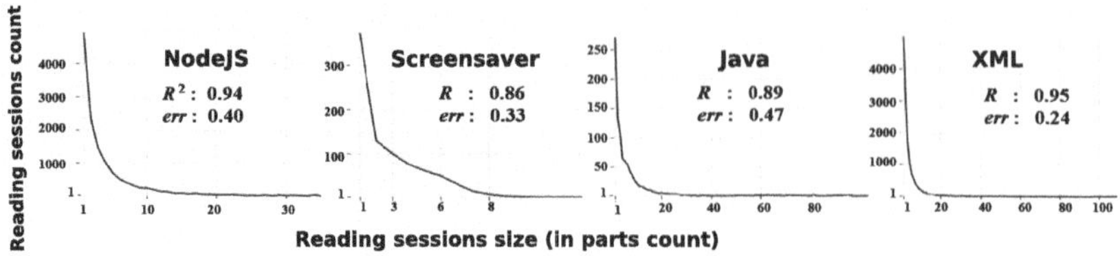

Fig. 6. Session size found by the power law distribution on the four courses

Table 2. Constructed sessions using three methods : our proposal, fixed page threshold (10-min) and fixed session threshold (30-min).

	Reading Session		10-min Page Thr.		30-min Session Thr.	
	R^2	*Err*	R^2	*Err*	R^2	*Err*
Nodejs	0.94	0.40	0.92	0.42	0.87	0.31
Screensaver	0.86	0.33	0.76	0.48	0.27	0.20
XML	0.89	0.47	0.82	0.45	0.79	0.51
Java	0.95	0.24	0.94	0.23	0.94	0.25

Compliance with Parts Size and Complexity. We estimated the size of each part of the courses by counting its significant words and in-line images (with each image considered as a short paragraph of 30 words). Pearson correlation coefficient between part size (computed as the words and figure count) and time threshold for that part is $r = 0.82$ ($p < 0.001$). This positive and significant correlation means that our method is actually generic and robust enough to take into account part size without needing to calculate it for each part. We can make the hypothesis that it is also the case for part complexity, even if part size does not directly indicates complexity level of the content. This also confirms the need to take into account characteristics of the parts for more accurate threshold values.

Comparison with Fixed Page Threshold Method. Following a per page reading time threshold approach for delimiting reading sessions based on learners reflects the actual usages and differentiates parts based on their content. Using a sole fix value would give imprecise results since we assume for each part the same maximum reading time. In fact, some parts may be read faster while others may need more than the fixed value time for reading, as exemplified by the four courses on Fig. 7. Whatever the selected threshold, there will always be parts which can be read in less than this time and others that may take more time.

Comparison with Fixed Session Threshold Method. Our method does not define constraints on the session size, which would cut many continuous long sessions and merge other short ones. We used a 30 min threshold on the data of about 2000 distinct readers of the `Java` course, which is known to be quite complex and having long parts (and hence, time-demanding). The results gave a median

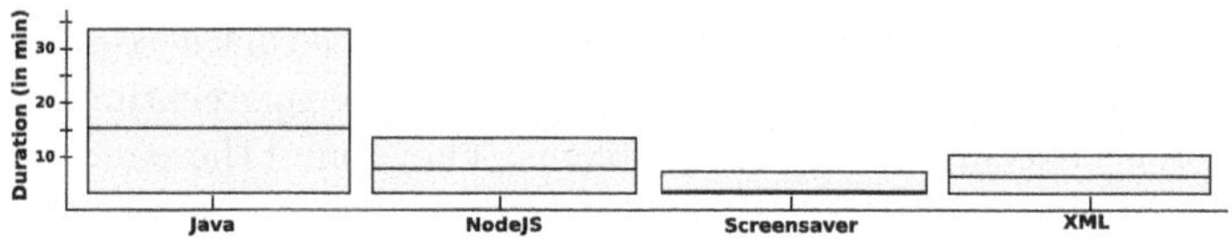

Fig. 7. Parts reading duration (boxplots): all are under 10 min for Screensaver.

of one (1) part – which mean that the half of sessions does not exceed one part – and a value of the 3rd quartile of 3 parts. The results using our method seem more realistic since they gave a median of 3 parts and 3rd quartile of 7 parts.

6.2 Reading Session Indicators Apprehension by Authors

To evaluate the relevance of the proposed indicators for course rewriting, we have conducted an exploratory study to gather OpenClassrooms course authors' opinions regarding our proposals. An online survey was set up that both contains *Likert scales* for rating indicators usefulness (very useful, useful, no opinion, somewhat useful or not useful) and free comment sections. At the time of writing, 105 out of hundreds authors had filled the online survey[3].

Indicators Rating. Figure 8 presents results of authors' ratings aggregated by category. All the proposed indicators were highly rated (useful), with the more contrasted results on the indicators related to parts distribution within sessions (*average number of parts per session*), rereading (*rereaders count* and *rereading – within and between-session – distribution on the parts* and interruption points (*definitive stops parts*). Indicators related to the *average reading speed per part* and *session count on the course* are the least rated ones.

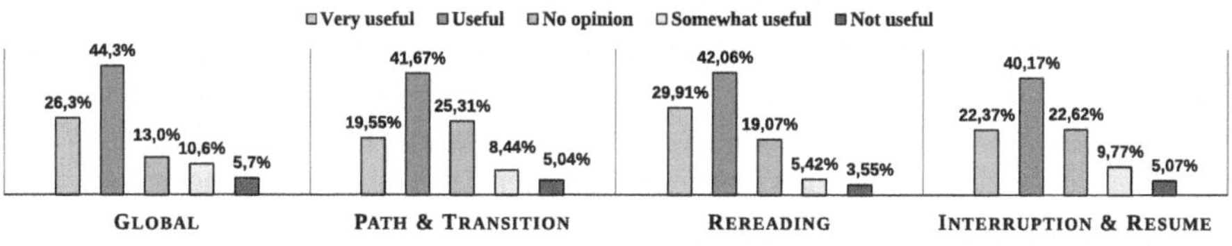

Fig. 8. Authors rating for the indicators, aggregated by categories

Comments and Opinions. The authors acknowledge that the exchanges between authors and readers are essential to build interesting and productive courses. The fact that readers' usages logs allow to consider the end-user perspective on consuming the course is deemed interesting. All the authors assess the usefulness

[3] The questionnaire and full results are available at http://bit.ly/authors-survey.

of reading usages to detect parts or aspects of the course that necessitate review. Many authors have appreciated indicators calculated by aggregating data, which may better reflect recurrent reading problems. They found these indicators judicious to give a good idea of the way learners read courses. While more than 73 authors estimate the set of indicators comprehensive enough to analyze reading, eight authors think that there are too many and without a judicious presentation to authors, this would be counterproductive. An author estimates that the approach seems complicated to implement technically and therefore may generate some unreliable results. Similarly, another author believes that we need a good level of abstraction so that authors will not be required to consult many tables and endless statistics. Another aspect reported by three authors is related to privacy; they suggested asking learners before logging them. Several authors proposed to consider the supplementation of computed indicators with explicit readers' feedback (courses and parts ratings, comments and annotations, etc.) that would help them to better understand readers' needs.

6.3 Conclusion and Future Work

In this paper, we use the concept of reading session as a means to model course reading. The proposed approach for session identification is grounded on data that represent learners' interactions with course parts and take into account each part characteristics. The computed threshold values for part reading-times are dynamic since they may be updated when new reading actions are logged. This allows their automatic adjustment 1/to precise their values with incoming reading data and 2/to take into account any evolution of the courses like pages restructuring and content update. Consequently, this approach seems a very plausible way to simulate learners reading and to fit the expected statistical behavior of real reading sessions. We plan to further verify this method capabilities by using/ defining appropriate metrics to characterize parts complexity and to compare the deduced sessions compliance with the real ones.

Several reading indicators based on reading sessions have been proposed and illustrated on courses from a major French eLearning provider. Reading session-based indicators intend to analyze reading from a behavioral perspective, a viewpoint that may efficiently reflect potential readers' needs and reading issues. This is acknowledged by authors whose survey responses indicate 1/ their understanding of the proposed set of indicators and 2/ the potential relevance of these indicators for course revision. Most of the gathered comments and suggestions actually correspond to aspects of our future work that we will address within our main project towards usage-based document reengineering : to further precise the reading indicators, supplement these with readers' annotations and build a simple and intuitive dashboard to assist authors.

References

1. Sadallah, M., Encelle, B, Maredj, A.-E., Prié, Y.: A Framework for usage-based document reengineering. In: 2013th ACM Symposium on Document Engineering DocEng 2013, pp. 99–102. ACM, New York (2013)
2. Hauger, D., Paramythis, A., Weibelzahl, S.: Using browser interaction data to determine page reading behavior. In: Konstan, J.A., Conejo, R., Marzo, J.L., Oliver, N. (eds.) UMAP 2011. LNCS, vol. 6787, pp. 147–158. Springer, Heidelberg (2011)
3. Zahoor, S., Rajput, D., Bedekar, M., Kosamkar, P.: Capturing, understanding and interpreting user interactions with the browser as implicit interest indicators. In: 2015th International Conference on Pervasive Computing (ICPC), pp. 1–6. IEEE Press, New York (2015)
4. Pahl, C., Donnellan, D.: Data mining technology for the evaluation of web-based teaching and learning systems. In: 7th International Conference on E-Learning in Business, Government and Higher Education, pp. 15–19. Dublin City University, Dublin (2002)
5. Arroyo, I., Murray, T., Park Woolf, B., Beal, C.R.: Inferring unobservable learning variables from students' help seeking behavior. In: Lester, J.C., Vicari, R.M., Paraguaçu, F. (eds.) ITS 2004. LNCS, vol. 3220, pp. 782–784. Springer, Heidelberg (2004)
6. Feng, M., Heffernan, N.T., Koedinger, K.R.: Looking for sources of error in predicting student's knowledge. In: 2005 AAAI Workshop on Educational Data Mining, pp. 54–61. AAAI Press, California (2005)
7. Hofmann, K., Reed, C., Holz, H.: Unobtrusive data collection for web-based social navigation. In: Workshop on the Social Navigation and Community based Adaptation Technologies, pp. 570–575. National College of Ireland, Dublin (2006)
8. Kovanović, V., Gašević, D., Dawson, S., Joksimović, S., Baker, R.S., Hatala, M.: Penetrating the black box of time-on-task estimation. In: 5th International Conference on Learning Analytics And Knowledge, pp. 184–193. ACM, New York (2015)
9. Mobasher, B.: Data mining for web personalization. In: Brusilovsky, P., Kobsa, A., Nejdl, W. (eds.) Adaptive Web 2007. LNCS, vol. 4321, pp. 90–135. Springer, Heidelberg (2007)
10. Marquardt, C.G., Becker, K., Ruiz, D.D.: A pre-processing tool for web usage mining in the distance education domain. In: Database Engineering and Applications Symposium IDEAS 2004, pp. 78–87. IEEE Press, New York (2004)
11. Aula, A., Khan, R.M., Guan., Z.: How does search behavior change as search becomes more difficult? In: SIGCHI Conference on Human Factors in Computing Systems, pp. 35–44. ACM, New York (2010)
12. Kazanidis, I., Valsamidis, S., Kontogiannis, S., Karakos, A.: Measuring and mining LMS data. In: 2012 16th Panhellenic Conference on Informatics (PCI), pp. 296–301. IEEE Press, New York (2012)
13. Bousbia, N., Rebaï, I., Labat, J.-M., Balla, A.: Learners' navigation behavior identification based on trace analysis. User Model. User-Adap. Inter. **20**(5), 455–494 (2010)
14. Zaíane, O.R.: Building a recommender agent for E-learning systems. In: International Conference on Computers in Education, pp. 55–59. IEEE Press, New York (2002)
15. Klašnja-Milićević, A., Vesin, B., Ivanović, M., Budimac, Z.: E-Learning personalization based on hybrid recommendation strategy and learning style identification. Comput. Educ. **56**(3), 885–899 (2011)

16. Brown, A.H., Green, T.: Time students spend reading threaded discussions in online graduate courses requiring asynchronous participation. Int. Rev. Res. Open Distrib. Learn. **10**(6), 51–64 (2009)
17. Romero, M., Barberà, E.: Quality of e-Learners' time and learning performance beyond quantitative time-on-task. Int. Rev. Res. Open Distrib Learn. **12**(5), 125–137 (2011)
18. Munk, M., Drlik, M.: Influence of different session timeouts thresholds on results of sequence rule analysis in educational data mining. In: Cherifi, H., Zain, J.M., El-Qawasmeh, E. (eds.) DICTAP 2011, Part I. CCIS, vol. 166, pp. 60–74. Springer, Heidelberg (2011)
19. Cooley, R., Mobasher, B., Srivastava, J.: Web mining: information and pattern discovery on the world wide web. In: 9th IEEE International Conference on Tools with Artificial Intelligence, pp. 558–567. IEEE Press, New York (1997)
20. Cooley, R., Mobasher, B., Srivastava, J.: Data preparation for mining world wide web browsing patterns. Knowl. Inf. Syst. **1**, 5–32 (1999)
21. Huynh, T., Miller, J.: Empirical observations on the session timeout threshold. Inf. Process. Manage. **45**(5), 513–528 (2009)
22. del Valle, R., Duffy, T.: Online learning: learner characteristics and their approaches to managing learning. Instr. Sci. **37**(2), 129–149 (2009)
23. Wise, A., Speer, J., Marbouti, F., Hsiao, Y.-T.: Broadening the notion of participation in online discussions: examining patterns in learners' online listening behaviors. Instr. Sci. **41**(2), 323–343 (2013)
24. Perera, D., Kay, J., Koprinska, I., Yacef, K., Zaïane, O.R.: Clustering and sequential pattern mining of online collaborative learning data. IEEE Trans. Knowl. Data Eng. **21**(6), 759–772 (2009)
25. Lehmann, J., Müller-Birn, C., Laniado, D., Lalmas, M., Kaltenbrunner, A.: Reader preferences and behavior on wikipedia. In: 25th ACM Conference on Hypertext and Social Media, pp. 88–97. ACM, New York (2014)
26. Ross, S.M.: Peirce's criterion for the elimination of suspect experimental data. J. Eng. Technol. **20**(2), 38–41 (2003)
27. McEneaney, J.E.: Graphic and numerical methods to assess navigation in hypertext. Int. J. Hum. Comput. Stud. **55**(5), 761–786 (2001)
28. Gwizdka, J., Spence, I.: Implicit measures of lostness and success in web navigation. Interact. Comput. **19**(3), 357–369 (2007)
29. Herder, E.: Revisitation patterns and disorientation. In: German Workshop on Adaptivity and User Modeling in Interactive Systems ABIS03, pp. 291–294. University of Karlsruhe, Germany (2003)
30. Berendt, B., Mobasher, B., Spiliopoulou, M., Wiltshire, J.: Measuring the accuracy of sessionizers for web usage analysis. In: Workshop on Web Mining at the 1st SIAM International Conference on Data Mining, pp. 7–14 (2001)
31. Vázquez, A., Oliveira, J.G., Dezsö, Z., Goh, K.-I., Kondor, I., Barabási, A.-L.: Modeling bursts and heavy tails in human dynamics. Physical Review E. 73(3), 036127–1:036127–19. American Physical Society, USA (2006)

Stand Tall and Raise Your Voice! A Study on the Presentation Trainer

Jan Schneider(✉), Dirk Börner, Peter van Rosmalen, and Marcus Specht

Welten Institute, Open University of the Netherlands, Heerlen, The Netherlands
{jan.schneider,dirk.boerner,peter.vanrosmalen,
marcus.specht}@ou.nl

Abstract. The increasing accessibility of sensors has made it possible to create instructional tools able to present immediate feedback to their users. In order to study how this type of instruction can have an effect on learning, we created the *Presentation Trainer*: a prototype designed to help users to develop their nonverbal communication skills for public speaking. In this paper we present our work in progress on the *Presentation Trainer*, which includes two user studies. The studies showed that participants would gladly use the *Presentation Trainer* to prepare for oral presentations, and pointed out to some considerations required for the design of tools able to effectively support a complex learning task through immediate feedback.

Keywords: Immediate feedback interface · Sensor-based learning support · Public speaking · Design-based research

1 Introduction

Public speaking is a subject that has been studied for ages. The earliest identified vestiges about a systematical study of the art of public speaking comes from the ancient Greeks and are about 2500 years old [1]. Nowadays public speaking is required for almost any profession [2] and has an influence on many aspects of our daily life [3].[1]

In a presentation, the speaker has the purpose to communicate her message to the audience. In order to do that successfully she has to be able to encode the message in the right format and deliver it effectively [3]. The nonverbal communication of the speaker plays an important role in the delivery of the message [4–6].

While currently it is possible to get access to different material such as seminars, courses, books, magazines, etc. that can teach us how to use our nonverbal communication effectively for public speaking, developing these skills requires practice and feedback. Having a human tutor to give us feedback is not always affordable or feasible, making it relevant to explore how technology can be used to solve this learning problem.

---

[1] http://www.nsaspeaker.org/.

© Springer International Publishing Switzerland 2015
G. Conole et al. (Eds.): EC-TEL 2015, LNCS 9307, pp. 311–324, 2015.
DOI: 10.1007/978-3-319-24258-3_23

Sensors have shown to be a technology able to provide learners with feedback for many different learning applications [7], therefore we use them to develop the *Presentation Trainer*: a sensor-based prototype designed to support the development of nonverbal communication skills for public speaking.

In order to create an effective trainer for a complex task such as the development of nonverbal public speaking skills, we need to overcome technical challenges such as how to accurately track and interpret the nonverbal communication of the user. As well as educational challenges such as how to use the analyzed information to provide users with the kind of feedback that will help them with the improvement of their skills. Therefore, we decided to follow a design-based research methodology [8], which includes user tests at the end of each iteration providing us with guidance for the upcoming ones. The purpose of this paper is to present our findings from the two studies that have been conducted in our process of developing the *Presentation Trainer.*

2 Presentation Trainer Application

The *Presentation Trainer* is a tool designed to support learners in the development of their nonverbal communication skills for public speaking, by giving them feedback and instruction about the use of their voice and body language. The approach followed for its development is an iterative one, where each iteration is evaluated through user tests. The two versions of the *Presentation Trainer* presented in this article were implemented in Processing 2.1[2], an open source JAVA-based programming language. It has an OpenGL integration that allows fast graphic manipulation making it suitable for 2D and 3D programs. To track the learner's performance the Presentation Trainer makes use of the Kinect Sensor[3] and the computer integrated microphone.

2.1 Feedback Framework

Feedback is one of the most influential learning tools; learners' achievements both positive and negative vastly depend on it [9]. The means to present feedback vary greatly and several dimensions of feedback have been identified. One of these dimensions refers to the timing of feedback, which can be delayed or immediate [10]. While training for public speaking, immediate feedback has been proven to have a superior influence in the development of the nonverbal communication skills [11]. The channel of feedback is another feedback dimension that we considered to be relevant for our designs. While giving a presentation, the presenter is constantly receiving feedback from the audience through the visual channel, also the most important nonverbal communication aspect while presenting is giving eye contact to the audience [6]. Therefore the *Presentation Trainer* gives immediate feedback that is transmitted through the visual channel, implicitly helping the user to learn how to receive feedback while giving a presentation.

[2] https://www.processing.org/.
[3] http://www.xbox.com/en-US/kinect.

2.2 Voice Analysis

To track the user's voice the *Presentation Trainer* uses the integrated microphone of the computer together with the Minim audio library.[4] By analyzing the volume input retrieved from the microphone it is possible to give instruction to the user regarding her voice volume and speaking cadence. Having a good voice volume modulation while public speaking is fundamental to transmit a clear message and keeping the audience attention [3]. Therefore the *Presentation Trainer* gives feedback to the user when the volume of her voice has been too loud, too low or has not been modulated for an extended period of time.

Pauses are referred as a stop while speaking. Mastering them is an important skill for public speaking [6]. When used correctly, pauses allow the audience to take a breathe when information is dense in content or emotion, create spaces for the audience to refocus on the given information, prepare the audience for the following subject, and can add dramatic emphasis during the presentation. To help with the improvement of this skill the *Presentation Trainer* gives feedback about the proper use of pauses, indicating the user when it is time to pause and start talking again. The default values used by the Presentation Trainer to give these indications have been obtained by analyzing the average speaking and pausing time of 15 different Ted Talks.[5]

2.3 Body Language Analysis

The *Presentation Trainer* uses the Microsoft Kinect sensor in conjunction with the OpenNI SDK[6] to track and analyze the body of the user. This fusion allows the creation of a skeleton representation of the user's body. With the use of this skeleton representation, the *Presentation Trainer* is able to analyze the user's body posture and movements in order to give feedback and instructions. While speaking to an audience it is important to project confidence, openness and attentiveness towards the audience. The body posture of the speaker is a tool to convey those qualities. Therefore it is recommended to stand up in an upright position facing the audience and with the hands inside of the acceptable box space; in front of the body without covering it, above the hips, and without the arms being completely extended [6]. We defined these rules in terms of the relative coordinates between the different tracked limbs of the user. Following these rules the Presentation Trainer is able to give feedback about the user's posture.

Hand gestures in public speaking enhance a speech in different ways such as: strengthening the audience's understanding of verbal messages, painting vivid pictures in the listeners' minds, conveying the speaker's feelings and attitudes, dissipate nervous tension, enhance audience attentiveness and retention, etc. [12] The current version of the *Presentation Trainer* does not identify specific gestures; nevertheless it gives feedback to the user whenever she is not using any gesture for a certain amount of time. In order to identify whether the user has been gesturing or not, the Presentation Trainer calculates the amount of movement of the user's hands.

4 http://code.compartmental.net/tools/minim/.
5 https://www.ted.com/talks.
6 http://www.openni.org.

3 First Study

The purpose of this first study was to explore the users' acceptance of the *Presentation Trainer* and to identify its usability challenges as an immediate feedback tool for learning. This section includes a description of the first version of the *Presentation Trainer's* output interface, a description of the setup used for our first user tests, and a report of our findings.

3.1 Output Interface Version 1

The output interface that has been used for the first user tests of the *Presentation Trainer,* was designed as a dashboard, it contains three columns with a total of seven different feedback modules (Fig. 1).

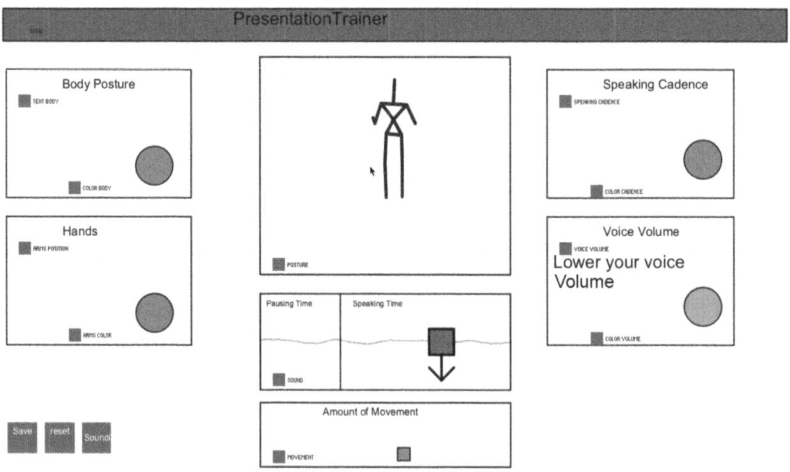

Fig. 1. Presentation Trainer interface showing that the user was speaking too loud.

Each of the feedback modules located on the columns at the left and the right side of the interface, provide feedback on only one aspect of the user's nonverbal communication. They present their feedback using a circle whose colors fade indicating whether the user is performing correctly or not. In the case when a mistake is detected, these modules show a written instruction on how to correct it. The modules on the left column give feedback about the user's body posture and hand movements; and the modules on the column give feedback about the user's voice volume and speaking cadence.

The center column contains three feedback modules that continuously reflect the user's actions, highlighting her mistakes. The module at the top shows a skeleton representation of the user, highlighting the limbs that are in an incorrect position. The module in the middle shows a graph mirroring the users voice. Finally the module at the bottom indicates the amount of hand movement performed by the user.

3.2 User Tests Setup

The test consisted on doing a trial short presentation while using the *Presentation Trainer* as a coach. The experimental setup sketched in Fig. 2 shows the participant standing at a distance of approximately 2.5 m in front of the Microsoft Kinect and 2 computer screens. One of the screens displayed the *Presentation Trainer;* the other displayed the slides that had to be presented. We deliberately chose to use two screens for the setup, because we wanted to simulate a real presentation scenario, where the presenter has to pay attention to the presented slides and to the audience.

After the trial presentation, participants were asked to fill in a System Usability Scale (SUS) [13] questionnaire followed by an interview. During the interview we showed the user interface of the Presentation Trainer to the participants and asked them questions to find out which components of the interface were the most used, helpful and interesting. We also asked questions on their general opinion about the Presentation Trainer and what they would like to get from it in the future.

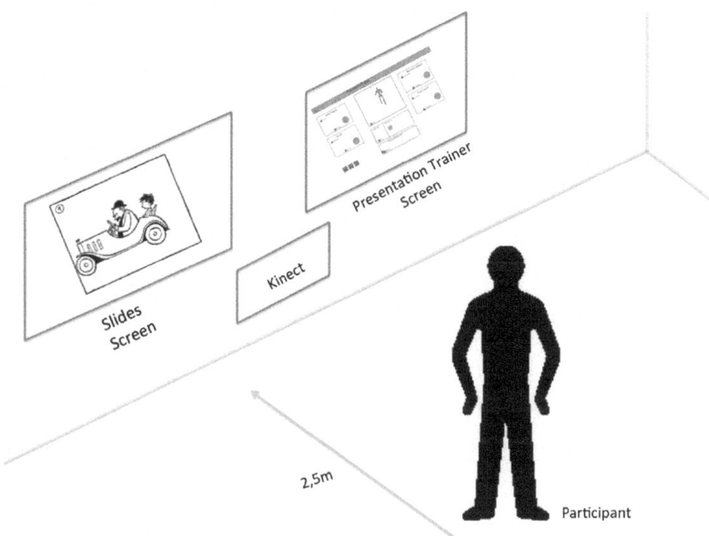

Fig. 2. The setup sketch of the first user test

3.3 Results of the First User Study

Six participants took part on the test we considered this amount reasonable since the recommended number of participants for user tests is five [14]. We had three female and three male participants, whose ages ranged from 24 to 45 years old. The working experience of all of them is in the field of learning or computer sciences. Moreover, as part of their work, they have to perform public presentations a couple of times a year. In a scale from 0 to 100 where 100 represents the best value, the average scores for the SUS were: 67.5 for SUS, 77.1 for learnability, and 65.1 for usability [15].

All participants concluded that the most observed modules where the ones located in the center column paying a special attention to the one showing the Skeleton. The colored circles were observed but participants did not know how to change their behavior based on them. The users did not observe the displayed texts with instructions. Some participants suggested using icons instead of the circles to make the feedback more explicit.

Participants remarked about the overload of attention required to give a presentation and be aware of all the feedback at the same time. Therefore it was suggested to use a learning strategy focusing on giving feedback only about on one aspect of the trained skills at the time.

3.4 Evaluation of First Results

Participants in the user tests show great enthusiasm towards using a tool such as the Presentation *Trainer* to practice for their future presentations. The observations executed during the user tests showed that participants did not always adapt their behavior according to the feedback presented by the tool. We attribute this lack of responsiveness mainly to the amount of cognitive load required to give a presentation, which constrains the amount of attention that can be paid to the tool. Hence, we can conclude that an immediate feedback interface for learning needs to be carefully designed, in order for it to be effective.

4 Second Study

For this study we created a second version of the *Presentation Trainer,* carefully redesigning it according to the challenges exposed by our first evaluation. In this second study we conducted again some user tests exploring the impressions, interactions and challenges of the second version of the *Presentation Trainer*. This section describes the approach used to improve our prototype, including the description and results of our second user study.

4.1 Tackling the Complexity

Our first study showed that the amount of attention that a learner can pay to feedback while giving a trial presentation is quite constrained. To tackle this problem we decided to follow two strategies. The first strategy was to make the task of training for a presentation simpler for the user by the implementation of an instructional design model on the *Presentation Trainer* that deals with the difficulty of learning complex tasks. The second strategy deals with the improvement of the interface so that users find it easier to act on its feedback.

Instructional Design for Complex Learning. Since developing nonverbal public speaking skills has shown to be a complex learning task, we decided to start implementing the four-component instructional design (4C-ID) model [16] in the design of the *Presentation Trainer*. In order to develop complex skills, instructional design models usually divide the complex skill, into sub-skills and teach these sub-skills separately. The 4C-ID also encourages a holistic approach with realistic, complete tasks so learners can understand the relevance of these sub-skills in the whole task [17].

To start with the implementation of the 4C-ID model, for this version of the trainer we created two modes:

- The *Freestyle Mode* with the purpose to allow learners to develop integrated knowledge while practicing a real life task, which is giving a presentation.
- The *Exercise Mode* for sub-skills practice.

Freestyle Mode. This mode has the purpose to let users practice the real life task (giving a presentation) while receiving feedback and instruction from the *Presentation Trainer*. It has the same functionality as the previous version of the tool, by standing in front of the Microsoft Kinect and speaking, the user will start to receive immediate feedback and instruction about her nonverbal communication. We called it *Freestyle Mode* because in this mode users are not restricted to perform specific tasks.

Our previous study showed us that the complexity of the previous version of the *Presentation Trainer* should be reduced in order for users to assimilate its feedback. Before making drastic changes on the interface, for this study we wanted to explore whether a nicely and clearly designed dashboard interface (Fig. 3) is practical for this type of learning scenarios.

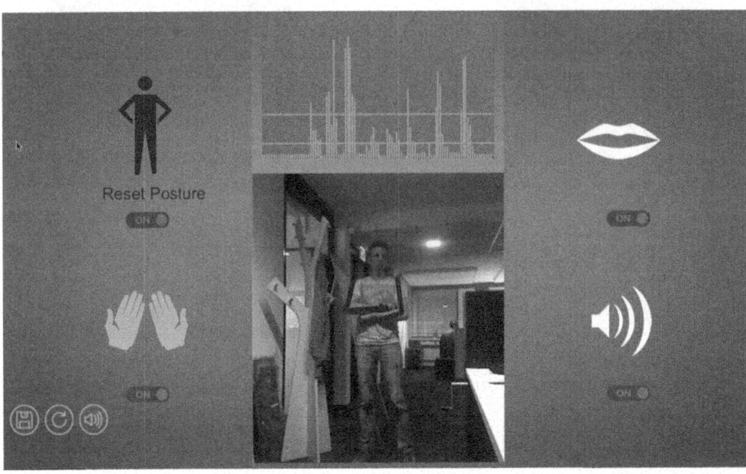

Fig. 3. Freestyle mode interface

To improve on the interface modules for Body Posture and Hands were merged into one module responsible to give instruction about the user's posture, including the posture of the hands and the body. In order to reduce the amount of possible instructions that the user can get about her posture, such as: uncross your arms, straighten up, look forward, do not hide your left hand behind your body, etc.; we decided to let the system tell the user to *Reset Posture*. The *Reset Posture* is a posture used by many public speakers, where they stand straight, facing the audience, with their legs uncrossed, their hands in front of their body, above their hips, and letting the fingers of the right hand touch the fingers of the left one (Fig. 4).

For immediate feedback the use of keywords have shown to be more effective than the use ad hoc explanations [18] therefore we shortened the text instructions from the feedback modules to maximum two word phrases such as: Reset Posture, Move More, Pause, Speak, Raise Volume, Lower Volume, and Modulate Volume.

In the first version the users commented that they noticed the color changes in the circles but did not understand how to respond. Additionally they suggested the use of icons instead of circles. Therefore this new version substituted the circles with icons fading their color from white when everything is correct to red when the user is making a mistake on the corresponding aspect of her nonverbal communication.

Additional changes in the interface deal with the skeleton representation, which changed into an enhanced mirrored image of the user. This image highlights user's limbs that are in a wrong position. Also the *Voice Feedback* module changed into a voice histogram, allowing the user to have an overview about the volume of her voice and how much has been talking.

Fig. 4. Examples of influential speakers standing in the Reset Posture

Exercise Mode. To implement the sub-skills practice defined in the 4C-ID model we created the exercise mode for the *Presentation Trainer*. This mode fractionates the task of developing nonverbal public speaking skills into different exercises or learning tasks. Each exercise is designed to train the user in a specific sub-skill of her nonverbal communication. Each exercise provides the user with information that highlights its relevance, instructions explaining the steps that the user is supposed to follow at the precise moment and feedback about her current performance (Fig. 5).

The exercises developed so far are: *Reset Posture*, *Voice Volume, Hands Gesticulation, Pause Control*, *Leaning in while speaking soft*, and *Questions and Answers* section. The *Reset Posture* exercise should get the user acquainted with the *Reset*

Posture, a posture that is commonly used by well-trained presenters that allows them to be perceived open and attentive towards the audience. During this exercise the user is asked to go back to the *Reset Posture* after speaking for a few moments.

The *Voice Volume* exercise intends to make the user aware of the importance of modulating her voice volume while public speaking. It asks the user to speak using different voice volumes for a predefined amount of time.

The *Hand Gesticulation* exercise aims at training the use of hand gestures that are inside of the acceptable box space, while teaching the importance of using these types of gestures. In these exercise the image mirror of the user is shown in the screen, and the user is asked to reach certain virtual targets with their hands while speaking, helping her to automate the use of hand gestures while doing a presentation.

The *Pause Control* exercise has the purpose to teach and train users about the proper way to use pauses while public speaking. In this exercise the user is instructed to speak for some seconds and then make a pause that is at least 2 s long, before instructing her to start speaking again.

In the previous exercises the purpose was to either train the body language or the voice. In the *leaning in while speaking soft* exercise we explore the combination of training both aspects at the same time. The *technique of leaning in and speaking soft* can be used in public speaking to help you to connect at a personal level with the audience while sharing some secrets or personal opinions [3]. So this exercises instructs the user to lean in and speak at a low voice volume for some seconds. After performing the exercise correctly the *Presentation Trainer* instructs the user to return to the *Reset Posture* in order to restart the exercise.

The purpose of the *Questions* exercise is to teach users to keep composure, while waiting for questions asked by an audience and answering them. During this exercise the user has to stand in the *Reset Posture* waiting for the *Presentation Trainer* to ask a question. The questions asked by the *Presentation Trainer* are related to the already trained nonverbal communication practices for public speaking. An example question is: "What are the benefits of pauses while public speaking?" Once the user answers the

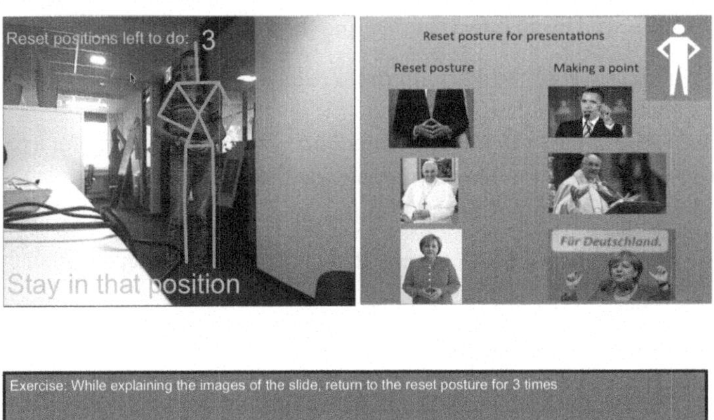

Fig. 5. Interface of Reset Posture exercise. Top left: enhanced mirror. Top right: sample slide to use for the exercise. Bottom: exercise instruction.

question, the *Presentation Trainer* instructs the user to stay quietly in the *Reset Posture* while waiting for the next question. The Presentation Trainer does not assess the answer to the questions; it only assesses the nonverbal communication of the user while waiting for the questions and answering them.

4.2 Second Study User Tests Setup

Prior to the test participants were asked to create six slides of a short presentation based on a template that was proportionated to them beforehand. The template includes topics such as the participant's origin, profession, personal hobbies and favorite movies.

Upon the arrival to the test, the participant was asked to sign up a form of consent to confirm the agreement that the recordings done during the test were going to be used only for academic purposes. After that we gave each participant a briefing about the purpose of the *Presentation Trainer* and explained the tasks to be done during the test.

Each user test consists of two phases. On the first phase the participant had a session using the *Exercise Mode* of the *Presentation Trainer.* In this session the participant followed the instructions provided by the Presentation Trainer, that guided him/her through the six different exercises: *Reset Posture, Voice Volume, Hand Gesticulation, Pause Control*, *Leaning in while speaking soft*, and *Questions.* In order to move from one exercise to the next the participant had to perform the exercise correctly three times. The experimental setup for this phase consisted on the participant standing at approximately 2.5 m in front of the Microsoft Kinect sensor and a 27-inch display displaying the *Presentation Trainer* interface. Once completing all the exercises, the participant was asked to start with the second phase of the test. For this second phase, the participant stood 2.5 m in front of the Microsoft Kinect sensor, a 27-inch display showing the *Presentation Trainer* interface on *Freestyle Mode,* and another screen showing the slides of the presentation (Fig. 2). During this phase of the test, the participant was asked to give a trial presentation of the prepared slides, while paying attention to the feedback from the *Presentation Trainer*.

After completing the two phases of the test, the participant was asked to fill in a SUS questionnaire followed by an interview. During the interview the examiner asked about:

- Personal impressions of the *Presentation Trainer.*
- Opinions about the *Exercise Mode*.
- The added value of the Presentation Trainer in contrast of preparing for a presentation in front of a mirror without any tool giving feedback.
- Additional comments and suggestions.

The tests and the interviews were recorded in order to make a proper analysis of the results.

4.3 Results of the Second Study

To make this study comparable with the previous one, we decided to recruit participants from the same age and background as in the first user test, and who never used the Presentation Trainer before. The amount of participants for these tests was five, three females, and two males. Once again the age of the participants ranged from 24 to 45 years old, they all worked also in the field of learning or computer sciences, and have to give oral presentations a couple of times a year. In a scale from 0 to 100 where 100 represents the best value, the results of the SUS questionnaire gave the Presentation Trainer an average of 57.0 in the SUS, 59.4 in usability and 47.5 in learnability [15].

All participants during the interviews stated that the load of attention for giving a presentation and using the system for the first time is too much to handle, therefore they all indicated that would need some time to get used to the tool before being able to assimilate the feedback and instructions provided by it. All participants pointed out that they perceived the Presentation Trainer as a useful tool and that they would like to use it in order to prepare for their upcoming presentations. Pointing out the relevance of receiving objective immediate feedback while preparing for them.

With regard to the Exercise Mode, all participants found this mode necessary to develop their nonverbal skills. Nonetheless, they remarked on improving the tutorial for each of the exercises. Two participants made a suggestion about making the feedback while performing the exercise more explicit, by giving clear indications on how to correct their current behavior when the exercise is being performed incorrectly.

During this user study we observed that the feedback provided by the *Presentation Trainer* had some effects on the participants' behavior, nevertheless this change of behavior was not always the desired one. For example when the *Move More* caption was presented, users shook their body or took one or two small steps to the sides, instead of gesticulating more with their arms while speaking. We also identified that all participants mastered the *Reset Posture* by using it throughout their trial presentation, providing us an indicator that some learning has happened while using the system.

4.4 Discussion of Second Study

The scores of the SUS questionnaire were considerably lower than in the previous study, this might give the impression that the older version of the trainer was more usable and learnable than the new version. However, in contrast with the tests of the previous study where participants did not change their behavior while receiving feedback from the trainer, during the tests of this second study participants modified their behavior when feedback and instruction was given to them. Also we found it very encouraging observing all participants using the *Reset Posture* while giving their presentation, suggesting us that some learning took place while using the *Presentation Trainer*. These observations indicate us that the trainer became more usable and learnable even when users perceived the opposite. We attribute the lower SUS scores to two different factors. The first one is that while giving the trial presentation, participants were able to identify in the feedback proportionated by the *Presentation Trainer* that there was something wrong with their performance, but that the feedback was not clear enough for them to know how to correct their mistakes. This led them to realize about the time needed to learn how to use the system correctly. The second factor deals with the expectations of the participants towards the Presentation Trainer. We explain these increasing expectations to the fact that the interface of this second tested version does not look like a prototype anymore, leading participants to expect from the *Presentation Trainer* to work as a commercial system and not as a experimental prototype.

Examining the impressions and observations of the use of the *Freestyle Mode*, we can conclude that the cognitive load is an important issue that needs to be further tackled. We observed that a clear interface allows users to perceive and adapt to some of its feedback. Showing us that a dashboard interface could be used to give immediate feedback for learning, but with some limitations. To make full use of this type of interfaces a user needs to pay attention to all the elements displayed on the screen and identify how to follow them; in order to be able to adapt her behavior and learn something, while performing a complex task. This requires an amount of a cognitive load that surpasses the capacity of the user.

We also observed that while using the Freestyle mode, in some cases participants were able to perceive the feedback, but adapted their behavior in an incorrect way. This pointed out the importance of adding a learning module to the system, explaining the meaning of the feedback and teaching users, the proper way to interpret it.

The Exercise Mode looks really promising; nonetheless it has room for improvement. Feedback showing whether the exercise is being performed correct or incorrect should become more explicit, and should give clear instructions on how to correct the mistakes. Exercises need to be well designed so that users are able to transfer the skills acquired during the exercises to the presentations. For example as shown during the tests, participants learned how to gesticulate, but not how to gesticulate while presenting. This was reflected during their trial presentations where none of them used enough hand gestures while presenting.

5 Conclusion and Future Work

The rising availability of sensors has created the space to design, develop and explore tutoring tools able to provide users with immediate feedback about their performance. In this article we present the findings of our ongoing studies on the *Presentation Trainer*: An example of a sensor-based tutoring system that by providing users with immediate feedback and instruction, is able to support them with acquisition and development of complex skills. The two studies described in this article showed us that users seem to be really enthusiastic and open towards the new learning experiences that this type of tools can provide. Furthermore, they also provided us with three findings that serve as guidelines for the design of this type of learning tools:

- Regardless of the explicitness of the feedback, the user requires an explanation on how to respond to it, before starting her training using the tool.
- The interface should be simple and clear; a dashboard giving feedback in multiple aspects at the same time is not optimal for learning.
- Decreasing the complexity of a learning task, by following the principles of an instructional design model helps users to assimilate the feedback given by the system, allowing them to learn specific skills. As the participants of our tests show by using the *Reset Posture*.

We consider that the learning effects of the *Presentation Trainer* and any other immediate feedback tool depend partly on their usability; therefore for near future work, we plan to continue with our current design-based research approach; keep on developing and conducting user test with the upcoming versions of the *Presentation Trainer*, until we consider it mature enough to test its learning effects on users. Furthermore we will conduct interviews with experts in the field of public speaking in order to come up with valid expertise model to analyze the nonverbal communication for presentations, and study the experts' opinion on how a tool such as the *Presentation Trainer* can be used to support the development nonverbal communication skills.

Acknowledgment. The underlying research project is partly funded by the METALOGUE project. METALOGUE is a Seventh Framework Programme collaborative project funded by the European Commission, grant agreement number: 611073 (http://www.metalogue.eu).

References

1. DeCaro, P.A.: Origins of public speaking. In: The Public Speaking Project, Chap. 2. http://www.publicspeakingproject.org/psvirtualtext.html (2011)
2. Parvis, L.F.: The importance of communication and public-speaking skills. J. Environ. Health 35–44 May 1 2001
3. DeVito, J.A.: The Essential Elements of Public Speaking. Pearson, Boston (2014)
4. DeCoske, M.A., White, S.J.: Public speaking revisited: delivery, structure, and style. Am. J. Health Syst. Pharm. **67**(15), 1225–1227 (2010)
5. Trimboli, A., Walker, M.B.: Nonverbal dominance in the communication of affect: a myth? J. Nonverbal Behav. **11**(3), 180–190 (1987)
6. Bjerregaard, M., Compton, E.: Public Speaking Handbook. Snow College, Supplement for Public Speaking (2011)
7. Schneider, J., Börner, D., van Rosmalen, P., Specht, M.: Augmenting the senses: a review on sensor-based learning support. Sensors **15**(2), 4097–4133 (2015)
8. Anderson, T., Shattuck, J.: Design-based research a decade of progress in education research? Educ. Researcher **41**(1), 16–25 (2012)
9. Hattie, J., Timperley, H.: The power of feedback. Rev. Educ. Res. **77**, 81–112 (2007)
10. Mory, E.H.: Feedback research revisited. In: Jonassen, D.H. (ed.) Handbook of Research on Educational Communications and Technology, 2nd edn, pp. 745–784. Lawrence Erlbaum, Mahwah (2004)
11. King, P., Young, M., Behnke, R.: Public speaking performance improvement as a function of information processing in immediate and delayed feedback interventions. Commun. Educ. **49**(4), 365–374 (2000)
12. Toastmasters International: Gestures: your body speaks. http://www.toastmasters.org/ (2011)
13. Brooke, J.: SUS: a "quick and dirty" usability scale. In: Jordan, P.W., Thomas, B., Weerdmeester, B.A., McClelland, A.L. (eds.) Usability Evaluation in Industry. Taylor and Francis, London (1996)
14. Nielsen, J., Landauer, T.K.: A mathematical model of the finding of usability problems. In: Proceedings of ACM INTERCHI 1993 Conference, pp. 206–213 (1993)
15. Lewis, J.R., Sauro, J.: The factor structure of the system usability scale. In: Kurosu, M. (ed.) HCD 2009. LNCS, vol. 5619, pp. 94–103. Springer, Heidelberg (2009)
16. Van Merriënboer, J.J.G.: Training Complex Cognitive Skills: A Four-Component Instructional Design Model for Technical Training. Educational Technology Publications, Englewood Cliffs (1997)

17. Van Merriënboer, J.J.G., Kirschner, P.A.: Ten Steps to Complex Learning, 2nd edn. Routledge, New York (2013)
18. Coninx, N., Kreijns, K., Jochems, W.: The use of keywords for delivering immediate performance feedback on teacher competence development. Eur. J. Teach. Educ. **36**(2), 164–182 (2013)

Displaying Teacher's Gaze in a MOOC: Effects on Students' Video Navigation Patterns

Kshitij Sharma[1(✉)], Patrick Jermann[2], and Pierre Dillenbourg[1]

[1] Computer Human Interaction in Learning and Instruction, École Polytechnique Fédérale de Lausanne, Lausanne, Switzrland
{kshitij.sharma,pierre.dillenbourg}@epfl.ch
[2] Center for Digital Education, École Polytechnique Fédérale de Lausanne, Lausanne, Switzrland
patrick.jermann@epfl.ch

Abstract. We present an eye-tracking study where we augment a Massive Open Online Course (MOOC) video with the gaze information of the teacher. We tracked the gaze of a teacher while he was recording the content for a MOOC lecture. Our working hypothesis is that displaying the gaze of the teacher will act as cues in crucial moments of dyadic conversation, the teacher-student dyad, such as reference disambiguation. We collected data about students' video interaction behaviour within a MOOC. The results show that the showing the teacher's gaze made the content easier to follow for the students even when complex visual stimulus present in the video lecture.

Keywords: Eye-tracking · MOOCs · Gaze contingency · Reference dissambiguation

1 Introduction

In the present decade, off the shelf eye-trackers have became readily available for use. With the advent in the mobile eye-tracking technology, eye-tracking researchers are no longer bound to laboratory based experiments. Eye-tracking provides direct access to users' attention which is useful in situations like MOOCs, where the major questions involve student engagement and learning processes.

We know from previous eye-tracking research that speakers look at the objects they refer to just before pointing and verbally naming the objects [6]. Listeners on the other hand, look at the referred objects shortly after seeing the speaker point and refer to the objects [2]. Richardson and colleagues [9] showed that the listeners who were better at attending the references made by the speaker were also better at understanding the context of the conversation. One way to aid the listeners attending the reference in a better way is to display where the speaker is looking at. This helps the listeners in a better disambiguation of the complex references [17,18]. In the case of complex stimulus displaying the gaze of speaker makes the disambiguation of the references even easier [19]. This motivated us

© Springer International Publishing Switzerland 2015
G. Conole et al. (Eds.): EC-TEL 2015, LNCS 9307, pp. 325–338, 2015.
DOI: 10.1007/978-3-319-24258-3_24

to study the effect of showing the gaze of the teacher in a MOOC video on the navigation patterns of the students.

Students' navigation styles can tell us a lot about their perception about the content. Li and colleagues [16] conducted a study with over 30,000 students and 100 videos across two courses where the authors asked students to rate the perceived difficulty of the content after the students watched the video. Based on students' rating and their video navigation behaviour [16] concluded that the students who perceived the video content as easy to understand did less frequent and shorter pauses, and replayed the video less frequently.

In this contribution, we show that displaying teacher's gaze in a MOOC video-lecture can help the students understand more easily the content of a MOOC video. Moreover, this effect remains consistent with the increasing complexity of the situation explained by the teacher.

2 Related Work

The literature on the use of eye-tracking methods for MOOCs is scarce. However, there is a lot to learn from the eye-tracking research carried out in various fields like online education, usability of the video content and gaze contingency (displaying the gaze of expert or one of the collaborators) studies. In this section we give a brief overview of the eye-tracking studies done in these different but related fields.

2.1 Eye-tracking and MOOCs

There are a few studies carried out in the MOOC context that have used eye-tracking as the process data source. Sharma and colleagues [10,11] proposed gaze measures to predict the learning outcome in MOOCs. [10] uses the low level gaze features (derived from the gaze directly on the stimulus) to predict the learning outcome; while [11] used the fact that how closely the students follow the teachers' deictic and verbal references to predict the learning outcomes [7].

2.2 Eye-tracking and Online Education

Use of eye-tracking in online education has provided the researchers with insights about the students' learning processes and outcomes. Van Gog [14] used eye-tracking data to provide feedback to the students about their action while troubleshooting an electrical circuit and found that the feedback improved the learning outcomes. In another contribution, Van Gog [13] found that displaying an experts gaze during problem solving guides the novices to invest more mental effort than when no gaze is displayed. Amadieu and colleagues [3] used eye-tracking data to find the affect of expertise, in a collaborative concept map task, on the cognitive load. The authors concluded that the average fixation duration was lower for the experts indicating more cognitive load on experts than novices. In an experiment, where the participants had to learn a game, [1] found that the good learners focus more on the contraption ares of the game while they think about the possible solutions. [12] found that the students spend more time on the complementary pictures in a presentation, than decorative pictures.

2.3 Gaze Contingency and Reference Disambiguation

Gaze contingent experiments are at the proactive side of the eye-tracking technology. These experiments consist in displaying the gaze of collaborating partners to each other; or displaying the gaze of an expert to a novice in order to teach the novice [5]. Another modality of gaze contingency is using gaze as a mode of communication. In a collaborative "Qs-in-Os" search [4] showed that the sharing gaze information between collaborating partners results in a strategy of division of labour as effective as if the partners were talking face to face. Using gaze as a communication modality [8] used gaze information to inform participants about the effectiveness of grounding process between a human and an infotainment presentation agent. In a multiparty video conference system [15] used gaze information to rotate the participants' virtual 3D representations to the persons they were talking to. Displaying the gaze of speaker helps the listener in deciphering the references [17,18]. Moreover, gaze of speaker makes it easier for the listener in deciphering the references in situations with high ambiguity [19].

3 The Present Work

In this section, we present the important details about the study we carried out to explore the effects of displaying gaze of the teacher on the students' video interaction patterns. The teacher's gaze was recorded when he was recording the MOOC video. Our prime hypothesis is that displaying teachers' gaze on the video will make the reference disambiguation easy in high ambiguous situations. Moreover, displaying teacher's gaze on the video will also make the students' behaviour more linear in terms of following the content.

3.1 Experiment Setup

We asked one of the teachers to track his eyes on the MOOC video he was going to record. We used SMI mobile eye-tracking glasses to record the gaze of the teacher. The main motivation to use mobile eye-trackers was to give the teacher as ecologically valid environment as possible. The setup of the MOOC recording studio is shown in Fig. 1. The teacher was equipped with the eye-tracking glasses. There was a screen capture software running on the tablet with the actual content to record every move of the teacher. Also, there was a camera on the ceiling of the studio to capture the external actions (external to tablet) on the tablet. We put 9 fiducial markers on the tablet so that later we can be able to re-locate the gaze pointer of the teacher on the tablet. The video was uploaded on Coursera as one of the video lectures during one of the weeks of the course "Villes africaines: Introduction à la planification urbaine" (African cities: an introduction to urban planning). The teacher explicitly chose the parts of the video where he wanted to display his gaze. None of the authors had control over this fact.

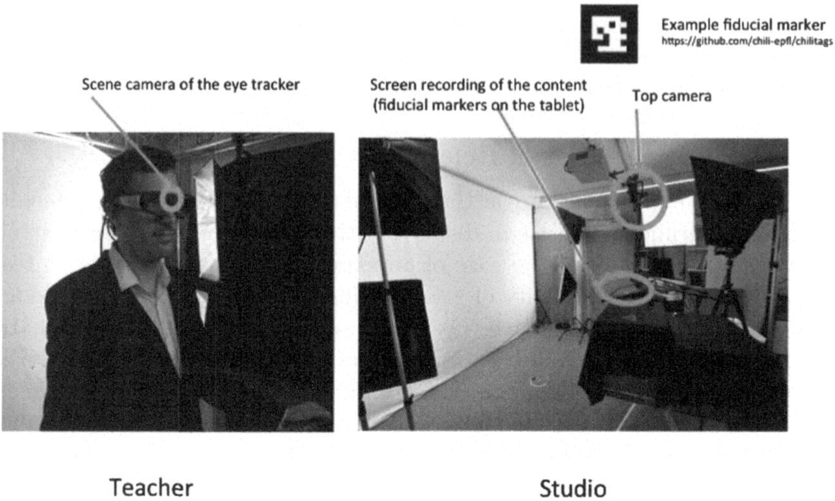

Fig. 1. Setup: The teacher is equipped with the SMI mobile eye-tracking glasses (left) and the MOOC recording studio (right) with the top camera on the ceiling and the tablet used by the teacher. The fiducial markers (top-right) are glued to the tablet to make the re-localisation of teacher's gaze on the actual content easy.

3.2 Research Questions

Through this experiment, we wanted to explore following two research questions:

1. What is the affect of displaying teachers' gaze on a MOOC lecture on students' video interaction patterns? Our hypothesis is that displaying teacher's gaze on the video will make the students' behaviour more linear in terms of following the content (*behavioural hypothesis*)
2. If there is a relation between the students' video interaction patterns and teacher's gaze, how is it effected by the ambiguity of the video? We hypothesise that displaying teachers' gaze on the video will make the reference disambiguation easy in ambiguous situations (*eye-tracking hypothesis*).

3.3 Re-localisation of Teacher's Gaze

We recorded three different video streams from the setup of Fig. 1. First, the video from scene camera of the eye-tracker. Second, from the top view camera in the studio. Finally, the third video stream comes from the screen capture software running on the teacher's tablet. We knew teacher's gaze positions in the frame of the video captured from the scene camera of the eye-tracker. The objective was to find the gaze positions on the video from the screen capture of the tablet. This is not a trivial task. Since the teacher was given full freedom to move, his field of the view of changes every instant. We compute the gaze positions on the actual content using following steps:

Step 1. We compute the relative position of the fiducial markers and the gaze positions in the video from the scene camera of the eye-tracker.

Step 2. We compute the relation between the positions of the fiducial markers in the video from the top camera and the video from the scene camera of the eye-tracker.

Step 3. Using the two relations, computed in steps 1 and 2,we compute the gaze positions on the video from the top camera. The output of this step is a video where the gaze pointers are shown on the video from the top camera.

Step 4. The video from the top camera is geometrically a distorted version of the video from the screen capture software running on the tablet. Hence, we remove the distortion from the resulting video of step 3 to get the video from the screen capture software with teachers' gaze pointers.

Fig. 2. Example of a high ambiguity image from the experimental video. The image is captured via satellite and the teacher is explaining the landscape captured. We rate these type of images because high ambiguity images as disambiguating a reference like "the cathedral" is difficult without a visual cue.

3.4 Ambiguity in Stimulus and Teacher's Gaze

To analyse the students' behaviour we divided the video into four episodes based on whether there was teacher's gaze present on the video and what was the level of ambiguity in the images shown in the video (high vs low ambiguity). The ambiguity in the image was determined by *how easy was it to disambiguate a simple verbal reference on any part of the image.* Simply put, how easy it was to locate what part of image/scene the speaker is talking about. Images with high ambiguity are satellite images and aerial images where the target reference are smaller in size and are not obviously present in front of the listeners' eyes. Whereas, images with low ambiguity are street views where the target references a bigger in size and are easily detectable by the listeners. Examples of images with high and low ambiguity are shown in Figs. 2 and 3 respectively. Examples of simple verbal references in both the images would be "the cathedral"(Fig. 2) and "the tree"(Fig. 3). This categorisation was done by the authors and later confirmed by the teacher himself. The main reason for this categorisation was to be able to segment the video in high and low ambiguity stimulus periods.

Fig. 3. Example of a low ambiguity image from the experimental video. The image is typical street view and the teacher is explaining the landscape captured. We rate these type of images as low ambiguity images because disambiguating a reference like "the tree" is easy without a visual cue.

3.5 Measures

In this subsection, we present the measures of students' behaviour we used to analyse the affect of displaying the teacher's gaze in the video. We compare the measures in two ways. First, we compare the values of the variable for the experimental video and other videos(*between videos variable*). Second, we compare the values of the variable within the experimental video for different episodes in the video (*within video variable*).

Proportion of Replayed Video Length: This is calculated by counting the number of video seconds that were played more than once. This primarily indicates the difficulty that student perceives during the video lecture. A high proportion of replayed video for a student suggest that the student was not able to understand some of the content properly in the first time going through the video. This is used only as a between video variable.

Number of Pauses: This is the average number of pauses that a student makes during one video. High number of pauses indicates the difficulty as well as frequent disengagements from the video. This variable is used as both a between and within video variable.

Ratio of Pause Time and Video Length: This is the ratio of the total time spent by the students while keeping the video in a pause state and the total video length. Longer pauses will result in a higher value of the ratio. Moreover, the higher ratio will indicate the difficulty in understanding the video as students will need more time to grasp the concept. This variable is used only as a between video variable.

Number of Seek Backs: This is the average number of backward jumps that a student makes during one video. The seek back event typically reflects two necessities from a student. First, a check for a reference that was made at a previous video point. Second, a complete section of the video being too difficult to understand and the student decided to re-watch the whole video segment. This variable is used as both the between and within video variable.

4 Results

As we mentioned in the Sect. 3.5, there are two levels of analysis to be presented in the paper. First, we compare students' behaviour across different videos in the weeks succeeding and the preceding the week of the experimental video. Second, we compare the students' behaviour across different episodes within the experimental video. The three weeks are weeks 10, 11 and 12, which also are the last weeks of the course. The main reasons behind selecting only three weeks to compare are that the size of student population is comparable for these three weeks and that the population is comparable in terms of motivation to finish the course and the levels of engagement.

4.1 Comparing User Behaviour Across Different Weeks

In this subsection we compare the number of pauses, seek backs, seek forwards, the pause time and replay time across different videos. The experimental video has "11.1" as the label. Moreover, in the Figs. 4 - 7 the variables corresponding to the experimental video are shown as a thicker bar than the other videos.

Proportion of Replayed Video Length: We observe that the proportion of the replayed length video is lowest (Fig. 4) for the experimental video ($F[9,4202] = 2.12$, $p = .03$).

Number of Pauses: We observe that the average number of pauses is second lowest (Fig. 5) for the experimental video ($F[9,4202] = 2.89$, $p = .002$). The reason for the video 12.3 having the least number of pauses is that the video 12.3 is the "end of course" video with only a few seconds of length.

Ratio of Pause Time and Video Length: We observe that the ratio of pause time and video length is lowest (Fig. 6) for the experimental video ($F[9,4202] = 2.58$, $p = .005$).

Number of Seek Backs: We observe that the average number of seek backs is second lowest (Fig. 7) for the experimental video ($F[9,4202] = 1.92$, $p = .04$). Again, 'end of course" video (12.3) is with only a few seconds of length.

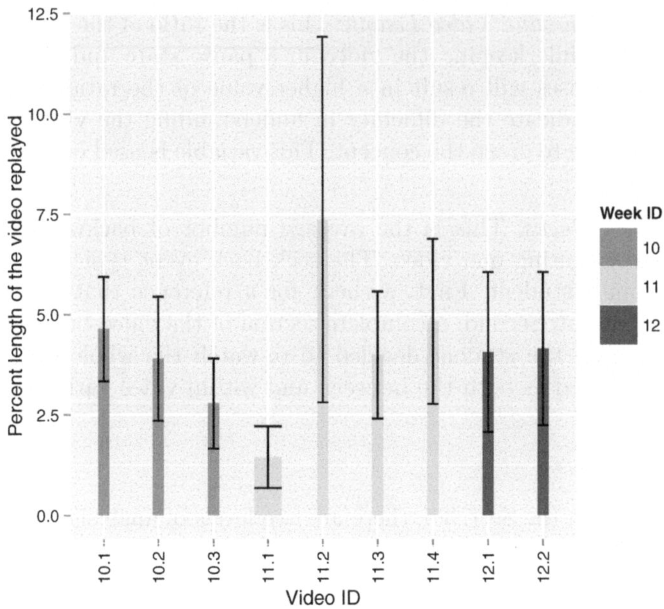

Fig. 4. Proportion of replayed video length compared across weeks 10, 11 and 12. The experimental video (thick bar, id 11.1) has significantly the lowest proportion of the replayed length among all the videos.

4.2 Comparing User Behaviour Within the Video

In this subsection, we compare the number of pauses, and seek back actions for different episodes within the experimental video (Figs. 8 and 9). As we explained in Sect. 3.4, the experimental video was divided in 4 different kinds of episodes based on two facts: (1) whether teacher's gaze is present or not; and (2) whether the ambiguity in the video has high or low ambiguity. In Table 1 we observe the following:

Number of pauses in "gaze-present" episodes is lower than that in "gaze-absent" episodes. Moreover, there are lower number of pauses in the high ambiguity situations than those in low ambiguity situations (χ^2 = 79.83, $p < .001$).

Number of seek backs in "gaze-present" episodes is lower than that in "gaze-absent" episodes. Moreover, there are lower number of seek backs in the high ambiguity situations than those in low ambiguity situations (χ^2 = 164.83, $p = .001$).

5 Discussion

The results in Sect. 4.1 show that the behavioural hypothesis (Sect. 3.2) comes out to be true. The fact that the students have less number of seek back events

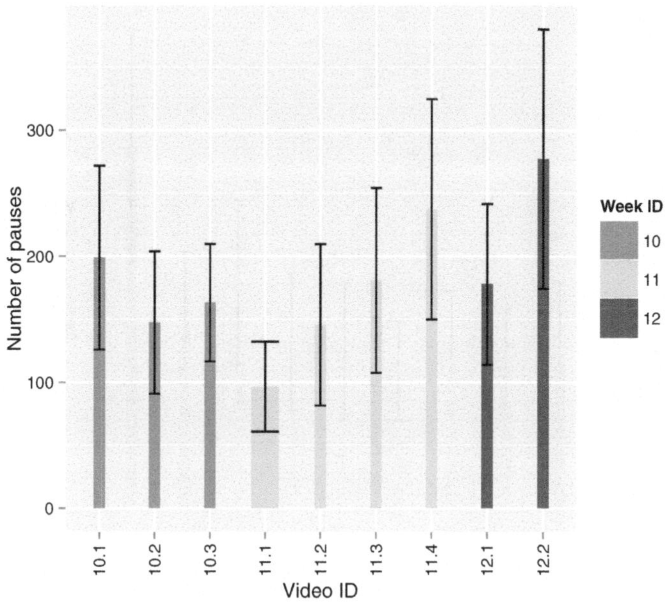

Fig. 5. Average number of pauses compared across weeks 10, 11 and 12. The experimental video (thick bar, id 11.1) has significantly lower number of pauses than other videos.

reflects the fact that they did not need to check back the previously told content because it was easy to understand for them once the teacher's gaze was displayed on the video. Moreover, the same fact is strongly supported with less amount of video content replayed for the experimental video. Similarly, less frequent and shorter pauses indicate that the content delivery was also easy due to the presence of additional cues to disambiguate complex references during the video. Li and colleagues [16] found similar video navigation patterns in their study for the students who perceived the video content as easy to understand.

The observation that there are less seek back and pauses during the experimental video also verifies our working hypothesis of making the learning experience more linear as compared to the video material. With less breaks in the

Table 1. Number of different types of events compared within the experiment video across different episodes.

Action	Pause		Seek-back	
Ambiguity level of the scene	High	Low	High	Low
Gaze-present	16(7.22)	64(-4.27)	18(-4.27)	23(-5.71)
Gaze-absent	94(-2.97)	232(-2.97)	52(1.21)	142(8.77)

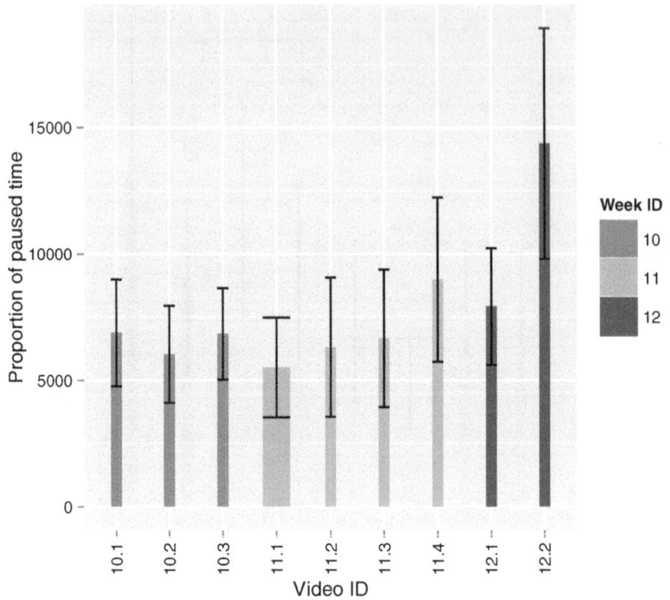

Fig. 6. Ratio of pause time and video length compared across weeks 10, 11 and 12. The experimental video (thick bar, id 11.1) has significantly the lowest ratio among all the videos.

content delivery and the less back references the student is well aligned with the video content in temporal space and hence the creation and maintenance of a mutual understanding between the teacher student dyad is effective and efficient.

The key difference between the experimental video and the videos from the other week was the augmentation of teacher's gaze on top of the video content. Since the students see where the teacher was looking and it is proved by eye-tracking research that people start looking at the point they are about to refer and hence it is easy to disambiguate the point of reference for the listener when(s)he sees the gaze of referee.

The results from the Sect. 4.2 proved our eye-tracking hypothesis (Sect. 3.2) to be true as well. The students make less pause and less seek backs in high ambiguity situations, such as the teacher describing complex images like satellite captured image (Fig. 2),when the gaze is present in the video as compared to when the gaze is absent on the video. This effect is present, although less pronounced, in situations with low ambiguity (for example when the teacher is explaining a street view, Fig. 3). Prasov and Chai [19] also found in their study about reference disambiguation in complex stimulus that the displaying the gaze of speaker makes it easy for the listener to disambiguate the reference.

Although the results support our hypothesis, more experimentation is required to find out whether displaying teacher's gaze helps in increasing the effectiveness of learning experiences. Moreover, further investigation is necessary to comment on the affect of augmenting multiple MOOC videos with teacher's gaze on the overall learning experience of students.

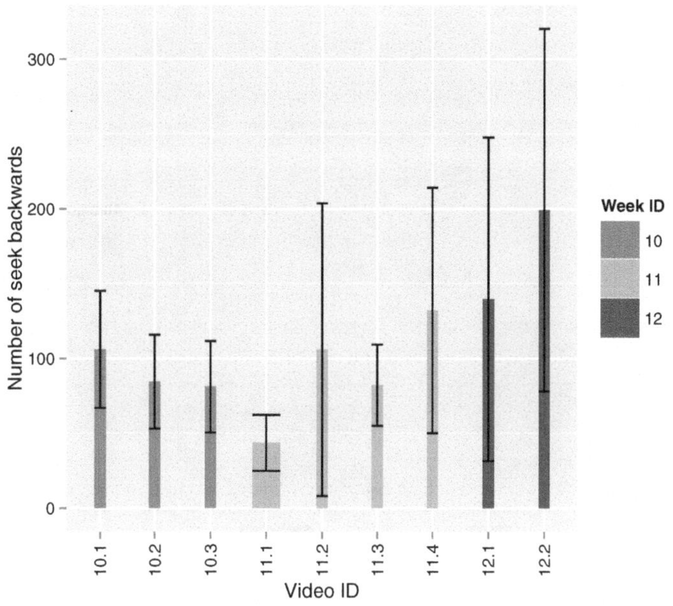

Fig. 7. Average number of seek back events compared across weeks 10, 11 and 12. The experimental video (thick bar, id 11.1) has significantly lower number of pauses than other videos.eps

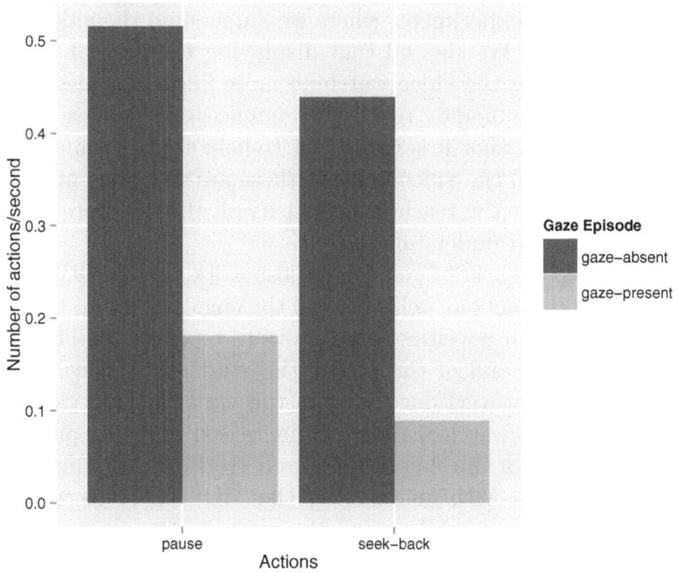

Fig. 8. Proportions of different types of events compared within the experiment video across different gaze episodes.

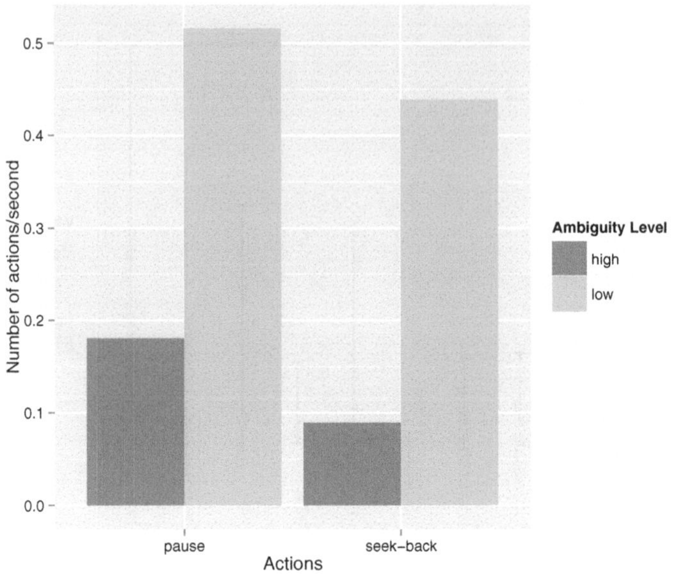

Fig. 9. Proportions of different types of events compared within the experiment video across different ambiguity episodes.

6 Conclusion

We presented a MOOC experiment, where we augmented the video lecture with the gaze of the teacher. We showed that displaying the gaze of the teacher on the video not only makes the video watching more linear but also makes it easy for the students to disambiguate teacher's references in complex situations. We put emphasis on the fact that it is important to help students understand where the teacher is referring in the video because these are the moments that create a shared understanding for the teacher student dyad. Having more such moments help maintain the shared understanding.

The introduction of teachers' gaze might also work as a novelty in the engagement process of the students as well. To keep the engagement up to a level which benefits the student, such novelties could prove to be effective. The results show that usually during the end of the course the students who watch the videos decrease drastically. However, once we put the experimental video online the number of students who watched the video increased from the previous week.

In a nutshell, both of our hypotheses were verified and this motivates us to continue experiments with augmenting the MOOC videos with the visual cues to help students better understand the content. Our future work includes experimentation with different eye-tracking data visualisations to augment the MOOC video and check how it affects the students' video navigation patterns and their learning processes. Also to perform a laboratory experiment to see how closely the students follow the gaze pointer of the teacher and how it affects their learning outcome.

Acknowledgement. This research was funded by Swiss National Science Foundation grants CR12I1_ 132996 and 206021_144975. We would also like to thank the teacher Prof. Jérôme Chenal, who agreed to let us experiment with his course on Coursera.

References

1. Alkan, S., Cagiltay, K.: Studying computer game learning experience through eye tracking. Br. J. Educ. Technol. **38**(3), 538–542 (2007)
2. Allopenna, P.D., Magnuson, J.S., Tanenhaus, M.K.: Tracking the time course of spoken word recognition using eye movements: evidence for continuous mapping models. J. Mem. Lang. **38**(4), 419–439 (1998)
3. Amadieu, F., Van Gog, T., Paas, F., Tricot, A., Marine, C.: Effects of prior knowledge and concept-map structure on disorientation, cognitive load, and learning. Learn. Instr. **19**(5), 376–386 (2009)
4. Brennan, S.E., Chen, X., Dickinson, C.A., Neider, M.B., Zelinsky, G.J.: Coordinating cognition: the costs and benefits of shared gaze during collaborative search. Cognition **106**(3), 1465–1477 (2008)
5. Chetwood, A.S., Kwok, K.-W., Sun, L.-W., Mylonas, G.P., Clark, J., Darzi, A., Yang, G.-Z.: Collaborative eye tracking: a potential training tool in laparoscopic surgery. Surg. Endosc. **26**(7), 2003–2009 (2012)
6. Griffin, Z.M., Bock, K.: What the eyes say about speaking. Psychol. Sci. **11**(4), 274–279 (2000)
7. Kizilcec, R. F., Papadopoulos, K., Sritanyaratana, L.: Showing face in video instruction: effects on information retention, visual attention, and affect. In: Proceedings of the 32nd Annual ACM Conference on Human Factors in Computing Systems, pp. 2095–2102. ACM (2014)
8. Prendinger, H., Eichner, T., Andre, E., Ishizuka, M.: Gaze-based infotainment agents. In: Proceedings of the International Conference on Advances in Computer Entertainment Technology, pp. 87–90. ACM (2007)
9. Richardson, D.C., Dale, R., Kirkham, N.Z.: The art of conversation is coordination common ground and the coupling of eye movements during dialogue. Psychol. Sci. **18**(5), 407–413 (2007)
10. Sharma, K., Jermann, P., Dillenbourg, P.: How students learn using moocs: An eye-tracking insight. In: EMOOCs 2014, The Second MOOC European Stakeholders Summit (2014)
11. Sharma, K., Jermann, P., and Dillenbourg, P.: "With-me-ness" : A gaze-measure for students? attention in moocs. In: International Conference of the Learning Sciences (2014)
12. Slykhuis, D.A., Wiebe, E.N., Annetta, L.A.: Eye-tracking students? attention to powerpoint photographs in a science education setting. J. Sci. Educ. Technol. **14**(5–6), 509–520 (2005)
13. Van Gog, T., Jarodzka, H.H., Scheiter, K., Gerjets, P., Paas, F.: Attention guidance during example study via the model's eye movements. Comput. Hum. Behav. **25**(3), 785–791 (2009)

14. Van Gog, T., Paas, F., van Merrienboer, J., Witte, P.: Uncovering the problem-solving process: cued retrospective reporting versus concurrent and retrospective reporting. J. Exp. Psychol. Appl. **11**(4), 237 (2005)
15. Vertegaal, R., Weevers, I., and Sohn, C.: Gaze-2: An attentive video conferencing system. In: CHI 2002 Extended Abstracts on Human Factors in Computing Systems, pp. 736–737. ACM (2002)
16. Li, N., Kidzinski, L., Jermann, P., Dillenbourg, P.: How do In-video interactions Reflect Perceived Video Difficulty. In: EMOOCs 2015,The Third MOOC European Stakeholders Summit (2015)
17. Hanna, J.E., Brennan, S.E.: Speakers' eye gaze disambiguates referring expressions early during face-to-face conversation. J. Mem. Lang. **57**(4), 596–615 (2007)
18. Gergle, D., Clark, A.T.: See what I'm saying? using Dyadic Mobile Eye tracking to study collaborative reference. In: Proceedings of the ACM 2011 Conference on Computer Supported Cooperative Work, pp. 435–444. ACM (2011)
19. Prasov, Z., Chai, J.Y.: What's in a gaze: the role of eye-gaze in reference resolution in multimodal conversational interfaces. In: Proceedings of the 13th International Conference on Intelligent User Interfaces, pp. 20–29. ACM (2008)

Reflexive Learning, Socio-cognitive Conflict and Peer-assessment to Improve the Quality of Feedbacks in Online Tests

Franck Silvestre(✉), Philippe Vidal, and Julien Broisin

Université Toulouse III Paul Sabatier,
Institut de Recherche en Informatique de Toulouse,
118 Route de Narbonne, 31062 Cedex 04 Toulouse, France
franck.silvestre@irit.fr

Abstract. Our previous works have introduced the Tsaap-notes platform dedicated to the semi automatic generation of multiple choice questionnaire providing feedbacks: it reuses interactive questions asked by teachers during lectures, as well as the notes taken by students after the presentation of the results as feedbacks integrated into the quizzes. In this paper, we introduce a new feature which aims at increasing the number of contributions of students in order to significantly improve the quality of the feedbacks used in the resulting quizzes. This feature splits the submission of an answer into several distinct phases to harvest explanations given by students, and then applies an algorithm to filter the best contributions to be integrated as feedbacks in the tests. Our approach has been validated by a first experimentation involving master students enrolled in a computer science course.

Keywords: Interactive questions · Quality of feedback · Reflexive learning · Peer-assessment · Socio-cognitive conflict

1 Introduction

Different studies [9,12] show that computer-based assessments facilitate the provision of frequent formative assessments to large groups of students. Also, the quality of the feedback provided to students in the context of their works or of their assessments results is a key factor for better learning [2,7,8]. David Nicol & DMD [10] recommend the use of online tests so the feedback is accessible to students anytime, from anywhere and as often as they wish. However, the feedback provided to students by traditional online learning management systems or other IMSQTI compliant platforms [11] is, by default, minimalist: for each question, it includes the student's score and the correct answer; additional and relevant feedback has to be produced by teachers manually, and this time consuming process is therefore not done very often.

We have described in [16] the approach "Note as Feedback" (NaF), implemented in our Tsaap-Notes platform [15]. Tsaap-Notes allows teachers to ask

© Springer International Publishing Switzerland 2015
G. Conole et al. (Eds.): EC-TEL 2015, LNCS 9307, pp. 339–351, 2015.
DOI: 10.1007/978-3-319-24258-3_25

interactive questions during lecture, and students to answer questions and to take notes on each of these questions in following the presentation of the results given by all the participants. As Tsaap-Notes questions are written using the Moodle gift format, the approach "NaF" allows the teacher to generate in an automatic way a Moodle compatible quiz composed of (1) the interactive questions asked by the teacher during the lecture, and (2) the notes taken by the students on those questions; these notes represent the feedback exposed to students when they perform the quiz within Moodle.

Despite the promising results of the first experimentation, two limits have been clearly identified in the current Tsaap-Notes implementation. 1- Every single note taken by students on a given question is automatically included into the feedback of the quiz; the notes are not evaluated nor filtered, there is no "quality check" of the feedback. 2- Only few students participate in the writing of explanations that are required to build relevant feedbacks. Thus, in this paper, we present a new feature to manage interactive questions called "question with submission of answer in n-phases" (NP-Q) dealing directly with the two limits mentioned above: interactions implemented in NP-Q maximize on one hand the students' participation in the writing of an explanation, and on the other hand enable students to assess the different analysis they made. In addition, the "best" contributions only are integrated as source of feedback into the Moodle quiz. The article is organized as follows : Sect. 2 presents the scientific sources which have inspired the making of NP-Q; Sect. 3 shows the implementation of NP-Q in Tsaap-Notes; Sect. 4 relates the results of the first experimentation made with a group of 51 Master students from Paul Sabatier University (Toulouse III). We conclude in Sect. 5 and present some future works.

2 Why the NP-Q Feature?

A limit highlighted by the first experimentation conducted with the NaF feature of Tsaap-Notes is the low engagement of students in the note-taking process. Indeed in [16], results show that only 25 % of students take notes, even though 75 % of students participate in interactive questions [15]. This limit affects the creation of revision tests because there are not enough feedbacks, and it affects the lecture itself as well. When three quarters of students answer multiple choice questions, why only one quarter participates in the writing of an explanation?

Scouller reminds that assessments influence the learning process considerably [13]: the way a student is assessed determines how, what, and how much he will learn. Most students put their efforts in acquiring knowledge and cognitive abilities on what they know they will be assessed on. In [1], Biggs and Tang explain that active educational methods, where students deal with activities aligned with the learning target and with the assessment tasks, stimulate a better and thorough learning approach for them. Both authors put forward the fact that "formative assessments" provide the student with the feedback allowing him to know where he stands. The positive impact of interactive vote systems on the involvement of students shown through different studies [4,6,14,18] is due mainly to the formative assessment function: during a lecture, students are able to notice in real time their level of knowledge or cognitive ability, whether individually or compared to a group.

Starting from these findings and to increase the participation rate in the writing of an explanation about a question during a lecture, our hypothesis stands on the fact that students should be provided with immediate feedback about their notes. Thus, the different phases of the NP-Q feature have been designed to promote reflexive learning, and expose to each student a feedback going from the comparison of alternative answers generating a socio-cognitive conflict, to the presentation of the assessment result of his explanation. In addition, as the quick assessment of a large number of explanations cannot be performed by a single teacher during a lecture, we have adopted a peer-assessment process whose properties have been demonstrated in different studies [3,5,17].

Finally, to tackle the other limit shown by the experimentation of the NaF feature (i.e. the integration of *all* contributions from the students in the feedbacks of the revision tests generated by Tsaap-Notes), the assessments of the notes by students are analysed by an algorithm to select the best contributions only.

Fig. 1. Submission of an answer with the NP-Q feature: first phase

3 Conception and Implementation of the NP-Q Feature

In this section, we describe how the NP-Q feature has been implemented into the Tsaap-Notes environment in order to integrate the writing of explanations within an activity allowing (1) students to get an immediate feedback about their contributions, and (2) a quick peer-assessment on the whole set of contributions.

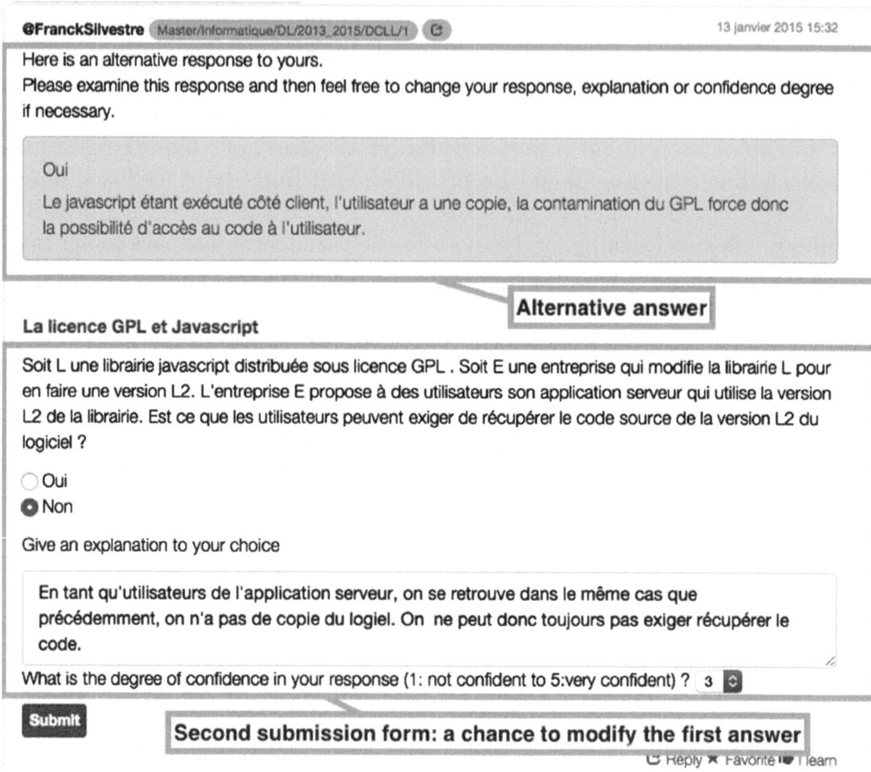

Fig. 2. Submission of an answer with the NP-Q feature: second phase

3.1 Main Principles

The activity we introduced consists in the separation of the submission of an answer of a multiple choice question in several phases. The first phase exposes a form illustrated in Fig. 1 and allows students to (1) answer a multiple choice question, (2) enter the explanation of their choice, and (3) indicate the confidence level of their answer. Thus, at this stage, the student turns into a reflective learning situation as he has to reflect on his own knowledge and abilities as soon as he indicates the level of confidence in his answer. This indicator represents also one of the key elements of the algorithm underlying the second phase. Although the example posed in Fig. 1 is a true/false question, the system supports general multiple choice questions.

The second phase of the submission process consists of providing the student with the form illustrated in Fig. 1, already filled in with his answer and explanation, together with an *alternative answer* submitted by another student participating in the same interactive session; the resulting interface is exposed on Fig. 2. This phase gives the student a first feedback through the suggestion of another answer and analysis, thus turning him into a situation of socio-cognitive

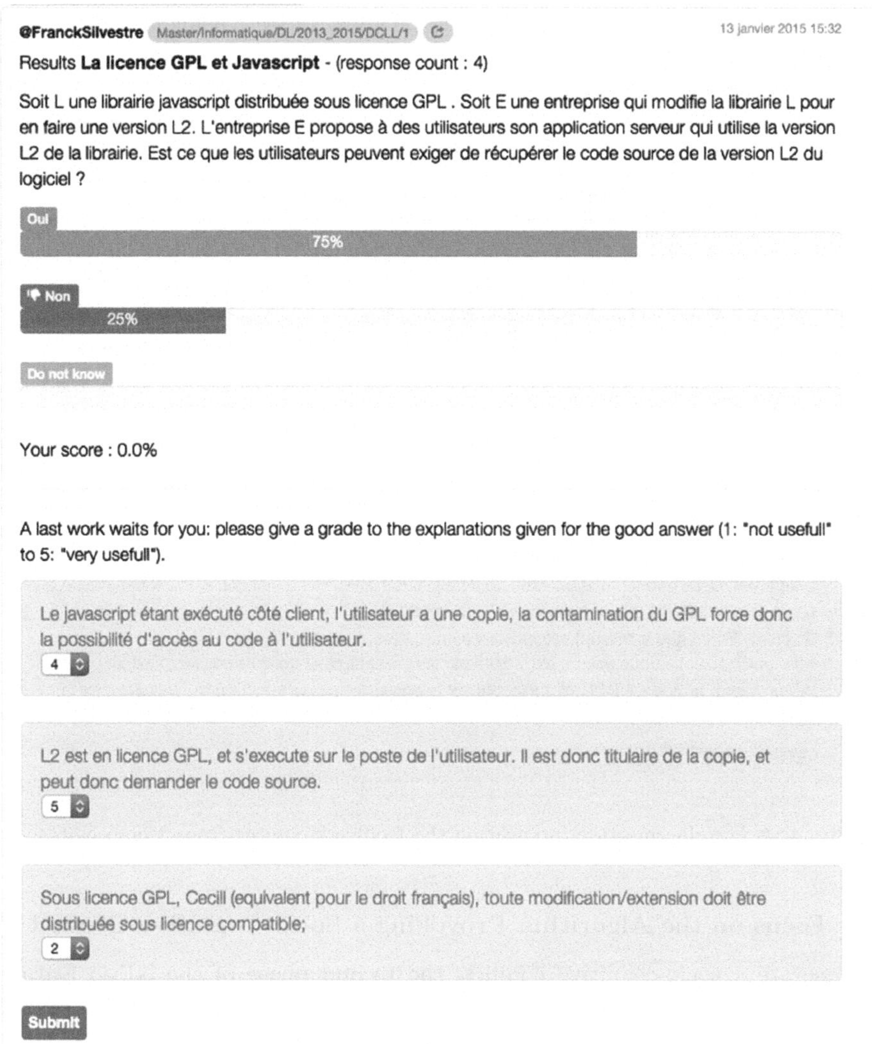

Fig. 3. Submission of an answer with the NP-Q feature: third phase

conflict as he has to compare his own answer with the one of his peers. The student can then confirm his choice and explanation, or he can modify his answer. Let us note that, in order to avoid relational influences, no information about the identity of the other peer is known by the student.

During the third and last phase, each student is provided with (1) the results of all students who answered the question, and (2) his own score on the question. In addition, the peer-assessment of the students' contributions takes place during this phase: through the interface illustrated in Fig. 3, each student is asked to assess three distinct explanations of the right answer using a Likert scale graduated from 1 to 5.

Once this phase is completed, Tsaap-Notes calculates the average rating for each assessed explanation, and presents to students the results of the assessment process in a descending order. Finally, the feedbacks integrated into the Moodle quizzes comprise the explanations characterised by an average value higher than 2.5 only; the resulting Moodle interface is shown in Fig. 4.

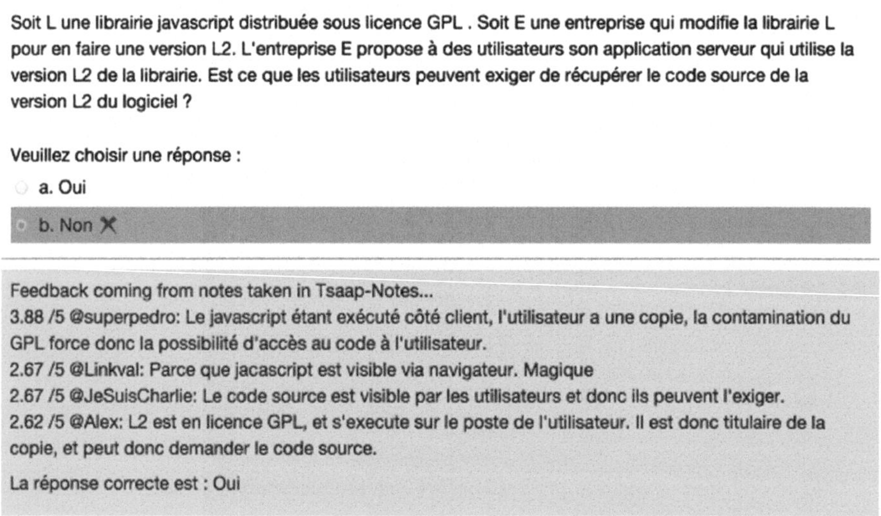

Fig. 4. A Moodle question integrating the feedback coming from Tsaap-Notes

3.2 Focus on the Algorithm Provoking a Socio-Cognitive Conflict

To generate a socio-cognitive conflict, the second phase of the NP-Q feature requires an algorithm capable of putting together two opposite and relevant answers given by students at the end of the first phase. Therefore, the main point of our algorithm consists in connecting an answer *ai* to an answer *aj*, where (i) both answers represent different choices, and (ii) the explanation associated with *ai* is of reasonable length. If several answers can be connected to *aj*, then the algorithm selects those characterised by the higher level of confidence, and encourages diversity by exposing different associations to students when possible. In order to present our algorithm, we propose a formal representation of the problem along with the most relevant parts of the solution.

In the remaining of the document, q represents a multiple choice question.

Definition 1. *An answer a to a multiple choice question q is a triplet*

$$a = (s; d; e)$$

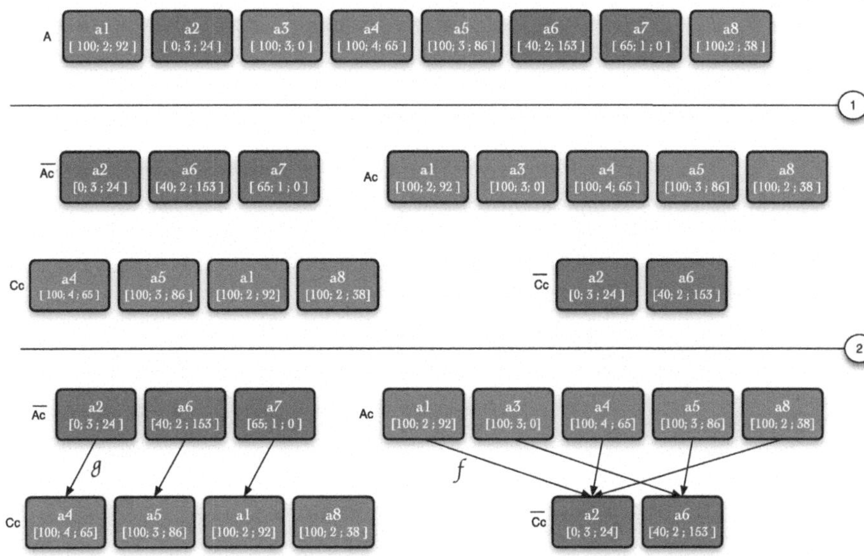

Fig. 5. The algorithm to generate a socio-cognitive conflict

where

- *s is the calculated score of the student;*
- *d is the level of confidence given by the student on his answer;*
- *e is the number of characters in the student's explanation.*

In the remaining of the document, q represents a multiple choice question.

Property 1. Given A the set of all answers got from q. The relation $\geq$ on A defined by

$$\forall (a_i = (s_i; d_i; e_i), a_j = (s_j; d_j; e_j)) \in A^2, \; a_i \geq a_j \Leftrightarrow d_i \geq d_j$$

is an order relation on A.

Definition 2. *The set A_c of all correct answers to q is defined as*

$$A_c = \{a_i = (s_i; d_i; e_i) \in A | s_i = MaxScore\}$$

where $MaxScore$ is the maximum score a student can obtain for a question q.

Definition 3. *The set $\overline{A_c}$ of all incorrect answers to q is the complementary of A_c in A.*

Definition 4. *All the answers to q able to generate a socio-cognitive conflict are included in the set C defined as follows*

$$C = \{a_i = (s_i; d_i; e_i) \in A | \; e_i > MinSizeExp\}$$

where $MinSizeExp$ is the minimum size of an explanation so that the associated answer can be selected to generate a socio-cognitive conflict.

Definition 5. *The set C_c of all correct answers to q able to generate a socio-cognitive conflict is defined as follows*

$$C_c = C \cap A_c$$

Definition 6. *The set $\overline{C_c}$ of all incorrect answers to q able to generate a socio-cognitive conflict is the complementary of C_c in C.*

Definition 7. *Given $A_c = \{a_1, a_2, a_3, ..., a_n\}$ where $\forall(i,j) \in \{1,..,n\} \quad i < j \Rightarrow a_i \geq a_j$ the ordered set of all correct answers to q.*

Given $\overline{C_c} = \{c_1, c_2, c_3, ..., c_p\}$ where $\forall(i,j) \in \{1,..,p\} \quad i < j \Rightarrow c_i \geq c_j$ the ordered set of all the incorrect answers to q able to generate a socio-cognitive conflict.

The function $f : A_c \to \overline{C_c}$ is the function which associates to each element $a_i \in A_c$ the element

$$f(a_i) = c_{i \mod p}$$

where $i \mod p$ is the remainder of the Euclidian division of i by p.

Definition 8. *Given $\overline{A_c} = \{a_1, a_2, a_3, ..., a_n\}$ where $\forall(i,j) \in \{1,..,n\} \quad i < j \Rightarrow a_i \geq a_j$ the ordered set of all incorrect answers to q.*

Given $C_c = \{c_1, c_2, c_3, ..., c_p\}$ where $\forall(i,j) \in \{1,..,p\} \quad i < j \Rightarrow c_i \geq c_j$ the ordered set of all the correct answers to q able to generate a socio-cognitive conflict.

The function $g : \overline{A_c} \to C_c$ is the function which associates to each element $a_i \in \overline{A_c}$ the element

$$g(a_i) = c_{i \mod p}$$

where $i \mod p$ is the remainder of the Euclidian division of i by p.

Starting from these definitions, Fig. 5 shows the different steps implemented within our algorithm. The first step takes the set A as input, and creates the four sets A_c, $\overline{A_c}$, C_c and $\overline{C_c}$; these sets are represented as ordered lists according to the relation introduced in Prop. 1. Since the maximum score that can be attributed to a question is always 100 in the current implementation of Tsaap-Notes, *MaxScore* has been set to this value as well; *MinSizeExp* (see Def. 4) has been arbitrary set to 10. The second stage of the algorithm gathers into a dictionary the results of the application of f (respectively g) on all the elements of A_c (respectively $\overline{A_c}$). This algorithm has been experimented with several groups of students; the results are detailed in the next section.

4 Results of the First Experimentation

The NP-Q feature offered by Tsaap-Notes has been experimented with two groups of students in two courses integrated in the first year of a Computer Science Master program. The experimentation took place during 3 sessions of 2 hours during which 5 NP-Q questions were asked to students. Table 1 shows that

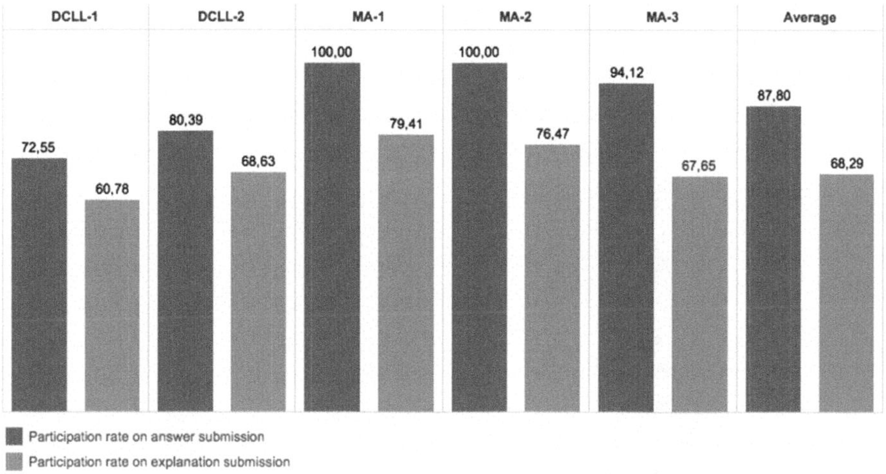

Fig. 6. Participation rates on answer submission/explanation submission

Table 1. Participation rates

Course label	Question code	Number of presents	Number of submitted answers	Participation rate
DCLL	DCLL-1	51	37	72.5 %
DCLL	DCLL-2	51	41	80.4 %
MA	MA-1	34	34	100 %
MA	MA-2	34	34	100 %
MA	MA-3	34	32	94.1 %
Average	NR	40.8	35.6	87.8 %

almost 88 % of students submitted an answer to each question; this high participation rate conforms to other studies related to audience response systems.

A more interesting indicator is the participation of students in the submission of an explanation: Fig. 6 shows that 68.29 % of students that answered a question also submitted an explanation to justify their answers. Even if this participation rate is below the observed rate on submitted answers (i.e. 87.8 %), it represents a very large increase compared to the values resulting from a previous experimentation conducted in 2014 [15]. In this experimentation that involved a group of 35 students, questions were exposed using the "traditional" way (i.e. without the NP-Q feature) and students were invited to submit explanations after the presentation of the results. Figure 7 shows that the NP-Q feature has strongly increased the participation rate in writing explanations: in average, only 5.7 % of students were engaged in this task in 2014, compared with 68.29 % of them in 2015. In addition, the number of contributions likely to be used as feedback in the Moodle quiz is much higher in 2015: 57.39 % of the students' input are selected, against 5.7 % in 2014 only.

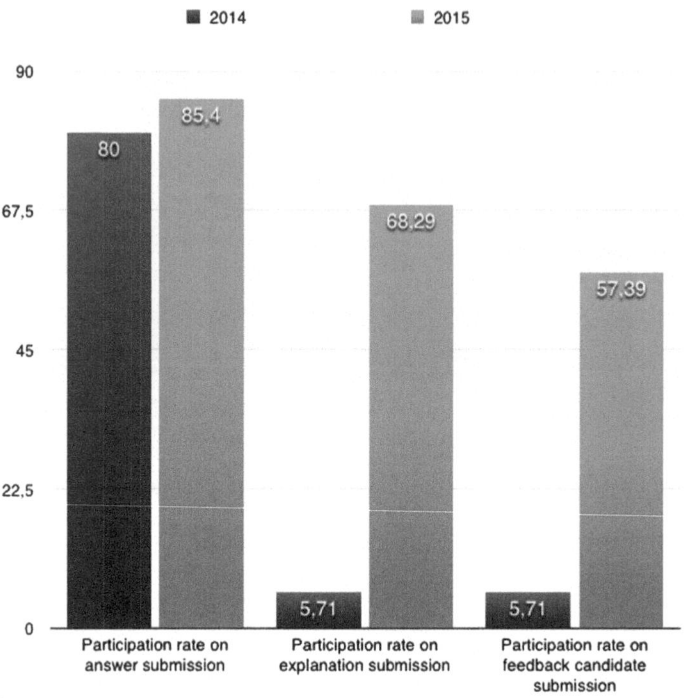

Fig. 7. Compared study on the participation rate for the writing of explanation

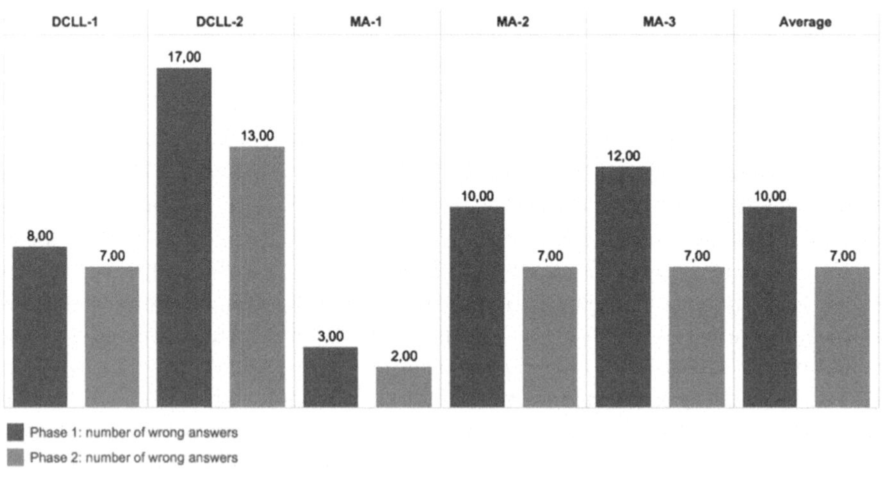

Fig. 8. Number of wrong answers in phase 1 and phase 2

Moreover, Fig. 8 shows that several students have altered their answer between the first and second phases: the socio-cognitive conflict made those students think about both their own and peers' knowledge. Since this conflictive approach brought 30 % of students having submitted a wrong answer to identify the right answer, we consider this result as a strong encouragement to further explore the ability to provoke socio-cognitive conflict through Tsaap-Notes.

Finally, Fig. 9 gives the results of the last NP-Q phase where students are asked (but not required) to evaluate three explanations, and shows that 75.6 % of them participated in this peer-assessment process. Thus, the average number of learners evaluating an explanation is 4.17, for an average of 40.8 attending students and 22.8 explanations to evaluate; we estimate this average as significant enough to obtain a representative grade for an explanation. Furthermore, the average of the standard deviation related to the rates given by students on an

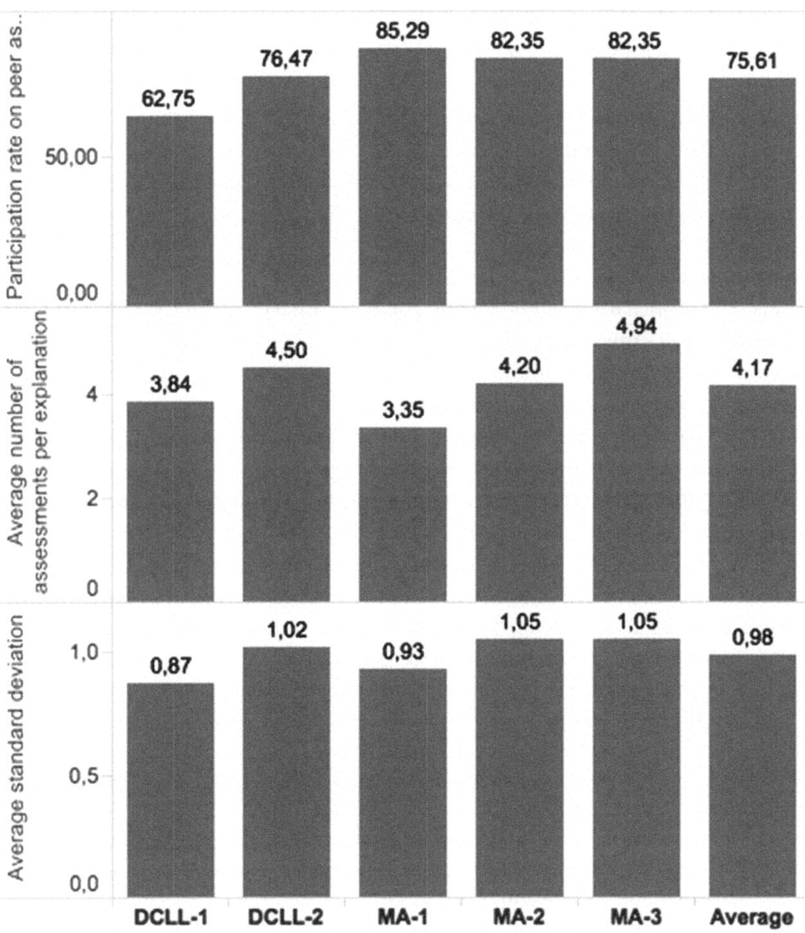

Fig. 9. Participation rate on peer assessment

explanation is 0.98. This standard deviation is quite significant as it shows that the rates vary by 20 % from one student to another, which is reasonable for our use (i.e. the selection of the highest rated explanations to build the feedback integrated into the Moodle quiz).

5 Conclusions and Perspectives

The Tsaap-Notes platform enables the semi-automatic generation of a multiple choice test questions providing feedbacks on the basis of (1) the interactive questions asked by teachers during face-to-face lectures, and (2) the notes taken by students to create the feedbacks presented to students within the quizzes. In this paper, we introduced the NP-Q feature in order to considerably increase the number of contributions made by students, and thus to significantly improve the quality of feedbacks integrated in the generated quizzes. Our proposal splits the submission of an answer in several phases and places students in three distinct situations: reflexive learning, socio-cognitive conflict, and peer assessment. The best rated explanations of correct answers are then used as feedbacks to improve the quality of the formative assessments. The results of the first experimentation conducted with two groups of students enrolled in a computer science Master course are very promising, as they show a very strong increase of the students' participation in the writing of explanations; the selection of the most appropriate contributions can thus apply to a significant amount of data and make the feedbacks integrated into the quizzes more relevant.

Today, the algorithm triggering the socio-cognitive conflict takes into account a few information concerning the learners: only the score, the size of the explanation and the level of confidence on a given question are used to influence an alternative answer. The results obtained at different questions or the ability to convince (i.e. to make another student change his mind during a socio-cognitive conflict) represent other data that could be used to improve this algorithm.

The NP-Q feature is currently used during face-to-face lectures, but it would be interesting to adapt and try it in the context of a Massive Online Open Course (MOOC). Indeed, MOOC often integrate platforms like forums allowing learners to help each other. However, this kind of platform doesn't guarantee the participation of all learners, and therefore doesn't ensure that they get support from their peers. On the other hand, the generation of a socio-cognitive conflict the way it is proposed in this paper makes use of the productions of all the learners, for all the learners.

References

1. Biggs, J., Tang, C.: Teaching for Quality Learning at University: What the Student Does. McGraw-Hill Education, UK (2011)
2. Black, P., Wiliam, D.: Assessment and classroom learning. Assess. Educ. **5**(1), 7–74 (1998)

3. Boud, D., Cohen, R., Sampson, J.: Peer Learning in Higher Education: Learning from and with Each Other. Routledge, New York (2014)
4. Caldwell, J.E.: Clickers in the large classroom: Current research and best-practice tips. CBE-Life Sci. Educ. **6**(1), 9–20 (2007)
5. Dochy, F., Segers, M., Sluijsmans, D.: The use of self-, peer and co-assessment in higher education: A review. Stud. High. Educ. **24**(3), 331–350 (1999)
6. Gauci, S.A., Dantas, A.M., Williams, D.A., Kemm, R.E.: Promoting student-centered active learning in lectures with a personal response system. Adv. Physiol. Educ. **33**(1), 60–71 (2009)
7. Hattie, J., Jaeger, R.: Assessment and classroom learning: a deductive approach. Assess. Educ. **5**(1), 111–122 (1998)
8. Higgins, R.: Be more critical: rethinking assessment feedback. DYE. V, PC4000 (2000)
9. Miller, T.: Formative computer-based assessment in higher education: the effectiveness of feedback in supporting student learning. Assess. Eval. High. Educ. **34**(2), 181–192 (2009)
10. Nicol, D., Milligan, C.: Rethinking technology-supported assessment practices in relation to the seven principles of good feedback practice. In: Innovative Assessment in Higher Education, pp. 64–77 (2006)
11. QTI, I.: Question and test interoperability (2006)
12. Ricketts, C., Wilks, S.: Improving student performance through computer-based assessment: Insights from recent research. Assess. Eval. High. Educ. **27**(5), 475–479 (2002)
13. Scouller, K.: The influence of assessment method on students' learning approaches: multiple choice question examination versus assignment essay. High. Educ. **35**(4), 453–472 (1998)
14. Shaffer, D.M., Collura, M.J.: Evaluating the effectiveness of a personal response system in the classroom. Teach. Psychol. **36**(4), 273–277 (2009)
15. Silvestre, F., Vidal, P., Broisin, J.: Tsaap-notes-an open micro-blogging tool for collaborative notetaking during face-to-face lectures. In: 2014 IEEE 14th International Conference on Advanced Learning Technologies (ICALT), pp. 39–43. IEEE (2014)
16. Silvestre, F., Vidal, P., Broisin, J.: Semi automatic generation of online tests providing feedbacks based on collaborative note taking. In: 2015 IEEE 15th International Conference on Advanced Learning Technologies (ICALT), IEEE (to appear)
17. Topping, K.: Peer assessment between students in colleges and universities. Rev. Educ. Res. **68**(3), 249–276 (1998)
18. Uhari, M., Renko, M., Soini, H.: Experiences of using an interactive audience response system in lectures. BMC Med. Educ. **3**(1), 12 (2003)

A Learning Analytics Approach to Correlate the Academic Achievements of Students with Interaction Data from an Educational Simulator

Mehrnoosh Vahdat[1,3](✉), Luca Oneto[1], Davide Anguita[2], Mathias Funk[3], and Matthias Rauterberg[3]

[1] DITEN - Università degli Studi di Genova, 16145 Genoa, Italy
mehrnoosh.vahdat@edu.unige.it, luca.oneto@unige.it
[2] DIBRIS - Università degli Studi di Genova, 16145 Genoa, Italy
davide.anguita@unige.it
[3] Department of Industrial Design, Eindhoven University of Technology, 5612AZ Eindhoven, The Netherlands
{m.funk,g.w.m.rauterberg}@tue.nl

Abstract. This paper presents a Learning Analytics approach for understanding the learning behavior of students while interacting with Technology Enhanced Learning tools. In this work we show that it is possible to gain insight into the learning processes of students from their interaction data. We base our study on data collected through six laboratory sessions where first-year students of Computer Engineering at the University of Genoa were using a digital electronics simulator. We exploit Process Mining methods to investigate and compare the learning processes of students. For this purpose, we measure the understandability of their process models through a complexity metric. Then we compare the various clusters of students based on their academic achievements. The results show that the measured complexity has positive correlation with the final grades of students and negative correlation with the difficulty of the laboratory sessions. Consequently, complexity of process models can be used as an indicator of variations of student learning paths.

Keywords: Learning analytics · Educational data mining · Technology Enhanced Learning · Process mining · Complexity · Interaction data · Educational simulator

1 Introduction

Learning Analytics (LA) and Educational Data Mining (EDM) have raised a lot of attention among researchers and practitioners of Technology Enhanced Learning (TEL) in the last decade. The aim is to gain more insight into the behavior of learners by building models based on data collected from learning

© Springer International Publishing Switzerland 2015
G. Conole et al. (Eds.): EC-TEL 2015, LNCS 9307, pp. 352–366, 2015.
DOI: 10.1007/978-3-319-24258-3_26

tools [1]. Consequently LA and EDM applied in educational settings enhance the understanding of various stakeholders (students, teachers, administrators, etc.) about the way people learn in a data-driven way. As a result, the TEL systems can be improved to be more personalized and adaptive, and learning can be optimized as one of the main goals [2–5].

In the environments where inquiry-guided learning is applied rather than traditional methods, e-tools can play an important role in providing guidance and principles to optimize learning. Inquiry-guided learning focuses on contexts where learners are meant to discover knowledge rather than passively memorizing the concepts [6–8]. In this way, the lesson begins with a set of observations to interpret, and the learner tries to analyze the data or solve the problem by the help of the guiding principles [9], resulting in a more effective educational approach [10]. In this context, simulation-based environments are efficient tools to improve learning [11]. The data gathered from these educational environments has special features of student-performed actions [12,13]. Therefore, to analyze this data we need to integrate methods that focus on learning processes in a more effective way. Among process related methods, Process Mining (PM) is emerging in TEL since it can enhance our understanding by building models of student actions and learning processes [14].

This paper is structured as follows. In Sect. 2, PM and its applications in education are described. We introduce a metric for measuring the understandability of process models, and the main contribution of this study is presented. In Sect. 3, PM tools and CM metric are described. In Sect. 4, we describe the protocol and how we collect the data. In Sect. 5, we report the results of this study and finally in Sect. 6, conclusions of this study are drawn.

2 Related Work and Contribution

2.1 Educational Process Mining

Process Mining is a method that has emerged from the business community to obtain valuable knowledge from a process. By adopting various PM techniques such as process model discovery and conformance checking, process-related knowledge from event logs can be extracted. In the context of LA and EDM, very few process-oriented approaches focus on the process as a whole [14]. Contrarily, educational PM allows obtaining a better insight on the underlying educational processes [15]. For example in [16], some applications of PM methods are shown and applied to online assessment data for analyzing the process of answering the questions or requesting feedback by students. In [15], a framework is introduced for integrating the domain knowledge in educational PM in order to facilitate interactive PM and help educators analyze educational processes based on formal modeling. Another study [17] analyzes student processes of self-regulated learning and shows the differences of learning behavior between successful students and less successful ones from their temporal patterns. For instance, it shows that successful students perform regulatory activities with a higher frequency and in a different order than the less successful ones.

2.2 Understanding Process Mining Through a Complexity Metric

In PM, many difficulties are on the way of understandability of process models. In [18] it is shown that, although process models help people have better understanding of processes, understanding complex models faces cognitive limits. In this context, complexity metrics can measure understandability and maintainability of a workflow net or a business process model extended from the metrics applied to measure the software complexity [19,20]. These metrics in PM have been introduced for petri nets or workflow nets but can be extended to other formalisms as well [21]. For instance, Cyclomatic Complexity of McCabe (CM) has been used as a metric to measure the complexity of a control-flow graph of a program [22], and usually applies to software complexity in the meaning of *the difficulty to maintain, change and understand software* [23]. CM is measured by calculating the number of linearly-independent paths through a graph [19]. Since complexity has strong relation with various concepts such as simplicity, ease of use, uncertainty and the context of application, it has been a topic of interest to the designers of Human-Computer Interaction (HCI) [24–27]. For instance in [28], this metric is applied into the context of HCI to measure the complexity of the observable behavior by analyzing the recorded task solving process, and obtained the behavioral complexity. In the educational context, CM is used in various studies to measure the complexity of the programming assignments of students while learning [29,30]. For instance, [29] compares CM of children programing tasks when using two interfaces among different age groups. In the next section, we explain how CM is adopted in the context of our study.

2.3 Cyclomatic Complexity as an Indicator of Student Behavior

Process Mining is emerging in the field of LA and EDM [15–17]. However, it is challenging to obtain knowledge from educational processes since they are usually very complex and unordered. Metrics like CM have been applied in PM for measuring the understandability of a process model [21]. We further propose to apply CM to understand the complex educational processes and compare them in particular, in the context of inquiry-based learning applications. We apply PM and CM metric in order to understand the differences between student clusters from their learning paths, while they interact with an educational simulator. For addressing these issues, we carried out our study over a simulation environment named Deeds (Digital Electronics Education and Design Suite) [31,32] which is used for e-learning in digital electronics. The environment provides learning materials through specialized browsers for the students, and asks them to solve various problems with different levels of difficulty. It has been effective, for over ten years, in teaching and improving the learning outcome of students since it provides a general-purpose simulator with a highly interactive e-learning environment. The course is organized in separated theoretical and laboratory sessions where students work with the Deeds simulator. Since we deal with a simulation-based environment, having access to the client side data plays an important role in understanding of how the user interacts with the simulator and uses it in problem solving. Therefore, data is gathered through a logging application called LA Data Collector (LADC), properly realized for our purposes. LADC is developed to log data from the client system, and currently can log the interaction data with Deeds browsers and external applications.

This study shows that CM can be used as an indicator of academic success of students. Additionally, it can be used as a predictor of the difficulty level of laboratory sessions for a group of students (e.g. from various engineering majors), and help instructors organize and adapt their lessons based on the needs of the students.

3 Analytics Methods

In this study, the data analytics process can be explained in two parts: creating the process models, and comparing them. We used fuzzy miner algorithm which is an effective tool to obtain the process models from the logs of students [17]. Indeed, it improved the abstraction of complex student processes. With this method, we detected the noise (irrelevant activities to the process of learning, for instance, when students setup programs, or visit web pages that are irrelevant to the course) in data and identified the various levels of granularity. Then, we used the obtained knowledge to measure CM effectively, which allowed us to compare the process models of students.

3.1 Creating the Process Models

In order to obtain the process models, we used Disco tool, which is developed for discovering models of complex processes through seamless abstraction and generalization [33]. This tool uses the fuzzy miner algorithm, which is effective when the events are unstructured, and the process model is not known beforehand. The fuzzy miner is capable of abstracting and aggregating the process in a way to highlight the most significant parts of the process by measuring the relative importance of behavior (for the formal description of fuzzy miner and its properties refer to [34]). This kind of modeling is required when dealing with so-called *spaghetti-like* processes since understanding them is very challenging [34]. Figure 1 shows the fuzzy miner capability in aggregating and abstracting a student process model during one of the sessions of the course. On the top, the process is shown with no aggregation, and on the bottom, fuzzy miner presents the most significant and correlated activities and paths by applying the node and edge cutoff parameters [34] to 20 % and 0 % respectively (0 % is the indicator of minimum number of paths throughout the process). These parameters are set in order to show a simple and yet meaningful process structure.

Applying fuzzy miner for process discovery, facilitated the detection of less significant behavior as well as less related events. By applying this miner to the first level of events, we discovered that out-of-task events (when students are not using the main applications relevant to exercises) are the least significant

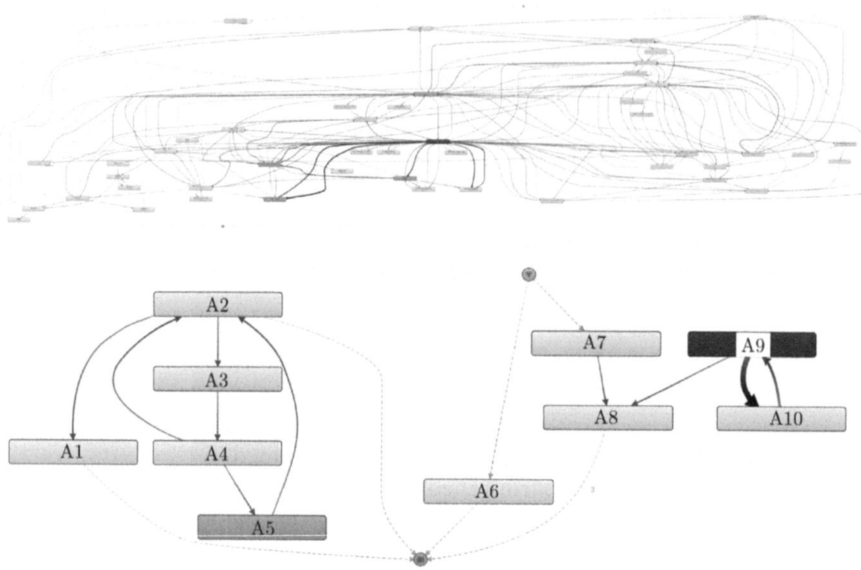

Fig. 1. An example of a student process model obtained by Disco tool and applying the fuzzy miner. Every *A* refers to an activity (light to dark blue: activities with low to high frequency) (Color figure online).

student behavior in the process of problem solving. In Fig. 2, the process models of a student are shown, considering the 20 % most significant activities. On the top, the process shows the most frequent activities (from light to dark blue) while on the lower image, the most timely activities of student performance are shown (from light to dark red). A comparison of the two showed that there is a lot of noise in data which needs to be reduced by filtering the irrelevant activities. For instance, *A4* that is represented with high frequency and low performance time, is an activity that occurs as noise when students switch between the applications.

3.2 Comparing the Process Models

In order to compare the process models of students, we measure the complexity of student processes and see if the difference in measured complexity is relevant to the learning achievement. There exist various complexity metrics among which CM [22] is the most widely used metric for measuring the testing efforts of structural programs [20]. CM measures *the number of binary decisions (for example IF-statements in a programming language) plus one* [19]. This metric is also used to measure the understandability of a process model [21]. In the context of our study, we measure CM of the process models of student interactions, in three levels of granularity, obtained from analysis of the created models. By level of granularity, we mean the way we consider the student performed-events in the context of process models. Events refer to activities and cases in a

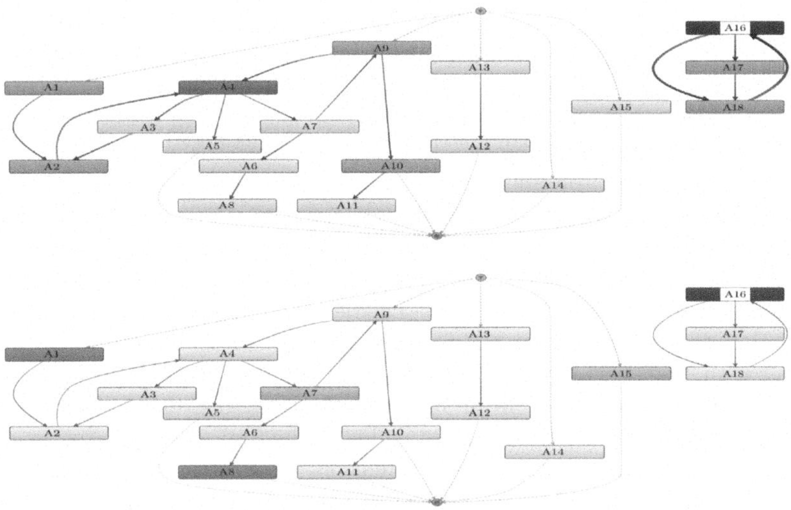

Fig. 2. Comparison of frequency versus performance of a student process model, obtained by Disco tool and applying the fuzzy miner. Every A refers to an activity (on the top, light to dark blue: activities with low to high frequency. On the bottom, light to dark red: activities with low to high performance time) (Color figure online).

workflow process, they are ordered, and obtained from an event log that is recorded sequentially [35]. In the first level, we consider all the events carried out by a student including both in-task and out-of-task events. In the second level, we calculate CM just based on in-task events. During the third level, we group the events based on meta-cognitive activities such that: studying the exercise content, model building, simulating, and reasoning for each specific exercise. Based on [22] for computing CM we need to define $G = (V, E)$ as a control-flow graph where E is the number of independent paths and V is the number of activities. The Cyclomatic metric CM is defined as: $CM = |E| - |V| + P$, where $|x|$ is the cardinality of the set and P is the number of connected components. P in our case is a constant with value of 1 since the process per session is one connected graph with no interruption.

4 Experimental Design

This study was carried out on two sets of BSc students during the laboratory sessions of a course of digital design at the University of Genoa. It is performed during the spring semester (March to June 2014) as a pilot experiment, and the autumn semester (October to December 2014). In the framework of this study, 125 students participated in a pilot study and 100 students participated in the real experiment. The structure of the experiment was modified after the pilot to limit the amount of noise in the collected data. For instance, during the pilot, students were free to continue working at home and submit their exercises with delay; while in the second round, we set more strict time limits to the process (the result of pilot study are not presented due to the space constraint). Additionally, two people were assigned to help the students during the data collection process in all the sessions. In this way, we ensured the accuracy of data collection by LADC and avoidance of data loss.

A comprehensive experiment has been designed and several activities have been conducted in parallel: semi-structured interviews with the instructors of the course; a demographic questionnaire designed to acquire the general information, motivation, and background knowledge from the learners; and a feedback questionnaire at the end of the course. The designed questionnaire captured the satisfaction of students about the teaching method in the laboratory sessions, working with Deeds simulator, and their feedback on our experiment. In addition, log data were collected from 100 students by LADC from six laboratory sessions. The final exam was designed to address the topics of laboratory sessions separately. In this way, intermediate evaluations of exercises, in addition to the final grade, can be related to the interaction data of each session.

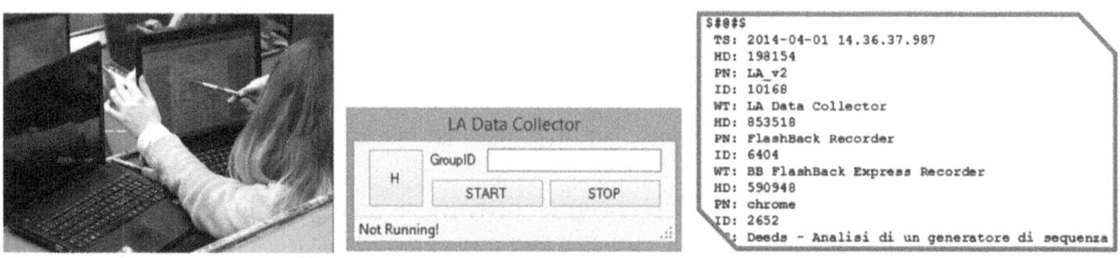

Fig. 3. Process of data collection by LADC in a laboratory session. From left to right: a student performing a task, LADC interface, raw data obtained from LADC.

The process of data collection was performed carefully to maintain the data accuracy and validity. Around 86 % of students in average were present and submitted their logs per session collected by LADC. After each session, testing algorithms were applied on the logs for detecting problems, and in this case, students were informed about their mistakes. In particular, we tested if the logs contained a minimum amount of data, and if data was relevant to the session exercises. Additionally, five students were asked to record their screen in order to have an explicable source for our logs. This data was collected from all the sessions and it was of great help to have more insight on raw data, as well as to understand the reason behind meaningless or irrelevant data in the log.

Figure 3 shows the process of data collection in the classroom by LADC. The raw data was collected as a text file, which contains data of one session per student (we tried to collect as much data as possible without re-engineering the simulator code). This data collects the user interaction every second. Each measure contains data in the following order: date and time, name of application in use on the system in combination with name of its window title, followed by title of the window in focus. Finally data present start and end time of the process, idle time, mouse clicks, mouse movements, and keystrokes. The raw data gives us valuable information on the activities per session, per student, and per exercise since each exercise is designed to contain a code in title which appears in the browser, the simulator title, and in the editor used for reasoning. Based on the titles in use, the activities, events and cases are withdrawn sequentially in order to discover the process model of each student through PM. The extracted events are later aggregated into three levels of granularity and CM is measured on each one.

5 Experimental Results

The results of this study can be summarized into four main contributions:

- CM is a predictor of difficulty of a session for students, since the average CM per course session has negative correlation with the average of student intermediate grades.
- CM can explain the interactive behavior of students, since the average CM of high-graded students is higher than the one of low-graded students, when calculated per session for two furthest clusters of students.
- CM explains the similarity of student behaviors depending on the level of granularity, and their behavior on out-of-task events.
- CM can raise awareness about the interactive and cognitive behavior of students, and improve the instructional design.

In this paper, we chose to present the results based on the second level of granularity, since from our experiment, this is the best trade-off between the accuracy and compression of the process models. The findings of this study are explained in more depth in the above-mentioned order.

5.1 Impact of Session Difficulty Over Cyclomatic Complexity

The results from comparing the average CM of various laboratory sessions, measured from the student processes, show that: CM depends extensively on the difficulty of the assignments given to the students. A comparison of average of intermediate grades ($\overline{IG}$) with average CM of total students ($\overline{CM}$) is performed. The result shows that $\overline{CM}$ per session has negative correlation with $\overline{IG}$. In Fig. 4, this relationship is shown for the second level of granularity: when $\overline{CM}$ increases, $\overline{IG}$ decreases. A similar result is obtained for the two other levels of granularity. This result can be used for predicting the perceived task difficulty by the students based on their interaction with Deeds simulator. In this way, instructors can spend more time and effort on the topics that are more complicated for the students. Additionally, this course is offered to many engineering majors in University of Genoa, and the students of various intakes have different backgrounds. Therefore, the complexity of the tasks and sessions is not the same for all the classes and majors. In this regard, $\overline{CM}$ shows how difficult or easy a session is for a particular class of students. Later, we compare these results with the interviews of the instructors, and show that the findings can be valuable for the teachers in order to organize their lessons and to balance the difficulty of the sessions for the students.

The simulator is new for all students since they are the first year students of computer science engineering. Based on the demographic questionnaire, 74 % of students did not have any experience with the simulator, and the rest had very few experience. So the background knowledge of students about the simulator is considered homogeneous. Additionally, during the first session of the course, complexity of students is relatively high while the average grade is the highest. This is due to the fact that interacting with the system was challenging for them in the beginning, while the assigned exercises were very simple.

5.2 Impact of Grades over Cyclomatic Complexity

Another contribution of this study shows the difference of interaction behavior of students when they are clustered into two groups based on their final grades: high-graded versus low-graded students. Our results show that the average of CM of high-graded students is higher than the one of low-graded students. This difference grows when the distance of student clusters increases. We incrementally re-cluster the students by increasing the difference of their grades: high-graded are the one with grades over the mean value of the grades (μ) plus n times the standard deviation of the grades sigma ($\mu + n\sigma$) while low-graded students are the ones below $\mu - n\sigma$ where n varies in $\{0, 2\}$. Figure 5 shows this difference when n is 0 (image on the top) versus 2 for the second level of granularity (the lower image). It means when n=2 we just consider the most and the least graded students. The results from the second and third level of granularity show a better separation in CM compared to the first level. This is due to the out-of-task events in the first level of granularity which plays as noise in the results. As future directions of this study, we aim to work on exploiting CM to predict the final outcome of each student.

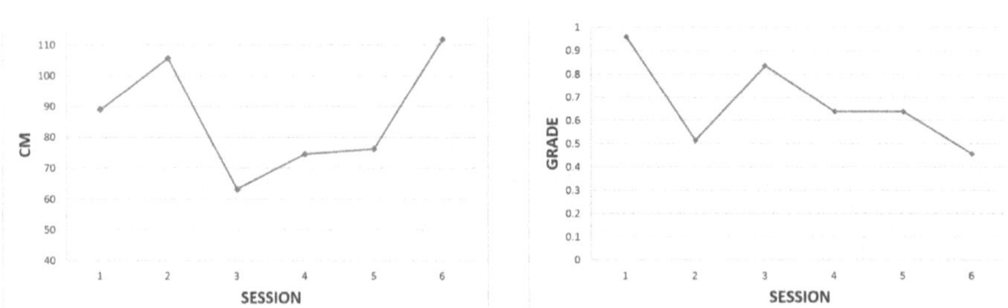

Fig. 4. Average of Cyclomatic Complexity (CM) per session (left), average of intermediate grades per session (right).

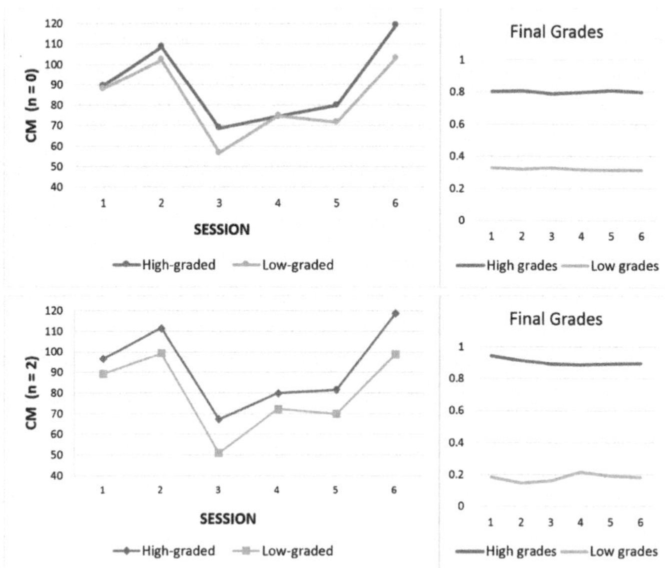

Fig. 5. Comparison of student clusters via the difference of average Cyclomatic Complexity (CM) for the second level of granularity. The average final grades are shown on the right (the grades are normalized due to the privacy issues).

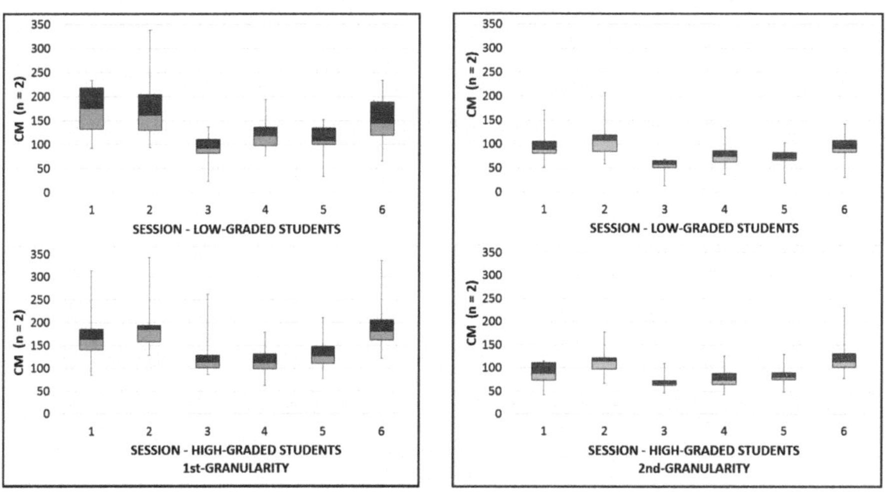

Fig. 6. The variance of average Cyclomatic Complexity (CM) for: Low-graded students (on the top) versus high-graded students (on the bottom), and first granularity level (on the left) versus second granularity level (on the right).

5.3 Impact of Granularity Level over Cyclomatic Complexity

We also compared the variance of students CM between the most and the least successful students. For this comparison we considered the first and second level of granularity since we can compare their behavior via in-task versus out-of-task events. The results show that when considering all the events (Fig. 6 on the left), the behavior of high-graded students are closer to each other than the low-graded ones for the majority of sessions. Whereas, when we exclude the out-of-task events in the second level (Fig. 6 on the right), the result is the opposite. The behavior of the least successful ones is closer to one another. And in both levels, this difference is higher in the sessions with more complex assignments. Additionally, a comparison of the two levels of granularity (Fig. 6) shows that the low-graded students perform more out-of-task activities that the better-graded students while interacting with Deeds.

5.4 Instructors Insight

The results obtained from a semi-structured interview of the instructors of the digital design course, are valuable for the interpretation of our findings. The interview questions ask them about: how difficult each course session was for the students, and how their experience was during the laboratory sessions. They were asked to sort the sessions based on the difficulty level from very difficult to very easy (Fig. 7). Also, the results of this study were shown to the instructors in order to get their interpretation and feedback.

Four instructors of the course were interviewed, each from 30 minutes to 1 hour. The instructors do not have the same level of experience. The major professor has over ten years experience of teaching with this particular course, and the experience of the rest varies from several years to several months. The results show that all agree on which sessions were the most difficult for the students (sessions 6 and 5) but their opinions varied about the difficulty level of

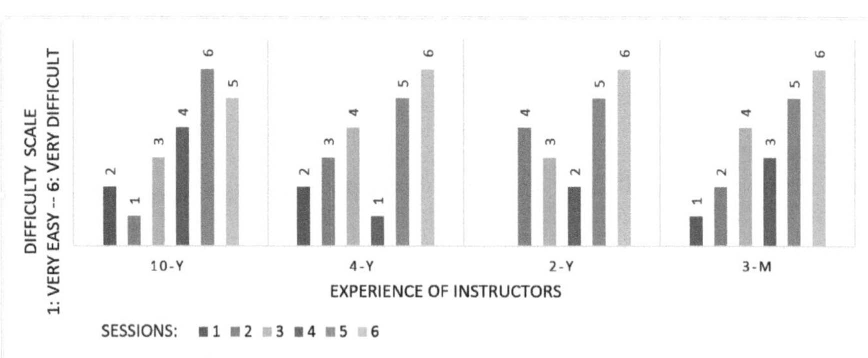

Fig. 7. The difficulty of sessions based on the instructors experience (from 10 years to 3 months).

the rest of the sessions (see Fig. 7). For example, two teachers indicated session 4 as medium difficult and the two other indicated it as an easy session.

Also we asked the instructors to draw an expected process model of a student, given the main events. We compared the models drawn by instructors and observed that their process models were different in size of events and linear paths. Also, their opinions varied about the significance of relationship between various events. For instance, two indicated that increasing of linear paths is an indicator of less successful behavior and the other two stated that it is not an indicator of learning. These results confirm that the average CM of students and the obtained process models can give valuable insights to the instructors of the course, in particular to those with less experience.

6 Discussion

LA and EDM methods aim to improve our understanding about the behavior of learners while interacting with TEL systems. Researchers of the field attempt to adapt the analytics methods to the educational goals and contexts in order to gain better insight about the learning behavior of students. In this regard, applying emerging methods like PM is valuable to abstract the learning processes, leads to better detection of problems, and improves the learning outcome.

In this paper, we applied PM methods and metrics to understand and compare the learning processes of students. We obtained the data from interactions of students while they were working with an educational simulator named Deeds during six sessions of a course of digital design. A data-set of temporal and sequential activities per student and per course session is aggregated by LADC developed for our research. We applied complexity metric of CM as an understandability metric of a process model in order to compare the processes of student learning. We compared average CM of various clusters of students based on their academic achievements, and interviewed the four instructors of the course for their interpretation and feedback.

Our findings show that process discovery and CM of the student models can give insight about the learning process of students, and give valuable information about how students act in a process of problem solving. It was shown that fuzzy miner is an effective algorithm of PM to abstract and simplify the process models, to detect the irrelevant activities to the learning process, and to define the granularity levels. Additionally we found that: CM is positively correlated with the average final grades of students and inversely correlated with the difficulty level of laboratory sessions. As a result, average CM of students can be used as a predictor of the difficulty level of laboratory sessions for a group of students (from various engineering majors or intakes), and help instructors organize and adapt their lessons based on the needs of every group. We discovered that the successful students have more similar CM than the less successful ones, when considering all the activities including both in-task and out-of-task. On the contrary, the low-graded students have more similar CM when we exclude out-of-task activities. We propose the following hypothesis to explain this result:

the better-graded students have more effortful cognitive activities and use more varied learning strategies in the process of problem solving.

In the future, we aim to use CM to predict the academic achievement of a group of students, and if possible, to predict for a single student. This can be done by adding other factors that influence the student success such as performance time, order of activities, etc. Such predictor can help teachers detect the students who deviate from the appropriate learning path so to provide help on time. Additionally, it can raise awareness of teachers to balance the difficulty of exercises based on the needs of the students with different academic backgrounds.

Acknowledgments. This work was supported in part by the Erasmus Mundus Joint Doctorate in Interactive and Cognitive Environments, which is funded by the EACEA Agency of the European Commission under EMJD ICE FPA n 2010-0012. Also, we thank professors Domenico Ponta and Giuliano Donzellini for providing support and help to our experiment.

References

1. Siemens, G.: Learning analytics: envisioning a research discipline and a domain of practice. In: International Conference on Learning Analytics and Knowledge (2012)
2. Chatti, M.A., Dyckhoff, A.L., Schroeder, U., Thüs, H.: A reference model for learning analytics. Int. J. Technol. Enhanced Learn. **4**(5), 318–331 (2012)
3. Romero, C., Ventura, S.: Educational data mining: a survey from 1995 to 2005. Expert Syst. Appl. **33**(1), 135–146 (2007)
4. Siemens, G., Long, P.: Penetrating the fog: analytics in learning and education. EDUCAUSE Rev. **46**(5), 30 (2011)
5. Vahdat, M., Ghio, A., Oneto, L., Anguita, D., Funk, M., Rauterberg, M.: Advances in learning analytics and educational data mining. In: European Symposium on Artificial Neural Networks, Computational Intelligence and Machine Learning (2015)
6. Kruse, A., Pongsajapan, R.: Student-centered learning analytics. In: CNDLS Thought Papers (2012)
7. Prince, M.J., Felder, R.M.: Inductive teaching and learning methods: Definitions, comparisons, and research bases. J. Eng. Educ. **95**(2), 123–138 (2006)
8. Vahdat, M., Oneto, L., Ghio, A., Anguita, D., Funk, M., Rauterberg, M.: Human algorithmic stability and human rademacher complexity. In: European Symposium on Artificial Neural Networks, Computational Intelligence and Machine Learning (2015)
9. Lee, V.S.: The power of inquiry as a way of learning. Innovative High. Educ. **36**(3), 149–160 (2011)
10. De Jong, T., Sotiriou, S., Gillet, D.: Innovations in stem education: the go-lab federation of online labs. Smart Learn. Environ. **1**(1), 1–16 (2014)
11. Donzellini, G., Ponta, D.: A simulation environment for e-learning in digital design. IEEE Trans. Ind. Electron. **54**(6), 3078–3085 (2007)
12. Bienkowski, M., Feng, M., Means, B.: Enhancing teaching and learning through educational data mining and learning analytics: An issue brief. In: US Department of Education, Office of Educational Technology (2012)

13. Del Blanco, A., Serrano, A., Freire, M., Martínez-Ortiz, I., Fernández-Manjón, B.: E-learning standards and learning analytics. can data collection be improved by using standard data models? In: IEEEGlobal Engineering Education Conference (2013)
14. Trčka, N., Pechenizkiy, M., van der Aalst, W.M.P.: Process mining from educational data. In: Robero, C., Ventura, S., Penchenizkiy, M., Baker, R., (eds.) Handbook of Educational Data Mining, pp. 123–142. Boca Raton: Chapman & Hall/CRC (2010). http://www.crcnetbase.com/doi/abs/10.1201/b10274-11
15. Trcka, N., Pechenizkiy, M.: From local patterns to global models: Towards domain driven educational process mining. In: International Conference on Intelligent Systems Design and Applications (2009)
16. Pechenizkiy, M., Trcka, N., Vasilyeva, E., Van Der Aalst, W., De Bra, P.: Process mining online assessment data. In: International Working Group on Educational Data Mining (2009)
17. Bannert, M., Reimann, P., Sonnenberg, C.: Process mining techniques for analysing patterns and strategies in students self-regulated learning. Metacognition Learn. **9**(2), 161–185 (2014)
18. Figl, K., Laue, R.: Cognitive complexity in business process modeling. In: Mouratidis, H., Rolland, C. (eds.) CAiSE 2011. LNCS, vol. 6741, pp. 452–466. Springer, Heidelberg (2011)
19. Gruhn, V., Laue, R.: Complexity metrics for business process models. In: International Conference on Business Information Systems (2006)
20. Štuikys, V., Damaševičius, R.: Complexity evaluation of feature models and meta-programs. In: Meta-Programming and Model-Driven Meta-Program Development (2013)
21. Lassen, K.B., Van Der Aalst, W.M.P.: Complexity metrics for workflow nets. Inf. Softw. Technol. **51**(3), 610–626 (2009)
22. McCabe, T.J.: A complexity measure. IEEE Trans. Softw. Eng. **4**, 308–320 (1976)
23. Zuse, H.: Softw. Complex. Walter de Cruyter, NY, USA (1991)
24. Thomas, J.C., Richards, J.T.: Achieving psychological simplicity: measures and methods to reduce cognitive complexity. In: Human-Computer Interaction: Design Issues, Solutions, and Applications (2009)
25. Rauterberg, M.: A method of a quantitative measurement of cognitive complexity. In: Human-Computer Interaction: Tasks and Organisation (1992)
26. Holzinger, A., Popova, E., Peischl, B., Ziefle, M.: On complexity reduction of user interfaces for safety-critical systems. In: Quirchmayr, G., Basl, J., You, I., Xu, L., Weippl, E. (eds.) CD-ARES 2012. LNCS, vol. 7465, pp. 108–122. Springer, Heidelberg (2012)
27. Ham, D.H., Park, J., Jung, W.: A framework-based approach to identifying and organizing the complexity factors of human-system interaction. IEEE Syst. J. **5**(2), 213–222 (2011)
28. Rauterberg, M.: How to measure cognitive complexity in human-computer interaction. In: Cybernetics and Systems Research (1996)
29. Sapounidis, T., Demetriadis, S., Stamelos, I.: Evaluating children performance with graphical and tangible robot programming tools. Pers. Ubiquit. Comput. **19**(1), 225–237 (2015)
30. Mohamed, N., Sulaiman, R.F., Endut, W.R.: The use of cyclomatic complexity metrics in programming performance's assessment. Procedia-Soc. Beha. Sci. **90**, 497–503 (2013)

31. Ponta, D., Anguita, D., Da Bormida, G., Donzellini, G.: Ten years of activity on computer-aided learning for electronics: Needs, experiences, field evaluation. In: Congreso sobre tecnologías aplicadas a la enseñanza de la electrónica (1998)
32. Vahdat, M., Oneto, L., Ghio, A., Donzellini, G., Anguita, D., Funk, M., Rauterberg, M.: A learning analytics methodology to profile students behavior and explore interactions with a digital electronics simulator. In: de Freitas, S., Rensing, C., Ley, T., Muñoz-Merino, P.J. (eds.) EC-TEL 2014. LNCS, vol. 8719, pp. 596–597. Springer, Heidelberg (2014)
33. Van Der Aalst, W.M.: Tool support. In: Process Mining (2011)
34. Günther, C.W., van der Aalst, W.M.P.: Fuzzy mining – adaptive process simplification based on multi-perspective metrics. In: Alonso, G., Dadam, P., Rosemann, M. (eds.) BPM 2007. LNCS, vol. 4714, pp. 328–343. Springer, Heidelberg (2007)
35. Van der Aalst, W., Weijters, T., Maruster, L.: Workflow mining: Discovering process models from event logs. IEEE Trans. Knowl. Data Eng. **16**(9), 1128–1142 (2004)

VisEN: Motivating Learner Engagement Through Explorable Visual Narratives

Bilal Yousuf(✉) and Owen Conlan

Adapt Center, School of Computer Science and Statistics,
Trinity College Dublin, Dublin, Ireland
{yousufbi, owen.conlan}@scss.tcd.ie

Abstract. Visualizations are increasingly being used to present student interactions and progress with online learning environments as motivations for student engagement with course content. Specifically, visualizations supporting data exploration and peer comparisons have yielded positive results in engagement. In addition, visual narratives have recently started to be used in learning environments to engage learners. This paper introduces VisEN, a visualization framework for semi-automatically constructing explorable visual narratives. VisEN was used during two successive academic years to construct individualized explorable visual narratives for undergraduate learners participating in an online Information Management course. The narratives presented engagement scores, time spent on activities and peer comparisons. This research evaluates the impact the explorable visual narratives had on student course engagement. This paper shows that the explorable visual narratives encouraged the majority of students (that were engaging poorly with course content) to engage with assigned tasks, and subsequently these students improved their engagement levels.

Keywords: Visual narratives · Learner engagement · Visual exploration

1 Introduction

In online learning environments, students' active involvement in the learning process is lower than traditional classroom settings, and hence they tend to get demotivated, leading to high dropout rates [1]. Such learning environments generate a large amount of logged data through student interactions with learning resources, discussion forums and course related quizzes. This data often contains valuable information that can highlight resource usage trends, reveal learner engagement levels and present peer comparisons. One of the aims of Learning Analytics is to present this data to learners in a consumable format to help motivate students to enhance their engagement with course content [2]. In addition, it is important that the logged data be displayed in a form that guides learners to understand and explore it, and thus support self-reflection [6]. One way of addressing this issue is to provide learners with visual stories that can be navigated and explored to help make sense of this data.

Information visualization provides a simple means to understand digitized data as it maps data attributes to visual properties [3]. Mapping appropriate visualizations to

© Springer International Publishing Switzerland 2015
G. Conole et al. (Eds.): EC-TEL 2015, LNCS 9307, pp. 367–380, 2015.
DOI: 10.1007/978-3-319-24258-3_27

datasets or segments of data is common in visual analysis and visual exploration tools [4, 5] where a chosen dataset or a selected segment of data is automatically visualized. Storytelling in information visualization or visual narrative can be defined as an ordered sequence of steps consisting of visualizations, which are linked or connected to make the communicated message more memorable [7]. Visual narratives also provide effective ways of highlighting facts, making points and passing on information [8]. In addition, visual data exploration supports end users in gaining a better understanding when little is known about the data and exploration goals are vague [9]. Visual drill downs allow end users to explore details behind the presented visualizations [10] as they render a more detailed view of a specific element within the visualization that is under examination.

This work aims to evaluate the effectiveness of explorable visual narratives in supporting learners to engage with online course content. In this work, supporting learners to engage refers to encouraging students to study course content, work through activities and submit deliverables within the time allocated. Studies were conducted using undergraduate students in Trinity College Dublin enrolled in the Information Management course. These students were presented with personalized explorable visual narratives. The course was delivered through AMAS [11], a Personalized Learning Environment (PLE) providing educational content and services to learners.

AMAS generates and sends students personalized notifications specifying the individual's level of engagement with the course and provides advice. Each learner has access to his/her own explorable visual narrative (hereafter, referred to as visual narrative), which uses the individuals logs, gathered by the AMAS PLE, to communicate a personalized message. The message provides the student with explorable visualizations presenting the level of engagement with the course, the time spent on activities and facilitates peer comparisons. The visual narratives are constructed using VisEN (Visual Exploration with Narrative), a generic visualization framework for generating explorable visual narratives. For AMAS, VisEN used student traces logged by the PLE to dynamically generate the visual narratives. In addition to providing personalized visual narratives, VisEN enables learners to drill down and explore data or explore related data to that shown in the view, hence making it an explorable visual narrative. The visual narratives also support anonymized peer comparisons, enabling learners to explore engagement; time spent on, and completed activities by peers. This paper analyzes the effect visual narratives had on the engagement of students using the AMAS PLE. It primarily focuses on students who improved their engagement levels. It was found that the visual narratives gave the majority of students that were engaging poorly with their course a strong motivational pull to engage with the PLE and motivated them to complete assigned activities and submit deliverables on time.

The remainder of this paper is structured as follows: Section 2 discusses related work. Section 3 describes an overview of the VisEN design. Section 4 introduces a use case of a typical student using the AMAS PLE. Section 5 evaluates the effectiveness of explorable visual narratives in enhancing student engagement over two academic years and Sect. 6 presents conclusions.

2 Related Work

Research on the use of Information Visualization in the Technology Enhanced Learning (TEL) domain has largely focused on three areas: Learning Analytics (LA) [2], Open Learner Modelling (OLM) [27] and Educational Data Mining (EDM) [23]. Across these three areas, visualizations have been used as a means of supporting reflection to promote learner motivation and engagement. In LA, visualizations have been used to present student activity data to either instructors to support the monitoring of students, or to students to promote a change in behavior or to both instructors and students [16, 17, 25]. In OLM, visualizations show student competencies and level of understanding using inferences from learner interactions to support reflection and assessment [21, 27]. EDM applies data mining algorithms to logged data to offer learners feedback and promote reflection [23]. The approach adopted by VisEN and discussed in this paper uses student activity data to generate explorable visual narratives to promote motivation and engagement amongst learners. Hence the remainder of this section analyzes systems that fall into the LA domain and specifically those that present logged data to learners in a format that enables self-reflection and behavioral change.

A number of systems [16, 17, 22] that present student traces facilitate exploration in the form of selecting elements within the visualizations and drilling down to view details. For example, SAM [16] provides visualizations of student activities to learners who can monitor what they have been working on and the time they spent on activities. The visualizations are interactive and facilitate drill down by clicking on visual elements, which reveal statistical details regarding resource usage and activity times. The CAM Dashboard [17] consists of goal-oriented visualizations for students to reflect on time spent on assigned activities and progress made towards goals. The explorations supported by the dashboard come in the form of drill down, where clicking a bar showing weekday activity numbers updates two visualizations to present actions and activities for the selected day. The StepUp dashboard [22] provides visualizations of student traces to promote reflection amongst learners. The dashboard contains sparklines showing overall activity per learner. Students can interact with the dashboard and explore a breakdown of their activities by clicking on the sparklines to load bar charts showing the time spent on activities and the distribution of forum posts.

From the above, it can be seen that there is a focus on providing visualizations that learners can interact with and explore to uncover details to support self-reflection. However, the exploration is predominantly selecting elements within the visualization and drilling down to explore details. VisEN supports visual exploration in two forms: the first is through drill down, where the student clicks on an element within the visualization, which loads a visualization showing details directly related to the element selected. The second form of exploration is manifested through links at the bottom of the visualization which, when clicked load data related to the data shown in the visualization. For example, if a visualization presents interaction timings showing individual student timings, then a related exploration could show the timings of the top engaging learners. In addition, the visualizations are offered through a narrative to enhance guidance and help make the communicated message more memorable [7].

Previous work has shown that visual narratives support students engage with study content in online learning environments [24].

While there are some indications [12] showing that students can at times be averse to peer comparisons, several systems [16, 17, 25] show that they can support learner motivations and engagement by allowing students to compare their own progress with peers. For example, Moodog [25] is a Moodle plug-in that uses the Course Management Systems logged data to visualize students' learning activities. It presents comparisons between students such as the number of times course material was viewed, the time spent on the course and forum activity. The eMUSE platform [26] provides learners with an integrated learning space to access a number of web tools, some of which include Twitter, Blogger and YouTube. It provides students with visualizations to compare their involvement and interactions with the tools against peers. TrAVis [13] provides learners with visualizations showing student tracking data on Computer Mediated Communications such as discussion forums, chat and blogs. Students can view peer comparisons at a number of communication levels through spiral graphs showing learner and peer activities. The systems facilitating visual exploration, discussed above, also support peer comparisons. For example, SAM provides a number of visualizations showing the number of documents used, average document usage time and average time spent on activities by peers. The CAM dashboard enables students to view comparisons with fellow learners regarding progress made towards goals. The StepUp dashboard presents the number of posts, time spent on course activities and tweets made by peers.

From the related work, it can be seen that there is also a strong emphasis on enabling peer comparisons amongst learners to support motivation and engagement. VisEN supports peer comparisons by enabling learners to select peer nodes through the visualization and explore detailed comparisons of engagement per activity and time spent on activities. In addition, it supports related data comparisons, which presents student comparisons related to the data shown in the visualization and these are offered through a visual narrative.

3 VisEN Design Overview

Users or narrative constructors use VisEN to build narratives that are automatically complemented with appropriate visualizations. In addition, VisEN enhances the visual narrative through explorations, called derivatives, which present data that is related to each section of the narrative. It supports end users (who are students in this deployment) in analyzing and exploring visual narratives and enables them to gain deeper insights into the visual narrative. This section describes an overview of the VisEN design by describing its architectural components and sub-components, shown in Fig. 1, used to generate explorative visual narratives. The design uses some of the principles discussed in sequencing in visual narratives [18], Template Editor and Shelf Configuration visual interface design approaches [19] and the visualization pipeline [3].

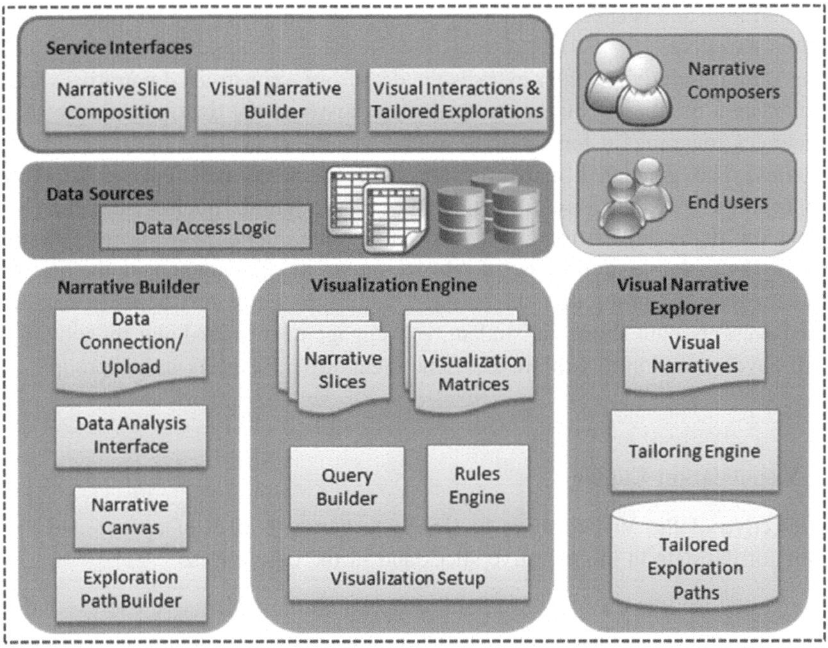

Fig. 1. VisEN architecture

3.1 Narrative Builder

The objective of the Narrative Builder is to enable narrative constructors (instructors, in this case) to connect to a data source, analyze the data and author narratives through a web-based interface.

- The Data Connection component is used to connect to data sources. Narrative constructors specify database connection parameters or select preconfigured data source parameters. For the AMAS deployment, a visual narrative template was created prior to the start of the course using test data, as logged data via student interactions was not available until the course started. Once the course commenced, the visual narratives used logged data generated by the PLE.
- The Data Analysis Interface displays the source tables and fields using the jQuery Accordion widget. The interface provides a Narrative Canvas with a number of panels to drop data fields and to specify filters. The jQuery Draggable widget is used to enable narrative constructors to drag and drop data fields onto relevant panels to build the narrative. When a field is dropped onto a filter panel, queries are generated to fetch data values and narrative constructors select the values to use in the filter. As data fields are dragged and dropped onto panels, the Visualization Engine is invoked to generate appropriate visualizations and render these to the narrative constructor. Narrative constructors enter captions to complement and explain the visualization, which can then be saved. This typically forms one part of

the narrative and is called a narrative slice and several slices can be linked to form a visual narrative.

- The Data Derivative Builder extracts the data from a constructed narrative slice and generates a number of queries to fetch derivatives of the data used in the slice. It generates mappings using the data source and these are used to create derivative queries. The generated mappings are used to create new queries to produce appropriate visualizations for the explorations. These queries are created by replacing fields and/or filters in the narrative slice queries with those in the mappings. For example, in the case of AMAS, one of the mappings pairs the individual student with the group that she belongs to. In this scenario, whenever a narrative slice presents data about the student, e.g. engagement breakdown by activity, she will have an option to explore the same breakdown for peers in her group.

3.2 Visualization Engine

The objective of the Visualization Engine is to generate a set of appropriate visualizations for the data in the narrative slices and in the derivatives.

- The Query Builder uses the data fields dropped onto the Narrative Canvas and filter data, if specified, to create and run SQL queries against the connected data source. The query results are formatted to specify the structure of the data, for example, univariate or multidimensional data, data types, etc. This formatting supports the Rules Engine to identify an appropriate set of visualizations for the narrative slice.
- VisEN uses visualization libraries to source visualization techniques. Research evaluating affordances and characteristics of visualization techniques [14, 15, 20] has shown the suitability of various visualizations against datasets. The Rules Engine consists of XML files (created by VisEN developers), which encode the characteristics and affordances of visualization techniques, which are used to map narratives slices to appropriate visualization techniques. In some cases, a few visualizations are appropriate for a narrative slice, in which case, all the matching techniques are made available to the narrative constructor to choose which one to use.
- The Visualization Builder generates the visualizations from the matching visualization technique(s) by fetching the templates from the appropriate visualization libraries and populating it using the formatted query results as JSON objects. The populated visualization techniques are then made available to the Narrative Constructor.

3.3 Visual Narrative Explorer

The Visual Narrative Explorer presents the visual narratives to end users (students in this deployment) through a web-based interface. This facilitates visual narrative consumption and tailored exploration.

- The visual narratives are presented to end users using JQuery tabs, where each tab represents a narrative slice, containing a title, visualization and a caption describing the data. End users are presented with the first narrative slice and they can view and analyze the entire narrative by navigating across the tabs, reading the descriptions and interacting with the visualizations.
- Derivative explorations are made available to end users to explore data related to the narrative slice. These are accessed by clicking on either elements within the visualization or links below it. When an end user wishes to explore a derivative, she clicks the element or link which fires an AJAX request loading a new visualization with the derivative data in a popup window. The exploration links at the bottom of the narrative slice are tailored to individual preferences. The Exploration Tailoring Engine analyzes how end users interact with the derivative links and infers preferences per individual. Exploration links are ordered by the level of exploration by the user as the engine computes the number of times the data presented in the exploration was viewed and time spent viewing it to determine the order.

4 Use Case

This section describes a use case of a student with typical learning and engagement behavior, and visual narrative usage shown by many learners using the AMAS PLE.

Joe is an Engineering student using the AMAS PLE to study Information Management. During the first month course, Joe has rarely used the PLE. During week 4 of the semester, Joe receives a notification by email informing him of his poor engagement with the course content and advising him of the upcoming deadline.

Joe is determined to improve his engagement and he immediately views his personal visual narrative through the PLE. He navigates through his visual narrative analyzing how he has engaged with the overall course and per activity. He explores the times spent by peers by clicking on activities and compares engagement levels. He also explores the time taken by peers to complete the next three activities that he is assigned. Having analyzed his visual narrative, Joe is motivated to start working through his activities. As he completes his tasks, Joe continuously revisits his visual narratives where he analyzes his engagement score and can see how it is increasing.

5 Evaluation

This section evaluates the impact that the explorative visual narratives had on learners' course engagement through three studies. Two of these studies use the logged data from students studying the Information Management course at Trinity College Dublin using the AMAS PLE over two academic years (2013–2014 and 2014–2015) and the third study analyzes student feedback. The system, including the visual narratives remained the same over the two years. The course was run for a period of three months (October - December) in each year with a total of over 120,000 student interactions logged over the two academic years. During the three months course, AMAS emailed personal engagement notifications at regular intervals (one every two to three weeks) to students informing them of their level of engagement with the course. These notifications described the learner's current engagement with the course (bad, poor, good, or excellent) and provided related advice. Course interactions (page clicks), study time (reading and reviewing durations), submissions and questionnaire scores were used by AMAS to calculate engagement. Course activity and grades from the preceding years' were used to determine thresholds for activities when calculating the level of engagement. The engagement notifications did not explicitly make any references to the visual narratives and interacting or viewing these narratives did not impact engagement scores. The home page of the PLE presented the current engagement score and students had the option to click 'view my progress' to load their visual narratives, which amongst other things includes how the engagement score was calculated. This evaluation primarily focusses on students who improved their engagement levels. Specifically those that received a bad or poor engagement notification, and following an improvement, received a good or excellent notification. It analyzes the impact the visual narratives had on encouraging these students to engage and subsequently improve their engagement. Figure 2 shows some of the visualizations from a learner's visual narrative.

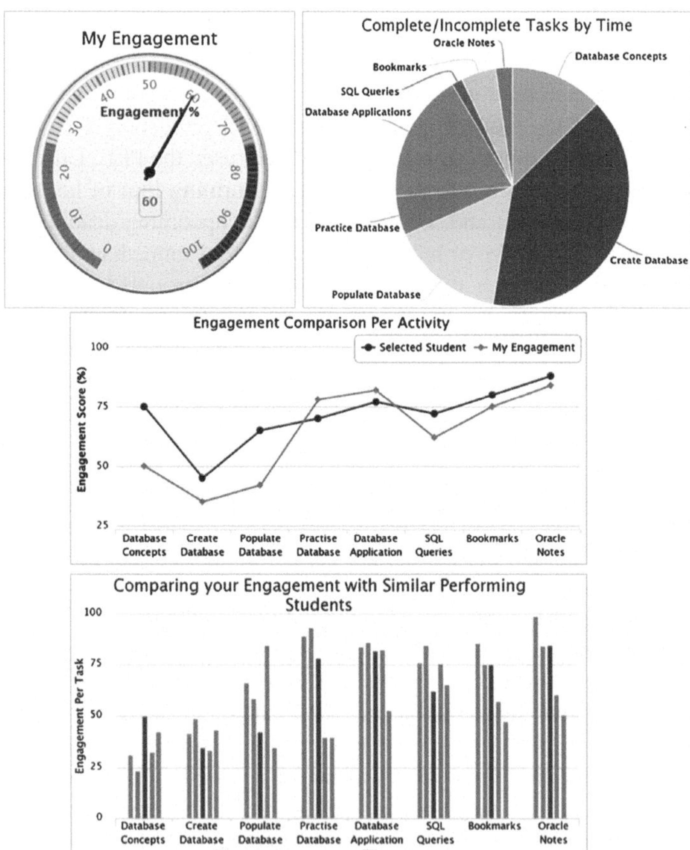

Fig. 2. Selected visualizations from a student's visual narrative

In total 233 students participated in the course over the two academic years. From these, a total of 125 students improved their engagement score from bad or poor to good or excellent. While the remaining students did not improve their engagement to the same degree, a relatively small number showed no improvements in engagement at all.

The first study analyzed the logged data to determine the correlation between students' course engagement and the number of times the learners revisited their visual narrative before and after receiving a bad or poor engagement notification. This study examined the extent to which the 125 students used their visual narratives to help them achieve a good or excellent engagement score. This study also analyzed the number of unique visual narrative visits by these students before and after receiving a bad or poor engagement notification. The second study used the logged data to assess if the visual narratives were immediately used by any of the 125 learners to understand a bad or poor engagement notification. It also examined the percentage of interactions these students had with their visual narrative versus the total course content interactions following such a notification. The third study assessed the responses to the AMAS course questionnaire completed by students once the course was over. The study examined the responses related to motivational factors and usefulness of the visual narratives.

5.1 Study 1: Visual Narrative Views Before and After Bad or Poor Engagement Notification

In the 2013–2014 academic year, 61 students improved their engagement to good or excellent following a bad or poor engagement notification and in 2014–2015, 64 students showed a similar improvement. Study 1 examined the number of times these students viewed their visual narratives before and after the notification by calculating the spread of the visual narrative revisits during both engagement periods. It also determined the correlation between course engagement and visual narratives visits using the Pearson correlation coefficient for both academic years during the study period leading to an improvement in engagement.

Increase in Visual Narrative Visits. The boxplot shown in Fig. 3 presents the spread in visual narrative revisits between a period of poor and bad engagement with the course and the subsequent period of good or excellent engagement for the same students. In 2013–2014, A and B in the figure show the increase in visual narrative visits, A showing the number of visits during low engagement and B showing the number of visits during improved engagement. The same holds true for 2014–2015, shown through C and D. The shift from A to B and from C to D clearly shows how these students increased their usage of their visual narratives as their course engagement improved. Study 1 also found that in the 2013–2014 academic year, 78 % of students who improved their engagement to good or excellent showed a minimum of a fourfold increase in their visual narrative views. In the 2014–2015 academic year, this figure was at 72 %. This finding showed that as the students worked through course content and improved engagement, they continuously returned to their visual narratives.

Strong Correlation Between Visual Narrative Views and Engagement. The Pearson correlation coefficient was used to determine if an improvement in course engagement correlated to increased visual narrative visits. In the 2013–2014 academic year, during the period of improved course engagement, the Pearson correlation coefficient was 0.74 and the 2014–2015 academic year, it was 0.76. This showed that an increase in visual narrative views was strongly correlated to an increase in learner engagement.

Finally, students who received a bad or poor engagement notification but did not improve to good or excellent engagement score (total of 86 students) across both academic years were analyzed. Of these students, 44 showed slight improvement in engagement and 37 of these had increased their visual narratives with the improvement in engagement.

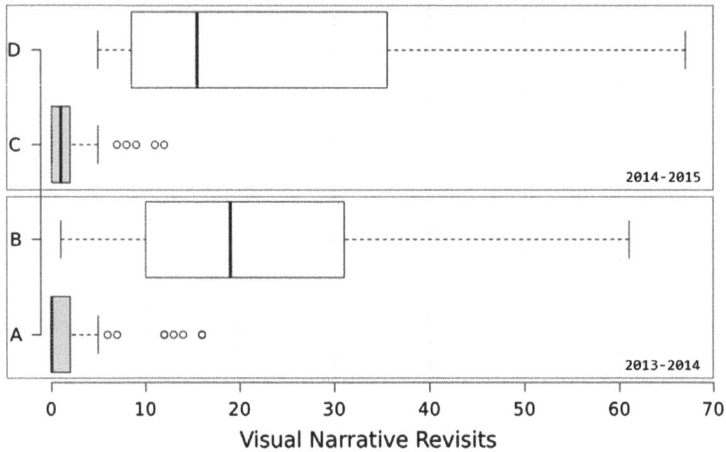

Fig. 3. Visual narrative revisits during low and high engagement

5.2 Study 2: Learners' Immediate Visual Narrative Interactions Following a Bad or Poor Engagement Notification

The second study analyzed how learners, who improved their course engagement from bad or poor to good or excellent, interacted with their visual narratives immediately after receiving a bad or poor engagement notification. It also examined the percentage of interactions these students had with their visual narrative against overall course interactions during the period when the engagement improved. The aim of this study was to determine if learners were drawn to their visual narratives to understand a poor engagement notification and weather these students continually visited their narratives as they worked through course content. It is important to remember that the notifications did not reference the visual narratives. Moreover, interacting with the visual narrative did not affect learner engagement scores, as these were calculated using course content interactions, study times and submitted deliverables.

Visual Narratives as a Means to Understand and Promote Engagement. This study found that in the 2014–2015 academic year 74 % of learners who improved their engagement to good or excellent executed at least half of their total visual narrative interactions on the first day after reading the bad or poor engagement notification. In the 2013–2014 academic year, this figure was 70 %. In addition, the study analyzed the percentage of these learners that repeatedly visited their visual narratives to understand their course engagement. It was found that at least one fifth of the total interactions with the system were with the visual narratives for 71 % of these students from 2014–2015. The same analysis found that this figure was 65 % for the 2013–2014 students. The study found a similar trend but to a much lesser degree for the students that received a bad or poor engagement notification and only slightly improved their engagement and still remained in the poor or bad engagement category.

From this study, it was concluded that the majority of students who improved their course engagement used their visual narrative as the first place to go to understand the reasons behind a bad or poor engagement notification. It also showed that a minimum of 20 % of overall interactions during the period when their engagement improved were dedicated to their visual narratives. This suggests that the visual narratives had an important role in encouraging and supporting engagement amongst these learners.

5.3 Study 3: Assessing Usefulness of Explorable Visual Narratives Through Feedback

The third study analyzed all the learner responses (including those that did and did not improve their engagement) to some of the questions related to the visual narrative from the AMAS questionnaire completed by students at the end of the course. This study analyzed the responses from all the students highlighting the responses from those who improved their engagement from bad or poor to good or excellent as they interacted with their visual narratives the most. In total 147 students completed the questionnaire, 79 in 2013–2014 and 68 in 2014–2015. Of these students, 85 were from the category of students that improved their engagement as mentioned above. The primary aim was to determine if the visual narratives had a role in motivating learners to engage with course content after interacting with their narratives. Hence this study analyzed student feedback from the following three statements.

Statement 1: The Engagement and Task Duration Visualizations Motivated me to Engage with the Course. Statement 1 incorporates all the visualization from the visual narrative presented to individual students. The figures in bold are from the students who improved engagement from bad or poor to good or excellent, with 80 % and 77 % strongly agreeing or agreeing from the 2013–2014 and 2014–2015 students respectively. This response confirms the findings from studies 1 and 2, that the visual narratives had an important role is motivating and supporting engagement of students who improved their engagement. The response from the entire class also suggests that the visual narratives motivated learner engagement, despite the fact over 40 % of these students used their visual narrative to a lesser degree (Table 1).

Table 1. Responses of the class and those whose engagement improved to good or higher (bold)

	S. agree	Agree	Undecided	Disagree	S. disagree
2013/14	28 %	37 %	5 %	20 %	10 %
2014/15	26 %	41 %	8 %	12 %	13 %
2013/14	**33 %**	**47 %**	**4 %**	**9 %**	**7 %**
2014/15	**33 %**	**44 %**	**3 %**	**13 %**	**7 %**

Statement 2: It was Useful to Explore Related Data Through Other Visualization. A core and novel component of the VisEN architecture are visual explorations of data related to what is shown in the visualizations of the narratives to enable users to gain a deeper insight into the data presented. The response (in bold) from statement 2 showed that 78 % (2013–2014) and 72 % (2014–2015) of the students who improved engagement from bad or poor to good or excellent found this feature beneficial for their study. The response from the entire class was also quite positive, which highlights the usefulness of related data exploration in the TEL domain (Table 2).

Table 2. Responses of the class and those whose engagement improved to good or higher (bold)

	S. agree	Agree	Undecided	Disagree	S. disagree
2013/14	14 %	47 %	10 %	23 %	6 %
2014/15	15 %	48 %	7 %	23 %	7 %
2013/14	**16 %**	**62 %**	**4 %**	**13 %**	**5 %**
2014/15	**21 %**	**51 %**	**0 %**	**26 %**	**2 %**

Statement 3: I Found it Beneficial to be able to Track my Progress and Compare it Against Other Class Students Through Personalized Visualization. Research [16, 17] has shown that peer comparisons can promote self-reflection and it has also shown that students can be averse to such comparisons [12]. The responses to this statement were quite spread, with 15 % and 9 % of the students (in bold), who improved their engagement from bad or poor to good or excellent and regularly used their visual narratives, undecided regarding the benefit of peer comparisons. Although the students agreeing with the statement were in majority, the responses suggest that some students were unsure about the benefit and others averse to such comparisons (Table 3).

Table 3. Responses of the class and those whose engagement improved to good or higher (bold)

	S. agree	Agree	Undecided	Disagree	S. disagree
2013/14	29 %	31 %	12 %	20 %	8 %
2014/15	7 %	47 %	16 %	20 %	10 %
2013/14	**25 %**	**38 %**	**9 %**	**13 %**	**5 %**
2014/15	**21 %**	**44 %**	**15 %**	**15 %**	**5 %**

6 Conclusions

This paper introduced the VisEN framework and described how explorative visual narratives can be constructed and used by end users to analyze and explore. The related work section showed how VisEN progresses the state of the art by introducing related data explorations within visual narratives. The paper focused on evaluating the effectiveness of students' individual explorative visual narratives, which were generated by VisEN, in supporting learners to engage with their course content using the AMAS PLE. Three studies were carried out using logged data and questionnaire responses from a total of 233 students over two academic years. The studies found that:

1. The visual narratives motivated learners to engage with course content.
2. The visual narratives were regularly used to understand course engagement and analyze progress, amongst learners who were improving their engagement.
3. An increase in engagement strongly correlated with an increase in visual narrative usage amongst students who were improving their engagement levels.
4. Students found it useful to explore their personal visual narratives through data related to what was shown in the visualizations.

These findings show that the visual narratives gave students a strong motivational pull to engage with course content, however, further work is required to accurately elicit the feelings of the students after viewing a narrative and connecting it to self-assessment.

Acknowledgements. This research is supported by the Science Foundation Ireland through the CNGL program (Grant 12/CE/I2267) in the ADAPT Center (www.adaptcentre.ie) at Trinity College Dublin.

References

1. Koutropoulos, A., Gallagher, M., Abajian, S., de Waard, I., Hogue, R., Keskin, N., Rodriguez, C.: Emotive vocabulary in MOOCs: context and participant retention. Eur. J. Open Distance E-Learn., **1** (2012). http://www.eurodl.org/?article=507
2. Duval, E.: Attention please!: learning analytics for visualization and recommendation. In: 1st International Conference on Learning Analytics and Knowledge, pp. 9–17. ACM, New York (2011)
3. Card, S., Mackinlay, J., Shneiderman, B.: Readings in Information Visualization: Using Vision to Think. Morgan Kaufmann, San Francisco (1999)
4. Gonzalez, H., Halevy, A., Jensen, C.S., Langen, A., Madhavan, J., Shapley, R., Shen, W.: Google fusion tables: data management, integration and collaboration in the cloud. In: 1st ACM Symposium on Cloud Computing, pp. 175–180. ACM, New York (2010)
5. Tableau Software: http://www.tableau.com
6. Zimmerman, B.J.: Becoming a self-regulated learner: an overview. Theor. Pract. **41**(2), 65–70 (2002)
7. Austin, M.: Useful Fictions: Evolution, Anxiety, and the Origins of Literature. University of Nebraska Press, Lincoln (2011)

8. Kosara, R., Mackinlay, J.: Storytelling: the next step for visualization. Computer **46**, 44–50 (2013)
9. Keim, D.A.: Visual exploration of large data sets. Commun. ACM **44**, 38–44 (2001)
10. Tibco Spotfire: http://spotfire.tibco.com
11. O'Keeffe, I., Staikopoulos, A., Rafter, R., Walsh, E., Yousuf, B., Conlan, O., Wade, V.: Personalized activity based eLearning. In: 12th International Conference on Knowledge Management and Knowledge Technologies, Article no. 2. ACM, New York (2012)
12. Burleson, K., Leach, C.W., Harrington, D.M.: Upward social comparison and self-concept: Inspiration and inferiority among art students in an advanced programme. Br. J. Soc. Psychol. **44**(1), 109–123 (2005)
13. May, M., George, S., Prévôt, P.: TrAVis to enhance students' self-monitoring in online learning supported by computer-mediated communication tools. Comput. Inf. Syst. Ind. Manage. Appl. **3**, 623–634 (2011)
14. Carr, D.B., Littlefield, R.J., Nicholson, W.L., Littlefield, J.S.: Scatterplot matrix techniques for large N. J. Am. Stat. Assoc. **82**, 424–436 (1987)
15. Dias, M.M., Franco, C., Rabelo, E., Yamaguchi, J.K.: Visualization Techniques: Which is the Most Appropriate in the Process of Knowledge Discovery in Data Base?. INTECH Open Access Publisher, Rijeka (2012)
16. Govaerts, S., Verbert, K., Duval, E., Pardo, A.: The student activity meter for awareness and self-reflection. In: CHI 2012 Extended Abstracts on Human Factors in Computing Systems, pp. 869–884. ACM, New York (2012)
17. Santos, J.L., Govaerts, S., Verbert, K., Duval, E.: Goal-oriented visualizations of activity tracking: a case study with engineering students. In: 2nd International Conference on Learning Analytics and Knowledge, pp. 143–152. ACM, New York (2012)
18. Hullman, J., Drucker, S., Riche, N.H., Lee, B., Fisher, D., Adar, E.: A deeper understanding of sequence in narrative visualization. IEEE Trans. Visual Comput. Graphics **19**, 2406–2415 (2013)
19. Grammel, L., Bennett, C., Tory, M., Storey, M.A.: A survey of visualization construction user interfaces. In: EuroVis-Short Papers, pp. 19–23 (2013)
20. Chi, E.H.: A taxonomy of visualization techniques using the data state reference model. In: IEEE Symposium on Information Visualization, pp. 69–75. IEEE (2000)
21. Hsiao, I.-H., Brusilovsky, P.: Motivational social visualizations for personalized E-learning. In: Ravenscroft, A., Lindstaedt, S., Kloos, C.D., Hernández-Leo, D. (eds.) EC-TEL 2012. LNCS, vol. 7563, pp. 153–165. Springer, Heidelberg (2012)
22. Santos, J.L., Verbert, K., Govaerts, S., Duval, E.: Addressing learner issues with StepUp!: an evaluation. In: Third International Conference on Learning Analytics and Knowledge, pp. 14–22. ACM, New York (2013)
23. Merceron, A., Yacef, K.: Educational data mining: a case study. In: 12th International Conference on Artificial Intelligence in Education. IOS Press, Amsterdam (2005)
24. Le, D.T.: Bringing data to life into an introductory statistics course with gapminder. Teach. Stat. **35**, 114–122 (2013)
25. Zhang, H., Almeroth, K.: Moodog: tracking student activity in online course management systems. J. Interact. Learn. Res. **21**, 407–429 (2010)
26. Popescu, E., Cioiu, D.: eMUSE - integrating web 2.0 tools in a social learning environment. In: Leung, H., Popescu, E., Cao, Y., Lau, R.W.H., Nejdl, W. (eds.) ICWL 2011. LNCS, vol. 7048, pp. 41–50. Springer, Heidelberg (2011)
27. Bull, S., Kay, J.: Open learner models as drivers for metacognitive processes. In: Azevedo, R., Aleven, V. (eds.) International Handbook on Metacognition and Learning Technologies. Springer, New York (2013)

Short Papers

ICT Supported Learning Rises Math Achievement in Low Socio Economic Status Schools

Roberto Araya(✉), Raúl Gormaz, Manuel Bahamondez, Carlos Aguirre, Patricio Calfucura, Paulina Jaure, and Camilo Laborda

Centro de Investigación Avanzada en Educación, Universidad de Chile, Periodista Carrasco 75, Santiago, Chile
roberto.araya.schulz@gmail.com

Abstract. Sustained improvement in student achievement on national standardized tests for low socio economic status (SES) districts is critical for reducing gaps in educational inequality. We report the results of 3 years of implementation of an ICT web-based learning environment in all 11 public schools of a low SES urban district in Chile. This includes 43 fourth grade classes and 1,355 students. This is a Computer Aided Instruction program that promotes whole class collaborative learning with peer support. Effect size on the national standardized fourth grade math test is 0.33, which is three times the national improvement level over the same period and five times the improvement made by a neighboring district with a similar population. On the other hand, the same students did not make any improvements on the national standardized language test. Since each class was taught by the same teacher, only without ICT, we can therefore discount the teacher effect.

Keywords: Computer aided instruction · Web-based learning · Effect sizes

1 Introduction

Sustained improvement in student achievement for low SES schools is critical for reducing gaps in educational inequality. This enormous challenge has several components. First, there is the difficulty of reliably measuring student achievement [7]. This requires being able to conduct annual national standardized tests. Furthermore, it is necessary to do large-scale, randomized control experiments. In the absence of such randomized trials, it is necessary to do non-experimental studies using statistical controls that include the relevant factors with which students are sorted by teachers and schools [13]. Next there is the difficulty of obtaining effects of an interesting size. Large-scale studies of the effect on student achievement for different factors do not reveal huge impacts. For example, factors such as the type of institution that educate the teachers [10], teacher certification [12], teacher professional development [13], change of teaching practices [6, 8, 14], textbooks [3], leadership strategies [17], use of computers [9, 22–24], and use of calculators [20], show impacts of a modest size or no

© Springer International Publishing Switzerland 2015
G. Conole et al. (Eds.): EC-TEL 2015, LNCS 9307, pp. 383–388, 2015.
DOI: 10.1007/978-3-319-24258-3_28

effect at all. In other cases, it is not clear how to change practices [6]. Moreover, most of these studies use pre- and post-tests designed or selected by the researchers and they are not necessarily aligned to the national standards, unlike national standardized tests.

Impact studies are much scarcer in developing countries. Firstly, there is a lack of resources for funding research projects, particularly if the study lasts several years. Secondly, resources for implementing Computer Aided Instruction (CAI) programs are very scarce. This is due in part to computer labs being less widely available, as well as there being less technical support for computer labs. There is also much less access to internet, narrower band width, as well as more unstable and unreliable internet services. Large-scale studies of the impact of ICT on student achievement in low SES schools in developing countries are even more difficult to find. On the other hand, there is extensive empirical research under laboratory conditions [11, 18], which shows that practice with feedback makes a big difference.

2 Methods

In this study we report 3 years using Supplemental CAI [5] on low SES schools. Teachers and lab coordinators track the students' progress with their smartphones. A real time early alert system lists students who are having more difficulties. The platform is designed to drive the progression of the entire class as a whole, and not to leave students alone by themselves. It has facilities to promote the cooperation and support of students that are ahead of their peers. We present evidence of 43 fourth grades classes from every urban public school in Lo Prado, a low SES municipality in Chile. This includes 16 fourth grade classes from 11 schools that used the CAI model in 2011, 16 classes from the same 11 schools that used the CAI during 2012, and 11 classes from 8 schools among the same 11 schools that used the CAI during 2013. This is a total of 1,355 fourth grade students which completed a total of 967,830 exercises on the CAI platform. Every year, fourth grade students have to take a national standardized test in mathematics, and another national standardized test in language. These tests are called the Mathematics SIMCE and the Language SIMCE, respectively. We will use the SIMCE test results to measure impact. Firstly, we compare yearly gains on the national standardized mathematics test. We define the yearly gain for each class as the difference between the score in a given year and the 2010 score for each school. The government publishes the scores for each school, but not the scores for individual students. Furthermore, if there are two or more fourth grade classes in a school, the government sends the score for each class to the corresponding school. However, not all of those class scores were obtained for this study. We use the class score when available, and the school score otherwise. As a control, we use the entire country, as well as a neighboring district with the same SES. Secondly, we compare the yearly gains on the mathematics test with the yearly gains on the language test in the same classes. In each class, both subjects are taught by the same teacher. Therefore, by comparing scores we can analyze the impact of the teacher and ultimately calculate whether the improvement was independent of the teacher.

3 Results

The yearly gains on the national standardized mathematics test for municipal schools in the municipality of Lo Prado was 0.33 standard deviations, which is greater (for a 99 % confidence level) than the 0.11 standard deviations witnessed by schools across the rest of the country, and the 0.07 standard deviations in the neighboring municipality of Pudahuel. These two municipalities are very similar. In fact, they used to be the same municipality until a few years ago and they have a similar SES [1].

It is important to note that attrition was very low. For example, in 2013 in Lo Prado, from the 332 students doing exercises at the beginning of the year, only 20 students did not finish the year at the school (i.e. 6.2 %). 11 of them (3.4 %) had scored below the average on the CAI platform and 9 of them (2.8 %) had scored above the average. In other words, attrition is low and it is equally distributed between high and low performing students. It is possible that the increase in the yearly gains on the mathematics test is due mainly to the contribution of the teachers and/or schools. Since in all the classes the teacher teaches all subjects, if the effect is due to specific characteristics of the teacher then one would expect that classes with an increase in yearly gains on the mathematics test would also see an increase on the language test. Conversely, if there is no clear relation in the increase or decrease across subjects, then the increase in mathematics is not just caused by the teacher. In Lo Prado, yearly gains on the mathematics test was 0.33 standard deviations, which is higher (99.9 % confidence level) than the yearly gains on the language test, which was −0.02 (a decrease). It is important to note that the Supplemental CAI model was only implemented for mathematics. In language, they implemented a different strategy.

It is also important to study the effect of the lab teacher in charge of the laboratory. Four lab coordinators took charge of the lab in the 11 schools, moving from one to another to assist classes during the sessions. We will look at the two lab coordinators with most classes in Lo Prado. The yearly gains on the mathematics test achieved by one lab teacher was 0.384 standard deviations, which corresponds to 5 classes. The increase achieved by the other lab teacher was 0.382 standard deviations, corresponding to 14 classes. They are similar for a 99 % confidence level.

How different is the impact obtained in Lo Prado municipal schools from the ones analyzed in the literature? For example, reference [22] reviewed 38 studies of the impact of Supplemental CAI programs, but only 15 of these studies used randomized or quasi-experimental designs. The median effect size was +0.19. In our implementation in the district of Lo Prado, the yearly gain on the SIMCE math test was +0.33. If we consider the neighbor municipality Pudahuel as control we get a net effect size of $0.33 - 0.07 = 0.26$. However, when using the assessment tests from the CAI platform between the beginning of the year and the end of the year, the improvement was +0.63 standard deviations. This effect is almost twice the yearly gain on the SIMCE math test. On the other hand, we have seen that it is reasonable to use the urban schools of the neighboring district of Pudahuel as a control group. They have a yearly gain on the SIMCE math test of +0.07. If we assume that the same relation holds true in Pudahuel as it did in Lo Prado, for the conversion between yearly SIMCE gain to the difference in the CAI test, then we can estimate the difference in the assessment test used in CAI for schools in the district of Pudahuel. If they would have taken the same assessment tests as those used with the CAI platform, then they would have obtained an effect size of +0.14. Both Lo Prado and Pudahuel use the "Ley Subvención Escolar Preferencial (SEP)" (the Law for Preferential School Subsidies) to fund its projects. SEP is a special government subsidy for schools with low SES students. All municipalities have access to a similar amount of funding per student and decide how to allocate its funding. Most of them use it for a blend of teacher training and support from external companies and universities. We can therefore use Pudahuel as a typical control group. After discounting the control group, the effect size for Lo Prado is 0.63 − 0.14 = +0.49 standard deviations. This effect is similar to the effect size of +0.39 obtained in [2] in India with a CAI program, but much higher than the effect of +0.16 obtained in [19] for rural school in China, and the effect size of +0.14 obtained in migrant schools in China [15, 16]. It is also higher than the median effect size of 0.19 found in [22].

The larger effect in Lo Prado compared to the other studies can be explained by the fact that in the case of Lo Prado, students attended one or two sessions per week that lasted 80 min (80 % of the time) and 40 min (20 % of the time), whereas in the study [22], most students attended the lab once a week for 30 min. Moreover, the yearly gains on the national standardized mathematics test by the classes from Lo Prado are correlated to the number of exercises with immediate feedback completed between the end of March and early October (just before the national test). There is an increase of 0.18 standards deviations on the math SIMCE test for every 100 extra exercises completed online per student (p-value of 0.006705, $R^2 = 0.2205$).

From each of the fourth grade classes in the 8 schools in Lo Prado using CAI in 2014, we took a sample of traditional material from 5 students. These were 5 notebooks, 5 worksheets and 5 other paper-based materials per class. With the CAI platform in Lo Prado, each student completed 10.2 exercises with feedback per session, whereas they only completed 3.2 exercises with feedback per session using traditional paper-based materials. The difference is huge. Only 50.9 % of the exercises assigned (copied by hand or printed on the worksheets) are completed by the students, with little feedback given on those that are completed. Only 3.8 % of the exercises that were assigned are completed and received feedback. This can explain why learning is faster [4] with a CAI model than in a regular classroom without computers.

It is also very important to compute separately the impact of CAI on strong and weak students. For each class, we define weak students as those who score below the class median for the test at the beginning of the year (March and April). The remaining students are classified as strong. Very similar tests were taken at the end of each year (October and November). The average improvement made by weak students is 1.08 standard deviations of the initial performance by the entire population, whereas the improvement by the strong students is 0.17 standard deviations. The average improvement for all students is therefore 0.63 standard deviations. Thus, the average improvement made by the weak students is 6.3 times more than the average improvement made by the strong students. These improvements are statistically significant for a 99.9 confidence level.

4 Conclusions

A critical question is: How does the use of technology in education can help increase student learning? [21] We have reviewed the data from three years of implementing the Supplemental CAI strategy. Students practice twice a week in computer labs throughout the school year. Each year we take the average score by the whole class on a national standardized test and compare it with the score by each school from the year before the implementation of the program. We have seen that the CAI program has produced a sustained impact. The effect size reached for a low SES district on the national standardized fourth grade math test is 0.33. This is much higher than the average improvement by the rest of the country. In fact, it is three times more than the improvement made by the rest of the country over the same period, and five times more than the improvement made by a neighboring district with a similar population. We have seen that a potential cause of the results is the intensity of practice. On average, classes that practice more achieve greater improvements. Another critical factor is that the students receive timely feedback. Students do a lot of exercises on paper but they receive very little immediate feedback. Using CAI, they receive three times as much feedback per session than they receive in a regular class. Improving student achievement is not easy. Several studies that have examined factors such as teacher education, certification, and professional development have shown little impact. However, the results reported from this low SES district are very promising. ICT supported learning can be very effective if properly implemented.

Acknowledgments. To Gonzalo Navarrete, President of the Education Commission for the Chilean Association of Municipalities; to Maximiliano Ríos, Director of the Lo Prado Education Department; to Basal Funds for the Centers of Excellence Project FB 0003 from the Associative Research Program of CONICYT.

References

1. Araya, R., Van der Molen, J.: Impact of a blended ICT adoption model on Chilean vulnerable schools correlates with amount of on online practice. In: Proceedings of the Workshops at the 16th International Conference on Artificial Intelligence in Education AIED 2013, Memphis, USA, 9–13 July 2013
2. Banerjee, A., Cole, S., Duflo, E., Linden, L.: Remedying education: evidence from two randomized experiments in India. Q. J. Econ. **122**, 1235–1264 (2007)
3. Banilower, E.R., Boyd, S.E., Pasley, J.D., Weiss, I.R.: Lessons from a decade of mathematics and science reform. A capstone report for the local systemic change through teacher enhancement initiative (2006)
4. Berlinski, S., Busso, M., Cristia, J., Severin, E.: Computers in schools: why governments should do their homework. In: Chong, A. (ed.) Development Connections: Unveiling the Impact of New Information Technologies. Palgrave MacMillan, London (2011)
5. Cheung, A., Slavin, R.: The effectiveness of educational technology applications on mathematics achievement in K-12 classrooms: a meta-analysis. Educ. Res. Rev. **9**, 88–111 (2013)

6. Cuban, L.: Inside the Black Box of Classroom Practice: Change without Reform in American Education. Harvard Education Press, Cambridge (2013)
7. Doran, H., Izumi, L.: Putting Education to the Test: A Value-Added Model for California. Pacific Research Institute, San Francisco (2004)
8. Garet, M., Wayne, A., Stancavage, F., Taylor, J., Walters, K., Song, M., Brown, S., Hurlburt, S., Zhu, P., Sepanik, S., Doolitle, F., Warner, E.: Middle School Mathematics Professional Development Impact Study Findings after the First Year of Implementation. US Department of Education, Washington, DC (2010)
9. Fuchs, T., Woessmann, L.: Computers and Student Learning: Bivariate and Multivariate Evidence on the Availability and Use of Computers at Home and at School. Ifo Institute for Economic Research, Munich (2004)
10. Harris, D., Sass, T.: Teacher Training: Teacher Quality and Student Achievement. University of Wisconsin and Florida State University, Tallahassee (2008)
11. Hattie, J., Timperley, H.: The power of feedback. Rev. Educ. Res. **77**(1), 81–112 (2007)
12. Kane, T.J., Rockoff, J., Staiger, D.O.: What does certification tell us about teacher effectiveness? Evidence from New York City. Econ. Educ. Rev. **27**, 615–631 (2008)
13. Kane, T.J.: Do Value-Added Estimates Identify Causal Effects of Teachers and Schools?. The Brown Center Chalkboard, Brookings Institution, Washington, DC (2014)
14. Labaree, D.: Someone Has to Fail. The Zero-Sum Game of Public Schooling. Harvard University Press, Cambridge (2010)
15. Lai, F., Zhang, L., Qu, Q., Hu, X., Shi, Y., Boswell, M., Rozelle, S.: Does computer-assisted learning improve learning outcomes? Evidence from a randomized experiment in public schools in rural minority areas in Qinghai. Working document N° 237. Rural Education Action Project, Stanford, CA (2012)
16. Lai, F., Luo, R., Zhang, L., Huang, X., Rozelle, S.: Does computer-assisted learning improve learning outcomes? Evidence from a randomized experiment in migrant schools in Beijing. Working document N° 228. Rural Education Action Project, Stanford, CA (2011)
17. Louis, K., Leithwood, K., Wahlstrom, K., Anderson, S.: Learning from leadership: investigating the links to improved student learning. Final report of research to the Wallace Foundation (2010)
18. Mayfield, K., Chase, P.: The effects of cumulative practice on mathematics problem solving. J. Appl. Behav. Anal. **35**, 105–123 (2002)
19. Mo, D., Zhang, L., Lui, R., Qu, Q., Huang, W., Wang, J., Qiao, Y., Boswell, M., Rozelle, S.: Integrating computer assisted learning into a regular curriculum: evidence from a randomized experiment in rural schools in Shaanxi. Working document N° 248. Rural Education Action Project, Stanford, CA (2013)
20. National Mathematics Advisory Panel: Report of the Task Group on Learning Processes, chap. 4. U.S. Department of Education, Washington, DC (2008)
21. Ortiz, E., Cristia, J.: The IDB and technology in education: how to promote effective programs? Tehnical Note IDB-TN_670 (2014)
22. Slavin, R., Lake, C.: Effective programs in elementary mathematics: a best-evidence synthesis. Rev. Educ. Res. **78**(3), 427–515 (2008)
23. Steenbergen-Hu, S., Cooper, H.: A meta-analysis of the effectiveness of intelligent tutoring systems on K-12 students' mathematical learning. J. Educ. Psychol. **105**(4), 970–987 (2013)
24. U.S. Department of Education: Effectiveness of Reading and Mathematics Software Products Findings from Two Student Cohorts. Institute of Education Sciences National Center for Education Evaluation and Regional Assistance, Washington, DC (2009)

Potentials of Gamification in Learning Management Systems: A Qualitative Evaluation

Jan Broer(✉) and Andreas Breiter

Institute for Information Management Bremen,
University of Bremen,
Bremen, Germany
{jbroer,abreiter}@ifib.de

Abstract. Besides game-based learning, gamification is an upcoming trend in education, studied in various empirical studies and found in many major learning management systems. Employing a newly developed qualitative instrument for assessing gamification in a system, we studied five popular LMS for their specific implementations. The instrument enabled experts to extract affordances for gamification in the five categories experiential, mechanics, rewards, goals, and social. Results show large similarities in all of the systems studied and few varieties in approaches to gamification.

Keywords: Gamification · LMS · Learning · Management

1 Introduction

Experiments of classroom gamification are becoming increasingly common (e.g. [1]). Gamification is likewise found in information systems, especially those supporting online communities (e.g. [2]). It is therefore not surprising that learning management systems (LMS) have been adopting gamification in some form or another. In a ranked list of the top 20 most popular LMS by Capterra [3], 10 systems are listed as including gamification. Unlike game-based learning (cf. [4]), gamification does not employ full-fledged games but game design elements in non-game contexts [5]. In most cases, this is done to improve user engagement [6], to motivate users [7], or to support value creation [8]. In education, goals of gamification are similar. Non-game systems, such as LMS, are enhanced with aspects of games in order to engage students with the content of the course. Outcomes reported in studies include higher performance on tasks, higher attention to reference materials, higher activity in a system, and self-reported satisfaction with the course or learning value. See [9] for a good overview. As in other contexts, reports on gamification in education and are generally positive, but empirical validation is limited to a small subset of possible contexts. In [10] we have shown the same phenomenon for gamification in general and discussed possible implications thereof.

© Springer International Publishing Switzerland 2015
G. Conole et al. (Eds.): EC-TEL 2015, LNCS 9307, pp. 389–394, 2015.
DOI: 10.1007/978-3-319-24258-3_29

2 Methods

Following Arjoranta's [11] suggestion of focusing definitions on Wittgensteinian family resemblances instead of a common core, we performed a survey among experts on gamification in order identify key terms that are relevant for describing gamification and, by corollary, indicators of the presence of gamification. A catalogue of questions was derived from the survey results and applied to five popular LMS. The instrument consists of 38 items, each with a standardized part categorizing the response into yes, no, or maybe and an open part detailing the reasoning for the answer. "Maybe" responses were reserved for cases in which a system had potential for gamification, but relied on user input for it. The items are divided into five categories – experiential, mechanics, rewards, goals, and social (see Table 1 for example items). Four evaluators applied the instrument to each of the five LMS – one expert and three evaluators with basic training in gamification. Agreement on the standardized part of each item was calculated to validate the instrument. Following Capterra's October 2014 [3] ranking, we analyzed the following five LMS focused on K-12 or higher education in this research (in order of ranking): Moodle, Edmodo, Blackboard Learn, Schoology, and Canvas.

Table 1. Example items from the instrument for evaluating gamification. Full instrument available at: https://db.tt/DaZNzaTA

#	Category	Subcategory	Question(s)
E3	Experiential	Challenge	Does the system include tasks designed to be challenging for the user to complete?
M1	Mechanics	Collecting	Does the system provide opportunities for the user to collect things?
M7	Mechanics	Storytelling	Does the system make use of storytelling?
R5	Rewards	Points	Does the system reward users with points of any kind?
G1	Goals	Clear goals	Does the system provide the user with clear goals/ideas about what to do next?
S1	Social	Fame/getting attention	Does the system provide means for the user to gain fame/attention?

3 Results

Experiential. The experiential items show a very high overlap of gamification in the five analyzed LMS. Accomplishment, autonomy, learning/mastery and positive emotions were found in all five systems. All systems had the potential to provide the user with a form of accomplishment through the successful completion of tasks and courses and through the awarding of badges and grades. These factors are also the causes of positive emotions - none of the systems was found to include additional elements specifically designed to afford positive emotions. Mechanics often found in games that give players a feeling of accomplishment even when they are not successful, are not obvious in the systems analyzed here. Challenge and competence were extreme examples of this, as they were uniformly coded as being potentially available but depending on instructor input.

Autonomy was reflected in the student's ability to choose when and where to complete their tasks. Depending on instructor input, they may still be bound to a strict syllabus, however. Learning/mastery was usually present in one of two ways: Users were allowed to re-take quizzes and assignments or there was a dedicated mastery system. Such systems were usually based on formative assessment and the alignment of tasks to goals. Affordances for curiosity, purpose, and concentration were not found in either platform (Fig. 1).

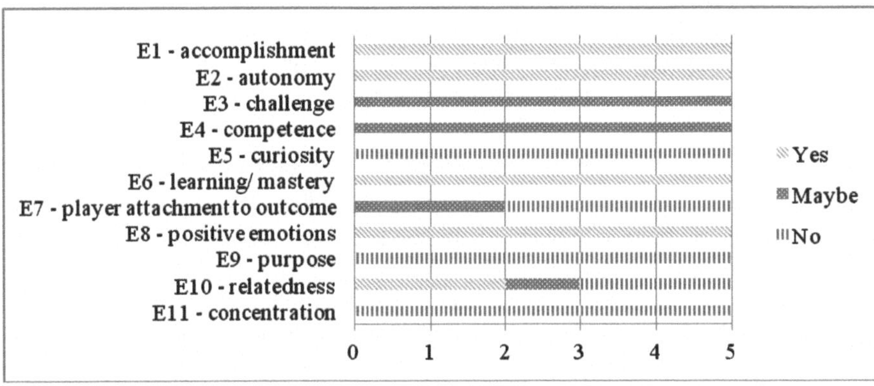

Fig. 1. Results in the "experiential" category, showing the number of LMS coded as expressing each subcategory (Yes), potentially expressing it (Maybe) and not expressing it (No). Results for all categories can be found at: https://db.tt/o4mRaeev

Mechanics. The major gamification mechanics found in the different LMS in the expert review were collecting, documentation of behavior, and player effort. Collecting can mostly be seen as an incidental result of the ubiquitous use of badges in these LMS. Documentation of behavior was generally available in different forms. Some systems provided activity streams for the users themselves, teachers, or parents.

Player effort was a difficult item to apply as the system needs to provide a measure of success that is distinct from outside measures of the same if it is to be coded in this way. This is directly related to the item of "variable outcome". All systems provided variable outcomes in so far as users could get different grades and potentially fail to complete the course. These are hardly different from the same mechanic in traditional courses, however, and therefore hard to ascribe to gamification.

Fixed rules were also rare beyond the norm provided by the frameworks of a school course and an information system. Blackboard Learn provided the ability to define rules for obtaining badges, which can be seen as similar to games. In all other systems, badges were handed out by the instructor, allowing for arbitrariness. Schoology and

Blackboard Learn were the only systems found to offer time pressure. Here, instructors can set time limits for specific questions/tasks. A common element in many games, time pressure seems to be rare in LMS. Nurturing/growing and storytelling are completely absent from the analyzed systems, even though both were thought to be highly relevant for gamification by the experts in the preceding survey.

Rewards. The rewards section is essentially identical for all five surveyed systems. All of them offer intangible rewards in the form of badges and some measure of progress. None made use of points or levels, which are equally commonly found in gamification literature. It should be noted that LMS with such features exist; they were simply not part of the sample analyzed here. Progress was shown through a mastery system in some cases, through general course completion in others. Some LMS allowed the sharing of badges outside the application through Mozilla's Open Badges program.

Goals. Goals were almost identically rated among all systems as well. In each case, instructors had the ability to subdivide coursework in such a way that the goals for the users are clear and potentially achievable. All systems show users in an understandable way, which next steps they should take, provided that the teacher has set up such steps. Some systems, such as Blackboard Learn, specifically encourage teachers to set up tasks that align with course goals, facilitating clear and achievable goals.

Social. The social category shows actual conceptual differences between the systems. Tools for collaboration were explicitly built into some systems (Blackboard Learn and Canvas), and possible in others through communication tools. Some systems, such as Edmodo, explicitly excluded communication between students from their features, while others even provided chat rooms and discussion boards (e.g. Blackboard Learn). Only Moodle allows for competition in the form of a leaderboard (through a third party plug-in), underlining an interesting result from the expert survey: Experts considered competition very important for a description of gamification in general, but most did not consider it important for their own chosen implementation of gamification. Finally, most systems did not make use of social incentives in general or social engagement loops in particular. Exceptions are Blackboard Learn and Canvas that provide notifications to users, when other users show activity.

4 Discussion

Probably the most interesting result of this study is the similarity of the implementation of gamification in different LMS. Only for 6 of 38 items was there a divergence of results that included more than one system. It is safe to assume that observation of the competition leads to a converging feature space. One could further postulate that experimental changes are more dangerous to a company with a large established user base than they would be to a new competitor. It would therefore be unwise to assume that this examination of the top five most popular LMS can give a complete overview over the variations of gamification used in LMS.

What, then, can we learn from such study? For one, it is very informative to study which known affordances for gamification are absent from our sample. Almost all authors on the topic agree that points, badges, levels, and leaderboards are the most commonly used of such affordances. Hamari et al. [12] as well as Dicheva et al. [9] have shown this in their reviews. While badges were found in all the LMS studied here, points, levels, and leaderboards were not. All of these are trivial to include on a technical level, making it likely that a conscious decision has led to their absence. The expert survey that this study was based on already revealed that most participants found competition to be important to describe gamification in general, but not to describe their own chosen gamified system. This implies that they made the conscious choice of not employing competition. Results from empirical studies on gamification, show that competition can be regarded negatively by a subset of users.

The lack of points and levels is harder to explain. One reason might be that students are already being given either points or grades for their assignments and that the addition of another set of points might be confusing. It is also difficult to reward leveling up in a LMS, as one cannot give material advantages to some students and not to others. Other affordances that are notably absent are those built on storytelling or nurturing/growing. Storytelling especially requires large content creation effort. Furthermore, both elements would likely require a lot of tailoring towards the content being delivered in the LMS. A LMS could only hope to implement tools that help instructors include storytelling or nurturing/growing into their courses, not provide complete packages.

5 Conclusion

Employing a catalog of 38 questions, we evaluated five popular learning management systems towards their use of gamification. Results show that all five systems are very similar in this aspect. All systems employ gamification but do so at a rather shallow level. Badges are ubiquitous, other affordances rare. In many cases, whether a learning management system affords gameful experiences is not so much dependent on the system, but the way it is set up by the instructor. Challenge and competence are two example items that completely depend on how the instructor sets up his or her course. For other items, support for gameful experiences could be identified, but was not necessarily linked to the use of game (design) mechanics. Autonomy, for example, was often afforded through the possibility to choose time and order of completing tasks and a sense of mastery through alignment of tasks to learning outcomes. Only very few affordances, mainly badges, can be directly tracked back to their use in games. Overall, gamification as offered in these learning management systems is still far behind even the approaches evaluated in research. There is a lot of room for additional gamification in learning management systems, but the effectiveness of those approaches has yet to be shown.

The reliance on instructor input for many items suggests a challenge for further implementations of gamification in educational settings. It will be interesting to see, how much gamification a learning management system can provide by default and how much can only be added through an instructor. One could further subdivide the discussion about possible affordances into two subsets - affordances for gameful experiences and affordances for creating affordances for gameful experiences. The former is likely to be cheaper due to its mass-market approach, while the latter is likely to be much more effective due to instructors tailoring gamification directly to their needs. This distinction brings forth the question of whether an evaluation of gamification at the system level even makes sense in systems that rely highly on user created content (i.e. LMS) or whether one has to evaluate the content within those systems instead. Goal alignment systems suggest the possibility for a combination of the two - learning goals would be adapted at the class level, for example, but gamified automated systems could make use of those goals to provide a more gameful experience.

References

1. Hanus, M.D., Fox, J.: Assessing the effects of gamification in the classroom: a longitudinal study on intrinsic motivation, social comparison, satisfaction, effort, and academic performance. Comput. Educ. **80**, 152–161 (2015)
2. Hamari, J.: Transforming homo economicus into homo ludens: A field experiment on gamification in a utilitarian peer-to-peer trading service. Electron. Comm. Res. Appl. **12**, 236–245 (2013)
3. Capterra: Top LMS software. http://www.capterra.com/learning-management-system-software/#infographic
4. Prensky, M.: Digital game-based learning. Comput. Entertainment **1**, 21 (2003)
5. Deterding, S., Dixon, D., Khaled, R., Nacke, L.: From game design elements to gamefulness: defining "gamification". In: Proceedings of MindTrek 2011, pp. 9–15. ACM, New York, NY, USA (2011)
6. Zichermann, G., Cunningham, C.: Gamification by Design: Implementing Game Mechanics in Web and Mobile Apps. O'Reilly Media, Sebastopol (2011)
7. Blohm, D.I., Leimeister, P.D.J.M.: Gamification. Bus. Inf. Syst. Eng. 1–4 (2013)
8. Huotari, K., Hamari, J.: Defining gamification: a service marketing perspective. In: Proceeding of the 16th International Academic MindTrek Conference, pp. 17–22. ACM, New York, NY, USA (2012)
9. Dicheva, D., Dichev, C., Agre, G., Angelova, G.: Gamification in education: a systematic mapping study. Educ. Technol. Soc. **18** (2015)
10. Broer, J.: Gamification and the trough of disillusionment. In: Butz, A., Koch, M., Schlichter, J. (eds.) Mensch and Computer-Workshopband, pp. 389–395. De Gruyter Oldenbourg, Berlin (2014)
11. Arjoranta, J.: Game definitions: a Wittgensteinian approach. Game Stud. **14** (2014)
12. Hamari, J., Koivisto, J., Sarsa, H.: Does gamification work?—a literature review of empirical studies on gamification. In: Proceedings of the 47th Hawaii International Conference on System Sciences (2014)

Investigating Self-directed Learning Dimensions: Adapting the Bouchard Framework

Inge de Waard(✉), Agnes Kukulska-Hulme, and Mike Sharples

The Open University, Milton Keynes, UK
{Inge.deWaard,Agnes.Kukulska-Hulme, Mike.Sharples}@open.ac.uk

Abstract. Self-Directed Learning (SDL) is gaining interest, as online learning is increasingly learner-centered. FutureLearn courses provide an array of online interactions and content deliveries, which have allowed the authors to investigate a diversity of SDL elements. This preliminary research examines the SDL taking place in three FutureLearn courses, and categorises those learner actions into meaningful elements and dimensions for the learners. The SDL framework by Bouchard [1] is used to interpret the self-reported findings coming from active learners. The research uses a grounded theory approach to look for learner experiences related to four dimensions (algorithmic, conative, semiotic, and economic) of the Bouchard [1] framework, and to discover new dimensions. Various research instruments are used: online surveys, learning logs, and one-on-one interviews, all collected pre-, during, or post-course. The initial adaptation of Bouchard's framework offers insights into SDL, its meaning, and value as perceived by the learners.

Keywords: Self-directed learning · MOOC · Futurelearn · Grounded theory

1 Introduction

This paper shares findings arising from the initial coding iteration of self-reported data from FutureLearn (MOOC) learners, to investigate the participants' Self-Directed Learning (SDL) experiences. The Bouchard framework [1] presents SDL dimensions using a specific terminology: algorithmic, conative, semiotic and economic. This allows SDL experiences to be categorized and interpreted from four important online learning angles: the pedagogical, psychological, infrastructural, and economic elements. As contemporary online learning is becoming increasingly learner-centered [2–4] it is becoming an increasingly important educational concept.

There is currently a research gap in understanding the full range of SDL dimensions that are used by the learner when s/he engages in an online course [4, 5].

© Springer International Publishing Switzerland 2015
G. Conole et al. (Eds.): EC-TEL 2015, LNCS 9307, pp. 395–400, 2015.
DOI: 10.1007/978-3-319-24258-3_30

2 Self-directed Learning

In this study, SDL relates to research into adult learning, based on the andragogy concept of Knowles [6], but also embedding technology as an influencing factor for SDL. Knowles [6] described SDL broadly as "a process in which individuals take the initiative, with or without the help of others, to diagnose their learning needs, formulate learning goals, identify resources for learning, select and implement learning strategies, and evaluate learning outcomes' (p. 18).

Students need to have a high level of self-direction to succeed in mLearning and online learning environments [7]. Learners themselves also consider that achieving the level of self-direction necessary for successful learning in a MOOC is related to prior experience and its resulting self-efficacy [8, 9].

Any SDL framework will need to take into account all these dimensions in a structured way. The Bouchard framework offers such a set of SDL dimensions.

3 The Bouchard Framework

Based on interviews with 40 professionals, Bouchard examined four dimensions of self-directed learning: the algorithmic, conative, semiotic, and economic. Bouchard [1] concluded that only through the careful application of multi-dimensional models can progress be made towards creating environments that truly support the emergence and development of SDL. The work of Bouchard builds upon research performed by Long [10] who provided two fundamental ways in which learning could be learner-controlled: psychological and pedagogical. Bouchard rethought the concepts of Long (psychological became the conative dimension, pedagogical became the algorithmic dimension) and he added two additional dimensions: a semiotic and economic dimension. As a result, Bouchard's framework [1] seemed well suited to use for a first iteration (bird's eye analysis), as it provided a schematic for SDL taking into account different dimensions related to online learning.

4 Methodology

To plan and analyse this study, a Grounded Theory (GT) methodology was chosen to organize the different stages of questioning the learners, and to set up research instruments [11]. GT fits research looking for meaning as perceived by the research subjects and permits data like learning experiences to be analysed [12].

4.1 Data Collection

The UK-led MOOC initiative FutureLearn was launched in 2013, and is offering free courses built upon a pedagogy that mixes mobile learning and social learning approaches [13]. This study collected data from three FutureLearn courses, which ran between 1 September and 15 November 2014. The 52 research participants were all experienced online learners. This was a decision based upon outcomes indicating that prior MOOC experience results in more efficient SDL [4, 8]. *Experienced online learner* covers learners that had prior MOOC and/or online learning experience, and had three or more years of social media experience.

This study uses elicited data (written, digitally delivered, and audio data) from 52 participants who gave full consent prior to the research. The research consisted of three phases to fully capture the SDL experience.

- Phase 1 – expectations (pre-course): gathering the expectations of the FutureLearn participants by collecting data through an online survey.
- Phase 2 –learning logs (during course): the participants kept learning logs: filled in every 2 weeks probing the actual learning experiences.
- Phase 3 – reflections (post-course): structured one-on-one interviews investigating differences between the learning expectations and the actual experiences in regard to SDL.

The data corpus consisted of 792 pages of text coming from learning logs, 115 pages of online survey answers, and 48 pages of interview transcript texts.

4.2 Data Analysis

The data analysis is in its initial coding stage following grounded theory coding suggestions [11], providing first impressions. Constructing theory and relating it to interactions was crucial for selecting GT as a method [11]. In order to analyse and interpret the rich, elicited data, memoing (making researcher assumptions transparent) and the following coding iteration was followed: initial coding, line-by-line coding and focused coding. Allowing the researcher to separate, sort and synthesize large amounts of data. Once the initial categories emerged, those categories were compared to the Bouchard Framework dimensions. The examples below are only a selection of the elements found, due to space restrictions.

5 Sharing Initial Findings

Following the analysis, two of the four dimensions (i.e. semiotic and economic dimension) needed to be revised to fit contemporary, massive online learning (e.g. adding collaborative learning). In addition to that, the algorithmic and conative dimensions harboured elements that needed some updating to match them with current FutureLearn options (e.g., pedagogy, available learner interactions). This resulted in additional dimensions, listed after Bouchard's known dimensions for each group of elements.

5.1 Algorithmic Dimension

The pedagogical options, and more specifically how the learner uses or interprets them for their own use, are gathered under the algorithmic dimension (Table 1).

Table 1. Algorithmic dimensions.

Dimensions	Examples from learner data
Pacing (ref. to the timing allowed by the learner to reach learning goals)	I watched the videos, read other people's comments and posted my results a few days early, since I am traveling overseas this week
Formulating objectives (ref. to formulating or stating learning objectives/goals)	I try to revive my memories related to scientific experiments, in order to demonstrate/practice with my son
Finding resources (ref. to materials, texts that allow learning to take place)	To find things out I use dictionaries – of science and of scientists in this case
Reformulated/added dimensions	
Finding human support in/outside course	I spoke to the lab technician at work
Collaborative peer learning (ref. to peer-to-peer interactions)	Some interesting discussions and insights from other learners especially about critiques of Fergusons analysis
Tutor-peer interactions	Jennifer's [tutor] enthusiasm worked stimulating

5.2 Conative Dimension

The conative dimension groups elements related to the social and psychological profile, as well as the context the learner is in (Table 2).

Table 2. Conative dimensions.

Dimension	Examples from learner data
Initiative (referring to the actions taken by the learner that starts and supports the learning process)	My interest goes beyond the course remit, so it will be a hobby to look into from time to time until I am satisfied
Motivation (ref. to learner actions undertaken to keep being motivated)	I admit that having to fill out this log prompted me to do this week's work on time
Context and transition (ref. to professional or personal new goals, needs or challenges as perceived by the learner)	I found it helped to discuss what I had learned with someone. It helped me realize what I did not understand… This is something I have avoided doing until now
Social environment (ref. to learners managing a useful network who act as learning resources or support)	I discussed what I had learned with my son as he has experience of me being on medication for depression
Adjusted/added dimensions	
Learner personality and identity (ref. to character or personal self-image)	I don't leave a commitment until I have achieved my goals. This was instilled in me by my parents and grandparents
Digital skills (ref. to online, electronic skills)	Using the online graph to record and display results of the phenomenon

5.3 Semiotic Dimension

In contemporary online learning each type of media possesses its own intrinsic characteristics that facilitate or hinder learning, depending on each individual's learning preference [1], which brings along a new, wide variety of semiotic dimensions (Table 3).

Table 3. Semiotic dimensions.

Dimension	Examples from learner data
Use of printed text (referring to PDF, documents, ...)	I no longer print all the course material as I did when starting with courses on FL, I only store the links
Reformulated/added dimensions	
Individualistic learning (ref. to learner interactions that are primarily undertaken on an individual basis)	I prefer looking up info on my own, but sometimes it is more efficient to just ask and not worry about looking stupid
Online resources (ref. to use of digital material)	I only store links to additional material, or links provided by fellow learners during discussions
Assessments provided in-course	Quizzes should be reasonably demanding in order to verify that the subject has been understood

5.4 Economic Dimension

Bouchard [1] saw the perceived economic value of its knowledge in the marketplace, either as an professional asset or as a means of production (Table 4).

Table 4. Economic dimensions.

Reformulated/added dimensions	Examples from learner data
Actual value of knowledge (referring to immediate return for the learner)	I've found that my brain wasn't so stiff and still opened for some new knowledge. I gained new softwares on my comp - NetLogo 5.1
Perceived value of knowledge, ref. to the symbolic value of learning	I choose the topics that seemed relevant in relation to my personal interests and/or as teacher
Cost of learning (ref. to cost of accreditation, infrastructure...)	Coming back from my work, I've purchased yeast for the experiment
Opportunity costs (ref. to hidden costs, e.g. learning versus earning wages)	I found out in September that I had plantar fasciitis and could not walk anymore until I had steroid injections in the sole of my foot. I enrolled into 10 online classes and loved it

6 Summary and Future Work

From these preliminary findings promising SDL dimensions were distilled coming from SDL experiences shared by FutureLearn participants. The Bouchard framework needs to be adapted once higher-level dimensions emerge from this on-going study. Once the full analysis is finished, it will potentially reshape Bouchard's framework, and offer a framework for SDL in FutureLearn courses and MOOCs.

References

1. Bouchard, P.: Pedagogy without a teacher: what are the limits. Int. J. Self-Directed Learn. **6**(2), 13–22 (2009)
2. Siemens, G.: Connectivism: a learning theory for the digital age. Int. J. Instr. Technol. Distance Learn. **2**(1), 3–10 (2005)
3. Downes, S.: Evaluating a MOOC [Web log post]. http://halfanhour.blogspot.ca/2013/03/evaluat-ing-mooc.html (2013). Accessed 14 June 2015
4. Kop, R., Fournier, H.: New dimensions to self-directed learning in an open networked learning environment. Int. J. Self-Directed Learn. **7**(2), 2–20 (2011)
5. de Waard, I., Kukulska-Hulme, A., Sharples, M.: Self-directed learning in trial FutureLearn courses. In: Proceedings of the European Stakeholder Summit 2015, pp. 234–243 (2015)
6. Knowles, M.S.: Self-Directed Learning. Association Press, New York (1975)
7. Song, L., Hill, J.R.: A conceptual model for understanding self-directed learning in online environments. J. Interact. Online Learn. **6**(1), 27–42 (2007)
8. Milligan, C., Margaryan, A., Littlejohn, A.: Patterns of engagement in massive open online courses. MERLOT J. Online Learn. Teach. **9**(2), 149–159 (2013)
9. de Waard, I.: Analyzing the Impact of Mobile Access on Learner Interactions in a MOOC. Masters dissertation, Athabasca University. https://dt.athabascau.ca/jspui/bitstream/10791/23/1/Master%20thesis%20Inge%20de%20Waard%20MEd%20publication%20final%20reviewed.pdf (2013)
10. Long, H.B.: Philosophical, psychological, and practical justifications for studying self-directed learning. In: Long, H.B., Associates, Self-directed Learning: Application and Research. Oklahoma Research Center, University of Oklahoma, Norman, OK 73037 (1992)
11. Charmaz, K.: Constructing grounded theory: a practical guide through qualitative analysis. Pine Forge Press, CA (2006)
12. Creswell, J.W.: Qualitative Inquiry And Research Design: Choosing Among Five Approaches. Sage Publications, London (2006)
13. Sharples, M.: FutureLearn and Pedagogy. Internal presentation circulated during Learning Fair, The Open University (2013)

Towards Hyper Activity Books for Children. Connecting Activity Books and Montessori-like Educational Materials

Raffaele Di Fuccio, Michela Ponticorvo(✉), Andrea Di Ferdinando, and Orazio Miglino

Nac Lab, Department of Humanistic Studies,
University of Naples "Federico II", Naples, Italy
{raffaele.difuccio,michela.ponticorvo,
andrea.diferdinando,orazio.miglino}@unina.it

Abstract. In the first years of school, activity books and Montessori-like educational materials are widespread. They satisfy children's precise psychological needs and result in funded educational practices based on game activity adopted by teachers. These materials are more effective for promoting learning if used in close interaction with an adult, they cannot be customised and the corrective feedback cannot be provided within the appropriate time frame. In this paper, we aim to overcome these limitations by exploiting a Technology Enhanced Learning (TEL) methodology to connect activity books and Montessori-like educational materials. We propose a general architecture for building hyper activity and exercise books called HAB, with three levels: multimedia, multimodality and computing; we describe a first implementation for validating this architecture, Block Magic, and outline development of the architecture under the INF@NZIA DIGI.Tales 3.6 project.

Keywords: Technology Enhanced Learning · Augmented reality systems · Embodied cognition · Natural interfaces · Hybrid educational materials · Montessori-like educational materials

1 Introduction and Background

In primary schools around the world, children and teachers spend much time playing with activity books and Montessori-like educational materials. A significant number of teaching/learning processes are therefore mediated by these tools. They exploit the child's natural involvement in games to promote learning.

Activity books are specifically addressed to children and include interactive content such as games, puzzles, pictures and other elements that require drawing or writing in the books. These interactive features can be supported by a narrative structure and contain elements such a mascots. In later school cycles, the activity book becomes an exercise book for a specific subject. Montessori-like educational materials [14] are manipulative, physical objects specifically designed to foster learning. These materials, introduced by Montessori, include logic blocks, cards, teaching tiles, etc.

These educational materials emerged among others because they meet important psychological needs of children that lead to educational outcomes for teaching adults.

© Springer International Publishing Switzerland 2015
G. Conole et al. (Eds.): EC-TEL 2015, LNCS 9307, pp. 401–406, 2015.
DOI: 10.1007/978-3-319-24258-3_31

These psychological needs are related to action, narration and forms of multiple intelligence. Action and interaction are crucial in children's development, as underlined by Piaget [15] and Bruner [2] and, in recent years, by Embodied and Situated Cognition Theory (ESCT) [3]. Especially for humans, these actions take place in a social and cultural context that proposes objects, artifacts, technologies, concrete or abstract cultural substrates [9] and narrative structures. Children need a narrative structure to understand the world around them [1]. The third need to be satisfied to support children's learning processes is feeding their multiple forms of intelligence [7].

These needs are reflected in educational outcomes, first of all the learning-by- doing [5] approach, that encourages active participation, active choice, manipulation of concrete objects and peer group cooperation. The second outcome is narration in an educational context that brings the learning dimension together with the emotional dimension. The third educational outcome is related to children's multiple forms of intelligence: each child should be seen by the teacher as a *unicum* requiring an individual learning path. These outcomes lead to practices which are aimed at focusing on the active participation of pupils as well as on customising educational interventions: the teacher prepares a tailored teaching approach for each child. Moreover it is important to underline that these practices rely on teacher/learner interaction, a fundamental relation that is universally recognised as the key for successful outcomes. But customisation is quite difficult in everyday school practice and the appropriate feedback cannot be delivered within the appropriate time frame. Moreover, as suggested before, ideal educational practice foresees a one-to-one ratio between teacher and learner. However, realising this educational utopia is quite difficult because it can be extremely expensive.

The psycho-pedagogical approach described implies constant supervision by adults. For this reason, mass diffusion of this kind of practice is considerably limited and the school reality is quite different.

Our proposal, described in detail in the next section, is to exploit technology to overcome these limitations and to support teachers, parents and learners in learning/teaching processes.

In particular, the technological starting point is represented by Game-based learning [18] that exploits the motivational qualities of digital games to create engaging educational and training tools [8]. This interest is motivated by the fact that games are carefully designed to stimulate user engagement [6, 10]. Moreover, games constitute an outstanding example of learning-by-doing, or experiential learning: learning by actually doing and being active in the learning process. This has led to many experiences in applying Technology Enhanced Learning (TEL), to children education. Considering the role of action introduced above, it is important to remember that a huge amount of research has been devoted to tangible interfaces [11, 16, 19] that transfer manipulatives into the digital domain.

2 An Architecture to Build Hyper Activity Books

To overcome the above-described problems, we propose the adoption of a general architecture to design and implement educational materials, namely Hyper Activity Books (HAB). This architecture exploits TEL methodology to connect activity books and Montessori-like educational materials. It is represented in Fig. 1.

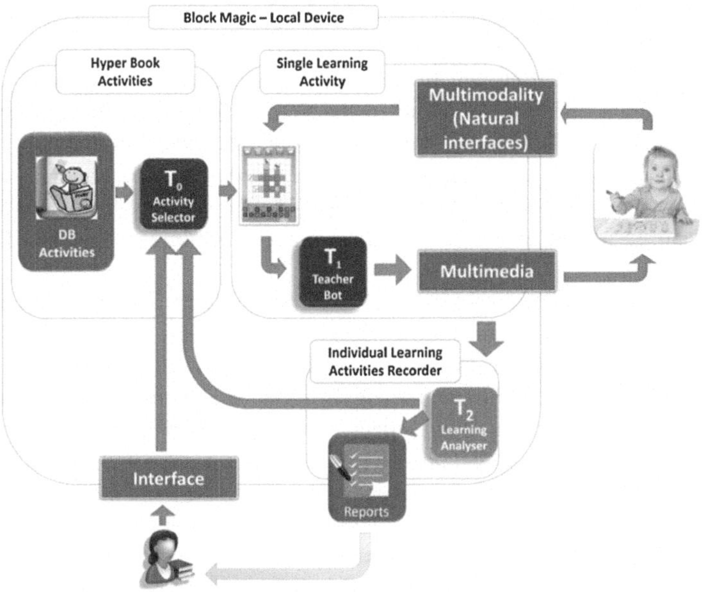

Fig. 1. HAB architecture. Brown boxes represent the three interaction levels of the architecture, where T represents Tutoring systems; the drawing represents the activity based on manipulatives (Color figure online)

Let us start from the database, on the left, where the various activities or exercises reside. It can be conceptualised as activity book pages, with every page representing a single activity. These activities stimulate a particular knowledge domain: to cite just a few, there are exercises about maths and logic, as well as activities to develop imagination and creativity. The activities to be played are chosen by T_0, that is to say the tutoring system with the task of selecting the activity to be proposed in accordance with two information sources: teacher hints and previous results. In the activity layer, the playing child interacts with physical materials, Montessori-like educational materials and T_1. T_1 it is the tutor who aims to maintain a high interaction level from the child. This is achieved through a particular kind of interaction that is multimedia and multimodal-based. In fact, HAB has three features - multimedia, multimodality and computing which govern interactions during activities.

2.1 Multimediality, Multimodality and Computing

During activities, children interact with the tool named T_1, both the trainer who proposes the task with a multimedia output (screen presentation, voice, images, pictures, videos, songs, etc.) and the child who interacts with it in a multimodal manner, using voice, hands, typing text. The answer from the child is tracked by T_1 which replies with a feedback based on the exercise performed and on its own artificial intelligence, the computing level. Feedback is fundamental for increasing child involvement in the activity. T_1 can offer various rewards for specific tasks, can name the child thus keeping him/her immerged in the activity layer. Feedback could be a success phrase like "Good! Well done! Play again" if the exercise is performed well or tips/suggestion in other cases. Multimediality is functional to the narrative and, by relying on appealing graphical solutions, it keeps the child in the fiction dimension, for example with a mascot character introducing and commenting on activities. Multimodality leads to natural interfaces which are invisible to the user and allow continuous interactions without using artificial control devices whose operation must be acquired. These interfaces can be implemented by exploiting various technologies such as RFID/NC, Smart Objects and Leap Motion.

What we have described up to now is HAB Stage 1, the activity experience. This platform also holds another stage, Stage 2, which is invisible to the child user, but is very important for the teacher. Stage 2 is based on T_2 work. This third tutor builds an individualised report on child interaction, records achievements and failures, and activity preferences in order to build a detailed user profile. This report comes back to the teacher who can further customise HAB/child interaction with a focused choice from the database and to T_0 that can better adapt itself to the child. In this way, the cycle can start again. It is evident that the role of tutors is fundamental, and for this reason we will describe them in more detail in the next subsection. We should stress that, in the HAB architecture, both Stages 1 and 2 run on a personal device.

2.2 HAB Tutoring Systems

In the HAB architecture, we have three different tutoring systems with different roles, implemented by Intelligent and Tutoring Systems [17] which exploit artificial intelligence techniques to provide instructions that are tailored to learners needs. They give the chance to customise didactic paths through the identification of specific goals for each pupil, and tracking of every child's learning achievement, which, in turn, offers feedback that can be used for redefinition of the didactic path along the path itself. They implement learning analytics by measuring, collecting, analysing and reporting data about learning in the activity layer, thus supporting learning processes. In HAB, Intelligent Tutoring Systems represent the computing level.

3 HAB Architecture Applied to Logic Blocks: Block Magic

Block Magic, for now BM, is a prototype for educational materials developed in a successful European research project under the framework of the LLP-Comenius programme. It builds a bridge between physical manipulation and digital technology [12] in education because it is an example of what we can call STELT (Smart Technologies to Enhance Learning and Teaching) [13] which links physical and digital applications. The project recovers above-mentioned Montessori-inspired psycho-pedagogical approach, based on active learning and teaching, exploiting current technology facilities to build a hybrid educational material. In particular, Block Magic has developed a functional prototypal system which has enhanced the Logic Blocks Box, a Montessori-like educational material widely used in kindergartens, primary schools, rehabilitation centers, homes, etc., dedicated to support learning and teaching processes in children aged 3 to 7.

Learning blocks were introduced by Dienes [4] and are a structured material formed by 48 classic pieces that vary in shape, color, thickness and size. BM is the first implementation of HAB architecture. At the single learning activity layer, the child runs an activity interacting with physical educational materials and T1, which is Blocki, the artificial trainer. The physical material consists of a set of magic blocks and a magic board/tablet device. A specific software implements multimediality, multimodality and computing. The first trials which involved 4 different schools, 257 students, 2 children with special needs and 10 teachers, and were devoted to an evaluation of BM impact, indicated that BM attractiveness emerged strongly. These preliminary trials indicate that HAB architecture can produce powerful tools to complement curricular activities. Block Magic has been accepted well by children and teachers because it is very appealing for children. This general architecture is currently inspiring an ongoing research project, INF@NZIA DIGI.Tales 3.6, the goal of which is to promote learning/teaching process, increasing hands-on practice with TEL methodologies.

4 Future Directions

Starting from the general HAB architecture and its first implementation, two pathways will be followed in the future. The first will be to develop HAB further. In particular, the platform will be extended by adding an authoring tool that will become an Open Educational Resource (OER). Moreover, a new tutor will be introduced with the specific task to build collective reports. These reports will contain data about children's groups with different characteristics: class, school, study course, region, nation.

The community will implement activities that are played individually or collectively by children on personal devices. The data collected by the personal devices are fed to the community to analyse learning achievements in a virtuous cycle. The second pathway will be devoted to deepening analysis about the effectiveness and usefulness of the HAB architecture in an attempt to understand which factors are relevant for improving learning and teaching processes.

Acknowledgments. This research is supported by INF@NZIA DIGI.Tales 3.6 project funded by MIUR (PON-Smart Cities) and ENACT skills project funded by EU Lifelong Learning programme.

References

1. Brockmeier, J.: Narrative psychology. Encycl. Crit. Psychol. 1218–1220 (2014)
2. Bruner, J.S.: The Culture of Education. Harvard University Press, Cambridge (1996)
3. Clark, A.: Supersizing the Mind: Embodiment, Action, and Cognitive Extension: Embodiment, Action, and Cognitive Extension. Oxford University Press, Oxford (2008)
4. Dienes, Z.P.: Large Plastic Set, and Learning Logic, Logical Games. Herder and Herder, New York (1972)
5. Dewey, J.: Democracy and Education. Courier Corporation, New York (2004)

6. Dondlinger, M.J.: Educational video game design: a review of the literature. J. Appl. Educ. Technol. **4**(1), 21–31 (2007)
7. Gardner, H.E.: Intelligence Reframed: Multiple Int. Perseus Books Group, Boston (2000)
8. Gee, J.P.: What video games have to teach us about learning and literacy. Comput. Entertainment (CIE) **1**(1), 20–20 (2003)
9. Jonassen, D., Land, S. (eds.): Theoretical Foundations of Learning Environments. Routledge, London (2012)
10. Mayo, M.J.: Games for science and engineering education. Commun. ACM **50**(7), 30–35 (2007)
11. Marshall, P.: Do tangible interfaces enhance learning?. In: Proceedings of the 1st International Conference on Tangible and Embedded Interaction, pp. 163–170 (2007)
12. Miglino, O., Di Ferdinando, A., Di Fuccio, R., Rega, A., Ricci, C.: Bridging digital and physical educational games using RFID/NFC technologies. J. e-Learn. Knowl. Soc. **10**(3), 89–106 (2014)
13. Miglino, O., Di Ferdinando, A., Schembri, M., Caretti, M., Rega, A., Ricci, C.: STELT (Smart Technologies to Enhance Learning and Teaching): una piattaforma per realizzare ambienti di realt aumentata per apprendere, insegnare e giocare. Sistemi intelligenti **25**(2), 397–404 (2013)
14. Montessori, M.: The Montessori Method. Transaction Publishers, Piscataway (2013)
15. Piaget, J.: Part I: cognitive development in children: piaget development and learning. J. Res. Sci. Teach. **2**(3), 176–186 (1964). UK
16. Revelle, G., Zuckerman, O., Druin, A., Bolas, M.: Tangible user interfaces for children. In CHI 2005 Extended Abstracts on Human Factors in Computing Systems, pp. 2051–2052. ACM (April 2005)
17. Sleeman, D., Brown, J.S.: Intelligent Tutoring Systems. Academic Press, London (1982)
18. Tobias, S., Fletcher, J.D., Wind, A.P.: Game-based learning. In: Spector, J.M., Merrill, M. D., Elen, J., Bishop, M.J. (eds.) Handbook of Research on Educational Communications and Technology, pp. 485–503. Springer, New York (2014)
19. Zuckerman, O., Arida, S., Resnick, M.: Extending tangible interfaces for education: digital Montessori-inspired manipulatives. In: Proceedings of the SIGCHI Conference on Human Factors in Computing Systems, pp. 859–868. ACM (April 2005)

A Framework to Design Educational Mobile-Based Games Across Multiple Spaces

Carmen Fernández-Panadero[1(✉)], Mar Pérez-Sanagustín[2], Abelardo Pardo[3], Raquel M. Crespo García[1], and Carlos Delgado Kloos[1]

[1] Department Ingeniería Telemática, Universidad Carlos III de Madrid, Madrid, Spain
{mcfp, rcrespo, cdk}@it.uc3m.es
[2] Department Ciencias de la Computación, Pontificia Universidad Católica de Chile, Santiago, Chile
mar.perez@ing.puc.cl
[3] School of Electrical and Information Engineering, University of Sydney, Sydney, Australia
abelardo.pardo@sydney.edu.au

Abstract. The adoption of mobile devices and context-aware technologies offers the opportunity of designing educational mobile-based games across multiple spaces that enrich the learners' experience. But producing these games is challenging from both the authoring and technical points of view. This paper proposes a framework to facilitate the design of these games. The framework consists of two elements: (1) a narrative structure, and (2) a platform for its deployment. Both elements defined as a set of templates to be completed for facilitating both the authoring of the narrative and the design of the platform. In order to show a usage example, the framework has been used to develop a mobile-based game for a museum. The game designed has been piloted with 10 students between 6 and 12 years old. The results of the pilot show that it is technically feasible to use this framework to design a mobile-base game across three spaces: a museum, home and a classroom. The students found the activity a good and engaging learning experience.

Keywords: Game-based learning · Museum · Augmented reality · Storytelling · Situated and embodied cognition

1 Introduction

In the past years, there has been a growth of mobile-based games for museums to enhance their visitors' experiences [1, 2]. These initiatives offer solutions limited in space and time to the location and the duration of the visit. Recent research on mobile learning suggests that learning activities in museums would be improved if integrated in a wider process that includes learners' personal experience not only during the visit (in the museum), but also before the visit (at home or school) and after it (also outside the museum) [3, 4].

© Springer International Publishing Switzerland 2015
G. Conole et al. (Eds.): EC-TEL 2015, LNCS 9307, pp. 407–413, 2015.
DOI: 10.1007/978-3-319-24258-3_32

However, the production of mobile-based education games across multiple spaces is a complex and challenging task from both the authoring and technical points of view [2]. Current models propose theoretical approaches for designing the game structural elements to maximize engagement and learning effectiveness [5–7], disregarding the technological support aspects of the game. Further, these models do not consider multiple spaces in their design. This paper proposes a framework to facilitate the design of these types of games from both the authoring and the technological perspectives.

2 The Framework

The framework consists of two elements: (1) a narrative structure, and (2) a platform for its deployment. Both elements defined as a set of templates to be completed for facilitating both the authoring of the narrative and the deployment of the platform. The framework allows integrating the narrative structure (game space) with content created by the students (digital space) and the exhibits in the museum (physical space). All the elements in the narrative and technical templates have been chosen to be reusable, interchangeable so that they are editable to be used in different spaces and contexts, allowing personalization of narrative and content without altering physical space.

2.1 The Narrative Structure

The narrative structure defines the **game structure**, **game mechanics**, and the **characters selection**. The templates designed to generate the narrative have been articulated around the narrative pattern of the "Hero Journey" [8] and PhyMEL methodology [9]. In this narrative pattern students travel from the world of common day into a new adventure in which they have to solve a set of challenges to win a decisive victory, that has impact in their fellows, and at the same time transform themselves.

The **game structure** (Fig. 1) is composed of the three acts typically defined in storytelling: Presentation, Conflict Rising and Denouement. The storytelling has been built upon the ideas proposed by Dickey [5]. The author argues that a gameplay should be composed by a backstory and a set of cut-scenes to combine in a balanced way the linear structure of the narrative with a non-linear structure typical from the game. The Backstory is the background story that provides the rigid skeleton that supports common dramatic context for the action. The Cut-scenes constitute the flexible cover that surrounds the skeleton. Accordingly, our framework proposes as backstory an adventure that is common to all the participants in the game. The backstory is enriched with a set of problems (the cut-scenes) that the students have to solve interacting with the exhibits in the museum (cut-scenes are different for each exhibit).

Additionally, the narrative introduces a new element: the missions. Missions are intermediate elements (between the background and the cut-scenes) that provide an overall objective that gives sense to the problems posed to a team. The missions are semi-rigid structures because they provide both a common fixed narrative structure for each team as adventure level (backstory), and the flexibility to introduce variations in

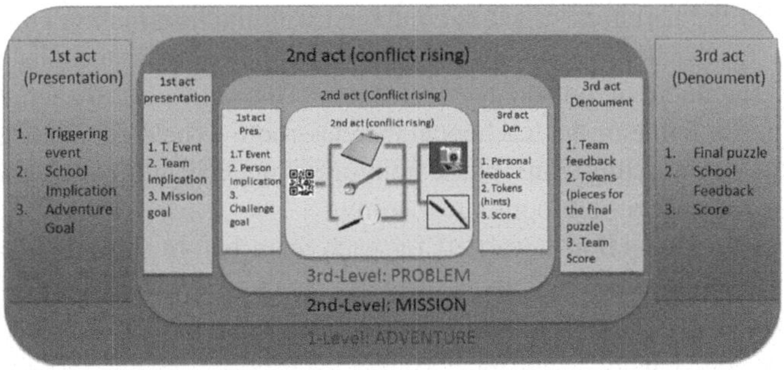

Fig. 1. Game narrative structure of the framework.

the storyline as problem level (cut-scene). These variations are needed so that teams may have different missions to construct the story in different ways.

The **game mechanics** have been designed to traverse Bloom's taxonomy in reverse order, beginning at the high order skills (creation) and ending with artifacts to facilitate remembering knowledge in the long term (memorize). The game is divided into three phases corresponding to the periods "before the visit", "during the visit" and "after the visit".

In the first place, "before the visit" students work in teams in traditional classroom science experiments to illustrate basic scientific principles. For example flying a ping-pong ball in the air stream of a hairdryer (Ventury effect) or attracting small pieces of paper with static electricity (Coulomb law). As a result of this classroom activity, students would produce a multimedia document about what they have learned (video or text). Content produced in this phase is independent of the narrative but it will be useful to solve some challenges that they have to face during the adventure. This content will be used to augment the exhibits in the museum. The objective of this phase is twofold: (1) to develop students' creativity, and (2) to promote the students sense of ownership of the experience in the museum to enhance their motivation.

In the phase "during the visit", each team is proposed a mission and receives a tablet that will help to solve it. Each mission corresponds to a path in the museum that visits three exhibits where students have to solve a problem. In each exhibit, the team reads a QR code and follows the instructions to solve the problem. The instructions will contain the media content generated in the previous phases and extra indications to help them solve the problem. Once the problem has been solved, the team receives message coded using Caesar cipher that they should write in a piece of paper and decode using a coding wheel to complete the challenge. Once all the teams have finished their missions, they need to join their messages to answer a final question. Once the game finishes, the teams have to report their results with photos and text messages. The objective in this phase is to develop the skills in the evaluation, analysis and application levels of Bloom's taxonomy.

During the phase "after the visit" students reflect about the entire activity. For this phase, students are provided with a set of automatically generated physical artifacts (a comic or a game board). These are personalized artifacts for each team, built collecting the text messages and pictures they produced in the previous phase.

The skeleton of the narrative structure combined with the information collected in log files and the feedback provided by the students (photographs and chat) allow this mechanical generation of personalized artifacts. This artifact can then be used by student families at home or the teachers at the classroom to help students reflect on the experience at the museum. This phase reinforces understanding and memorization skills at the lower levels of Bloom's taxonomy.

The **characters selection** is carried for each team before starting a mission. The characters selection is also based on a semi-rigid structure. On the one hand it provides a fixed set of characters with a clear role that small variations can adapt to different stories. On the other hand it allows players to choose the character they prefer and personalize the story with their own photograph. Each team member has a to select characters, whose specific functions in the adventure are shown in Table 1.

Table 1. Characters and team roles.

Role	Mission in the team	Gadget	Icon
Leader	Coordinate the team take decisions about next role to act	Leadership skills and tablet	Hand
Tracker	Take the team to its physical destination finding the shortest path	Map (paper and tablet)	Magnifying glass
Handyman	Solve problems that require manual interaction	Everything is a tool in his hands	Wrench
Photographer	Capture essence of the moment	Camera (tablet)	Camera
Reporter	Report the progress feedback and lesson learned during the mission	Logbook (tablet-chat)	Pencil

2.2 The Platform

The platform to support this game structure is composed by a mobile app and a web-based backed structure to collect the pictures and text messages produced by the learners and generate the final artifacts after the missions.

The app was developed using PhoneGap framework and web-based TouchDB as database engine. PhoneGap was chosen because it allows generating apps for any platform. The platform uses two kind of tags (XML tags and QR codes) to connect three different spaces (game, digital and physical). XML tags are used to identify unambiguously each narrative element: characters, locations, hints, goals and challenges that will be the links that connect the narrative structure (game space) with the content generated by the student (digital space). QR-codes act as anchoring points to link the customized narrative (game + digital spaces) with the exhibits (physical space).

3 The Pilot Experience: Discovering the Kidnapped Scientist

This section describes the game "Discovering the kidnapped scientist", as an example of the types of games that can be instantiated using the framework proposed. The aim of this pilot was to test whether the structure designed for the game supported the creation and deployment of mobile-based games across multiple spaces.

The goal of the game is to foster scientific skills. It proposes six missions that students need to solve to discover six scientists that have been kidnapped by the malevolent organization ECNEICS. The artifact generated at the end of the missions is a comic summarizing the missions using their text messages and pictures.

The participants were 10 children between 6 and 12 years old (50 % male and 50 % female) most of them (80 %) enrolled in 5th grade of primary school. A mixed methods approach was used to analyze the experience. The game was analyzed using a survey with 36 questions asking the students about: their game and museum habits, and their opinion about the different elements of the game narrative. Students' survey includes open questions and close questions with a 5-point Likert scale. Additionally, the video recordings and observations collected by 3 researchers of three of the teams participating in the experience are considered.

Regarding the students' **game and museum habits**, the results show that all students (100 %) have experience in the use of game consoles, mobile devices and personal computers. They report spending 3.5 h per week playing electronic games. They visit museums with a frequency ranging from 1 per month to 1 per year (50 % once a year, 30 % every 3 months and 20 % monthly).

Regarding the **students' opinion about the activity** we obtained 6 different results. (**Result 1**) *The game is effective for engaging students in a learning experience.* First, students rate whole experience with an average of 4.5/5, being 5 the maximum score. Second, students rated with 4.3/5 this experience compared with other previous activities in museums. Finally, 100 % of the students were willing to repeat the experience. (**Result 2**) *The game is effective for learning.* The activities that had the biggest impact on learning were: Interacting with the exhibits (4.5/5), decrypting the secret messages (4.1/5), watching the video hints (4.1/5) and answering the challenge questions (4/5). The less formative activities according to students opinions were reading text accompanying exhibits (3.2/5) because they were not suitable for their age, listening instructions about game mechanics (3/5), and solving the final puzzle among all the teams (2.7/5). (**Result 3**) *Students liked the game structure and understood their function in the team and the team dynamics.* Observations and open questions confirm that the students understood their function in the team and team dynamics. They liked their role in the team (4.4/5), and the fact that there were different roles (4.4/5). However, the interaction among team members was preferred over the interaction with other teams to solve the final puzzle (3.2/5). (**Result 4**) *The students enjoyed all the game activities.* All the activities were rated over 2.5/5. The most engaging activity was deciphering secret messages (5/5) and interact with the museum exhibits (4.6/5). The activity with the lowest rating was reading text accompanying exhibits because they were very long (2.8/5). (**Result 5**) *Students enjoy very much the fact that content is hidden.* They enjoy both mechanisms used during game mechanics coded messages using Caesar cipher (4.8/5) and QR codes (4.1/5). Students used the adjectives "entertained", "amused", "surprised" and "happy" to describe their emotional state during the game. (**Result 6**) *Students like to participate in content creation.* Observation and survey shows a great willingness of students to participate in content authoring. The activity of video recording received the higher scored (4.6/5), and creation of questions for challenges (evaluation) was the poor rated (3.8/5). (**Result 7**) *The students value the comic as positive to summarize the experience.* They rated above 4/5 the comic content.

4 Conclusions and Future Work

This paper has presented a framework to support the design of mobile-based games across multiple spaces. The framework consists of two elements, a narrative structure and a platform. Both elements are defined as a set of templates to be completed for facilitating both the authoring the game and of the platform for its support. In addition, this paper has presented, as an example, the results of a pilot experience of a game designed with this framework. The results of the experience are positive and encouraging.

As future work, we plan using the results of this preliminary pilot study to adjust the framework. In addition, we plan to analyze how this framework is useful for designing other types of mobile-based games.

Acknowledgments. Work partially funded by the EEE (TIN2008-05163/TSI), RESET (TIN2014-53199-C3-1-R) eMadrid projects (S2013/ICE-2715) and the PhyMEL strategic action. The authors would also like to thank especially A. Martínez, I. Quiñones, A. García, J. Hidalgo, D. Novillo and R. Alonso.

References

1. Avouris, N., Yiannoutsou, N.: A review of mobile location-based games for learning across physical and virtual spaces. J. UCS **18**(15), 2120–2142 (2012)
2. Wei, T., Li, Y.: Design of educational game: a literature review. In: Pan, Z., Cheok, A.D., Müller, W., Zhang, X., Wong, K. (eds.) Transactions on Edutainment IV. LNCS, vol. 6250, pp. 266–276. Springer, Heidelberg (2010)
3. Vavoula, G., et al.: Design and evaluation of support for learning with multimedia phones between classrooms and museums. Comput. Educ. **53**(2), 286–299 (2009)
4. Pérez-Sanagustín, M., Hernández-Leo, D., Santos, P., Delgado-Kloos, C., Blat, J.: Augmenting reality and formality of informal and non-formal settings to enhance blended learning. Trans. Learn. Technol. (TLT) **7**(2), 118–131 (2014)
5. Dickey, M.: Engaging by design: how engagement strategies in popular computer and video games can inform instructional design. Educ. Tech. Res. Dev. **53**(2), 67–83 (2005)
6. Garris, R., Ahlers, R., Driskell, J.: Games motivation, and learning: a research and practice model. Simul. Gaming **33**, 441–467 (2002)
7. Amory, A.: Game object model version II: a theoretical framework for educational game development. Educ. Technol. Res. Dev. **55**, 51–77 (2007)

8. Campbell, J.: The Hero with a Thousand Faces. Pantheon Books, New York (2008). ISBN 978-1-57731-593-3
9. Fernández-Panadero, C., Delgado Kloos, C.: PhyMEL. A framework to integrate physical, mental and emotional learning in meaningful experiences and multidimensional reports. In: Proceedings of 3rd European Immersive Education Summit, London, UK, pp. 203–209 (2013)

Predicting Results from Interaction Patterns During Online Group Work

Alvaro Figueira(✉)

CRACS & INESC TEC, University of Porto, Rua do Campo Alegre, 1021/1055, 4169-007 Porto, Portugal
arf@dcc.fc.up.pt

Abstract. Group work is an essential activity during both graduate and undergraduate formation. Although there is a vast theoretical literature and numerous case studies about group work, we haven't yet seen much development concerning the assessment of individual group participants. The problem relies on the difficulty to have the perception of each student's contribution towards the whole work. We propose and describe a novel tool to manage and assess individual group. Using the collected interactions from the tool usage we create a model for predicting ill-conditioned interactions which generate alerts. We also describe a functionality to predict the final activity grading, based on the interaction patterns and on an automatic classification of these interactions.

Keywords: Group work · Individual assessment · Interaction pattern · Grading prediction · Online tool

1 Introduction

During the last decade, in many European countries the student/teacher ratio has continuously and systematically being increased. This situation is due to a more rational use of resources, as some would say; or due to measures to cut off public expenses, as another might also say. Apart from the reasons, there is a clear need for the use of other pedagogical resources and pedagogical means in order to promote a more decentralized education. In this article we present and describe a tool to manage, promote, predict behavior, and help to assess, learning activities developed in a group. Our view is that those activities should be increased because they are certainly a possible, simple solution, to circumvent this ratio problem.

The interaction between students, while undertaking a joint project, provides them an opportunity to have a more active role in their learning, and the possibility to develop their social skills. In fact, group work is a teaching strategy that makes students become more responsible for their learning and for the learning of their group fellows. Although the concept of "collaborative learning", also called "group work", is quite attractive in the first instance, it appears that it presents several difficulties for the teacher [1], especially at the time of evaluating and grading the students, as it is not always easy to have the perception of the contribution of each student to the whole group work. Accordingly,

© Springer International Publishing Switzerland 2015
G. Conole et al. (Eds.): EC-TEL 2015, LNCS 9307, pp. 414–419, 2015.
DOI: 10.1007/978-3-319-24258-3_33

the adoption of this kind of pedagogical activity justifies the need for reliable instruments and techniques to provide a greater accuracy (and legitimacy) when assigning the student's final grading.

In the following sections we describe the problems and perspectives related with group work (Sect. 2); in Sect. 3 we give a brief overview our tool. In Sect. 4 we describe the interactions and the pattern mining to predict grading and, we conclude the article (Sect. 5) with a brief synthesis of the work.

2 Group Work

Modern pedagogy [1, 2] takes into account the need to expose students to collaborative work. However, group work is still far from being consensual and reluctance to its adoption derives from many handicaps of the respective assessment procedure.

One of the advantages of group work is that it provides students with an opportunity to improve their "social component" [3], which is essential given that we are in the "social networks generation". Other more objective aspect of the group work is the fact that every student has the opportunity to acquire new learnings, according to their knowledge/experiences and to the knowledge/experiences of the colleagues.

However, there are also disadvantages in conducting group work strategies. The main ones occur due to the large discrepancy with respect to the workload, or the engagement of each of the participants. To minimize these disadvantages some tools are used to analyse the development of the work, and to record which interactions are made [4].

2.1 Assessment of Group Work

Assessment is many times one of the most influential aspects when creating a new pedagogical activity. The way the work is evaluated and assessed largely depends on the purpose of it [5]. Taking into account the characteristics inherent in group work, it is essential to consider not just the final work but also the contribution of each element in the preparation of this work. We believe that there is a general consensus on respect to the need for differentiating the grades of participants in a group work. However, the same is not true when we discuss how this differentiation should be made. For example, three aspects have been proposed in [6]. Unfortunately, all of these characteristics are very hard to be objectively assessed in a short period of time.

However, there are many objective suggestions, for instance through auto and hetero evaluation [7]; through the creation of individual portfolios [8] and even through the use of basic level generic log-files, trace data, and "digests" to determine the interactivity degree in the course of the collaborative activity [9].

Knowing which strategy to adopt is still an open question, since every task has its own characteristics, namely on the *modus operandi* of group work, which makes it difficult to find a way that can be considered simultaneously advantageous to all the different cases. Despite the relevance of each of the aspects mentioned, it is important that the assessment should be as objective as possible. The problem is that some of aforementioned parameters are inherently subjective. Recently, we have seen an interesting proposal [10] which is based on relations between peers, and teachers.

2.2 Group Work in Online Environments

The Moodle system is perhaps the most well-known and most-used worldwide, open source, learning management system. In Moodle there are activities which can be performed simultaneously by several students, whereas activities such as the Test, or the Survey, which typically require an individualized participation. It is curious to note that while it is possible to monitor the students' work in most Moodle activities, in none of them (except the Wiki) is possible to monitor the participation of each student individually. If we consider other LMSs which feature collaboration tools, we get essentially the same problems [2].

3 Overview of the Philosophy of Our Proposed Tool

We have proposed a tool to promote group work that is able to operate on two different modes, which correspond to different pedagogical situations. The first one, the "sequential activity" is based on the assumption that a group work is previously structured in tasks, one task per student. The second one if based on the view that students should structure themselves the work and organize them to be productive and accomplish the activity without further guidance. The tool works as a Moodle module and its management and usage characteristics have been described in [11].

4 Pattern Mining from the Tool Usage

While students use our tool in an online environment, provided by the Moodle LMS, their interactions are being stored in a new table, as log data, in the standard Moodle database. These interactions are atomic actions that a user performs in the context of the group tool usage.

We equipped the tool with the capability to distinguish, and identify up to eight different types of interactions (as listed in Table 1).

Table 1. List of the eight interactions.

1. Upload of a file	5. Read a comment in a file
2. Download of a file	6. Grade a peer submission
3. Edit/change a file	7. Vote for accomplishment
4. Register a comment in a file	8. Grant permission for final submission

It is important to stress that a change to a file (interaction 3) can be done without doing a previous download (2), followed by a upload (1). In fact, a change to a file is an atomic operation which creates a new version of the same filename. On the other hand, a file upload is always the addition of a new file to the system, whereas, a file download means the access of a file without the immediate purpose of changing it.

Examples of Interactions. Not only the interactions are important but also the order in which they appear. Sometimes there is a "logic" sequence of interactions. For example, it is expected that a student revises, or gets to know what a peer has done, before grading him/her. Nevertheless, illogic situations may arise from the interactions' sequence. For the sake of clarity, we present some examples:

- 5-5-3-4: the student read the comments of two different files, then decided to change one file and then updated a comment on the changed file.
- 2-2-6-6: the student downloaded two files and, without reading a single comment, graded two of his peers.
- 1-8: one student did an upload of a file, probably thought that he/she did his part of the work and granted permission for submission of the whole group work without looking at the peer's work.

4.1 Data Analysis Moments

Despite all user interactions with the tool being stored in the database immediately after being triggered, the system does not operate on "real-time". Actually, the automatic analysis of the interactions is triggered only on three moments, which seem to us of importance for pedagogical reasons: the first one occurs 48 h after the first use of the tool by the students; the second one, occurs halfway of the time period defined for the whole group work, and; the last one occurs immediately after completion of the whole group job. We must say that the system is tuned for activities that last for at least one week.

The choice of these three stages is, respectively, due to:

First stage: was created due to the need to check if every student is motivated to perform the assigned job and understands what he/she is supposed to do;
Second stage: acts as a preliminary assessment stage, where early problematic situations may be detected providing the teacher with information for an eventual intervention/assistance;
Third stage: during the last stage all the data is collected, analysed, and stored in the Moodle database to be consulted during the next use of the tool.

4.2 Data Mining and Analysis

A stored database of previous interactions is provided to the system in order to have a starting point for the upcoming and future analysis and predictions.

There are two important analyses that must be considered: (1) the detection of an "illogical" pattern in a sequence, and; (2) the categorization of each sequence into a set of pre-defined categories for grade prediction. We illustrate the process of creating the clusters and of assigning a sequence of interactions to each cluster. To allow graphic representation of the dimensions we assume that each vector belongs to a 2-dimensional space, say dimension V1 and dimension V2. This restriction of the illustration does not loose generality to the 8-dimensional model. On the left side of Fig. 1 (A) we depict three test-data vectors. Those vectors are manually picked as seeds for the creation of a particular cluster (either the "worst", "medium" or "best"). From these vectors, the system computes the centroid (P1) of the cluster. The process is repeated to create the three centroids (part B of the figure). Finally, in part C) of the figure we depict what happens when a vector (D1 or D2) is presented to the system: computing the distance to the nearest centroid the vector is assigned to a particular cluster. In Fig. 1, D1 was assigned to P1 and D2 to P3.

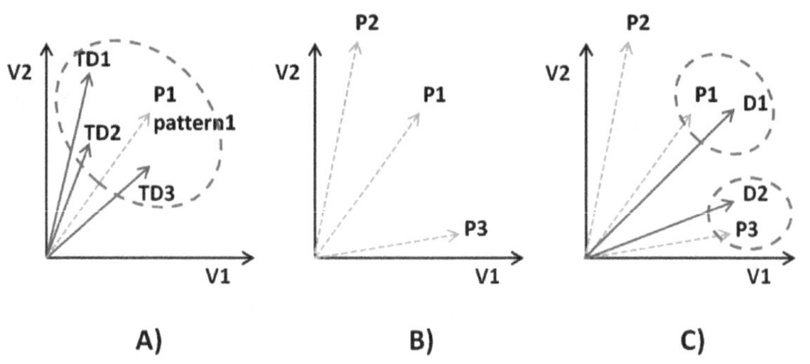

Fig. 1. Clustering the interactions.

As a result of the processing phases (A) and (B) we get three groups: the group of students whose interaction patterns may lead to a higher grade, to a medium grade and to a lower grade. As a result of processing phase (C) the system classifies each interaction in a cluster, therefore predicting the final grade. The system evolves by using the "medoids" (the vector that is the most close to geometric centre) of each resulting cluster, in each stage, and storing them in the Moodle database. These patterns are only made available for future system analysis when the final corresponding grade, given by the teacher, becomes available.

This is a self-feedback system that evolves as it is used. As the database increases and more patterns are acquired and by the system, its prediction accuracy gets improved.

5 Conclusions

Sometimes group assignments are a set of individual tasks, which later on are gathered and assessed as a single activity, where the participation of each group participant is seen as part of a "black box". More than frequently, the grading of each participant for the developed work is not meritocratic, but just the same as the mark given to the whole group work.

Our system can help overcome the difficulties to evaluate the work and involvement of each group participant by allowing the teacher to verify the participation of each student. The tool allows the teacher to follow the progress of the group work and receive notification whenever a student creates a sequence of interactions with the tool that don't make sense or are clearly illogic. Moreover, at three specified stages, during the group work, the tool automatically predicts the final grade of each participant based on their interactions and on a database of previous interaction patterns.

Acknowledgements. This work is financed by ERDF – European Regional Development Fund through the COMPETE Programme (operational programme for competitiveness) and by National Funds through the FCT (Portuguese Foundation for Science and Technology) within project «Reminds»/UTAP-ICDT/EEI-CTP/0022/2014.

References

1. Swan, K., Shen, J., Hiltz, S.R.: Assessment and collaboration in online learning. J. Asynchronous Learn. Netw. **10**(1), 45–61 (2006)
2. Burnett, B., Roberts, A.: Online collaborative assessment: unpacking process and product. In: Comeaux, P. (ed.) Assessing Online Learning, pp. 55–71. Jossey-Bass, San Francisco (2005)
3. Hoffman, J., Rogelberg, S.: All together now? College students' preferred project group grading procedures. Group Dyn. Theor. Res. Pract. **5**(1), 33–40 (2001)
4. Chyng, Y.J., Steinfeld, C., Pfaff, B.: Supporting awareness among virtual teams in a web-based collaborative system: the TeamSCOPE system. ACM SIGGROUP Bull. **21**(3), 28–34 (2000)
5. Boud, D., Cohen, R., Sampson, A.J.: Peer learning and assessment. Assess. Eval. High. Educ. **24**(4), 413–426 (1999)
6. Strijos, J.W.: Assessment of (computer-supported) collaborative learning. IEEE Trans. Learn. Technol. **4**(1), 59–70 (2011)
7. Gilies, R.M.: Cooperative Learning: Integrating Theory and Practice. Sage, Beverley Hills (2007)
8. Lee, E., Chan, C., Aalst, J.: Students assessing their own collaborative knowledge building. Int. J. Comput. Support. Collab. Learn. **1**(1), 57–87 (2006)
9. Schummer, T., Strijos, J., Berkel, T.: Measuring group interaction during CSCL. In: Proceedings of Computer Supported Collaborative Learning: Learning (CSCL 2005), pp. 567–576 (2005)
10. Fidalgo-Blanco, Á., Sein-Echaluce, M.L., García-Peñalvo, F.J., Conde, M.Á.: Using learning analytics to improve teamwork assessment. Comput. Hum. Behav. **47**, 149–156 (2015)
11. Figueira, A.: Orchestrating online group work while assessing individual participations. In: Proceedings of INTED 2015, pp. 2996–3005. Madrid (2015)

Teachers' Perceptions About the HANDSON MOOC: A Learning Design Studio Case

Muriel Garreta-Domingo[1], Davinia Hernández-Leo[2(✉)], Yishay Mor[3], and Peter Sloep[4]

[1] Universitat Oberta de Catalunya, Barcelona, Spain
murielgd@uoc.edu
[2] Serra Hunter Fellow, ICT Department, Universitat Pompeu Fabra, Barcelona, Spain
davinia.hernandez@upf.edu
[3] P.A.U. Education, Barcelona, Spain
yishaym@gmail.com
[4] OUNL, Heerlen, The Netherlands
Peter.Sloep@ou.nl

Abstract. Recently, Massive Open Online Courses (MOOCs) have been proposed as relevant instruments for professional development. This paper reports on two editions of the HANDSON MOOC for teacher professional development. The MOOCs use the Learning Design Studio methodology as a pedagogical framework, the Integrated Learning Design Environment (ILDE) as the design infrastructure, and Moodle and Canvas as delivery platforms. The paper summarizes the design of both MOOCs, including the supporting technologies, and presents an analysis of the evolution of teachers' perceived level of conform with approach and tooling. Data is collected in weekly and final surveys. The results show a general satisfactory level of conform in both MOOCs, which is especially high the last two weeks.

Keywords: Learning design · MOOC · Continuous Professional Development

1 Introduction

The learning design field focuses on the importance of training teachers as designers that reflect on their particular learning contexts and analyse the characteristics of their learners as well as the contextual constraints and targeted learning objectives [1, 2]. As a field, learning design boasts over a decade of rich activity in research, development and practice [1]. However, despite this 'certain maturity', the lack of widespread adoption indicates that additional efforts are needed to better understand how to best develop teachers' design skills and what technological form such support should take [2–4].

This paper focuses on the design and tools used for a Continuous Professional Development (CPD) [4, 5] action-based learning design approach. The action is framed in the HANDSON project (http://handsonict.eu/). Characteristic of the case is that it uses a Massive Open Online Course (MOOC) to support teachers' professional development in the use of ICT in class. Using MOOCs for professional development is a growing trend [6, 7]. This also applies to the professional development of teachers, particularly relating

© Springer International Publishing Switzerland 2015
G. Conole et al. (Eds.): EC-TEL 2015, LNCS 9307, pp. 420–427, 2015.
DOI: 10.1007/978-3-319-24258-3_34

to their ICT skills [7, 8]. HANDSON MOOC's activities follow the Learning Design Studio (LDS) methodology [9]. The LDS methodology leads participants through a design inquiry cycle in which they identify an educational challenge, investigate the context in which it is situated and the relevant pedagogical approaches, review examples of past innovations for inspiration, conceptualise a solution, prototype and evaluate it, and reflect on the process and its outcomes. Two pilots of the MOOC have been delivered using different MOOC platforms and the Integrated Learning Design Environment (ILDE) as the tool supporting the design activities [10], developed in METIS project (http://www.metis-project.org). Section 2 describes the MOOC, listing the LDS activities, tools used and the implementation approach. Evaluation results are discussed in Sect. 3.

2 The HANDSON MOOC

The 'Learning Design Studio for ICT-based learning activities' is the title of the HANDSON MOOC. Main features characterizing the MOOC are: (1) Emphasis on a hands-on approach based on a design process that brings together educators with wide and diverse backgrounds from around the world. (2) Focus on the LDS approach to help educators design learning activities. (3) Involve facilitators with expertise in Online Learning, Creativity and Learning Design. (4) Offer an opportunity to observe and practice methods for peer review and mentoring. (5) Creation of practical artefacts that can be used by the participants in their classrooms.

To accomplish this, the HANDSON MOOC combines a set of tools to support the LDS activities. Table 1 shows a list of them organized per pilot. Differences include the usage of Moodle (1st pilot) and Canvas (2nd pilot) as the MOOC platforms, and the use of additional learning design tools in the second pilot.

HANDSON MOOC chose ILDE as the environment for participants' learning design activities because its flexibility and social approach. ILDE provides a number of tools that support learning design from conceptualization to implementation, and using different representation and pedagogies [10]. The tools are provided in the context community platform where members can share and co-create learning designs. It also makes easy for MOOC facilitators to follow participants' activity. The LDS activities involved use of ILDE conceptualization tools (Dream, Persona Card, Factors & Concerns, Learning Objectives, Heuristic Evaluation, Scenario) together with additional tools for prototyping (participants were free to choose any tool).

Because the activities were based on the LDS approach, the HANDSON MOOC is a project-based course, closer to a cMOOC than an xMOOC [6]. So there were no pre-recorded video lectures. Video is used, however through Google Hangouts in order to run the convergence sessions. These were recoded and made available as OERs for public viewing. This approach provided an engaging and interactive experience for those who could attend in real time, and a reference resource for those who could not. The main characteristics of the two MOOC pilots are summarized in Table 2. The 2nd LDS pilot was accessible to a more global community of educators since participants could communicate in seven different languages. Even though all materials and interfaces were in English, the seven languages had separate discussion and peer-mentoring spaces so participants could write in the language they felt most comfortable with. ILDE was also extended with automatic language tagging for an easy management of the designs created in ILDE. To support this diversity, volunteer facilitators were recruited, trained and accompanied before and during the MOOC.

Table 1. LDS activities, course and learning design tooling

Tools (2nd LDS pilot)	Tools (1st LDS pilot)	Activities	Week
Canvas, GHO (Google Hangout), ILDE (Dream tool)	Moodle, GHO, ILDE (open conceptualization tools)	Design Studio Journal	Week 1
		Dream Bazaar	
		Convergence session	
Canvas, GHO, ILDE (Persona Card, Factors and Concerns, Learning Objectives tools)	Moodle, GHO, ILDE (Persona Card, Factors and Concerns tools)	Get familiar with persona concept	Week 2
		Create your own persona	
		Analysing context	
		Objective of your learning activities	
		Revisit your dream	
		Convergence session	
Canvas, GHO, ILDE (Heuristic Evaluation, Scenario tools)	Moodle, GHO, ILDE (Heuristic Evaluation, open conceptualization tools)	Search for other learning activities	Week 3
		Define the heuristics	
		Learn about scenarios	
		Create scenario	
		Convergence session	
Canvas, GHO, Web2.0 tools	Moodle, GHO, Web2.0 tools	Prototype your artefact	Week 4
		Test your prototype	
		Consolidate your prototype	
		Convergence session	
Canvas, GHO, ILDE (Design Narrative, Comment tool)	Moodle, GHO, ILDE (Design Narrative, Comment tool)	Publish your learning activity	Week 5
		Peer feedback	
		Convergence session	

Table 2. Implementation details of the two LDS HANDSON MOOC editions

2nd LDS pilot	1st LDS pilot
5 weeks (Oct, 28th to Nov. 28th 2014) + 3 weeks extension	5 weeks (May 19th to Jun. 20th 2014)
Bulgarian, Catalan, English, French, Greek, Slovenian, Spanish	English
Guided through rubrics and with the peer-review Canvas option	Not-guided, via forums and ILDE
Certificate of assistance + badges + certificate for some local groups (Catalan, Greek, Bulgarian)	Certificate of assistance +

3 Results from Two HANSON MOOC Pilots

3.1 Methodology

The focus of the study are the general LDS approach, the supporting technologies and the learning design tools as a mechanism to understand its probability for adoption and as indicators to assess the value of tools [11]. Data was collected by weekly surveys, which elicited specific feedback on activities completed and tools used each week and at the same time tracked the evolution of teachers' perception along the weeks. Additional global questions were included the last week and in a post-survey in the 2nd LDS pilot. The 2nd pilot used a traceability system that allows analysing and comparing the responses from participants that finished against those that did not.

3.2 Key Figures and Level of Activity Reached

Table 3 summarizes the key figures characterizing both pilots. Overall, there was more activity going on in the second pilot than in the first one, both in terms of number active participants in ILDE, the number of comments added, and especially the number of designs created. In the second pilot, the activity was also more stable as the weeks went by (e.g. 288 Design Narratives created the fifth week). All the produced designs are available in the ILDE installations for both pilots (links at http://ilde.upf.edu/about/).

3.3 Teachers' Perceived Comfort with MOOC Approach and Tools

Weekly surveys included questions to assess the comfort level with the global LDS approach and the different tooling used in the two MOOC editions. Figures 1 and 2 show the evolution of teachers' ratings for the MOOC platform, ILDE, Converge sessions and Hangouts, and other ICT tools used, in each pilot. The number of participants completing the survey varied every week (see horizontal axis in figures), having higher participation the first two weeks. The data visualized in both Figures indicate similar trends in

Table 3. Key figures for the two pilots

	2nd LDS pilot	1st LDS pilot
Facilitators	2 dedicated facilitators + 32 volunteer facilitators + 1 technical support	3 dedicated facilitators + 1 technical support
Registered participants in MOOC	1690	743
Registered participants in ILDE	396	323
Designs created in ILDE	2294	1472
	(644 in Bulgarian, 455 in Catalan, 411 in English, 317 in Greek, 240 in Spanish, 153 in French, 23 in Slovenian, 51 untagged language)	(no differentiation of languages in this pilot)
	Week 1: 424 Dream;	Week 1: N/A Dreams;
	Week 2: 380 Persona card, 290 Factors and concerns, 298 Learning objectives;	Week 2: 199 Persona card, 152 Factors and concerns;
	Week 3: 315 Heuristic evaluation, 296 Scenario;	Week 3: 124 Heuristic evaluation;
	Week 4: N/A prototypes;	Week 4: N/A prototypes;
	Week 5: 288 Design Narrative	Week 5: 39 Design narrative
Comments to designs (ILDE)	889	603

teachers' perceptions. Yet, the behaviour in the evolution of their opinions varies in both pilots. It is important to say that if we only consider the data of participants finishing the MOOC, probably more highly motivated, the observed trends in data are similar.

The impact on the comfort level with ICT tools in general unfolds differently if we look at the two pilots. The 1st pilot attracted a community of teachers initially less comfortable with ICT tools in general; though at the end their perceived level of comfort had increased it did so less than for the 2nd LDS pilot. This contrasts with the 2nd LDS

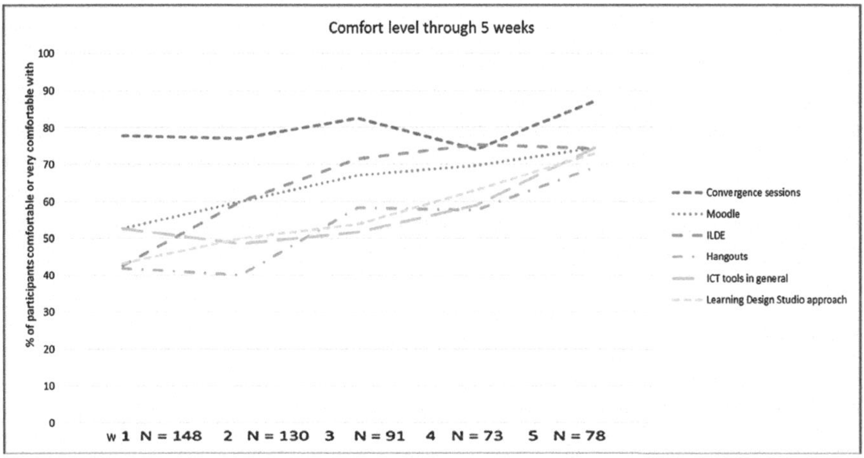

Fig. 1. Comfort (comfortable and very comfortable) with approach and tools, 1st pilot

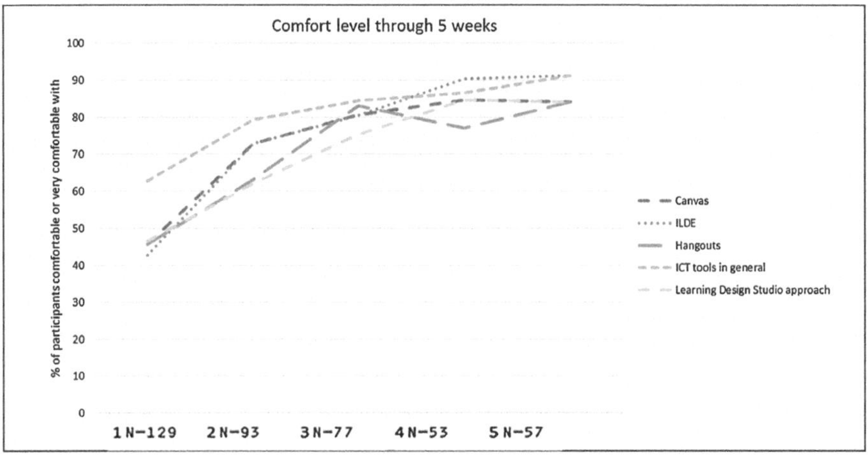

Fig. 2. Comfort (comfortable and very comfortable) with approach and tools, 2nd pilot

pilot, in which the initial level was higher and at the end it had increased nearly 30 points. Therefore in both MOOC editions participants perceived an increase of comfort level - one of the aims of the HANDSON project - but it seems to be more effective if the comfort level is already high. Note the difference between the Moodle and Canvas MOOC platforms. The comfort level with Moodle started at a higher position at the beginning of the MOOC but finished in a lower position than Canvas. The comfort level with ILDE started at the same level for both pilots and increased more for the 2nd LDS pilot; the level of comfort at the end of the 2nd pilot reaches 90 % for ILDE as the learning design environment.

In both MOOC editions, the comfort level with the Learning Design Studio, as the methodology behind the proposed activities, started at a similar level - around 40 % -

and again increased more for participants in the 2nd pilot. This tallies with the fact that the originated activity in the 2nd LDS pilot was higher (more designs created, more comments). The post-survey used in the 2nd LDS pilot also shows this positive level of perceived usability and utility of LDS and technological support as a whole approach: 78.1 % of respondents agreed with "The Learning Design Studio is a valuable resource to include ICT in education", 74.4 % agreed that "The tools and templates provided to work with Learning Design Studio were appropriate" and 73.1 % said that "Using Learning Design Studio can help me improve my educational practices".

4 Conclusions

This preliminary analysis of the HANDSON MOOC results show that despite the different tools used during the implementation of the course the perceived comfort levels with LDS approach and the technological setup for the MOOC delivery as well as the learning design environment (ILDE) increased, especially for the teachers participating during the second half of the MOOC and when they reached a certain familiarity with the technologies. The second edition showed that increased engagement of practitioners in learning design training can be achieved with strong facilitation, if possible in the language of the participants. A complete analysis of pre and post surveys as well as the log files from Moodle and Canvas is currently being done. These analyses will provide a deeper understanding of the MOOC impact and the type of engagement and follow-up activities that participants may need to continue with to hone the skills developed during the MOOC.

Acknowledgments. This work has been partially funded by EACEA, Hands-On ICT Project 531086-LLP-1-2012-1-ES-KA3-KA3MP, with the collaboration of the METIS Project 531262-LLP-2012-ES-KA3-KA3MP.

References

1. Mor, Y., Craft, B., Hernández-Leo, D.: Editorial: the art and science of learning design. Res. Learn. Technol. **21** (2013)
2. Bennett, S., Agostinho, S., Lockyer, L.: Technology tools to support learning design: implications derived from an investigation of university teachers' design practices. Comput. Educ. **81**, 211–220 (2015)
3. Lawless, K.A., Pellegrino, J.W.: Professional development in integrating technology into teaching and learning: knowns, unknowns, and ways to pursue better questions and answers. Rev. Educ. Res. **77**, 575–614 (2007)
4. Fetter, S., Berlanga, A.J., Sloep, P.B., Vuorikari, R.: Major trends arising from the network, Tellnet deliverable 3.1, Brussels, Belgium (2011)
5. Daly, C., Pachler, N., Pelletier, C.: Continuing Professional Development in ICT for teachers. WLE Centre, Institute of Education, University of London (2009)
6. Margaryan, A., Bianco, M., Littlejohn, A.: Instructional quality of massive open online courses (MOOCs). Comput. Educ. **80**, 77–83 (2015)

7. Cross, S.: Evaluation of the OLDS MOOC curriculum design course: participant perspectives, expectations and experiences, Milton Keynes, UK (2013)
8. Laurillard, D.: Anatomy of a MOOC for Teacher CPD, Technical report. UCL Institute of Education (2014)
9. Mor, Y., Mogilevsky, O.: The learning design studio: collaborative design inquiry as teachers' professional development. Res. Learn. Technol. **21**, 1–15 (2013)
10. Hernández-Leo, D., Asensio-Pérez, J.I., Derntl, M., Prieto, L.P., Chacón, J.: ILDE: community environment for conceptualizing, authoring and deploying learning activities. In: de Freitas, S., Rensing, C., Ley, T., Muñoz-Merino, P.J. (eds.) EC-TEL 2014. LNCS, vol. 8719, pp. 490–493. Springer, Heidelberg (2014)
11. Venkatesh, V., Morris, M., Davis, G., Davis, F.: User acceptance of information technology: toward a unified view. MIS Q. **27**, 425–478 (2003)

Learners' Attitudes Toward Using Wikis and Forums for Collaboration on Case Problems

Andri Ioannou[1(✉)], Anthony R. Artino[2], and Scott W. Brown[3]

[1] Department of Multimedia and Graphic Arts, Cyprus University of Technology, Limassol, Cyprus
andri.i.ioannou@cut.ac.cy

[2] Uniformed Services University of the Health Sciences, Bethesda, MD, USA
anthony.artino@usuhs.edu

[3] Educational Psychology Department, University of Connecticut, Storrs, CT, USA
scott.brown@uconn.edu

Abstract. In a case study using quasi-experimental methods (within-subject repeated measures with counterbalancing), differences in students' attitudes were assessed when they used a wiki with discussion (i.e., an enhanced wiki) and a forum with attached MS Word documents for virtual collaboration on case problems. Data from 63 online learners working with both tools was collected. Statistically significant differences were found on a technology experience measure, in favor of the wiki tool. Further, qualitative data supported this finding. This study is an extension of the authors' previous work, adding to a holistic picture of collaborative learning using wikis and forums in online learning settings.

Keywords: Wiki · MediaWiki · Forum · Threaded discussion · Collaborative learning · Online learning · Attitudes · Technology experience

1 Introduction

The era of online learning is characterized by student-centered pedagogies and an abundance of Web 2.0 tools. Particular interest has been given to collaborative problem-based pedagogies, such the case method, that situate learning in meaningful tasks and emphasize the importance of practical experience in learning. Their implementation requires the use of collaboration technologies that enable the discussion of alternative views and support the co-construction of group artifacts (e.g., an essay, a diagram). Wikis and forums are perhaps the most widely used technologies in this case. They made their way into online learning environments more than a decade ago, continue to be used extensively, and an abundance of research literature discusses their effectiveness and limitations in supporting collaborative learning.

Forums have been found to be effective in promoting participation and diversifying of ideas, while enabling learners to reflect on their peers' contributions and analyze their own ideas before articulating them [1]. Nevertheless, forums are associated with

© Springer International Publishing Switzerland 2015
G. Conole et al. (Eds.): EC-TEL 2015, LNCS 9307, pp. 428–434, 2015.
DOI: 10.1007/978-3-319-24258-3_35

problems such as incoherence (i.e., ideas not being tied together, drifting away from the original intention of the thread) and lack of convergence (i.e., synthesizing, summarizing) [2]. Additionally, in typical forums, conversation and artifacts are disjoined (displayed on different screens), which is not conducive to artifact-centered discourse [3]. As argued, discussion tools should allow the inclusion of artifacts outside of individual messages (not as attachments) so that collaborators can change them [4].

Wikis have become very popular as collaborative editing tools for supporting the creation of complex, cohesive artifacts authored by many individuals [7]. Four design elements in wikis seem to support collaboration: (1) The existence of a group-owned document with editing capabilities; (2) The tracking mechanism/history documentation for modifications to the group document; (3) The alert features which give the collaborators the option of receiving automatic reports when the group document is modified; and (4) The inclusion of meta-level communication supports, such as a discussion page associated with the group document, for collaborators to identify problems, resolve disagreements, and negotiate consensus. Yet, these kinds of wiki supports often do not adequately facilitate rich collaborative learning; in fact, [5] argued that a dialogic perspective is needed in wikis in order to accomplish collaboration on a shared problem.

Considering the wide adoption of wikis and forums, we sought to compare them through the lens of learners' perceived experiences, in the context of virtual collaboration on case problems. Very few studies compare the technologies from the learners' point of view. When available, these studies compare different groups of learners using *either* wiki *or* forum e.g., [6, 7]. This study addresses learners' perceived experiences after they have collaborated on case problems using *both* technologies. This is an extension of our own previous investigation of wikis and forums grounded on the quantitative content analysis of learners' interactions as an objective account of the differences in learners' use of the technologies [8]. Nevertheless, here we argue that subjective measures, such as leaners' perceptions and attitudes, are equally important to examine, for a holistic view of forum-enhanced and wiki-enhanced collaborative learning.

2 Method

Participants. Data was collected from 63 graduate students, over a two-year period. The students were enrolled in one of three sections (Sects. 1–3) of an online course on learning theories, at a public university in the northeast USA, and one section (Sect. 4) of an online course on educational psychology at a private university in northeast Europe. Each section was taught by a different instructor; however, all four used identical procedures for the investigation and applied similar weekly activities and pedagogy. Students completed all activities as part of their class work. The sample was composed of students pursuing a MA in educational technology (Sect. 1, n = 20), a 6th-year professional certificate in educational leadership (Sect. 2, n = 14; Sect. 3, n = 19), or a MA in educational psychology (Sect. 4, n = 10) and included 50 (80 %) women between 22–54 years old (M = 34, SD = 8.0). Approximately 80 % were in-service K-12 teachers.

Technologies. The wiki was built in the open-source, MediaWiki, and provided a group-owned document with editing capabilities, a (wiki-type) discussion page associated with each document (i.e., an enhanced wiki), history documentation and alert features. The forum was provided by the Blackboard® (for Sects. 1–3) and Moodle's (for Sect. 4) discussion board, where MS Word documents can be attached within threads.

Case Problems. Two case problems (see [8]) were used in this study (Case A and Case B); three educational psychology experts agreed on their equivalency in terms of complexity. Students were to apply concepts learned in the course, as well as their professional practice, to suggest solutions to the case problems, in the form of an essay. To mitigate the instructor effect, the instructors of all sessions monitored the groups' progress during the activity, but their intervention was deliberately limited.

Research Design and Procedures. This case study used quasi-experimental design methods, specifically a within-subject (repeated measures) design with counterbalancing. The power of the within-subject design is that it allows the researcher to study every single participant (or group) in all treatments (i.e., wiki vs. forum). This design controls the variance due to individual (or group) differences and increases the likelihood that any differences found across conditions are the result of the treatment and not characteristics of the students. At the same time, this design requires fewer participants, since participants serve as their own control. A power analysis conducted for this design indicated that a minimum of 34 learners would be needed to obtain a power of .80 (at alpha = .05) with a moderate effect size (partial $\eta 2 = .06$). To avoid an order effect, the order of using wiki and forum was counterbalanced; that is, some groups used the wiki 1st - forum 2nd, and other groups used the forum 1st - wiki 2nd. For nine weeks, students were exposed to both wikis and forums through weekly class-wide activities. During weeks 10–11, students in each section were randomly assigned to groups of 3–4 students to work on Case A. Nine groups (Group A) used the wiki for their collaboration on Case A, and eight groups (Group B) used the forum. During weeks 12–13, the same groups worked on Case B, but the technologies were reversed. Students were instructed not to use any other technologies for their collaboration. A questionnaire was administrated at the completion of Case A and again at the completion of Case B. The questionnaire addressed students' experiences with the wiki or forum as appropriate.

Questionnaire. The questionnaire included 21 Likert-type items (Response scale: 1 = strongly disagree to 7 = strongly agree), measuring four constructs of interest, three of which were adapted from previous studies reporting good psychometric properties in terms of factor structure and internal consistency (see Fig. 1): (1) communication and interaction, (2) satisfaction, (3) frustration, and (4) technology experience. Two additional essay questions assessed perceived experiences in regards to "positive/negative aspects of using each tool" and "how each tool promoted/hindered collaboration."

1. Communication and Interaction (C&I): 6-item subscale assessing the extent to which students interacted with their teammates during the activity (adapted from [10]) o C&I-1 I explained my ideas to other students. o C&I-2 I asked other students to explain their ideas. o C&I-3 Other students responded to my ideas. o C&I-4 I related my work to other students' work. o C&I-5 I made good sense of other students' contributions. o C&I-6 I sought to improve the group product.	4. Technology Experience (TE): 6-items subscale assessing the extent to which students thought the technology supported their collaboration. o TE-1 The technology met my needs as a collaborator. o TE-2 The technology helped me work effectively in my group. o TE-3 The technology encouraged my participation in the activity. o TE-4 The technology was successful in promoting collaboration. o TE-5 If I were teaching an online course, I would use this technology for collaborative activities. o TE-6 I would recommend this technology to an instructor who needs to support online collaborative learning.
3. Frustration (F): 4-item negatively worded (-), subscale assessing the extent to which students were frustrated with the technology (adapted from [11]) o F-1 I felt frustrated. o F-2 I was angry. o F-3 I felt as though I was wasting my time. o F-4 I was irritated.	2. Satisfaction (S): 5-item subscale assessing the extent to which students were satisfied with their collaborative learning experience (adapted from [11]) o S-1 Overall, my collaborative learning experience was positive. o S-2 The activity met my needs as a learner. o S-3 I am satisfied with my experience through this activity. o S-4 Collaboration added value to the group product. o S-5 I would recommend this activity to another instructor.

Fig. 1. Questionnaire subscales and individual items

3 Results

Quantitative Data Analysis. The students (N = 63) responded to the questionnaire twice – at the completion of each case. Cronbach's coefficient alpha reliabilities were calculated for each subscale and for each administration of the questionnaire; all subscales had acceptable internal consistency reliability (Cronbach's alphas > .80; Fig. 2). To create variables, we calculated mean scores for the participants by calculating an un-weighted mean score for the items in each subscale. Figure 2 summarizes the mean statistics for Group A (wiki 1st, forum 2nd) and Group B (forum 1st, wiki 2nd). Next, to examine differences in students' attitudes across technologies, six repeated measures (RM)ANOVAs were conducted – one for each variable. For each RM-ANOVA: (a) the dependent variable was a within-subjects factor with two levels – score at the completion of Case A and score at the completion of Case B, (b) order of the treatment was a between-subjects factor with two levels (Group A: wiki 1st vs. Group B: forum 1st).

	Cronbach's Alpha		Group A (wiki 1st)		Group B (forum 1st)	
	End_Case A	End_Case B	Wiki	Forum	Wiki	Forum
1. C&I	.77	.89	5.88	5.59	5.71	5.81
2. S	.97	.95	5.66	5.64	5.26	5.00
3. F (-)	.91	.91	2.41	2.76	2.49	3.03
4. TE	.95	.96	5.50	4.77	5.30	4.69

Fig. 2. Subscales reliabilities and variable mean statistics (N = 63)

Statistically significant differences were found for the technology experience variable. Specifically, we found a statistically significant (technology experience x order) interaction (Fig. 3), showing that students using the wiki, for either Case A or Case B, scored higher on the technology experience subscale than when using the forum, $F(1,61) = 7.50$, $p = .008$, partial $\eta^2 = .12$ (i.e., a medium to large effect). To counteract the problem of multiple comparisons (i.e., six separate RM-ANOVAs) a Bonferroni correction was used to adjust the alpha level to alpha = .05/6 = .0083. The F-test for the interaction effect remained significant ($p = .008 < .0083$). For the other variables, the analysis revealed no significant differences in learners' attitudes between wiki and forum use, although means marginally favored the wiki. Means were generally above the mid-point of the scales, suggesting that both technologies were perceived positively by the learners.

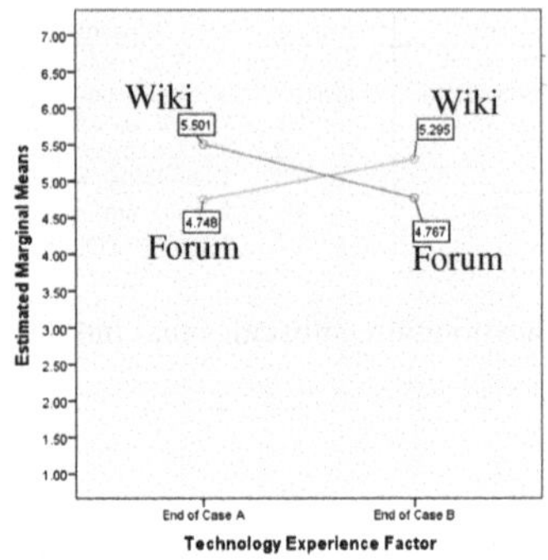

Fig. 3. Technology experience in favor of the wiki

Qualitative Data Analysis. A simple pattern-seeking method was used to identify commonalities among students' responses related to the perceived value and difficulties in using both tools. The analysis was conducted by two investigators independently, who then met to discuss the patterns, concluding to six themes. This data supported the quantitative results; students generally thought the wiki was more appropriate for their

Theme 1. *The wiki functionality enables collaboration on a shared artifact.* G2/Sec 3 member: "In the wiki, we were all able to add ideas, easily move them around, copy and paste from the discussion to the document, write comments and then easily delete them, and fixed mistakes by editing right on the page. We used headings to organize our thoughts and highlighting to get members' attention and all this made it easy to collaborate."
Theme 2. *The wiki discussion page was need.* G1/Sec 1 member: "I liked having the wiki discussion page to discuss/comment on issues and the shared document where we wrote the essay. If there were questions or issues we could check the discussion before editing the essay. I thought this helped us come to a consensus."
Theme 3: *The forum supports communication.* G2/Sec 2 member: "I liked the discussion board venue as it allows you to post ideas, questions, and comments and wait for feedback. The bolded posts and replies immediately notify you."
Theme 4: *The forum suffers from incoherence.* G3/Sec 3 member: "I feel that the forum hindered our collaboration. I found it difficult to follow the discussion as it started to take off and evolve. It was hard to find people's posts; I spent a lot of time searching for individual posts that I wanted to comment on."
Theme 5: *The forum lacks support for collaborative co-construction of artifacts.* G2/Sec 2 member: Forum was good for discussion and consensus, but bad to develop a product. We could discuss in theory but in writing our plan it was hard to show our consensus.
Theme 6: *The wiki was preferred.* G1/Sec 2 member: "The wiki was an ideal technology for this activity. Forum was restrictive as far as collaboration is concerned. In wiki we had one document to look at, build upon, revise, etc. Everything was in the same place which made us feel more like we were building it together. It did get a bit difficult though to find new additions when the pages got long." G3/Sec 1 member: "There are a number of things I liked about using the wiki: All posts were in one spot, writing was grouped by subtopics, easy to find subtopics, ability to edit within another person's post, ability to cut and paste thoughts from our discussion into the essay. I felt as though the wiki provided more opportunities for collaboration compared to the forum."

Fig. 4. Themes from qualitative data

collaboration on case problems, although both technologies were appreciated for different reasons. In Fig. 4, we present the themes and examples of direct student quotes.

4 Discussion and Conclusion

The study examined (within-subject) differences in learners' perceived experiences in using a wiki and forum for online collaboration on case problems. Students scored significantly higher on a technology experience measure in favor of the wiki. The moderate effect suggests that this difference in attitudes is meaningful and may have practical implications for researchers, instructors and students using these tools [9].

Qualitative patterns supported the quantitative results, but also revealed how both tools were appreciated for different reasons. Students valued the capability to edit each other's work in the wiki and felt that having a discussion page associated with a group-owned document (i.e., an enhanced wiki) was conducive to collaboration. Students also valued the communication capabilities of the forum (particularly the 'reply' option and the 'bolding' of new messages) yet, there were barriers associated with its use, including incoherence in the threads and difficulty in co-constructing a group artifact. Overall, these findings reinforce previous work on wikis and forums as discussed in our introduction. Moreover, these results confirm the findings of our previous work [8], in which the quantitative content analysis of learners' interactions (i.e., a more objective account) allowed us to document differences in learners' use of the technologies such as, the expanding nature of forums vs. condensing nature of wikis, collaborative nature of wikis vs. cooperative nature of forums, efficiency of wiki collaboration etc. Thus, results from the self-reported (subjective) data of the present study improve the validity of our findings in [8].

Given the limitations of this work, the results should be interpreted and evaluated with caution. The questionnaire used in this study has limited validity evidence, although the internal consistency reliabilities of the subscales were acceptable. Also, the study used a sample of convenience and thus findings cannot be generalized beyond learners and contexts that are similar to our study (i.e., graduate students in asynchronous courses working on case problems). Closing, overall our results favor the use of wikis for online collaboration on case problems. These findings, as well as findings from our earlier work in the same context [8], may be of interest to instructors who use wikis and/or forums in their courses to support collaborative learning.

References

1. Hammond, M.: A review of recent papers on online discussion in teaching and learning. J. Asynchronous Learn. Netw. **9**(3), 9–23 (2005)
2. Hewitt, J.: Beyond threaded discourse. Int. J. Educ. Telecommun. **7**(3), 207–221 (2001)
3. Suthers, D., Xu, J.: Kukakuka: An online environment for artifact-centered discourse. In: Education Track of the Eleventh WorldWideWeb (WWW 2002), pp. 7–11, May 2002
4. Suthers, D.D.: Collaborative representations: Supporting face to face and online knowledge-building discourse. In: Proceedings of the 34th Annual Hawaii International Conference on System Sciences, 2001, p. 10. IEEE, January 2001

5. Larusson, J.A., Alterman, R.: Wikis to support the "collaborative" part of collaborative learning. Int. J. CSCL **4**(4), 371–402 (2009). Springer
6. Ioannou, A.: Online collaborative learning: the Promise of wikis. Int. J. Instr. Media **38**(3), 213–223 (2011)
7. Ioannou, A., Artino, A.R.: Wiki and forum for online collaborative activities: Students' perceptions and use. Emerg. Technol. Web Intell. **1**(1), 97–105 (2009)
8. Ioannou, A., Brown, S.W., Artino, A.R.: Wikis and forums for collaborative problem-based activity: a systematic comparison of learners' interactions. Internet High. Educ. **24**, 35–45 (2015)
9. LeCroy, C.W., Krysik, J.: Understanding and interpreting effect size measures. Soc. Work Res. **31**, 243–250 (2007)
10. Yeo, S., Taylor, P., Kulski, M.: Internationalising a learning environment instrument for evaluating transnational online university courses. Learn. Environ. Res. **9**, 179–194 (2006)
11. Artino, A.R.: Think, feel, act: Motivational and emotional influences on military students' online academic success. J. Comput. High. Educ. **21**, 146–166 (2009)

Students' Deep and Surface Approach: Links to Interaction in Learning Environments

Maria Margeti[1,2(✉)] and Manolis Mavrikis[2]

[1] University of Westminster, London, UK
M.Margeti@westminster.ac.uk
[2] UCL-Institute of Education, London, UK
M.Mavrikis@ioe.ac.uk

Abstract. This paper presents the initial results of a study where we embrace and test Entwistle's theory in order to explain the students' interaction when using interactive learning environments (ILEs) in real conditions. In contrast to others who seek ways of adapting a system to students' specific learning style, our aim is to find ways of designing an ILE that encourages students' adoption of a deep approach to studying and discourages a surface approach. In this paper we focus only on the relationship between two subscales of the Approaches and Study Skills Inventory for Students (the deep subscale of interest in ideas and surface subscale of fear of failure), and metrics occurring from usage in a specific ILE. The results point to insights for instructors regarding the integration of ILEs in classrooms, as well as suggestions regarding the design of features which encourage a deep approach to studying.

Keywords: Deep and surface approach to studying · Fear of failure · Intrinsic motivation · Entwistle's approaches and study skills inventory for students

1 Introduction

As more interactive and intelligent learning environments (ILEs) are getting employed in real settings it is paramount to understand better how learners interact with them, and to identify ways to support them as well as provide information about their interaction to their instructors.

In education, one of the areas which has been involved in this type of investigation, is the theory of learning styles. In the 1990's, there was a gradual increase in studies that examine various style constructs in relation to the way students use ILEs. The main aim of most studies was to eventually propose ILEs which can be adapted to suit students' style [1, 2]. However, certain criticisms arise from such an application: whether the proposed measurements capture subtleties and complexities of individual human behavior in real educational settings; whether they measure what they claim to measure; and whether their psychometric standards are sound [3]. In addition, the wider debate on the wisdom of matching or mismatching style to instruction and the lack of solid empirical evidence about the effect on performance [3, 4], led us to examine the application of the learning style theory in the context of ILEs from a different perspective.

© Springer International Publishing Switzerland 2015
G. Conole et al. (Eds.): EC-TEL 2015, LNCS 9307, pp. 435–440, 2015.
DOI: 10.1007/978-3-319-24258-3_36

This study, in contrast, does not seek ways of adapting a system to a specific learning style, but it rather aims to find ways of designing an ILE that encourages students' adoption of a deep approach to studying and discourages a surface approach. This is reinforced by evidence that adoption of a deep approach to studying by first-year undergraduate students correlates positively to their performance; whereas a surface approach correlates negatively to their performance [5, 6]. Therefore, for this study, we employ a learning style approach which suits exactly this context and purpose. We rely on the theory behind Entwistle Approaches and Study Skills Inventory for Students (ASSIST), as it can contribute to creating more sophisticated ILEs where the emphasis is on a more explorative and meaningful approach to learning. We seek therefore to develop metrics that act as 'proxies' for the identification of students with deep or surface approach and enable instructor intervention, particularly in settings where an ILE is used in the classroom, assessment or other decision making.

This can give us insights on how students' approach to learning is linked to usage of an ILE for a specific learning scenario; and what factors occurring in a natural learning setting (e.g. tutor intervention) may influence this relationship. Henceforth, hypotheses are formed about the relationship between deep and surface approaches, as measured through ASSIST, and the specific metrics that emerge from students' usage of an ILE for mathematics when practicing in tutorial sessions in the classroom.

2 Methodology

2.1 Description of Study

The sample consists of 233 undergraduate students from a London-based university who attended at the common core module of mathematics in the School of Computer Science that takes place during the first semester of the first year of their studies. In the sample, there are 190 males and 43 females, aged 18 to 46 years. The study was carried out over the course of four weeks under real learning conditions -during the two-hour tutorials of the module-. During the first two weeks students were introduced to and registered in an ILE for mathematics: ActiveMath (AM). During the third and fourth week, AM was used for the first time for learning purposes, specifically for the chapters of 'Functions-Graphs', and 'Matrices' respectively. ASSIST was also administered to students who completed it voluntarily. Finally, observations were made in class to record and identify issues, such as tutors' interventions, which naturally occur in real learning environments, and may influence the results of study.

2.2 ActiveMath

AM is an interactive learning environment which presents mathematical concepts, procedures, examples and exercises in verbal (text and numerical) and visual form. The AM interface and features were customized to integrate the learning material as defined by the syllabus, and the learning outcomes of the specific university course. 'Reading pages' allow students to view concepts, theory, and working examples for mathematical procedures, with hyperlinks to other concepts. 'Exercise pages' contain groups of exercises, allowing students to select which exercise to work on such as multiple choice, and fill-in-the-blank. Students can explore further concepts by submitting a query for math terms in search and getting results from sites such as Wikipedia and Math World. As the purpose of the study is to examine students' approaches to studying in relation to the way they interact in ILE, AM has been designed in a way that doesn't influence students' decisions or studying approach (e.g. it doesn't provide intelligent guidance). So in that sense AM is a fairly typical ILE for mathematics in which allows students to control which theory, example, and exercise they study.

2.3 Metrics of Usage in AM Learning Environment

Previous studies looking at the relationship between styles and students' interaction when using ILEs have examined metrics such as: the number of pages visited and revisited, the time they spend on the system; and the use of navigational options that allow them to have a more global or detailed view of the learning material [7, 8]. Metrics were chosen according to: whether they enable us to capture how students move around and what students do in AM, and whether the metrics can have empirical and conceptual connections to the ASSIST deep and surface scales and subscales.

2.4 The ASSIST Instrument and Hypothesized Relationships with AM Metrics

We employed the second part of the questionnaire that provides a student's 'Approaches to studying' and consists of 52 items [9]. ASSIST consists of 3 main approaches: deep, surface, and strategic. In this paper we focus on two subscales of the deep and surface approaches respectively and investigate their relationship with interaction metrics as discussed below.

First, the 'deep' approach regards the intention to understand for oneself, and the 'interest in ideas' subscale (one of its four subscales) measures whether there is an interest in the subject [10]. Accordingly, we developed the hypothesis that interest in content is likely to encourage a more exploratory search when students retrieve information and go beyond the syllabus [11, 12]. In AM this would be manifested by the number of submitted queries in search option, the number of search results visited in search option and any number of contextual hyperlinks that allow students to visit new concepts or revisit previous ones.

The 'surface' approach regards the extent to which students have the intention to complete a task with very little engagement, and the 'fear of failure' subscale (one of its four subscales) measure whether there is motivation to avoid failure [5, 9]. Students perceive the learning environment as threatening [11]. Accordingly, we develop the hypothesis that fear of failing may have a negative impact on students' performance when practicing their exercises. In AM students can evaluate their answers and receive feedback. If the answer is incorrect, they are encouraged to try again, and are allowed three attempts in all. As indicated in similar systems [13, 14], students' interaction with the exercises can indicate whether students are simply abusing the affordances of the environment to achieve good results but with questionable learning gains. Students with high degree of fear of failure may well exhibit gaming behavior, because it allows them to succeed without risking failure [15]. In addition, studies with first-year undergraduates show that there is a statistically significant, negative correlation between the factor of fear of failure and performance [5, 6]. This leads us to the general assumption that students with high fear of failure scores are not likely to perform well in our context. We use proportional metrics which make it easier to compare performance, than metrics based on raw accounts. We expect: a negative association between fear of failure subscale and the ratio of exercises solved on the first effort over the number of exercises attempted by the student; and positive associations between fear of failure subscale and the metrics of the ratio of exercises solved on the second or third effort over the number of exercises attempted by the student.

3 Results

The analysis concerns the usage of AM during the third week of the study (when students were studying 'Functions-Graphs'). The analysis was carried out on 114 students of the sample (out of the 223 described in 2.1), who attended and used AM during the third and fourth weeks of the study, and who also completed ASSIST.

3.1 The Deep Subscale 'Interest in Ideas' and Students' Usage Metrics

Based on the results of the bivariate analysis, we did expect to find and actually did find, a statistically significant relationship between the interest in ideas subscale and the use of contextual hyperlinks ($r_s = 0.185$, $p < 0.05$). On the other hand, we did expect to find and did not find, a statistically significant relationship between the interest in ideas subscale and the metrics of: number of submitted queries in search option; and number of search results visited in search option.

3.2 The Surface Subscale 'Fear of Failure' and Students' Usage Metrics

Based on the results from the bivariate analysis, we did expect to find and actually did find, a statistically significant relationship between the fear of failure subscale and the metric of ratio of exercised solved on the: first effort over the number of exercises attempted by the student ($rs = -0.220$, $p < 0.05$); second effort over the number of exercises attempted by the student ($rs = 0.260$, $p < 0.05$); third effort over the number of the exercises attempted by the student ($rs = 0.215$, $p < 0.05$).

4 Discussion and Conclusion

The results suggest that the studying approaches of interest in ideas and fear of failure can relate to some aspects of students' usage in the mathematical learning environment AM. However, these relationships seem to have been influenced by the way AM is designed, and tutors' interventions and the practical nature of the tutorial sessions.

Intrinsic interest in mathematics can be related to use of tools such as hyperlinks which assist students in following up the mathematical term or procedure they are interested in. The results indicated, however, that the practical significance –the magnitude of the observed effect– is very small. The majority of hyperlinks are placed on the reading pages. It is possible that the practical nature of the tutorials did not encourage students with an interest in ideas to view the reading pages of the application. The classroom observations suggest that the majority of students only visited the reading pages when tutors would advise them to examine topics that would help them to solve a specific type of exercise. Other research findings suggest that science students examine relationships between topics or concepts within the context of a task, when it is made obvious to them that they need to understand certain relationships between concepts in order to solve specific problems [5].

On the other hand, the results do not agree with our prediction concerning the association between the interest in ideas subscales and the metrics of the number of submission of queries and the number of visits on the search results in the search option. It seems that intrinsic motivation is not enough to promote the usage of features which encourage further exploration of the learning material. ILEs should be designed in a way that can gratify students' intrinsic interest in mathematics, thus encouraging a deep approach. Intrinsic interest in a subject is not so much something one creates but rather something one finds; so if we want to utilize students' intrinsic motivation, we must focus on what they are interested in and link the study material to it [11]. Following this suggestion, the search option in ILEs could be designed in a way that would trigger the curiosity of the students with an interest in ideas approach, as they are likely to explore the parts of a program that gratify their curiosity [12]. A possible solution is to make ILEs more responsive, so the search option is not simply a choice placed statically at the navigation bar, but an option that can suggest a search at a 'crucial' moment that is likely to be noticed. For example, when students fail to solve exercises after the first effort, a suggestion could emerge to explore a mathematical concept or an example related to the specific exercise.

Furthermore, fear of failure is related to poor performance in the tutorial exercises. It seems that students who report to be overanxious about failing in mathematics, are not likely to solve an exercise on the first effort and they are more likely to solve an exercise on the second or third effort. The results indicate, however, that the practical significance –the magnitude of the observed effect– for these results is small, which can be explained as students with high fear of failure scores work with such effort and persistence which can be rewarded in their academic work [16]. This association between fear of failure and performance metrics can aid towards identifying a surface approach towards studying, and therefore may improve the integration of ILEs in class and enrich further the learning-teaching experience. For example, an intelligent tutoring system that indicates poor performance in exercises may 'flag up' a student who seems to demonstrate a surface approach in a specific tutoring session.

Further analysis on the relationship of other subscales and AM usage metrics (involving also data from the fourth week) will show whether the above indications are consistent and help us to further clarify the issues highlighted in this paper.

Acknowledgements. We would like to acknowledge: the ActiveMath group for the help and support in pre-processing the log files; Harvey Mellar for supervising part of the work; and Vasos Pavlikas for providing the math content for AM.

References

1. Papanikolaou, K., Grigoriadou, M., Kornilakis, H., Magoulias, G.: Personalising the interaction in a web-based educational hypermedia system: the case of INSPIRE. User Model. User-Adap. Inter. **13**, 213–267 (2003)
2. Stash, N., Cristea, A., De Bra, P.: Authoring of learning styles in adaptive hypermedia: problems and solutions. In: 13th International Conference on World Wide Web, New York, pp. 114–123 (2004)
3. Coffield, F., Moseley, D., Hall, E., Ecclestone, K.: Learning Styles and Pedagogy in Post-16 Learning. A Systematic and Critical Review. Learning and Skills Research Centre, London (2004)
4. Curry, L.: A critique of the research on learning styles. Educ. Leadersh. **48**, 50–56 (1990)
5. Entwistle, N., Ramsden, P.: Understanding Students Learning. Nichols, New York (1983)
6. Tait, H., Entwistle, N.: Identifying students at risk through ineffective study strategies. High. Educ. **31**, 97–116 (1996)
7. Chen, S., Macredie, R.: Cognitive styles and hypermedia navigation: development of a learning model. J. Am. Soc. Inform. Sci. Technol. **53**, 3–15 (2002)
8. Mimirinis, M., Dafoulas, G.: Patterns of use of virtual learning environments and students' approaches to learning: a case study of undergraduate students. In: Proceedings of World Conference on Educational Multimedia Hypermedia and Telecommunications, Vienna, pp. 6349–6356 (2008)
9. ETL Project. http://www.etl.tla.ed.ac.uk/questionnaires/ASSIST.pdf
10. Entwistle, N.: Contrasting perspectives on learning. In: Marton, F., Hounsell, D., Entwistle, N. (eds.) The Experience of Learning - Implication for Teaching and Studying in Higher Education. Scottish Academic Press, Edinburgh (1997)
11. Fransson, A.: Test anxiety and motivation to learn. Department of Education, Acta Univertsitatis Gothoburgensis (1978)
12. Martens, R.L., Gulikersw, J., Bastiaensw, T.: The impact of intrinsic motivation on e-learning in authentic computer tasks. J. Comput. Assist. Learn. **20**, 368–376 (2004)
13. Baker, R., Walonoski, J., Heffernan, N., Roll, I., Corbett, A., Koedinger, K.: Why Students in "gaming the system" behavior in interactive learning environments. J. Interact. Learn. Res. **19**, 185–224 (2008)
14. Mavrikis, M.: Modelling student interactions in intelligent learning environments: constructing bayesian networks from data. Int. J. Artif. Intell. Tools **19**, 733–753 (2010)
15. Entwistle, N., Hanley, M., Hounsell, D.: Identifying distinctive approaches to studying. High. Educ. **8**, 365–389 (1979)
16. Entwistle, N.: Styles of Learning and Teaching- An Integrated Outline of Educational Psychology. Wiley, Chichester (1981)

Grounding Serious Game Design on Scientific Findings: The Case of ENACT on Soft Skills Training and Assessment

Davide Marocco[1(✉)], Daniela Pacella[1], Elena Dell'Aquila[1], and Andrea Di Ferdinando[2]

[1] Plymouth University, Plymouth, UK
{davide.marocco,daniela.pacella,e.dellaquila}@plymouth.ac.uk
[2] AIDVANCED Srl, Rome, Italy
andrea.diferdinando@aidvanced.com

Abstract. The lack of open-access tool for the enhancement and promotion of soft skills is bringing the e-learning community to new educational challenges. The paper describes the implementation of ENACT, an online serious game for the standardised psychometric assessment and training of users' negotiation skills through the interaction with virtual artificial agents. The assessment process is divided into 8 scenarios based on real life situations and investigates the user negotiation styles in relation to Rahim's conceptualization of five different styles of handling conflict. Need analysis data and preliminary testing results of the platform are presented.

Keywords: e-Learning · Technology-enhanced eearning · Serious games · Simulation-based learning · Psychometric assessment · Negotiation · Soft skills

1 Introduction

In recent years the attention of e-learning is progressively moving from the classical view, assuming that learning involves knowledge acquisition and transfer, with a main focus on hard skills, to a more comprehensive approach that involves the domain of soft skills training. Soft skills, also commonly referred as "people skills", are personal attributes or a cluster of personal traits that contribute to how people know and manage themselves, as well as their relationships with others. They include skills such as proficiencies in the area of communication, conflict resolution and negotiation, leadership, and team building, to name a few. Today soft skills are recognized as transversal competencies existing in reciprocal relationship with hard skills, as it is testified by the numerous documents produced by the European Union about the enhancement of social and entrepreneurial skills (e.g. the Key Competences for Lifelong Learning [1]) and by the US Accreditation Board for Engineering and Technology (ABET), which is explicitly demanding the improvement of soft skills training in the IT sector [2], with a particular focus on communication and negotiation skills.

A crucial feature of soft competencies is that they can be assessed and developed through training, education and development programs. The most effective training

© Springer International Publishing Switzerland 2015
G. Conole et al. (Eds.): EC-TEL 2015, LNCS 9307, pp. 441–446, 2015.
DOI: 10.1007/978-3-319-24258-3_37

method for soft skills development is considered to be role-playing, usually performed by trainees face-to-face, with the guidance of a professional trainer acting as facilitator. In general terms, the act of "role-playing" describes an experience in which two or more people are involved in "as-if" or simulated actions and circumstances [3] that project participants into an imaginative-creative process established through the interpretation of a real or fictional role in a specific given situation. Derived from the psychodrama and sociodrama methods introduced by Moreno [4], role- playing is an active pedagogical method to learn about social roles and interactions.

The porting of soft skills training and assessment into technology enhanced environments is relatively recent and current examples of technology-enhanced role-playing simulations are usually based on 2D or 3D chat rooms, where users can interact online by voice or text messages. In some cases they portray emotional states [5]. In other limited cases the interactions can also happen between humans and artificial agents controlled by Artificial Intelligent algorithms [6, 7].

In this paper we describe the methodology for the development of an educational tool in the form of a 3D game-based intelligent platform to assess and train the user's negotiation and communication skills in realistic scenarios. The ENACT (Enhancing Negotiation Skills through On-Line Assessment of Competencies and Interactive Mobile Training) platform aims at crossing the boundaries between educational games and tutoring systems, merging the importance of an standardised, online user assessment with the motivating environment of serious games. Within the ENACT project *negotiation* has been identified as a crucial competence for learning and personal development, as it helps to communicate constructively in different contexts and directly affect people's social environment. The paper will present the process of porting soft skill assessment and training from classroom to digital environments.

2 Psychological Modelling and Platform Design

The negotiation model adopted in ENACT is based on the five styles of handling interpersonal conflict proposed by Rahim [8, 9], which is the most recognised model by occupational psychologists. This model differentiates 5 styles of negotiation based upon two basic dimensions: *concern for self*, the degree (high or low) to which a person attempts to satisfy his or her own concern; and *concern for others*, the degree (high or low) to which a person attempts to satisfy the concern of others. The combination produces the following styles of conflict management: (1) *Integrating* (high concern for self and others); (2) *Obliging* (low concern for self and high concern for others); (3) *Dominating* (high concern for self and low concern for others); (4) *Avoiding* (low concern for self and others); and (5) *Compromising* (intermediate in concern for self and others).

Each style manifests itself in a pattern of observable behavioural indicators that we have identified in the communication model of assertiveness, passivity and aggression [10]. For each of the 5 styles, we have distinguished verbal, non-verbal and paraverbal variables, grouped in the two dimensions proposed by Rahim, i.e., concern for self and for others.

The final goal of ENACT game is to return an assessment and provide training opportunities. The assessment of the player is based on the preferred negotiation styles used during a series of negotiation scenarios, based on the description of the 5 styles provided by Rahim. The assessment should be comparable to a professional assessment conducted with traditional "pen and pencil" methods (i.e. the ROCI-II questionnaire designed by Rahim [9]). Based on the assessment, the system automatically elaborates a training strategy tailored to the specific development areas of the player, in order to create an effective learner-centred environment, where the user activity is focused on the areas of behaviour that mostly require improvements.

The web platform has been designed to bring the model into a 3D virtual environment. The game is organized in scenarios, each independent from the others, where the user will play a different character and will negotiate with various virtual agents in real and everyday life situations. The main game components are the virtual agents and the interface (Fig. 1).

Fig. 1. The user interface of one scenario in the assessment mode. The foreground avatar is controlled by the computer and the avatar in the smaller windows at the top-left corner represents the player's avatar. The sentences on the left represent the choices of the player in response to the actions of the computer avatar.

The artificial agents are implemented as virtual 3D characters inside the game scenarios developed within the Unity3D framework. They interact dynamically with the user and are able to perform a range of basic expressions using verbal cues: Vocal tone and structure of the sentence; and non-verbal indicators: Facial expression, eye contact, body posture and gestures. The user character is also shown to the player, and it is represented by a 3D model inside the scenario. The sex of the characters is a variable related to the gender specified by the user at the registration, mandatory for accessing the platform. The virtual agent-user interaction is divided into states, which include one turn of speech for each party. In every state, the user can choose one among 4 possible sentences, each of which is correlated to a gesture and/or facial expression that shows the way the sentence will be told to the agent.

The interface is designed to be as intuitive as possible. The two characters are shown on the screen along with their gestures, while the sentences are shown in bubbles over the head of the agents. When the mouse is over one of the user sentences (Fig. 1, left side), the animation related to that sentence is shown in the top-left rectangle. In order to choose a sentence, the user needs to click on it.

Two game sessions are planned: *Assessment*, where the user negotiation attitude are measured and *Training*, where the user will be individually taught about her adopted negotiation styles. The training session is still in development.

The assessment session is a game mode for the user to be assessed in a standardized way according to Rahim's model. In this session, the system collects the data about the user's behavior and choices and creates a model of the player that will then be used for generating tailored information in a subsequent training session. The assessment environment is composed by a series of 8 different scenarios that concern a negotiation situation between two peers. The virtual agent's behavior shows a specific negotiation style for each of the scenarios. The user does not get any feedback between the scenarios, and there is no right or wrong answer.

Three parameters according to which the scenarios were designed are: (i)The negotiation style adopted by the virtual agent; (b) If the player and the agent have the same or opposite gender, so the interactions can be male-male (or female-female) and male-female (or female-male); (3) If the negotiation concerns a decision about two different possibilities (divergence) or concerns a single object which must be exclusively assigned to one of the two characters (convergence).

3 Results

In order to design and develop the ENACT learning scenarios a systematic investigation and analysis of the training needs of target groups across 3 countries participating in the project has been conducted. Multiple methods of data collection have been used: (1) completion of a scoping questionnaire from 9 pivotal group target stakeholders (to gather information regarding existing training policy and practices of soft skills); (2) completion of 10 face-to-face semi-structured interviews (to identifies different cultural definitions of the concept of negotiation); (3) utilisation of an online survey completed by 56 respondents (to elicit views and gain useful insights and nuanced opinions on the training needs). Results show that there is a gap between (a) recommended educational practice of national guidelines and current practice in schools and training institution about soft skills related subject; and (b) national practice guidelines of technology application and the training provided to teachers in the use of technology. Few projects and training activities have been developed for promoting the use of computer games for soft skills development, with exception of Italy that in the last decade has been forefront of innovative role-playing and simulation tools for soft skills training, e.g. [4]. Results also show that key elements related to the concept of negotiation varies between target groups and age range. In business, for example, problem-solving and effective time management are the aspects more appreciated within negotiation. Teachers consider essential the ability to positively manage a conflict. For students, interpersonal relationships are the key for a successful negotiation. Moreover, findings from the online questionnaires have identified the relational competencies considered being more characteristic of negotiation:

- Spain: effective communication (90 %), empathy (70 %) decision making (65 %);
- Turkey: effective communication (80 %), problem solving (50 %), empathy (50 %) and creative thinking (50 %);
- Italy: critical thinking (64 %) and active listening (64 %).

The platform prototype has been tested in two public occasions. The first set of data were collected at Plymouth University in September 2014. 152 subjects tested the game, of which 72 in the age 6–10. A total of 79 subjects between the age of 11 and 60 completed the questionnaire, with a mean age $\approx$ 20.6, of which 41 males and 38 females. The questionnaire was made of 8 questions about the game content and interface. The first 7 items had 5 possible answers based on a 5 point Likert scale, where 1 stood for "Extremely bad" and 5 "Extremely Good"; the last question, instead, asked the participant if she would have played the game again in different scenarios. Data showed that the overall feedback was positive, the average rating for each of the question never scored below 3.5 points except for Question 2 (regarding the realism of the conversations) and 5 (about the game graphics) which scored a mean of 3.4 and 3.3. 95.3 % of the subjects answered "Yes" to Question 8, showing an overall interest in the future development of the game.

Another set of data about a second prototype with the full assessment system in place were collected at Plymouth University in March 2015, where subjects were asked to play 4 different scenarios and to provide a feedback about the platform. The pool was composed of 39 people, in the age 11–28, of which 18 males and 21 females. The questionnaire was composed by 13 questions, of which 12 of them had a 5 points Likert scale as possible responses that ranged from "Totally Disagree" (represented as 1 point) to "Totally Agree" (represented as 5). All the questions asked in the previous test showed at least a slight improvement, and in this case only Question 5, about how modern the graphics look, scored less than 3.5. Two questions even scored above 4, and, in particular, the highest score was reached by Question 12, about if users had a positive experience in using ENACT game, while that same question had scored 3.9 on the previous demo. 94.7 % of the subjects answered that they would play the game again with different scenarios.

4 Conclusions

The final aim of ENACT is twofold. On one hand, it is to apply role-playing techniques in a digital context in order to obtain comparable information provided by the administration of the ROCI-II, as well as investigate possible relationships between the scores from the questionnaire about the different styles, and the styles shown by the users during the interaction with the artificial agents. This aims to provide a reliable alternative to traditional psychometric assessment methodologies based on questionnaires and tests. On the other hand, it is to provide a personalised, learner-centred and protected environment, where the user can build up from the assessment and gain awareness of her own negotiation and communication in a constructive and experienced-based environment. Therefore, we are proposing a methodology that focuses on the complementarity with traditional assessment and training tools, and offers alternatives and inclusive training processes of soft skill to the often expensive assessment centres provided by professional consultancy firms.

We believe that technology can offer a new and positive model for approaching the fundamental domain that involves the personal sphere of individual, not only through well know social networks dynamics, often difficult to control, but thanks to a rational and scientific approach that tries to bridge the past to the present with modern, accessible and effective tools, that can be comparable with previous assessment and training methods. This is the case of ENACT in comparison with the ROCI-II test. We believe that the validation process which is currently in place will add a fundamental dimension to the current use of technology and serious games in education, by grounding learning analytics and player's behaviours in frameworks that are accepted and recognised by psychologists and professional trainers.

Acknowledgments. This research has been supported by the European Commission, project ENACT (43301-LLP-1-2013-1-UK-KA3-KA3MP) from the LLP 2013 Key Activity 3.

References

1. European Union, Recommendation of the European Parliament and of the Council of 18 December 2006 on key competences for lifelong learning (2006)
2. ABET, Criteria for Accrediting Engineering Programs (2015)
3. Yardley-Matwiejczuk, K.M.: Role Play: Theory and Practice. Sage, London (1997)
4. Moreno, J.L.: Psychodrama, Fourth Edition with New Introduction, vol. 1, Beacon House Inc., Beacon N.Y. 1977 (1946)
5. Miglino, O., Di Ferdinando, A., Rega, A., Benincasa, B.: SISINE: Teaching negotiation through a multiplayer online role playing game. In: Proceedings of the 6th European Conference on E-Learning, pp. 439– 448. Academic Conferences Limited (2007)
6. Zhang, L., Gillies, M., Dhaliwal, K., Gower, A., Robertson, D., Crabtree, B.: E-Drama: facilitating online role-play using an AI actor and emotionally expressive characters. Int. J. Artif. Intell. Edu. **19**(1), 5–38 (2009). Goldsmiths Research Online
7. Johnson, W.L.: Using virtual role-play to prepare for cross-cultural communication. In: Proceedings of the 5th International Conference on Applied Human Factors and Ergonomics AHFE 2014, Poland (2014)
8. Rahim, M.A., Bonoma, T.V.: Managing organizational conflict: a model for diagnosis and intervention. Psychol. Rep. **44**, 1323–1344 (1979)
9. Rahim, M.A.: A measure of styles of handling interpersonal conflict. Acad. Manag. J. **26**, 368–376 (1983)
10. Dryden, W., Constantinou, D.: Assertiveness step by step. Sheldon Press, London (2004)

Informal Learning in Online Knowledge Communities: Predicting Community Response to Visitor Inquiries

Nicolae Nistor[1,2,3(✉)], Mihai Dascălu[4], Lucia Larise Stavarache[4], Yvonne Serafin[2], and Ștefan Trăușan-Matu[4]

[1] Faculty of Psychology and Educational Sciences, Ludwig-Maximilians-Universität, Leopoldstr. 13, 80802 Munich, Germany
nic.nistor@uni-muenchen.de

[2] Faculty of Human Sciences, Universität der Bundeswehr München, Werner-Heisenberg-Weg. 39, 85577 Neubiberg, Germany
yvonne.serafin@unibw.de

[3] Richard W. Riley College of Education and Leadership Walden University, 100 Washington Avenue South, Suite 900, Minneapolis, MN 55401, USA

[4] Faculty of Automatic Control and Computers, University "Politehnica" Bucharest, Splaiul Independenţei 313, 60042 Bucharest, Romania
{mihai.dascalu,stefan.trausan}@cs.pub.ro, larise.stavarache@ro.ibm.com

Abstract. Informal learning in online knowledge communities (OKCs) comprises visitor inquiries on specific topics. Learning can occur only if the OKC adequately respond. This study aims to predict OKC response, using a social learning analytics approach based on computational linguistics and Bakhtin's theory of dialogism. Observing the blog topic (cooking vs. politics & economics) and the visitor inquiry format (off-topic vs. on-topic), a field experiment with a 2×2 factorial design was conducted on a sample of $N = 68$ blogger communities with a total of 25,303 members. For the entire sample, the community response was influenced only by the inquiry format. In a separate examination of experimental groups, only for one examined topic (cooking) this remained true, while for the other (politics & economics) the community response only depended on the previously established dialog quality. The findings suggest identification criteria for responsive communities, which can support OKC integration in learning environments.

Keywords: Social learning analytics · Computational linguistics · Informal learning · Online knowledge communities

1 Introduction

People search and visit online knowledge communities (OKC) to ask questions, and clarify problems encountered in their daily life. From an educational perspective, this can be regarded as informal learning. However, it cannot be taken for granted that an OKC will adequately respond. Successful informal learning in OKCs would strongly benefit from OKC responsiveness. Social learning analytics can provide an automated

© Springer International Publishing Switzerland 2015
G. Conole et al. (Eds.): EC-TEL 2015, LNCS 9307, pp. 447–452, 2015.
DOI: 10.1007/978-3-319-24258-3_38

means to predict OKC responsiveness [1]. A first step towards this endeavor was taken by Nistor, Dascălu, Tarnai, Bresser and Trăuşan-Matu [2]. This paper proposes a refinement and empirical validation of their approach.

2 Theoretical Framework

OKCs are groups of mutually engaged people, sharing interests, knowledge and "ways of doing things", and sustaining a joint computer-mediated discourse over longer periods of time [3, 4]. A central aspect of OKCs resides in the socio-cognitive structure that includes central, active and peripheral members [4]. Central participants assume more responsibility and perform more difficult tasks than peripheral participants; therefore, their identity is that of an expert. Identity within the community typically develops from newcomer and novice to old-timer and expert, and is negotiated in the community discourse (ibid.). The inseparability of knowledge, identity and social practice on the one hand, and community discourse on the other (ibid.), suggests that adequate discourse analysis may inform the researcher about the socio-cognitive structures of OKCs, and predict the probability of new member integration.

In this vein, Nistor and colelagues [2] conducted an automated discourse analysis based on Bakhtin's dialogism [5] and on the polyphonic discourse model [6, 7]. Measuring participants' involvement has been computed as follows. Firstly, the relevance of each contribution is identified using the aggregate score of each constituent word. Each word score considers three analysis dimensions [8]: (1) statistical presence, (2) semantic relatedness, and (3) semantic coverage derived from the importance of the semantic chain covering the given concept and spanning throughout the conversation thread. Secondly, each post or comment is assigned an individual score equal to the normalized term frequency of each word multiplied by its relevance [9]. Finally, the overall contribution score (either for the initial post or of the corresponding comments) is computed according to its on-topic relevance. Additionally, each contribution score is augmented through its connections or cohesive links to other posts or comments, thus emphasizing the information transfer between utterances [9].

Transposing the local importance of each concept with respect to other inter-linked utterances models the inter-animation of 'voices' or opinions [10]. Furthermore, in order to measure the participation engagement in the discussion thread, the voices of different participants have been overlapped in a polyphonic manner [11]. Thus, by applying a pointwise mutual information (PMI) model on the moving averages of voice distributions [9] from different participants, a reliable estimator of the degree of inter-animation between voices results [10].

Altogether, the resulting score per community member is computed as the aggregated of the above from each individual conversation thread where the members contributed, thus generating a global overview of member participation in an OKC. The automated computational measurements have been implemented in the ReaderBench tool, described in detail by Dascălu [9] and validated by Nistor et al. [2]. Several indicators describing the personal and social quality dimensions of a collaborative dialog, emphasizing discourse cohesion and the overall coverage of given topics have been used in order to compute the scores.

Employing this discourse analysis tool, Nistor and colleagues [2] propose a prediction criterion of OKC responsiveness and integrativity; however, their study has some limitations related to its quasi-experimental approach, the operationalization of community response, and sample size. Further research is needed to overcome these limitations.

3 Research Questions and Methodology

The research addressed above suggests that the OKC response to visitor inquiries may depend on the visitor inquiry format, in addition to the socio-cognitive OKC structure, and the collaborative dialog quality previously established in the community. This assumption is explored through the following research questions:

RQ1. What is the effect of the socio-cognitive structure on the collaborative dialog quality in blogger communities?
RQ2. What is the effect of visitor inquiry format, blog topic, collaborative dialog quality, and socio-cognitive structure of blogger communities on the community response?

Accordingly, a field experiment with a 2 × 2 factorial design was conducted within blogger communities on the Internet. One of the factors was the treatment, i.e., the *visitor inquiry format*. This consisted of either an off-topic inquiry (a request for participation in a questionnaire survey); or an on-topic inquiry consisting of a short dialog (three question-answer or answer-comment sequences), followed by the same request for participation in a questionnaire survey. The second factor was the *blog topic*. Two different topics were chosen: cooking, and politics & economics, with the expectation that participants would employ different communication, argumentation and knowledge construction strategies for each topic [12].

A sample of $N = 68$ blogger communities was analyzed, for a total of 25,303 members distributed between 1 and 1844 per community (in average $M = 7.54$, $SD = 9.55$ participants per month of blog lifetime). The blogs were distributed across experimental groups as shown in Table 1.

Table 1. Distribution of blogs across the 2 × 2 factorial design.

Blog topics	Treatment 1: off-topic inquiry	Treatment 2: on-topic inquiry
Cooking	20	17
Politics & economics	16	15

Besides treatment and blog topic, several covariates were further considered. Seven indicators of the *quality of collaborative dialog* at the blog level were provided by the ReaderBench tool [9, 13]. From these indicators, the *socio-cognitive structure* of the examined OKCs, i.e., the number of central, active and peripheral members, was subsequently extracted according to the procedure defined by Nistor et al. [2]. The dependent variable was *community response*, defined on a scale with five values: 1 = no reaction, 2 = deleted comment, 3 = approved comment (in moderated blogs), 4 = single answers, 5 = discussion on visitor's inquiry. This was regarded as an interval scale.

The blogger communities were randomly selected from the Internet. One of the researchers posted the inquiries according to the experimental design. Subsequently, the community response was followed and recorded for the two weeks after the inquiries had been posted. The comments posted during the entire lifetime of each blog were locally saved, and analyzed with the ReaderBench tool [2, 9]. Finally, all collected data were statistically processed employing IBM SPSS Statistics version 22 for Mac.

4 Findings

The measured *collaborative dialog quality* indicators varied within very large limits and were strongly correlated with each other. Hence, they were normalized (z values were calculated) and a main component analysis with oblimin rotation was performed. Two components were extracted (by means of the Anderson-Rubin method) and used in the further analysis to describe the collaborative community dialog quality. These components explained 79 % of the total variance. The first factor (in the following referred to as 'overall discourse quality') corresponds to the dialog quality in the entire community's discourse, including the voice inter-animation. The second factor (referred to as 'comments quality') corresponds to the dialog quality in single comments. No significant differences were found between blog topics in terms of overall discourse quality. A marginally significant difference was found in the comments quality ($F = 3.98$, $p = .050$), such that the comments quality was higher in politics & economy ($M = .26$, $SD = 1.36$) than in cooking blogs ($M = -.22$, $SD = .47$).

To determine the *socio-cognitive structure* of the examined OKCs, a similar dimension reduction procedure was performed for each community discourse. Subsequently, the participants of each community were hierarchically clustered according to the Ward method, extracting three clusters that corresponded to the community layers: central participants ($M = 3$, $SD = 11$), active participants ($M = 159$, $SD = 292$) and peripheral participants ($M = 1322$, $SD = 319$).

To answer RQ1, the *effects of the socio-cognitive structure on the established dialog quality* in the OKCs were tested by means of multiple regression analysis. The overall discourse quality was significantly impacted by the number of active members ($\beta = .51$, $p < .000$), peripheral members ($\beta = .47$, $p < .000$) and central members ($\beta = .25$, $p < .01$), which cleared corr. $R^2 = .55$ of the total variance in overall discourse quality.

Community response covered the entire scale range from 1 to 5, with $M = 2.76$ and $SD = 1.34$. To answer RQ2, a variance analysis (UNIANOVA) corresponding to the 2×2 factorial design, was performed. This revealed a strong, significant main effect of the visitor inquiry format: $F(1, 65) = 39.83$, $p < .000$, partial $\eta^2 = .41$, explaining corr. $R^2 = .45$ of the total variance in community response. The blog topic effect, the interaction and covariate effects were not significant.

Additionally, these effects were examined separately, by multiple regression analysis in the two blog topic groups. For cooking blogs only, the community response was strongly impacted by the visitor inquiry format ($\beta = .72, p < .000$). This model explained corr. $R^2 = .62$ of the total variance. For politics & economics blogs, the community response was only influenced by dialog quality, i.e., by the percentage of social knowledge building per utterance scores ($\beta = 1.00, p < .05$), which explained corr. $R^2 = 0.43$ of the total variance. In this case, neither the visitor inquiry format, nor the socio-cognitive community structure had significant effects on the OKC response.

5 Discussion and Conclusions

This study examined the effects of visitor inquiry format, topic, established collaborative dialog quality and socio-cognitive structure on the response of a blogger OKC. As expected, the visitor inquiry format had a significant impact on community response, meaning that OKCs were more likely to respond to on-topic than to off-topic inquiries. This relationship was connected with the established blog topics. In the examined cooking blogs, the community response was strongly influenced by the inquiry format only. In contrast, in the politics & economics blogs, the community response depended only on the collaborative dialog quality, i.e., on social knowledge building. This difference may be caused by a difference in the specific knowledge construction process and employed communication strategies, which in turn may be given by the difference in topic. While discussing politics and economy, OKC members are likely to elaborate more, and create more knowledge [3] than while exchanging cooking recipes. Consequently, the success of a visitor inquiry may be a matter of netiquette in cooking blogs (i.e., of on-topic comments), and a matter of knowledge and argumentation (i.e., interanimation of voices [5]) in politics & economy blogs.

Remarkably, the community structure impacted the overall dialog quality, but it had no direct effect on the community response. This seems to contradict the findings reported by Nistor and colleagues [2], who provided empirical evidence for a significant effect of socio-cognitive structure on OKC response.

The results of this study suggest a shift in the initial research model. Initially, it was assumed that the visitor inquiry format, the blog topic, the established collaborative dialog quality, and the socio-cognitive OKC structure of the examined communities would have direct effects on the community response. The presented results suggest that only two factors may have direct effects on community response, namely the visitor inquiry format, and the established dialog quality. The latter may be further impacted by the socio-cognitive OKC structure, i.e., collaborative dialogue quality may mediate the effect of socio-cognitive structure on community response. Such a model would reconcile the findings reported above with those reported by Nistor and colleagues [2]. This would be worth verifying in follow-up research.

For the practice of technology-enhanced learning, this study suggests that social learning analytics can support informal learning in OKCs by automatically assessing the quality of the collaborative dialog in various OKCs, and subsequently recommending those with higher dialog quality as more likely to be responsive and integrative communities [2, 13]. At the same time, OKC visitors should have a minimum of insight in community's knowledge and "ways of doing things" [4], observing the interaction rules and strategies that are specific to the chosen OKC.

Acknowledgements. This work has been partially funded by the 644187 RAGE H2020-ICT-2014 project, as well as by the Sectorial Operational Program Human Resources Development 2007-2013 of the Romanian Ministry of European Funds according to the Financial Agreements POSDRU/159/1.5/S/134397 and 134398.

References

1. Baker, R., Siemens, G.: Educational data mining and learning analytics. In: Sawyer, K. (ed.) Cambridge handbook of the learning sciences. Cambridge University Press, Cambridge (in press) (2014)
2. Nistor, N., Dascălu, M., Tarnai, C., Bresser, N., Trăuşan-Matu, S.: Online knowledge communities as student-centered open learning environments: how likely will they be to integrate learners as new members? In: 11th International Conference on Computer-Supported Collaborative Learning (CSCL 2015). ISLS, Gothenburg, Sweden (in press) (2015)
3. Bereiter, C., Scardamalia, M.: Knowledge building and knowledge creation: one concept, two hills to climb. In: Tan, S.C., So, H.J., Yeo, J. (eds.) Knowledge Creation in Education, pp. 35–52. Springer, New York (2014)
4. Lave, J., Wenger, E.: Situated Learning: Legitimate Peripheral Participation. Cambridge University Press, Cambridge (1991)
5. Bakhtin, M.M.: The Dialogic Imagination: Four Essays. The University of Texas Press, Austin and London (1981)
6. Trăuşan-Matu, S., Stahl, G., Sarmiento, J.: Polyphonic support for collaborative learning. In: Dimitriadis, Yannis A., Zigurs, I., Gómez-Sánchez, Eduardo (eds.) CRIWG 2006. LNCS, vol. 4154, pp. 132–139. Springer, Heidelberg (2006)
7. Trăuşan-Matu, S.: The polyphonic model of hybrid and collaborative learning. In: Wang, F.L., Fong., J., Kwan, R.C. (eds.) Handbook of Research on Hybrid Learning Models: Advanced Tools, Technologies, and Applications, pp. 466–486. Information Science Publishing, Hershey, NY (2010)
8. Dascălu, M., Trăuşan-Matu, S., Dessus, P., McNamara, D.S.: Discourse cohesion: a signature of collaboration. In: 5th International Learning Analytics & Knowledge Conference (LAK 2015). ACM, Poughkeepsie, NY (in press) (2015)
9. Dascălu, M.: Analyzing discourse and text complexity for learning and collaborating. Studies in Computational Intelligence, vol. 534. Springer, Switzerland (2014)
10. Dascălu, M., Trăuşan-Matu, S., Dessus, P., McNamara, D.S.: Dialogism: a framework for CSCL and a signature of collaboration. In: 11th International Conference on Computer-Supported Collaborative Learning (CSCL 2015). ISLS, Gothenburg, Sweden (in press) (2015)
11. Bakhtin, M.M.: Problems of Dostoevsky's Poetics. University of Minnesota Press, Minneapolis (1984)
12. Schmidt, J.: Blogging practices: An analytical framework. J. Comput. Mediated Commun. **12**(4), 1409–1427 (2007)
13. Nistor, N., Trăuşan-Matu, S., Dascălu, M., Duttweiler, H., Chiru, C., Baltes, B., Smeaton, G.: Finding student-centered open learning environments on the internet: Automated dialogue assessment in academic virtual communities of practice. Comput. Hum. Behav. **47**(1), 119–127 (2015)

Learning Analytics: Trends and Issues of the Empirical Research of the Years 2011–2014

Nicolae Nistor[1,2,3(✉)], Michael Derntl[4], and Ralf Klamma[4]

[1] Faculty of Psychology and Educational Sciences, Ludwig-Maximilians-Universität, Leopoldstr. 13, 80802 Munich, Germany
nic.nistor@uni-muenchen.de
[2] Faculty of Human Sciences, Universität der Bundeswehr München, Werner-Heisenberg-Weg 39, 85577 Neubiberg, Germany
[3] Richard W. Riley College of Education and Leadership, Walden University, 100 Washington Avenue South, Suite 900, Minneapolis, MN 55401, USA
[4] Advanced Community Information Systems (ACIS) Group, RWTH Aachen University, Informatik 5, Ahornstr. 55, Aachen, Germany
{derntl,klamma}@dbis.rwth-aachen.de

Abstract. In very recent years, the advent of Learning Analytics (LA) has resulted in a number of publications reporting on empirical research. This literature overview identifies the mainstream of empirical LA research, and emphasizes insufficiently investigated directions that display a higher innovation potential. The mainstream consists of learning trajectory visualizations aimed to predict learner success. Single studies prove innovative by addressing in particular: informal educational settings, video and audio records as data sources, automated assessment and error/misconception analysis. A central issue of empirical LA research consists of the frequent lack of an explicit theoretical framework from educational perspective. We maintain that educational and psychological theories are urgently needed for significant progress of upcoming LA research.

Keywords: Learning analytics · Empirical educational research · Literature review

1 Introduction

Learning Analytics (LA) was officially born around 2010, as a new domain at the intersection of computer science and educational science. Baker and Siemens [1] defined the main tasks and methods of LA: predicting learning behavior and output, structure discovery, including clustering learner types and actions, factor analysis, social network analysis and domain structure discovery, relationship mining, distillation of data for human judgment (including monitoring, visualizing), discovery with models, and method and tool development for LA. However, if we look at the empirical research connected with LA, the applicability of this classification is an open issue. Basic aspects of empirical educational research, such as data sources or theoretical frameworks are

© Springer International Publishing Switzerland 2015
G. Conole et al. (Eds.): EC-TEL 2015, LNCS 9307, pp. 453–459, 2015.
DOI: 10.1007/978-3-319-24258-3_39

not addressed. Moreover, some categories may describe the LA mainstream, while others may find little application so far.

Relying on Baker and Siemens' classification, this paper proposes an overview of the empirical LA research of the years 2011–2014, addressing the following points: the educational setting, data sources, the theoretical framework from educational perspective, the purpose of data processing, and the associated computational methods. The conclusions pertain to the current state of the art in empirical LA research, identifying the mainstream, and emphasizing research directions that have been insufficiently investigated so far, thus displaying a higher innovation potential.

2 Paper Selection Procedure

To identify the most representative empirical LA studies, we considered for analysis a body of literature comprising 480 papers published in proceedings of the EC-TEL conference (298 papers) and LAK conference (182 papers) between 2011 and 2014. The process of selecting the key papers for thorough analysis was performed as follows. First, three coders (the authors of this paper) independently flagged each paper as being relevant or not. A paper was flagged as relevant if it contained empirical research on learning analytics. We used the definition of learning analytics included in the 2011 Horizon Report, which reads as follows: "Learning analytics loosely joins a variety of data-gathering tools and analytic techniques to study student engagement, performance, and progress in practice, with the goal of using what is learned to revise curricula, teaching, and assessment in real time. Building on the kinds of information generated by Google Analytics and other similar tools, learning analytics aims to mobilize the power of data-mining tools in the service of learning, and embracing the complexity, diversity, and abundance of information that dynamic learning environments can generate" [2].

As a result, unanimous relevance ratings were obtained for 421 papers (88 %). Of those, 138 were unanimously coded as relevant and 283 as irrelevant. The latter 283 were then reviewed by the coders once again, and agreement of two coders was achieved for 31 papers (6 %) (11 %?), and the remaining 28 papers (6 %) (10 %?) were rated as relevant by just one coder. Instead of reaching a consensus on the 59 (should this be 224?) conflicting papers, we decided to include those in the analysis.

With the resulting set of 197 relevant papers (71 from EC-TEL and 126 from LAK) we built a dynamic topic model using the topic modeling toolkit D-VITA[1] [3]. A topic model is a mathematical model about how a text corpus is generated by distributing words over documents [4]. It can be used for finding the latent thematic structure in document collections. There are various methods to obtain a topic model, with the most prominent and simple being Latent Dirichlet Allocation (LDA) [5]. LDA assumes that a document corpus exhibits latent topics. The number of topics to obtain as an input to LDA can be freely set by the user. All documents will share the same set of topics, but the proportion of each topic in the documents varies. Essentially, topics are distributions over words from a shared vocabulary. Some words will be more relevant and some less

[1] The model can be explored online at http://monet.informatik.rwth-aachen.de/DVita?id=3001

relevant to a topic. A dynamic topic model factors in the epoch in which a document was created. The time window of an epoch can be defined by the topic modeler; it can be a year, a day, or any other time period, depending on the nature of the document collection. The dynamic topic model explains how the relevance of topics in the model changes when transitioning to the subsequent epoch.

We chose to build a topic model with 24 topics. We think that this is a sufficiently large number of topics to account for the breadth of learning analytics research, and it is sufficiently small for efficient further processing of the papers. We then selected the most relevant paper for each topic in the year 2014, i.e., from the proceedings of LAK 2014 [6] and EC-TEL 2014 [7]. In the topic model the relevance of a paper is reflected by a fraction that expresses the topic's share of the paper's topic distribution. One paper had the highest relevance for two topics, and four more papers were excluded because of a lack of details on empirical data. Hence, the final set of papers that we selected for analysis includes 19 papers, including 12 from LAK 2014 [8–19] and 7 from EC-TEL 2014 [20–26].

3 Educational Settings

The LA studies were conducted in three basic settings: university/college, school and informal settings.

University/College. The majority of the studies were conducted in universities or colleges, involving undergraduate, graduate and doctoral students. Total: 12 cases, [8–10, 12, 13, 15, 17–19, 21, 23, 25]

School. Further studies took place in schools, including isolated cases of at-risk or special education students. Total: 6 cases, [11, 14, 16, 20, 22, 24]

Informal Settings. As an exception, one study involved informal users of an information system. Total: Total: 1 case, [26]

4 Data Sources in LA Research

The same LA studies used different data sources. In all categories, sample sizes ranged from isolated cases that could potentially be scaled up to Big Data, e.g., N = 2 [20], to ten or hundred thousands of involved learners [9, 18].

Learning management system log data. In most studies, log file data of various platforms or learning management systems were processed. Total: 11 cases, [8, 9, 11, 13, 14, 18–20, 23–25] **Learner-generated data.** A smaller number of studies employed data that were actively generated by users, e.g., response to assignments. This included generic text, annotations or other kinds of user-processed material. Total: 4 cases, [10, 12, 21, 26] **Additionally collected data.** In some studies, additional data was collected, e.g., video or audio records of groups or individuals involved in learning activities. Total: 3 cases, [16, 17, 22] **Available academic administration data.** One study used data that was already available at the student record office. Total: 1 case, [15].

5 Theoretical Framework from an Educational Perspective

Empirical research is mostly supposed to be positioned in a specific theoretical framework, which was in some cases not explicitly named, therefore recognizing and classifying these in separate categories was sometimes an issue.

No Specific Educational Theoretical Framework Acknowledged. A relatively large part of the reviewed studies named no explicit theoretical framework, or were atheoretical from an educational perspective. Total: 7 cases, [8, 13, 15, 18, 23–25] **Linguistic/ Logic Approach.** A further category of studies was built on linguistic or logic approaches, such as those dealing with domain knowledge, learning contents, and corresponding learning objects. Total: 3 cases, [10, 21, 26] **Situated Learning/Community of Practice.** Some studies addressed situated learning, or community of practice approach. Against possible expectations, these were not the studies conducted in informal educational settings. Total: 2 cases, [9, 16] **Vygotsky's Zone of Proximal Development.** Further studies were based on Vygotsky's concept of Zone of Proximal Development. Total: 2 cases, [14, 22] **Various Approaches.** Further approaches were self-regulated learning [12], adaptive learning environments [11], peer assessment [19], autism [20], or the instructional design concept of learning orchestration [17]. Total: 5 single cases.

6 Purpose of Data Processing

Data were processed according to different purposes, sometimes also combining, e.g. the visualization of learning trajectories with success predictions. These categories were also named by Baker and Siemens [1] in their LA overview.

Learning Trajectory Visualization. Many studies follow the learning process and offer teachers or instructors a visualization that can be used for adequate instructional support. Total: 7 cases, [9, 10, 12, 13, 21, 23, 25] **Predicting Learning Success or Failure/ Dropout.** Several studies predict learner success, and indicate the cases were educational interventions may be necessary. Total: 5 cases, [8, 14, 15, 18, 22] **Diagnosis.** Some LA studies include error diagnosis or learner diagnosis, e.g., for autism. Total: 3 cases, [17, 20, 24] **Assessment.** In few cases, the learning outcome is assessed, e.g. in order to provide an easy way of grading. Total: 2 cases, [16, 19] **Intervention.** In a strict sense, educational interventions were rather uncommon in the reviewed material, although they would have been enabled by the LA results. However, LA output was used for interventions in a wider sense, such as automatically adapting or recommending learning material. Total: 2 cases, [11, 26].

7 Computational Methods

Baker and Siemens [1] differentiate several key methods and tools for LA and in this section we focus on the computational methods applied to them.

Prediction. The goal of these methods is to predict certain variables from observed variables. The goal is typically to facilitate interventions based on the observed data. Different prediction models can be used, in our data set the primary model is based on classifiers [10, 15, 16, 18, 21, 22, 24]. Total: 7 cases. **Structure Discovery.** The goal here is to identify the structure that emerges in the data. Methods used include clustering [8, 26] and social network analysis [13]. Total: 3 cases. **Relationship Mining.** The aim here is to identify relationships between variables in the data, and many techniques can be used for that. In our papers, we find correlation mining [12, 17, 19], association rule mining [11] and others with mixed approaches [20, 25]. Total: 6 cases. **Visualization.** This refers to ways of distilling and presenting data for human judgment using various visualization techniques like histograms, grids and others [9, 14, 23]. Total: 3 cases.

8 Conclusions

This study aimed at identifying trends and shortcomings of LA-based empirical research. The relatively simple analysis provided above includes the most representative conference presentations of the years 2011–2014, and points to mainstream tends on the one hand, and at potentially interesting themes that are largely unexplored on the other hand. Evidently, the vast majority of LA studies examine log data to visualize learning trajectories and predict the success or failure of university students.

Apart from the mainstream, single studies prove innovative by applying alternative approaches. Learning and collaborating in *informal settings*, e.g., in virtual communities on the Internet, is nowadays a ubiquitous phenomenon and probably one of the most important producers of Big Data. However, there is still a shortage of related LA research. Further on, *video and audio records* are traditionally very rich data sources, however few studies exploit them in the sense of Big Data, although automated analysis systems, e.g., for emotion recognition are increasingly available as commercial software. Of course, privacy and human subjects protection issues must be additionally addressed while exploring various data sources for LA. As for the purpose of the LA studies, both *automated assessment*, at least as an addition to manual assessment, and *error or misconception diagnosis* may be very helpful for teachers and instructors dealing with large student groups.

A challenging aspect of LA research lies in the theoretical framework it is embedded in. It is widely accepted that the explicit and coherent application of educational and psychological theories substantiates empirical studies. On the other hand, this overview shows that many empirical studies provide significant results without being positioned in any explicit theoretical framework. To put it in a more provoking way, it seems that LA research can do very well without educational theories, too. Nevertheless, we maintain that educational and psychological theories are urgently needed for in-depth understanding of educational phenomena, and for significant progress of upcoming LA research.

References

1. Baker, R., Siemens, G.: Educational data mining and learning analytics. In: Sawyer, R.K. (ed.) The Cambridge Handbook of the Learning Sciences, 2nd edn, pp. 253–274. Cambridge University Press, Cambridge (2015)
2. Johnson, L., Smith, R., Willis, H., et al.: The 2011 Horizon Report. The New Media Consortium, Austin (2011)
3. Günnemann, N., Derntl, M., Klamma, R., et al.: An interactive system for visual analytics of dynamic topic models. Datenbank Spektrum **13**(3), 213–223 (2013)
4. Blei, D.M.: Probabilistic topic models. Commun. ACM **55**(4), 77–84 (2012)
5. Blei, D.M., Ng, A.Y., Jordan, M.I.: Latent dirichlet allocation. J. Mach. Learn. Res. **3**(1), 993–1022 (2003)
6. Pistilli, M.D., Willis, J., Koch, D., et al. (eds.): Proceedings of Learning Analytics and Knowledge Conference 2014, LAK 2014. ACM, New York (2014)
7. Rensing, C., de Freitas, S., Ley, T., Muñoz-Merino, P.J.: Open learning and teaching in educational communities. In: Rensing, C., de Freitas, S., Ley, T., Muñoz-Merino, P.J. (eds.) EC-TEL 2014. LNCS, vol. 8719. Springer, Switzerland (2014)
8. Bogarín, A., Romero, C., Cerezo, R., et al.: Clustering for improving educational process mining. In: [6], pp. 11–15 (2014)
9. Clow, D.: Data wranglers: human interpreters to help close the feedback loop. In: [6], pp. 49–53 (2014)
10. Coopey, E., Shapiro, R.B., Danahy, E.: Collaborative spatial classification. In: [6], pp. 138–142 (2014)
11. Fancsali, S.E., Ritter, S.: Context personalization, preferences, and performance in an intelligent tutoring system for middle school mathematics. In: [6], pp. 73–77 (2014)
12. Gasevicm, D., Mirriahi, N., Dawson, S.: Analytics of the effects of video use and instruction to support reflective learning. In: [6], pp. 123–132 (2014)
13. Hecking, T., Ziebarth, S., Hoppe, H.U.: Analysis of dynamic resource access patterns in a blended learning course. In: [6], pp. 173–182 (2014)
14. Mendiburo, M., Sulcer, B., Hasselbring, T.S.: Interaction design for improved analytics. In: [6], pp. 78–82 (2014)
15. Nam, S., Lonn, S., Brown, T., et al.: Customized course advising: investigating engineering student success with incoming profiles and patterns of concurrent course enrollment. In: [6], pp. 16–25 (2014)
16. Okada, M., Tada, M.: Formative assessment method of real-world learning by integrating heterogeneous elements of behavior, knowledge, and the environment. In: [6], pp. 1–10 (2014)
17. Raca, M., Tormey, R., Dillenbourg, P.: Sleepers' lag - study on motion and attention. In: [6], pp. 36–43 (2014)
18. Santos, J.L., Klerkx, J., Duval, E., et al.: Success, activity and drop-outs in MOOCs an exploratory study on the UNED COMA courses. In: [6], pp. 98–102 (2014)
19. Vozniuk, A., Holzer, A., Gillet, D.: Peer assessment based on ratings in a social media course. In: [6], pp. 133–137 (2014)
20. Cabielles-Hernández, D., Pérez Pérez, J.R., Paule-Ruiz, M.P., et al.: dmTEA: mobile learning to aid in the diagnosis of autism spectrum disorders. In: [7], pp. 29–41 (2014)
21. González López, S., López-López, A.: Analysis of concept sequencing in student drafts. In: [7], pp. 422–427 (2014)

22. Janning, R., Schatten, C., Schmidt-Thieme, L.: Feature analysis for affect recognition supporting task sequencing in adaptive intelligent tutoring systems. In: [7], pp. 179–192 (2014)
23. Loboda, T.D., Guerra, J., Hosseini, R., et al.: Mastery grids: an open source social educational progress visualization. In: [7], pp. 235–248 (2014)
24. McTavish, T.S., Larusson, J.A.: Labeling mathematical errors to reveal cognitive states. In: [7], pp. 446–451 (2014)
25. Vahdat, M., Oneto, L., Ghio, A., et al.: A learning analytics methodology to profile students behavior and explore interactions with a digital electronics simulator. In: [7], pp. 596–597 (2014)
26. Niemann, K., Wolpers, M.: Usage-based clustering of learning resources to improve recommendations. In: [7], pp. 317–330 (2014)

Towards an Intelligent Tutoring System for Logical Reasoning in Multiple Contexts

Roger Nkambou[1(✉)], Janie Brisson[1], Clauvice Kenfack[1,2], Serge Robert[1], Pamela Kissok[1], and Ange Tato[1]

[1] Université du Québec à Montréal, Montréal, Canada
{nkambou.roger, robert.serge}@uqam.ca
[2] University of Yaoundé, Yaoundé, Cameroun

Abstract. In this paper we present a participatory approach to design Logic-Muse, an Intelligent Tutoring System that helps learners develop reasoning skills in multiple contexts (situations). The study was conducted jointly with the active participation of experts in the field of logic and the psychology of reasoning. An explicit catalogue of systematic errors in classical logic is built, followed by an explicit representation and encoding of the semantic knowledge behind reasoning as well as reasoning procedural structures and meta-structures. Logic-Muse innovates through its design rationale, which leads to strong structures on which learning is based. It also innovates with the projection of reasoning skills in a variety of well-defined classes of situations to ensure an absolute mastery of reasoning skills regardless of the content effect.

Keywords: Intelligent tutoring system · Reasoning skills · Formal logic learning

1 Introduction

Many experiments in cognitive science have shown that systematic errors are common in human logical reasoning [5]. A number of questions are raised when looking for solutions to improve human skills in this domain: What are the phenomena involved in learning logical reasoning skills? Does modeling allow to elicit them? What are the adaptive strategies to foster the development of logical competence? What are the characteristics of an Intelligent Tutoring System (ITS) to support this learning?

Answers cannot be brought to these questions without an appropriate elicitation and understanding of the knowledge behind logical reasoning and errors made by humans. Logic-Muse project aims at studying the fundamentals of learning logical reasoning skills, to understand the difficulties in such learning and to build an ITS that can detect, diagnose and correct reasoning errors in various situations. To do so, we have adopted a participatory design approach aiming at: (1) providing a catalog of current logical reasoning errors; (2) developing an original theory of the causes of these errors including a logical reasoning competence theory; (3) analyzing the formal structures of information processing we find in logical systems; (4) developing an intelligent tutoring system for helping learners improve their reasoning skills and (5) helping

© Springer International Publishing Switzerland 2015
G. Conole et al. (Eds.): EC-TEL 2015, LNCS 9307, pp. 460–466, 2015.
DOI: 10.1007/978-3-319-24258-3_40

experts to redefine the nature of human rationality using the ITS as a test bed for the testing of other assumptions in the cognitive science of reasoning.

This paper describes some results of this unique approach. It is organized as follow: Sect. 2 presents the theoretical background of our work, which highlights the main differences with some related works. Section 3 describes the system as well as the approach that leads to its main building blocks.

2 Logical Reasoning and Intelligent Tutoring Systems

Multiple Standpoints on Reasoning Learning. The theoretical standpoint used in the development of Logic-Muse is correctionist in the sense that learning to reason is learning to correct creative inferences, so that our deductive skills improve [10]. Integrating an explicit catalog of reasoning errors and developing effective services to detect and address errors patterns in learner reasoning is our way to support this standpoint. Moreover, dual processes of inference [4, 7] is another standpoint of Logic-Muse. To become logically more competent, one needs to recognize errors generated by type 1 processes (rapid, implicit, unconscious, independent of working memory) and to learn how to inhibit them. However, inhibition of type 1 processes isn't sufficient to reason logically. Because of their high cognitive cost, type 2 processes (low, conscious, explicit, dependent of working memory) are also prone to errors. Thus, reasoners must learn how to use them properly, which requires time, practice and effort. This view is close to the thesis in education which defines the learning of a science, like physics, as an inhibition of naive physics, in order to allow the construction of a sophisticated one. This also highlights the adaptive character of logical competence. Our primary focus in respect with this standpoint is the detection and improvement of type 2 processes that lead to logical reasoning.

Need of Technological Support. Our goal is to bring together the latest developments in the field of ITS, Cognitive Science and AI to build an expert reasoner able to help students improve their reasoning skills. ITSs aim at providing every student with an individual and adaptable tutor, and to rely on cognitive diagnosis to determine specific learner' needs. Although many ITSs have been developed since the early 70 s, few dealt with logic as a learning domain [1, 9, 12], and they are limited in terms of strong semantic grounding in explicit reasoning knowledge structures and lack of metacognitive support in reasoning skills learning. Some eLearning tutorials also exist (e.g. Logic Learning Tools, Logic Tutor and Power of Logic Web Tutor) but fail to explicitly encode the reasoning knowledge. None of these systems addresses some key issues such as the dual processes of inferences or the correctionist theory of reasoning learning.

3 Participatory Design of Logic-Muse

Logic-Muse's architecture looks like a classical ITS including the three usual components: the logic expert, the learner model and the tutor. The learning environment includes a database of reasoning problems in six types of situations (or contexts).

3.1 Participatory Building of Logic-Muse Expert of Propositional Reasoning

Logic-Muse expert module implements logical reasoning skills and knowledge as well as related reasoning mechanisms (syntaxic and semantic rules of the given logical system). In fact, because we plan to cover several logical systems, Logic-Muse has a general controller component which goal is to select the most relevant logic in which the situation (current problem statement) fits. This is done thanks to meta-knowledge that the system uses to find some patterns (markers of each logic system provided by the experts) in the situation which represents good prediction of the need expressivity degree, leading to the selection of the appropriate logic system. In this paper, we focus only on one logic system (the propositional logic).

Specifying Propositional Logic Semantics and Procedural Memories. The participatory design of each component of the expert module was carefully carried out in the team. First, we studied the propositional logic domain and came up with a thorough specification of all concepts related to it, which led to a domain ontology that we implemented as a OWL model. The formal ontology was then validated in another round with the logicians.

The team then went through the elicitation process of procedural knowledge which led to the specification of all logical inference rules in propositional logic including valid and non-valid rules. Logicians suggested to consider four possible inferences for three logical connectives, namely the conditional, the disjunction and the incompatibility connectives. The reason is that, they are the ones that lead to two valid and two invalid inferences. Since humans have great difficulties in recognizing the uncertainty of an invalid conclusion, these inferences are the most challenging ones. Other connectives, like the conjunction, lead to four valid and more obvious inferences. All inference rules were explicitly encoded with JESS (Table 1).

Error diagnosis and tutoring strategies (in response to leaner's reasoning error) are based on recommendations came out from thorough discussions involving a logician expert with 40 years logic teaching experience and a reasoning psychologist.

Multiple Reasoning Situations. Reasoning is not an absolute process. Many studies have shown that reasoners give different conclusions for formally identical inferences that only differ in premise content [3, 8]. Our experts identified four main classes of reasoning situations, which gradually increase in difficulty, given the nature of the content: Concrete, Contrary-to-fact, Abstract Informal and Abstract Formal. The Concrete and Contrary-to-fact classes were refined into two sub-classes (e.g. *Concrete with Many Alternatives* (CMA); *Concrete with Few Alternatives* (CFA), *Contrary-to-fact with Many Alternatives* (CFMA), *Contrary-to-fact with Few Alternatives* (CFFA). This refinement is based on empirical findings in reasoning psychology [6]. In fact, one can clearly be evaluated as skilled in a CMA content but fails to be in CFA. This claim is supported by the results of many studies carried out by our team members [2]. The reasoning situation categorization provides not only a framework for classifying reasoning skills, but also a way to organize reasoning learning activities.

Table 1. Examples of valid and invalid inferences

Conditional inference	
Valid	JESS rule
Major premise: *If I throw a rock in a window, then it will break.*	defrule MTTvalid
	"Modus tolendo tollens $((P \supset Q) \,\&\, \sim Q) \supset \sim P$."
	?problem < - (Problemes (operateur ?op) (consequent ?q) (antecedent ?p) (information ?o ?q))
Minor premise: *The window is not broken*	(test (eq ?op "Implication"))
	(test (eq ?o "not"))
Conclusion: *I didn't trow a rok*	=>
	(modify ?problem (conclusion ?o ?p))
Disjunctive inference	
Invalid	JESS rule
Major premise: *I choose soup or I choose salad.*	defrule MPTinvalid $((P \vee Q) \,\&\, Q) \supset \sim P$
	?problem < - (Problemes (operateur ?op) (consequent ?q) (antecedent ?p) (information ?q) (conclusion "not" ?p))
Minor premise: *I choose salad.*	?reponse < - (Reponse (reponse ?x))
	(test (eq ?op "Ou"))
Conclusion: *I don't choose soup.*	=>
	(modify ?reponse (reponse "invalid") (mode "MPT") (conclusion "")))

3.2 The Learner Model

The learner model has several dimensions. The episodic memory keeps track of all the exercises performed by the learner. The cognitive model basically represents the state of the learner's knowledge (mastery of the reasoning skills in each of the six reasoning situations). It is a Bayesian network built from the domain knowledge, where influence relationships between nodes (reasoning skills) as well as prior probabilities are provided by the experts [11]. The nodes are directly connected to the reasoning activities (items) selected for the learner.

The Bayesian network represents a cognitive state for the reasoning skills with conditional probabilities. The skills are those pointed out by mental models theory in order to reason in conformity to the logical rules, namely the inhibition of exceptions to the premises, the generation of counterexamples to the conclusion and the ability to manage all the relevant models for the concrete, contrary to fact, abstract informal and abstract formal situations. The items nodes (bottom of the structure) represent inferences about each of the logical rules in each of the reasoning situations.

Statistics regarding learner performance on items are estimated using the episodic memory that contains the learning traces. Furthermore, A CDM-Based psychometric model is built using the item bank, a Q-Matrix (items/skills), as well as data related to all student responses on items. The Q-Matrix connects items categories to the involved skills. The resulting model is part of the learner model and allows for initial predictions about the learner strengths and weaknesses regarding reasoning skills given his/her performance on items (pretest).

3.3 Tutoring Feedback

The main goal in Logic-Muse is to help the learner to become a better logical reasoner in several situations. Logic-Muse Tutor should diagnose the learner reasoning mental model to detect reasoning errors and to help him to correct it. To do this, together with the experts, we specified the tutor interventions when errors are detected and the way the tutor will help to correct it. For instance, in a simple syllogism problem in causal concrete situation with many alternatives (CMA content), if the learner decides not to conclude, the system should check if this is because he or she didn't considered other possible alternatives of the subject mentioned in the premises. Then, the tutor can ask for the reason of that inference suppression. If it appears that it is clearly due to that fact, the tutor will tackle the learner by making him/her aware about the existence of other alternatives that can hold (see an example of tutor's intervention in Fig. 1). The experts describes an intervention rule for each possible error in respect to the situation in which the reasoning is carrying out. Furthermore, one of our goals was to set up some metacognitive support to the learner. We carefully examine logical meta-structures and analyse how they could be used to provide visual feedback to the learner so that he or she is aware about his/her own reasoning errors.

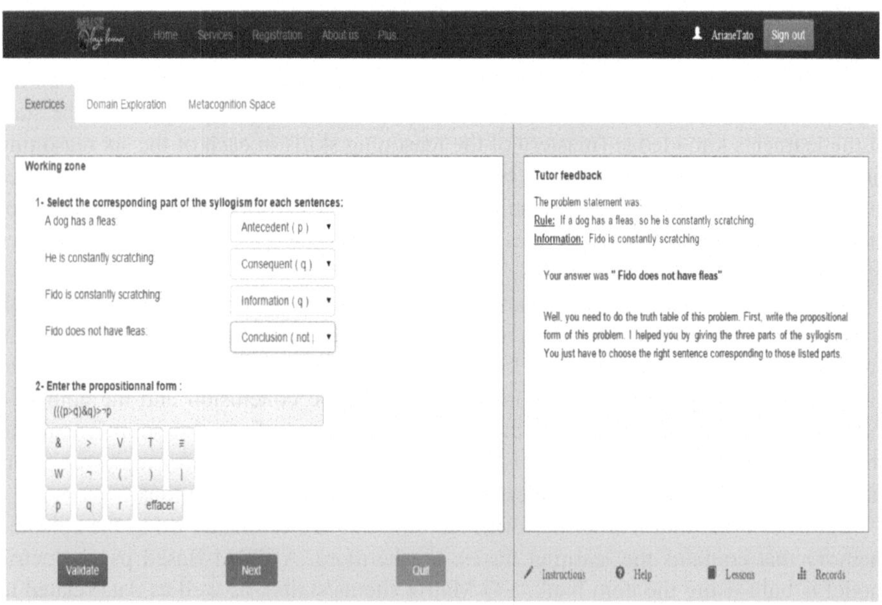

Fig. 1. Logic-muse reasoning service

3.4 Logic-Muse Main Services

Logic-Muse provides three levels of learning activity to the learner organized into services: (1) Domain exploration service using the domain ontology encoded in OWL; (2) General exercises on basic logic concepts including logic formula conversion, well-formed formulas (wff) checking, truth table building, etc. and Reasoning procedural learning service (e.g. syllogism and polysyllogism problem solving); (3) Metacognitive reasoning (logical meta-structure exploration).

Logic-Muse is a responsive Web-based application implemented using Bootstrap. Domain rules (logical rules) are encoded in the expert component with JESS (Rule Engine for the Java platform) as well as the pedagogical rules used by the tutor component. The Bayesian network was implemented in the student model and is initialized thanks to some parameters provided by the CDM component after a new learner took a pre-test.

4 Conclusion

The Logic-Muse development is a multidisciplinary initiative which enabled us to enroll in a perspective of participatory design that has led to a set of valid components of logical reasoning implemented within an ITS. This paper was intended to share this unique experience with the reader. We have presented the elements that led us to propose such a system. We also presented the process undertaken to define and explain the reference components we have used in Logic-Muse. We have presented an overview of the system modules, which provide a number of relevant services for logical reasoning learning. The system has been implemented for propositional logic with a fully functional and valid (internal) Expert module (which demonstrates all valid reasoning skills and detects and explains reasoning errors), plus a Tutor that helps learners in various reasoning situations.

The next step is the external evaluation of this first version of Logic-Muse in a logic course offered to first year students at the University of Quebec in Montreal. This experiment will enable us to collect data in order to better assess the add-value of the system in terms of learning gains. We will then proceed in the same way with the integration of other logics by extending the current propositional reasoning system in order to reach a Logic-Muse ITS capable of selecting the best logical system relevant to the reasoning situation at hand.

Acknowledgement. We would like to thank all Logic-Muse team members (J. Bourdeau, M. Bélanger, A, Cloutier, J-B Plouhinec, H. Markovits and M. Sainte-Marie) for their contribution to this work.

References

1. Barnes, T., Stamper, J.: Automatic hint generation for logic proof tutoring using historical data. Educ. Technol. Soc. **13**(1), 3–12 (2010)

2. Brisson, J., de Chantal, P.-L., Lortie-Forgues, H., Markovits, H.: Belief bias is stronger when reasoning is more difficult. Think. Reasoning **20**(3), 385–403 (2014)
3. Cummins, D.D., Lubart, T., Alksnis, O., Rist, R.: Conditional reasoning and causation. Mem. Cogn. **19**(3), 274–282 (1991)
4. Evans, J.S.B.: On the resolution of conflict in dual process theories of reasoning. Think. Reason. **13**, 321–339 (2007)
5. Evans, J.S.B.T., Newstead, S.E., Byrne, R.M.J.: Human Reasoning. Lawrence Erlbaum Publishers, Hove (1993)
6. Markovits, H.: On the road toward formal reasoning: reasoning with factual causal and contrary-to-fact causal premises during early adolescence. J. Exp. Child Psychol. **128**, 37–51 (2014)
7. Stanovich, K.E.: Rationality and the Reflexive Mind. Oxford University Press, Oxford (2011)
8. Thompson, V.A.: Conditional reasoning: the necessary and sufficient conditions. Can. J. Exp. Psychol. **49**(1), 1–60 (1995)
9. Lesta, L., Yacef, K.: An intelligent teaching assistant system for logic. In: Cerri, S.A., Gouardéres, G., Paraguaçu, F. (eds.) ITS 2002. LNCS, vol. 2363, pp. 421–431. Springer, Heidelberg (2002)
10. Robert, S.: Logique de la découverte et naturalisation de la connaissance: L'épistémologie historique d'Imre Lakatos. Presses de l'Université Laval, Québec (2009)
11. Tchétagni, J.M., Nkambou, R.: Hierarchical representation and evaluation of the student in an intelligent tutoring system. In: Cerri, S.A., Gouardéres, G., Paraguaçu, F. (eds.) ITS 2002. LNCS, vol. 2363, pp. 708–717. Springer, Heidelberg (2002)
12. Tchetagni, J., Nkambou, R., Bourdeau, J.: Explicit reflection in prolog-tutor. Int. J. Artif. Intell. Educ. **17**(2), 169–217 (2007)

The Value of Self-tracking and the Added Value of Coaching in the Case of Improving Time Management

Viktoria Pammer[1(✉)], Marina Bratic[2], Sandra Feyertag[2], and Nils Faltin[3]

[1] Knowledge Technologies Institute, Graz University of Technology, Graz, Austria
viktoria.pammer@tugraz.at
[2] Know-Center, Graz, Austria
[3] IMC AG, Saarbrücken, Germany

Abstract. We report two 6-week studies, each with 10 participants, on improving time management. In each study a different interventions was administered, in parallel to otherwise regular work: In the self-tracking setting, participants used only an activity logging tool to track their time use and a reflective practice, namely daily review of time use, to improve time management. In the coaching setting, participants did the same, but additionally received weekly bilateral coaching. In both settings, participants reported learning about time management. This is encouraging, as such self-directed learning is clearly cheaper than coaching. Only participants in the coaching setting however improved their self-assessment with respect to predefined time management best practices.

Keywords: Time management · Workplace learning · Activity logging · Time tracking · Self-tracking · Personal informatics · Quantified self · Coaching

1 Introduction

The ability to self-manage time is one of the key challenges for knowledge workers [e.g., 21]. Time management (TM) means activities like assessing, planning and monitoring time use with the goal to organize time use in a productive and healthy manner [e.g., 5]. Commercial activity logging tools like ManicTime, RescueTime or SLife already claim to support time management. Scientifically however, the usefulness of activity logging tools for (learning about in the sense of improving) time management is surprisingly unexplored. Automatic activity logging has often been used to measure the behavior of study subjects, investigating for instance the cost of task interruption [4] or work patterns dependent on daytime, weekday or location [1]. Only more recently, time-stamped data have been investigated also as means to support time management. The authors of [7] explored which visualizations and analyses of calendar data would be helpful for time management (21 participants). In study described in [12], we found that people were consistently surprised about their actual time use as automatically logged, in particular about the extent of work time fragmentation (7 participants). In both settings, participants were looking not only for insights on data, but for "actionable analytics", i.e. analyses and interpretations of data that would help them decide on future behavior.

© Springer International Publishing Switzerland 2015
G. Conole et al. (Eds.): EC-TEL 2015, LNCS 9307, pp. 467–472, 2015.
DOI: 10.1007/978-3-319-24258-3_41

Activity logging as computer support for time management is related to the wider research on personal informatics and quantified self. Under these names [3, 9, 10] people measure (quantify) their own behavior. Popular areas of interest are behavioral patterns related to health or sustainable living, and typical goals are to gain insights and to change (improve) the behavior under scrutiny [3, 10]. Manually or automatically created activity logs in this context serve the purpose to provide a data basis beyond memory for re-evaluating experiences [3, 8–10]. Such reconstruction and re-evaluation with the goal to learn for the future can then be understood as reflective practice, where learning could mean new insights, change in behavior as well as a change in perception (e.g., [2, 13]).

2 User Study

2.1 Method

We conducted two field studies of 6 weeks each. Each was designed to show the effects of an intervention with respect to improving time management.

The studies took place in two companies with similar characteristics: Both are medium-sized IT consulting and development companies in Germany. The intervention was different though in each company. At one company, only self-tracking was used (ST-setting), while in the other, additional coaching was provided (C-setting). Note that both studies took place in parallel to otherwise regular work.

All participants (i.e. in both settings) were instructed to have an activity logging tool (AL tool) running in the background throughout the study and to manually label time whenever they found this useful (self-tracking). The used AL tools were KnowSelf[1] (used by all participants in the ST setting, and half of participants in the C-setting) and ManicTime[2] (used by half of participants in the C-setting). Participants were further instructed to review their time use in the AL tool daily and to write down insights and plans for change (reflective practice). The suggested daily time was ten minutes at most for the reflective practice. In the self-tracking setting (ST-setting), participants received no further information or instruction with respect to time management.

In the coaching setting (C-setting), participants received bilateral coaching in addition. All participants in the C-setting had a weekly 1-hour bilateral coaching meeting with the same coach for everyone. The overall goal of coaching was predefined: Coaching was intended to support the improvement of time management. The coaching was paid for by the company.

2.2 Evaluation Tools

TM skills and behavior were measured with a 12-item scale (TM scale - by Hansen, taken from [14]). The TM scale asks for compliance with typical time management

1 http://www.know-center.tugraz.at/en/knowself/.
2 http://www.manictime.com/.

practices. Additionally, we asked for gained insights (learning), changes in TM and the perceived benefit of AL tools on a 17-item scale (TM Learning and Change). Example items are "*I gained a deeper understanding of my TM behavior*" or "*I made a conscious decision to change my behavior*". Measurements were self-assessments before and after the study with both open and closed items (5-point Likert scales: 1 = strongly disagree; 5 = strongly agree). Bilateral interviews were conducted after the study with all 20 participants plus the coach from the C-setting.

2.3 Participants

All participants were volunteers. Overall, 20 study participants completed the study (2 drop-outs in the ST setting filled only the pre-questionnaire). 5 participants were female, 15 male. One was younger than 19, eight were aged between 20 and 29, ten between 30 and 39, and three between 40 and 49. At the time of the study a majority of study participants were employed full-time in their respective company (19 out of 20). A majority of participants were experienced and skilled knowledge workers, in terms of their job description (18 out of 20). These were team managers or experts required to essentially work on their own towards a specified goal; typically they would be given only a project or a customer and the overall goal such as "*to acquire a new contract with a potential customer*" or "*to implement a strategy for a customer*".

3 Results

Questionnaire and interview data were analyzed with respect to learning and behavior change, as well as with respect to the contribution of activity logging tools.

In both settings, participants were positive that **learning in terms of gaining insights with regard to TM had occurred**. There was no statistically significant difference between the ST-setting and the C-setting in any item related to learning (TM Learning and Behavior scale).

There was a single item in the TM Learning and Change scale that showed a significant, namely "I made a conscious decision to change my TM behavior" (independent samples t-test $t(18) = 2.52$ $p = 0.022$). Participants of the ST-setting reported significantly lower values for this conscious decision to change ($M = 3.3$; $SD = 1.059$) than participants in the C-setting ($M = 4.3$; $SD = 0.675$).

Additionally, we had measured compliance with TM best practices before and after the study with the TM scale (see Table 1). At the beginning of the study, participants in the ST-setting rated their TM skills and behavior significantly better than participants in the C-setting (independent samples t-test: $t(18) = 2.32$, $p = 0.032$). However, **participants in the C-setting reported significant improvements over time** (repeated measures t-test: $t(9) = 3.4$, $p = 0.007$), **while participants in the ST-setting reported essentially no changes**. A mixed-design ANOVA (within subjects: pre/post; between subjects: ST-setting/C-setting) shows as interaction effect $F(1,18) = 4.34$, $p = 0.0518$, $\eta_p^2 = 0.194$. This closely misses the $p < 0.05$ level of significance, but shows a large effect size despite a relatively small number of participants. We therefore assume the different patterns of change originate in the different interventions given to the two groups (self-tracking vs. coaching).

The **usefulness of activity logging** (automatic plus manual labeling) was stated to lie in **providing accurate information about time use with very little extra effort** (manual recording tasks if necessary/required) by six participants in the self-tracking setting (out of 7 interviewed) and seven in the coaching setting. This is in line with the key claim underlying research in the quantified self and personal informatics community.

In both settings, participants missed peer support. While participants were of course free to discuss their TM efforts with colleagues informally (in each study, all participants knew of each other), we had not instructed participants to do so, and neither AL tool had social software features like sharing and comparing one's data with peer's data, messaging, or discussion forums. One participant in the ST-setting, for example, suggested some sort of sharing one's plans and progress for improving TM in order to make visible to others whether "*you are holding up your part of the deal or not*". Note that we did not specifically ask about social software features but rather generically inquired about what had been missed, what could be improved, etc.

4 Discussion and Conclusion

4.1 Limitations of Study Methodology

The two studies we compare within this paper are field studies – they are by nature more messy than lab studies. In an endeavor to allow readers to judge for themselves on the validity of results, we discuss the shortcomings of our methodology.

Firstly, we are reasonably sure about the quality of interventions in relation to typical similar interventions: The activity logging tools did not differ significantly in terms of used evaluation tools. However, the study is not a comparative study of two different tools. A second point of critique could be that only subjective data about time management behaviour are available. Although KnowSelf would have allowed us to collect anonymised data about work activities (only application names and timestamps in clear-text; file names and full-text like note would have been hashed), most study participants did not share their data with us. Finally, we used the two studies in this work also in a comparative manner (mixed-design ANOVA). We did this, because the two companies are comparable with respect to the kind of work (IT consulting and development) and the culture (both in the same area in Germany). Differences found between the two settings (ST-setting, C-setting) could therefore come not only in the different intervention but also in the different organizational culture.

4.2 Insights

The value of self-tracking lies in gaining self knowledge: Participants in both studies gained insights on their personal time management, decided on and implemented reasonable changes in their time management strategies with no significant difference between the two settings. Mentioned TM strategies were for instance "saying no", "planning more time buffers", "create priorities for tasks" or "focus on priorities" (translated quotes from German). This result is interesting and relevant, as it confirms what marketing of commercial time tracking tools already claims, i.e. they support time. This result is also novel, as nothing similar is to date available in literature on improving time management aided by activity logging tools. In addition, this result supports the assumption and claim of the quantified self and personal informatics community, namely that self-tracking can indeed foster learning and ultimately behavior change. This result also indicates that there might be quite enough to gain from the cheaper solution of self-directed learning aided with self-tracking when compared to the definitely more expensive solution of paying a coach to give additional support.

The added value of coaching lies in supporting behavior change: Participants in the C-setting decided on changing their behavior more consciously than participants in the ST-setting and rated their compliance with predefined TM best practices (TM scale) significantly better after the intervention study, while participants in the ST-setting essentially did not change their respective self-assessment. As underlying mechanisms we draw out the following from background literature and qualitative data (from interviews): Firstly, interpretation of activity logging data requires background knowledge, in our case of time management. In the C-setting the participants were supported in this task by the coach, in particular via explicitly setting goals, and experimenting with concrete solution approaches. Indeed, self-tracking approaches often experience data interpretation as a key hurdle [3, 9]. This has also been expressed as design challenge for software to provide actionable knowledge (see [4, 13] in the case of time management). Secondly, there is a social norm to keep promises. The underlying psychological mechanism is emotional commitment and/or guilt aversion (which it is, is under discussion [5, 6]). In the C-setting, the participants had agreed with the coach to review their time use and achievement of goals on a daily basis, as well as to spend significant time reflecting on their progress in the weekly coaching meeting.

Social software features to the rescue: Social software features in activity logging tools for improving time management could address the latter, in that they could provide a platform for making "promises". In addition, they could provide the means to identify systemic time management issues within an organization.

Acknowledgements. This work was partially funded under the FP7 of the European Commission (project number 257617). The Know-Center is funded within the Austrian COMET Program - Competence Centers for Excellent Technologies - under the auspices of the Austrian Federal Ministry of Transport, Innovation and Technology, the Austrian Federal Ministry of Economy, Family and Youth and by the State of Styria. COMET is managed by the Austrian Research Promotion Agency FFG.

References

1. Begole, J.B., Tang, J.C., Smith, R.B., Yankelovich, N.: Work rhythms: analyzing visualizations of awareness histories of distributed groups. In: Proceedings of CSCW 2002, pp. 334–343. ACM
2. Boud, D., et al.: Reflection: Turning Experience into Learning. Kogan Page, London (1985)
3. Choe, E.K., Lee, N.B., Lee, B., Pratt, W., Kientz, J.A.: Understanding quantified-selfers' practices in collecting and exploring personal data. In: Proceedings of SIGCHI 2014, pp. 1143–1152. ACM
4. Dugan, C., Geyer, W., Muller, M., Valente, A.N., James, K., Levy, S., Cheng, L.-T., Daly, E., Brownholtz, B.: "I'd never get out of this !?% office": redesigning time management for the enterprise. In: Proceedings of SIGCHI 2012, pp. 1755–1764. ACM (2012)
5. Dufwenberg, M., Gneezy, U.: Measuring beliefs in an experimental lost wallet game. Games Econ. Behav. **30**(2), 163–182 (2000)
6. Ellingsen, T., Johannesson, M.: Promises, threats and fairness*. Econ. J. **114**, 397–420 (2004)
7. Iqbal, S.T., Horvitz, E.: Disruption and recovery of computing tasks: field study, analysis, and directions. In: Proceedings of SIGCHI 2007, pp. 677–686. ACM
8. Krogstie, B., Prilla, M., Knipfer, K., Wessl, D., Pammer, V.: Computer support for reflective learning in the workplace: a model. In: Proceedings of ICALT 2012, pp. 151–153
9. Li, I., Dey, A., Forlizzi, J.: A stage-based model of personal informatics systems. In: Proceedings of SIGCHI 2010, pp. 557–566. ACM
10. Li, I., Dey, A., Forlizzi, J.: Understanding my data, myself: supporting self-reflection with ubicomp technologies. In: Proceedings of UbiComp 2011, pp. 405–414. ACM
11. Mackenzie, A., Nickerson, P.: The Time Trap: The Classic Book on Time Management. AMACOM, New York (2009)
12. Pammer, V., Bratic, M.: Surprise, surprise: activity log based time analytics for time management. In: CHI Extended Abstracts 2013, pp. 211–216. ACM
13. Schön, D.: The Reflective Practitioner. Basic Books Inc., New York (1983)
14. Seiwert, L.J.: Das neue 1×1 des Zeitmanagement. Gräfe und Unzer, München (2005)

Screen or Tabletop: An Eye-Tracking Study of the Effect of Representation Location in a Tangible User Interface System

Mina Shirvani Boroujeni(✉), Sébastien Cuendet, Lorenzo Lucignano, Beat Adrian Schwendimann, and Pierre Dillenbourg

CHILI, École polytechnique fédérale de Lausanne, Lausanne, Switzerland
{mina.shirvaniboroujeni,lorenzo.lucignano,beat.schwendimann, pierre.dillenbourg}@epfl.ch, sebastien.cuendet@gmail.com

Abstract. This article presents a comparison of the effects of input-output location (co-located versus discrete) on user performance in a tangible user interface (TUI) system. We conducted a mobile eye-tracking study with two different versions of a TUI system and, despite similar performances in both conditions, our findings revealed differences in the users gaze patterns, shedding new light on the underlying cognitive processes.

Keywords: Tangible interface · Eye-tracking · Representation location

1 Introduction

The potential benefits of tangible user interfaces (TUIs) and the related new possibilities for the design of learning experiences drew the attention of HCI and education research communities in recent years [12]. Training spatial skills is one of the areas in which TUIs are shown to be effective and this could be explained by the physicality of the tools towards the development of mental models [2]. TapaCarp Fig. 1a is a recent augmented tabletop system developed by Cuendet for improving spatial skills [1]. However, the high hardware and maintenance costs of TapaCarp prevent widespread application by educational institutes. To reduce the costs, the author developed a web-based version, named eTapaCarp, which does not rely on any dedicated hardware components but uses off-the-shelf web-cams. As a consequence, in eTapaCarp the digital feedback is not co-located within the manipulation space, but it is represented on a discrete plane (i.e. a monitor, Fig. 1a and b).

The goal of this user study is to discern the differences in user performances and gaze patterns brought by the design of the two systems, identifying to what extent it affects the users experience with TUI systems.

2 Related Work

Price and colleagues [9] provided a comprehensive framework to classify TUIs, which features the location of input and output as a discriminative parameter.

© Springer International Publishing Switzerland 2015
G. Conole et al. (Eds.): EC-TEL 2015, LNCS 9307, pp. 473–478, 2015.
DOI: 10.1007/978-3-319-24258-3_42

It refers to the relative spatial positioning of physical and digital components of the system. Three modalities have been proposed for location: discrete, co-located, or embedded. Location can impact attention demands [5], potential for representing multiple levels of abstraction [8], as well as the collaborative group working [10]. The investigation of those aspects of designing TUIs has rarely exploited the eye-tracking methodology, although it has been successfully employed in interaction and usability research [7]. Recently, authors in [4] have used eye-tracking data to compare the user experience in a TUI environment and GUI counterpart. Results of this study suggest some cognitive advantages in using TUIs as the gaze values in the tangible condition indicated less demanding mental efforts. In [11], Schneider and colleagues reported how the use of eye-tracker data could reveal some information regarding the underlying mental processes of the user while performing a task. Those works encouraged us to investigate the effect of location from the novel perspective of gaze behaviors.

3 Experimental Setup

The experimental setup distinguished two conditions: discrete (eTapaCarp) and co-located (TapaCarp) displays. We will refer to these two conditions by the system titles. TapaCarp (Fig. 1a) is a tabletop user interface system. Users interact with the system through manipulating small wooden blocks equipped with fiducial markers. The system dynamically projects the three orthographic projections (*top*, *front* and *side* views) of the blocks on the tabletop. In eTapaCarp (Fig. 1b), users manipulate the objects in the horizontal workspace and see the feedback on an external vertical screen.

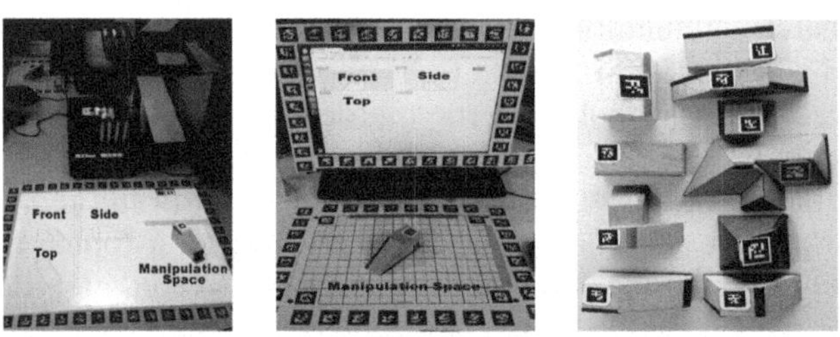

(a) TapaCarp (b) eTapaCarp (c) Blocks set

Fig. 1. Experimental setup

Research Questions: There are two main research questions we address in this paper. Q_1: *"Does the separation of input and output spaces in eTapaCarp affect the user performance?"* Our initial hypothesis is that this design choice in eTapaCarp could lead to a split of attention, which in turn might affect the task performance, for example by lowering the accuracy or interaction speed. Q_2: *"Does the eye gaze data provide insight into differences of representational* *location and user interaction?*" Previous works such as [2,3] often came short explaining the observed differences, whereas the use of eye-tracker data might enable us to go a step further into understanding how users are thinking.

Task: The experimental task was a set of 10 edge finding questions. In an edge finding question, three edges are highlighted using colored tapes on the physical block (Fig. 1c). The user is given the task of identifying and selecting the corresponding edges on each of the three orthographic projections. The edge selection is performed by a mouse click.

Participants: A total of 18 university students (16 men, 2 women) from the 2nd and 4th academic year in Mechanical Engineering and Microtechnique sections participated in the experiment. Their average age was 21.4 years and 9 participants were randomly assigned to each of the two conditions.

Procedure: The experiment was composed of two parts: (1) A pretest on spatial skills, consisting of a mental rotation and a paper folding task [6] with a time limit of 3 min for each test, (2) the set of 10 edge finding questions, performed on TapaCarp or eTapaCarp, depending on the condition. There was no time limit for completing this part and participants gaze data was collected employing SMI Eye-Tracking Glasses with binocular pupil tracking at 30 Hz.

4 Results

The statistical tests were made using ANOVAs on linear models. Repetitions were taken into account using mixed effect models when needed. For the eye-tracking data analysis, the workspace is divided into four areas of interest (AOIs) corresponding to the physical block (*object*) and the three orthographic views. The unit for the eye tracking analysis is the dwell, defined as one visit in an AOI from entry to exit.

Pretest Scores: The 18 participants got an average score of 73.61 % (SD: 24.63 %) in the mental rotation test and 85.55 % (SD: 12.47 %) in the paper folding test. According to the literature [1], these scores indicate well-developed spatial reasoning skills.

Activity Duration: The average time to complete all the edge finding questions was 9.5 min (SD: 3.12 min). Comparing the two conditions, in eTapaCarp completion of all questions took slightly less time than in TapaCarp (8.6 min vs. 10.3). However this difference was not statistically significant ($F[1,16]=1.40$, $p > .1$).

Performance Accuracy: Participants on average completed 8.11 (SD: 1.97) out of 10 questions with no mistake in any of the views. Analysis of the number of correctly answered questions in the two conditions reveals no significant difference (8.33 in TapaCarp vs. 7.89 in eTapaCarp, $F[1,16]=0.22$, $p=.65$). The total number of mistakes (missing or excess edges) made by each user was also not significantly different between the two conditions (around 7.15 mistakes, over

90 edges to be found in total, in both conditions). In general, most mistakes occurred in the *side* view (4.3 in TapaCarp and 5.11 in eTapaCarp) and the number of mistakes in *front* and especially *top* view were relatively low.

Strategy: All participants in the experiment preferred to find all edges in one view before switching to next view, which we call a "group-by-view" strategy. Most of the participants adopted this strategy starting from the first question, but 4 in TapaCarp and 3 in eTapaCarp started with a "group-by-edge" strategy and after one or two questions, they also switched to group-by-view since they found their initial approach quite confusing. The most common order for completing the views was *front*, *side* and *top* which can be related to the positioning of the views in the output plane, where the *front* view is in the top-left area.

Dwell Percentage, Duration and Revisit Time: As depicted in Fig. 2, in both systems the largest proportion of dwells was related to the physical block (42 % in TapaCarp and 34 % in eTapaCarp), and the smallest to the *top* view (12 % in TapaCarp and 19 % in eTapaCarp). In TapaCarp the percentage of dwells on the physical block was higher than eTapaCarp (marginally significant $F[1,16]=4.04$, $p<.06$), while in TapaCarp dwells on the *top* view were significantly lower in proportion ($F[1,16]=38.41$, $p<.0001$). For the other two AOIs (*front* and *side* views), participants in both conditions had quite equal dwell ratios. Moreover, TapaCarp participants showed shorter dwell duration ($F[1,16]=14.41$, $p=.001$), especially on the *side* view for which the average dwell duration was significantly smaller than eTapaCarp ($F[1,16]=21.68$, $p<.001$). The revisit times for each AOI, namely the time between two consecutive entries in an AOI, were shorter in TapaCarp condition ($F[1,16]=13.21$, $p=.002$). Moreover, there was a stronger significant difference between the revisit times on the *object* in the two conditions: the revisit time for the *object* in TapaCarp was shorter ($F[1,16]=15.11$, $p=.001$).

Gaze Transitions Among AOIs: According to Fig. 2, transitions among views and *object* were generally more prevalent in TapaCarp (except for *top* view) whereas transitions within the orthographic views were more frequent in eTapaCarp. However transitions in both graphs exhibit an *object* centric distribution. In TapaCarp transitions between *object* and 2D views account for around 85 % of total transitions and this value in eTapaCarp is around 70 % which are both considerably large proportions. Furthermore, transitions back and forth between *side* view and *object* were significantly higher in TapaCarp ($F[1,16]=4.96$, $p<0.5$), whereas the same value for the *top* view was significantly higher in eTapaCarp ($F[1,16]=10.36$, $p<.001$).

5 Discussion and Conclusion

Regarding our first research question (user performance), participants in both conditions performed equally well. Moreover, the absence of a significant difference in the task duration implies that there was no considerable time overhead imposed by the separation of input and output planes in eTapaCarp. Considering the task completion strategies, the group-by-view approach was preferred

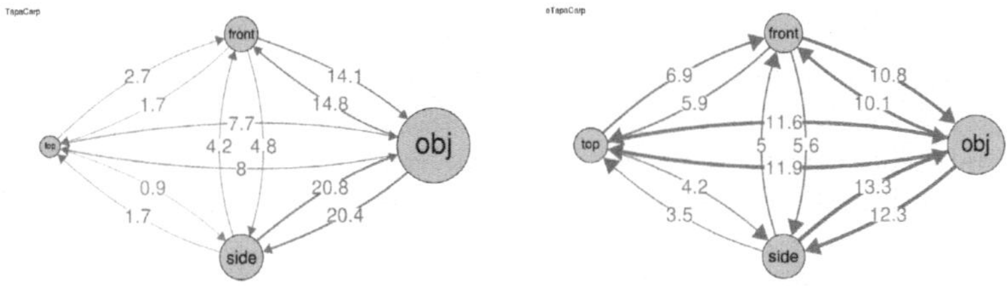

(a) TapaCarp (b) eTapaCarp

Fig. 2. Transition between AOIs: Nodes size are proportional to the average percentage of dwells on the AOIs, and edge labels indicate the average percentage of transitions among AOIs.

since the cognitive cost imposed by switching the views in the group-by-edge approach is higher than switching the edges in group-by-view strategy.

Regarding our second research question (can eye-tracking tell us more?), the eye-tracking data provided more insights about the completion strategies between the two conditions. In both conditions, *object* absorbed most of the dwells and the transition graphs showed the centrality of this area. This indicates that relating views with the physical blocks was preferred by the participants probably due to the ease of extracting spatial information from the 3D block as compared to the 2D representations. However, two main results characterized the two conditions: in Tapacarp, the short revisit time and the higher dwell proportion on the *object* suggest that the users referred more often to the physical block, frequently exploiting the scaffold provided by the external representation rather than referring to their mental model; in eTapaCarp, the lower percentage of transitions among views and block could be resulting from the separation of input and output planes which increases the cost of switching between the two parts of the interface. This resulted in mapping the orthographic view of interest to another orthographic projection in which the participant had already identified the edge and implies the use of a partially internalized mental model. Extracting information in this way requires more effort and this is probably the reason why participants in eTapacarp reported longer dwell duration. Another point coming from the transition analysis is the higher connectivity level between the *side* view and the *object* in TapaCarp, and between the *top* view and the block in eTapaCarp. A possible explanation for this can be the proximity effect. In TapaCarp the spatially closest view to the block zone is the *side* view, while in eTapaCarp it is the *front* view. According to the high ratio of references to the *object* and the relatively higher difficulty level of the *side* view, placing this view next to the block zone is a rational choice in the interface design of TapaCarp.

In conclusion, although this study presents some limitation due to the laboratory setting and a relatively small number of participants who belonged to a specific population, it contributes to the TUIs research providing design hints based on quantitative eye-tracking measurements, which provided a new insight on the problem and enabled us to go a step further in the explanation of the differences caused by the variation of output location. Despite the absence of significant differences in the performance measures between the two systems, co-located representation could be more appropriate for training low skilled users, thanks to the facilitation in accessing the physical 3D model and in linking it to the digital information; Discrete location discourages the reference to the tangible model, in favor of relying on the mental model. Consequently, splitting the input-output is more suitable for users with better developed visual-spatial abilities. Future researches is encouraged to explore deeply the impact of design choices and extend design rules for tangible interface and their applications in learning activities.

References

1. Cuendet, S.: Tangible interfaces for learning: training spatial skills in vocational classrooms. Ph.D. thesis, EPFL (2013)
2. Cuendet, S., Bumbacher, E., Dillenbourg, P.: Tangible vs. virtual representations: when tangibles benefit the training of spatial skills. In: Proceedings of the 7th Nordic Conference on Human-Computer Interaction: Making Sense Through Design, pp. 99–108. ACM (2012)
3. Cuendet, S., Jermann, P., Dillenbourg, P.: Tangible interfaces: when physical-virtual coupling may be detrimental to learning. In: Proceedings of the 26th Annual BCS Interaction Specialist Group Conference on People and Computers, pp. 49–58. British Computer Society (2012)
4. Lucignano, L., Cuendet, S., Schwendimann, B.A., Shirvani Boroujeni, M., Dehler, J., Dillenbourg, P.: My hands or my mouse: comparing a tangible and graphical user interface using eye-tracking data. In: Fablearn 2014. No. EPFL-CONF-204226 (2014)
5. Patten, J., Ishii, H., Hines, J., Pangaro, G.: Sensetable: a wireless object tracking platform for tangible user interfaces. In: Proceedings of the SIGCHI Conference on Human Factors in Computing Systems, pp. 253–260. ACM (2001)
6. Peters, M., Laeng, B., Latham, K., Jackson, M., Zaiyouna, R., Richardson, C.: A redrawn vandenberg and kuse mental rotations test-different versions and factors that affect performance. Brain Cogn. **28**(1), 39–58 (1995)
7. Poole, A., Ball, L.J.: Eye tracking in HCI and usability research. Encycl. Hum. Comput. Interact. **1**, 211–219 (2006)
8. Price, S., Falcão, T.P., Sheridan, J.G., Roussos, G.: The effect of representation location on interaction in a tangible learning environment. In: Proceedings of the 3rd International Conference on Tangible and Embedded Interaction, pp. 85–92. ACM (2009)
9. Price, S., Sheridan, J.G., Falcão, T.P., Roussos, G.: Towards a framework for investigating tangible environments for learning. Int. J. Arts Technol. **1**(3–4), 351–368 (2008)
10. Rogers, Y., Lindley, S.: Collaborating around vertical and horizontal large interactive displays: which way is best? Interact. Comput. **16**(6), 1133–1152 (2004)
11. Schneider, B., Sharma, K., Cuendet, S., Zufferey, G., Dillenbourg, P., Pea, A.D.: 3D tangibles facilitate joint visual attention in dyads. In: International Conference on Computer Supported Collaborative Learning (CSCL), pp. 158–165 (2015)
12. Shaer, O., Hornecker, E.: Tangible user interfaces: past, present, and future directions. Found. Trends Hum. Comput. Interact. **3**(1–2), 1–137 (2010)

Evolution of Interests in the Learning Context Data Model

Hendrik Thüs(✉), Mohamed Amine Chatti, Roman Brandt, and Ulrik Schroeder

Informatik 9 (Learning Technologies), RWTH Aachen University, Aachen, Germany
{thues,Chatti,schroeder}@cs.rwth-aachen.de,
roman.brandt@cs.rwth-aachen.de

Abstract. A key area of application for Learning Analytics (LA) and Educational Data Mining (EDM) is lifelong learner modeling. The aim is that data gathered from different learning environments would be fed into a personal lifelong learner model that can be used to foster personalized learning experiences. As learning is increasingly happening in open and networked environments beyond the classroom and access to knowledge in these environments is mostly context-sensitive and interest-driven, learner's contexts and interests need to constitute important features to be modeled. The context data of a learner as it is already represented by the Learning Context Data Model (LCDM) specification, describes the learner's activities, her biological conditions, as well as the characteristics of the learning environment. Towards a lifelong learner model, a model consisting of context data can further be refined with an evolving set of interests. This paper describes an approach to extend the existing LCDM specification with interests, taking into account the importance of the interests as well as their evolution over time.

Keywords: Interests · Mobile learning · Data model · Lifelong learner model · Open learner model

1 Introduction

Learning modeling is a crucial task in the emerging research areas of learning analytics (LA) and educational data mining (EDM) [5]. A learner model represents information about a learner's characteristics or states, such as knowledge, motivation, meta-cognition, and attitudes [1]. A learner model is also a representation of information about an individual learner that is essential for adaptation and personalization tasks [1]. A big challenge to tackle here is lifelong learner modeling. Kay and Kummerfeld [7] define a lifelong learner model as a store for the collection of learning data about an individual learner. They note that to be useful, a lifelong learner model should be able to hold many forms of learning data from diverse sources.

The six most popular and useful features in (lifelong) learner modeling include the learner's knowledge, interests, goals, background, individual traits, and context [2]. Context is a central topic of research in the area of learner modeling. The capacity to build a detailed picture of the learner across a broader learning context would provide

© Springer International Publishing Switzerland 2015
G. Conole et al. (Eds.): EC-TEL 2015, LNCS 9307, pp. 479–484, 2015.
DOI: 10.1007/978-3-319-24258-3_43

more effective personalized learning experiences. A context model should reflect a complete picture of the learner's context information [4].

In the frame of the Learning Context Project[1], we proposed the Learning Context Data Model (LCDM) specification as a possible standard representation of context data, thus enabling the interoperability and reusability of context models [10].

In addition to context, learner interests build another important aspect in learning modeling. As access to information in today's open and networked learning environments is mostly interest-driven, learner interests need to constitute an important learner feature to be modeled in order to help learners overcome the information overload problem. The capacity to mine learner's interests across different learning contexts would provide more effective personalized learning experiences for lifelong learners.

Recognizing the importance of the interest dimension in the learner modeling task, we implemented an extension of LCDM which is able to hold weighted interests of the learners towards a lifelong learner model.

2 Interest Modeling and Development

According to Krapp [8], an interest represents "a more or less enduring specific relationship between a person and an object in his or her life-space". An object of interest can be any type of content like a certain topic, an abstract idea, or a concrete object which is somehow connected with the person's life-space. A learner may have multiple interests at the same time but at each point in time, she can only have a deeper interest in some of those objects, topics or activities. Such a closer relationship may last over a longer period of time and can be seen as a consolidated interest of the person. The personal importance of interests may also change over time; some will be more important while other interests loose importance or disappear completely [8].

The three stage model described by Krapp explains the evolution from the first occurrence of a certain interest to a longer-lasting individual interest. In general, interests are divided into two main types: situational and individual interests. A Situational interest is mostly triggered externally in a given learning environment. Such interests can develop to individual interests when the person spends a lot of time on them and identifies herself with them. The already mentioned three stage model additionally divides the situational interest into two different stages while the individual interest is described by the last of the three stages. The first stage defines the first occurrence of an individual interest while the second stage describes a stabilized situational interest that lasts through a particular learning phase. In general, a learner has more interests on stage one than individual interests on stage three.

3 Implementation

The implementation of the extension of LCDM with interests was done in four steps. The first step was to define the new version of the model itself by considering different

[1] http://www.learning-context.de.

quality requirements. Step two defined the weighting of the different interests, how they affect each other and when the transition between the different stages happens. For adding new interests to the model and for requesting the resulting data, the already existing RESTful API has been extended in step three. For exhibiting the different stages of an interest enriched model, the step four described how a prototypic visualization can look like. These four steps are addressed in the following sections.

3.1 Interest Data Model

The underlying data model of the Learning Context Project has a high impact on the complete system because the flexibility and the complexity depend on the quality of the data model [9]. Besides the semantic requirements of the data model, general requirements for an entity relation model need to be fulfilled to develop a high quality data model. Moody [9] describes eight general requirements of a data model (completeness, integrity, flexibility, understandability, correctness, simplicity, integration and implementability) which are the foundation of any modification of this model.

All interests are specified by the relationship between a person and a certain object which can be represented by a topic, an idea, or by a term. Interests are not static and may develop or ascend to/descent from the described three stages. The model also needs to contain information about the point in time when the learner is interacting with an interest related object. This information is necessary to be able to specify the importance of an interest and also to specify to which stage the interest belongs to. If the user was interested in an object over a certain time period and engaged frequently enough with this interest, it can ascent to the next stage. The model should also distinguish between different types of interests. Persons can e.g. have private, academic and work related interests. Every interest is influenced by all other interests and vice versa. If a learner suddenly gets interested in a new topic A, the importance of all the other interests will drop, while interest A is rising in importance. So the modeled interests need to have a weight, which can be adapted, based on the importance of the events that are related to those interests.

The following list gives a summarizing overview over all interest related requirements:

- Interests are represented as relationships between a person and an object
- Multi-stage model of interests
- Different interest types: private, work, academic
- Every interest has a weight to describe its importance and development
- Ranking of interests

Driven by these requirements, the interest-enriched version of LCDM (see Fig. 1) has been implemented in several iterations. Interests are linked to events because they are the central objects. Events could be actions like opening a learning resource or like writing a scientific paper. They may have zero to n related interests, for example if someone writes a paper, it normally covers more than one interest.

3.2 Weighting

The general idea behind the calculation of the weight for each interest is that a learner only has limited time and attention which can be seen as a resource, a learner can assign to her different interests. The weight of a new interest is calculated by multiplying a user-defined value for initial weightings of new interests with an – also user-defined – factor for the application which wants to add the new interest. We introduced such an app-based factor to let the learner decide which applications generates more important interests or which generate less important ones.

All the events which have effects on the weighting of interests are collected for one day to be normalized. After this re-calculation of the weights of all the interests, a new history entry is added to the database. The advantage of this procedure is that the runtime of the atomic event of adding, deleting and merging can be decreased a lot if the new weights are not calculated in real time.

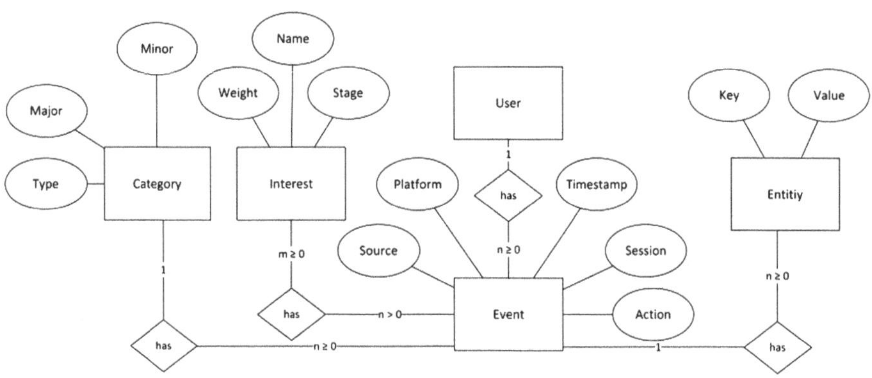

Fig. 1. The current version 4 of LCDM

Since interests may lose their importance if they are not refreshed regularly, a *Forgetting Function* has been introduced. It decreases the weight of an interest based on the time interval between the last date the learner interacted with this interest and the current date. Cheng et al. [6] introduced a function to describe the attenuation of human interests. It was also used as a basis to model the decreasing weight of non-refreshed interests by changing the used half-life *hl* to control the speed of forgetting.

$$F(d) = e - \frac{\ln(2) * d}{hl}$$

The parameter d represents the difference between the date of the last occurrence of the interest and the date, where the new interest weight is calculated. Difference d and half-life hl are both expressed in days.

3.3 LCDM API

We implemented an extension of the existing LCDM API to make the data model accessible by third-party applications. The interest-related subset of the API provides full access to the interest model with a complete set of CRUD (create, read, update, delete) functions that enable requesting, adding, updating and deleting interests including their complete history. As an example, sending a GET request to the interface *interests* will return all interests of the current learner with *name*, *weight*, *stage*, *type*, and the *timestamp* of the last update sorted by weight. By using the parameter *top*, only the top n interests are returned. For deleting interests, the names of all interests that should be deleted have to be sent to the server via a DELETE request. The corresponding interest with the complete history and the connection to the events are deleted.

Another important functionality of the API is merging two interests when two interest names are stored in the system which have the same meaning but which are probably spelled differently. The first interest is used as the base for the new merged interest. All events and history entries related to the second interest are related to the base interest after merging. To combine the two weights, each of them is decreased with the Forgetting Function. After calculating the sum, the second interest is deleted and the first one is updated.

3.4 Visualization

For an open learner model [3], the learner should be able to inspect and manage the data which is stored about her. The first module (see Fig. 2) which visualizes the development of different interests over time makes the available interest data easier to grasp for the learner. Moreover, it enables self-reflection about the own interests and to set or alter the personal priorities.

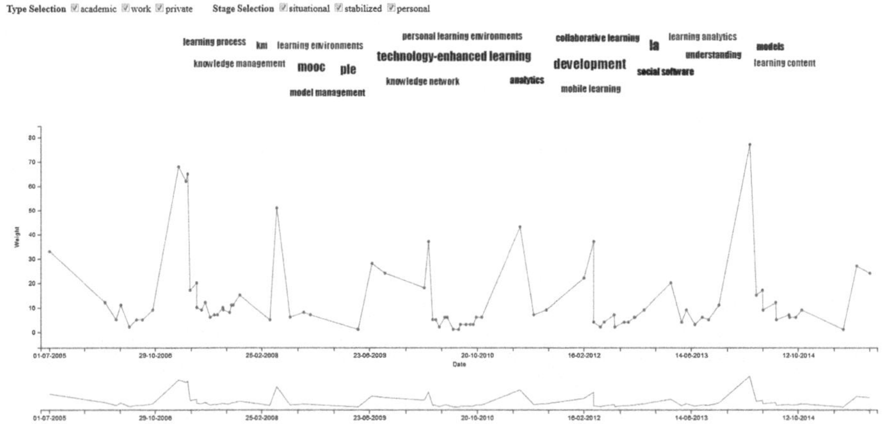

Fig. 2. Visualization for the evolution of different interests

The second module is for managing the existing learners' interest. It contains an overview of all interests with the related information about the weight, stage and type of the interest. This module further supports open learner modeling by enabling the learner to edit, merge and delete her interests.

4 Conclusion

Lifelong learner modeling is crucial to achieve personalized learning experiences. Context and interests represent important features in the lifelong learner model. Towards a lifelong learner model, we proposed in this paper an extension of the existing Learning Context Data Model (LCDM) specification with interests, taking into account the weights of the interests as well as their evolution over time. We followed an iterative approach to develop a new version of LCDM which satisfies specific interest-related requirements from a psychological perspective. We further provided an API which enables requesting, adding, deleting, updating, merging, and visualizing interests.

The current version of LCDM which encompasses context and interest information about a learner can further be extended with other attributes of a learner model such as knowledge, goals, background, and individual traits in order to build a complete lifelong learner model.

References

1. Baker, R.S.J.D., Yacef, K.: The state of educational data mining in 2009: A review and future visions. J. Educ. Data Min. **1**, 3–17 (2009)
2. Brusilovsky, P., Millán, E.: User models for adaptive hypermedia and adaptive educational systems. In: Brusilovsky, P., Kobsa, A., Nejdl, W. (eds.) Adaptive Web 2007. LNCS, vol. 4321, pp. 3–53. Springer, Heidelberg (2007)
3. Bull, S., Kay, J.: Open learner models. In: Nkambou, R., Bourdeau, J., Mizoguchi, R. (eds.) Advances in Intelligent Tutoring Systems. SCI, vol. 308, pp. 301–322. Springer, Heidelberg (2010)
4. Chatti, M.A., Lukarov, V., Thüs, H., Muslim, A., Yousef, A.M.F., Wahid, U., Greven, C., Chakrabarti, A., Schroeder, U.: Learning analytics: challenges and future research directions. eleed (10) (2104)
5. Chatti, M.A., Dyckhoff, A.L., Schroeder, U., Thüs, H.: A reference model for learning analytics. Int. J. Technol. Enhanced Learn. (IJTEL) **4**(5/6), 318–331 (2012)
6. Cheng, Y., Qiu, G, Bu, J., Liu, K., Han, Y., Wang, C., Chen, C.: Model bloggers' interests based on forgetting mechanism. In: Proceedings of the 17th International Conference on World Wide Web 2008, pp. 1129–1130. ACM, New York
7. Kay, J., Kummerfeld, B.: Lifelong learner modeling. In: Durlach, P.J., Lesgold, A.M. (eds.) Adaptive Technologies for Training and Education, pp. 140–164. Cambridge University Press, New York (2011)
8. Krapp, A.: Structural and dynamic aspects of interest development: theoretical considerations from an ontogenetic perspective. Learn. Instr. **12**(4), 383–409 (2002)
9. Moody, D.L.: Metrics for evaluating the quality of entity relationship models. In: Ling, T.-W., Ram, S., Li Lee, M. (eds.) ER 1998. LNCS, vol. 1507, pp. 211–225. Springer, Heidelberg (1998)
10. Thüs, H., Chatti, M.A., Greven, C., Schroeder, U.: Kontexterfassung, -modellierung und -auswertung in Lernumgebungen. In: Proceedings of the 12. e-Learning Fachtagung Informatik, DeLFI 2014, pp. 157–162 (2014)

Efficient Generation of High-Quality Multilingual Subtitles for Video Lecture Repositories

Juan Daniel Valor Miró(✉), Joan Albert Silvestre-Cerdà, Jorge Civera, Carlos Turró, and Alfons Juan

Universitat Politècnica de València, Camino de Vera s/n, 46022 Valencia, Spain
{jvalor,jsilvestre,jcivera,ajuan}@dsic.upv.es, turro@cc.upv.es

Abstract. Video lectures are a valuable educational tool in higher education to support or replace face-to-face lectures in active learning strategies. In 2007 the Universitat Politècnica de València (UPV) implemented its video lecture capture system, resulting in a high quality educational video repository, called poliMedia, with more than 10.000 mini lectures created by 1.373 lecturers. Also, in the framework of the European project transLectures, UPV has automatically generated transcriptions and translations in Spanish, Catalan and English for all videos included in the poliMedia video repository. transLectures's objective responds to the widely-recognised need for subtitles to be provided with video lectures, as an essential service for non-native speakers and hearing impaired persons, and to allow advanced repository functionalities. Although high-quality automatic transcriptions and translations were generated in transLectures, they were not error-free. For this reason, lecturers need to manually review video subtitles to guarantee the absence of errors. The aim of this study is to evaluate the efficiency of the manual review process from automatic subtitles in comparison with the conventional generation of video subtitles from scratch. The reported results clearly indicate the convenience of providing automatic subtitles as a first step in the generation of video subtitles and the significant savings in time of up to almost 75 % involved in reviewing subtitles.

Keywords: Video lecture repositories · Automatic speech recognition · Machine translation · Efficient video subtitling

1 Introduction

Video lectures are fast becoming an everyday educational resource in higher education used to supplement and complement face-to-face lectures [6], and are being incorporated into existing university curricula around the world with enthusiastic response from students [8].

However, the utility of these audiovisual assets could be further extended by adding subtitles that can be exploited to incorporate added-value functionalities such as searchability, accessibility, and discovery of content-related videos,

© Springer International Publishing Switzerland 2015
G. Conole et al. (Eds.): EC-TEL 2015, LNCS 9307, pp. 485–490, 2015.
DOI: 10.1007/978-3-319-24258-3_44

among others. In fact, most of the video lectures available in university large repositories are neither transcribed nor translated, despite the clear need to make their content accessible to speakers of different languages and people with disabilities ([10]). Also, the subtitles can be used to develop advanced educational functionalities like content summarisation to assist student note-taking ([2]). For this reason, it is important to develop a cost-effective solution that can do so to a reasonable degree of accuracy. In this work, we propose the application of state-of-the-art techniques in Automatic Speech Recognition (ASR) and Statistical Machine Translation (SMT) to generate high-quality video subtitles under the supervision of lecturers involved in this process.

This paper is organised as follows. Next section is devoted to present poliMedia [5], a video lecture repository of the Universitat Politènica de València (UPV), and transLectures [7], the European project under which framework ASR and SMT technology was developed to be applied for video subtitling. Section 3 describes the user evaluation campaign performed at UPV to review video transcription and translations, and its results. Finally, conclusions are drawn in Sect. 4.

2 poliMedia and transLectures

In 2007 the UPV implemented its poliMedia lecture capture system for the cost-effective creation and publication of quality educational video content. It now has a collection of over 10,000 video objects created by 1373 lecturers, in part incentivised by the *Docència en Xarxa* (DeX) action plan. poliMedia is primarily designed to allow UPV lecturers to record pre-prepared mini lectures for use by students in supplement to the traditional live lecture. For the most part they consist of concise overviews of a given topic and have a typical duration of around ten minutes.

In addition, in 2011 the UPV embarked on the EU-subsidised project transLectures to generate automatic subtitles in Spanish, English and Catalan for all videos in the poliMedia repository. These poliMedia videos were automatically transcribed using the TLK toolkit for ASR [1], which consists of a set of tools that allows acoustic model training and speech decoding. The language model of these ASR systems was a linear mixture trained on the poliMedia manual transcriptions along with other external resources. Then, poliMedia videos were automatically translated into other languages (Spanish, English and Catalan) using the well-known SMT toolkit Moses [3] trained on large parallel external resources. Also, we apply adaptation techniques based on a selection of topic-specific sentences related to the topic of the videos being translated.

A conventional post-editing protocol was adopted for both, transcription and translation review using a web interface called transLectures player [9], an innovative web player with editing capabilities. As shown in Fig. 1, the player plays a video lecture and its corresponding transcription in synchrony, allowing the user to correct the transcription while watching the video.

Similarly, an interface for the review of video translations was designed in order to show the original transcription, the corresponding translation and the

Fig. 1. transLectures web player for the review of a video transcription.

video in synchrony (see Fig. 2). It is important to note that the transLectures player is able to log precise user interaction statistics that will be useful to analyse users' behaviour or develop a user model.

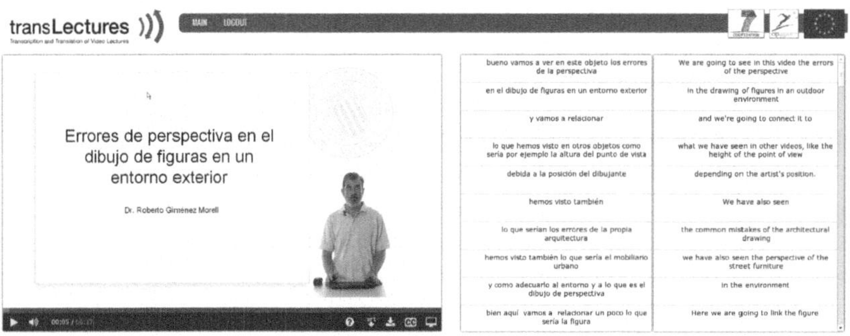

Fig. 2. transLectures web player for the review of a video translation.

3 User Evaluations

In this section we describe user evaluations carried out under UPV 2013–2014 DeX programme. User evaluations are considered from two viewpoints, the transcription or translation quality of the subtitles automatically generated and how much time takes for lecturers to review these automatic subtitles. Lecturers' background is diverse but mainly grounded on engineering studies, however a few lecturers were related to other areas, such as business management, social science, and biology. Lecturers committed to reviewing the automatic transcriptions of five poliMedia videos or the automatic translations of three poliMedia videos. The topics of the video lectures reviewed had also different topics, but we had not found any influence in the results arising from this variety.

Transcription and translation errors are automatically gauged according to Word Error Rate (WER) and Translation Edit Rate (TER), respectively.

These measures are widely accepted in the ASR and SMT fields. WER is the ratio, expressed as a percentage, of the number of basic word editing operations required to convert the automatic transcription into the correct reviewed transcription, and the total number of words in the reviewed transcription. Similarly, TER is the ratio, expressed as a percentage, of the number of edit operations (including phrasal shifts) required to convert the automatic translation into the correct reviewed translation, and the total number of words in the reviewed translation. So if, for example, a user needs to correct 20 words in a transcription (or translation) containing 100 words, the WER (or TER) is 20 %.

The time required for lecturers to review automatic transcriptions or translations is computed in terms of Real Time Factor (RTF). RTF is the ratio between the time devoted to reviewing the transcription or translation of a video and the duration of said video. So if, for example, a video lasts 20 min and its review takes, by way of example, one hour, then the RTF for this video would be 3.

Next sections report the results obtained on the review of Spanish, English and Catalan transcriptions and Spanish into English translations.

3.1 Review of Spanish Transcriptions

Spanish automatic transcriptions were reviewed by 39 lecturers accounting for 18.3 hours (135 videos). A simple linear regression model $RTF = \beta \cdot WER$ was fitted to all collected data that resulted in a statistically significant (β=0.184, Sig$< 2.2*10^{-16}$) dependency between RTF and WER. On average, WER was as low as 12 WER points (high transcription quality) and RTF was 2.7. In practical terms, the review of an average length poliMedia video of 10 min takes approximately 100 min (non-expert users usually needs 10 RTF [4]) to do it from scratch, but using the post-editing protocol with our high-quality ASR system, the review time would be less than 30 min.

3.2 Review of English Transcriptions

In English, 57 video transcriptions accounting for 7.9 hrs were reviewed by 12 non-native volunteers. The process was the same as in the Spanish review.

As in Spanish, there is a statistically significant linear dependency between WER and RTF (β=0.168, Sig$< 2.2*10^{-16}$). The average RTF was 6.2 still far below 10 RTF achieved by non-expert users. The reason behind this higher RTF was the transcription quality, since the ASR English system trained attained 36.0 WER points in this evaluation. Since this user evaluation was performed, the English ASR system has notably improved up to reaching 21.4 WER points.

In terms of more qualitative feedback, volunteers valued the simplicity and efficiency of the player interface. Volunteers agreed that the quality of the English automatic transcription must increase to reduce review time. In summary, results were largely positive and, as desired, volunteers prefered this system than transcribing videos from scratch.

3.3 Review of Catalan Transcriptions

The review of Catalan transcriptions was carried out by 5 lecturers that reviewed 19 video transcriptions accounting for 1.5 hrs. The review process was the same described in the Spanish and English reviews. It is important to note that, in this case, Catalan transcriptions had a significantly lower quality than those of Spanish, since this transcription system was at the first stages of development.

The average RTF was 5.6, while the average WER of automatic transcriptions was 40.4. As in Spanish and English, there is a clearly statistically significant linear dependency between WER and RTF (β=0.138, Sig$< 2.2*10^{-16}$). Lecturers expose the idea that the transcription quality must be improved.

Fortunately, the Catalan transcription system has significantly improved since these evaluations were carried out, and nowadays Catalan WER figures are 17.4 points, decreasing the review time to attain correct transcriptions.

3.4 Review of Spanish into English Translations

Ten lecturers took part in the review of Spanish into English translations accounting for 13 video translations fully reviewed (about 2.1 hrs of video). The average RTF was 12.2, while the average TER was 41.9. If we compare this RTF to that achieved by manual translations (about 30 RTF), we observe a significant relative decrease in user effort. As with WER, there is a statistically significant linear dependency between RTF and TER (β=0.255, Sig=$3.73*10^{-7}$).

As in transcription evaluations, generally speaking, lecturers were satisfied with the interface, however they requested that the player stopped at the end of each segment to have more time to review the translation. This request was not necessary while reviewing transcription, since the cognitive load is notably lower than when translating. Finally, lecturers demanded higher translation quality.

4 Conclusions

This work describes the efficient generation of high-quality multilingual subtitles for the poliMedia video repository. Our results on user evaluations with lecturers reflect significant reductions in review time to generate subtitles. As expected, review times depend on the automatic transcription or translation quality and user expertise. However, WER figures achieved by our ASR systems provided automatic transcriptions whose review was already more efficient than transcribing from scratch with significant effort reductions about 70 %, 40 % and 35 % for Spanish, English and Catalan, respectively. The Spanish-English translation review task also proved to save time compared to translating from scratch. No evidence exists regarding the difference in quality between subtitles (transcriptions and translations) generated after reviewing automatic subtitles and those that were obtained from scratch.

In practical terms, the review of transcription and translation for an average length poliMedia video of 10 min takes approximately 400 min (approximately 10

RTF for transcription plus 30 RTF for translation) to do it from scratch. Using transLectures technology, the user would need about 30 min (2.7 RTF) to review the transcription plus about 120 min (RTF 12.2) to correct the translation, that is, 150 min. This means a user time-saving of approximately two thirds with respect to do it from scratch.

The system presented in this work is currently in production and available at the poliMedia site [5]. Nowadays, all video lectures generated by UPV lecturers are automatically transcribed and translated into Spanish, English and Catalan, being available for review using the transLectures player.

Acknowledgments. The research leading to these results has received funding from the European Union FP7/2007-2013 under grant agreement no 287755 (transLectures) and ICT PSP/2007-2013 under grant agreement no 621030 (EMMA), and the Spanish MINECO Active2Trans (TIN2012-31723) research project.

References

1. del-Agua, M.A., Giménez, A., Serrano, N., Andrés-Ferrer, J., Civera, J., Sanchis, A., Juan, A.: The translectures-UPV toolkit. In: Navarro Mesa, J.L., Ortega, A., Teixeira, A., Hernández Pérez, E., Quintana Morales, P., Ravelo García, A., Guerra Moreno, I., Toledano, D.T. (eds.) IberSPEECH 2014. LNCS, vol. 8854, pp. 269–278. Springer, Heidelberg (2014)
2. Glass, J., et al.: Recent progress in the MIT spoken lecture processing project. In: Proceedings of Interspeech 2007, vol. 3, pp. 2553–2556 (2007)
3. Koehn, P., et al.: Moses: open source toolkit for statistical machine translation. In: Proceedings of ACL, pp. 177–180 (2007)
4. Munteanu, C., et al.: Improving ASR for lectures through transformation-based rules learned from minimal data. In: Proceedings of ACL-AFNLP, pp. 764–772 (2009)
5. poliMedia: polimedia platform (2007). http://media.upv.es/
6. Ross, T., Bell, P.: No significant difference only on the surface. Int. J. Instr. Technol. Distance Learn. **4**(7), 3–13 (2007)
7. Silvestre, J.A. et al.: Translectures. In: Proceedings of IberSPEECH 2012 (2012)
8. Soong, S.K.A., Chan, L.K., Cheers, C., Hu, C.: Impact of video recorded lectures among students. In: Who's Learning, pp. 789–793 (2006)
9. Valor Miró, J.D., Pérez González de Martos, A., Civera, J., Juan, A.: Integrating a state-of-the-art ASR system into the opencast matterhorn platform. In: Torre Toledano, D., Ortega Giménez, A., Teixeira, A., González Rodríguez, J., Hernández Gómez, L., San Segundo Hernández, R., Ramos Castro, D. (eds.) IberSPEECH 2012. CCIS, vol. 328, pp. 237–246. Springer, Heidelberg (2012)
10. Wald, M.: Creating accessible educational multimedia through editing automatic speech recognition captioning in real time. Inter. Technol. Smart Educ. **3**(2), 131–141 (2006)

A Model to Support Monitoring for Classroom Orchestration in a Tablet-Based CSCL Activity

Patrick Wang[1(✉)], Pierre Tchounikine[1], and Matthieu Quignard[2]

[1] Université Grenoble Alpes, LIG, F-38000, Grenoble, France
{patrick.wang,pierre.tchounikine}@imag.fr
[2] CNRS, ICAR, Lyon, France
matthieu.quignard@ens-lyon.fr

Abstract. The work presented in this article addresses CSCL settings in which students work with tablets in classrooms. The objective is to study how to equip teachers with tablets to monitor students' progress and intervene when required. We propose a model that provides teachers with both quantitative and qualitative run-time feedback based on the students' progress. An implementation of this model was tested in the context of an activity called negotiated dictation. The results suggest that the model and associated tools are easy for teachers to use and allow them to satisfactorily monitor the progress of both the class and individual students or groups.

Keywords: Classroom orchestration · Monitoring CSCL activities · Quantitative and qualitative progress · Tablets

1 Introduction

Orchestrating Computer-Supported Collaborative Learning (CSCL) scripts may be seen as intertwining scripting, i.e., making a priori design decisions and then adapting them at run-time as necessary, and conducting, i.e., monitoring the students' progress and helping students when required [7]. In this article, we introduce a simple model to design *monitoring* tools for tablet-based CSCL scripts in classrooms. The model is based on the idea that orchestration in classroom is both digital and physical: teachers are provided with quantitative and qualitative data captured from students' activities that they can use to physically go and help the students. The model is voluntarily simple because teacher adoption of new technologies depends on the ability to appropriate and integrate the tools in their classrooms [5]; tools should thus be designed to be user-friendly and intuitive.

The model has been tested by developing and testing monitoring tools for a tablet-based negotiated dictation CSCL script, which setting is as follows (see [8] for details). In the initial individual phase, students listen to a dictation (audio-recorded) and type it on tablets. Then, teachers align students' dictations to facilitate word by word comparisons and create groups of two or three students. Finally, in the collective phase, groups are asked to discuss on specific words for which they have to choose a spelling and

© Springer International Publishing Switzerland 2015
G. Conole et al. (Eds.): EC-TEL 2015, LNCS 9307, pp. 491–496, 2015.
DOI: 10.1007/978-3-319-24258-3_45

justify it. The research question we considered is: does the model support (1) defining what should be displayed on the teacher's tablet and (2) implementing tools that are simple enough to be easily used by not-specifically-trained teachers while allowing them to satisfactorily monitor and conduct the activity?

2 A Model to Support Monitoring for Orchestration

The activity and monitoring model we propose is illustrated in Fig. 1. With respect to the learning activity, we adopt a model that builds on the classic CSCL script structure. An activity is composed of several phases associated with actors (students or groups). In each phase, one or several tasks are performed by the corresponding actor, who produces some data (productions). With respect to monitoring, the design rationale is to provide teachers with information related to the actors' progress and productions, being respectively quantitative and qualitative data. This double perspective is consistent with our idea that monitoring requires both a coarse-grained view (a synthesized overall classroom view) and a fine-grained view of how the activity is unfolding. "Additional data" corresponds to other monitoring data made available to teachers and which is not directly related to the progress of the activity.

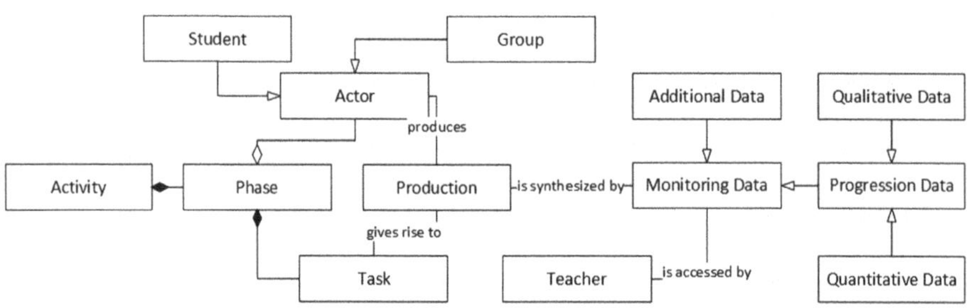

Fig. 1. The model: offering both quantitative and qualitative monitoring data.

In the case of negotiated dictations, the model is instantiated as follows. For the individual dictation phase (see Fig. 2): quantitative data corresponds to the part of the dictation completed by students (displayed as a progress bar); qualitative data corresponds to the dictation itself; additional data corresponds to the number of student corrections and the number of times each audio track was played. For the collective phase: quantitative data corresponds to the number of words justified by each group; qualitative data corresponds to the different students' votes and their justifications; additional data is the time spent voting and justifying each word (duration of a few seconds may denote limited interactions).

Figure 2 illustrates the abstract interfaces and the implementation we developed for the individual phase and, to some extent, the general look and feel. By swiping the screen left or right, the teacher can have a quick glance at the quantitative data (classroom progress) and qualitative data (each student's dictation). Additional information is made available by touching the corresponding row, which opens a pop-up window. The monitoring tools for the collective phase follow the same pattern. As dictations are linear exercises, it may seem that qualitative data would be sufficient to monitor the activity as the dictation itself can illustrate the students' progress. However, with a larger set of students and multi-line dictations, separating quantitative and qualitative information proves necessary to offer an immediately clear perception of the students' progress and avoid overwhelming teachers with too much data. If the list of students does not fit on the screen, the teacher simply has to swipe the screen up and down.

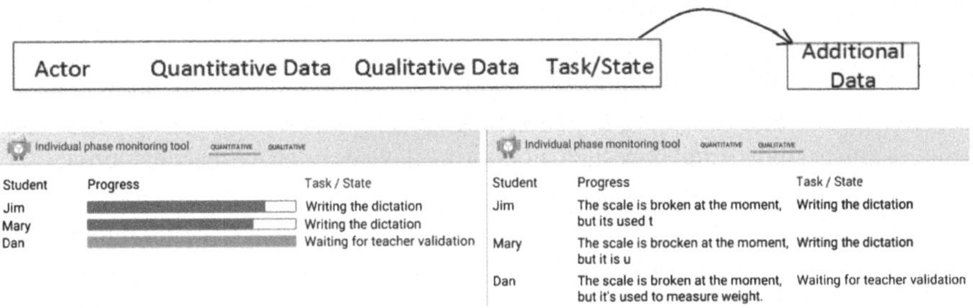

Fig. 2. The abstract interface (top) is instantiated to provide quantitative and qualitative perspectives for the individual phase of the negotiated dictation (bottom).

From a technical perspective, each tablet is connected to a dedicated WLAN and the MQ Telemetry Transport (MQTT) protocol is used to enable communication between the devices. Using this protocol, the students' tablets continuously send feedback about the ongoing activity to the teacher's tablet, and vice-versa when the teacher needs to send instructions to students. A MySQL server is used to log each user's actions, outputs and progress in the activity. This feature is essential for the research (analyzing data), but also allows recovery of a student's activity in case of failure.

3 Tests and Results

Tests were conducted with four teachers in two Grade 4 (age 9-10) and two Grade 5 (age 10-11) classes. Classrooms ranged from 20 to 29 students for a total of exactly 100 students. Though the tools were designed with the help of teachers, the ones involved in the tests had actually no part in the design decisions. Hence, they were quickly briefed on how to use the tablet and the monitoring tools before the session. The class was split in halves with one engaged in the negotiated dictation and the other one on another task, and the activity was conducted twice so each half could participate. After the second session, teachers were asked via a questionnaire if and how they had satisfactorily monitored and conducted the sessions, and how they perceived the usability and efficiency of the tools offered (using a Likert scale). Three points were studied: usability of the student application, usability of tablets for monitoring the activity and usability and efficiency of the monitoring tools. As the results related to our concerns (usability and efficiency) were consistent, no more tests were run after these eight sessions.

We first considered the usability of the student application, which may influence teacher monitoring. Actually, students encountered no major difficulty in using the system. All four teachers agreed that the individual phase went smoothly and that the collective phase produced interesting justifications, which supports the idea that students were comfortable with the device and focused on the pedagogical tasks.

Regarding usability of tablets for monitoring the activity, three features were analyzed: the general look-and-feel of the tablets and the interest of touch screen interfaces, the size of the screen (we used "10.5" tablets) and the interest of the mobility offered by tablets. All four teachers fully agreed that tablets were easy to use and that the screen was big enough for the tools offered with only two of them being familiar with tablets. With respect to mobility, they all mentioned that it was an advantage as they all benefited from it by walking around the classroom during the individual and collective phases and providing hints to students. This behavior suggests that it could be interesting to study if and how such monitoring devices improve teachers' proactivity, in opposition to solving issues only.

Our central research question was about usability and efficiency of the monitoring tools. Many differences in students' task performance and individual behavior emerged from both the individual phase and the collective phase, which resulted in various durations required to finish each task. Such contrast provided enough occasions for teachers to use the tools and conduct the setting. A first general question addressed the usefulness of the tools offered for monitoring the students, in particular given these differences. All four teachers strongly agreed that the monitoring tools were necessary as they could simultaneously help students or groups in trouble and keep an eye on the overall course of the activity. A second question addressed if teachers had satisfactorily monitored the quantitative and qualitative progress of each actor (student by student and group by group). Altogether, the answer was positive (three strongly agreed and one agreed) for 99 out of the 100 students and for all 37 groups. The usability of the different tools was demonstrated by the ease with which the teachers used the tools right from the first session, and confirmed by the open discussion during the debriefing session. These findings suggest the different tools are highly usable and demonstrate the efficiency of both these tools (collectively) and the underlying model.

Additional questions addressed the usefulness of each individual tool. Here, some answers differ. For instance, one teacher found the qualitative monitoring tool very helpful and the quantitative one rather superfluous. Another did not use the diagnosis information. The debriefing discussion allowed us to understand that this was related to different monitoring strategies (see discussion in next section).

4 Discussion

The results suggest that the model and its implementation for negotiated dictations provide easy-to-use and efficient monitoring tools for teachers. It also validates the interest of our approach to monitoring as a mixed (digital and non-digital) activity and the usefulness of tablet mobility for this purpose.

The model of activity we used is fairly general and traditional in CSCL. Our future research agenda includes developing and testing instantiation with other learning scenarios. This implies identifying, for the considered scenario, a way to describe the actors' progress and productions with quantitative and qualitative information. Depending on the nature of the tasks, an actor's quantitative data can be illustrated with either a continuous or discrete (in the mathematical sense) progress bar while the qualitative data can reuse the same type of interface to show the answers. For instance, for a scenario based on a suite of exercises to be addressed individually and then collectively, reusing a discrete representation to display the quantitative and qualitative information of each exercise seems appropriate.

Another aspect to be further considered is the extent to which the model can be scaled, i.e., the maximum number of students or groups that can be managed simultaneously and the quality of the management. With more students, tablets might be too small to provide efficient monitoring tools. At this level, however, let us recall that we are considering monitoring for *classroom* orchestration.

An interesting observation that became apparent during the experiment, and was confirmed by the questionnaire and the debriefing session, is that teachers implemented different monitoring strategies. These different monitoring strategies can be explained by the teachers own work practices [6] (let us remember that they were not involved in the design process of the tools nor trained to use them). Given our research goals, this observation suggests that teachers seemed to succeed in using the tools according to their strategy and were satisfied with the way they monitored the activity. This also suggests that the simplicity of the model and tools, coupled with the overall mixed perspective of monitoring, allows for a variety of strategies. Keeping in mind this diversity of teacher own practices is a crucial issue when designing orchestration tools, and more generally, when designing educational software [6].

The work presented in this article is in line with other works having shown that mobile technologies may be used in classrooms to scaffold face-to-face interactions and foster social interactions between students [9]. This is the rationale for using technology to enhance an activity with which teachers are already familiar (here, dictation). Using tablets provides teachers with the necessary mobility to move around the classroom and intervene among students, which would be more difficult if computers were used. With respect to orchestration research themes presented by the synthesis proposed in [4], our work addresses regulation issues and awareness. With respect to the orchestration design principles presented in [1], our work implements control, visibility, physicality and, last but not least, minimalism. The design principle of proposing a dual perspective (progress bars and students' productions) is a well-founded pattern. For instance, the monitoring tool presented in [3] uses progress bars to show the students' relative involvement in their groups during a collective phase. In [2], the groups' actions are shown on a public display allowing both teacher and students to be aware of all the productions. The work presented distinguishes itself from these by using a single model to monitor both individual and collective phases and by delivering both quantitative and qualitative feedback to ensure whole class and individual monitoring.

5 Conclusions and Perspectives

In this article, we presented a model to support teachers' monitoring actions for the orchestration of CSCL activities in a classroom. An instantiation has been implemented and tested, and results suggest the value of the approach. The experiments also suggest that it would be worth studying teachers' monitoring strategies and the interplay between these strategies and the model and tools. The model, the abstract interfaces and the implementation architecture and framework are generic. Our research agenda also includes developing other instances with other tablet-based CSCL activities consistent with our activity model. Developing new instances will help define the precise scope of application of the model and framework. Finally, another perspective of this work is to enhance the monitoring device with orchestration tools, such as means to move students from one group to another at run-time.

Acknowledgements. This work is partially funded by the ARC6 action of the Rhône Alpes region (France).

References

1. Dillenbourg, P.: Design for classroom orchestration. Comput. Educ. **69**, 485–492 (2013)
2. Kreitmayer, S., Rogers, Y., Laney, R., Peake, S.: Unipad: orchestrating collaborative activities through shared tablets and an integrated wall display. In: Proceedings of the 2013 ACM International Joint Conference on Pervasive and Ubiquitous Computing, pp. 801–810. ACM (2013)
3. Martinez Maldonado, R., Dimitriadis, Y., Kay, J., Yacef, K., Edbauer, M.T.: Orchestrating a multi-tabletop classroom: from activity design to enactment and reflection. In: Proceedings of the 2012 ACM International Conference on Interactive Tabletops and Surfaces, pp. 119–128. ACM (2012)
4. Prieto, L.P., Dlab, M.H., Gutiérrez, I., Abdulwahed, M., Balid, W.: Orchestrating technology enhanced learning: a literature review and a conceptual framework. Int. J. Technol. Enhanc. Learn. **3**(6), 583–598 (2011)
5. Roschelle, J., Dimitriadis, Y., Hoppe, U.: Classroom orchestration: synthesis. Comput. Educ. **69**, 523–526 (2013)
6. Tchounikine, P.: Computer Science and Educational Software Design. Springer-Verlag, Heidelberg (2011)
7. Tchounikine, P.: Clarifying design for orchestration: orchestration and orchestrable technology, scripting and conducting. Comput. Educ. **69**, 500–503 (2013)
8. Wang, P., Tchounikine, P., Quignard, M.: Orchestration issues raised by transposing an individual paper-based activity into a tablet-based CSCL activity: an example. In: Proceedings of the 11th International Conference on Computer Supported Collaborative Learning. International Society of the Learning Sciences (ISLS) (2015)
9. Zurita, G., Nussbaum, M.: Computer supported collaborative learning using wirelessly interconnected handheld computers. Comput. Educ. **42**(3), 289–314 (2004)

Resource Access Patterns in Exam Preparation Activities

Sabrina Ziebarth[(✉)], Irene-Angelica Chounta, and H. Ulrich Hoppe

University of Duisburg-Essen, Essen, Germany
{ziebarth,chounta,hoppe}@collide.info
http://www.collide.info/

Abstract. In this paper we investigate patterns of resource usage for exam preparation based on a resource intensive blended learning course. To this end, we analyzed a blended learning, online course facilitated by Moodle. During the course, the students had to work individually and in teams. Furthermore, they were given access to a broad spectrum of learning resources such as videos, slides, wiki articles and quizzes. The logfiles obtained from Moodle were further processed and analyzed. Our analysis approach is based on association rule as well as sequential pattern mining. The results indicate that students' activity with respect to resource usage follows common patterns during exam preparation either on the individual or the group level. These patterns also relate to the performance of students and to reflect their prior collaborative experience.

Keywords: Small private online courses · Moodle · Exam preparation · Sequential pattern mining · Association rule mining

1 Introduction

There are numerous examples of enhancing traditional learning scenarios with online and interactive elements, usually subsumed under the notion of "blended learning". Armando Fox [5] argues for complementing traditional university courses with concepts and materials from Massive Open Online Courses (MOOCs) to "increase instructor leverage, student throughput, student mastery, and student engagement". He calls this concept "Small Private Online Course" (SPOCs). To investigate the effectiveness of complementing traditional university courses with SPOCs, in 2013 we redesigned an existing Master level lecture on user/task modeling and models of interactive and collaborative learning environments [13]. The main idea was to shift the focus of the classroom experience from teacher centered lecturing to student centered interactions. To achieve that, the lecture was redefined in the sense of providing orientation knowledge ("advance organizer") and core definitions with a limited number of characteristic examples. The presence based exercise was "virtualized", i.e. replaced by a combination of individual and group assignments with reporting

© Springer International Publishing Switzerland 2015
G. Conole et al. (Eds.): EC-TEL 2015, LNCS 9307, pp. 497–502, 2015.
DOI: 10.1007/978-3-319-24258-3_46

back into the learning management system (a Moodle 2 plattform). Additionally, the plenary face-to-face setting of the lecture was used as a forum to take up and discuss results from the virtual exercise activities. An important assignment was the collaborative creation of wiki articles. Each group focused on another topic, thus the combination of all wiki articles also provided the course with a collaboratively created script of the lecture for exam preparation. Based on the experiences of the 2013 course, in 2014 we repeated the course with some changes, e.g. regarding group formation and size, and added exercises involving virtual labs for supporting the better understanding of complex, theoretical concepts.

This kind of blended learning course results in a broad spectrum of learning resources (lecture slides and videos, papers, wiki articles and quizzes). First results of analyzing the Moodle log files of the 2013 course show that during lecture time the resource usage depends highly on the exercises, while there are different patterns of resource usage in the exam preparation phase [7]. Thus, to analyze how the different types of resources are used for learning we focus on the exam preparation phase. Furthermore, the students of the 2013 course stated that they regarded both teacher as well as student created material as beneficial for learning (with a slight preference for teacher generated content) [13]. Therefore, we want to analyze to which extent this is reflected in their resource access patterns during exam preparation. While this paper only focuses on the log analysis of the Moodle data, we plan to survey additional information in the next instance of the course to allow for triangulation of the results. Our research questions are:

- Are there typical patterns in resource usage for exam preparation?
- Do members of groups portray similar behavior with respect to resource usage during the exam preparation phase and is this reflected on the overall results?

2 Related Work

The analysis of learning activities aims to identify the meaningful episodes that take place when a group of learners interact with the instructor, their peers or the available resources within a learning context. The use of computers allows the detailed recording of user activity in log files and provides access to vast resources for further analysis [3]. The analysis of learning activities usually focuses on user activity and user interaction [12]. However, we can gain valuable information not only from the way users interact with each other but also from the way they interact with the learning material. To that end, Learning Analytics can be applied in order to investigate the relations between learners and learning resources. The use of learning resources in MOOCs and online communities has been widely studied in order to define common learning styles [2] and contributor's profiles for user-created learning material [6]. There is also research demonstrating dependencies between the LMS usage in blended learning courses and the achieved learning results, e.g. [9]. Data-mining algorithms are widely applied in order to discover patterns on resource usage and consequently for further assessment of good practices [11]. Resource usage has been proposed as a method for clustering learning objects in a way that reflects their semantic similarity [10].

3 Methodology

As basis for this analysis the Moodle log files of the course, that was conducted in summer term 2014, have been used. 33 students participated in the course, but two deleted their accounts and thus were not considered. The students formed eight groups of four students on average and these groups were maintained over the complete lecture time. Twenty-six students took their exam. The exams were conducted orally over a time span of one week, starting 18 days after the last lecture. In this analysis we focus on these 18 days as well as the exam week. Of course, only the behavior on the Moodle platform can be observed. Students could easily download lecture slides and scientific papers, thus they would not need to go back to the platform. However, it was much harder to download the lecture videos, since they were provided in a player that did not offer downloads. Furthermore, Moodle does not offer a download function for wiki articles and quizzes could only be attempted in the Moodle platform.

3.1 Association Rule Analysis

This section focuses on the research question regarding patterns in resource usage for exam preparation. We consider resources used together in one Moodle session to reflect the student's learning goal of that session (and thus a part of his/her learning strategy). Such a goal could be to recapitulate a certain subtopic using different types of relevant resources, to recapitulate a broader topic using only specific types of resources or to use quizzes or slides with exam questions for self-testing. Based on this assumption, resources that often occur together in one session can be considered to be associated in the students learning strategies.

To detect associations between resources based on their co-occurrence in sessions, the Apriori algorithm [1] was applied. Table 1 shows examples for association rules found in the Moodle sessions of the exam preparation phase. The rules with the highest support are between resources of the same media type and of the same topic. All of the 68 rules with a minimal support of 0.05 and a minimal confidence of 0.5 consist of resources that belong to the same topic. Most of them only refer to slides, but there are also four rules on wiki articles, two rules on videos and two referring to one slide set and one of the papers highlighted for exam preparation.

The Apriori algorithm can also be used to create (undirected) associations between resources that are weighted by the support value ("co-occurrences"). The results of analyzing the 185 co-occurrences with a minimal support of 3 % of learning objects support the observation that students mainly use resources of the same media type and topic in one session. But while there are some interconnections between different types of teacher generated content (slides, papers, videos), the student generated wiki articles are only linked to other wiki articles. This indicates that while wiki articles are used for exam preparation, they take another role than the teacher generated material. While there are typically few links between resources on different topics, the accessed lecture slides are more often linked with slides of other topics. This could e.g. be an indicator for downloading slides to have a local copy, getting an overview or searching for some specific information. Reducing the minimal support to 2 % shows a triad consisting of the three quizzes. This indicates that the quizzes are used together, but separately from the other resources. Since they cover the three main topics of the lecture, there is no connection by topic. A typical goal for using the three question might be self-testing, which fits with the observation that quizzes are only used in the second part of the exam preparation phase.

Table 1. Examples for association rules

Rule	Support	Confidence
Slides: Cognitive Task Models Q&A-2 → Slides: Cognitive (Task) Models Q&A	0.085	0.848
Paper: Understanding Interactivity → Slides: Interactivity, Direct Manipulation and User Centered System Design	0.057	0.613
Wiki article: GOMS → Wiki article: Model Human Processor	0.051	0.739

3.2 Sequential Pattern Mining Analysis

Learners with common interests are expected to interact with thematically-related learning material [8]. We aim to explore the sequential patterns of resource usage among the members of student groups. The research hypothesis is that groups who collaborated successfully during a course, will also portray similar behaviour during the exam preparations with respect to resource usage. Moreover, we explore the relation of resource usage and the learning outcome as assessed by the teacher of the course. For the purpose of our study, we portrayed the activity of groups as sets of sequences. Each sequence maps the activity of individual users with respect to resource usage. A sequence is composed of itemsets that represent the resources accessed within one user session. According to the hypothesis, successful collaborative practice should lead to similar patterns of resource usage. Therefore, the activity of each student is compared to the activity of his team mates. To discover potential frequent sequential patterns in user activity, we used the PrefixSpan algorithm [4] and looked for patterns that occur for all the students of one group (100 % pattern matching). We argue that frequent patterns of resource usage characterize groups that share common ground and have adopted common working styles. The PrefixSpan algorithm discovered frequent patterns for all eight groups. This means that all members per group accessed the same resources in the same sequence. The number of sequential patterns ranges from 2 to 45 and their length ranges from 1 to 3 itemsets (2 to 13 objects). Group 1 scored the lowest average group grade and the frequent sequential patterns consisted only of video resources. The same is true for groups 3 and 4; group members accessed in common only wiki articles. For Group 6, that scored the higher group grade, the frequent patterns of resource usage consisted of 6 objects from four different categories: two scientific papers, one lecture slides, one video and 2 wiki articles. The group grade appears to correlate with the number of categories of resources. Groups that use resources from more categories also score higher grades, thus students who spread over various resources achieve better results in the exam. However, the overall number of accessed resources is similar for all groups and there is no indication that groups with higher grades access more resources in general. To further study whether user behavior in exam preparation is affected by group dynamics, we divided groups in two categories: heterogeneous and homogeneous. We define homogeneity (hf) as the deviation of the individual highest grade within the group to the group's average grade. Heterogeneous groups (Group 3 with hf = 0.87 and Group 4 with hf = 2.68) portrayed the minimum number of frequent patterns on a 100 % level (i.e. for all the users). For these two groups, there were indeed two students (one per group) that had limited activity in comparison to their team members. Thus, it was difficult to discover sequential patterns that would appear in all users activity. Additionally, homogeneous groups have more sequential patterns that consist of more resources from various categories. This pinpoints that students of the same level access similar resources in the same way. Furthermore, students of different levels use different kinds of resources. This consequently can serve as an indication that particular group members do not share a common ground with the rest of the group. However, in the current study we could not establish statistical significance or relevance due to the small size of the dataset. Therefore, further exploration is necessary in order to establish general conclusions.

4 Conclusions

In this paper we study the activity of students during the exam preparation phase of a resource-intensive, blended-learning course. The course was supported by an LMS platform (Moodle) and a wide variety of learning resources was provided to and partially created by students. We assume that the resource usage will reflect the practice of students, thus providing valuable information on how students prepare for the exams. To test this assumption we are applying questionnaires regarding the usage of sources and exam preparation strategies in the current summer term and plan to triangulate the results with the log analysis. We hope to use the detected practices to predict success of and recommend resource usage strategies for students in future. The analysis of student activity with respect to resource usage was carried out on both the individual and the group level. Our main objective was to explore whether there are typical patterns in resource usage during the exam preparation phase and if the members of the same group portray similar behaviour regarding resource usage. To that end we used association rule analysis and sequential pattern mining. The results indicate there are common patterns of resource usage on both the individual and the group level that relate to the performance of students, to the type of resources and to their prior collaborative experience. However, it is necessary to conduct further, large scale studies in order to provide well-established conclusions. Additionally these studies should not only address log analysis but also surveys of the students (e.g. regarding learning attitudes and strategies, motivation, group interaction, etc.) to complement the results and to allow for triangulation.

References

1. Agrawal, R., Mannila, H., Srikant, R., Toivonen, H., Verkamo, A.I.: Knowledge Discovery and Data Mining, Chap. 12, pp. 307–328. AAI Press / The MIT Press (1996)
2. Breslow, L., Pritchard, D.E., DeBoer, J., Stump, G.S., Ho, A.D., Seaton, D.: Studying learning in the worldwide classroom: research into EDXS first MOOC. Res. & Pract. Assess. **8**, 13–25 (2013)
3. Dillenbourg, P., Baker, M.J., Blaye, A., O'Malley, C., et al.: The evolution of research on collaborative learning. In: Spada, E., Reiman, P. (eds.) Learning in Humans and Machine: Towards an interdisciplinary learning science, pp. 189–211. Elsevier, Oxford (1995)
4. Fournier-Viger, P., Gomariz, A., Soltani, A., Lam, H., Gueniche, T.: Spmf: Open-source data mining platform (2014). http://www.philippe-fournier-viger.com/spmf/
5. Fox, A.: From MOOCS to SPOCS. Commun. ACM **56**(12), 38–40 (2013)
6. Halatchliyski, I., Hecking, T., Goehnert, T., Hoppe, H.U.: Analyzing the path of ideas and activity of contributors in an open learning community. J. Learn. Analytics **1**(2), 72–93 (2014)
7. Hecking, T., Ziebarth, S., Hoppe, H.U.: Analysis of dynamic resource access patterns in a blended learning course. In: The 4th International Conference on Learning Analytics and Knowledge. pp. 173–182. ACM, New York (2014)
8. Hoppe, U., Pinkwart, N., Oelinger, M., Zeini, S., Verdejo, F., Barros, B., Mayorga, J.I.: Building bridges within learning communities through ontologies and thematic objects. In: Proceedings of the International Conference on Computer Supported Collaborative Learning. pp. 211–220 (2005)
9. Mödritscher, F., Andergassen, M., Neumann, G.: Dependencies between e-learning usage patterns and learning results. In: Proceedings of the 13th International Conference on Knowledge Management and Knowledge Technologies. ACM (2013)
10. Niemann, K., Schmitz, H.C., Kirschenmann, U., Wolpers, M., Schmidt, A., Krones, T.: Clustering by usage: higher order co-occurrences of learning objects. In: Proceedings of the 2nd International Conference on Learning Analytics and Knowledge. pp. 238–247. ACM (2012)
11. Perera, D., Kay, J., Koprinska, I., Yacef, K., Zaïane, O.R.: Clustering and sequential pattern mining of online collaborative learning data. IEEE Trans. Knowl. Data Eng. **21**(6), 759–772 (2009)
12. Suthers, D.D., Dwyer, N., Medina, R., Vatrapu, R.: A framework for conceptualizing, representing, and analyzing distributed interaction. Int. J. Comput. Support. Collaborative Learn. **5**(1), 5–42 (2010)
13. Ziebarth, S., Ulrich Hoppe, H.: Moodle4SPOC: A resource-intensive blended learning course. In: de Freitas, S., Rensing, C., Ley, T., Muñoz-Merino, P.J. (eds.) EC-TEL 2014. LNCS, vol. 8719, pp. 359–372. Springer, Heidelberg (2014)

Demo Papers

ReaderBench: An Integrated Cohesion-Centered Framework

Mihai Dascalu[1(✉)], Larise L. Stavarache[1], Philippe Dessus[2], Stefan Trausan-Matu[1], Danielle S. McNamara[3], and Maryse Bianco[2]

[1] Computer Science Department, University Politehnica of Bucharest, Bucharest, Romania
mihai.dascalu@cs.pub.ro, larise.stavarache@ro.ibm.com, stefan.trausan@cs.pub.ro

[2] LSE, Université Grenoble Alpes, Grenoble, France
{philippe.dessus,maryse.bianco}@upmf-grenoble.fr

[3] LSI, Arizona State University, Tempe, USA
dsmcnama@asu.edu

Abstract. *ReaderBench* is an automated software framework designed to support both students and tutors by making use of text mining techniques, advanced natural language processing, and social network analysis tools. *ReaderBench* is centered on comprehension prediction and assessment based on a cohesion-based representation of the discourse applied on different sources (e.g., textual materials, behavior tracks, metacognitive explanations, Computer Supported Collaborative Learning – CSCL – conversations). Therefore, *ReaderBench* can act as a Personal Learning Environment (PLE) which incorporates both individual and collaborative assessments. Besides the a priori evaluation of textual materials' complexity presented to learners, our system supports the identification of reading strategies evident within the learners' self-explanations or summaries. Moreover, *ReaderBench* integrates a dedicated cohesion-based module to assess participation and collaboration in CSCL conversations.

Keywords: Textual complexity assessment · Identification of reading strategies · Comprehension prediction · Participation and collaboration evaluation

1 ReaderBench's Purpose

Designed as support for both tutors and students, our implemented system, *ReaderBench* [1, 2], can be best described as an educational learning helper tool to enhance the quality of the learning process. *ReaderBench* is a fully functional framework that enhances learning using various techniques such as textual complexity assessment [1, 2], voice modeling for CSCL discourse analysis [3], topics modeling using Latent Semantic Analysis and Latent Dirichlet Allocation [2], and virtual communities of practice analysis [4]. Our system was developed building upon indices provided in renowned systems such as *E-rater, iSTART, and Coh-Metrix. However, ReaderBench* provides an

© Springer International Publishing Switzerland 2015
G. Conole et al. (Eds.): EC-TEL 2015, LNCS 9307, pp. 505–508, 2015.
DOI: 10.1007/978-3-319-24258-3_47

integration of these systems. *ReaderBench* includes multi-lingual comprehension-centered analyses focused on semantics, cohesion and dialogism [5]. For *tutors*, *ReaderBench* provides (a) the evaluation of reading material's textual complexity, (b) the measurement of social collaboration within a group endeavors, and (c) the evaluation of learners' summaries and self-explanations. For *learners*, *ReaderBench* provides (a) the improvement of learning capabilities through the use of reading strategies, and (b) the evaluation of students' comprehension levels and performance with respect to other students. *ReaderBench* maps directly onto classroom education, combining individual learning methods with Computer Supported Collaborative Learning (CSCL) techniques.

2 Envisioned Educational Scenarios

ReaderBench (RB) targets both tutors and students by addressing individual and collaborative learning methods through a cohesion-based discourse analysis and dialogical discourse model [1]. Overall, its design is not meant to replace the tutor, but to act as support for both tutors and students by enabling continuous assessment. Learners can assess their self-explanations or collaborative contributions within chat forums. Tutors, on the other hand, have the opportunity to analyze the proposed reading materials in order to best match the student's reading level. They can also easily grade student summaries or evaluate students' participation and collaboration within CSCL conversations. In order to better grasp the potential implementation of our system, the generic learning flows behind *ReaderBench*, which are easily adaptable to a wide range of educational scenarios, are presented in Figs. 1 and 2.

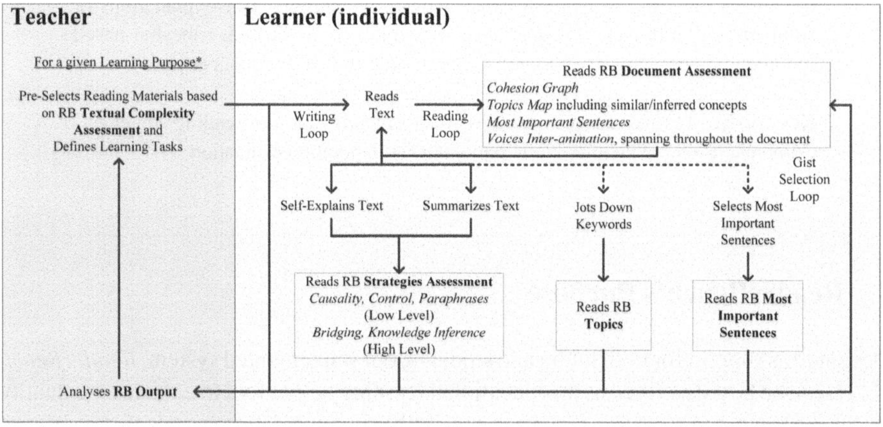

Fig. 1. Generic individual learning scenario integrating the use of *ReaderBench* (RB).

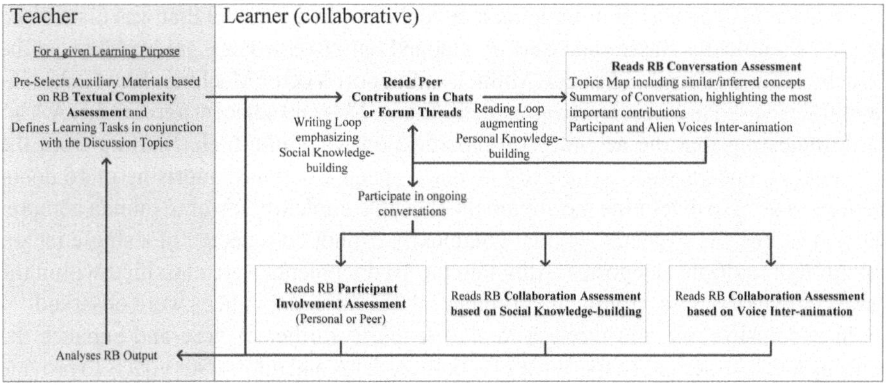

Fig. 2. Generic collaborative learning scenario integrating the use of *ReaderBench* (RB).

3 Validation Experiments

Multiple experiments have been performed, out of which only three are selected for brief presentation. Overall, various input sources were used for validating *ReaderBench* as a reliable educational software framework.

Experiment 1 [6] included 80 students between 8 and 11 years old (3rd– 5th grade), uniformly distributed in terms of their age who were asked to explain what they understood from two French stories of about 450 words. The students' oral self-explanations and their summaries were recorded and transcribed. Additionally, the students completed a posttest to assess their comprehension of the reading materials. The results indicated that paraphrases and the frequency of rhetorical phrases related to metacognition and self-regulation (e.g., "*il me semble*", "*je ne sais*", "*je comprends*") and causality (e.g., "*puisque*", "*à cause de*") were easier to identify than information or events stemming from students' experiences. Furthermore, cohesion with the initial text, as well as specific textual complexity factors, increased accuracy for the prediction of learners' comprehension.

Experiment 2 [3] included 110 students who were each asked to manually annotate 3 chats out of 10 selected conversations. We opted to distribute the evaluation of each conversation due to the high amount of time it takes to manually assess a single discussion (on average, users reported 1.5 - 4 h for a deep understanding). The results indicated a reliable automatic evaluation of both participation and collaboration. We validated the machine vs. human agreement by computing intra-class correlations between raters for each chat (avg $ICC_{participation}$ = .97; avg $ICC_{collaboration}$ = .90) and non-parametric correlations to the automatic scores (avg $Rho_{participation}$ = .84; avg $Rho_{collaboration}$ = .74). Overall, the validations supported the accuracy of the models built on cohesion and dialogism, whereas the proposed methods emphasized the dialogical perspective of collaboration in CSCL conversations.

Experiment 3 [7] consisted of building a textual complexity model that was distributed into five complexity classes and directly mapped onto five primary grade classes of the French national education system. Multiclass Support Vector Machine (SVM) classifications were used to assess exact agreement (EA = .733) and adjacent agreement (AA = .933), indicating that the accuracy of classification was quite high. Starting from the previously trained textual complexity model, a specific corpus comprising of 16 documents was used to determine the alignment of each complexity factor to human comprehension scores. As expected, textual complexity cannot be reflected in a single factor, but through multiple categories. Although the 16 documents were classified within the same complexity class, significant differences for individual indices were observed.

In conclusion, we aim through *ReaderBench* to further explore and enhance the learning and instructional experiences for both students and tutors. Our goal is to provide more rapid assessment, encourage collaboration and expertise sharing, while tracking the learners' progress with the support of our integrated framework.

Acknowledgments. This research was partially supported by the 644187 RAGE H2020-ICT-2014 and the 2008-212578 LTfLL FP7 projects, by the NSF grants 1417997 and 1418378 to ASU, as well as by the POSDRU/159/1.5/S/132397 and 134398 projects by ANR DEVCOMP Project ANR-10-blan-1907-01. We are also grateful to Cecile Perret for her help in preparing this paper.

References

1. Dascalu, M.: Analyzing Discourse and Text Complexity For Learning and Collaborating. Studies in Computational Intelligence, vol. 534. Springer, Switzerland (2014)
2. Dascalu, M., Dessus, P., Bianco, M., Trausan-Matu, S., Nardy, A.: Mining texts, learners productions and strategies with Reader Bench. In: Peña-Ayala, A. (ed.) Educational Data Mining: Applications and Trends, pp. 335–377. Springer, Switzerland (2014)
3. Dascalu, M., Trausan-Matu, Ş., Dessus, P.: Validating the automated assessment of participation and of collaboration in chat conversations. In: Trausan-Matu, S., Boyer, K.E., Crosby, M., Panourgia, K. (eds.) ITS 2014. LNCS, vol. 8474, pp. 230–235. Springer, Heidelberg (2014)
4. Nistor, N., Trausan-Matu, S., Dascalu, M., Duttweiler, H., Chiru, C., Baltes, B., Smeaton, G.: Finding student-centered open learning environments on the internet. Comput. Hum. Behav. **47**(1), 119–127 (2015)
5. Dascalu, M., Trausan-Matu, S., Dessus, P., McNamara, D.S.: Discourse cohesion: A signature of collaboration. In: 5th International Learning Analytics and Knowledge Conference (LAK 2015), pp. 350–354. ACM, Poughkeepsie, NY (2015)
6. Dascalu, M., Dessus, P., Bianco, M., Trausan-Matu, S.: Are automatically identified reading strategies reliable predictors of comprehension? In: Trausan-Matu, S., Boyer, K.E., Crosby, M., Panourgia, K. (eds.) ITS 2014. LNCS, vol. 8474, pp. 456–465. Springer, Heidelberg (2014)
7. Dascalu, M., Stavarache, L.L., Trausan-Matu, S., Dessus, P., Bianco, M.: Reflecting comprehension through French textual complexity factors. In: ICTAI 2014, pp. 615–619. IEEE, Limassol, Cyprus (2014)

KnowBrain: An Online Social Knowledge Repository for Informal Workplace Learning

Sebastian Dennerlein[1](✉), Dieter Theiler[2], Peter Marton[2], Patricia Santos Rodriguez[3], John Cook[3], Stefanie Lindstaedt[2], and Elisabeth Lex[1]

[1] Knowledge Technologies Institute, Graz University of Technology, Graz, Austria
{sdennerlein,dtheiler,elisabeth.lex}@tugraz.at
[2] Know-Center GmbH, Graz, Austria
{pmarton,slind}@know-center.at
[3] University of the West of England, Bristol, UK
{patricia.santosrodriguez,john2.cook}@uwe.ac.uk

Abstract. We present KnowBrain (KB), an open source Dropbox-like knowledge repository with social features for informal workplace learning. KB enables users (i) to share and collaboratively structure knowledge (ii) to access knowledge via sophisticated content- and metadata-based search and recommendation, and (iii) to discuss artefacts by means of multimedia-enriched Q&A. As such, KB can support, integrate and foster various collaborative learning processes related to daily work-tasks.

Keywords: Collaborative learning · Meaning making · Informal learning · Workplace learning

1 Introduction

Today's challenges in industry and research require workers and learners to effectively and efficiently communicate and collaborate with different disciplines in the digital world. Hence, tools are needed that facilitate social and collaborative learning or working in informal settings by supporting underlying meaning making processes [1]. KnowBrain (KB) aims to do just that. It is a social Dropbox-like system representing an online knowledge repository enriched with social features beyond sharing and organizing mechanisms: e.g., multimedia question-answer (Q&A) functionality, activity stream, grouping, or social recommenders. Since KB is self-hosted, i.e., it can be hosted on the own servers within an enterprise, which ensures data privacy and gives direct control over the whole system. Together, those features aim for unfolding the potential of meaning making to enable collaboration in an online social knowledge repository for organizational learning contexts.

2 Background

Informal workplace learning takes place alongside the daily work-tasks on a just-in-time basis. It is problem based, contextualized, episodic and includes the

© Springer International Publishing Switzerland 2015
G. Conole et al. (Eds.): EC-TEL 2015, LNCS 9307, pp. 509–512, 2015.
DOI: 10.1007/978-3-319-24258-3_48

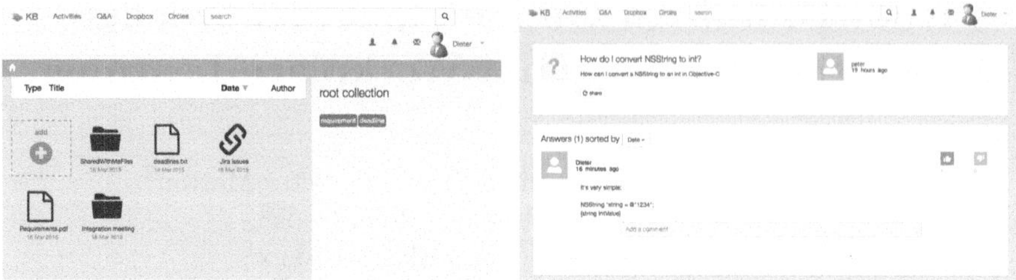

(a) Dropbox-like online knowledge repository (b) Answered question in Q&A

Fig. 1. KnowBrain's knowledge repository and question-answer (Q&A)

communication and transfer of knowledge and experiences [2–4]. Hence, informal learning experiences often involve other persons and lead to a social context [5]. In other words, informal workplace learning reflects complex situations with many interwoven actors and artefacts (e.g., documents, links, pictures). This situation requires that we repeatedly establish a shared understanding to be able to collaboratively solve problems and arrive at an agreed solution. This can be achieved through meaning making, which takes place when multiple collaborators contribute to a composition of interrelated manipulations of digital artefacts [6]. Hence, meaning making processes have to be considered, supported, reflected and exploited as part of social and collaborative learning tools [7]. KB builds the ground for such meaning making processes by enabling manifold ways of sharing and collaboratively manipulating artefacts, which are a necessary prerequisite for collaborative and organisational learning [8]. In addition, KB makes use of respective outcomes (i.e., metadata) via recommendations such as collaborative filtering to further stimulate meaning making.

3 KnowBrain: Prototype Description

KB provides an integrated solution to (collaboratively) collect and structure knowledge; to reuse and share information within a single platform; to access information via search and intelligent recommendation mechanisms; and to enable multimedia-enriched Q&A, discussions and chats. It opts for openness and loose coupling of functionality by decoupling client-side business (i.e., solely relying on HTML, CSS and Javascript backed-up by the AngularJS framework) from server-side REST-based infrastructure (i.e., the SocialSemanticServer - SSS - a service-framework for social semantic network data [9]), in comparison to monolithic and closed systems as they can be found in (organisational) knowledge repositories (e.g., Moodle or Blackboard from within the e-learning scene, or Sharepoint from within the enterprise content management area). Thus, KB is easily extendable, if new affordances are required to fully support informal workplace learning. It aims to integrate popular approaches of otherwise separated environments such as content management platforms (e.g., Dropbox or Google Drive), social platforms (e.g., Facebook or Google+) and help seeking platforms (e.g., StackExchange) with research findings in the area of recommendation, search and meaning making. Figures 1 and 2 show the current status of the prototype which enables sharing, social tagging and collaboratively organizing of (uploaded) artefacts such as learning or working material, in addition to hierarchically structuring the same in folders (see Fig. 1a). Thereby, sharing can be done directly with colleagues, friends, groups or the whole community. Collaboratively enriching artefacts with more or less formal concepts (i.e., tags or categories) is inherent to meaning making driven by technology. Hence, KB also supports learners in their needs to discuss artefacts or to raise questions with regard to particular topics of interest as shown by Fig. 1b. Interaction threads in KB can not only be enriched with comments and metadata, but also with multimedia artefacts from the local file system, or from already organized content in the platform. To scaffold learners with the task at hand, KB recommends similar threads or answers before new communication threads are created (see Fig. 2a). These threads can in turn be shared with others to make them visible to a broader community. To allow KB users to keep track of meaning making outcomes and their evolution, activities of collaborators can be followed via user- and group-based profiles as shown in Fig. 2b. These profiles also provide insights into the interdependency of artefacts, users, metadata, activities and communication threads. This way, users can better understand their learning or working groups and acquire relevant knowledge to further minimize interruptions of the ongoing meaning making process. Search can be utilized to find (multimedia) artefacts, users, groups and metadata using metadata and content-based keywords. On top of this, KB offers recommendations to enrich search results with interesting and relevant learning materials. Thus, the emerged traces of meaning making are reused and exploited to scaffold community members.

(a) Recommendations in Q&A (b) Activities within a grouping

Fig. 2. Example for KnowBrain's recommendations and activity stream

4 Conclusion and Future Work

The current prototype of KB leverages essential meaning making processes via collaborative (re)structuring, discussing and enriching of learning materials to enable online social learning and collaboration. In the future, we will integrate further intelligent services that take into account research in technology enhanced learning from within various areas such as sense making or expert and community identification. Planned features include graphical interaction mechanisms facilitating social categorization processes, as well as opportunities for collaborative writing to formalize and mature ideas into other formats. All these efforts aim for a seamless connection of workers and learners via thoughtful integrated features in a self-hosted knowledge repository that shall also effect real-life working processes in the long run.

Acknowledgements. This work is funded by the Know-Center and Learning Layers. Learning Layers is funded by the European Commission within the 7th Framework Programme (Grant Agreement 318209). The Know-Center is funded by the Austrian COMET Program under the auspices of the Austrian Ministry of Transport, Innovation and Technology, the Austrian Ministry of Economics and Labor and by the State of Styria. COMET is managed by the Austrian Research Promotion Agency FFG. We thank Viktoria Pammer-Schindler for her valuable feedback on the paper and Christoph Trattner for his work in the context of Learning Layers in the first 1.5 years of the project.

References

1. Stahl, G., Koschmann, T., Suthers, D.: Computer-supported collaboratives learning: an historical perspective. In: Sawyer, R.K. (ed.) Cambridge Handbook of the Learning Sciences, pp. 409–426. Cambridge University Press, Cambridge (2006)
2. Attwell, G., Baumgartl, B.: Creating Learning Spaces: Training and Professional Development for Trainers. Navreme, Vienna (2008)
3. Eraut, M.: Non-formal learning and tacit knowledge in professional work. Br. J. Educ. Psychol. **70**(1), 113–136 (2000)
4. Kooken, J., Ley, T., De Hoog, R.: How do people learn at the workplace? investigating fourworkplace learning assumptions. In: Duval, E., Klamma, R., Wolpers, M. (eds.) EC-TEL 2007. LNCS, vol. 4753, pp. 158–171. Springer, Heidelberg (2007)
5. Marsick, V.J., Volpe, M.: The nature and need for informal learning. Adv. Developing Hum. Resour. **1**(3), 1–9 (1999)
6. Suthers, D.D.: Technology affordances for intersubjective meaning making: a research agenda for CSCL. Int. J. Comput. Support. Collaborative Learn. **1**(3), 315–337 (2006)
7. Dennerlein, S.: Understanding and Supporting Intersubjective Meaning Making in Socio-Technical Systems. EC-TEL Doctoral Consortium (2013)
8. Pammer, V., Prilla, M., Divitini, M.: The functions of sharing experiences, observations and insights for reflective learning at work. In: Proceedings of the 2nd Workshop on Awareness and Reflection in Technology-Enhanced Learning (ARETL 2012) at EC-TEL 2012 (2012)
9. Kowald, D., Dennerlein, S., Theiler, D., Walk, S., Trattner, C.: The social semantic server a framework to provide services on social semantic network data. In: Proceedings of I-Semantics (2013)

Communicate! — A Serious Game for Communication Skills —

Johan Jeuring[1,3(✉)], Frans Grosfeld[2], Bastiaan Heeren[3], Michiel Hulsbergen[1], Richta IJntema[1], Vincent Jonker[1], Nicole Mastenbroek[1], Maarten van der Smagt[1], Frank Wijmans[1], Majanne Wolters[1], and Henk van Zeijts[4]

[1] Utrecht University, Utrecht, The Netherlands
{J.T.Jeuring,r.ijntema,v.jonker,n.j.j.m.mastenbroek, M.J.vanderSmagt,M.J.Wolters}@uu.nl

[2] University Medical Centre Utrecht, Utrecht, The Netherlands
F.J.M.Grosfeld@umcutrecht.nl

[3] Faculty of MST, Open University of the Netherlands, Heerlen, The Netherlands
Bastiaan.Heeren@ou.nl, m.hulsbergen@rhythmtraining.nl, fswijmans@gmail.com, henk@vrijeruimte.org

[4] Utrecht, The Netherlands

Abstract. Communicate! is a serious game for practicing communication skills. It supports practicing interpersonal communication skills between a health care professional such as a doctor or a pharmacist, or a (business) psychologist, and a patient or client. A player selects a scenario, and holds a consultation with a virtual character. In the consultation, the player chooses between the various options offered in the scenario. The player scores on the learning goals addressed by the scenario, and gets immediate feedback through the effect of the choice between the answer options on the utterance and emotion of the virtual character. Communicate! also offers an editor for scenarios. A scenario is a graph-like structure, extended with several constructs to avoid the development of repetitive structures. We have performed several experiments with Communicate!, both with students to evaluate the use of Communicate! in various programs at Utrecht University, and with teachers to evaluate the development of scenarios for Communicate!

Keywords: Communication skills · Scenarios · Authoring scenarios

1 Communicate

Good communication skills are essential for health care professionals such as doctors [1] and veterinarians [2], and (business) psychologists. At Utrecht University the programs Psychology, Medicine, Veterinary medicine, and Pharmacy offer introductory communication skills courses, in which yearly about 1500 students practice and learn communication skills. Practicing communication

© Springer International Publishing Switzerland 2015
G. Conole et al. (Eds.): EC-TEL 2015, LNCS 9307, pp. 513–517, 2015.
DOI: 10.1007/978-3-319-24258-3_49

Fig. 1. Screenshot of a consultation in Communicate!

skills is labour-intensive and requires quite a bit of organisation: students practice in pairs, together with an observer, or a student practices with an actor, again together with an observer. To offer better possibilities for practicing interpersonal communication skills between a health care professional and a client we have developed Communicate!, a serious game for practicing communication skills.

In Communicate!, a player selects a scenario, and holds a consultation with a virtual character. See Fig. 1 for a screenshot of the game. For example, Communicate! offers scenarios for practicing dispensing drugs to a client for the first time, and for bad news consultations. In the consultation, the player chooses between the various options offered in the scenario. For example, in the bad news consultation the player can choose between amongst others:

1. Rita, I'd like to discuss something with you, but first I want to make sure you won't get angry.
2. Rita, I have bad news for you. I'm very sorry, but I think it is better if you are treated by another psychologist.

The player scores on the learning goals addressed by the scenario, which in this case are clarity and empathy, and gets immediate feedback through the effect of the choices on the utterance and emotion of the virtual character, which in this case are anger, fear, contempt, and happiness. For example, if the player chooses the first option, Rita responds defensively, and Rita's fear, anger, and contempt increase. The player scores negatively on empathy and clarity. The second choice is the preferred one [3], and although Rita reacts angrily, the player scores positively on empathy and clarity.

After playing a scenario, a player gets feedback in the form of a score on the various learning goals of the scenario, and the consultation annotated with textual feedback at the choices the player took.

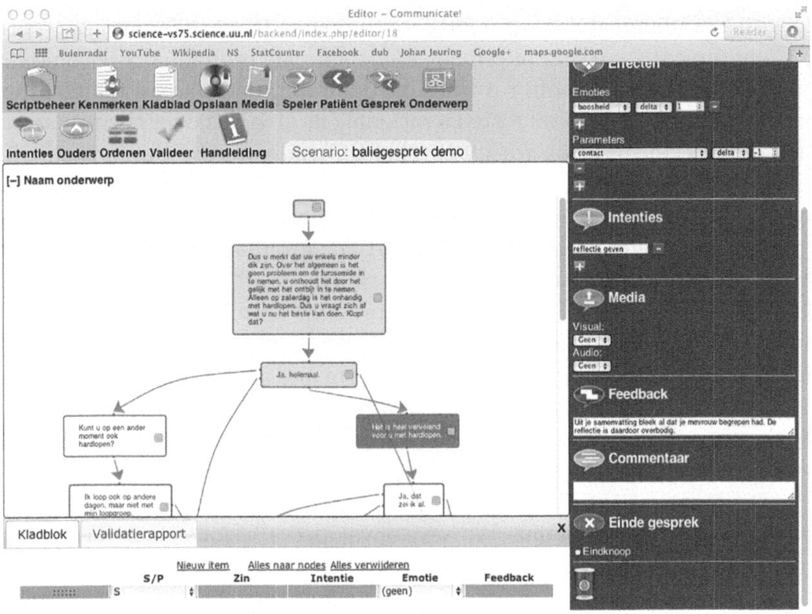

Fig. 2. Screenshot of the scenario editor for Communicate!

Scenarios. To use Communicate!, teachers develop scenarios that fit their curriculum. The teachers have various requirements for the development of scenarios: they want to have fine control over the form and structure of the consultation, avoid repetition in the scenarios as much as possible, and annotate each choice in the scenario with scores on the learning goals, emotional effect on the client, and feedback to the player. We developed a scenario editor for Communicate!, see Fig. 2. A teacher specifies the learning goals of a scenario, selects a virtual character, and then develops a graph-like structure for the consultation. In the scenario, a teacher can specify a sequence of choices for the player, but also conditions under which certain options are offered or not, parts of consultations that may be interleaved in any order, or that a (part of a) consultation may be stopped at any point. In the leaves of the graph are sentences, and the choices of the player are annotated with scores on learning goals and emotions of the client. A scenario developer can choose to replace the text of the client by audio.

In the back-end of the game we use a so-called domain reasoner [4,5] for scenarios to calculate the choices for the player. We use a domain reasoner for scenarios instead of dialog trees [6] or a virtual agent approach using beliefs, desires, and intentions [7] to offer fine control over the form and structure of the consultation, and to avoid repeating subtrees of scenarios as much as possible.

Experiments. To evaluate the current version of the tool, and obtain requirements for how to improve it, we performed several play tests and small experiments with Communicate! In april 2014 we compared three different interventions using Communicate! with 42 pharmacy students: play individually with no introduction, play individually after a brief introduction, and play in teams after an introduction. Later in 2014 we tested a rational emotive behavior therapy scenario and a bad news consultation with 9 psychology students. On March 13, 2015, we organised a think-aloud session with 5 veterinary medicine students: one individual, and two pairs. Besides with students, we performed several tests with health care professionals, and with several other ad-hoc groups of people. Students generally see added value in the game, and say things like: "This is much better than watching videos, because I really have to practice here," or "Nice to see how a patient reacts on the choices I make". Their main comments are related to recognizing the emotions in the client, and to the form and structure of some of the scenarios, which sometimes force a player in a particular direction, or which are set up to encourage discussions. The teachers think that the discussions after playing the scenarios are very fruitful.

Conclusions and Related Work. We have developed a serious game for practicing interpersonal communication skills between a professional and a client. When playing a scenario, the choices of the player have an effect on the utterances and emotions of the virtual client. This distinguishes Communicate! from for example the KAVE [8], which does not deal with emotions.

We have also developed a scenario editor that supports the easy development of scenarios for the game. The distinguishing features of the scenario editor are the fine control offered over the structure and form of scenarios, and the several constructs for avoiding repetitive work in the development of scenarios.

References

1. Silverman, J., Kurtz, S., Draper, J.: Skills For Communicating With Patients, 3rd edn. Radcliffe Publishing Limited, Milton Keynes (2013)
2. Gray, C., Moffet, J.: Handbook of Veterinary Communication Skills. Wiley-Blackwell, Hoboken (2010)
3. van der Molen, H.T., Kluytmans, F., Kramer, M.: Gespreksvoering. Vaardigheden en modellen (in Dutch). Wolters-Noordhoff (1995)
4. Heeren, B., Jeuring, J., Gerdes, A.: Specifying rewrite strategies for interactive exercises. Math. Comput. Sci. **3**(3), 349–370 (2010)
5. Heeren, B., Jeuring, J.: Feedback services for stepwise exercises. Sci. Comput. Program. **88**, 110–129 (2014)
6. Despain, W. (ed.): Writing for Video Games: From FPS to RPG. A.K. Peters, Natick (2008)

7. Muller, T.J., Heuvelink, A., van den Bosch, K., Swartjes, I.: Glengarry glen ross: using BDI for sales game dialogues. In: Artificial Intelligence and Interactive Digital Entertainment, pp. 167–172 (2012)
8. Richardson, A., Bracegirdle, L., McLachlan, S.I.H., Chapman, S.R.: Use of a three-dimensional virtual environment to teach drug-receptor interactions. Am. J. Pharm. Educ. **77**(1), 11 (2013)

Bucket-Server: A System for Including Teacher-Controlled Flexibility in the Management of Learning Artifacts in Across-Spaces Learning Situations

Juan A. Muñoz-Cristóbal[1], Juan I. Asensio-Pérez[1(✉)], Alejandra Martínez-Monés[1], Luis P. Prieto[2], Iván M. Jorrín-Abellán[3], and Yannis Dimitriadis[1]

[1] GSIC-EMIC Group, Universidad de Valladolid, Valladolid, Spain
juanmunoz@gsic.uva.es, amartine@infor.uva.es, {juaase,yannis}@tel.uva.es
[2] CHILI Research Lab, École Polytechnique Fédérale de Lausanne, Lausanne, Switzerland
luis.prieto@epfl.ch
[3] Bagwell College of Education, Kennesaw State University, Kennesaw, GA, USA
ijorrina@kennesaw.edu

Abstract. Recent technological advances in mobile devices enable the connection of classrooms with other virtual and physical spaces. Some approaches aim at helping teachers carry out learning situations across such spaces. However, these proposals tend to be isolated from other activities in teachers' current common practices, and do not allow teacher-controlled flexibility of what students do during the enactment. Aiming to overcome such limitations, the Bucket-Server is a system that enables teachers to include *learning buckets* in their learning situations: containers of learning artifacts generated and/or consumed across-spaces by students during the enactment. Teachers create *learning buckets* at design time, configuring them with constraints to regulate the degree of freedom offered to the students. These *learning buckets* can be integrated into multiple existing technologies used in different educational spaces (e.g., web, physical and 3D virtual world spaces), thus helping embed buckets in the teachers' current common practices.

Keywords: Across-spaces · Flexibility · Augmented reality · VLE · Virtual world

1 Introduction

Besides the physical classroom, many different virtual and physical spaces have shown affordances for learning. That is the case, for instance, of Virtual Learning Environments (VLEs), which enable both distance and face-to-face learning [1]; outdoor spaces, allowing contextual and experiential learning [2]; and even 3D virtual worlds (3DVWs), enabling the perception of objects from multiple perspectives [3]. Recent advances in technologies such as mobile devices and Augmented Reality (AR) [4] are allowing to merge such physical and virtual spaces into environments wherein a continuity of learning is possible [5]. Helping teachers achieve seamless learning across-spaces has been marked by the Technology Enhanced

© Springer International Publishing Switzerland 2015
G. Conole et al. (Eds.): EC-TEL 2015, LNCS 9307, pp. 518–521, 2015.
DOI: 10.1007/978-3-319-24258-3_50

Learning research community as a key challenge to explore [6]. Thus, multiple authors have proposed solutions aimed to extend education beyond the walls of the classroom and outside the windows of VLEs [7–9]. However, such proposals tend to limit the possibilities for teachers to regulate the degree of flexibility offered to students (e.g., to choose the tools to use). Such flexibility, as well as the teachers' capability of regulating the balance between guidance and freedom offered, are important concerns in some pedagogies, such as CSCL [10]. In addition, the across-spaces learning situations supported by such proposals are typically isolated from other activities and technologies of the teachers current practice. This may negatively affect teachers' orchestration load (what some authors call the "classroom usability" [11]). The *Bucket-Server* system aims at aiding in such challenge, by enabling teachers to embed *learning buckets* in their activities, which may be carried out using several existing technologies focused on different web, physical and 3DVW spaces. The next section describes the learning bucket notion and the Bucket-Server system, and Sect. 3 outlines the main implications of this work.

2 The Bucket-Server System

The notion of *learning bucket* [12] was proposed with the aim of introducing flexibility in the management of learning artifacts during the enactment of across-spaces learning situations (e.g., regarding technological, contextual or arbitrary decisions). A learning bucket is a container of learning artifacts that is created by the teacher at design time, and configured with *constraints*. Such constraints define what the students will be able to do at enactment time within the bucket (e.g., tools allowed, maximum number of artifacts to insert, etc.), thus enabling the teacher to regulate the degree of flexibility (and coercion) provided. During the enactment, the students can use the bucket to create learning artifacts of multiple types, e.g., using existing Web 2.0 tools such as Google Drive[1]. The students can also *position* the artifacts in different spaces (e.g., web, physical and 3DVW) using a variety of positioning types (e.g., geographical coordinates, AR markers, or any other coordinates system). The buckets and the artifacts they contain can be accessed from different spaces by means of technologies commonly used in each space (e.g., VLEs in web spaces, AR apps in physical spaces and Virtual Globes [13], VGs, in 3DVW spaces).

The *Bucket-Server* (Fig. 1, top) is a system that implements the learning bucket notion. The Bucket-Server can be integrated with multiple existing *artifact providers* (including several Web 2.0 tools, widgets servers, etc.), thus enabling the population of the learning buckets with multiple kinds of artifacts. The Bucket-Server can be also integrated with multiple existing technologies focused on web (VLEs), physical (mobile AR apps) and 3DVW (VGs) spaces. This integration enables the creation of buckets from any of the aforementioned spaces (e.g., using a VLE), and access them as well as their artifacts, using other technologies in other spaces (e.g., AR apps and VGs). Figure 1 (down) shows a basic example of the use of a learning bucket. A teacher creates

[1] https://www.google.com/drive/. Last access June 30, 2015.

a learning bucket at design time from within a Moodle[2] course and configures it with a set of constraints. During the enactment, a group of students create different learning artifacts in the bucket (in this case, Google Drive documents and presentations) regarding types of trees and monuments of the world, and position them in specific geolocations. Later on, another group of students (and also the teacher from the VLE) can access the artifacts using the Junaio[3] AR app, and the 3D view of the Google Earth[4] VG.

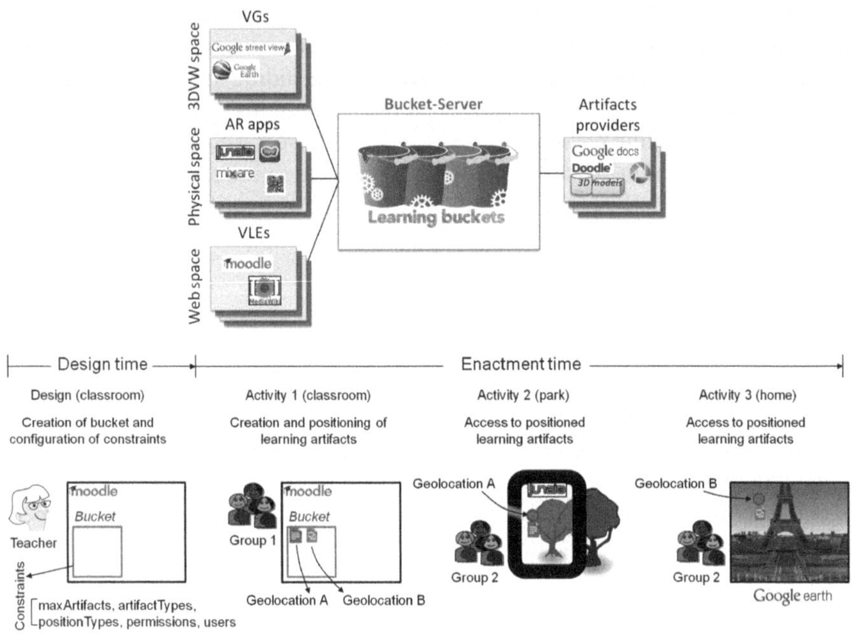

Fig. 1. The Bucket-Server system (top) and example of the use of a learning bucket (down)

3 Conclusions

The Bucket-Server helps solve the challenge initially described, since it enables teachers to include multiple learning buckets in the different activities of their across-spaces learning situations, thus allowing the flexible creation and positioning of student-generated content. The Bucket-Server architecture allows teachers to choose among a wide range of technologies (of different types and for different spaces), including those of commonly used (e.g., VLEs), that are integrated in a single across-spaces learning environment.

[2] https://moodle.org. Last access June 30, 2015.
[3] http://www.junaio.com. Last access June 30, 2015.
[4] https://www.google.com/earth/. Last access June 30, 2015.

Acknowledgements. This research has been partially supported by the Spanish Projects TIN2011-28308-C03-02, VA277U14, the European Project 531262-LLP-2012-ES-KA3-KA3MP, and the Marie Curie Fellowship FP7-PEOPLE-2012-IEF (project no. 327384). The authors thank the rest of the GSIC/EMIC research team for their ideas and support.

References

1. Keller, C.: Virtual learning environments: three implementation perspectives. Learn. Media Technol. **30**(3), 299–311 (2005)
2. Dyson, L.E., Litchfield, A., Lawrence, E., Raban, R., Leijdekkers, P.: Advancing the m-learning research agenda for active, experiential learning: four case studies. Australas. J. Educ. Technol. **25**(2), 250–267 (2009)
3. Dede, C.: Immersive interfaces for engagement and learning. Science **323**(5910), 66–69 (2009)
4. Wu, H.-K., Lee, S.W.-Y., Chang, H.-Y., Liang, J.-C.: Current status, opportunities and challenges of augmented reality in education. Comput. Educ. **62**, 41–49 (2013)
5. Li, L., Zheng, Y., Ogata, H., Yano, Y.: A framework of ubiquitous learning environment. In: The Fourth International Conference on Computer and Information Technology (CIT 2004), pp. 345–350. Wuhan, China (2004)
6. Milrad, M., Wong, L.-H., Sharples, M., Hwang, G.-J., Looi, C.-K., Ogata, H.: Seamless learning: an international perspective on next-generation technology-enhanced learning. In: Berge, Z.L., Muilenburg, L.Y. (eds.) Handbook of Mobile Learning, pp. 95–108. Routledge, Abingdon (2013)
7. Casany, M.J., Alier, M., Mayol, E., Piguillem, J., Galanis, N., García-Peñalvo, F.J., Conde, M.Á.: Moodbile: a framework to integrate m-learning applications with the LMS. J. Res. Pract. Inf. Technol. **44**(2), 129–149 (2012)
8. Wong, L.-H., Looi, C.-K.: What Seams Do We Remove in Mobile-assisted Seamless Learning? a critical review of the literature. Comput. Educ. **57**(4), 2364–2381 (2011)
9. Muñoz-Cristóbal, J.A., Prieto, L.P., Asensio-Pérez, J.I., Martínez-Monés, A., Jorrín-Abellán, I.M., Dimitriadis, Y.: Coming down to earth: helping teachers use 3D virtual worlds in across-spaces learning situations. Educ. Technol. Soc. **18**(1), 13–26 (2015)
10. Dillenbourg, P., Tchounikine, P.: Flexibility in macro-scripts for computer-supported collaborative learning. J. Comput. Assist. Learn. **23**(1), 1–13 (2007)
11. Cuendet, S., Bonnard, Q., Do-Lenh, S., Dillenbourg, P.: Designing augmented reality for the classroom. Comput. Educ. **68**, 557–569 (2013)
12. Muñoz-Cristóbal, J.A., Prieto, L.P., Asensio-Pérez, J.I., Jorrín-Abellán, I.M., Martínez-Monés, A., Dimitriadis, Y.: Sharing the burden: introducing student-centered orchestration in across-spaces learning situations. In: Hernández-Leo, D., Ley, T., Klamma, R., Harrer, A. (eds.) EC-TEL 2013. LNCS, vol. 8095, pp. 621–622. Springer, Heidelberg (2013)
13. Rakshit, R., Ogneva-Himmelberger, Y.: Application of Virtual Globes in education. Geography Compass **2**(6), 1995–2010 (2008)

Using Video Visualizations in Open edX to Understand Learning Interactions of Students

Héctor J. Pijeira Díaz[1,2], Javier Santofimia Ruiz[1], José A. Ruipérez-Valiente[1,3(✉)], Pedro J. Muñoz-Merino[1], and Carlos Delgado Kloos[1]

[1] Universidad Carlos III de Madrid, Madrid, Spain
{100075697,100060449}@alumnos.uc3m.es,
{jruipere,pedmume,cdk}@it.uc3m.es
[2] Oulun yliopisto, Oulu, Finland
[3] IMDEA Networks Institute, Madrid, Spain

Abstract. The emergence of Massive Open Online Courses (MOOCs) has caused a high disrupting effect on online education. One of the most extended MOOC platforms is Open edX. There is a demanding necessity by the instructors and students of these courses to provide timely analytics tools that can help understand the learning process at any moment. In this direction we have developed the Add-on of learNing AnaLYtics Support for open Edx (ANALYSE), which is our learning analytics contribution for Open edX. In this demonstration paper we will provide guidelines on how to use some of the ANALYSE video visualizations in order to detect problems in video resources, so that the learning process can be improved.

Keywords: Moocs · Open edx · Learning analytics · Visualizations

1 Introduction

MOOCs have had quite an important impact on education in the last years. These courses usually have thousands of students, which makes them particularly difficult to control and have a feeling about what is actually happening. Learning analytics functionality is a key factor in these virtual environments for allowing students self-reflection and facilitating teachers to make decisions based on data. However, most of the MOOC platforms are not providing yet the learning analytics functionalities to support these courses. Therefore, as an example, instructors might feel a little bit lost about how their students are progressing in the course or whether some learning resources are causing problems due to a bad design. The use of visualizations with the objective of transmitting information is a common tool in learning analytics. We can find several learning analytics developments for different platforms such as ALAS-KA [1] for Khan Academy which also include visualizations for video activity.

Currently our efforts are focused on Open edX platform. Most of the MOOC data analyses in the literature are performed over the static data after course completion. As

© Springer International Publishing Switzerland 2015
G. Conole et al. (Eds.): EC-TEL 2015, LNCS 9307, pp. 522–525, 2015.
DOI: 10.1007/978-3-319-24258-3_51

an example we can find several post-hoc analysis papers[1] by the MIT Office of Digital Learning. However, there is not much work developed in Open edX aimed at providing timely information for both students and instructors while taking and teaching a course respectively. The current support for learning analytics in Open edX is at an early stage providing a single visualization about the progress in problems. In this direction we have developed ANALYSE, which currently incorporates 12 brand new visualizations that were not present previously in Open edX. In this paper we provide guidelines on how to use some of the video visualizations included in ANALYSE to detect problems in educational video resources.

2 Detecting Problems in Video Resources with Visualizations

Information regarding the use of videos is often not provided by MOOC platforms, an exception can be Khan Academy[2] which provides several visualizations regarding video activity for students and instructors. In this section we use three of the visualizations provided by ANALYSE to study how these charts can be interpreted in order to obtain further insight about problems in video resources. In MOOCs such as the ones delivered in edX, video resources are one of the most used components by students, as reported initial research on this matter [2]. Therefore we want to point out the importance of providing tools that support such type of analysis, for example to find out which designs are better in order to improve the effectiveness of video resources. The data of these examples have been prepared for the sole purpose of creating a case study for this scientific contribution.

Figure 1 shows in dark blue the *Different Video Time* in each video (from 0 to 100) and in light blue *Total Video Time* (from 0 to infinite). The difference between these two values is that the *Different Video Time* can be seen as the percentage of progress in a video whereas the *Total Video Time* can contain parts that have been reproduced repetitively by the students. Therefore if the difference between these two values is very high, it might indicate that there are problems in that video because students are repeating the video more than once. Analyzing Fig. 1 we can detect two videos where the difference between the two values is very high, which are "Correlations" and "Algorithms" and we want to look more in depth. Figure 2 shows for these two videos the *Repetition of Video Intervals* visualization, where we can see the number of times that each second of a video has been reproduced and Fig. 3 shows the *Distribution of Video Events* visualization where it is represented the second in which each video event was triggered.

Figure 2 shows for each one of these two videos the *Repetition of Video Intervals* visualization, where we can see the number of times that each video second has been reproduced. Additionally, the second in which each video event was triggered is represented by the *Distribution of Video Events* visualization shown in Fig. 3. We analyze first the video "Correlations". We can see in Fig. 2 that there is an approximate interval from second 15 to 70 that has been reproduced many more times than the rest of the

---

[1] http://odl.mit.edu/mitx-working-papers. (visited on 07/01/2015).

[2] https://www.khanacademy.org (visited on 07/01/2015).

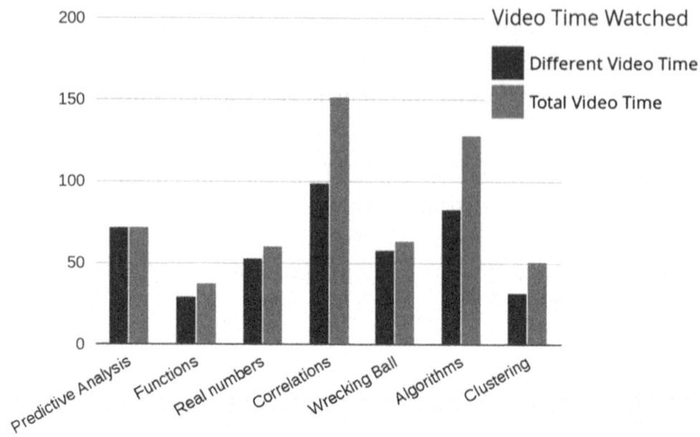

Fig. 1. *Video Time Watched* visualization by all the students in the course

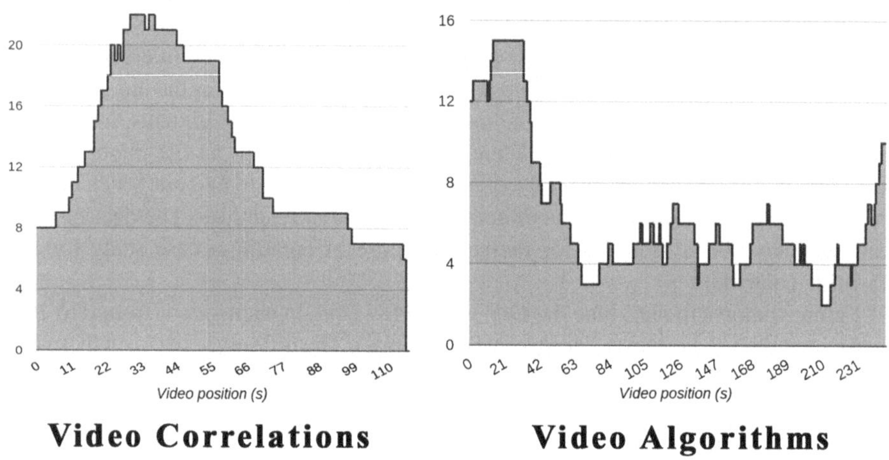

Fig. 2. *Repetition of Video Intervals* comparison between the two videos

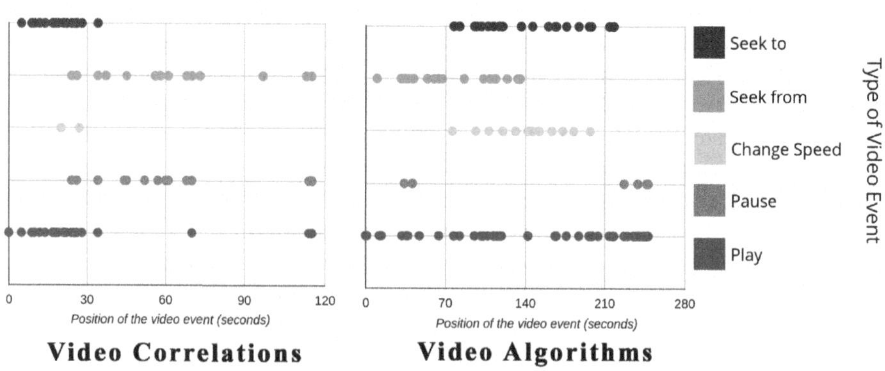

Fig. 3. *Distribution of Video Events* in the two problematic videos

video. In addition, if we inspect Fig. 3 we can check that there are many "seek to" events approximately in the start of that time interval (around second 15). A possible interpretation of these results could be that the video interval might be very hard to understand for the students and they are seeking to the start of the interval to watch it repetitively.

In the case of the video "Algorithms", Fig. 2 shows that students start watching the video a lot, but then it gradually drops out to a much lower level of reproduction times after second 60. The additional information provided by Fig. 3 shows that the video "Algorithms" have many "seek from" events around second 70 to a later time, as we can also find many "seek to" events around second 140. Therefore, a possible explanation for these results is that the video has a normal start but around second 60 some kind of problem is arising in the video and that is causing students to seek to a later time of the video; maybe this part of the video is not an important one, and that might be the reason why students are forwarding time. Previous works have also analyzed the possible meanings of peaks in the number of views in certain segments of videos with similar conclusions [3].

Acknowledgements. This work has been supported by the "eMadrid" project (Regional Government of Madrid) under grant S2013/ICE-2715 and the EEE project (Spanish Ministry of Science and Innovation, "Plan Nacional de I + D+I") under grant TIN2011-28308-C03-01.

References

1. Ruipérez-Valiente, J.A., Muñoz-Merino, P.J., Leony, D., DelgadoKloos, C.: ALAS-KA: A learning analytics extension for better understanding the learning process in the Khan Academy platform. Comput. Hum. Behav. **47**, 139–148 (2015)
2. Seaton, D.T., Bergner, Y., Chuang, I., Mitros, P., Pritchard, D.E.: Who does what in a massive open online course? Commun. ACM **57**, 58–65 (2014)
3. Kim, J., Guo, P.J., Seaton, D.T., Mitros, P., Gajos, K.Z., Miller, R.C.: Understanding in-video dropouts and interaction peaks in online lecture videos. In: Proceedings of the First ACM Conference on Learning @ scale conference, pp. 31–40 (2014)

Presentation Trainer: Polishing Your Communication Skills

Jan Schneider(✉), Dirk Börner, Peter van Rosmalen, and Marcus Specht

Welten Institute, Open University of the Netherlands, Heerlen, The Netherlands
{jan.schneider,dirk.boerner,peter.vanrosmalen,
marcus.specht}@ou.nl

Abstract. The paper presents the evolution of Presentation Trainer, a prototypical sensor-based toolkit that works as a public speaking instructor. It tracks the learner's body posture, movements and voice in order to provide instructional feedback on nonverbal communication skills. Based on our design-based research the current version of the Presentation Trainer is able to provide the learner with the type of feedback that it considers to be appropriate according to the learner's performance; it includes haptic feedback helping to reduce the learner's cognitive load.

Keywords: Sensor-based learning · Immediate feedback · Demonstration

1 Introduction

"There is no such thing as failure, only feedback." Is a common motivational phrase, whose truth appears to be undisputed. However, knowing how to correctly interpret this feedback is not always a straightforward task. This is the case of public speaking, where the feedback provided by a tutor has proven to have a big influence in the development of the learners' public speaking skills [1]. The timing, in which this feedback is given, delayed or immediate [2], has also shown to be an important factor regarding the learning outcomes. Revealing that immediate feedback is far more efficient for aspects that can be corrected immediately, such as the nonverbal communication of the speaker [3]. The implementation of immediate feedback in general, not only for public speaking, is still a challenge. Hence, it requires personal tutors to be constantly evaluating the learner. Sensor technologies seem to be suitable solution for this challenge, since they have the innate capability to continuously track the learner. Furthermore they have already shown to support learning by providing learners with feedback in a vast number of learning applications [4]. To study how sensors can be used to provide learners with immediate feedback for public speaking we conducted a design-based research approach [5] on the *Presentation Trainer*, a tool designed to support learners on the development of their public speaking skills. In this paper we describe the evolution of the *Presentation Trainer* up to its current 3rd version.

© Springer International Publishing Switzerland 2015
G. Conole et al. (Eds.): EC-TEL 2015, LNCS 9307, pp. 526–529, 2015.
DOI: 10.1007/978-3-319-24258-3_52

2 Presentation Trainer Iterations

The *Presentation Trainer* is a sensor-based system that works as a public speaker instructor for nonverbal communication. For its development we followed a design-based research methodology, creating a different version of the tool on each iteration of our research. This section describes the main characteristics of the different versions of the *Presentation Trainer.*

2.1 First Version

The first version of the *Presentation Trainer* was developed in Processing 2.1[1]. It uses the Microsoft Kinect Sensor V1[2] to track the body language of the learner and the computer's integrated microphone to track the learner's voice.

This version of the trainer provides feedback through a computer monitor using a dashboard interface (Fig. 1). This interface contains eight feedback modules including: A skeleton representation that highlights the limbs of the learner placed in a wrong position, a volume graph mirroring the learner's usage of her voice, an amount of movement indicator, four modules that get highlighted giving feedback about specific mistakes, and a general feedback module that gets highlighted when a mistake is tracked.

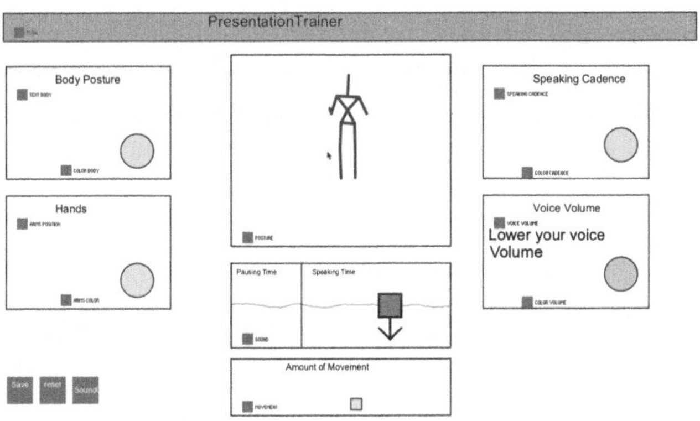

Fig. 1. Presentation trainer V1.

2.2 Second Version

The second version of the Presentation Trainer was also developed in Processing 2.1 and it also uses the first version of the Microsoft Kinect and the computer's integrated microphone to track the users body language and use of voice.

[1] Processing: http://processing.org. [Accessed 13 March 2015].
[2] http://www.xbox.com/en-US/kinect. [Accessed 13 March 2015].

It contains two different modes: the freestyle, and the Exercise mode. The freestyle mode (Fig. 2) allows learner's to practice for their presentations while receiving feedback from a clear dashboard interface. This interface contains an enhanced mirror that highlights important aspects of the learner's body language, a voice histogram and four modules represented by icons, that when highlighted shortly instruct the learner how to correct her performance.

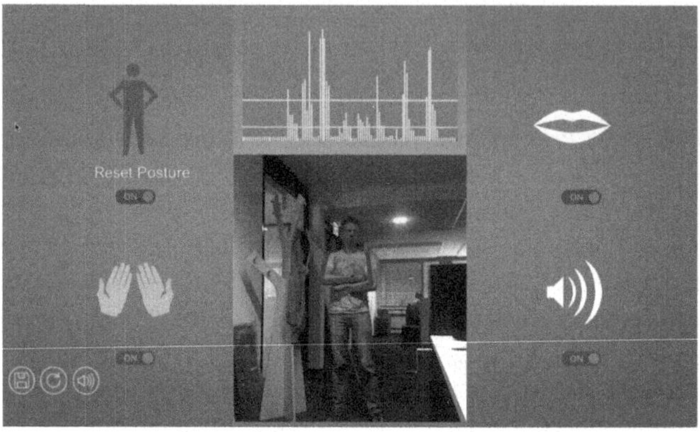

Fig. 2. Freestyle mode interface

The exercise mode contains six different exercises, each one of them designed to train a specific skill such as: standing in a proper posture, using different volume ranges, proper use of hand gestures, proper use of pauses, leaning in and speaking soft, and keeping composure while answering questions.

2.3 Third Version

This third version of the Presentation Trainer was developed using the.Net Framework[3] and the Microsoft Kinect for Windows V2[4] to track the learner's body language and voice.

It contains an immersive interface that continuously shows a mirrored image of the learner and showing at maximum feedback about one specific aspect at the time (Fig. 3). It uses an intelligent algorithm that decides the appropriate time and type of feedback to be provided to the learner. The type of feedback can be continuous without interrupting the learner's flow, or interruptive when the tool infers that the learner needs to stop and reflect about her performance. According to the learner's performance it suggests the learner to focus on working on a specific communication aspect at the time, and guides her through it. To ensure that the learner receives the right feedback at the right time while training, this version the *Presentation Trainer* also provides feedback to the learner through the haptic channel.

---

[3] http://www.microsoft.com/net. [Accessed 13 March 2015].

[4] http://www.microsoft.com/en-us/kinectforwindows/. [Accessed 13 March 2015].

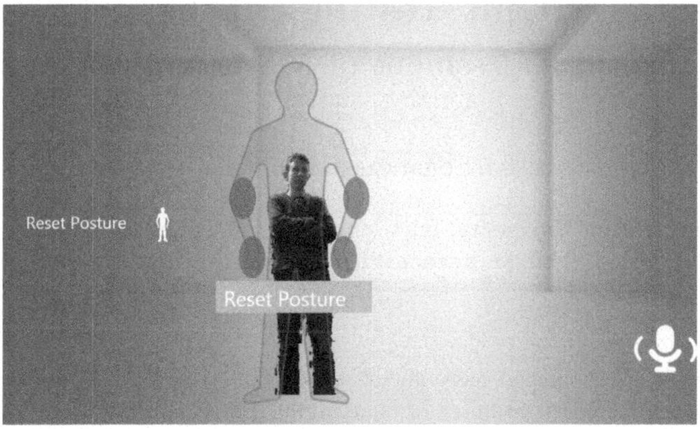

Fig. 3. Presentation trainer V3

3 Conclusions and Future Work

The Presentation Trainer is a sensor-based tool that works as public speaker instructor. It has been evolving to its third version so far based on observations coming from user tests. The general findings of the tests have shown that providing the learners with the type of immediate feedback that can be easily assimilated and therefore help them to develop their skills, is a quite challenging task that requires a meticulous design.

For future work we will continue our design-research approach, to improve the feedback of the Presentation Trainer, exploring how to personalized it.

Acknowledgement. The underlying research project is partly funded by the METALOGUE project. METALOGUE is a Seventh Framework Programme collaborative project funded by the European Commission, grant agreement number: 611073 (http://www.metalogue.eu).

References

1. Kerby, D., Romine, J.: Develop oral presentation skills through accounting curriculum design and course-embedded assessment. J. Educ. Bus. **85**(3), 172–179 (2009)
2. Mory, E.H.: Feedback research revisited. In: Handbook of Research on Educational Communications, pp. 745–784. (2004)
3. King, P., Young, M., Behnke, R.: Public speaking performance improvement as a function of information processing in immediate and delayed feedback interventions. Commun. Educ. **49**(4), 365–374 (2000)
4. Schneider, J., Börner, D., van Rosmalen, P., Specht, M.: Augmenting the senses: a review on sensor-based learning support. Sensors **15**(2), 4097–4133 (2015)
5. Anderson, T., Shattuck, J.: Design-based research a decade of progress in education research? Educ. Res. **41**(1), 16–25 (2012)

Unit Testing Maths
Automated Assessment of Mathematic Exercises

Edgar Seemann(✉)

Furtwangen University, Furtwangen im Schwarzwald, Germany
edgar.seemann@hs-furtwangen.de

Abstract. Automated assessment systems for the field of mathematics need to tackle a number of challenging problems. Existing systems focus on the processing of mathematic expressions and their different representations (e.g. $x^{1/2}$ vs. $\sqrt{x}$). In order to correctly assess a student's solution approach, a system has to check intermediate steps and conclusions. Typically, this assessment fails completely in the presence of a small oversight error at the beginning of an exercise. In this paper, we will show, how the idea of unit testing from the field of computer science may be used to detect and handle follow up and cascading errors in mathematic exercises. Thus, resulting in a fairer grading outcome, which is closer to manual grading. The developed technique may be used for large scale (online) courses or acceptance tests.

Keywords: Mathematics · Assessment · Grading · Tutoring

1 Introduction

The adoption of automated assessment techniques for both exercises and exams has become more and more common in recent years. The main drivers of this development are increasing student numbers, the rise of online courses and more user-friendly testing tools. In Germany e.g. the number of students rose by nearly 35 % from 2007 till 2013, whereas university budgets typically lag (see University World News 2014). Regular manual grading in large courses or even MOOCs becomes impractical for the teaching staff. Thus, it is impossible to provide students with an adequate and prompt feedback on their learning success. Modern E-Learning systems (e.g. Moodle) incorporate software modules, which allow even less tech-savvy teachers to create simple electronic tests. e The adoption of automated tests can be relatively straight forward for some domains which focus on memorizing tasks with closed-ended questions, e.g. medicine. For other domains, which traditionally use open-ended questions (e.g. the humanities) or have a focus on technical understanding, this is a more challenging task.

In technical domains as e.g. engineering or mathematics automated tests are not commonly used. While there are e-learning and e-teaching systems tailored towards technical and mathematical education and math tutoring (e.g. [1,3,5,8]), those are, to our knowledge, not used to a larger extent at universities.

© Springer International Publishing Switzerland 2015
G. Conole et al. (Eds.): EC-TEL 2015, LNCS 9307, pp. 530–534, 2015.
DOI: 10.1007/978-3-319-24258-3_53

In fact, the development and active use of many of those systems seem to have halted. Despite promising results (e.g. [7]) the same holds true for many automatic grading systems, which have been developed specifically for the field of mathematics (e.g. [4,9]). Peer grading systems (e.g. [2]) also try to address automatic grading by delegating the process from teachers to peers. Their obvious drawbacks are in the areas of possibly unbalanced and non-immediate feedback.

In this paper we present a novel technique for the automatic assessment of technical and in particular mathematic exercises. In order to be able to analyze more complex exercises we draw inspiration from the concept of unit testing, which is popular in the field of computer science [6]. The idea is to think of a mathematical exercise as an algorithm. These algorithms are typically multi-step processes with successive intermediate results. In order to assure a fair assessment result, all of these steps should be taken into account. Small computer programs (unit tests) allow us to detect follow up or cascading errors and handle them accordingly. By applying this technique, we avoid an all-or-nothing style grading, where students only succeed, when all steps are correct.

2 Unit Testing

In computer science unit testing is a technique to validate the functionality of a software program. In order to implement and validate the functionality of an algorithm, a programmer proceeds in the following steps:

1. Split the algorithm into meaningful parts
2. Define input/output parameters for the individual parts
3. Implement test cases for each part

For the automatic assessment of math exercises, we treat the exercise problem as an algorithm. Similar to a computer program, we then divide the algorithm into multiple parts. An exercise to compute the distance of a point P to a given plane E could e.g. be divided into one part, which computes an orthogonal vector to E, another part which computes a connecting vector between the plane E and the point P and a third part, which executes the projection onto the orthogonal vector. A test case would be constructed by defining:

- Input data
- An algorithmic implementation
  (known to be correct)
- Output data

The output data of a test case always corresponds to a student's response. We cannot assume this output data to be valid. Instead we need to provide an algorithmic implementation which is known to be correct. Thus, instead of testing the algorithm, we are testing the output data.

In order to detect follow up or cascading errors, however, we need to modify this procedure. Imagine e.g. that a student makes a mistake in the computation of the orthogonal vector. Then, all subsequent test cases would fail as well, since the student's results depend on this first computed value. If a test case is dependent on the output of a previous test case, we therefore can use this output as an input value of the test case. That is, instead of using precomputed valid input values for each test case, we use the outputs of earlier test cases as input for subsequent test cases. Note that, we obtain a directed acyclic graph of test cases which needs to be evaluated.

3 Exercise Design

When phrasing a problem or question, teachers have to keep in mind that the students' responses need to be covered by a test case. In particular, this means that they need to clearly specify not only the input information given in the exercise, but also the required intermediate results a student needs to provide.

An exercise problem could be specified in the following manner:

> Compute the distance between the point $P = (3, 3, -2)$ and the plane E using an orthogonal projection. The plane E is given as
>
> $$E : \boldsymbol{x} = \begin{pmatrix} 1 \\ 1 \\ 0 \end{pmatrix} + s \begin{pmatrix} 1 \\ 0 \\ 1 \end{pmatrix} + t \begin{pmatrix} 0 \\ 1 \\ 1 \end{pmatrix}.$$
>
> (a) Compute a vector $\boldsymbol{n}$ orthogonal to E
> (b) Which vector $\boldsymbol{v}$ can you use for this projection?
> (c) What is the absolute value d of the distance?

That is, the exercise problem is split into three steps. For each step the students have to provide an intermediate solution, which will be used as output or input data for the unit tests. Each subquestion (a), (b) and (c) correspond to one test case.

4 Exercise Implementation

Test cases may be implemented in any programming language, but mathematic languages like Matlab or Maxima are the obvious choice due to their large libraries of mathematical functions and of course due to their convenient syntax. It is important to realize, that test cases may leverage the full power of the programming language and the implementations of test cases may range from a simple numeric comparison to complex algorithms.

For the sample question given in Sect. 3, there are three test cases. The first test case needs to verify that the vector $\boldsymbol{n}$ provided by the student is indeed orthogonal to the given plane. This could e.g. be solved by the following program:

```
function isValid = testCase1()
    // input data
    r1 = [1; 0; 1];
    r2 = [0; 1; 1];
    // reference solution
    o = cross(r1,r2);
    // output data
    n = userField1();
    // result
    isValid = rank([n o])==1;
```

That is, once the input data is specified, the program computes a reference solution o, which is used to compare to the student response. Obviously, the sub-question has not one, but an infinite number of possible solutions. Any multiple of an orthogonal vector is again orthogonal.

The third test case in our example, depends on the results of the first two steps. This could be implemented as follows:

```
function isValid = testCase3()
    // input data
    eps = 0.01;
    n = userField1();
    v = userField2();
    // reference solution
    p = v'*n/norm(n);
    // output data
    d = userField3();
    // result
    isValid = (p-d)<eps;
```

Note, that the test case uses the input provided by the student instead of correct reference values. This allows the system to handle follow up errors. That is, a student's solution is correct, if it is correct based on his/her previous intermediate results. Consequently a mistake early in the solution process does not necessarily result in mistakes for subsequent steps.

5 Conclusion

In this paper, we have described a novel grading system for the assessment of mathematic or engineering exercises. The idea is to use small but sophisticated computer programs to validate the correctness of a student response. These computer programs are inspired by the concept of unit tests, which are popular in software engineering.

Our systems requires teachers to implement an algorithmic test case for each exercise using a programming language. This additional effort, however, results in a new flexibility. Teachers may use a much larger variety of questions, since the system "understands" mathematical expressions and can compare different representations of numbers and functions. For the students the benefit lies in a fairer grading result. Follow up errors can be detected and handled appropriately. Thus, avoiding the all-or-nothing style grading of most other assessment systems.

References

1. Beal, C., Beck, J., Woolf, B.: Impact of intelligent computer instruction on girls' math self concept and beliefs in the value of math. In: Annual meeting of the American Educational Research Association (1998)
2. Caprotti, O., Ojalainen, J., Pauna, M., Seppl, M.: Weps peer and automatic assessment in online math courses (2013)
3. Cheung, B., Hui, L., Zhang, J., Yiu, S.: Smarttutor: An intelligent tutoring system in web-based adult education. J. Syst. Softw. **68**(1), 11–25 (2003)
4. Joglar, N., Risco, J.L., Snchez, R., Colmenar, J.M., Daz, A.: Testing in Math courses a new tool for online exams automatically graded: a teaching and learning experience. Research Report Universidad de Madrid (2013)
5. Koedinger, K., Corbett, A.: Cognitive tutors: Technology bringing learning science to the classroom. In: Sawyer, K. (ed.) The Cambridge Handbook of the Learning Sciences, pp. 61–78. Cambridge University Press, Cambridge (2006)
6. Kolawa, A., Huizinga, D.: Automated Defect Prevention: Best Practices in Software Management. Wiley-IEEE Computer Society Press, New York (2007)
7. Livne, N., Livne, O., Wright, C.: Can automated scoring surpass hand grading of students' constructed responses and error patterns in mathematics. MERLOT J. Online Learn. Teach. **3**(3), 295–306 (2007)
8. Melis, E., Siekmann, J.: Activemath: An intelligent tutoring system for mathematics. In: International Conference on AI and Soft Computing (2004)
9. Sandene, B., Bennett, R., Braswell, J., Oranje, A.: Online assessment in mathematics. Reports from the NAEP Technology-based Assessment Project (NCES 2005457) (2005)

User-Modelled Ambient Feedback for Self-regulated Learning

Bernardo Tabuenca(✉), Dirk Börner, Marco Kalz, and Marcus Specht

Open University of the Netherlands, Valkenburgerweg 177,
6401 DL Heerlen, The Netherlands
{bernardo.tabuenca, dirk.boerner, marco.kalz,
marcus.specht}@ou.nl

Abstract. A fundamental objective of human-computer interaction research is to make systems that are seamlessly integrated into daily life activities. Hence, the challenge is not only to make information available to people at any time, at any place, and in any form, but specifically to say the right thing at the right time in the right way. On the other hand, the proliferation of sensor technology is facilitating the scaffolding and customization of smart learning environments. This manuscript presents an ecology of resources comprising NFC, BLE and Arduino technology, orchestrated in the context of a learning environment to provide smoothly integrated feedback via ambient displays. This ecology is proposed as a suitable solution for self-regulated learning, providing support for setting goals, setting aside time to learn, tracking study time and monitoring the progress. Hereby, the ecology is described and intriguing research questions are introduced.

Keywords: Feedback · Near-field-communication · BLE-beacons · Arduino · Time-management · Learning analytics · Ambient display

1 Introduction

Providing in-context support and feedback is key to identify the best learning moments and self-organize the learning day. Lifelong learning implies setting aside regular time for learning during the day as well as combining learning activities with daily life activities (i.e. family, work, leisure). Nevertheless, daily contingencies and their varying priorities make specially challenging to provide technological support for lifelong learners in the task to set realistic goals, set aside daily time to learn, track the time devoted to learn, and monitor learning progress. In previous research, we investigated different ways to provide feedback services fostering the competence of *learning to learn*, using SMSs [1] and mobile chart visualizations [2] as channels to provide guidance from the teacher. The differentiation among external and internal feedback is crucial if one investigates the effects of feedback on the basis of recent instructional models viewing the process of knowledge acquisition as a self-regulated learning process [3]. Hence, hereby we present a smart learning ecology in which lifelong learners are able to customize internal feedback based on their own occasional learning priorities and contingencies.

© Springer International Publishing Switzerland 2015
G. Conole et al. (Eds.): EC-TEL 2015, LNCS 9307, pp. 535–539, 2015.
DOI: 10.1007/978-3-319-24258-3_54

2 Smart Ecology of Resources for Time Management

Candy [4] summarized four components of self-directed lifelong learning: self-monitoring, self-awareness, self-management and meta-learning. The challenge in an information-rich world is not only to make information available at any time, at any place, and in any form, but specifically to say the right thing at the right time in the right way [5]. This ecology provides self-regulated support for lifelong learners tracking time devoted to learn, orchestrating sensor technology, and modelling ambient feedback.

The NFC-LearnTracker [6] is an open source mobile application developed for NFC-enabled devices that features learning analytics of time devoted to learn based on the timestamps recorded every time the user starts *check-in* and stops *check-out* a self-defined learning goal. The evaluation of the NFC-LearnTracker [7] concluded that it is a useful tool to set and adjust mini-goals, to foster awareness on preferred learning environments, and to integrate2 learning in daily activities.

Fig. 1. Feedback cube & BLE-beacon

Fig. 2. NFC-Tags bound to learning activities

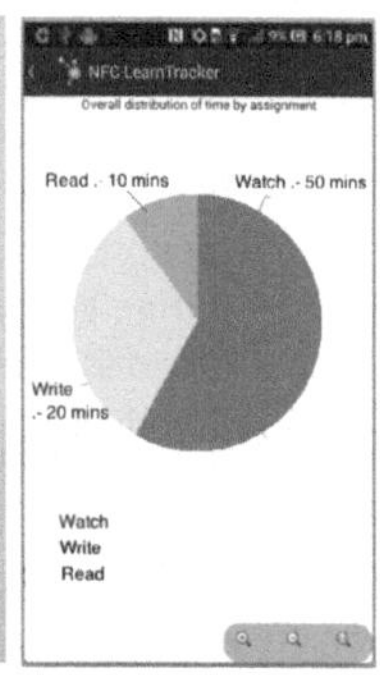

Fig. 3. NFC Learn-Tracker

The NFC-LearnTracker interprets the information provided by the following sensors:

- NFC tags (Fig. 2 See blue squared). As illustrated in Fig. 3, an overall learning goal (i.e. learn Dutch) comprises a set of sub-goals (watch videos; write texts: read news) that are assigned a coloured tag (blue; orange; green), an estimated daily time in minutes (50; 20; 10), and a deadline date to accomplish each sub-goal.
- Bluetooth Low Energy (BLE) beacons (Fig. 1a. See green hexagon). BLE-beacons are being novelty used to provide proximity-adapted feedback in the field of shopping[1], access control, and home entertainment. Hereby, we use BLE-beacons to monitor student's progress when he approaches or moves away from the beacon.

[1] Estimote Beacons. https://www.youtube.com/watch?v=sUIqfjpInxY.(Last accessed 29/06/2015).

The Feedback Cube [8] (Fig. 1) is an ambient learning display [9] built-on an Arduino microcontroller that provides visual and audio feedback (Fig. 3). The used LEDs are capable of displaying the full RGB colour space with 16777216 colours at 256 brightness levels (Fig. 5). All 16 RGB LEDs on the ring can be controlled individually, which allows programming various visual patterns (i.e. Fig. 6 matches pie chart in Fig. 3) and effects, such as fading, blinking, or colour transitions. The used mini speaker can reproduce programmatically created audio patterns and effects, such as playing single tones, complex melodies, or even encoded audio files.

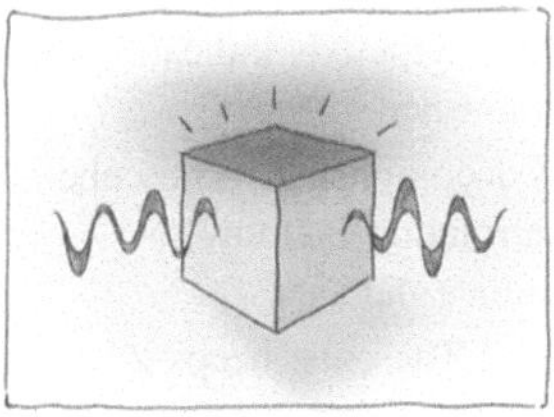

Fig. 4. Visual and audio effects

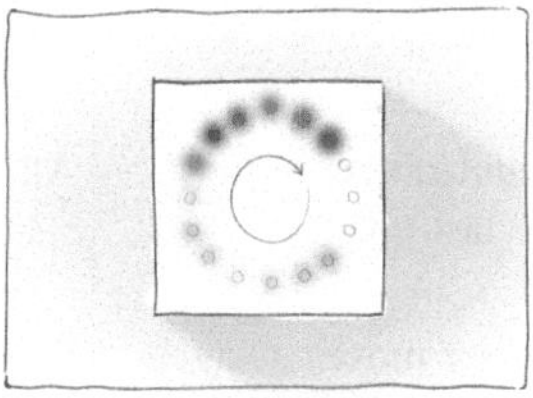

Fig. 5. Rainbow effect

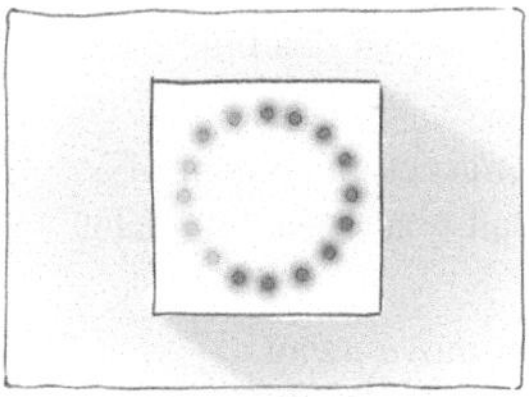

Fig. 6. Piechart effect

3 Mapping Events and Feedback

The NFC-LearnTracker lets the user configure which feedback signal fits better each one of the events listed below. Hereby we present the events supported and their default set-up: (Table 1).

Table 1. Default configuration of the ecology

Event	Action	Feedback
On approach	The user moves closer to the BLE beacon	Summarize! The cube lights a pie chart indicating the distribution of time for pending tasks (Fig. 6)
On check-in	The user taps on the NFC tag every time an activity is started.	Start! The cube lights the blue colour (Fig. 1) to indicate your are working on the blue learning goal
On check-out	The user taps on the NFC tag to stop a learning activity.	Stop! The cube switches off the existing light
X minutes before expiring the estimated time for a goal in a day	X minutes before time expires	Time to wrap up! The cube slowly fades X' times to gently advice that time will expire in X minutes.
On expiry estimated time for a goal in a day	Time expired	Time just expired! The cube beeps once providing a more intrusive notification

(*Continued*)

Table 1. (*Continued*)

Event	Action	Feedback
Y minutes after expiring the estimated time for a goal in a day	Y minutes after expiring	Overworking! The cube fades faster Y' times warning that you exceeded Y minutes your scheduled time.
On accomplishment of all goals in a day	On check-out the last goal	All daily goals accomplished! The cube lights a rainbow to congratulate the user
On accomplishment of one-goal deadline date	Scheduled date to finish one goal	Learning goal accomplished! The cube plays a melody indicating the goal is finished
On accomplishment of all-goals deadline date	Scheduled date to finish the last goal	All goals accomplished! The cube lights a rotating rainbow to congratulate the user
On move away	The user moves away from the BLE beacon	Summarize! The cube beeps Z' times summarizing pending study time (e.g. 30 min pending beeps 3 times)

Feedback Cube effects in video: https://sites.google.com/site/lifelonglearninghubproject/home/feedback-cube. (Last accessed 29/06/2015).

4 Future Work

In further research, the quality of the learning analytics via mobile visualizations (Fig. 3) and displays (Figs. 4–6) will be contrasted and evaluated [10]. Additionally, we will explore whether internal feedback services might improve self-regulated learning.

References

1. Tabuenca, B., Kalz, M., Ternier, S., Specht, M.: Stop and think: exploring mobile notifications to foster reflective practice on meta-learning. IEEE Trans. Learn. Technol. **8**, 124–135 (2015)
2. Tabuenca, B., Kalz, M., Drachsler, H., Specht, M.: Time Will Tell: the role of mobile learning analytics in self-regulated learning. Comput. Educ. (2015, In Press)
3. Narciss, S.: Feedback strategies for interactive learning tasks. Handb. Res. Educ. Commun. Technol. **3**, 125–144 (2008)
4. Candy, P., Brookfield, S.: Self-direction for Lifelong Learning: A Comprehensive Guide to Theory and Practice. John Wiley & Sons, San Francisco (1991)
5. Fischer, G.: User modeling in human computer interaction. User Model. User-adapt. Interact. **11**, 65–86 (2001)
6. Tabuenca, B., Kalz, M., Specht, M.: Lifelong learning hub: a seamless tracking tool for mobile learning. In: de Freitas, S., Rensing, C., Ley, T., Muñoz-Merino, P.J. (eds.) EC-TEL 2014. LNCS, vol. 8719, pp. 534–537. Springer, Heidelberg (2014)

7. Tabuenca, B., Kalz, M., Specht, M.: Binding daily physical environments to learning activities with mobile and sensor technology. In: Ebner, M., Erenli, K., Malaka, R., Pirker, J., Walsh, A. (eds.) EiED 2014. CCIS, vol. 486, pp. 73–84. Springer International Publishing, Switzerland (2015)
8. Börner, D., Tabuenca, B., Storm, J., Happe, S., Specht, M.: Tangible interactive ambient display prototypes to support learning scenarios. In: Proceedings of the Ninth International Conference on Tangible, Embedded, and Embodied Interaction, pp. 721–726. ACM, New York (2015)
9. Börner, D., Kalz, M., Specht, M.: Beyond the channel: a literature review on ambient displays for learning. Comput. Educ. **60**, 426–435 (2013)
10. Scheffel, M., Drachsler, H., Stoyanov, S., Specht, M.: Quality indicators for learning analytics. J. Educ. Technol. Soc **17**, 117–132 (2014)

Augmented Reality-Based Simulations Embedded in Problem Based Learning Courses

Diego Villarán(✉), María Blanca Ibáñez, and Carlos Delgado Kloos

Departamento de Ingeniería Telemática, Universidad Carlos III de Madrid, Madrid, Spain
diego.villaran@uc3m.es, {mbibanez,cdk}@it.uc3m.es

Abstract. Augmented reality is a technology that can be used to deploy Problem Based Learning activities that immerse students into meaningful learning activities by overlaying digital information; such as audio, video, 3D simulations, etc., to the vision of the real world. This paper explores the integration of augmented reality based activities in web courses providers and proposes a communication flow between an augmented reality application and a web based learning course provider.

Keywords: Augmented reality · Problem based learning · E-learning

1 Introduction

The term augmented reality (AR) refers to technology that enhances user's sensory perception of real world with a computer-assisted contextual layer of information [1]. Among the possible educational benefits of AR technology are its capabilities to provide contextualized information, to allow the visualization of invisible phenomena and to promote certain psychological states in learners - such as immersion, sense of presence and motivation [2, 3]. A growing number of pilot experiences are being deployed by researchers to explore AR's affordances and their impact on learning outcomes. However, there is a lack of effort to integrate augmented reality learning activities into learning management systems, few technological attempts have been carried out to orchestrate learning activities following instructional designs, and there is no online assessment nor learning support according to students profile.

The main goal of this paper is to present a technological initial solution to the problem of integration AR activities into a web course provider, and to show the feasibility of this integration through a demonstration. The paper is structured as follows: the Sect. 2 describes the AR application using Problem Based Learning as instructional design and the Sect. 3 describes the integration of the application in a web course provider.

2 Augmented Reality Application

The learning activity based on Problem Based Learning used in this work allows students to explore the effect of a magnetic field on a current-carrying wire, and to determine

© Springer International Publishing Switzerland 2015
G. Conole et al. (Eds.): EC-TEL 2015, LNCS 9307, pp. 540–543, 2015.
DOI: 10.1007/978-3-319-24258-3_55

both the magnitude of the magnetic force on the wire and its direction. To this end, students are asked to solve a problem that involves the knowledge of basic concepts of electricity, magnetism, and Lorentz's law. Students are guided through the resolution of the problem in five sequential stages. Each stage is associated with one element of the electromagnetic circuit together with the problem, which students have to solve: Cable, Battery, Magnet_1, Magnet_2, and Magnet_3. These are 3D objects wrapped with a fiducial marker that the AR browser will recognize. The augmented simulations will provide the behavior of real electric-magnetic components. The narrative of the activity consists of the construction of the circuit by adding a new element in each stage. A pilot study using this AR-based application was presented in [4].

3 Problem Based Learning Course Activities Based on Augmented Reality

This section gives an overview of the behavior of functional instances of AR-based experimental activities deployed and managed through a web-server. Two main actors will be considered: (1) the Problem-Based Learning Course Provider (PBLCP), a web-based service hosted in a server, and (2) the AR-Based Learning Application (ARBLA), a client AR-based application running on mobile devices. The PBLCP will be responsible for providing the problem to solve and the guidelines of the information required for assessment to ARBLA, whereas ARBLA will be in charge of the coordination of the tasks students must do to solve the problem and to recollect assessment information for the PBLCP (see Fig. 1).

Instructional designers will be in charge of choosing the problem that students will solve and specifying the Capturing Interaction Model according to assessment and recommendation purposes. The definition of the Capturing Interaction Model becomes specially important when using emergent technologies with a strong Human Computer Interaction (HCI) component. The model might include parameters such as time, localization, type of object. For example, in the case study presented students must build an electromagnetic circuit as part of the solution of the proposed problem which implies that students will be required to choose a particular element (e.g. an object that mimics a magnet) and to place it in a specific place with the right polarity. For the instructor, if a student chooses a wrong element it might indicate a distraction but if student places it using a wrong polarity might advise about a conceptual problem. On the other hand, every indicator to be recollected imposes a time overhead over the system. Hence, a tradeoff must be established for instructional designers when defining the indicators in the Capturing Interaction Model.

The PBLCP will send the problem to solve and the Capturing Interaction Model to the mobile device triggering and running the ARBLA, which will take the necessary actions to recognize, capture and store the students' interactions established in the Capturing Interaction Model. Once the ARBLA has been set up, students will be able to perform the activity.

Once the problem to solve is established and the Capturing Interaction Model is specified, the PBLCP will send that as input to the mobile device. As result, ARBLA is

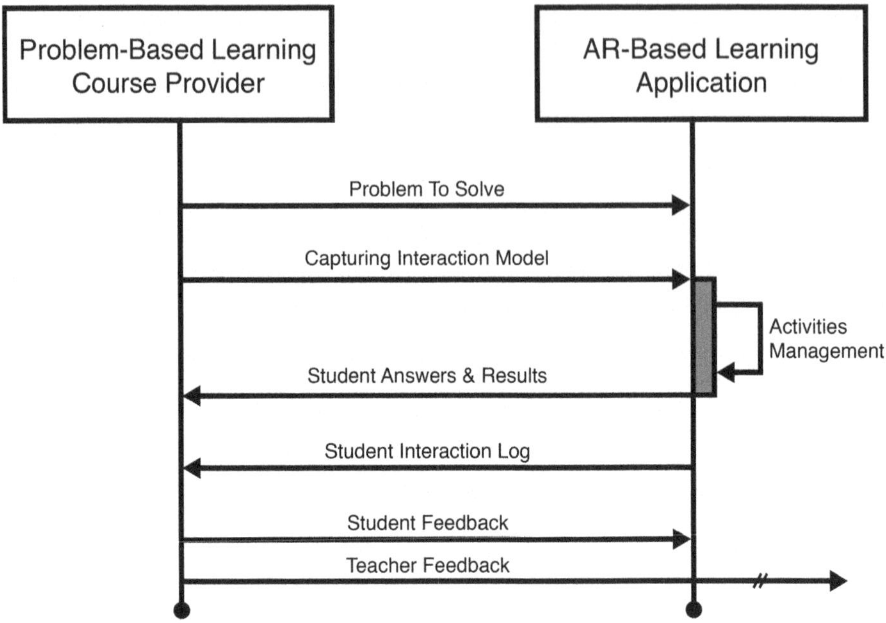

Fig. 1. Sequence diagram interactions between PBLCP and ARBLA

triggered and auto-configured according to the data sent by the PBLCP, starting the orchestration of learners' activities. This orchestration is carried out by ARBLA, which will manage the AR activity on the students' mobile devices and comprises the working flow of tasks such as reading, where students will be able to get a theoretical knowledge about electromagnetism; AR-based simulations, where ARBLA provides students visualizations of simulations and allows students to perform experiments by manipulating real objects through AR; and assessment questions, where the students will be asked to answer several questions about the performed activities to demonstrate their acquired knowledge.

Students are invited to follow the learning tasks recommended by ARBLA in a step-by-step process that will guide them toward the solution of the proposed problem. Recommendations are based on the students' actions within the learning flow and they will have the possibility to take different paths on their own. ARBLA registers and stores all the interactions generated and the students' answers.

In the following step, ARBLA will send back to the PBLCP both students' answers to the assessment questions and the log comprising students' interactions as specified by the Capturing Interaction Model. Then, the PBLCP will analyze the data received in order to send feedback about the student activity to the ARBLA module which in turns will provide it to the student and eventually, to the instructor.

Acknowledgements. This work was supported in part by the Spanish project EEE under Grant TIN2011-28308-C03-01 and the Spanish project eMadrid under the grant S2009/TIC-1650.

References

1. Azuma, R., Baillot, Y., Behringer, R., Feiner, S., Julier, S., MacIntyre, B.: Recent advances in augmented reality. IEEE Comput. Graphics Appl. **21**(6), 34–47 (2001)
2. Cheng, K.H., Tsai, C.C.: Affordances of augmented reality in science learning: suggestions for future research. J. Sci. Educ. Technol. **22**(4), 449–462 (2013)
3. Dunleavy, M., Dede, C., Mitchell, R.: Affordances and limitations of immersive participatory augmented reality simulations for teaching and learning. J. Sci. Educ. Technol. **18**(1), 7–22 (2009)
4. Ibáñez, M.B., Di Serio, A., Villarán, D., Delgado-Kloos, C.: Experimenting with electromagnetism using augmented reality: impact on flow student experience and educational effectiveness. Comput. Educ. **71**, 1–13 (2014)

Poster Papers

Managing Time Through a Self-regulated Oriented ePortfolio for Undergraduate Students

Aikaterini Alexiou(✉) and Fotini Paraskeva

Department of Digital Systems, University of Piraeus,
Karaoli & Dimitriou 80, 185 34 Piraeus, Greece
katialex@webmail.unipi.gr, fparaske@unipi.gr

Abstract. A self-regulated oriented ePortfolio as a dynamic social networking tool, orchestrated along the processes of Self-Regulated Learning (SRL) with career management skills was designed. The aim of this study is to examine how time management can be positively influenced through the implementation of the ePortfolio. We conducted a quasi-experimental research with comparison groups in pre/post-tests in order to examine time management as a behavioral self-regulatory process for academic performance. The findings revealed that students tend to manage time effectively, make schedules and allocate time after the completion of the ePortfolio. Further research should measure students' SRL and the relations among cognitive, affective, behavior and context processes.

Keywords: Time management · Self-Regulated learning · ePortfolio · Social networking tool · Career management skills

1 Introduction

Research in academic context indicates relationships among time management, academic achievement, goal setting, self-efficacy beliefs and achievement emotions and suggests that scholarly productivity is maintained [1]. Furthermore, it is stated that many undergraduate students often complain about the lack of time to deliver all the programmed learning tasks, prepare for exams in last-minute cramming, and most of them cannot estimate the study time needed [2]. This means that students should, therefore, be engaged in life designing and building processes that help them acquire skills and knowledge they value throughout their academic and career development [3]. A self-regulated oriented ePortfolio, as a dynamic social networking tool, orchestrated along the processes of Self-Regulated Learning (SRL) with career management skills was, thus, designed to support learners in regulating their learning. We suggest open source code-based with elements of social networking, ePortfolios that are adaptable for modification or distribution and provide various benefits such as web-data sharing, collaboration, reflection and can combine informal and formal education. Following pedagogical considerations, ePortfolios should be able to accommodate learner-centered pedagogical models like Self-Regulated learning (SRL) [4]. SRL is defined as an active, constructive process whereby learners set goals and then attempt to plan, monitor and

© Springer International Publishing Switzerland 2015
G. Conole et al. (Eds.): EC-TEL 2015, LNCS 9307, pp. 547–550, 2015.
DOI: 10.1007/978-3-319-24258-3_56

control their cognition, motivation, and behavior [5, 6]. Time planning and management constitute a self-regulatory process where individuals' attempt to control their own overt behavior so as to bolster their performance.

2 The Method: αpt²iMySelf ePortfolio

We introduce αpt²iMySelf ePortfolio, which is part of an on-going research aligns the aspects (cognitive, affective, behavior and context) of SRL with career management skills with the aim of developing specific aspects and instilling a learning culture in students [7, 8]. Apt²iMySelf ePortfolio is based on open-source social networking engine Elgg, which enables students to construct and update their profile, articulate a list of other students with whom they share a connection, and build their own pages. This tool fosters a sense of community between users, strengthens interactions and supports academic and career management (Fig. 1).

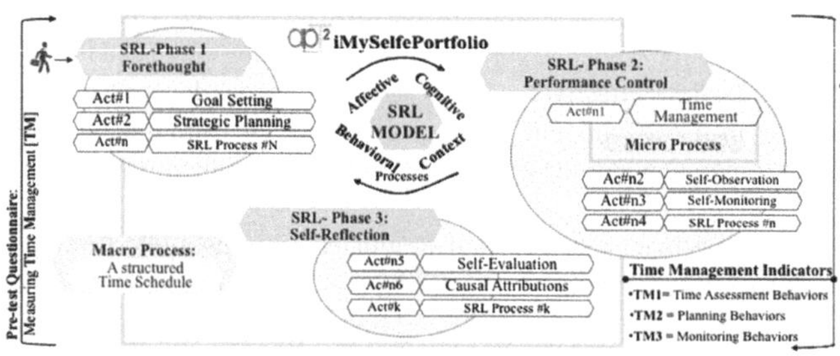

Fig. 1. The rationale of αpt²iMySelf ePortfolio

We conducted an experimental research (one group only) within a computer science department of a Greek university, throughout a course titled "IT -centric Professional Development". The sample of the study consisted of 41 undergraduate students (30 males and 11 females) who participated voluntarily. The research question was: "How can time management be positively impacted through the implementation of αpt²iMySelf ePortfolio in order to enhance academic and career skills? Participants completed a self-developed questionnaire (The self-report based on an adapted version of the Motivated Strategies for Learning Questionnaire – MSLQ. It is used the scale of resource management strategies which includes time management) [5] as a pre and post-test to render the measurement of their time management skills on ePortfolio plausible. Through this process, an attempt to shed light on the participants' beliefs about their use of strategies for time management (monitoring, setting goals, prioritizing, planning, delegating, and analysis of time spent) was made [1]. The self-report consists of 23 close-ended divided in sub-scales (three-fold categorization of Time Management (TM): TM1: time assessment behaviors, TM2: planning behaviors and TM3: monitoring behaviors). During the experimental procedure, students engaged in the αpt²iMySelf ePortfolio activities following a structured time schedule and attempting to learn how to manage their time (macro-process). In more detail, participants followed the SRL phases for structuring αpt²iMySelf ePortfolio [6] (Fig. 1): **'Forethought' Phase:** Students enter the SRL cycle for planning their learning efforts (goal setting, strategic planning activities). In this phase students organize their learning path for constructing the content and context of their ePortfolio. **'Performance Control' Phase:** Students get engaged in specific learning activities such as familiarizing with learning strategies, note taking and activities for recognizing their capacity to manage time. Especially, students participated in a time management activity entitled 'Be an effective manager of your time' (micro-process) so as to engage in a set of strategies for time management: time assessment behaviors, planning behaviors, and monitoring behaviors. **'Self-Reflection' Phase:** Whilst in the third phase, students reflect on the learning activities performed to evaluate their performance. They evaluate their ePortfolio, performance and time management.

3 Results

A paired-samples t-test was taken to explore statistical differences (pre and post-test) on participants' time management. Results indicate that the experimental group appeared to have a significant increase on the means across the sub-scales of Time Management (TM). In detail, the contrast in Time Assessment Behaviors (TM1) between the pre-test and post-test was significant, $t(40) = -6.927$, $p < 0.01$. Results show that after the completion of 'αpt²iMySelf ePortfolio', students' time assessment behaviors improved, the mean score of the post-test (3.699, SD = 0.575) was greater than that of the pre-test (2.890 SD = 0.526). This means that students engaged in learning activities, which advance their ability to manage time effectively and realize the difficulties they may face unless they follow a well-organized time schedule. The contrast in Planning Behaviors (TM2) between the pre-test and post-test was significant, $t(40) = -5.280$, $p < 0.01$. Results reveal that after the completion of the procedure students' planning behaviors also improved, the mean score of the post-test (3.829, SD = 0.654) was greater than that of the pre-test (2.878, SD = 0.927). This is also an important finding, as TM2 can be directly linked to SRL processes (cognitive, affective, behavioral and context). Students succeed in understanding the advantages of a well-organized time schedule and engaged in the process of setting goals and planning their study time. Finally, the contrast in monitoring behaviors (TM3) which is divided in TM3.1: Monitoring Schedule and TM3.2: Monitoring Behaviors between the pre-test and post-test was significant, $t(40) = -9.240$, $p < 0.01$ (TM3.1) and, $t(40) = -3.517$, $p < 0.01$ (TM3.2). Results depict that the mean score of the post-test (3.670, SD = 0.554) was greater than that of the pre-test (2.682, SD = 0.521) which shows that students engaged in a time management activity and realized the potential of monitoring time schedule (TM3.1). Participants are convinced that the process of monitoring the time spent offered them the opportunity to conceptualize specific strategies such as prioritizing and delegating time spent. Furthermore, students monitor their behaviors (For TM3.2, the mean score of the post-test (4.120, SD = 0.630) was greater than that of the pre-test (3.569, SD = 0.757) and try to identify whether they engage in procrastination, minimize opportunities for interruptions and have lack of discipline.

4 Conclusion

The process of αpt²iMySelf ePortfolio urged learners to realize the need of effective time management, recognize their own patterns of planning and managing time and learn how to utilize time management strategies and applications (evernote, remember the milk, google calendar, notes, reminders etc.); it encouraged learners to, engage in structured and unstructured time management activities so as to apply their knowledge and create feasible time schedules. Finally, the implementation of αpt²iMySelf ePortfolio has a positive impact on participants' time management strategies such as time assessment, planning, and monitoring behavior, setting goals, prioritizing, planning, delegating, and analysis of time spent. Considering that this study is part of an on-going research, our future intentions entail testing the reliability and validity of the proposed conceptual framework in prospective experimental procedures. Further research should focus on measuring students' SRL and career management skills as well as the relations among cognitive, affective, behavior and context processes of SRL.

Acknowledgements. This work was supported by the University of Piraeus Research Centre (UPRC). We acknowledge the UPRC contribution to this research paper.

References

1. Chase, J.A., Topp, R., Smith, C., Cohen, Z.M., et al.: Time management strategies for research productivity. West. J. Nurs. Res. **35**(2), 155–176 (2013)
2. Garcia-Ros, R., Perez-Gonzalez, F., Hinojosa, E.: Assessing time management skills as an important aspect of student learning. The construction and evaluation of a time management scale with Spanish high school students. Sch. Psychol. Int. **25**(2), 167–183 (2004)
3. Daloglu, A., Vural, S.: The effects of training on pre-service english teachers' regulation of their study time. Aust. J. Teach. Educ., **38**(6), 26 p. (2013). http://dx.doi.org/10.14221/ajte.2013v38n6.2
4. Wade, A., Abrami, P.C., Sclater, J.: An electronic portfolio for learning. Can. J. Learn. Technol. **31**(3), 33–50 (2005)
5. Pintrich, P.R., Smith, D.A.F., Garcia, T., McKeachie, W.J.: A Manual for the use of the Motivated Strategies for Learning Questionnaire (MSLQ). National Center for Research to Improve Postsecondary Teaching and Learning, University of Michigan, Ann Arbor, MI (1991)
6. Zimmerman, B.J.: Attaining self-regulation: a social-cognitive perspective. In: Boekaerts, M., Pintrich, P.R., Seidner, M. (eds.) Handbook of Self-regulation, pp. 13–39. Academic Press, San Diego, CA (2000)
7. Alexiou, A., Paraskeva, F.: Enhancing self-regulated learning skills through the implementation of an e-portfolio tool. Procedia Soc. Behav. Sci. **2**(2), 3048–3054 (2010)
8. Alexiou, A., Paraskeva, F.: Exploiting Motivation and Self-efficacy through the Implementation of a Self-Regulated Oriented ePortfolio. Paper presented at the International Conference on E-Learning in the Workplace, NY, USA, 12–14th June 2013

Detecting Sarcasm from Students' Feedback in Twitter

Nabeela Altrabsheh(✉), Mihaela Cocea, and Sanaz Fallahkhair

School of Computing, University of Portsmouth, Lion Terrace, Portsmouth, UK
{nabeela.altrabsheh,mihaela.cocea,sanaz.fallahkhair}@port.ac.uk

Abstract. Sarcasm is a sophisticated form of act where one says or writes the opposite of what they mean. Sarcasm is a common issue in sentiment analysis and detecting it is a challenge. While models for sarcasm detection have been proposed for general purposes (e.g. Twitter data, Amazon reviews), there is no research addressing this issue in an educational context, despite the increased use of social media in education. In this paper we experiment with several machine learning techniques, features and preprocessing levels to identify sarcasm from students' feedback collected via Twitter.

Keywords: Sentiment analysis · Sarcasm detection · Students feedback

1 Introduction

Students' feedback can be a valuable data source for detecting students' emotions. Detecting students' emotions is important because previous research highlights that positive emotions increase students' interest in learning, increase engagement in the classroom and motivate students. Moreover, students who are happy are generally more motivated to accomplish their learning goals.

Students' feedback can be analysed using sentiment analysis, which is also known as opinion mining. Sentiment analysis can help the lecturer by analysing large amounts of feedback and summarising it, thus giving a complete picture of what students' opinions are. Unfortunately, students sometimes use sarcasm in their feedback leading to inaccurate results when analysing the data.

Sarcasm is a form of irony conveying criticism in an indirect way. It could also cover up embarrassment in a way that is dramatic or humorous [4]. Unlike lying, sarcasm is used to highlight reality rather than hide it, and it is perceived as being more polite and less aggressive than direct confrontation [4].

In education, sarcasm has been studied from the perspective of the teacher/lecturer. More specifically, studies looked at the use of sarcasm when communicating with or giving feedback to students. It was found to be negative when sarcasm was used to belittle students, but also found to be positive when sarcasm was used with humour and not targeted at particular students. To the best of our knowledge, there is no research looking at sarcasm in students' feedback.

© Springer International Publishing Switzerland 2015
G. Conole et al. (Eds.): EC-TEL 2015, LNCS 9307, pp. 551–555, 2015.
DOI: 10.1007/978-3-319-24258-3_57

Detection of sarcasm for text is a difficult problem and there are only a few approaches looking at this problem [2,3,6]. None of these approaches, however, look at sarcasm in an educational context.

2 Related Work

Detection of sarcasm received increased attention from the research community, with several works reported for the detection of sarcasm from text only [2,3,6]. Unlike previous research, our experiments focus on data from an educational context, and more specifically, from students' feedback. We experiment with several classifiers to investigate the reliability of the prediction. In the following we give an overview of the several processes involved in the development of prediction models: preprocessing, feature selection and machine learning techniques.

Preprocessing involves cleaning the data from unwanted elements which may negatively affect the performance of the machine learning techniques. The most common techniques are: tokenization, removing punctuation, removing numbers, and converting text to lower or upper case. Most research about sarcasm in sentiment analysis has been on tweets. Some examples of preprocessing Twitted data are removal of Twitter special characters [6] and removal the HTML links [6].

Feature selection is the process of selecting relevant features for the particular prediction problem. The most commonly feature is unigrams, i.e. individual words. In sarcasm, n-grams are commonly used as well [2].

A variety of *machine learning techniques* were used for sentiment analysis in general and sarcasm detection in particular. We experimented with classifiers that have previously performed well for polarity, emotion prediction, and sarcasm detection [5]: Naive Bayes (NB), Multinomial Naive Bayes (MNB), Complement Naive Bayes (CNB), Maximum Entropy (ME), Support Vector Machines (SVM), Sequential Minimal Optimization (SMO), and Random Forest (RF).

3 Predicting Sarcasm from Students' Feedback

Twitter was used to collect students feedback about the lecture. For each tweet, students were asked to choose an emotion from a set of 19 learning-related emotions provided, e.g. amused, bored, confused, frustrated, and to provide a polarity label (positive/ negative/ neutral). A list of all the emotions can be found in [1]. 1522 tweets were collected with their corresponding emotion and polarity labels.

We identified sarcasm in the tweets by: (a) detecting the word or hashtag "sarcasm" (or other variants such as "sarcastic"), e.g. "Nothing great than doing some vectors on sunday morning #vectors #lecture #sarcasm #justuniversitythings", and (b) detecting if the tweets were labeled an emotion that was opposite to the tweet's meaning, e.g. "in need of some inspiration #literature #lecture #boring #feelingdown" with label amused. Using these two methods, we found 194 sarcastic tweets; all the other tweets were labeled as non-sarcastic.

We tested three preprocessing levels using different techniques which were chosen due to their popularity in previous studies: (a) P1, i.e. the baseline, includes converting text to lower case; (b) P2, includes P1 plus removal of numbers, punctuation, spaces and blanks, and special characters; (c) P3, which includes P2 plus the removal of hashtags, emoticons and Twitter special characters.

Like most researchers, we focus on n-grams, and in particular on unigrams. Unigrams have been widely used in previous sentiment analysis research, as well as for detecting sarcasm [2]. We also explored other features in combination with unigrams (U): (a) emotion label (E) (from students); (b) polarity label (P) (from students); (c) number of all punctuation characters (PC) (e.g. commas, semicolons, brackets, apostrophes, etc.); (d) number of question and exclamation marks (QE); (e) number of emoticons (NE); (f) number of hashtags (H); (g) time of the tweet during the lecture (T), i.e. beginning, middle, end. All combinations of these additional features with unigrams were experimented with.

4 Results and Discussion

All models were tested using 10-fold cross-validation; accuracy, precision, recall, F-score, and error rate are used to evaluate the models. Precision, recall, F-score and Area Under Curve (AUC) of Receiver Operating Characteristic (ROC) for the sarcasm class are also reported. The best models for sarcasm detection are displayed in Table 1.

Table 1. Best models for sarcasm prediction

	NB	MNB	CNB	RB	LIN	ME	SMO	RF
Features	All	U+E+P	E+P	U	All	E+P	All	U+H
Accuracy	0.82	0.78	0.72	0.87	0.80	0.85	0.86	0.84
Precision	0.84	0.84	0.84	0.76	0.82	0.84	0.84	0.81
Recall	0.82	0.78	0.72	0.87	0.80	0.85	0.86	0.84
F-score	0.83	0.80	0.76	0.81	0.81	0.85	0.84	0.82
Error rate	0.18	0.22	0.28	0.13	0.20	0.15	0.14	0.16
Precision (Sarcasm)	0.34	0.30	0.26	0.00	0.28	0.42	0.43	0.30
Recall (Sarcasm)	0.47	0.51	**0.63**	0.00	0.35	0.33	0.25	0.22
F-score (Sarcasm)	0.39	0.37	0.36	0.00	0.31	0.36	0.31	0.25
AUC	0.76	0.71	0.68	0.50	0.61	0.75	0.60	0.68

Regarding *preprocessing*, we first experimented with unigrams only and found that most of the models showed higher performance in terms of sarcasm detection when using the lowest level of preprocessing (P1), which could be due to hashtags, numbers, and punctuation holding value to the prediction of sarcasm. In previous work, punctuation was used by Tsur et al. [6], where they showed that on its own it is not a good predictor, but that in combination with other features it can increase the performance. Consequently, for the unigrams combinations with the other features, we only experimented with level P1 of preprocessing.

Regarding the *features*, we found that adding the emotion and polarity labels to the unigrams led to an increase of 1 to 6 % in sarcasm detection, i.e. recall, in five out of the eight classifiers (NB, MNB, CNB, ME and SMO). We found that overall, the punctuation features (PC and QE), the emoticons count (NE) and the time of the lecture (T) made little difference to the performance, and in some cases led to a small decrease of 1 % to 2 %. Using all the features led to an increase for the recall of the sarcasm class for the NB, LIN and SMO classifiers by 7 %, 4 % and 9 %, respectively.

In terms of *machine learning techniques*, we found that the best classifiers to detect sarcasm are Complement Naive Bayes, Multinomial Naive Bayes and Naive Bayes, mainly due to their high recall rate. Naive Bayes has not been used before to detect sarcasm, however, previous research shows that it is performs well in sentiment analysis [1]. Multimonial Naive Bayes has been used in sarcasm detection by Justo et al. [3], obtaining a recall of 77 %. We notice that interestingly, CNB performs the lowest in terms of accuracy, despite previous research showing that it performs well with uneven classes [1], which is applicable to our dataset as the sarcasm class represents only 13 % of the data; however, CNB led to the highest sarcasm recall of 63 %.

We found that the worst classifiers to detect sarcasm are RB, SMO and RF. However, these algorithms are prone to overfitting. Despite the high accuracies of these classifiers, the recall and other measures for the sarcasm class were low, indicating that the good performance is due to the recognition of the majority class, i.e. non-sarcasm. Similarly, research by González-Ibánez et al. [2] to identify sarcasm from tweets showed that SMO led to a high accuracy of 71 % using unigrams as features. They did not, however, report the measures for the sarcasm class; consequently, we do not know how much of the accuracy performance is due to the recognition of sarcasm.

Although the results we reported in this paper are relatively low for what is considered a good performance for a classifier, when looking at the previous results on sarcasm detection, we can see that our results are comparable, and on some metrics even better than previous research. In future work we will investigate the use of lexicons and other features such as POS tagging.

References

1. Altrabsheh, N., Cocea, M., Fallahkhair, S.: Predicting students' emotions using machine learning techniques. In: Conati, C., Heffernan, N., Mitrovic, A., Verdejo, M.F. (eds.) AIED 2015. LNCS, vol. 9112, pp. 537–540. Springer, Heidelberg (2015)
2. González-Ibánez, R., Muresan, S., Wacholder, N.: Identifying sarcasm in twitter: a closer look. In: Proceedings of the 49th Annual Meeting of the Association for Computational Linguistics: Human Language Technologies, pp. 581–586 (2011)
3. Justo, R., Corcoran, T., Lukin, S.M., Walker, M., Torres, M.I.: Extracting relevant knowledge for the detection of sarcasm and nastiness in the social web. Knowl.-Based Syst. **69**, 124–133 (2014)

4. Shany-Ur, T., Poorzand, P., Grossman, S.N., Growdon, M.E., Jang, J.Y., Ketelle, R.S., Miller, B.L., Rankin, K.P.: Comprehension of insincere communication in neurodegenerative disease: lies, sarcasm, and theory of mind. Cortex **48**(10), 1329–1341 (2012)
5. Tian, F., Gao, P., Li, L., Zhang, W., Liang, H., Qian, Y., Zhao, R.: Recognizing and regulating e-learners' emotions based on interactive chinese texts in e-learning systems. Knowl.-Based Syst. **55**, 148–164 (2014)
6. Tsur, O., Davidov, D., Rappoport, A.: ICWSM-a great catchy name: semi-supervised recognition of sarcastic sentences in online product reviews. In: The 4th International AAAI Conference on Weblogs and Social Media, pp. 162–169 (2010)

Motivation and Engagement in MOOCs: How to Increase Learning Motivation by Adapting Pedagogical Scenarios?

Aicha Bakki[1,2(✉)], Lahcen Oubahssi[1], Chihab Cherkaoui[2], and Sebastien George[1]

[1] LUNAM University, University of Maine, EA 4023, LIUM, 72085 Le Mans, France
{aicha.bakki,lahcen.oubahssi,sebastien.george}@univ-lemans.fr
[2] FSA, IRF-SIC Laboratory, Ibn Zohr University, Agadir, Morocco
ccherkaoui@yahoo.fr

Abstract. With the MOOC movement, education stakeholders are taking part of a pedagogical renewal. These dynamics present different advantages such as: massiveness, openness, accessibility, etc. However, it raises particular issues related to the dropout. To remedy to this issue, a promising lead resides in supporting learners' motivation and engagement. To reach this goal, innovative pedagogic strategies and /or sophisticated Instructional design, personalization or even adaptability are needed. The purpose of this paper is to examine the point of view of literature, the dropout issue and possible solutions to motivate learners.

Keywords: MOOC · Motivation · Dropout · Personalization · Adaptivity · Pedagogical scenario · Engagement · Learning model · Learning design

1 Introduction

MOOCs are distinguished from E-Learning platforms by different characteristics such as the massiveness, openness, accessibility, certification, the nature and programming of content, assessment modalities, etc.

All of these characteristics offer added value to education in general and to major stakeholders involved in online learning process (teachers, learners and tutors). For teachers for example, it is a question to think about the learning activity by formalizing pedagogical scenarios and implementing them through new technologies and modalities. This allow us experimenting although different educational approaches and content, but also promoting sharing and reusing content and best practices. For the learner, many benefits can be distinguished namely: flexibility, accessibility, openness, collaboration, autonomy, etc.

The aim of our work is to conceive and develop various tools that consider complementary and plural aspects of online learning, through individual and/or adaptive, collaborative, fun and massive dimensions. We consider particularly the dropout issue and we propose a synthesis of approaches to reduce the dropout rate. Therefore, the perspective of our work is to refine these approaches to provide models, tools and techniques enhancing MOOCs centric scenarios by trying to capture the issues of motivation and adaptation.

© Springer International Publishing Switzerland 2015
G. Conole et al. (Eds.): EC-TEL 2015, LNCS 9307, pp. 556–559, 2015.
DOI: 10.1007/978-3-319-24258-3_58

The main purpose of this communication is to not examine the contribution of MOOCs in achieving the guidelines traced at the beginning, but to discuss new issues raised, especially dropout rates. Indeed, for reference, most authors point out a success rate that not exceed 10 % [1]. In a deeper analysis of this issue, several authors link this dropout to a lack of learners' motivation, or a lack of learners' engagement [2–4]. These dropout rates are also associated with an insufficiency of tools and methods that allow personalization and/or adaptation of learning activities, in order to motivate learners in these environments [4].

2 Dropout Issue in MOOCs

Many researchers have examined the dropout issue in MOOCs. Clow [3] explains the dropout rate by the demotivation of learners. Anderson [2] emphasized that several participants "enroll" just to satisfy their curiosity without any intention to complete the course. Other researches are around the engagement of learners in a MOOC, we cite in particular: the work of Kizilcec et al. [4]. They explore an empirical study about the lack of engagement of learners and its causes in MOOCs; but also the lack of interaction between participants in MOOC. In the same sense, the fact participants' isolation is considered by many authors as one of the main reasons behind the weak engagement of the participants [5].

To study the dropout issue in MOOCs, we examined the work related to learner's profiles in MOOCs. In this sense, we note the work of Kizilcec et al. [4] and Hill [6]. They introduce classifications of learners that interacting with the platform. For illustration, we summarize Hill's work [6]. He proposed a classification of participants in a MOOC according to their degree of involvement in five categories: **Active, passive, Drop-ins, Observers & No-shows**.

3 Some Possible Solutions to Minimize Dropout

Based on a literature review, we can distinguish four different approaches to minimize the dropout rate:

Pedagogical Strategies Approach. It is a number of theoretical strategies validated by empirical studies. Among the pedagogical strategies discussed in the literature, we highlight the work of Williams [7] of adding motivational messages to students when they solve mathematics problems [8].

Personalization and/or Adaptivity Approach. Several researches focus on the importance of personalization to avoid dropout. In this context, we can mention PERSUA2MOOC project [9]. This project provides a system for personalization of learning outcomes in MOOCs. PERSUA2MOOC is a project that aims to "adapt" the learning activities considering the individualities and teachers educational activities.

Gamification Approach. Integrating games into the learning process is a solution to capture a larger audience. Indeed, the coupling of learning, virtual reality and video games allow to consider the integration of serious games in the online learning process. We can mention the work of [10, 11].

Technological Approach. Finally, we note that in addition to video, MOOCs also follow technological ascent implementing other tools web2.0, namely, social networks, wikis, forums, etc.

4 Discussion

First observations in MOOCs: a revolutionary platform, a new educational reform and a very high dropout rates. A learner-centered approach reveals several difficulties. In the first place, defining the learners' profiles that enroll in MOOC and their initial motivations. Second, massiveness, which constitutes a major issue when we talk about monitoring, mentoring or coaching: how to handle a huge number of learners? Especially as the MOOCs do not offer proximity between teachers and learners. We also highlight the importance of considering two fundamental aspects MOOC: massiveness and openness in the process of elaboration of pedagogical scenarios. We speak more and more about personalization and adaptivity to reduce dropout rates. Moreover, many researches have been specified in this sense. Research works in TEL, in this context, have allowed the development of different approaches and methods; that have been recovered under the MOOCs. We have specified, the project PERSUA2MOOC [9] which presents a personalization in MOOC according to Learners' profiles.

Our work focuses on supporting learners' motivation through instructional scenario building, by implementing tools and models specific to the field of TEL but also cognitive science and educational sciences. Indeed, the elaboration of our work spread over several layers. The principal layer includes different TEL platforms and tools. It integrates also different works specified in: instructional scenario building, learners' profiles and different motivation theories.

However, we must consider the different types of MOOCs. We distinguish two principal types: xMOOCs and cMOOCs, each having their own technological and pedagogical characteristics. They represent two pedagogical models that consider the video as primary course support, but disjoining in instructional scenario building models that they offer. So many other types are emerging nowadays, to prevent some dysfunctions in MOOCs, but the purposes of this paper will be limited to xMOOCs and cMOOCs. xMOOC is most of the time comprising traditional approaches of teaching and learning, it places the teacher as the main leader in the pedagogical scenario process, whereas cMOOC is more collaborative. It integrates the learner in a dynamic multi-actors process of instructional scenario building. According to this, we believe that cMOOCs are adapted to our research vision and approach.

Our approach consists to study instructional scenario building process, in cMOOCs, according to three points of view: massiveness, openness and motivation. Our research problematic can be summarized in three questions:

Which pedagogical context model to comply with learning rhythm in a massive environment? Our objective is to be able to manage and adapt the pedagogical activities in MOOCs in order to create a favorable environment for learning and personal development.

Which model or approach of the motivational theory should be used? Our goal is to identify and adapt the various existing motivation approaches, models and theories to reduce dropout rates.

Which model to adopt to organize and sequence teaching activities? Our goal is to manage and adapt pedagogical scenario in MOOCs in order to respect the aspects of opening (a specificity of MOOCs).

5 Conclusion

Following the various issues presented, we posed a first draft of the current problems related to the issue of dropout in MOOCs. The synthesis of the literature highlights our views on the approach of dropout along three dimensions: possible causes of dropout, research related to the types of participants and solutions to minimize the dropout rate. All points are complementary. The objective of our work is to propose an approach, models, methods and techniques to users of MOOCs, to take into account motivation concept in the design and / or adaptation of their pedagogical scenarios.

References

1. Liyanagunawardena, T.R., Adams, A.A., Williams, S.A.: MOOCs: A systematic study of the published literature 2008–2012. Int. Rev. Res. Open Dis. Learn. **14**(3), 202–227 (2013)
2. Anderson, T.: Promise and/or Peril: MOOCs and open and distance education. Commonwealth of Learning (2013)
3. Clow, D.: MOOCs and the funnel of participation. In: Proceedings of the Third International Conference on Learning Analytics and Knowledge, pp. 185–189 (2013)
4. Kizilcec, R.F., Piech, C., Schneider, E.: Deconstructing disengagement: analyzing learner subpopulations in massive open online courses. In: Proceedings of the Third International Conference on Learning Analytics and Knowledge, pp. 170–179 (2013)
5. Cisel, M.: Etudier les interactions dans les MOOCs. Blog de Matthieu Cisel (2014)
6. Hill, P.: Some validation of MOOC student patterns graphic (2013). http://mfeldstein.com/validation-mooc-student-patterns-graphic
7. Williams, J.J.: Applying cognitive science to online learning. NIPS Data-Driven Education Workshop (2013)
8. Khan Academy platform. http://www.KhanAcademy.org
9. Clerc, F.: Mise en Place de la Personnalisation Dans le Cadre des MOOCs. Mémoire de master, Université Claude Bernard Lyon 1 - LIRIS (2014)
10. Romero, M., Usart, M.: Serious games integration in an entrepreneurship massive online open course (MOOC). In: Ma, M., Oliveira, M.F., Petersen, S., Hauge, J.B. (eds.) SGDA 2013. LNCS, vol. 8101, pp. 212–225. Springer, Heidelberg (2013)
11. Freire, M., Del Blanco, A., Fernández-Manjón, B.: Serious games as edX MOOC activities. In: Global Engineering Education Conference (EDUCON), pp. 867–871. IEEE (2014)

A Literature Review of Serious Games for Intellectual Disabilities

Ana R. Cano[1(✉)], Álvaro J. García-Tejedor[2], and Baltasar Fernández-Manjón[1]

[1] Universidad Complutense de Madrid, Madrid, Spain
anarcano@ucm.es, balta@fdi.ucm.es
[2] Universidad Francisco de Vitoria, Madrid, Spain
a.gtejedor@ceiec.es

Abstract. Our review examines the literature on Serious Games used as learning tools for people with intellectual disabilities. Although intellectual disabilities are a very broad field where each individual has very specific characteristics, it would be beneficial to have general evidence-based recommendations about how to design videogames adapted to their cognitive requirements. Thus, the first step of our investigation is to identify and review the available literature on Serious Games for intellectual disabilities classifying them according to the learning outcomes associated. Search terms identified 43 papers covering this topic and our review presents the initial results. A second aim is to understand the mechanics designed, the methods used in the investigation and the data obtained. The final goal is to identify what is working in this kind of games and how this can be generalized into a methodology to simplify the creation of more effective games for people with intellectual disabilities.

Keywords: Serious games · Intellectual disabilities · Cognitive disabilities · Educational games · Autism spectrum disorder · Down syndrome

1 Introduction

The use of educational or therapeutic videogames for people with intellectual disabilities is still a relatively unexplored field. Even though intellectual disabilities are a very broad and diverse field where each individual has very specific characteristics, it would be beneficial to have general evidence-based recommendations about how to design videogames adapted to their cognitive features. To pursue this goal, the purpose of this paper is to identify and review the available literature on Serious Games for intellectual disabilities and classify the research found according to the learning outcomes associated to them. A second aim would be to understand the mechanics designed, the methods used in the investigation and the data obtained.

© Springer International Publishing Switzerland 2015
G. Conole et al. (Eds.): EC-TEL 2015, LNCS 9307, pp. 560–563, 2015.
DOI: 10.1007/978-3-319-24258-3_59

2 Serious Games for Intellectual Disabilities

Even though the different intellectual disabilities have similarities, it is not possible to standardize common requiremenmts of all impairments and reflect them in the design of a videogame's mechanics. The result is that not all Serious Games are suitable as learning tools for all disabled game players [1, 2] so we are interested in identifying those articles referred to two concrete disabilities: ASD (Autistic Spectrum Disorder) and DS (Down Syndrome) for three reasons:

1. Down Syndrome is the most common genetic disorder found in newborns and the most common intellectual disability associated with mental impairments. The prevalence of Down syndrome has been reported to occur in about 1 out of every 600 live births [3].
2. ASD comprises a group of conditions within the category of developmental disorders. Due to its heterogeneity of symptoms, ASD is the disorder with the largest number of scientific investigations among the intellectual disabilities [4].
3. There are a large number of associations in Spain and US dedicated to ASD and DS (separately) that can provide us advice about the characteristics, skills, attitudes and behavior of each group and provide users for the actual game testing.

3 Method

To examine the available literature in Serious Games we applied a similar approach to the used by Connolly et al. [5]. First, we selected the databases that are relevant in the topic of this article: Computer Science, Psychology, Medicine and Science in general. All of them were accessed in their electronic format.

Secondly, we identified three groups of search terms that combined helps us to perform an accurate search in databases referred to the technology, the subject and our particular interest in game design and development methodologies. The final query used in the databases included terms like "videogame", "intellectual disability", "down syndrome" or "autism"[1]

As a result of the search we obtained 498 studies but not all of them were relevant for the purpose of our investigation so we applied the following selection criteria in order to choose which articles include in our review:

1. The purpose of the study is to test the acquisition of knowledge through videogames designed or adapted considering specific needs of a particular intellectual disability or a common feature in people with intellectual disabilities in general.
2. The purpose of the study is to identify patterns and behaviors in the use of videogames in people with intellectual disabilities.
3. The purpose of the study is to apply a methodology in the design or development of videogames for a particular intellectual disability or intellectual disabilities in general.

---

[1] Note that each database has its own nomenclature. We adapted the query to each database's search requirements without removing any search term.

In addition, we discarded the studies that do not appear in scientific publications and those published before 2005. Those papers that do not report an empirical evidence of the results has been included only when the results show relevant behaviors of the users or when best practices are identified.

We obtained 43 papers to include in our review following the method previously described.

4 Classification of the Studies and Future Work

The studies included in our review are classified as follows: First, we determined the purpose of the investigation in accordance to one of our three inclusion criteria. Second, we applied the taxonomy described by Wouters [6] to those studies which purpose is to learn a skill (Fig. 1).

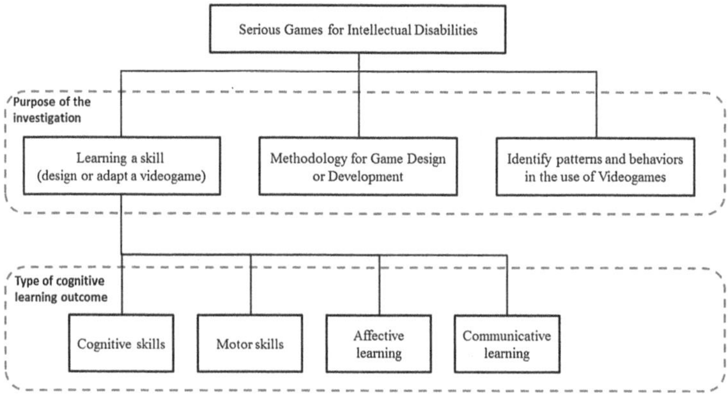

Fig. 1. Classification scheme of the studies included in the review

We provide an outline of the research available on Serious Games for intellectual disabilities by reviewing and classifying these 43 studies according to the purpose of the investigation and the learning outcomes associated to them. We think that the literature available is still insufficient because the majority of the studies do not provide empirical results that can be collected in a best-practice guide for developing Serious Games for intellectual-disabled people.

Our review is only a first step to obtain guidelines for creating more effective games for users with intellectual disabilities. Next step would be the identification, compilation, implementation and test of the best practices using a proof of concept. These best practices will be a mix of lessons learned identified in the review and our own assumptions.

Once we test the mock-up with our design assumptions, our final goal consists on describing a methodology that can be generalized to simplify the development of more effective Serious Games for people with intellectual disabilities.

Acknowledgments. The e-UCM research group has been partially funded by Regional Government of Madrid (eMadrid S2013/ICE-2715), by the Complutense University of Madrid (GR3/14-921340), by the Ministry of Education (TIN2013-46149-C2-1-R), by the RIURE Network (CYTED 513RT0471) and by the European Commission (RAGE H2020-ICT-2014-1-644187).

References

1. Alves, S., Marques, A., Queirós, C., Orvalho, V.: LIFEisGAME prototype: a serious game about emotions for children with autism spectrum disorders. PsychNology J. **11**(3), 191–211 (2013)
2. Karal, H., Kokoç, M., Ayyıldız, U.: Educational computer games for developing psychomotor ability in children with mild mental impairment. Procedia Soc. Behav. Sci. **9**, 996–1000 (2010)
3. Davis, A.: Children with Down Syndrome: implications fos asessment and intervention in the school. Sch. Psychol. Q. **23**(2), 271–281 (2008)
4. Lecavalier, L., Snow, A., Norris, M.: Autism spectrum disorders and intellectual disability. In: Matson, J.L., Sturmey, P. (eds.) International Handbook of Autism and Pervasive Developmental Disorders. Autism and Child Psychopathology Series, pp. 37–51. Springer, Heidelberg (2011)
5. Connolly, T.M. et al.: A systematic literature review of empirical evidence on computer games and serious games. Comput. Educ. **59**(2), 661–686 (2012)
6. Wouters, P., van der Spek, D., van Oostendorp, H.: Current practices in serious game research: a review from a learning outcomes perspective. In Games-Based Learning Advancements for Multi-Sensory Human Computer Interfaces: Techniques and Effective Practices, pp. 232–250. IGI Global (2009)

Towards Teacher-Managed Deployment and Integration of Non-SaaS Tools in Virtual Learning Environments

Rafael Cano-Parra(✉), Eduardo Gómez-Sánchez, Miguel L. Bote-Lorenzo, and José A. González-Martínez

GSIC/EMIC Research Group, Universidad de Valladolid, Valladolid, Spain
{rafcano,jgonmar}@gsic.uva.es
{edugom,migbot}@tel.uva.es

Abstract. Virtual Learning Environments (VLEs) such as Moodle or Sakai are now commonplace in many educational settings, but the limited set of built-in tools (e.g. chats or forums) is often mentioned as a drawback. While successful solutions to integrate Software as a Service (SaaS) tools are reported in the literature (e.g. IMS Basic LTI and GLUE!), there are other non-SaaS tools with potential for education that cannot be integrated in VLEs. These include single-user standalone tools that are run on local computers without a web-based interface (e.g. Matlab), but also virtual machines and laboratories that are common in Computer Science-related disciplines. This paper addresses the integration of these non-SaaS tools in VLEs, proposing an architecture to help teachers to select and configure non-SaaS tools using existing integration approaches from VLEs, but that also relies on cloud infrastructures for provisioning and deploying these tools transparently to the end users.

Keywords: Architecture · Cloud computing · e-learning · Educational tools · Integration · Software as a service · Virtual Learning Environments

1 Introduction

Virtual Learning Environments (VLEs) typically allow educators to structure the learning activities in courses or lessons, describing for each activity a set of predefined learning objectives, and including some built-in tools and artifacts (e.g. chats, forums, or documents) to help students to reach these objectives [4]. Several authors, like Pätzold [7], argue that the support of learning activities with VLEs has benefits both for educators and students in some learning contexts. But one of the limitations in current VLEs, such as Moodle[1], LAMS[2], or Sakai[3],

[1] https://moodle.org/.
[2] http://lamsinternational.com/.
[3] https://www.sakaiproject.org/.

© Springer International Publishing Switzerland 2015
G. Conole et al. (Eds.): EC-TEL 2015, LNCS 9307, pp. 564–567, 2015.
DOI: 10.1007/978-3-319-24258-3_60

is the lack of tools beyond the built-in tools [1,2]. Educators want to find in VLEs those tools that they are already using in their classes (e.g. Eclipse or Matlab) to implement learning situations using these tools inside of the VLE [9].

The integration of Software as a Service (SaaS) tools in VLEs is now a reality thanks to some proposals such as IMS Basic LTI[4] or GLUE! [1]. Under a predefined contract between the VLE and the SaaS tool, and including a small module in the VLE that allows to embed its web-based interface, these proposals can integrate instances of external tools while supporting educators in the management of their life-cycle (i.e. selection, configuration, and deletion).

Unfortunately, the integration of non-SaaS tools in VLEs is not supported by any of the existing proposals using an easy and generic way. However, there is a wide range of non-SaaS tools that are frequently used in various educational contexts, such as single-user standalone software commonly installed in personal computers (e.g. Matlab to do mathematical calculations), terminals of operating systems (e.g. a GNU/Linux terminal to compile and execute a program in C), and virtual laboratories (e.g. a virtual laboratory to conduct experiments on simulated networks using ns-3 simulator and Eclipse as a scripting environment).

There are several works in the literature related with the problem of integrating non-SaaS tools in VLEs. Mulfari *et al.* [6] propose an architecture for running assistive technology tools (software for disabled people) in a cloud and offering access to them through simple web browsers. Despotovic-Zrakic *et al.* [3] propose ELABCloud, a system that allows the allocation and deployment of virtual machines associated to Moodle courses and users. Students can use preconfigured images that contain tools or platforms required by teachers, but this configuration must be done by specialized administration staff and out of the Moodle environment. Radulescu's work [8] proposes the use of a middleware to fill the gap between Cloud Management Systems, employed in this study to facilitate the creation and management of virtual laboratories, and VLEs.

These works share two important limitations. First, both teachers and students need to go outside of the VLE to configure and interact with non-SaaS tools because there is no interface integration in the VLE. Even some non-SaaS tools require to work with third-party applications that have no access from a web browser. Second, teachers cannot manage the non-SaaS tool instance life-cycle as they can do with SaaS tools, so the selection, configuration, and deletion of one or more non-SaaS tool instances can be a complex and time-consuming task that cannot be handled by most educators.

Taking into account previous works and the relevance of using external tools inside of a VLE, we propose an architecture that enables the integration of non-SaaS tools in VLEs to help teachers to implement and deploy their current and new learning scenarios directly from the VLE, and using the cloud infrastructure to manage these tools.

[4] http://www.imsglobal.org/lti/.

2 Architecture

Consider a real scenario on which an educator wants his students to use Eclipse as a standalone tool to practice with Java language within the context of Moodle as a VLE that already employs GLUE! as a SaaS integration solution. He wants that their students can collaboratively work with Eclipse in pairs, using a preconfigured environment which meets the teacher's requirements. There are no solutions that integrate Eclipse in a similar way as Google Docs, already used by students to write reports collaboratively. Also, the teacher could gain time and reduce complexity if the preconfigured environment can be automatically replicated for each students' group.

The architecture proposed in the Fig. 1 has been conceived to enable the integration of non-SaaS tools, such as Eclipse, either employing existing SaaS integration solutions, such as GLUE!, or developing ad-hoc adapters for VLEs. In this way, different integration options will be available for VLE administrators, so that it is more likely that they find one suitable for their needs. Furthermore, the architecture has been designed to enable the integration of non-SaaS tools deployed in cloud infrastructures. This allows the possibility of having a wide range of non-SaaS tools available for integration as well as of scaling the tools if it is necessary to cope with the load generated by students [5].

Following the previous scenario, the educator can now choose to add an external tool in Moodle, which uses GLUE! to retrieve a list of non-SaaS tools available in the proposed architecture. The teacher selects Eclipse and fills a *configuration template* also provided by the proposed architecture that is stored in the *data model* databases. Once the Eclipse tool instance is configured, the architecture creates a cloud-independent script that is the translated by a *cloud adapter* into a sequence of commands that is required to launch the virtual machine(s), hosting the Eclipse tool in a specific *cloud infrastructure* (e.g. OpenStack) used by the tool provider. The virtual machine includes a *visualization mode* that translates the Eclipse interface to HTML5 and JavaScript using a web-socket proxy such as Guacamole or noVNC [6], so that the Eclipse interface can be seamlessly integrated in Moodle (or other VLE) course activity web page.

Other learning scenarios that require to use different non-SaaS tools, such as *virtual machines or laboratories* can be deployed and integrated in a similar way.

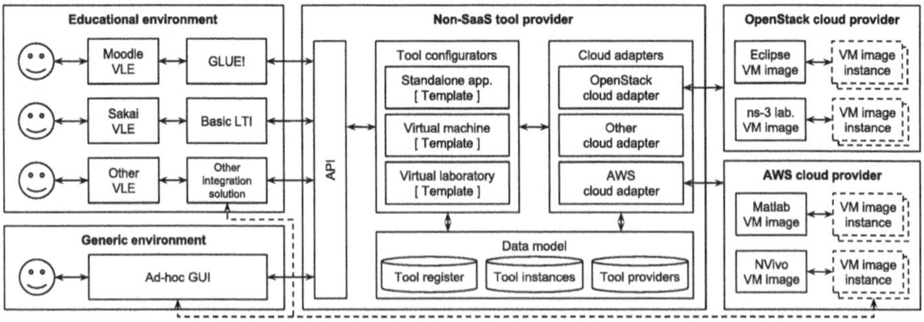

Fig. 1. The architecture that supports the integration of non-SaaS tools in VLEs.

The educator should fill out the template with his configuration needs (e.g. type of operating system, required services, network connection), and this information will be injected into the cloud adapters that will set up and launch the virtual infrastructure. Then, the console(s) interface(s) will be translated as a web-based content for their integration in the VLE, but also a simple access URI (e.g. IP address for SSH or VNC connection) can be passed, so that only the tool instance life-cycle management is used.

In summary, the proposed architecture will allow educators to manage themselves the configuration and integration in their VLEs of non-SaaS tools deployed in cloud infrastructures. This proposal will be prototyped in the short term using GLUE! middleware for integration in Moodle, OpenStack cloud infrastructure for deployment, and noVNC for serving standalone-tool web-based interfaces of standalone tools. Mid term efforts will extend this prototype, and will also be evaluated in diverse real scenarios.

Acknowledgements. This research has been partially funded by the European project 531262-LLP-2012-ES-KA3-KA3MP, the Regional project VA277U14, and the predoctoral fellowship FPI-UVa 2012.

References

1. Alario-Hoyos, C., Bote-Lorenzo, M.L., Gómez-Sánchez, E., Asensio-Pérez, J.I., Vega-Gorgojo, G., Ruiz-Calleja, A.: GLUE!: An architecture for the integration of external tools in Virtual Learning Environments. Comput. Educ. **60**(2013), 122–137 (2013)
2. Bower, M., Wittmann, M.: A comparison of LAMS and Moodle as learning design technologies - Teacher education students' perspective. Teach. Engl. Technol. Spec. Issue LAMS Learn. Des. **11**(1), 62–80 (2011)
3. Despotović-Zrakić, M., Simić, K., Labus, A., Milić, A., Jovanić, B.: Scaffolding environment for e-learning through cloud computing. Educ. Technol. Soc. **16**(3), 301–314 (2013)
4. Dillenbourg, P., Schneider, D., Synteta, P.: Virtual learning environments. In: Proceedings of 3rd Hellenic Conference with International Participation "Information & Communication Technologies in Education" (EICT 2002), Rhodes, Greece, pp. 3–18, September 2002
5. González-Martínez, J.A., Bote-Lorenzo, M.L., Gómez-Sánchez, E., Cano-Parra, R.: Cloud computing and education: a state-of-the-art survey. Comput. Educ. **80**(2015), 132–151 (2015)
6. Mulfari, D., Celesti, A., Villari, M., Puliafito, A.: Using Virtualization and noVNC to Support Assistive Technology in Cloud Computing. In: Proceedings of 2014 IEEE 3rd Symposium on Network Cloud Computing and Applications (NCCA 2014), Rome, Italy, pp. 125–132, February 2014
7. Pätzold, H.: Increasing value without increasing effort? The use of WebCT in accompanying face-to-face lectures under the constraint of low budget. Int. J. e-Learn. Distance Educ. **20**(2), 78–84 (2005)
8. Rădulescu, S.A.: A perspective on E-learning and Cloud Computing. Procedia - Soc. Behav. Sci. **141**(2014), 1084–1088 (2014)
9. Weller, M.: Virtual Learning Environments: Using Choosing and Developing your VLE. Routledge, Abingdon (2007)

Validating Gamification Mechanics and Player Types in an E-learning Environment

Borja Gil[1(✉)], Iván Cantador[1], and Andrzej Marczewski[2]

[1] Escuela Politécnica Superior, Universidad Autónoma de Madrid, 28049 Madrid, Spain
{borja.gil,ivan.cantador}@uam.es
[2] Digital Solutions Unit, Capgemini, London, EC1N 2PB, UK
andrzej.marczewski@capgemini.com

Abstract. We present a preliminary user study in an e-learning environment aimed to adapt and validate generic mechanics and player types proposed in the gamification literature. We incorporate well-known gamification mechanics into a number learning activities, implemented them as functionalities of an e-learning system, and investigate the learning effectiveness of the proposed mechanics, as well as the relations between the mechanics and their assumed player types.

Keywords: E-learning · Gamification · Learning style · Motivation · Engagement

1 Introduction

Gamification is defined as the application of game-design elements to non-game contexts with the intention of modifying behaviours, increasing fidelity or motivating and engaging people [3], by leveraging human motivations present in games, e.g. competition, rewards and socializing. In the literature, these motivations have been identified and associated to the so called types of players [1, 6]. Specifically, four main player types may be considered: *achievers*, who are motivated by mastery and rewards, *explorers* or *free spirits*, who are motivated by autonomy and self-expression, *socializers*, who are motivated by social relatedness and status, and *philanthropists*, who are motivated by altruism and care-taking. For each of these player types, particular gamification mechanics have been proposed to support the corresponding motivations [5]. Hence, for example, mechanics that may suit an achiever's motivations are the achievement of certain challenges and levels, and the gain of points and badges.

Although gamification has already been applied successfully in a large number of cases [7], to the best of our knowledge, it still pending the study on how to effectively acquire the users' motivations and player types, and how to select the appropriate gamification mechanics, and translate them into tasks and actions for a given application or domain [2, 8]. As in [4], we focus on Higher Education, and start addressing the above issues through a preliminary user study aimed to validate existing gamification mechanics and player types, addressing the following research questions:

© Springer International Publishing Switzerland 2015
G. Conole et al. (Eds.): EC-TEL 2015, LNCS 9307, pp. 568–572, 2015.
DOI: 10.1007/978-3-319-24258-3_61

- **RQ1**: Which gamification mechanics are effective in e-learning, and how can they be implemented by means of generic learning activities?
- **RQ2**: Do the considered gamification mechanics really correspond to the students' inferred types of player?

2 Gamification-Based E-Learning Framework

In the classroom and during several lectures, students were requested to solve a number of assignments related to topics of a subject, working in different ways (alone, in pairs, or in teams) and performing various actions, which were related to certain gamification mechanics and player types. All the actions were supported and recorded by an e-learning system, accessible via web though the students' mobile phones. As shown in

Table 1. Considered student actions, gamification mechanics, and assumed player types.

Student action		Mechanic	Player type
A1	Choosing to work alone for solving the assignments	Challenge	Achiever
A2	Receiving a "victory badge" for being the first student who solved certain assignment		
A3	Receiving a "quest badge" for solving certain number of assignments	Quest	
A4	Receiving a "level-X expertise badge" for solving certain number of assignments with difficulty level X	Level /Progression	
A5	Receiving a "mastery certificate" for obtaining certain number of victory, quest and/or expertise badges	Certificate	
E1	Choosing to work alone for solving the assignments	Exploration	Explorer
E2	Receiving an "explorer badge" for asking (the teacher/system) and solving hidden assignments of high difficulty		
E3	Receiving an "adventurer badge" for asking (the teacher/system) and solving assignments out of the study topics	Unlockable /Rare Content	
E4	Receiving a "customizer badge" for proposing and solving adaptations or modifications of an assignment	Customization	
E5	Receiving a "creator badge" for proposing and solving new assignments	Creativity	
S1	Choosing to work in a team for solving the assignments	Team /Guild	Socializer
S2	Receiving points for the competition ranking by solving assignments	Competition	
S3	Receiving a "colleague badge" (from a member of my team) for being very participative and cooperative	Social status	
S4	Creating a "twinning link" with a student I enjoyed working with	Social networking	
S5	Giving a "gentleman badge" to a student to whom I asked for help on solving an assignment	Social discovery	
P1	Receiving a "gentleman badge" from a student I helped on solving an assignment	Meaning /Purpose	Philanthropist
P2	Helping a student to solve an assignment	Care taking	
P3	Presenting an assignment solution on the blackboard	Sharing knowledge	
P4	Ask (the teacher/system) for an assignment solution	Access	
P5	Interchanging a "ring" with other student	Collecting & Trading	
P6	Giving one of my rings to a student	Gifting	

Table 1, a total of 21 actions were considered, which were specific implementations of existing gamification mechanics [5] for our particular learning scenario. At the beginning of the study and each lecture, the students were presented with the description of the different activities, and they were allowed to freely choose and perform (record) any of them during the study.

3 User Study

The study was conducted in a subject belonging to the 1st-year course of Computer Science studies, which is an introduction to Abstract Data Types and the C programming language. It was done within the classroom and took five 1-hour lectures in which students were presented with a large number of assignments of different (marked) difficulty degrees, and were asked to freely choose and solve any of them. They were also requested to freely perform and record actions (Table 1) available in the system. A total of 40 students participated in the study. A week before the starting of the study, they filled a questionnaire [6] with which their assumed player types were inferred. From their responses, 31.1 % of the students were assigned to *achiever* as their main player type, 15.6 % to *explorer*, 22.2 % to *socializer*, and the remaining 31.1 % to *philanthropist*.

3.1 Effectiveness of Actions and Gamification Mechanics

To obtain initial insights about which of the tested actions and mechanics are more effective (RQ1), we briefly present here two sets of analysis results. First, after the study, the students evaluated several issues about the system and the activity. They stated that, with respect a "typical" assignment solving lecture: they felt to learn more (73.7 %) or the same (26.3 %); they had more (80.0 %), much more (10.5 %), or the same (9.5 %) fun; and would like to have similar activities in the future (84.2 %) or not (15.8 %). Most of them found the system easy or very easy to use (89.5 %), but a significant percentage felt *a bit* stressed (52.6 %), mostly explorers and achievers, who worked alone. This may be due to the fact that the study took place in 1-hour lectures.

Second, we checked the number of times each action was recorded. Most of the used actions were related to the achievement of goals and progression–challenge and certificate–, collaborative work–team and social networking–, and knowledge access. This is in concordance with the students' most preferred mechanics, namely teams (57.9 %), levels (52.6 %), challenges (47.4 %) and quests (36.8 %).

3.2 Relations Between Actions, Gamification Mechanics, and Player Types

To preliminary validate if the freely chosen actions and gamification mechanics really corresponded to the students' inferred player types (RQ2), in Fig. 1 we show the number of students who performed each action, grouped by the main player types assigned to them. Each of the questions had a manually set weight representing the relevance of the question to derive a user's player type. The figure shows the curves of inferred player types applying (a) and not applying (b) such weights. We observe that the students' actions and mechanics relate quite well with the corresponding player types, except for the *explorer* case. The students neither wanted to spend time accessing to assignments of other topics (E3), nor modifying the given assignments (E4) or creating new ones (E5). Exploration (E2), which was implemented as solving hidden assignments of high difficulty, was conducted by *achievers*, who were motivated to achieve challenges (A1, A2), quests (A3) and certificates (A5) for solving as many (difficult) assignments as possible. *Socializers* decided to use all their assumed mechanics except competition (S2) and social discovery (S5), which did not receive too much interest in the activity. Finally, *philanthropists* not only performed their assumed mechanics (P1-P4 especially), but also decided to work in teams (S1).

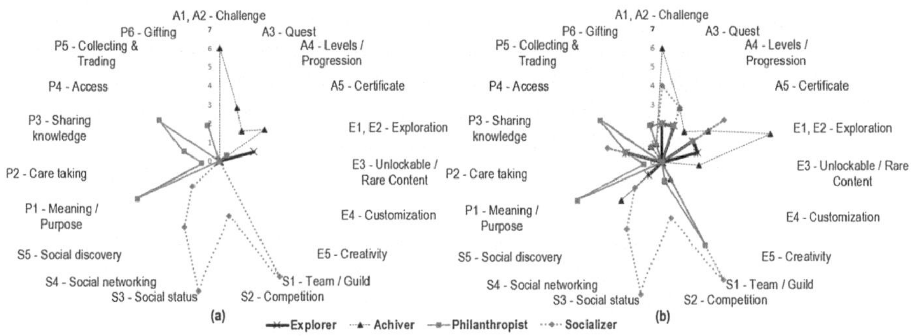

Fig. 1. Number of students who performed each action, grouped by their inferred player types.

4 Conclusions and Future Work

In this paper we have preliminary validated gamification mechanics and player types in education. We have shown that, in an e-learning environment, students freely performed learning actions that really corresponded to inferred *achiever*, *socializer* and *philanthropist* player types, but did not fit with the *explorer* player type. The study has allowed us to identify certain gamification mechanics that are more relevant in terms of their use and student assessments, namely *collaborative-* and *challenge-based mechanics*. Nonetheless, a more rigorous and exhaustive experimentation and analysis is needed to prove the above claims, and work is required to understand and exploit the relationships between the player types with well-known learning styles and personality types.

Acknowledgements. This work has been supported by the Spanish Government through its Ministry of Science and Innovation (RTC-2014-2089-7).

References

1. Bartle, R.: Hearts, clubs, diamonds, spades: players who suit MUDs. J. MUD Res. **1**(1), 19 (1996)

2. Butler, C.: A framework for evaluating the effectiveness of gamification techniques by personality type. In: Nah, F.F.-H. (ed.) HCIB 2014. LNCS, vol. 8527, pp. 381–389. Springer, Heidelberg (2014)
3. Deterding, S., Sicart, M., Nacke, L., O'Hara, K., Dixon, D.: Gamification: using game-design elements in non-gaming contexts. In: CHI 2011 Extended Abstracts on Human Factors in Computing Systems, pp. 2425–2428 (2011)
4. Iosup, A., Epema, D.: An experience report on using gamification in technical higher education. In: Proceedings of the 45th ACM Technical Symposium on Computer Science Education, pp. 27–32 (2014)
5. Marczewki, A.: Game Mechanics in Gamification. Gamified UK (2013). http://www.gamified.uk/2013/01/14/game-mechanics-in-gamification
6. Marczewki, A.: Six User Types for Gamification Design – Hexad. Gamified UK (2013). http://www.gamified.uk/user-types
7. Merino, B.: Gamification: A System to Improve Sustainability Efforts. MSc thesis. School of Computer Science, University of Manchester, UK (2013)
8. Nicholson, S.: A User-centered theoretical framework for meaningful gamification. In: Proceedings of the 8th Games Learning and Society Conference (2012)

Integrating Teacher and Student Workspaces in a Technology-Enhanced Mathematics Lecture

Giorgi Goguadze(✉)

Leuphana University of Lüneburg, Lüneburg, Germany
goguadze@leuphana.de

Abstract. Recent introduction of modern computer technology into schools and universities presented new challenges to mathematics teachers. On one hand, powerful computer tools have emerged that allow for rich animation and visualization. On the other hand, the teachers are not ready to give up using the blackboard, which is still their main workspace. This work presents a tool for teachers, that allows for more freedom than the fixed lecture slides and helps illustrating rules for transforming mathematical expressions and solving equations. Using this tool, the teacher can automatically generate solutions for mathematical problems on the fly and interactively present these to the students step by step. The solution is then blended out and the students are offered to solve similar problems on their computers interactively using the system.

This tool is a part of a larger toolkit used within several innovative Blended Learning Bridging Courses in Mathematics at Leuphana University in Lüneburg, held in a computer-equipped classroom.

Keywords: Intelligent tutoring systems · Worked solutions · Interactive exercises · Technology enhanced teaching

1 Introduction

Since early age of computers there have been attempts to use them in education. Most of the developed intelligent systems are aiming to replace the teacher by providing intelligent guidance of a learning process without the participation of a human tutor. On their way to achieve this goal, Intelligent Tutoring Systems have established a deep on-to-one interaction with each student via intelligent diagnosis of the user's actions and adaptive feedback [1]. Some modules of these systems such as intelligent mathematical rule engines, capable of automatically generating solutions of problems could be of a good use for teachers. However those systems were never intended to assist a teacher, they just served the goals of an intelligent tutoring system as back-engines.

The goal of our work is to employ intelligent production engines of an ITS system to build a tool for mathematics teachers enhancing their performance with the help of a computer environment and providing the students with an interface for interacting with the lecture materials and training the learned skills on the spot.

© Springer International Publishing Switzerland 2015
G. Conole et al. (Eds.): EC-TEL 2015, LNCS 9307, pp. 573–576, 2015.
DOI: 10.1007/978-3-319-24258-3_62

In order to achieve this goal we have built an extension of EXAMAT - a web-based system for intelligent interactive exercises, introduced in [2]. This system can be used by the teacher and the students in different ways. The teacher can generate sample problems on the fly and present their solutions to the audience step by step, and the students can then directly train the learned skills by solving the same problems as interactive exercises in the system. The system is running on the central server and the teacher and students only need a web-browser to access it.

This tool covers most of the school mathematics topics dealing with algebraic transformations and equation solving. It is also suitable for some introductory university courses and is being currently tested within several bridging courses in mathematics at Leuphana University in Lüneburg, Germany.

2 Framework Tools and Instructional Approach

The EXAMAT learning environment offers a tool for authoring and executing interactive exercises for multiple mathematical topics for which the system can provide intelligent feedback to students' actions on their own solution path. A basis for such adaptation is a rich diagnosis provided by external AI engines performing rule based reasoning in the corresponding domains. These so-called *domain reasoners* can solve mathematical problems step by step and provide diagnosis on student's own solutions.

A valuable functionality for the teacher would be an opportunity to present a worked out solution of a problem visualizing the application of concepts he/she teaches. This functionality is now enabled within a component called TERMANIA which aims at allowing the teacher to interactively demonstrate various examples of term manipulation in an illustrative way without the need to actually perform the handwriting on the blackboard. This approach offers an illustrative process triggering a mental effort of understanding the transition of participating terms from one state to another. Such process should have a similar effect to watching teacher interacting with the blackboard and producing information piece by piece as opposed to looking at a ready solution on a static slide. By visualizing in more detail the transformation of expressions we show the student not only what the next step is, but also how we obtained it, which could be even more illustrative than the traditional way of just writing down the ready solution steps. This is the first approach of the kind to teaching algebraic transformations, known to the author.

Thanks to the integrated domain reasoner components, the system can generate complete worked solutions automatically, the teacher only has to select the type of the task and enter the actual problem statement, represented as a formula.

Thanks to the usage of IDEAS domain reasoners, specifically designed for the needs of interactive exercises, as described in [3], the generated knowledge representation contains enough information about the structure of the solution in order to be able to generate the needed interactive elements automatically.

For example, in each step the system delivers information which rule was applied to obtain this step from the previous one alongside with its arguments.

The solution is presented in a stepwise manner, as shown in Fig. 1 (left). In the first step, a copy of the problem statement is presented, and the teacher can transform or manipulate the participating terms by clicking on them or dragging their parts to obtain the next step. In order to produce the following step, the teacher clicks on the next step button, represented by a '+' sign in the right upper corner. The current step is left on the screen and copied once again in the next line. The teacher then modifies it by clicking or dragging its parts to produce the following step. This procedure is repeated until the final step is performed and the solution is completed. The resulting worked solution is stored in the system as a video, so that the students can not only revisit the solution at home, but recreate the process of its generation.

In our Blended Learning approach we implement a new instructional strategy we call *teach-&-train* in which we combine the elements of a lecture and a practical work with the computer system. The lecturer introduces a topic by means of presenting definitions and interactive examples and worked solutions. Then the students are requested to work with the system solving the corresponding interactive exercises. We believe that this style of lecture has given students better understanding of concepts and processes behind the formal definitions, and an opportunity to directly use the freshly learned rules in praxis.

A novel instructional paradigm here is also the fact that the EXAMAT environment becomes a technology platform for communication between the teacher and students. The teacher workspace is shared with the students and adapted to their task. Each of the participants of the tutorial dialogue has his/her own role and there is a clear turn taking strategy. The teacher explains a worked example interactively using the tool and afterwards blends away the solution and offers the same problem as an exercise to the students. Students then solve this exercise step by step using the system, that gives automatic intelligent feedback to each step and supports the students on their own solution path, as shown in Fig. 1 (right).

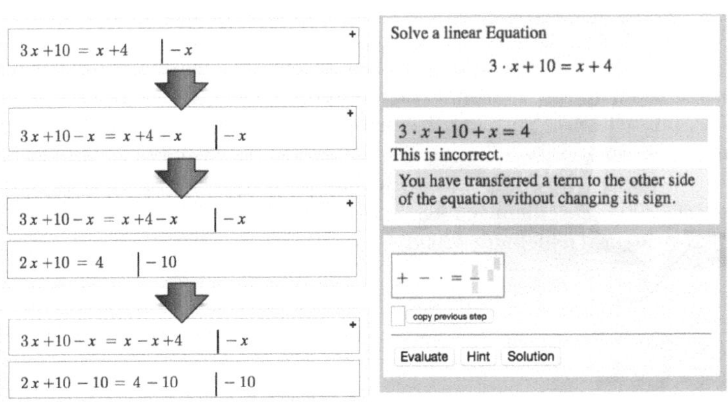

Fig. 1. Step by step solution by the teacher (left), exercise for the learner (right)

The students can also continue working with the system at home. The lecture materials are available in the same form as during the lecture and the interactive solutions are offered in the form of videos, replaying the same process the teacher would show in the presence hour. The students can continue solving exercises at home using the system and replay the worked examples if they need to recall the solution process.

3 Conclusion and Future Work

The goal of our research is to develop new instruments for teachers and students that support more interactive tutorial dialogue and innovative teaching and learning scenarios. We present an extension of the learning environment EXAMAT that gives an opportunity to the teacher to interactively present structured worked solutions to the students. Moreover, the students can train the acquired skills directly after being presented with the solution by solving similar problems as interactive exercises in the system.

One of the interesting future developments would be to be able to apply different presentation strategies to the worked solutions and allow the teachers to configure presented solutions depending on their instructional goals. For example, the same solution can be presented with different level of detail within a single step, also larger steps could be allowed for advanced audience, and so on.

Finally, it is necessary to evaluate the learning effect of the suggested instructional approach in comparison to learning only using non-animated worked solutions and to the condition without solving interactive exercises right after learning from a worked solution.

References

1. Corbett, A.T., Koedinger, K.R., Anderson, J.R.: Intelligent tutoring systems. In: Helander, M., Landauer, T.K., Prabhu, P.V. (eds.) Handbook of Human-Computer Interaction, Chap. 37, pp. 849–874. Elsevier Science B.V., Amsterdam (1997). second, completely revised edition
2. Goguadze, G.: Examat: Intelligent exercise services for mathematics learning. In: de Freitas, S., Rensing, C., Ley, T., Muñoz-Merino, P.J. (eds.) EC-TEL 2014. LNCS, vol. 8719, pp. 566–567. Springer, Heidelberg (2014)
3. Heeren, B., Jeuring, J., van Leeuwen, A., Gerdes, A.: Specifying strategies for exercises. In: Autexier, S., Campbell, J., Rubio, J., Sorge, V., Suzuki, M., Wiedijk, F. (eds.) AISC 2008, Calculemus 2008, and MKM 2008. LNCS (LNAI), vol. 5144, pp. 430–445. Springer, Heidelberg (2008)

Using Cloud Computing for E-assessment Process Integration

Fahima Hajjej[(✉)], Yousra Bendaly Hlaoui, and Leila Jemni Ben Ayed

Laboratory LaTICE, University of Tunis, Tunis, Tunisia
hajjejfahima@gmail.com, yousra.bendalyhlaoui@esstt.rnu.tn, Leila.jemni@fsegt.rnu.tn

Abstract. Currently, there are many problems of the application development of E-Assessment such as the difficulty to use the assessment object from a platform to another one. In addition, the domain model reuse rate is very low in various application systems, and hardness to guarantee the consistency between designs and codes. Therefore, to resolve these problems, we need an approach aiming to automate the modeling and coding processes in e-assessment system. The present study describes an approach, based on service cloud computing, for integrating e-assessment functionalities of candidate LMS systems into a generalized e-assessment process.

Keywords: E-assessment · Cloud computing · LMS · Flexibility

1 Introduction

We propose to develop a generic and adaptable e-assessment process. The e-assessment approach could not be suitable for all types of learners as they present different knowledge profiles and learning behaviors. Some of them need to be assessed on the complete learning materials to evaluate their overall knowledge. Others may only need to estimate their knowledge at a particular stage of the learning process in order to access to the suitable learning material. There is why, we are brought about adapting the generic e-assessment process to the learner behavior. In fact, to ensure this adaptation, we present a set of mapping rules defined as a composite cloud service. The use of cloud technology in our e-assessment approach offers for us many benefits such as: interoperability, scalability and flexibility.

2 Generic E-Assessment Process Development

We present in this section the development of a generic e-assessment process using the LMS [8, 10] and based on the LTSA [6] which we extend by some features required to such development. The generated e-assessment model is specified by UML AD [1]. To build this generic e-assessment process, we are brought about following steps.

© Springer International Publishing Switzerland 2015
G. Conole et al. (Eds.): EC-TEL 2015, LNCS 9307, pp. 577–581, 2015.
DOI: 10.1007/978-3-319-24258-3_63

2.1 Analyze and Study the Existing LMSs Functionality

We have studied and analyzed a set of existing LMSs (Learning Management System) such as Moodle [3], OLAT [2] and LAMS [4] … These LMSs provide several e-assessment tools and not a global e-assessment process. In fact, we have explored the functionalities that they offer to realize the e-assessment (Fig. 1).

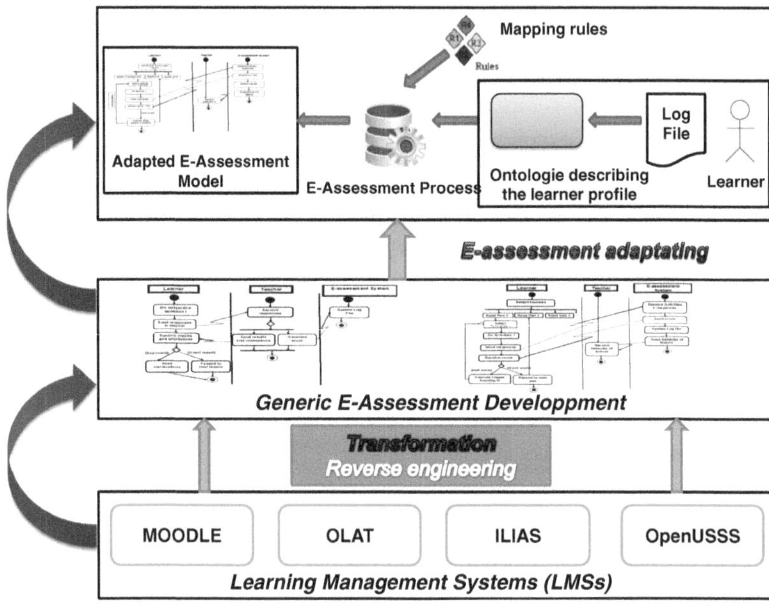

Fig. 1. Generic e-assessment process development

2.2 Create the Generic E-Assessment Activities from Existing LMSs E-Assessment Tasks Using the Reverse Engineering

In this step we have collected the e-assessment tasks and concepts used by several LMSs to specify and define generic e-assessment activities. Using the reverse engineering [9], we propose a set of transformation from the LMS specific e-assessment tasks to LMS independent e-assessment activities corresponding to our generic e-assessment activities. We present the set of the elaborated transformations. Practically it means to create translation tables for data structures of a LMS system to the generalized system. Such relations or mapping rules can have forms of **1 to1** (*simple mapping)*, **1 to n** (*refining* mapping) or **n to 1** (abstracting mapping).

2.3 Create the Generic E-Assessment Process

We have defined the e-assessment process by coordinating the generic e-assessment activities, generated from the previous step, in a workflow structure. We use workflow technology to have abstract, generic and flexible e- assessment process. This e-assessment workflow model should be a good communication axe between teachers, learners and the e-assessment system. We try to test learner on each level of training to guarantee its comprehension and to help him to reach a high level of knowledge. In fact our e-assessment process is not independent from the e-learning process. To design our e-assessment process, we are based on the learning cycle described in LTSA layer II by combining two methods of evaluation: the e-assessment part method and the e-assessment lesson method.

3 Adapt the Generic E-Assessment Process to the Leaner Profile

Once the generic e-assessment process is built, it will be personalized according to a learner profile defining her\his level of knowledge. Using the generated log file, the tutor will define and adapt the learning and assessment material to the behavior of the learner. If the learner's performance does not meet the pre-defined expectations, the presentation of the course content is adapted to his level of knowledge and the selection of the appropriate assessment content is then performed. Thus, each learner will be able to get a highly personalized course which will be appropriate to his level of knowledge. In fact, to specify an adaptive and flexible e-assessment workflow, we propose to refine the generic e-assessment workflow by adding, deleting or editing specific e-assessment activities according to each learner profile. We define three refinement rules: add activity (***AddAC***), delete activity (***DelAC***) and edit activity (***EditAC***). Applying these rules on a generic workflow, we provide an adapted e-assessment workflow relatively to the learner profile.

4 From Traditional E-Assessment to Cloud E-Assessment

In our approach, we specify the adaptation process and the e-assessment process as cloud services. Therefore, we are brought to identify the interfaces, the messages and the operations of each built cloud service. The innovation that this cloud e-assessment system defines the resulting generic and adapted e-assessment process as a composite cloud service allowing flexibility and interoperability between any LMS e-assessment. Our e-assessment cloud is composed by two main composite services. The first composite cloud service, presented in Fig. 2, is called *E-assessment generic model*. This service is composed of a set of simple cloud services. Each simple service invokes a generic e-assessment activity. The second composite cloud service, presented in Fig. 3, is called *Adaptation process*. This service is composed of a set of simple cloud services. Each simple service invokes an adaptation function presented in the previous section.

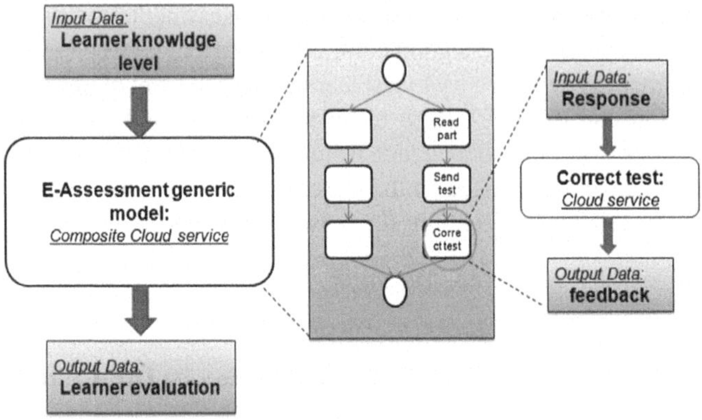

Fig. 2. E-Assessment generic model: composite service cloud process

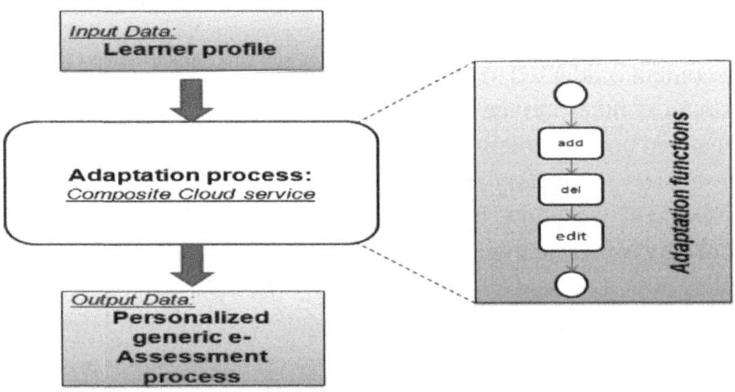

Fig. 3. Adaptation process: composite service cloud

5 Conclusion

In this paper, we have presented a novel approach for developing generic and personalized e-assessment process for different existing LMSs. This approach is based on the reverse engineering to develop this generic e-assessment process using existing LMS's e-assessment functionality and the LTSA architecture. In addition, this approach uses service cloud computing to improve the interoperability of the use of the adaptation process and the personalized generic e-assessment process.

References

1. OMG: Unified Modeling Language Specification. http://www.omg.org
2. OLAT Project. http://www.olat.org
3. Moodle project. http://docs.moodle.org
4. LAMS Project. http://www.lamsinternational.com

5. Hua, R.: Teaching information system based on cloud computing. Comput. Telecommun. **2**, 42–43 (2010)
6. ZhongmeiZheng, H., Ye, F., Tong, S.: The Applied Research of Cloud Computing in the Construction of Collaborative Learning Platform under E-learning Environment. 978-0-7695-4223-2
7. Corbiere, A., Choquet, C.: Designer integration in training cycles: IEEE LTSA model adaptation, CALIE. In: International Conference on Computer Aided Learning in Engineering Education, Grenoble, France, p. 12 (2004)
8. Chikofsky, E.J., Cross, J.H.: Reverse engineering and design recovery: a taxonomy. IEEE Softw. **7**(1), 13–17 (2009)
9. Petrina, S.: Sidney Pressey and the automation of education, 1924–1934. Technology and Culture, pp. 305–330 (2004)
10. Stalljohann, P., Herding, D., Schroeder, U.: Utilizing a workflow engine to manage semi-automatic correction processes across domains. In: 14th International Conference on Interactive Collaborative Learning (ICL 2011): Piestany, Slovakia, 21–23 September 2011

Querying Repositories of OER Descriptions: The Challenge of Educational Metadata Schemas Diversity

Hiba Hajri(✉), Yolaine Bourda, and Fabrice Popineau

LRI, CentraleSupélec, bat. 650 (PCRI), 91405 Orsay, France
{hiba.hajri,yolaine.bourda,fabrice.popineau}@centralesupelec.fr

Abstract. Personalized applications like recommendation systems or open adaptive hypermedia require to facilitate reuse and interoperability of educational resources. Thus we have to solve the problem of discovering educational datasets and the problem of the fragmented landscape of competing metadata schemas. In this paper, we compare a subset of metadata schemas used by educational datasets obeying the Linked Open Data principles and we propose mappings between them.

Keywords: Linked open data · Educational datasets · Metadata schemas

1 Introduction

The efficiency of personalized applications of Technology-Enhanced Learning (TEL) depends in particular on the quality of the metadata describing the education open resources (OER) [6]. In this article we are interested in personalization based on OER and especially on those supporting interoperability [3] with descriptions following the Linked Open Data principles (LOD) [1].

We start by searching for repositories accessible on the Web, which contain descriptions of OER and which provide SPARQL endpoints [10] for data access. Therefore we look for the *Linked Education Catalog*[1] provided by the Linked Up Project[2]. It is a catalog of data sets relevant to educational applications with SPARQL endpoint for each one and also a common SPARQL endpoint that provides access to VOID[3] descriptions of currently included datasets [2]. There are also other repositories in the literature not referenced in the Linked Up Project like SemUNT [7] which is a project of French digital thematic universities.

Once we have found accessible repositories and in order to be able to interrogate them with one SPARQL query for a given question (e.g. finding exercises about calculus for undergraduate students), we have to study closely the distinct metadata schemas used. We start with comparing a subset of metadata schemas.

[1] http://data.linkededucation.org/linkedup/catalog/.
[2] http://linkedup-project.eu/.
[3] http://www.w3.org/TR/void/.

© Springer International Publishing Switzerland 2015
G. Conole et al. (Eds.): EC-TEL 2015, LNCS 9307, pp. 582–586, 2015.
DOI: 10.1007/978-3-319-24258-3_64

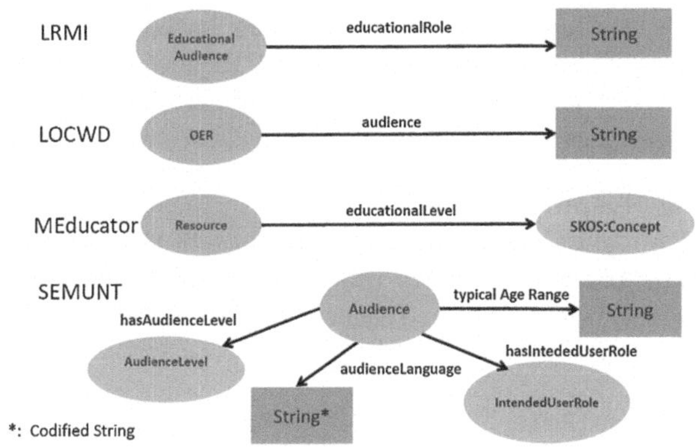

Fig. 1. Elements describing the audience

Actually the schemas specific to education and more preciously OER are either the LOM [8] and its applications profiles or extensions of generic schemas such as Dublin Core (DC)[4] and FOAF[5].

In our comparison, we focus on a subset of schemas which have complete RDF or OWL bindings and which are specific for OER description. We choose firstly Learning Resource initiative(LRMI)[6]: a schema based on DC. Secondly, Linked OpenCourseWare Data (LOCWD) [9]: it describes OER in the OpenCourseWare context. Thirdly mEducator [5]: a LOM application profile for the health sector. And the last one SemUNT [7]: a schema defined from an application profile of the LOM for French UNT.

The principle of our comparison is to take all educational aspects and to study how they are described in each one of these schemas. An example of educational aspects is the description of the audience (for whom is the OER?). In Fig. 1, we detail the elements used by each schema to specify this aspect.

2 Definition of Mappings and SPARQL Queries

The study of schemas enabled us to define mappings or SPARQL queries, as the case may be, based on our comparison results. The problem of schema mapping has been pointed out as one of the big challenges when interlinking educational resources and LOD. Many approaches have been proposed. Fully automated approaches are more scalable than manual approaches, but they perform lower in terms of precision [4]. Thus we choose to use a manual approach in our work because personalized applications need to be based on precision and also because we don't have a large number of classes and properties to deal with. To this end we define the LOOM: *Learning Object Ontology of Mapping* devoted to the specification of mappings. We note that the defined mappings have, as unique

[4] http://dublincore.org/documents/dces/.
[5] http://xmlns.com/foaf/spec/.
[6] http://dublincore.org/dcx/lrmi-terms/2015-02-09/.

purpose, to allow writing queries for repositories based on diverse educational metadata schemas. Consequently when one of the used metadata schemas is changed, we have just to change the mapping defined in our ontology.

Our LOOM ontology provides the following classes and properties:

loom:Learning Resource a class representing educational resources;
loom:Audience a class representing the audience of the learning resource;
loom:educationalRole a property used to describe the role of the audience intended by the resource (e.g. Teacher, Author, Learner, etc.). Here is its definition:

```
loom:educationalRole     owl:datatypeProperty;
                         rdfs:domain loom:LearningResource.
```

loom:educationalLevel a property used to describe the level of the audience intended by the resource (e.g. Master, License, etc.). Here is its definition:

```
loom:educationalLevel    owl:datatypeProperty;
                         rdfs:domain loom:Audience.
```

The next step is to define mappings with the elements of the educational metadata schemas cited in our comparison. First, we define mappings between the classes representing the resource:

```
loom:Learning Resource  owl:EquivalentClasses  mEducator:Resource
loom:Learning Resource  owl:EquivalentClasses  semunt:LearningResource
loom:Learning Resource  owl:EquivalentClasses  locwd:OER
loom:Learning Resource  owl:EquivalentClasses  lrmi:CreativeWork
```

Secondly we define mappings between the classes representing the audience:

```
loom:Audience  owl:EquivalentClasses  lrmi:Educational Audience
loom:Audience  owl:EquivalentClasses  semunt:Audience
```

Thirdly, we define mappings between properties describing the audience level:

```
loom:educationalLevel  owl:equivalentProperty  semunt:hasAudienceLevel
loom:educationalLevel  owl:equivalentProperty mEducator:educationallevel
```

The property *educationalLevel* of mEducator is a property of the class *Resource* while *hasAudienceLevel* of SemUNT is a property of the class *Audience*. Thus we propose the following SPARQL query to select the resources and the educational levels of SEMUNT and mEducator.

```
SELECT ?lr ?el
WHERE {
     ?lr a loom:LearningResource;
         hasAudience?/loom:educationalLevel ?el}
```

Concerning the properties dealing with the audience role, we propose the following mappings:

```
loom:educationalRole  owl:equivalentProperty  lrmi:educationlRole
loom:educationalRole  owl:equivalentProperty  semunt:hasIntentedUserRole
loom:educationalRole  owl:equivalentProperty  locwd:audience
```

While, on the one hand, *educationalRole* of LRMI and *hasIntendedUserRole* of SemUNT are properties of the classes representing the audience, on the other hand, *audience* of LOCWD is a property of the class *OER*. So we propose the following SPARQL query.

```
SELECT ?lr ?er
WHERE {
    ?lr a loom:LearningResource;
        hasAudience?/loom:educationalRole ?er}
```

3 Future Work

This work is only the beginning and there is still a range of shortcomings that need to be addressed. It is important to continue the study with other used metadata schemas and to compare them on the basis of all educational aspects. Another future work is to use the results of this comparison in order to complete our LOOM ontology. As longcomings, we have to benefit from all these outcomes to integrate a personalized application to a platform of MOOC or LMS such as the OpenEdx platform.

References

1. Bizer, C., Heath, T., Berners-Lee, T.: Linked data: principles and state of the art. In: World Wide Web Conference, pp. 1–40 (2008)
2. d'Aquin, M., Adamou, A., Dietze, S.: Assessing the educational linked data landscape. In: Proceedings of the 5th Annual ACM Web Science Conference, pp. 43–46. ACM (2013)
3. Dietze, S., Drachsler, H., Giordano, D.: A survey on linked data and the social web as facilitators for TEL recommender systems. In: Manouselis, N., Drachsler, H., Verbert, K., Santos, O.C. (eds.) Recommender Systems for Technology Enhanced Learning, pp. 47–75. Springer, New York (2014)
4. Dietze, S., Yu, H.Q., Giordano, D., Kaldoudi, E., Dovrolis, N., Taibi, D.: Linked education: interlinking educational resources and the web of data. In: Proceedings of the 27th Annual ACM Symposium on Applied Computing, pp. 366–371. ACM (2012)
5. Evangelia, M., Taibi, D., Giordano, D., Dietze, S., Yu, H.Q., Bamidis, P., Bratsas, C., Woodham, L.: Connecting medical educational resources to the linked data cloud: the mEducator RDF schema, store and API (2011)
6. Hylén, J.: Open educational resources: opportunities and challenges. In: Proceedings of Open Education, pp. 49–63 (2006)

7. Isaac, Y., Bourda, Y., Grandbastien, M.: Semunit-french unt and linked data. In: LiLe-2012 at WWW-2012, vol. 840, pp. 1–6. CEUR workshop proceedings (2012)
8. Nilsson, M., Palmér, M., Brase, J.: The LOM RDF binding: principles and implementation. In: Proceedings of the Third Annual ARIADNE Conference, Leuven, Belgium (2003)
9. Piedra, N., Tovar, E., Colomo-Palacios, R., Lopez-Vargas, J., Chicaiza, A.J.: Consuming and producing linked open data: the case of opencourseware. Progr. Electron. Libr. Inf. Syst. **48**(1), 16–40 (2014)
10. Quilitz, B., Leser, U.: Querying distributed RDF data sources with SPARQL. In: Bechhofer, S., Hauswirth, M., Hoffmann, J., Koubarakis, M. (eds.) ESWC 2008. LNCS, vol. 5021, pp. 524–538. Springer, Heidelberg (2008)

Linked Data-enabled Gamification in EPUB 3 for Educational Digital Textbooks

Pieter Heyvaert(✉), Ruben Verborgh, Erik Mannens, and Rik Van de Walle

Ghent University - iMinds - Multimedia Lab, Ghent, Belgium
{pheyvaer.heyvaert,Ruben.Verborgh,Erik.Mannens,rik.vandewalle}@ugent.be

Abstract. Interest in eLearning environments is increasing, as well as in digital textbooks and gamification. The advantages of gamification in the context of education have been proven. However, gamified educational material, such as gamified digital textbooks and systems, are scarce. As an answer to the need for such material, the framework GEL (Gamification for EPUB using Linked Data) has been developed. GEL allows to incorporate gamification concepts in a digital textbook, using EPUB 3 and Linked Data. As part of GEL, we created the ontology Gamification Ontology (GO), representing the different gamification concepts, and a JavaScript library. Using GO allows to discover other gamified books, to share gamification concepts between applications and to separate the processing and representation of the gamification concepts.

Keywords: Digital textbooks · Education · EPUB 3 · Gamification · GEL · GO · Linked Data · Ontology

1 Introduction

Integrating games and education has been the topic of the several research efforts in the past, and their interest will only grow in the future. Game-based learning, that is, learning through games, is a high-potential [1] method to facilitate this integration. Another way is gamification, which is the use of game design elements in non-game contexts, products and services to motivate desired behavior [2]. Hamari et al. [3] perceived gamification, in the context of education, to have positive impact on motivation, engagement and enjoyment.

A large part of education material consists of print textbooks. However, digital alternatives are being considered [4,5]. The use of digital textbooks allows authors and publishers to create an enhanced publication, that is, a publication enriched with multimedia and/or interactive features. A concept using such features is *gamification*, which is considered beneficial for educational material – such as gamified digital textbooks – by González and Area [6]. EPUB 3[1] is the preferred digital book format for both enhanced publications [7], and educational textbooks [8]. However to assess the effects of digital gamification on students, gamified digital systems need to be created, as Hanus and Fox [9] point out.

[1] http://www.idpf.org/epub/301/spec/epub-overview.html.

© Springer International Publishing Switzerland 2015
G. Conole et al. (Eds.): EC-TEL 2015, LNCS 9307, pp. 587–591, 2015.
DOI: 10.1007/978-3-319-24258-3_65

In this paper we introduce GEL[2] (Gamification for EPUB using Linked Data) to adhere to the need for gamified education material, more specific: digital textbooks and digital systems. GEL is a framework that allows to add gamification to a digital textbook in the EPUB 3 format. Linked Data refers to a set of best practices for publishing and connecting structured data on the Web [10]. It is introduced to facilitate the interoperability of gamification concepts. GEL has the following characteristics: (1) it works with a JavaScript-based e-reader, by offering a JavaScript library, (2) it structures its gamification data as defined by our newly proposed ontology GO[3] (Gamification Ontology) and (3) it allows to add gamification with minimal modifications to the e-book and the e-reader.

2 Related Work

Duolingo[4] is a free cross-platform application that allows you to learn languages, while incorporating gamification in every lesson, i.e., through points, hearts, and so on. Duolingo shows the benefits of gamification in the context of education. However, it is a (custom) application, and not an (open) format, such as EPUB. Hence, its reusability is limited.

When applying gamification some caution should be taken, as explained by Hamari et al. [3]. The effects of (1) the context being gamified and (2) the qualities of the user should be considered. However, GEL does not make any assumptions regarding these aspects, because this is decided outside our framework by the user.

Several gamification services, frameworks and libraries exist (e.g., UserInfuser[5]). However, they are focused on gamifying websites and not digital books, and use their own non-interoperable representations for gamification concepts. Our framework does not have these limitations.

3 Framework: GEL

First, in Sect. 3.1 we will discuss the architecture of GEL, combining our library, our ontology GO, the e-reader Epub.js and an example EPUB 3 file. Next, we will elaborate on GO, which models the gamification concepts used by our library and the EPUB 3 file, in Sect. 3.2.

3.1 Architecture

The architecture of GEL is shown in Fig. 1, where the original EPUB file is extended with a Turtle file. Turtle[6] is a format for Resource Description Framework[7] (RDF). RDF is a standard model for data interchange on the Web. Hence,

[2] http://www.go-gel.org.
[3] GO can be found at http://semweb.mmlab.be/ns/go.
[4] http://www.duolingo.com.
[5] http://code.google.com/p/userinfuser/.
[6] http://www.w3.org/TR/turtle/.
[7] http://www.w3.org/TR/REC-rdf-syntax/.

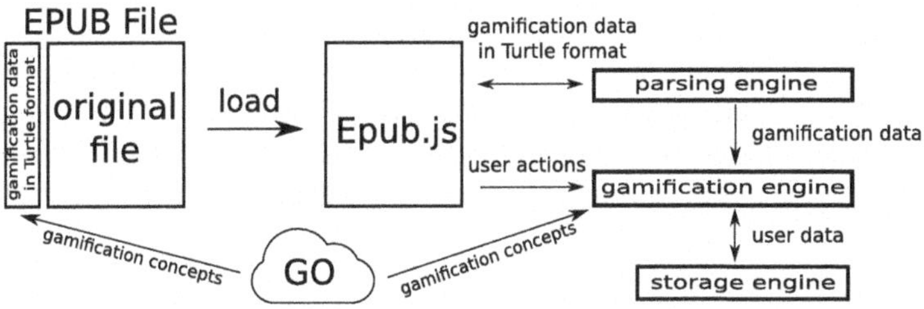

Fig. 1. The architecture of GEL.

the file is used to facilitate the Linked Data best practices. It contains the gamification information relevant to the EPUB file. The EPUB file is read using Epub.js[8], which is a JavaScript library that allows for reading EPUB files in a browser. Epub.js is extended with our Gamification Engine (GE) and Parsing Engine (PE). The former makes use of our PE and our Storage Engine (SE). The GE contains all the logic to handle the gamification concepts. The PE allows to read the gamification information, structured using GO, from the EPUB file, and allows to add this information to the GE. The SE is used to persistently save the user data. All three engines are part of our library.

3.2 Gamification Ontology

Towards connecting gamified educational material, the format to represent the gamification information should offer (1) support for discovering other (educational) books using similar gamification elements (e.g., books using the same leaderboard), (2) support for easy sharing of these elements between other applications, aside from digital books and (3) separation between the representation of these elements and their processing. To this extent, following the Linked Data best practices, we have created the ontology GO, because to the best of our knowledge there exists no ontology representing the needed gamification concepts, as indicated by Zichermann and Cunningham [11]. GO consists of the following basic concepts: challenges, rewards and points systems. Ontologies allow to reuse domain knowledge, hence, fulfilling the first and second requirement. They separate the domain knowledge from the operational knowledge, which fulfills the third requirement.

4 Conclusion and Future Work

The GEL framework targets four types of users: readers, authors, developers and researchers. The readers can enjoy gamified education material without needing to know any of the implementation details. Authors are able to enrich their books with gamification concepts. Though, currently GEL does not support editing the

[8] https://github.com/futurepress/epub.js/.

gamification information. This is a topic of future work. Developers are able to build upon the GEL framework or can create their own applications that work together with our framework if they follow the Linked Data practices and use GO. Researchers are able to evaluate the influence of gamification in digital systems using GEL. The uniques of GEL lays within the use of Linked Data. That is, by using GO we enable educational material, and not only textbooks, to be more connected (on a gamification level). This allows to motivate readers across different materials. Because we have created the library without any preference for a specific JavaScript-based e-reader, it is usable with every JavaScript-based e-reader. Our choice for Epub.js is arbitrary, and other e-readers, such as Readium[9], could also be used. A demo with the e-reader and a web application using GO and Linked Data can be found at http://www.go-gel.org/#demo.

Acknowledgments. The research activities were funded by Ghent University, iMinds, the Institute for the Promotion of Innovation by Science and Technology in Flanders (IWT), the Fund for Scientific Research Flanders (FWO Flanders), and the European Union.

References

1. Moreno-Ger, P., Burgos, D., Torrente, J.: Digital games in elearning environments current uses and emerging trends. Simul. Gaming **40**(5), 669–687 (2009)
2. Deterding, S.: Gamification: designing for motivation. Interactions **19**(4), 14–17 (2012)
3. Hamari, J., Koivisto, J., Sarsa, H.: Does gamification work?-a literature review of empirical studies on gamification. In: 2014 47th Hawaii International Conference on System Sciences (HICSS), pp. 3025–3034. IEEE (2014)
4. Reynolds, R.: Trends influencing the growth of digital textbooks in us higher education. Publishing Res. Q. **27**(2), 178–187 (2011)
5. Weisberg, M.: Student attitudes and behaviors towards digital textbooks. Publishing Res. Q. **27**(2), 188–196 (2011)
6. González, C., Area, M.: Breaking the rules: gamification of learning and educational materials. In: Proceedings of the 2nd international workshop on interaction design in educational environments, pp. 7–53 (2013)
7. Sigarchian, H.G., De Meester, B., De Nies, T., Verborgh, R., De Neve, W., Mannens, E., Van de Walle, R.: EPUB 3 for integrated and customizable representation of a scientific publication and its associated resources. In: Proceedings of the 4th Workshop on Linked Science, October 2014. URL http://ceur-ws.org/Vol-1282/lisc2014_submission_3.pdf
8. Gailer, C., Ebner, M., Kopp, M., Lackner, E., Raunig, M., Scerbakov, A.: Potential of EPUB3 for digital textbooks in higher education. In: de Freitas, S., Rensing, C., Ley, T., Muñoz-Merino, P.J. (eds.) EC-TEL 2014. LNCS, vol. 8719, pp. 564–565. Springer, Heidelberg (2014)
9. Hanus, M.D., Fox, J.: Assessing the effects of gamification in the classroom: A longitudinal study on intrinsic motivation, social comparison, satisfaction, effort, and academic performance. Comput. Educ. **80**, 152–161 (2015)

[9] http://readium.org/.

10. Bizer, C., Heath, T., Berners-Lee, T.: Linked data-the story so far. Semant. Serv. Interoperability Web Appl. Emerg. Concepts, 205–227 (2009)
11. Zichermann, G., Cunningham, C.: Gamification by design: implementing game mechanics in web and mobile apps, 1st edn. O'Reilly Media Inc, Sebastopol (2011). ISBN 1449397670, 9781449397678

Authoring Tools Supporting Novice Teachers Identifying Student Problems

Pablo Llinás[1(✉)], Estefanía Martín[1], Isidoro Hernán-Losada[1], Miguel A. Gutiérrez[1], Gill Clough[2], and Anne Adams[2]

[1] Universidad Rey Juan Carlos, Madrid, Spain
{pablo.llinas,estefania.martin,isidoro.hernan,
miguelangel.gutierrez}@urjc.es
[2] Open University, Milton Keynes, UK
{gill.clough,anne.adams}@open.ac.uk

Abstract. We live immersed in a technological world. Learning is not an exception; most classrooms are equipped with multiple devices intended to improve the learning process for students. Especially for novice teachers, there is a need to provide usable technological tools that help them with their counterpart teaching tasks. This paper presents a set of teacher authoring tools to facilitate the tasks of identifying learning *tricky topics*, noting student difficulties, and creating quizzes for knowledge evaluation. The resulting quizzes, generated by these tools, are used at the start of learning activities, where students explain *tricky topics* by creating educational videos that use juxtaposition, and which are then shared and commented among peers.

Keywords: Threshold concepts · Authoring tools · Knowledge construction · Video-based learning

1 Motivation

Web-based learning is the preferred e-learning option due to universal access, increased flexibility and multimedia capabilities [1]. However, facilitating access to learning resources is not enough to acquire a meaningful understanding. As it is well known learning performance depends on student's motivation [2]. The JuxtaLearn project[1] provides a pedagogical and technological framework that encourages students to perform creative activities, in particular video-making, to help them understand topics they find difficult to grasp (also known as threshold concepts). This approach provokes student reflection combining "learning by teaching" and "learning by doing". This is particularly valuable for novice teachers who are seeking to develop their application of learning theories into practice.

In a typical e-learning environment, the two most extended roles are the "learner" and the "author". However, a trending type of Learning Management System (LMS)

[1] http://juxtalearn.eu/project-overview.

© Springer International Publishing Switzerland 2015
G. Conole et al. (Eds.): EC-TEL 2015, LNCS 9307, pp. 592–595, 2015.
DOI: 10.1007/978-3-319-24258-3_66

called Personal Learning Environment (PLE) [3] is changing these fixed roles allowing for users themselves to become producers, through creating and sharing. The learner has an active role based on a constructivism approach that takes place in social environments [4].

2 ClipIt: Authoring Tools

ClipIt[2] is the central Web space which serves as data hub for the JuxtaLearn process [5]. As well as storing information, it offers a Web interface from which teachers and students carry out the different tasks. Regarding the theme of this paper, ClipIt provides teachers with authoring tools which help them create and manage all of the pedagogical material and student guidance required to carry out activities. This includes *tricky topics*, a teacher-defined set of threshold concepts [6], example student problems, quizzes and teaching materials.

- **Tricky Topics:** They are the linking glue in ClipIt, as they are tagged to everything which has relation to them: student problems, quizzes, teaching materials, and all subsequent work that students perform. Teachers, and in particular novice teachers, begin by identifying the main *tricky topic* and the contained *stumbling blocks*. When teachers have problems doing this, they are guided to reflecting on the student problems reported on students acquiring knowledge. To support this activity teachers need a tool to create, manage and explore them easily, with the possibility to reuse and share *tricky topics* with other teachers to use them in activities.
- **Example Student Problems:** In particular for novice teachers, there is a great value in identifying student problems and reviewing student problems identified by other teachers. ClipIt support this activity by enabling teachers to document student difficulties and adding example student problems. The example student problems describe how the *stumbling blocks* from a *tricky topic* become an obstacle to students on their normal learning progress. Upon creation, problems are tagged with the *stumbling blocks* they refer to, and also items from a list of problem types which cover the universal reasons why student problems occur. Each problem type is well described and catalogued. The list is open for extension in case a teacher wants to add new problem types. The example student problems are for teacher use, and the information contained is shared among them to contrast and enrich the pinpointing of student difficulties. Teachers will need a tool to create, edit and share example student problems to use as reference for attacking *stumbling blocks* by performing ClipIt activities around them.
- **Quizzes:** After teaching the topic, teachers can prepare for activities by creating knowledge-assessment quizzes. ClipIt will provide the necessary tool to create and manage these quizzes, which are each aimed at a single *tricky topic* and its related *stumbling blocks*. During the creation of quizzes, each question must be linked to related *stumbling blocks*, and must be filled in with the main question, its type (multiple choice, checkboxes, true/false or numeric), the possible options, and the

[2] http://clipit.es.

correct combination of options for verifying answers—this will obviously not be shown to students. Example student problems will be used to give guidance to teachers towards creating quizzes which focus on them. While creating a new quiz, and tagging it with related *stumbling blocks*, student problems tagged with those same *stumbling blocks* will show up to refresh the teacher's memory on how students struggled with the *tricky topic*. Teachers can go on to review student problems so that their quiz questions are profiled towards them, and also towards the problem types they represent. Quizzes will be taken by students, which will submit their results. These will be also saved into ClipIt, and automatically evaluated to obtain metrics about individual and group results, based on the individual questions or summarised by *stumbling blocks* covered. Therefore, the quiz results will need to be automatically marked as correct or incorrect, ideally without the intervention of the teacher.

The teacher authoring tools analysed previously were developed as plugins for ClipIt, adding the functionality described in the previous section to the existing platform. The technology used for the back-end development was mainly PHP and MySQL, while the front-end Web interface (see Fig. 1) was developed using PHP, JavaScript (jQuery), Ajax, CSS and HTML (including HTML5).

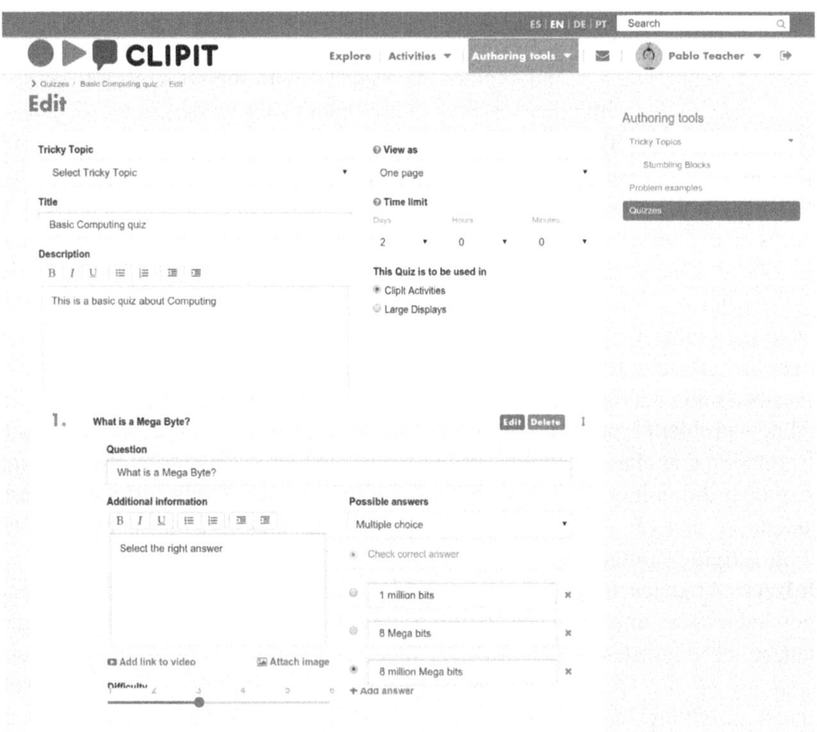

Fig. 1. ClipIt quiz authoring tool screenshot.

3 Conclusions

This paper presents teacher authoring tools inside ClipIt—a social educational platform—supporting identification of learning *tricky topics*, documenting student difficulties, and creating quizzes for knowledge evaluation. Further evaluations are being currently conducted with both experienced and novice teachers in schools across different countries in Europe, in order to develop and improve the tools for a more general use. We propose that developers of other learning tools should consider the advantages of evaluating their systems by novice professionals, prior to practice-based application of the tools. On one hand, this pragmatically supports early TEL evaluations increasing the rigour and applicability of the tools functionality. On the other, it increases the potential for uptake within the practice-based contexts, in this case schools. Ultimately if we want to develop teaching tools for the future we should start to develop these tools with the teachers for the future.

Acknowledgement. The research leading to these results has received funding from the European Community's Seventh Framework Programme (FP7/2007-2013) under grant agreement n° 317964 JUXTALEARN.

References

1. Horton, W.K.: Designing Web-Based Training: How to Teach Anyone Anything Anywhere Anytime, vol. 1. Wiley, Hoboken (2000)
2. Adams, A., Rogers, Y., Coughlan, T., Van-der-Linden, J., Clough, G., Martin, E., Haya, P., Collins, T.: Teenager needs in technology enhanced learning. In: Workshop on Methods of Working with Teenagers in Interaction Design, CHI 2013, Paris (2013)
3. Attwell, G.: Personal learning environments-the future of eLearning? e-Learn. papers **2**(1), 1–8 (2007)
4. Vygotsky, L.S.: Mind in Society: The Development of Higher Psychological Processes. Harvard University Press, Cambridge (1980)
5. Llinás, P., Haya, P., Gutierrez, M.A., Martín, E., Castellanos, J., Hernán, I., Urquiza, J.: ClipIt: supporting social reflective learning through student-made educational videos. In: de Freitas, S., Rensing, C., Ley, T., Muñoz-Merino, P.J. (eds.) EC-TEL 2014. LNCS, vol. 8719, pp. 502–505. Springer, Heidelberg (2014)
6. Meyer, J.H.F., Land, R.: Threshold concepts and troublesome knowledge 1 – linkages to ways of thinking and practising' in improving student learning – ten years on. In: Rust, C. (ed.) OCSLD, Oxford (2003)

Collaborative Learning Orchestration Using Smart Displays and Personal Devices

Kalpani Manathunga[1(✉)], Davinia Hernández-Leo[1], Jaime Caicedo[2], Jhon Jairo Ibarra[2], Francisco Martinez-Pabon[2], and Gustavo Ramirez-Gonzalez[2]

[1] ICT Department, Universitat Pompeu Fabra, Barcelona, Spain
{kalpani.manathunga,davinia.hernandez}@upf.edu
[2] Departamento de Telemática, Universidad del Cauca, Popayán, Colombia
{jcaicedo,jjibarra,fomarti,gramirez}@unicauca.edu.co

Abstract. Pervasive classroom environments with interconnected smart devices permit enacting diverse pedagogical models in education. This paper proposes an extensible architecture integrating smart display, smart phones and wearable devices to support flexible orchestration of dynamic collaborative learning activities in face-to-face educational scenarios. The paper motivates an architectural design and describes its main components based on existing systems like Signal Orchestration System (SOS) and a multi-screen cooperation middleware. An applicable scenario illustrates the usage of proposed architecture in which wearable devices are used to indicate orchestration mechanisms (group formation, change of activity), a shared display visualizes tasks with summary of the orchestration and activity progress for collective awareness and smart phones are used to interact with the shared display and complete the activities.

Keywords: CSCL · Classroom orchestration · Devices for seamless learning

1 Introduction

Learning in groups or collaborative learning (CL) leads to effective learning when mediated by productive social interactions as many studies had shown [1–3]. In recent past research on integrating collaborative activities within physical classrooms and blended learning scenarios had drawn attention in the domain of Computer Supported Collaborative Learning (CSCL) [1]. Collaborative Learning Flow Patterns (CLFP) like Jigsaw or Pyramid are known as best practices [2] that specify how to structure (orchestrate) the CL activities on aspects like group formation based on policies, role allocation and resource distribution. When enacting CL activities, a traditional classroom could be converted into a smart space by seamlessly integrating interactive displays and devices [3]. Live didactic mechanisms and dynamic orchestration approaches catch student's attention and interest [2, 4, 5] if addressed with sufficient flexibility [6]. Existing classrooms are already equipped with shared display units like projectors and smart boards. Yet, converting these displays to be smart awareness boards that can be used to orchestrate activities in cooperation with smart phones and wearable devices has been addressed less [1, 3].

© Springer International Publishing Switzerland 2015
G. Conole et al. (Eds.): EC-TEL 2015, LNCS 9307, pp. 596–600, 2015.
DOI: 10.1007/978-3-319-24258-3_67

This paper proposes an architectural solution to enact CL activities forming a smart classroom with prevailing artifacts and previously proposed technologies.

2 Opportunities for Smart Classrooms: CL Orchestration

Smart classrooms have been devised for different purposes including enabling extended tele-education, diverse learning activities and facilitating implementation of classroom dynamics. For example, Shi et al. [4] proposed a smart classroom design integrating voice-recognition, computer vision and other smart devices to provide tele-education experience in a real class. Another attempt used smartphones to enact an innovative collaborative activity to teach physics within a classroom [7]. Wearable devices and interactive furniture have been proposed as physical computing approaches to enhance classroom orchestration by indicating organizational aspects to students [3] or visualizing feedback about their progress to the teachers [5]. Yet, support for dynamic orchestration taking advantage holistically of smart classroom technology (including collective display devices, personal devices, etc.) has not being addressed. This paper highlights potential opportunities of integrating different devices (smart phones, wearable devices, collective displays, etc.) seamlessly with CL orchestration services implying pervasive computing methods to organize face-to-face CL activities in the classroom. These opportunities include displaying activity details and configurations to clarify tasks (e.g., in mobile phones); promote social awareness of progress among students and teachers (e.g., via shared classroom displays); indicate CL flow mechanisms, such as group formation, distribution of roles and resources, see for instance the CLFPs [2] (e.g., in wearable devices); facilitating dynamic modifications when required [8] supported by the transfer of the activity status and automatic configuration of the devices (through orchestration services comprising a "classroom middleware" interconnecting the devices).

3 Architectural Elements

The proposed architecture for holistic CL classroom orchestration is composed of systems proposed by the authors in previous research [3, 9] which are already devised [3] or has potential [9] to support classroom orchestration. The architecture proposes CL orchestration services with open APIs, enabling the extension of the architecture with the integration of additional classroom technologies [5]. Figure 1 shows the main components which relies on features of two service layers. First, orchestration services of the Signal Orchestration System (SOS) [3], which compute orchestration mechanisms to be transmitted as orchestration signals to SOS wearable devices (physical forearm bracelets rendering e.g., color signals indicating grouping, vibration signals for change of activities). Second, the Smart TV–Smart phone interaction middleware [9] enables a multi-screen cooperation model [10] based on loosely coupled publish/subscribe paradigm for message exchange. The Smart TV screen (or any HDMI-compliant display in the classroom) is complemented by mobile devices bringing seamless interaction capabilities rather than being only a display unit. The middleware integration enables coherent global orchestration of CL activities replicating relevant orchestration indications in different displays, when appropriate, or showing complementary information as suitable considering the affordances of the displays and the characteristics of the activities. The seamless transfer of orchestration status between devices enables dynamic modifications of the CL flow.

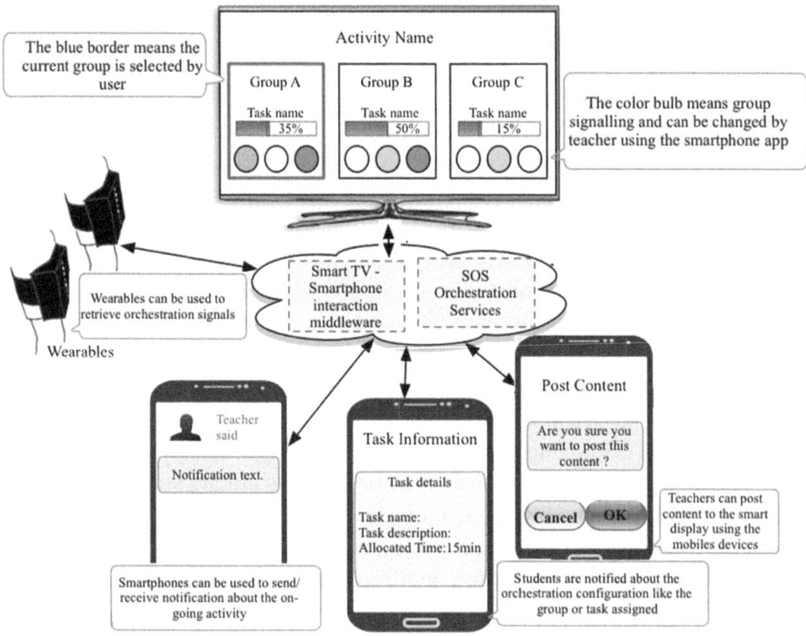

Fig. 1. Components of SOS and smart devices integration

4 Illustrative Scenario

Following scenario illustrates applicability of proposed architecture using Jigsaw CLFP [2] at a secondary educational context; yet can be extrapolated to other subject matters and educational levels. The application of the architecture is also of interest with other CLFPs. Jigsaw pattern promotes positive interdependence and individual accountability by dividing a problem into sub-problems, allocating sub-problems to individuals, forming expert groups (to address sub-problems) and jigsaw groups (groups with experts on each sub-problem, addressing the global problem).

In a secondary school curriculum students are required to gain knowledge while being able to critically contrast the three main different climates in Spain. To achieve this learning objective, the teacher designs a Jigsaw-inspired learning activity that spans for two classes which requires individuals do prepare at home for assigned climate zone provided they know their groups on the first day. The activity continues next day with the expert and jigsaw phases (supported by SOS wearable devices, mobile phones and smart display). When teacher configures sub tasks (3, in this) and uploads student list (30) using SOS manager, the services compute distribution of sub-problems and groupings (10 students read each sub-problem; 3 or 6 expert groups with 10 or 5 members with same sub-problem; 5 or 10 jigsaw groups with 3 or 6 members). In the class groupings are illustrated in the smart display for students to know peers. Further details required for the activity can also be visualized in the display and students can interact using smart phones. During activity enactment, expert groups are displayed enabling quick grouping, but teacher notices that 2 students are absent from previous class and requires regrouping to comply with Jigsaw constraints. SOS manager facilitates this and new expert groups would be 6 groups – 2 with 4 members and 5 with 5 members, and only 7 jigsaw groups with 3 or 4 members being at least one of them an expert on a sub-problem and these dynamic changes are reflected on-the-fly to the smart display. Students are not confused if peers are missing and they see the new group structure. Orchestration indications (vibration signal to indicate change of activity or color signals for phase changes or space allocation) are propagated to the wearable devices. Teacher posts questions to the experts to monitor knowledge and students answer using smart phones and their progress/performance is indicated in the smart display. Students make annotations of their discussions in phones, which are, later visualized in the shared display for a collective discussion.

5 Conclusion

This paper proposes a holistic view of technology-supported CL orchestration in the classroom that exploits use of personal devices (smart phones, wearable devices) and shared displays. The paper describes elements of an extensible architecture with services (computing CL orchestration mechanisms) and a multi-screen cooperation middleware (interaction and data flow with/between screens) based on previous work. The illustrated scenario shows the integrative use of wearable devices to indicate group formation, mobile phones to inform and support tasks, smart displays to offer awareness about activity progress and visualize individual and collective assignments with interactions. Future work includes evaluation and extensions of the architecture considering other classroom technologies and virtual learning environments.

Acknowledgments. This work was supported by the Spanish Government (EEE TIN2011-28308-C03-03) and the University of Cauca (VRI 4045 "MANTISS").

References

1. Dillenbourg, P., Järvelä, S., Fischer, F.: The evolution of research on computer-supported collaborative learning. In: Balacheff, N., Ludvigsen, S. (eds.) Technology- Enhanced Learning: Principle and Products, pp. 3–19. Springer, The Netherlands (2009)
2. Hernández-Leo, D., Villasclaras-Fernández, E.D., Jorrín-Abellán, I.M., Asensio-Pérez, J.I., Dimitriadis, Y., Ruiz-Requies, I., Rubia-Avi, B.: Collage, a collaborative learning design editor based on patterns. J. Educ. Technol. Soc. **9**(1), 58–71 (2006)

3. Hernández-leo, D., Nieves, R., Arroyo, E., Rosales, A., Melero, J., Blat, J.: SOS : orchestrating collaborative activities across digital and physical spaces using wearable signaling devices. J. Univers. Comput. Sci. **18**(15), 2165–2186 (2012). doi:10.3217/jucs-018-15-2165
4. Shi, Y., Xie, W., Xu, G., Shi, R., Mao, Y., Liu, F.: The Smart Classroom: merging technologies for seamless tele-education. IEEE Pervasive Comput. **2**(2), 47–55 (2003)
5. Alavi, H.S., Dillenbourg, P.: An ambient awareness tool for supporting supervised collaborative problem solving. IEEE Trans. Learn. Technol. **5**(3), 264–274 (2012)
6. Dillenbourg, P., Tchounikine, P.: Flexibility in macro-scripts for computer supported collaborative learning. J. Comput. Assist. Learn. **23**(1), 1–13 (2007)
7. Echeverría, A., Nussbaum, M., Calderón, J.F., Bravo, C., Infante, C.: Face-to-face collaborative learning supported by mobile phones. Interact. Learn. Environ. **19**(4), 351–363 (2011)
8. Pérez-Sanagustín, M., Burgos, J., Hernández-Leo, D., Blat, J.: CLFP intrinsic constraints-based group management of blended learning situations. In: Daradoumis, T., Caballé, S., Juan, A.A., Xhafa, F. (eds.) Technology-Enhanced Systems and Tools for Collaborative Learning Scaffolding. SCI, vol. 350, pp. 115–133. Springer, Heidelberg (2011)
9. Martinez-Pabon, F., Caicedo, J., Ibarra, J.J., Gonzalez, G.R., Organero, M.M., Astaiza, A.C.: Smart TV-smartphone corporation model on digital signage environments: an implementation approach. In: 4th International Conference on Mobile Services, Resources and Users, pp. 25–31, Paris (2014)
10. Yoon, C., Um, T., Lee, H.: Classification of N-Screen services and its standardization. In: 14th International Conference on Advanced Communication Technology, pp. 597–602 (2012)

Project-Based Learning: Methodology and Assessment Learning Technologies and Assessment Criteria

Iratxe Menchaca[1], Mariluz Guenaga[1(✉)], and Josu Solabarrieta[2]

[1] DeustoTech Learning, Deusto Institute of Technology, University of Deusto, Bilbao, Spain
{iratxe.mentxaka,mlguenaga}@deusto.es

[2] Faculty of Psychology and Education, University of Deusto, Avda. Universidades 24, 48007 Bilbao, Spain
josu.solabarrieta@deusto.es

Abstract. This paper uses a project-based learning methodology in higher education to analyse its relation to a theoretical framework of competency. Based on this analysis, we propose a set of technological tools to support the development of competency at the university level as well as a set of indicators to systematize the assessment process. Finally, indicators are related to data that can be obtained from these technological tools. This is the basis for additional work on learning analytics that is used to support the assessment of a project-based learning approach.

Keywords: Project-based learning · Competence-based learning · Project management · Competency assessment · Learning technology · Cloud technology

1 Introduction

The PBL method consists of a continuous and progressive learning process in which several competencies are developed through the fulfilment of a complex and meaningful project during inter-related phases [1]. It is also defined as a learning model in which students plan, implement and evaluate a project, which is then applied to the real world beyond the classroom [2]. The socio-constructivist learning paradigm exercises great influence in the definition of the method. This way, it is understood as an active learning process in which the student interacts with the environment and solves real problems both individually or in groups.

Currently, new learning and teaching processes following PBL are consolidating in the European Higher Education Area (EHEA). The innovation in learning methodologies emerges from the concern about enabling students with skills and competencies that prepare them for adult and professional life. This is why learning in real contexts is especially relevant. In the following text, we describe the pedagogical principles of the PBL methodological approach as well as its strengths and the objectives of its curricular integration.

© Springer International Publishing Switzerland 2015
G. Conole et al. (Eds.): EC-TEL 2015, LNCS 9307, pp. 601–604, 2015.
DOI: 10.1007/978-3-319-24258-3_68

2 Project-Based Learning Methodology

Authors have proven that the implementation of PBL methodology improves active and self-directed learning, the understanding of the multidimensional dimension of real problems, management development, responsibility and collaboration, as well as communication capacities [3]. A learning experience designed following the PBL methodology enables the development of transversal skills as a workgroup, cooperative learning, and effective communication. The aim of this methodological approach is to prepare the individual to integrate knowledge and skills while promoting his or her autonomous learning, group behaviour, and self-assessment. Based on the fundamentals of PBL, we defined a series of learning objectives:

- Plan and manage a project.
- Increase the knowledge and skills in an interdisciplinary area.
- Develop groupware skills, interpersonal communication, problem solving, mathematical, time management, and planning and project management competencies.
- Improve research capabilities.
- Improve information management and synthesis capacity.
- Assume individual and shared responsibility.
- Use technological tools that support the development of the project.
- Self-evaluate and evaluate other members in the project team.
- Carry out continuous control and monitoring of the project.

The PBL methodology fundamentals fit exactly with the bases of the project management competency. Project management is the application of knowledge, skills, and techniques to carry out projects in an efficient and effective way [4]. It refers to the capacity of the individual to organize his activity and objectives, have resources available, and evaluate self-development all in an effort to complete a project. The theoretical framework of project management competency has three relevant models: PMBOK from the Project Management Institute (PMI) in 1987 [4], ICB3 "International Competence Baseline" from the International Project Management Association (IPMA) in 1999 [5], and the PRINCE 2 "Projects In Controlled Environments" from the Office of Government Commerce (OGC) in 1996 [6].

Based on the previously defined objectives of the PBL methodology as well as analysis of project management competency, we elaborated a catalogue of technological tools to support different phases of project development. These include:

- Basic tools such as word processing, spread sheets, databases and image processing software. These can be integrated in a software package or be separate. They can be available offline or through the Cloud.
- Specific tools to plan, manage, and prioritize tasks and resources in a project such as Microsoft Project, Gantter or Google Calendar.
- Programs to manage tasks similar to personal assistants including Ever note or Remember the Milk.
- Internal communication services like chat, video or audio conference, email, online forums, etc. Chat, Skype or Hang-out may also be useful.

- Document storage and sharing systems in the Cloud, e.g. Google Drive, Drop box.
- Social bookmarks and citation managers such as Delicious or Refworks.
- E-portfolio tools, e.g. Google Sites, Blogger or Wordpress.

3 The Assessment of Project-Based Learning

Given the complexity of this methodological approach, the assessment should be planned and based on the acquisition of competencies. The assessment of competencies is a dynamic evaluation that places the action in its context. It includes knowledge of intellectual content and behavioural norms [7]. This assessment approach enables the evaluation of different phases in a project, the interaction among members, acquired skills, knowledge, etc. The complexity of these approaches involves a barrier to its integration in education. Teachers need sufficient evidence about students' work progress, activities performed, resources used, and decisions taken during the project development. However, they often lack data that records these processes.

After analysing PMBOK [4], ICB3 [5], and PRINCE2 [6] theoretical frameworks as well as the Competency Model developed by Villa and Poblete [8] (main reference in the University of Deusto (UD), we elaborated a common list of indicators and some descriptors that integrate all phases, elements, and objectives in a PBL approach:

- **I1**. Definition of objectives: Establishes clear objectives for the project; objectives are coherent with identified needs; ranks the projects' objectives and needs.
- **I3**. Definition of tasks: Plans the actions in relationship to the objectives; estimates the efficiency and effectiveness of the actions; sequences the activities.
- **I4**. Temporal planning: Foresees and assigns time to achieve each task.
- **I5**. Management of resources: Distributes responsibilities and tasks according to the profile of each team member; estimates the cost of resources.
- **I6**. Risk estimation and management: Identifies risks inherent to the project.
- **I7**. Track changes: Plans the evaluation of project results; adapts actions and the person responsible to incidences and changes that may arise.
- **I8**. Communication and collaboration: Plans the team management; plans communication management; establishes communication mechanisms and systems.
- **I9**. Leadership: Makes decisions about the project; has an overall view of the project; promote and uses the team to share ideas.

As described before, the assessment of PBL is a complex task that requires a great effort from teachers to collect data. Even with a detailed recording of daily activities in the project, teachers do not have access much relevant information. Thus, they ignore how some processes have been developed. With this challenge in mind, and applying results from Learning Analytics research area, we propose an assessment model based on the analysis of data gathered from the interaction between students and technological tools used to carry out their learning [9, 10].

Thanks to previously-described technological tools, we can obtain data about the students' performance in project management. This results in impartial evidence about their learning. For example, we can obtain data about the interaction among project members, resources studied, contributions to a document, the level of progress of tasks in a concrete moment, members that have contributed to a deliverable, communications in a chat forum, etc. Tools available for the project management provide data that can feed the indicators to assess PBL competency. For instance, data obtained automatically, with no user intervention, from Google Calendar can tell us if the student plans activities or not and if in those activities other members are involved. Comments in a shared document among project members can give the teacher information about the contribution of each student to the group who behaves as a leader. It can also detail the most valuable contributions. These are only some examples of how data provided by technological tools can be processed and converted to higher-order indicators to assess competency.

4 Conclusions and Future Work

In addition to other assessment techniques such as self- or peer-assessment, evidence gathering is necessary in the assessment of PBL. It can be eased through technological resources. These tools also enrich students' work through different phases of the project and provide students and teachers information about the project progress. Currently, some preliminary experiences have been performed with the UD using learning analytics and the aforementioned indicators to assess PBL competency. In the future, we aim to introduce this assessment support system in different PBL scenarios at the UD using learning analytics to provide feedback to teachers about students' progress as well as to students about their own learning.

References

1. Boss, S., Krauss, J.: Reinventing Project-Based Learning: Your Field Guide to Real-World Projects in the Digital Age. International Society for Technology in Education 480 Charnelton Street, Eugene, OR 97401-2626 (2007)
2. Harwell, S.: Project-based learning. In: Blank, W.E., Harwell, S. (eds.) Promising Practices for Connecting High School to the Real World. University of Tampa, Tampa (1997)
3. Kolmos, A. et al. (eds): Facilitation in a PBL environment. Aalborg: UNESCO Chair in Problem Based Leaning in Engineering Education. Aalborg University (2008)
4. Guide, A.: Project Management Body of Knowledge (PMBOK® Guide). In Project Management Institute (2001)
5. IPMA, I.: IPMA Competence Baseline Version 3. Nijkerk, The Netherlands (2006)
6. Bentley, C.: Prince 2: A practical handbook. Routledge, New York (2009)
7. Bravo Arteaga, A., Fernández del Valle, F.: La evaluación convencional frente a los nuevos modelos de evaluación auténtica. Psicothema **12**(2), 95–99 (2000)
8. Villa, A., Poblete, M.: Evaluación de competencias genéricas: principios, oportunidades y limitaciones. Bordón: Revista de Pedagogía **63**(1), 147–170 (2011)
9. Campbell, J.P., Oblinger, D.G.: Academic analytics. EDUCAUSE, Quarterly (2007)
10. LAK: 1st International Conference on Learning Analytics and Knowledge, Banff, Alberta February 27–March 1 (2011)

Patterns of Practice and Design: Towards an Agile Methodology for Educational Design Research

Yishay Mor[1(✉)], John Cook[2], Patricia Santos[2], Tamsin Treasure-Jones[3], Raymond Elferink[4], Debbie Holley[5], and James Griffin[2]

[1] Consultant, London, UK
yishaym@gmail.com
[2] University of the West of England, Bristol, England
{john2.cook,Patricia.Santosrodriguez}@uwe.ac.uk,
j.ben.griffin@gmail.com
[3] University of Leeds, Leeds, UK
T.Treasure-Jones@leeds.ac.uk
[4] Raycom, Utrech, The Netherlands
raymond@raycom.com
[5] Anglia Ruskin University, Cambridge, UK
debbie.holley@anglia.ac.uk

Abstract. This paper proposes a framework which attempts to address the barriers to the development of successful educational design research through a process which identifies gaps in current practices and devises innovations to target them. Educational design research assumes an ambitious position: a dual commitment to understand and contribute to both theory and practice. This task is confounded by the complexity of the domain and the inherent multi-stakeholder nature of most initiatives. Three barriers to success are identified: the shortage of mechanisms for cross-stakeholder dialogue, the failure to account for existing practices and contexts, and the rigid processes dictated by the dynamics of research projects. We report early findings from an attempt to address these barriers, based on an extension and adaptation of the Participatory Pattern Workshop (PPW) methodology (This paper has received the support of the Learning Layers project co-funded by the European Commission; Grant Agreement Number 318209; http://learning-layers.eu/).

Keywords: Learning design · Educational design research · Design patterns · Design narratives · Patterned practices · Stakeholder participation

1 Introduction

Educational design research (EDR) [1], or Design-based research [2, 3] emerged over a decade ago as an alternative paradigm for education science [4, 5]. EDR is a change-oriented paradigm: its emphasis goes beyond understanding the world as it is, to ask "how do we make it better?" This entails a dual commitment to advance theory and practice

© Springer International Publishing Switzerland 2015
G. Conole et al. (Eds.): EC-TEL 2015, LNCS 9307, pp. 605–608, 2015.
DOI: 10.1007/978-3-319-24258-3_69

simultaneously. It dictates a highly interventionist, inherently multi-disciplinary, iterative and situated methodology, which holds the promise of producing theory relevant to practice and practical innovations informed by theory. It is interventionist in the sense that researchers introduce innovations into the environment they study to observe their effects, iterative because these innovations evolve in tandem with their theoretical underpinnings, situated meaning that interventions are introduced into real-life settings, rather than laboratory conditions. Research questions are unashamedly value-driven: when asking "how do we make the world better?" researchers are compelled to take a stance on what is "better". EDR shares some of the features of the learning design approach [6]. However, the latter is much more focused on improving practice – without an equal commitment to advancing theory. On the other hand, research in learning design has yielded a wealth of tools [7] and representations [8], which could potentially benefit EDR.

1.1 The Layers Project and the Theory of Hybrid Social Networks

The Learning Layers Project (http://learning-layers.eu/), funded by the EU FP7 programme, is developing technologies to support informal learning in the workplace, specifically in the healthcare and construction sectors. The project team identified EDR as an appropriate approach, given the commitment to advance both the professional practice in hybrid social networks of healthcare practitioners and the theoretical understanding of emergent learning in such networks. Specifically, we identified the Participatory Pattern Workshop methodology (described below) as appropriate to our work. However, we found it necessary to extend and elaborate this methodology for two reasons. First, we noticed parallels and potential synergies with agile software development methodologies, and wanted to leverage these. Second, we observed a need for a closer account of the existing (pre-intervention) professional practices, which would allow our designs to blend into the current situation.

1.2 SNaP!, PPW and LDS

The Participatory Pattern Workshop (PPW) methodology [9] is a framework for engaging multi-disciplinary communities in collaborative reflection on educational innovation in a given domain. This methodology leads participants through a process of articulating their experience in the form of Design Narratives, eliciting from those Design Patterns, and using these to generate testable future design conjectures, in the form of Design Scenarios [10]. This methodology is mirrored by the Learning Design Studio approach, which guides practitioners through a reflective process of designing, prototyping and evaluating new innovations [11]. The synergies between the two are discussed in [12].

2 The Patterns of Practice and Design (PPD) Approach

When considering the PPW approach for the Layers project, we observed several limitations of the methodology:

1. Design patterns encode practitioner experiences in a form that can be calibrated with theory and then re-applied to new situations. Yet, they do not provide a pathway directly from theory into practice. A pattern always originates in experience. How do we represent directives for design derived from theory?
2. Any innovation we introduce will need to blend in and then modulate existing practices. How do we describe these practices, and how do we bind them into the design cycle?
3. The PPW methodology has been shown to be effective in establishing cross-disciplinary design-level discourse. However, when developers proceed to translate the outcomes of such a discourse to a development plan, they need to represent them in a suitable language. We needed boundary objects to bridge the research and reflection dynamics and the development processes.

Consequently, we extended the PPW methodology by including design principles [13] as boundary objects translating theory into practice, and agile user stories as boundary objects bridging the EDR language with that of software engineering. The resulting methodology (Fig. 1), which we call "Patterns of Practice and Design" (PPD), leads practitioners and researchers through a cycle in which they: (1) Understand existing epistemic practices (2) Identify gaps in those practices (3) Consider relevant theories as well as existing /previous attempts to address these gaps (4) Conceptualise a novel solution (5) Define the evaluation protocols for this solution.

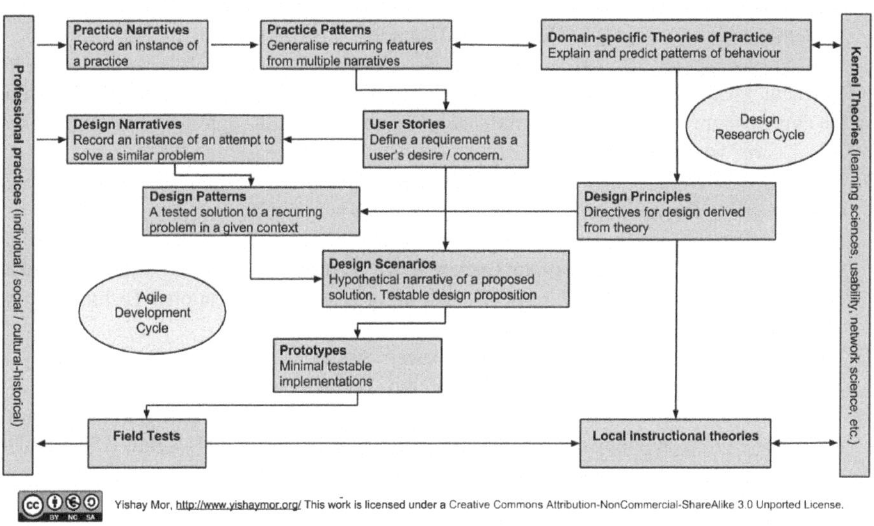

Fig. 1. Schematic diagram of the PPD methodology

To support this process, we use a platform called ILDE (Integrated Learning Design Environment), developed by Universitat Pompeu Fabra, Barcelona [14]. ILDE has built-in support for design narratives and design patterns, as well as other learning design representations. It also supports a simple yet powerful mechanism for ad-hoc templates, which allowed us to add support for all the other constructs we used.

The elements of this methodology, and the results of the initial pilot, are described in detail in an extended version of this paper, available at: http://figshare.com/articles/Patterns_of_Practice_and_Design_Towards_an_Agile_Methodology_for_Educational_Design_Research/1456055.

References

1. McKenney, S., Reeves, T.: Conducting Educational Design Research. Routledge, London (2012)
2. Bannan, B., Cook, J., Pachler, N.: Re-conceptualizing design research in the age of mobile learning. Interactive Learning Environments, 1–16 (2015) (in press)
3. Mor, Y., Winters, N.: Design approaches in technology enhanced learning. Interact. Learn. Environ. **15**, 61–75 (2007)
4. Barab, S., Squire, K.: Design-based research: putting a stake in the ground. J. Learn. Sci. **13**, 1–14 (2004)
5. Disessa, A.A., Cobb, P.: Ontological innovation and the role of theory in design experiments. J. Learn. Sci. **13**, 77–103 (2004)
6. Mor, Y., Craft, B., Hernández-Leo, D.: Editorial: The art and science of learning design. Res. Learn. Technol. vol. 21 (2013)
7. Prieto, L. P., Dimitriadis, Y., Craft, B., Derntl, M., Émin, V., Katsamani, M., Laurillard, D., Masterman, E., Retalis, S., Villasclaras, E.: Learning Design Rashomon II - exploring one lesson through multiple tools. Res. Learn. Technol. vol. 21 (2013)
8. Persico, D., Pozzi, F., Anastopoulou, S., Conole, G., Craft, B., Dimitriadis, Y., Hernández-Leo, D., Kali, Y., Mor, Y., Pérez-Sanagustín, M., Walmsley, H.: Learning Design Rashomon I - supporting the design of one lesson through different approaches. Res. Learn. Technol. vol. 21 (2013)
9. Mor, Y., Warburton, S., Winters, N.: Participatory Pattern Workshops: A Methodology for Open Learning Design Inquiry. Res. Learn. Technol. vol. 20 (2012)
10. Mor, Y.: SNaP! re-using, sharing and communicating designs and design knowledge using scenarios, narratives and patterns. In: Luckin, R., Goodyear, P., Grabowski, B., Puntambekar, S., Winters, N., Underwood, J. (eds.) Handbook of Design in Educational Technology, pp. 189–200. Routledge, London (2013)
11. Mor, Y., Mogilevsky, O.: The Learning Design Studio: Collaborative Design Inquiry as Teachers' Professional Development. Res. Learn. Technol. vol. 21 (2013)
12. Warburton, S., Mor, Y.: Double loop design: configuring narratives, patterns and scenarios in the design of technology enhanced learning. In: Mor, Y., Maina, M., Craft, B. (eds.), The Art and Science of Learning Design. Sense publishers, Dordrecht (2015) (in press)
13. Kali, Y.: Collaborative knowledge building using a design principles database. IJCSCL **1**, 187–201 (2006)
14. Hernández-Leo, D., Asensio-Pérez, J.I., Derntl, M., Prieto, L.P., Chacón, J.: ILDE: community environment for conceptualizing, authoring and deploying learning activities. In: de Freitas, S., Rensing, C., Ley, T., Muñoz-Merino, P.J. (eds.) EC-TEL 2014. LNCS, vol. 8719, pp. 490–493. Springer, Heidelberg (2014)

Teaching Syllogistics Through Gamification and Interactive Proofs

Peter Øhrstrøm[1(✉)], Ulrik Sandborg-Petersen[1], Steinar Thorvaldsen[2], and Thomas Ploug[1]

[1] Department of Communication and Psychology, Aalborg University, 9000 Aalborg, Denmark
{poe,ulrikp,ploug}@hum.aau.dk

[2] Department of Education, University of Tromsø, 9037 Tromsø, Norway
steinar.thorvaldsen@uit.no

Abstract. This paper is a continuation of earlier studies involving experiments with Communication students using a Java-Applet running in the student's browser, developed using the Prolog programming language as embodied in a Java implementation called Prolog+CG. This makes it possible to support logic teaching through the use of interactive systems and also to do learning analytics based on the log-data from the use of the systems. The aim of the present paper is to investigate whether the use of gamification and an interactive proof system formulated in terms of controlled natural language can be helpful in logic teaching in order to obtain a better understanding of syllogistic reasoning.

Keywords: Syllogistics · Argumentation · Logical proofs · Logic teaching

1 Introduction

Aristotelian syllogistics have been an essential part of almost all courses in basic logic since the rise of the European university in the 11th century; cf. [1,8]. Syllogisms may be discussed in various ways (e.g., Euler circles, Venn diagrams, etc.). In modern logic teaching we may take advantage of the fact that the system of syllogisms can be conceived as a deductive system. This makes it possible to introduce the idea of a logical proof in terms of syllogistic arguments. The present study is a continuation of earlier studies concerning logic teaching of students from the humanities, mainly from Communication (including Humanistic Informatics); cf. [5–7].

2 The Experiments in the Present Study

The present study has been conducted as part of a logic course for 2nd year Communication students at Aalborg University (Aalborg and Copenhagen) in February and March of 2015. The course was organised in four course days, each consisting of 3 lessons of 45 min each.

© Springer International Publishing Switzerland 2015
G. Conole et al. (Eds.): EC-TEL 2015, LNCS 9307, pp. 609–612, 2015.
DOI: 10.1007/978-3-319-24258-3_70

- 1st **course day:** General introduction to logic and argumentation. Introduction to classical syllogistics.
- 2nd **course day:** Classical syllogistics and propositional logic.
- 3rd **course day:** The idea of a logical proof. Group work with interactive proofs using a system based on [7] and with a natural language interface.
- 4th **course day:** The idea of formal reasoning. Experiments 1 and 2.

The experiments have been carried out using a revised version of the so-called Syllog system [4]. This system is implemented as a Java-Applet running in the student's browser, developed using the Prolog programming language as embodied in a Java implementation called Prolog+CG; cf. [2,3,9]. Syllog generates syllogisms at random, and the user is supposed to evaluate them using the system. The activities of the students while working with the system can be logged, and the log-data from the use of the system may give rise to very interesting learning analytics. The source code to the Syllog system can be downloaded as Open Source software from SourceForge.Net [10]. The documentation is also available from the same site. An online version of the versions of Syllog system used in Experiments 1 and 2 can be tested online [11].

On the fourth course day, the students were asked to run the Syllog system in groups of 2–4. They were informed that all test results would be logged by Syllog and stored anonymously. Participation in the experiments was not obligatory. However, almost all students chose to participate. In the user interface shown in Fig. 1 the element of gamification is present in the indication of "The number of correct answers in a row". From the observation of the students during their work with the system, it is obvious that they accept the element of competition, and that this rather simple gamification element actually works as a motivating factor in the practical setting.

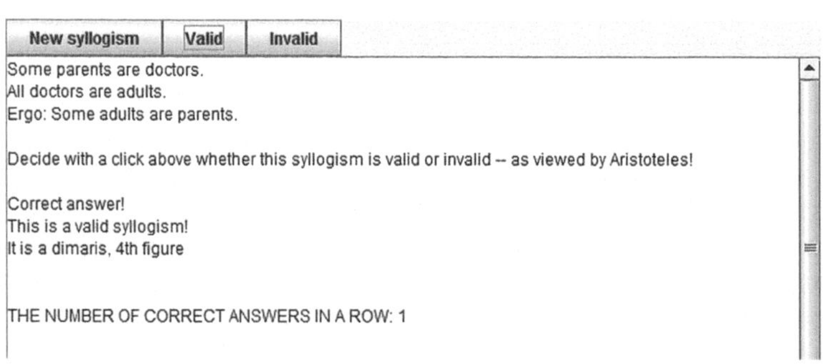

Fig. 1. The user can click on "New syllogism" to get a new syllogism presented on the screen. Then the user can choose between "Valid" and "Invalid". — In the example shown here, the user finds that the syllogism which has been displayed is valid and he clicks accordingly. The system answers that this is correct, and the medieval name of the syllogism is given.

Table 1. This table summarizes the characteristics of the two experiments. The two versions of the system were used for 15 min each.

Terms in Experiment 1	Terms in Experiment 2
"males", "females", "adults", "mothers",	"plarfeebs", "habzoops", "kloojarbs",
"fathers", "parents", "students",	"greegarfs", "zeefs", "troofklejoobs",
"teachers", "doctors"	"meefjarbs, "bloogs", "flarkjerbs"

Table 2. This table summarizes counts of how often students in Aalborg and Copenhagen replied correctly on the last course day, as compared to a pre-test carried out before the logic teaching itself begins, obtained from earlier studies, cf. [5].

	Correct	Incorrect	Score
Earlier findings [5]	921	595	0.608
Experiment 1	1112	462	0.706
Experiment 2 (nonsenical terms)	794	378	0.677

The outcome of the experiments is analysed in terms of a score which is based on log-data from the experiments. This score is calculated as:

$$\text{Score} = \frac{\text{correctanswers}}{\text{answercount}}$$

The score measures how well the user is doing in evaluating the validity of syllogistic arguments. Logic teaching is at least in part aimed at raising this score. We tested whether such a raise occurred in Experiment 1. On the fourth course day we also measured the score when the usual real-world terms were substituted with nonsensical terms (Experiment 2). The characteristics of the two experiments are summarized in Table 1, and the mesurements are given in Table 2.

3 Results and Discussion

The aggregated results of the score before the course and on the last course day (Experiment 1) are presented in Table 2, together with the results from Experiment 2. The data concerning Experiment 1 support strong statistical evidence against the presumption that students in the two situations will handle syllogisms equally well (p-value < 0.001 by the χ^2-test). This means that the students have improved their ability to evaluate syllogistic arguments significantly at the end of this course.

Concerning Experiment 2 the results show that there is a tendency to a lower score (0.677) in arguments based on nonsensical terms as compared with the score in arguments based on meaningful terms from natural language (0.706).

However, the difference in favour of the terms from natural language is not significant (p-value = 0.10 by the χ^2-test). This may be taken to indicate that many students probably during the course have obtained a somewhat clear understanding of logical validity as a purely abstract and formal notion.

On the other hand, it should be admitted that more information is needed in order to give a full account. Among other things, it would be nice to have data from Experiment 2 when carried out before the beginning of the logic course. Furthermore, it should be noted that what is measured in this study is the effect of the logic course as a whole (i.e., lectures and exercises using gamification and interactive proofs in total). However, by looking into the data from the use the interactive proofs on the third course day, we may be able to point to more detailed results. Finally, it would also be interesting to known to what extent the (apparent) effects from the course regarding the understanding of logical validity are lasting.

References

1. Aristotle: Prior analytics (1994–2000), translated by A.J. Jenkinson. The Internet Classics Archive. http://classics.mit.edu/Aristotle/prior.html
2. Kabbaj, A., Janta-Polczynski, M.: From prolog++ to prolog+cg: A cg object-oriented logic programming language. In: Ganter, B., Mineau, G.W. (eds.) ICCS 2000. LNCS, vol. 1867, pp. 540–554. Springer, Heidelberg (2000)
3. Kabbaj, A., Moulin, B., Gancet, J., Nadeau, D., Rouleau, O.: Uses, improvements, and extensions of Prolog+CG : case studies. In: Delugach, H.S., Stumme, G. (eds.) ICCS 2001. LNCS (LNAI), vol. 2120, pp. 346–359. Springer, Heidelberg (2001)
4. Øhrstrøm, P., Sandborg-Petersen, U., Ploug, T.: Syllog - a tool for logic teaching. In: Proceedings of Artificial Intelligence Workshops 2010 (AIW 2010), pp. 42–55. Mimos Berhad (2010)
5. Øhrstrøm, P., Sandborg-Petersen, U., Thorvaldsen, S., Ploug, T.: Classical syllogisms in logic teaching. In: Pfeiffer, H.D., Ignatov, D.I., Poelmans, J., Gadiraju, N. (eds.) ICCS 2013. LNCS, vol. 7735, pp. 31–43. Springer, Heidelberg (2013)
6. Øhrstrøm, P., Sandborg-Petersen, U., Thorvaldsen, S., Ploug, T.: Teaching logic through web-based and gamified quizzing of formal arguments. In: Hernández-Leo, D., Ley, T., Klamma, R., Harrer, A. (eds.) EC-TEL 2013. LNCS, vol. 8095, pp. 410–423. Springer, Heidelberg (2013)
7. Øhrstrøm, P., Sandborg-Petersen, U., Thorvaldsen, S., Ploug, T.: Teaching syllogistics using conceptual graphs. In: Hernandez, N., Jäschke, R., Croitoru, M. (eds.) ICCS 2014. LNCS, vol. 8577, pp. 217–230. Springer, Heidelberg (2014)
8. Parry, W., Hacker, E.: Aristotelian Logic. State University of New York Press, Albany (1991)
9. Petersen, U.: Prolog+CG: a maintainer's perspective. In: de Moor, A., Polovina, S., Delugach, H. (eds.) First Conceptual Structures Interoperability Workshop (CS-TIW 2006), Proceedings, Aalborg University Press (2006)
10. Sandborg-Petersen, U., Øhrstrøm, P.: The syllog code, open Source Software. http://syllog.sourceforge.net/
11. Sandborg-Petersen, U., Øhrstrøm, P., Ploug, T., Thorvaldsen, S.: Two experiments using syllog. http://syllog.emergence.dk/2015/

Combining Virtual Reality and Relaxation Techniques to Improve Attention Levels in Students from an Initial Vocational Qualification Program

Helena Olmos[1], Soledad Gómez[2], Mariano Alcañiz[1], Manuel Contero[1](✉), M. Puig Andrés-Sebastiá[2], and Norena Martín-Dorta[3]

[1] I3BH, Universitat Politècnica de València, Camino de Vera s/n, 46022 Valencia, Spain
{eolmos,malcaniz,mcontero}@i3bh.es
[2] Facultad de Psicología, Magisterio y Ciencias de la Educación, Universidad Católica de Valencia, C/Sagrado Corazón, 5, 46110 Godella, Spain
{soledad.gomez,mpuig.andres}@ucv.es
[3] Departamento de Técnicas y Proyectos en Ingeniería y Arquitectura, Universidad de La Laguna, Avda. Ángel Guimerá Jorge, s/n, 38204 La Laguna, Spain
nmartin@ull.edu.es

Abstract. The objective of this study is to verify whether Virtual Reality together with relaxation techniques incorporated into it improve the students' attention levels. To do so we made an intervention in an "Initial Vocational Qualification Program" group of Spanish high school in the Valencia metropolitan area. We had 13 students aged between 16 and 19 that participated in the study using an Oculus Rift virtual reality headset. These students were subject to an experimental environment that simulates a beach sunset. They had to perform breathing exercises and concentrate their attention on their breathing, the rhythm of the waves and on flowers of different colors that were appearing in the environment. Experimental results have revealed that levels of attention measured with the Trail Making Test (TMT) were improved when participants had the help of the virtual environment.

Keywords: Virtual reality · Attention · Relaxation · Schoolwork

1 Introduction

School failure is present in many educational systems in developed countries. Low performance within the school is caused, among other factors, by the environment or an unfavorable personal or emotional environment. As a response to these situations, the Spanish education system has created the Initial Vocational Qualification Program (PQPI per its Spanish initials). This program is geared toward students who, after spending 16 years in school, have not been able to graduate from secondary education. It is in this context where the present research work fits and it aims to develop interventions that can reverse this problem. In this particular case, the application of virtual reality has been studied along with meditation and relaxation techniques in order to

© Springer International Publishing Switzerland 2015
G. Conole et al. (Eds.): EC-TEL 2015, LNCS 9307, pp. 613–616, 2015.
DOI: 10.1007/978-3-319-24258-3_71

improve care in the completion of homework and study as well as to contribute to personal relaxation of the student.

There are many scientific studies that have addressed the impact of relaxation and meditation techniques in different life situations [1–3]. If we place the focus on the field of education, we note that studies on yoga, meditation and relaxation in educational environments are relatively recent [4–6]. However, reviewing of the state of the art we observe that there are practically no studies reported on the use of Virtual Reality and relaxation techniques in the field of education, and more specifically in environments with students with special needs such as those described in the introduction to this article. This work aims to make a first approximation to this field.

2 Materials and Methods

This study uses a virtual 3D environment (see Fig. 1) as a supporting tool for the improvement in attention through relaxation exercises. The virtual environment consists of a beach at dusk where, in addition to the landscape view, the sound of the waves of the sea accompanied by relaxing music can be heard through headphones. The environment is shown by the Oculus Rift DK1 system.

Fig. 1. Virtual environment for relaxation.

The method for intervention (VR intervention) with students was as follows: for one minute, we let the student become familiar with the virtual environment. Then we ask them to focus their attention on the waves and their movement given that they emulate the abdominal movement of breathing. This is intended to have a duration of 4 times for inhalation and 4 times for exhalation. Once these eight breaths are completed, the subject visualized a soap bubble inside which flowers of different colors (seven different flowers) appeared. We combined abdominal breathing in the aforementioned times with air retentions for 8 s each. With four flowers, they performed abdominal breaths and with three of them air retentions. Almost by the end of the exercise, all the flowers together appeared within the soap bubble. At that moment, the student was asked to focus on them and to try to remember in which order they appeared as well as the bodily sensations that he/she might have had. We tell the student to refocus their attention on the waves and later on the beach in general. The exercise lasts for 4–5 min. During the entire session, the presence of the teacher was important given that he/she guides the activity actively both during relaxation and during the execution of the tasks and the tests.

2.1 Participants, Instrument and Procedure

The pilot study was conducted with a class of an Initial Vocational Qualification Program (level 2) of a public high school in the city of Valencia (Spain) with 13 students (5 males and 8 females) aged between 16 and 19 in a period of 4 weeks. The initial conditions for all were similar: they had had no contact with 3D virtual environments and had not taken part in any study related to the improvement of their skills at the academic level or relaxation and concentration techniques. None of the subjects knew how the procedure would unfold. Students and their parents received a text document defining the purpose of the investigation and their right to withdraw at any time. Consent was obtained from all participants. Level of attention has been evaluated with the Trail Making Test (TMT) part A [7]. This is an easily administered and widely used test that requires a subject to draw lines connecting a set of 25 dots as fast as possible while still maintaining accuracy. It is a neuropsychological test of visual attention and task switching. Score is based on the total time it takes to complete. It was originally developed by the U.S. Army and is considered to be in the public domain. It can thus be reproduced without obtaining permission.

Table 1. Experimental design and results

Intervention	VR & relax. tech		Regular activities	
Session	1	2	3	4
Sequence of tasks	Pretest VR relax. Activities Postest	Pretest VR relax. Activities Postest	Pretest — Activities Postest	Pretest — Activities Postest
Pre-test mean	3.8923	3.0546	2.8962	2.8977
Post-test mean	3.2646	2.5723	2.9023	2.8446
Mean difference	0.6277	0.4823	−0.0062	0.0531
(std. dev.)	(0.4900)	(0.4751)	(0.2802)	(0.1903)

The study was conducted over four weeks, and each student participated in an individual session per week. The first phase, corresponding to the first two weeks, involved the use of relaxation techniques with the virtual reality application described previously (VR condition). As detailed in Table 1, at the beginning of the session a TMT-A test was administered to the student (pretest). Then the relaxation exercises wearing the Oculus Rift headset were carried out. Afterwards, the student followed the regular tutoring routine with the help of the teacher. At the end of the session, a TMT-A test (postest) was administered again. During the second two weeks the same protocol was followed, not including the VR relaxation exercises in the procedure.

3 Results and Conclusions

Pre and post TMT-A scores and mean differences are shown in Table 1. Data was analyzed with IBM SPSS Statistics 21 for Windows. The hypotheses of this study were: (H1) Relaxation techniques with a Virtual Reality environment (VR intervention) would improve levels of attention in learning tasks in contrast with those following only the regular activities; (H2) The time did not affect the results.

Two-way analysis of variance (ANOVA) with repeated measures was conducted to evaluate hypotheses H1 and H2. Considered factors were: session (week 1/week 2) and intervention condition (VR intervention/regular activities). Results showed no statistically significant difference between sessions (week 1 & 2) ($F(1,12) = .090$, $p = .769$; Wilk's $\Lambda = .993$). Significant differences were found between intervention conditions ($F(1,12) = 140.38$, $p < .001$; Wilk's $\Lambda = .079$). Intervention with Virtual Reality and relaxation techniques showed a significant improvement in the students' attention levels. Mean difference scores in TMT test were remarkably higher for the sessions which used Virtual Reality based relaxation techniques to improve attention. Although no significant differences were found between sessions in each intervention (Interaction Condition = Session*VR: $F(1, 12) = 1.026$, $p = .331$, Wilk's $\Lambda = .921$).

The analysis of results reveals a promising application of combining virtual reality with relaxation exercises to improve attention levels. Nowadays, lack of concentration is an important problem for many students to conduct regular academic activities due to their over exposure to multitude of digital stimuli. The small amount of time dedicated to this relaxation exercises, and its positive impact on attention levels must lead to consider seriously this option as a tool to cope with the lack of concentration in many students.

References

1. Benson, H., Proctor, W.: Relaxation Revolution: The Science and Genetics of Mind Body Healing. Scribner, New York (2010)
2. Kabat-Zinn, J.: La Práctica de la Atención Plena. Editorial Kairós (2013)
3. Jain, S., Shapiro, S.L., Swanick, S., Roesch, S.C., Mills, P.J., Bell, I., Schwartz, G.E.: A randomized controlled trial of mindfulness meditation versus relaxation training. Ann. Behav. Med. **33**(1), 11–21 (2007)
4. Noggle, J.: Benefits of yoga for pshycosocial well-being in US high school curriculum. J. Dev. Behav. Pediatr. **33**, 193–201 (2002)
5. Sharma, S.: Anxiety in students. Psychol. Stud. **47**(1–3), 49–53 (2002)
6. Harrison, J.L., Manocha, L., Rubia, K.: Sahaja: yoga meditation as family treament programme for children with ADHD hyperactivity disorder. J. Emotional Behav. Disord. **1**(15), 56–63 (2007)
7. War Department, Adjutant General's Office: Army Individual Test Battery. Manual of directions and scoring, Washington, DC (1944)

Investigating Learners' Views of Assessment Types in Massive Open Online Courses (MOOCs)

Tina Papathoma(✉), Canan Blake, Doug Clow, and Eileen Scanlon

Institute of Educational Technology, The Open University, Milton Keynes, UK
{Tina.Papathoma,Canan.Blake,Doug.Clow,Eileen.Scanlon}@open.ac.uk

Abstract. Massive Open Online Courses (MOOCs) are changing the contours of the teaching and learning landscape. Assessment covers an important part of this landscape and may be a key driver for learning. This paper presents preliminary results of a qualitative study that investigated learners' views on assessment types within a MOOC. A thematic analysis of learners' interactions in a MOOC Facebook Group and twelve online interviews of learners in the same MOOC reveal that participants identify benefits in peer assessment but they prefer automated assessment as an already-known type. Self-assessment was not preferred by these learners. They reported that clear guidance assists them to carry out peer assessment more effectively. Some learners favored the combination of assessment types, as each of them serves a different purpose for their learning. The learners' socio-cultural context emerged as a theme affecting both their learning and assessment activities and will be considered for future research.

Keywords: Assessment · Moocs · Learners' views · Peer assessment · Self-assessment · Automated assessment

1 Overview

MOOCs are a fast-growing phenomenon which attract continuous research and discourse as their numbers grow and they are of interest to the educational community [1]. MOOCs are used globally to provide millions of learners with access to education [2]. Assessment is also part of the learning process as it motivates learners and provides the necessary feedback on their performance so that they can track their learning progress [3]. Along the same lines assessment is considered as a process of measuring a person's knowledge, comprehension and skills [4]. The purpose of assessment in MOOCs is mainly formative (self/peer/auto assessment) and therefore used to assist students to take the next steps in their learning rather than to report their achievement with a particular grade.

The types of assessment, in the MOOC context, that are mostly discussed in the existing literature are auto-assessment (machine scored objective type questions), peer-assessment and self-assessment [5–8] and therefore are the types under investigation in this study. The voice and the standpoint of learners about the different assessment types in MOOCs are not prominent in the current literature and further research is required. Therefore, the aim of this study was to answer the following research questions:

© Springer International Publishing Switzerland 2015
G. Conole et al. (Eds.): EC-TEL 2015, LNCS 9307, pp. 617–621, 2015.
DOI: 10.1007/978-3-319-24258-3_72

- How do learners view the different types of assessment in MOOCs?
- How effective do learners feel each type of assessment is in their learning?

This study took a qualitative approach, employing thirteen observations of online interactions in a MOOC Facebook Group of a Behavioral Economics course set up by the course educators, as well as twelve online interviews with learners on the same course. Further information of interviewees is shown in Table 1. This study followed the Ethical Guidelines from the British Educational Research Association and Association of Internet Researchers, and sought and obtained approval from the Open University Human Research Ethics Committee.

Table 1. Participants information

Participant identifier (pseudonyms)	Age range	Country of origin	Higher education qualifications	Level of experience – number of courses completed	Courses enrolled and dropped out
Filippos	20–30	India	MBA	High/10	None
Orestis	20–30	Brazil	BA	High/14	None
Aris	51+	Canada	MA	High/20	None
Danae	31–40	Australia	MA	Moderate /4	None
Maya	20–30	Greece	MA	Moderate/3	2
Dionysus	31–40	Russia	MA	Moderate/3	None
Niobe	20–30	Greece	MA	Limited/2	Several in the past before completing these 2
Antigone	31–40	Venezuela	MA	Limited/2	None
Elpi	51+	US	MA	Limited/1	None
Melpo	51+	Denmark	BA	Limited/1	None
Calypso	20–30	US	BA	Limited/1	Several in the past
Hermes	20–30	Colombia	BA	Limited/2	None

This small sample of interviewees is not necessarily representative of the many millions of learners and the diversity of their contexts, but themes and issues were investigated to be explored in more detail later. The data collected from the interviews and observations were analysed using thematic analysis [9]. The Facebook Group where the online interactions were observed had more than 200 posts when the course was live and the analysis was carried at the end of the course. The first author was a member of this group. Facebook posts from the course that were related to assessment were manually filtered and saved in separate files. As well as a complete read of the posts to find assessment related posts, key words such as 'assessment', 'peer', 'self', 'automated' and 'assessment issues' were used to filter the Facebook posts. Only 13 posts were related to assessment. The data from these posts and interviews were read repeatedly by one researcher, initial codes were generated and quotes of the participants were highlighted. The codes contributed to creating themes that were then reviewed. The Behavioral Economics Course in which all the participants were enrolled ran for six weeks and consisted of video lectures, automated quizzes (no time limitation, with multiple attempts), peer-assessed writing assignments, self-assessment, and a final exam (with just one attempt with time limit). Some of the themes -from the interviews and observations- that captured data in relation to the research questions are:

- Assessment value
- Types of assessment
  - Automated Assessment
  - Peer Assessment
  - Self-Assessment
- Assessment preference
- Peer Assessment Issues

2 Preliminary Results

The preliminary results of the interviews and the observations of this qualitative study show that the majority of the interviewees made statements indicating that assessment drives their learning [3] and they valued each type in various ways. Each assessment type served a different purpose for learners. They reported that automated methods tested their memory and knowledge, giving them the opportunity to revise and see wrong and correct answers, crystallizing what they learned while giving them a feeling of accomplishment. They reported that peer assessment exposed them to others' ideas and was a powerful way to understand some concepts more deeply, despite the fact that some learners were negative about the process of assessing their peers' work because they found it time consuming, unfair or they felt that a language barrier made it hard to assess their peers' work. Finally, learners reported fewer benefits in self-assessment. The benefits they reported were related to self-assessment's role in assisting the improvement of their own work and in contributing to the enhancement of their learning experience. Interviewees also reported that the combination of different assessment types could also have positive effects on students' learning because each of them serves a different purpose and provided that each assessment type is well designed, they can reinforce each other. Most students reported that they preferred automated methods while only a couple preferred peer assessment and none had self-assessment as a first preference.

Some interviewees also reported the view that expertise is needed for peers to assess other peer's work, with a notion that papers should be marked by a "respected superior". Learners came from different countries (as shown in Table 1) and educational systems, and may have been expecting a certain set of conventions based on their previous educational experiences. It is clear that their socio cultural experiences on education affected how learners responded to assessment. MOOCs learners from various educational systems may have different expectations. It is reasonable to assume that educational systems in different countries have specific norms or conventions that are used in teaching and learning environments. As a result, assessment may elicit different responses and needs to be considered in the next steps of this study in the context of the global offer of MOOCs. When designing assessment (as with designing learning opportunities) in MOOCs it is important to also take into account the cultural differences of the students without implying that different assessment types should be applied according to the culture of each learner. MOOCs designers need to examine students' views and prepare them for learning in a global setting.

3 Conclusions

The preliminary findings of this study suggest that assessment in MOOCs can be considered from different perspectives (i.e. learners' expectations, prior educational experience, prior MOOCs experience etc.) and that learners perceive different benefits depending on whether they are assessing, being assessed, or are self-assessing. Moreover, learners from different backgrounds and intentions may respond to assessment in various ways. MOOCs designers and educational researchers need a better understanding of how learners perceive the different assessment types and this will enable them to tailor assessment to learners' needs to enhance the learning experience.

References

1. Clow, D.: MOOCs and the funnel of participation. In: Proceedings of the Third Learning Analytics and Knowledge Conference, Leuven, Belgium, pp. 185–189 (2013)
2. Ferguson, R., Clow, D.: Examining engagement: analysing learner subpopulations in massive open online courses (MOOCs). In: Proceedings of the Fifth Learning Analytics and Knowledge Conference, Poughkeepsie, NY, USA, pp. 51–58 (2015)
3. Rowntree, D.: Assessing Students: How Shall We Know Them? Kogan Page, London (1987)
4. Chao, K.J., Hung, I.C., Chen, N.S.: On the design of online synchronous assessment in a synchronous cyber classroom. J. Comput. Assist. Learn. **28**(4), 379–395 (2011)
5. Vogelsang, T., Ryppertz, L.: On the validity of peer grading and a cloud teaching assistant system. In: Proceedings of the Fifth Learning Analytics and Knowledge Conference, Poughkeepsie, NY, USA pp. 41–50 (2015)
6. Raman, K., Joachims, T.: Bayesian ordinal peer grading. In: Proceedings of the Second Learning @ Scale Conference, Vancouver, BC, Canada, pp. 149–156 (2015)
7. Balfour, S.P.: Assessing writing in MOOCs: automated essay scoring and calibrated peer review. Res. Pract. Assess. **8**(1), 40–48 (2013)

8. Wilkowski, J., Russel, D. M., Deutsch, A.: Self-evaluation in advanced power searching and mapping with google MOOCs. In: Proceedings of the First Learning @ Scale Conference, New York, USA, pp. 109–116 (2014)
9. Braun, V., Clark, V.: Using thematic analysis in psychology. Qual. Res. Psychol. **3**(2), 77–101 (2006)

Designing and Evaluating Personalised Courses with LAMS: The Designer Perspective

Eva Papazoi[1(✉)], Kyparisia Papanikolaou[2], and Evangelia Gouli[2]

[1] Hellenic Open University, Patras, Greece
eva3x7@gmail.com
[2] School of Pedagogical and Technological Education, Athens, Greece
kpapanikolaou@aspete.gr, lilag@di.uoa.gr

Abstract. This study explores approaches of implementing adaptation with the Learning Activity Management System (LAMS) as well as the technological knowledge and skills that designers develop through the creation of personalised lessons in LAMS. Postgraduate students used LAMS to design and personalise courses. To determine the ways in which adaptation was implemented, we conducted a comparative analysis among the personalised courses. To explore the technological knowledge that designers develop through course personalisation, we used specific criteria inspired by the Technological Pedagogical Content Knowledge framework (TPACK). Concluding, all participants enriched personalised courses and elaborated on various adaptation design issues.

Keywords: Adaptation · Personalisation · LAMS · TPACK

1 Introduction

Adaptation to learner characteristics in the educational process is based on the fact that different individuals learn in different ways. Adaptation can be viewed as moving between two extremes, the one being the complete control of adaptation features by the system itself (adaptivity) and the other being the complete control of adaptation features by the learner himself (adaptability) [1]. The latter is considered a crucial characteristic of the learning process [2].

Aiming at investigating how personalisation can be implemented in contemporary learning management platforms widely used, such as the Learning Activity Management System (LAMS) [3], we conducted an empirical study with postgraduate students. In this study students undertook the role of learning designers creating lessons as sequences of activities, which they transformed in adaptive ones.

The lessons created were analysed in order to explore the approaches adopted, the means by which adaptation was implemented in LAMS, as well as the appropriateness and adequacy of the available tools. We further investigated the added value of developing personalised lessons for the students-designers; an approach considered promising for training in technology enhanced learning [4]. To this end, we used Technological Pedagogical Content Knowledge (TPACK) [5] as a framework for analysing the lessons

© Springer International Publishing Switzerland 2015
G. Conole et al. (Eds.): EC-TEL 2015, LNCS 9307, pp. 622–625, 2015.
DOI: 10.1007/978-3-319-24258-3_73

created by students. TPACK stresses that the educational process is a particularly complex process that draws from the diverse and interacting knowledge areas of Technology, Pedagogy and Content [5]. The various types of knowledge proposed by TPACK were used as the basis for evaluating and comparing the adaptive and non-adaptive versions of learning designs created by students (features of adaptivity and adaptability). In this paper the focus is on the technological knowledge cultivated with the aim to address the following research questions:

- Which are the technological characteristics of personalised courses created in LAMS?
- How does the technological knowledge develop while a designer creates personalised courses in LAMS?

2 Study Design

The study was conducted in the context of a post graduate course on Distance Learning organised at the University of Athens. Twenty-five students were assigned to design a lesson in LAMS. In phase A, twenty students worked in groups of two and five students worked individually in order to design a lesson for distance learning. In phase B, students were asked to transform their lesson to an adaptive one according to specific learner characteristics of their choice.

The *data of the study* consist of the two versions of the lessons authored in the LAMS environment, namely the initial version (phase A) and the adaptive version (phase B). During phase A, 15 lessons were created on various topics. Figure 1 presents how an excerpt of the non-adaptive version (left, a preview of the authoring environment of LAMS) of the lesson entitled "Databases", was transformed into an adaptive one (right) in phase B. In total, 14 adaptive lessons were created (due to member changes in the initial groups).

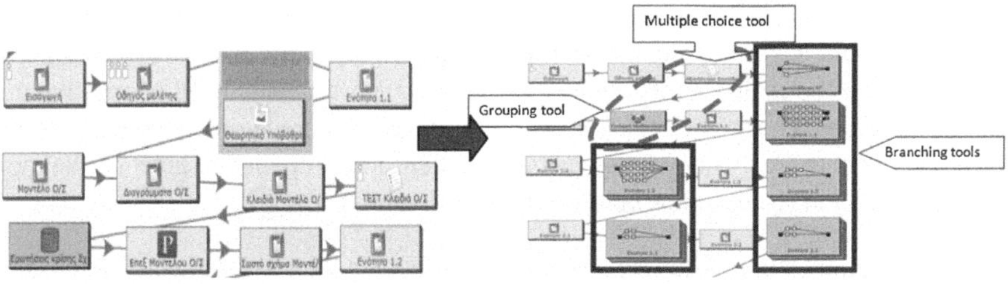

Fig. 1. Excerpt of the authors' perspective of the initial version of the lesson in LAMS (left) and the adaptive one (right) with annotations of the LAMS tools used for implementing adaptation: branching, grouping and multiple choice tools (Source: Adaptive lesson on "Databases")

The *data analysis* performed in order to answer research question 1 and identify the ways in which adaptation was implemented included a comparative analysis among the adaptive versions of all the lessons concerning (a) learner characteristics used as adaptation sources, (b) system characteristics differentiated according to learner's profile and (c) adaptability features.

The *data analysis* performed to answer research question 2 used the TPACK framework to identify instances of the initial and adaptive versions of the lessons that reflect the knowledge areas that were developed. In particular we selected specific questions from the TPACK questionnaire [6] which we reformulated into 23 evaluation criteria that were then used to assess the lessons. The 15 initial and the 14 adaptive lessons were analysed and evaluated with these 23 criteria and scored with a five-point rating scale.

3 Results and Discussion

Research Question 1: Which are the technological characteristics of personalised learning sequences developed in LAMS?

Regarding the learner characteristics and traits selected as *sources of adaptation*, we observed that in all the lessons designed in phase B, adaptation was implemented based on learning style; in eleven of them the Honey & Mumford learning style theory was adopted. In phase A, although it was not required, 4 lessons were designed with adaptive features based on learners prior knowledge, while in phase B the adaptive lessons based on the same feature rose to 10. Two lessons took into account learners preferences on how the material was presented and one lesson gave the learners the choice of following a different sequence based on the stereotype category they belonged to, i.e. parents or teachers.

Regarding the *adaptation method*, the most prominent implementation one was the presentation of learning units (e.g. activity, theory) in various orderings based on the learning style. The sources of adaptation used were the learning style (in 14 lessons), learner preferences, performance in assessment tests and combinations of the above. The second most promising method was the provision of different material with the use of different tools according to the learners' learning style (in 5 lessons). Regarding *adaptability*, in the majority of lessons (12 lessons), participants used supportive and optional activities. The method that the designers used in order to implement adaptability allowed learners to freely choose or change: (a) their prior knowledge level on the topic (in 10 lessons) and (b) their learning style (in 13 lessons).

Research Question 2: How does the technological knowledge develop while a designer is creating personalised content in LAMS?

The main result of the analysis was that the second version of all lessons scored higher points according to the 23 evaluation criteria assessing the various types of TPACK knowledge. Below we discuss the results for selected criteria assessing elements of the lessons that reflect specific facets of the technological knowledge and specifically the ability to integrate various types of tools in learning activities such as tools of the authoring environment (LAMS) and Web 2.0 tools

Criterion 1: Ability to use the various types of tools of the authoring environment (LAMS) for designing a lesson. All participants enriched the adaptive versions by adding more activities and tools compared to the initial one. In all lessons there was a rise in the number of tools used in the adaptive version, from 2 to 16 extra tools. Adaptation was implemented with the LAMS branching tool, allowing the design of various learning paths within the main sequence, matching students' characteristics. Additionally, grouping tools were also used, allowing grouping students based on learning style or other characteristics, as well as tools for creating multiple choice questions and evaluation tools. Overall, the tools used for the design of learning activities in both phases were mostly tools that LAMS offers.
Criterion 2: Ability to create learning objects using Web 2.0 tools: In phase A, the lessons developed included a small number of Web 2.0 tools and multimedia elements. In phase B there was a rise in the use of Web 2.0 tools leading to increase of interactivity. The most popular category of Web 2.0 tools were quiz tools that were used in 10 lessons, followed by presentation tools.

Regarding LAMS functionality, the students considered that LAMS offers appropriate tools for the creation of adaptive lessons even though it is a general purpose e-learning environment. However, it has less potential when developing lessons with adaptability due to its sequential nature. Students made several proposals for extending LAMS with functionalities that could facilitate the creation of adaptive lessons such as the possibility of creating a learner profile/model to guide adaptation decisions.

4 Conclusions

This study highlighted various approaches of implementing adaptation in LAMS. This is also a first step providing important evidence about the development of all the TPACK knowledge areas during the transformation of a non-adaptive to an adaptive lesson. The research on defining evaluation criteria for students' artifacts based on the TPACK framework is a work in progress.

References

1. Brusilovsky, P.: Adaptive hypermedia. User Model. User-Adap. Inter. **11**, 87–110 (2001)
2. Vosniadou, S.: How children learn. International Academy of Education and the International Bureau of Education (UNESCO) (2001)
3. LAMS Foundation. http://lamsfoundation.org/index.htm
4. Papanikolaou, K.: How authoring content for personalised learning may cultivate learning design skills? In: 14th IEEE International Conference on Advanced Learning Technologies (ICALT2014), pp.94–98. IEEE Computer Society, Washington (2014)
5. Mishra, P., Koehler, M.J.: Technological pedagogical content knowledge: a new framework for teacher knowledge. Teachers Coll. Rec. **108**, 1017–1054 (2006)
6. Schmidt, D.A., Baran, E., Thompson, A.D., Mishra, P., Koehler, M.J., Shin, T.S.: Technological pedagogical content knowledge (TPACK): the development and validation of an assessment instrument for preservice teachers. Res. Technol. Educ. **42**, 123–149 (2009)

Reflective TEL: Augmenting Learning Tools with Reflection Support

Michael Prilla(✉) and Oliver Blunk

Ruhr University of Bochum, Bochum, Germany
{michael.prilla,oliver.blunk}@rub.de

Abstract. Reflection and collaborative reflection are common means for learning at work. Based on four studies on tool supported collaborative reflection, which created insights on barriers and opportunities for such support, we describe a concept of augmenting tools with reflection and a prototype showing how the concept can be implemented in typical TEL environments.

Keywords: Reflection · Collaborative reflection · Plugin reflection

1 Introduction

Reflection can be understood as returning to experiences, re-assessing them and deriving insights for future behavior [1]. Reflection occurs "when our existing conceptual schema do not apply (or do not apply well) and thus we need to reschematize nature in order to come to a (better) understanding of it." [2] and is necessary in modern workplaces [3]. It has a social dimension, as workers often exchange experiences and try to learn from it together. Such *collaborative reflection* can create results transcending results of individuals [4]. Collaborative reflection has been neglected in past research and most work is on individual reflection [5], but recent work has taken it up [2, 6]. Concepts for applying collaborative reflection in practice, however, are missing.

Support for collaborative reflection needs an understanding of how reflective practice can be supported, that is, which tasks need to be supported and how. We created [5, 7, 8] a model of collaborative reflection, which we used for the design of reflection support (see Fig. 1). The three basic steps in the model are *creating data and documenting experience* to reflect upon, *reflection on experiences* and *sustaining results* from reflection. Reflection includes *individual and collaborative reflection*, as each situation of collaborative reflection also contains individual reflection.

Baumer [2] has suggested three dimensions of "reflective informatics", which resonate with our model. These include *breakdowns* (situations in which the reality diverges from expectations), *inquiry* (people critically examine their experiences), and *transformation* (results from reflection are put into practice).

While the work described above provides information on *what* to support in collaborative reflection, the problem remains *how* to support it. Following we analyze outcomes from studies on tool supported collaborative reflection to frame a concept.

© Springer International Publishing Switzerland 2015
G. Conole et al. (Eds.): EC-TEL 2015, LNCS 9307, pp. 626–629, 2015.
DOI: 10.1007/978-3-319-24258-3_74

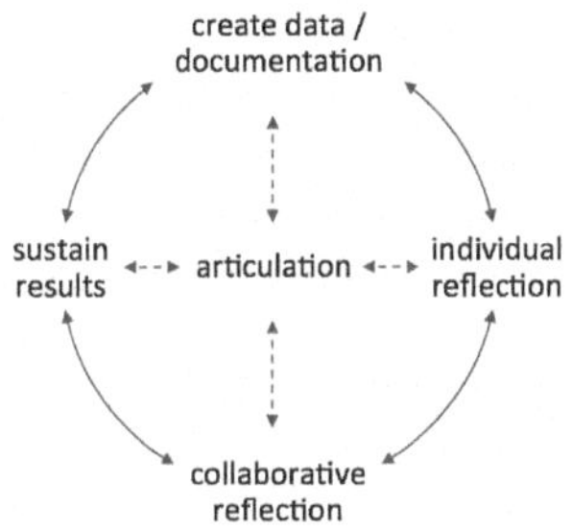

Fig. 1. Model of collaborative reflection introduced by Prilla et al. in [7], adapted in [8].

2 Supporting Collaborative Reflection in Practice: A Study

Using the model shown in Fig. 1 we created the "TalkReflect App" to support reflection on social interaction at work [7]. It supports users in reporting experiences by creating notes, sharing these notes and reflecting on them by creating comments that contain similar experiences, viewpoints and ideas for learning from the discussion.

The TalkReflect App was used in four studies in different workplaces with different constraints: a *care home*, a *hospital*, a *group of interns* in public administration and a *department* in the same organization. The studies were run for 50–80 days and with user groups of 6–18 users and gave us insights on the usage of the tool [8, 9]:

- **Spatial Arrangement of User Group (Co-located vs. Remote):** For users working in different locations the app provided value as a new channel enabling exchange. This was different when users were co-located, as in the hospital and care home.
- **Support by a Facilitator:** Users used the app more often if others encouraged participation or asked for comments. However this does not scale for large groups.
- **Duration of App Usage:** In all studies activity started slowly, reached its peak after the slow start and decreased shortly after. This suggests that the effects caused by the tool were short to mid-term only, even if there was a facilitator present.

A content analysis [9] shows that in the interns and public administration cases the tool was used (as intended) for sharing experiences, reflecting on them and creating learning outcomes. In the other two cases it was used only for sharing experiences and (in the hospital case) for seeking guidance from a superior (the facilitator of the group). We attribute these differences to the location (see above) and facilitator activities – the facilitator in the hospital case provided advice rather than supporting reflection [9]. Based on correlations and cross tables we also found three types of articulations likely to positively influence the creation of outcomes in a thread:

- **Mentioning Emotions:** Some participants explicitly described that they were (un)happy with certain situations they shared with others, e.g. "Was not fun man".
- **Asking Questions Triggering Reflection:** Such as "what do people think about …".
- **Exchanging Experiences**: Participants often pointed to similar experiences or even included descriptions of them, e.g. "I have been through similar situations. I (…)".

Regression analysis was used for further investigation. We found an effect of exchanging experiences on the number of results being documented ($R2 = 0.515$, $F = 37.2$, Sig. $<= 0.01$), while questions and emotions had minor effects on this. Therefore we conclude that actively supporting experience exchange may foster the results documented in tools, and that using questions or emotions may provide additional support.

3 Augmenting Tools to Support Collaborative Reflection

Our studies suggest that two aspects may enable successful reflection support:

- Activity decline and low usage happened mostly in co-located groups and when it was used as a short-term intervention. We thus suggest *embedding reflection into existing or wider communication contexts* to enable long term usage.
- Facilitator support was helpful for tool usage and we found that certain articulations led to more outcomes being documented. Therefore we suggest that reflection and supportive articulations should be *supported actively by facilitation.*

These aspects can be supported if systems already used in organizations are augmented with reflection features. This includes (but is not limited to) the following features:

- **Prompting Users:** Providing *prompts* (e.g. questions and instructions) to users can support them in contributing to collaborative reflection [8, 10, 11]. Adding reflective prompts to communication tools such as forums (e.g., asking users to share experiences) encourages reflective articulations. This also scales for large groups.
- **Asking Questions in Conversations:** A system can provide users with *support for actively asking others for support* such as choosing from a list of helpful questions.
- **Connecting Users:** A tool can provide users with suggestions of other users, who share similar experiences or are interest in similar topics, to support cases in which reflection between people who could not reflect in face-to-face situations regularly.

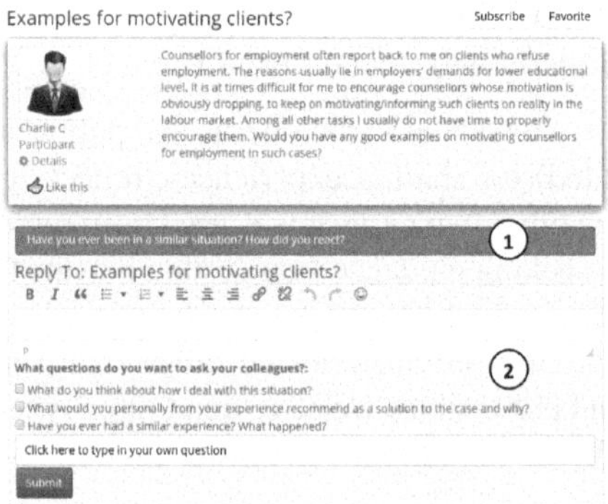

Fig. 2. Snippet from our community of practice platform augmented by reflection features.

As part of a large project we are developing a prototype of a community of practice augmented by reflection features. As an example for the features mentioned above Fig. 2 shows that the prototype uses prompts (no. 1 in Fig. 2) and questions to be chosen by the user (no. 2) to encourage commenting on a shared experience (top). This transforms a common feature (threaded discussions) into a reflective feature.

4 Conclusion and Outlook

We have suggested the concept of *augmenting existing communication and learning tools with features supporting reflection* to implement collaborative reflection in practice. Our work adds to the community by describing a conceptual and technical approach for the implementation of reflective learning at work. We are aware of the fact that there might be other concepts, but we are convinced that ours is a good way to go forward with development and research on reflective learning. In further work we will evaluate the prototype in real workplace scenarios to explore the concept further, asking questions such as how augmented reflection features change the use of tools and how much reflective content is created as opposed to no reflection support.

Acknowledgements. This work is part of the EmployID (http://employid.eu) project on "Scalable & cost-effective facilitation of professional identity transformation in public employment services" supported by the EC in FP 7 (project no. 619619). We thank all colleagues and associated partners for their cooperation and our fruitful discussions.

References

1. Boud, D.: Reflection: Turning Experience into Learning. Kogan Page, London (1985)
2. Baumer, E.P.: Reflective informatics: conceptual dimensions for designing technologies of reflection. In: Proceedings of CHI 2015 (2015)
3. Schön, D.A.: The Reflective Practitioner. Basic books, New York (1983)
4. Hoyrup, S.: Reflection as a core process in organisational learning. J. Workplace Learn. **16**, 442–454 (2004)
5. Prilla, M., Pammer, V., Krogstie, B.: Fostering collaborative redesign of work practice: challenges for tools supporting reflection at work. In: Bertelsen, O.W., Ciolfi, L., Grasso, M.A., Papadopoulos, G.A. (eds.) ECSCW 2013, pp. 241–260. Springer, London (2013)
6. Porges, Z., Yang, X., Desai, A., Ho, C., Pallegedara, R., Razzaque, R., Cosley, D.: Achieve: evaluating the impact of progress logging and social feedback on goal achievement. In: Proceedings of the Companion Publication of CSCW 2014, pp. 221–224. ACM, Baltimore, Maryland, USA (2014)
7. Prilla, M., Degeling, M., Herrmann, T.: Collaborative reflection at work: supporting informal learning at a healthcare workplace. In: Proceedings of the ACM International Conference on Supporting Group Work (GROUP 2012), pp. 55–64 (2012)
8. Prilla, M.: Collaborative reflection support at work: a socio-technical design task. In: Proceedings of European Conference on Information Systems (ECIS 2014) (2014)
9. Prilla, M., Renner, B.: Supporting collaborative reflection at work: a comparative case analysis. In: Proceedings of ACM Conference on Group Work (GROUP 2014). ACM (2014)
10. Davis, E.A.: Scaffolding students' knowledge integration: prompts for reflection in KIE. Int. J. Sci. Educ. **22**, 819–837 (2000)
11. Thillmann, H., Künsting, J., Wirth, J., Leutner, D.: Is it merely a question of "what" to prompt or also "when" to prompt? Zeitschrift für Pädagogische Psychol. **23**, 105–115 (2009)

Visualizing Students' Performance in the Classroom: Towards Effective F2F Interaction Modelling

Samara Ruiz(✉), Maite Urretavizcaya, Isabel Fernández-Castro, and Juan-Miguel López-Gil

Department of Languages and Computer Systems, University of the Basque Country, UPV/EHU, Donostia-San Sebastián, Spain
{samara.ruiz,maite.urretavizcaya,isabel.fernandez, juanmiguel.lopez}@ehu.eus

Abstract. Students are supposed to work and learn when they are in the classroom, but how are they learning? Answering this question is not so easy, but perhaps knowing the learning activities of the student and following his or her learning progress can be good supporting mechanisms. The PresenceClick environment is intended to let teachers and students nimbly capture what happens in class to provide them, in return, with information about students' behavior during class. The system involves two platforms −a web system and a mobile application− that working together allow recording of students' interactions and provide updated graphical visualizations about their behavior.

Keywords: Technology in classrooms · F2F interactions · Learning analytics

1 Introduction

Nowadays, the teaching learning process is considered an exchange of information in two directions: student-teacher-student [1], so learning is more a continuous interaction than a master class [2]. In this sense, developing new educational models, where students turn into active agents of their own formation, becomes necessary. Thus, students would benefit from supporting tools that let them manage their own active learning while in and out of classroom [3]. At present, personal computers and laptops are widespread learning-supporting tools, although the students' mastery also makes the current mobile technologies into good candidates [4].

The proposal here presented aims to enrich the face-to-face (F2F) educational models with *knowledge about what happens in classroom*. This knowledge could be inferred from behaviour data captured by means of suitable supporting tools. The more interactions registered and analysed, the more information can be given to teachers and students to enrich the teaching-learning process. *PresenceClick* is a learning-supporting tool that allows collaboratively capturing students' interaction information, and visualizing just-in-time the students' learning evolution as inferred from recorded data. It is composed of a web system, a mobile application and a data server to maintain learners' and groups' models. The platform *WebClick* lets teachers and students follow the

© Springer International Publishing Switzerland 2015
G. Conole et al. (Eds.): EC-TEL 2015, LNCS 9307, pp. 630–633, 2015.
DOI: 10.1007/978-3-319-24258-3_75

students' progress during the course by means of visualizations; its web responsive characteristic allows accessing from any device, i.e. PC, laptops, tablets or smartphones. It manages and visualizes the data captured during the F2F interactions, and conveniently updates the Learner and Group Models by inferring the students' knowledge from their behaviour in class, e.g. attendance, participation and activity. On the other hand, the mobile app *pClick* captures the students' interaction that occur to *answer questions* or *surveys* that teachers openly launch in class, and those related to their status during *exercise performance −done* or *with doubts*. The information captured and integrated in the Learner and Group Models allows teachers to visualize students' activities, knowledge and behaviour. Reflecting on this idea, this paper aims to answer the next research questions: (a) *Is it possible to use mobile devices in class to catch F2F learning interactions?* (b) *Can we deduce the learning process and state of each student from the modelled interactions and their visualizations?* Taking these questions as starting point, the paper is structured as follows: Sects. 2 and 3 present the design and evaluation of the web platform *WebClick* and the mobile application *pClick*, respectively. Finally, the conclusions and further work are drawn.

2 PresenceClick Web Platform: *WebClick*

The monitoring of attendance is an interesting, and frequently compulsory, activity for managing and control of regular F2F education. It has been also valued as beneficial for both individual learners and universities [5], what suggests automating this process. *WebClick* captures the list of classroom attendees in real time [6] by using a control device and the student's personal identification card −provided by the university. This process is effortless for teachers, and students only have to pass their card when entering the class. The *attendance* functionality of *WebClick* (Fig. 1) has been evaluated during two academic years.

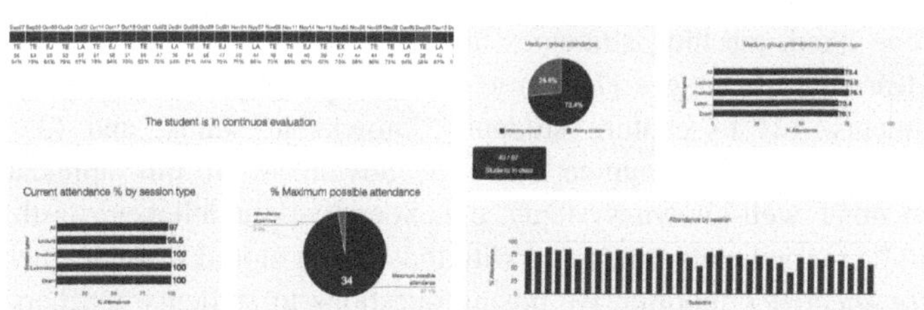

Fig. 1. Some *WebClick* visualizations

During the 2013/2014 academic year, 12 teachers covering 10 subjects and 182 students participated in the study; 9 teachers of 7 subjects, and 200 students participated in the 2014/2015 experience. A total of 7 presence control devices connected through TCP/IP protocol were used. Besides, several questionnaires were run to collect the voluntary opinion of both students and teachers at the end of each semester. The evaluation experience was very positive, and the system *utility* and *usability* were highly rated by the participants. They highlighted *"the information presented is interesting"* and that they *"wish to continue registering the attendance"*. Students also indicated that *"comparing their attendance with the one of rest of the group"* would be an interesting feature to develop.

3 PresenceClick Mobil Application: *pClick*

pClick is a multi device mobile application[1] which involves two modules for: *audience response* and *exercise monitoring* (Fig. 2). Both functionalities feed the Learner and Group Models with shallow information about students' actions, e.g. questions answered, finished exercises, number of doubts, learning speed while solving exercises or answering questions, etc. This information will be later analysed by *webClick* to infer deep aspects of the students' behaviour, e.g. students' participation or knowledge.

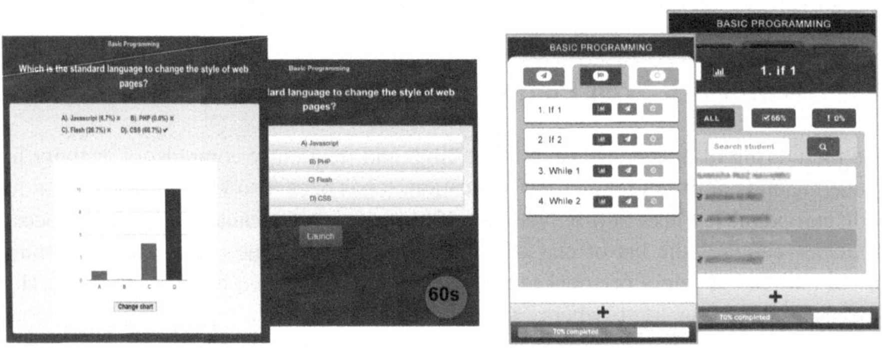

Fig. 2. *pClick*: audience response (left) and student's exercise monitoring system (right)

On the one hand, teaching strategies that use audience response systems involve some main learning advantages [7]: (1) to facilitate participation to especially shy or reserved students, (2) to capture students' knowledge status, and (3) to record teacher-students-teacher communications. The advantage of this application when compared to other well-known systems, e.g. Socrative[2] or iclicker[3], is that all data captured will be immediately integrated with those other stored in the learner model by whatever *PresenceClick* module. By posing questions to students, teachers know the student's knowledge status and participation, and also can promote open discussion in class. The *question* functionality has been evaluated with 64 attendees: 52 participants answered and their response was very positive; students were highly motivated to use mobile devices in classroom.

---

[1] It has been built with Apache Cordova to be used as a native app in different mobile operative systems (iOS, Android, Windows Mobile and BlackBerry). http://cordova.apache.org.

[2] http://www.socrative.com

[3] https://www1.iclicker.com

On the other hand, when teachers launch an exercise to be done (it can be previously planned), students receive a notification on their device and then communicate whether they have finished it or found difficulties. So, teachers clearly observe the exercises performance and may decide to add new information when presenting solutions. This functionality aims at: (1) monitoring students activities in classroom, individually or in groups, (2) helping teachers to develop more adaptable sessions even when student groups are large, and (3) providing a new communication channel to students with problems.

4 Conclusions

Supported on the use of new technologies, we have designed the *PresenceClick* system to monitor the interactions among teachers and students that happen in classroom. This tool is distributed on two subsystems: a web platform and a mobile application. The first and preliminary evaluation shows that *teachers and students show a high interest in registering the class interactions* to *follow the learning progress*. According to these results, we are developing new experiences to verify its real impact on learning. As previous studies point out, mobile devices are powerful platforms that can be used in classroom to exploit new learning strategies based on their agility and dynamism. In addition, due to the contrasted high interest and motivation of students on the use of these technologies, the possibility of using them in class not only becomes real but also a necessity.

Acknowledgements. This work has been supported by the Govern of the Basque Country (IT722-13), the University of the Basque Country (PPV12/09, UFI11/45) and Gipuzkoako Foru Aldundia (FA-208/2014-B).

References

1. Parsons, D., Ryu, H., Cranshaw, M.: A study of design requirements for mobile learning environments. In: 2006 Sixth International Conference on Advanced Learning Technologies, pp. 96–100 (2006)
2. Sharples, M., Taylor, J., Vavoula, G.: A theory of learning for the mobile age. In: Bachmair, B. (ed.) Medienbildung in neuen Kulturräumen, pp. 87–99. VS Verlag für Sozialwissenschaften (2010)
3. Dunlap, J.C., Grabinger, S.: Preparing students for lifelong learning: a review of instructional features and teaching methodologies. Perform. Improv. Q. **16**, 6–25 (2003)
4. Aljohani, N.R., Davis, H.C.: Learning analytics in mobile and ubiquitous learning environments. In: 11th World Conference on Mobile and Contextual Learning: mLearn 2012 (2012)
5. Bowen, E., Price, T., Lloyd, S., Thomas, S.: Improving the quantity and quality of attendance data to enhance student retention. J. Furth. High. Educ. **29**, 375–385 (2005)
6. Ruiz, S., Urretavizcaya, M., Fernandez-Castro, I.: Monitoring F2F interactions through attendance control. In: 2013 IEEE Frontiers in Education Conference (FIE) 0, pp. 226–232 (2013)
7. Kay, R., LeSage, A.: A strategic assessment of audience response systems used in higher education. Australas. J. Educ. Technol. **25**(2), 235–249 (2009)

Supporting Learning Analytics for Informal Workplace Learning with a Social Semantic Infrastructure

Adolfo Ruiz-Calleja[1(✉)], Sebastian Dennerlein[2], Vladimir Tomberg[1], Kai Pata[1], Tobias Ley[1], Dieter Theiler[2], and Elisabeth Lex[2]

[1] Tallinn University, Narva Road 29, 10120 Tallinn, Estonia
{adolfo,vtomberg,kpata,tley}@tlu.ee
[2] Graz University of Technology, Inffeldgasse 13, 8010 Graz, Austria
{sdennerlein,dtheiler,elex}@know-center.at

Abstract. This paper presents the potential of a social semantic infrastructure that implements an Actor Artifact Network (AAN) with the final goal of supporting learning analytics at the workplace. Two applications were built on top of such infrastructure and make use of the emerging relations of such a AAN. A preliminary evaluation shows that an AAN can be created out of the usage of both applications, thus opening the possibility to implement learning analytics at the workplace.

Keywords: Informal learning · Workplace learning · Social-semantic technologies · Artifact-Actor Network · Data integration

1 Introduction

Informal learning at the workplace is a multi-episodic activity that is often connected to current demands and tasks at the workplace. This fact makes the knowledge to be easily applicable but hinders individual learning experiences to be further taken up in systematic organizational learning practices [1]. Supporting such unplannable learning experiences with technology has proven to be a major challenge that is far from being solved.

The Learning Layers project is devoted to tackle with these learning processes. Several applications have been developed in this project, as well as an infrastructure that enables their technical integration [2]. This infrastructure relies on a semantically-enriched Artifact-Actor Network (AAN) [3] to describe the relationships among actors and artifacts in different learning contexts. This AAN can be useful to support learning activities or to monitor the learning processes [2]. But how to take advantage of this AAN to monitor and to feed back on these learning processes is still a problem that could be approached using learning analytics techniques [4]. This paper reports a first step exploring how an AAN can be exploited for learning analytics using a social-semantic infrastructure.

© Springer International Publishing Switzerland 2015
G. Conole et al. (Eds.): EC-TEL 2015, LNCS 9307, pp. 634–637, 2015.
DOI: 10.1007/978-3-319-24258-3_76

2 A Social Semantic Infrastructure to Support Workplace Learning

The Social Semantic Server (SSS) is an infrastructure specially developed to integrate workplace-learning applications. From a data perspective, its key idea is to log the interactions between actors and artifacts-including some meta-data that describes the context where this interaction takes place- and then offer an abstraction of this data as a semantically-enriched AAN. Thus, the relationships between the SSS entities are explicit. In addition, as the relationships of this AAN have a semantic meaning, they can be based on different characteristics of the entities that may depend on their associated context. For example, some artifacts may be related because they are frequently accessed from the same place (a contextual characteristic) while two actors may be related because they chatted together or one read a document published by other.

Besides, it is not possible to foresee all the possible applications that can potentially be integrated into this infrastructure. For this reason we developed the SSS as a framework that implements an AAN via the provision and respective usage of a set of core services, such as discussion activities or users and artifacts recommendations [2]. These services can then be extended to satisfy the requirements of the applications integrated. Additionally, purpose-specific services can also be developed for some applications that require some extra functionality. Figure 1 graphically depicts the integration of learning applications into the SSS.

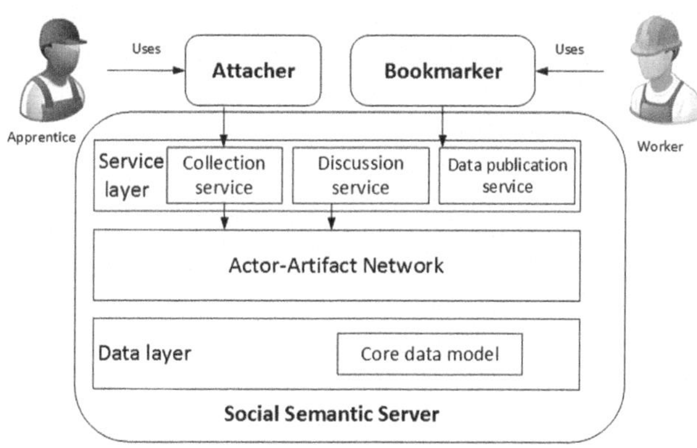

Fig. 1. Integration of learning applications into the social semantic infrastructure.

3 Attacher and Bookmarker

One of the applications that make use of the SSS is **Bookmarker**. It is a Chrome extension that simply allows users to submit bookmarks to the SSS while browsing. Each bookmark may include a title and a set of tags that describe it. Another application is **Attacher**, a WordPress plugin that integrates a blog editor to the SSS. Attacher displays a tagcloud in the blog publishing interface that includes the tags registered in the SSS. With this tagcloud the blog publisher can browse the artifacts published in the SSS, filter them by their authorship and easily cite them in the blog post using a drag-and-drop interface. In turn, Attacher automatically registers the published blog posts in the infrastructure, including some additional meta-data to capture the context of the creation (authorship, publication time and tags related).

There was no need to extend the services available on the SSS to develop Attacher and Bookmarker. In this sense, these applications exemplify how well-known and massively used applications, as WordPress and Chrome, can easily be integrated into the SSS and thus share information among them.

4 Experience Using Attacher and Bookmarker

Attacher and Bookmarker have been used in a master course for training future teachers at Tallinn University. Ten students were asked to bookmark web resources they considered relevant using Bookmarker. Then, they wrote a blog post about their reflections of the subject using WordPress and Attacher to browse the bookmarks published in the social semantic infrastructure.

The SSS registered the tags employed by the users (both to describe and browse them), the blog publications and their citations. These events were used to create a semantically-enriched AAN that had three different types of elements: actors, which represented the students; artifacts, which represented the blog posts and the bookmarks; and tags, which are meta-data related to the artifacts. The actors and artifacts could have several types of relationships. For example, there can be “assigned” or “used to browse” relationships between actors and tags. The resulting AAN had 11 actors, 53 resources and 116 tags.

The teacher suggested to extract three social networks out of this AAN: the students who cited a resourced bookmarked by other student; the students who used the same tags to describe resources; and the students who used to browse the tags assigned by other students. Only one student cited once a bookmark published by other student. The other two resulting social networks are represented in Fig. 2. Several conclusions can be extracted analyzing these social

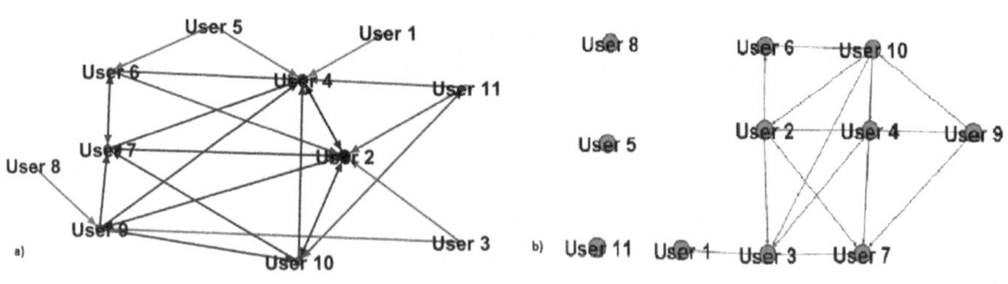

Fig. 2. Social networks of the students who browsed tags created by other students (left) and the students who used same tags to describe resources (right).

networks. For example, in the left graph we can see that some students influenced (e.g. user 2 or 9) their classmates more than others (e.g. user 5 or 9), since the tags they assigned to resources were used later on for browsing by other students. The second network indicates that three students did not tag any resource using a tag that was also used by other student, which indicates that their topics of interest were not shared with the rest of the class.

5 Conclusions and Future Work

This paper presented a first step on how to support learning analytics at the workplace exploiting an AAN that was implemented by the SSS. The experiment done with students shows the technical viability of this approach. It is also promising how the SSS can create semantically-enriched AAN. In this experiment the meta-data related to the artifacts was reduced to tags, but still three different social networks were extracted with different semantic relationships between the actors. These networks helped the teacher to analyze the learning of the students and to understand their behavior. It exemplifies how the SSS can integrate the data from different applications and coherently combine it to support learning analytics at the workplace. Further research is required to understand which of these contextual relationships are meaningful for the domain and how can they be exploited to explain learning processes at the workplace.

Acknowledgements. This research has been partially funded by the FP7 ICT Workprogramme of the European Community: "Learning Layers - Scaling up Technologies for Informal Learning in SME Clusters" (http://www.learning-layers.eu/, grant no: 318209).

References

1. Ley, T., Cook, J., Dennerlein, S., Kravcik, M., Kunzmann, C., Pata, K., Purma, J., Sandars, J., Santos, P., Schmidt, A., Al-Smadi, M., Trattner, C.: Scaling informal learning at the workplace: a model and four designs from a large-scale design-based research effort. Br. J. Educ. Technol. **45**(6), 1036–1048 (2014)
2. Kowald, D., Dennerlein, S., Theiler, D., Walk, S., Trattner, C.: The social semantic server a framework to provide services on social semantic network data. In: Proceedings of the I-SEMANTICS 2013 Posters & Demonstrations Track co-Located with 9th International Conference on Semantic Systems, pp. 50–54. Citeseer, Graz (2013)
3. Reinhardt, W., Moi, M., Varlemann, T.: Artefact-Actor-Networks as tie between social networks and artefact networks. In: Proceedings of the 5th International Conference on Collaborative Computing: Networking, Applications and Worksharing, pp. 1–10. IEEE Press, Washington (2009)
4. Duval, E.: Attention please!: learning analytics for visualization and recommendation. In: Proceedings of the 1st International Conference on Learning Analytics and Knowledge (LAK), pp. 9–17. ACM, Banff (2011)

Boosting the Learning Process with Progressive Performance Prediction

Carlos Villagra-Arnedo, Francisco J. Gallego-Durán, Rafael Molina-Carmona(✉), and Faraón Llorens-Largo

Departamento de Ciencia de la Computación e Inteligencia Artificial, Universidad de Alicante, Alicante, Spain
{villagra,fgallego,rmolina,faraon}@dccia.ua.es

Abstract. A prediction system to early detect learning problems is presented. The starting point is a gamified learning system from which a massive set of usage and learning data is collected. They are analyzed using Machine Learning techniques and a prediction of each student's performance is obtained. The information is weekly presented as a progression chart, with valuable information about students' progression. The system has a high degree of automation, is progressive, uses learning outcomes as well as usage data, allows the evaluation and prediction of the acquired skills, and contributes to a truly formative assessment.

Keywords: Performance prediction · Machine learning · Gamified systems · Automatic assessment · Learning process

1 Introduction

This paper presents a prediction system to detect learning problems, using Gamification and Machine Learning. Gamification [1,2] is usually mentioned as a means of boosting student motivation. Immediate feedback, game dynamics, automatic assessment and learning customization are important points in gamification considered to have great impact on students. Machine Learning has also been used to determine if the students are at risk of failing [3].

Section 2 presents a gamified system called PLMan. The prediction system is presented in Sect. 3, the experiments and results in Sect. 4 and the conclusions and future work in Sect. 5.

2 Gamified, Automatic Learning System with PLMan

PLMan [4] is a game to learn Prolog. Students program the AI of a Pac-Man like character, using a Prolog knowledge base. Each exercise comes in the form of a new maze, for which students have to program an AI able to get all the dots, dodging the perils, using simple rules in the form *"If you see an enemy to your*

© Springer International Publishing Switzerland 2015
G. Conole et al. (Eds.): EC-TEL 2015, LNCS 9307, pp. 638–641, 2015.
DOI: 10.1007/978-3-319-24258-3_77

right, move left"[1]. Mazes increase in complexity and programming requirements, encouraging students to learn more about Prolog and to be creative in their solutions. More than 400 different mazes with different layouts, objects, enemies and obstacles, organized into 4 stages and 5 levels of difficulty per stage have been created. They are included into a gamified, automatic, web-based platform.

Students have to beat the 4 stages and a checkpoint in the system to get the maximum grade. At each stage, students have to solve several random mazes, picking up the desired difficulty level (1 to 5). The same maze cannot be assigned to two different students. Then, they use the PLMan software to construct and test their AI for the maze. When they think their AI is ready, they send it to the system and get an automatic assessment in percentage. When they achieve more than 75 % on a given maze, they unlock the next one and can continue. Errors do not penalize and there is not a limit of submissions for a given maze: the system always consider the best solution. Students can also follow their own path by selecting difficulty levels: the greater the difficulty level, the more the contribution to the final grade. They may also stop whenever they want.

The use of this system generates a huge amount of data. The main aim of this work is to transform this data into valuable information that can help to predict the students' performance at the end of term. A list of features that are input for a Machine Learning algorithm of prediction is built from some use events and learning information: number of frontpage visits, number of maze downloads, number of submissions by stage, average marks in percentage by stage, time to finish each stage, time to finish each maze, and difficulty levels selected by maze.

3 Progressive Prediction System

The prediction system is based on a standard C-parameterized margin, SVM classifier (C-SVC) [5] with Radial Basis Function (RBF) kernel [6,7], adding probability estimates using Pairwise Coupling [8]. The prediction system classifies expected student performance in 1 out of 3 possible classes, depending on the ***e**xpected final **m**arks* out of 10 points (em): (1) Great students ($em > 8.05$), (2) Normal students ($em \geq 5.75$) and (3) Underperforming students ($em < 5.75$). Since the sample is small (336 students), only 3 classes are defined.

For each week, all the information in the event database is processed. The features are scaled to $[0, 1]$ range, preserving the values that are 0 and maintaining matrix scarcity. The SVM gets a 42-dimensional input and 3 probabilities as ouput. With the scaled features, a model selection is conducted to boost the performance of the SVM by picking up the best set of parameters. As 2 parameters must be selected (C regularization parameter, γ amplitude of RBF), a 2D grid-search is performed, with parameter varying exponentially in powers of 2.

$$C \in \{2^i : i \in [-15, 15] \cap \mathbb{Z}\}, \gamma \in \{2^j : j \in [-15, 5] \cap \mathbb{Z}\}$$

For each pair of parameters, a leave-one-out Cross-Validation training gives its accuracy estimation. Parameters for the best accuracy estimation are selected.

[1] in Prolog: `rule :- see(normal, right, 'E'), doAction(move(left)).`.

Using the best set of parameters, 10 SVM are trained, one for each week. This improves expected performance by having specialized SVMs for each week. The data used to train SVMs has to be from past, closed terms, because the actual final performance is required to train SVMs. Once SVMs are trained, real-time predictions for an undergoing term can be done. These final predictions are added to the prediction stack, where all previous predictions are stored. Then, graphs are elaborated and presented to teachers for student evaluation.

4 Experiments and Results

The system has been tested with data from 336 students and 11 weekly lessons. So, 10 weeks of predictions are given and the final marks in week 11. The accuracy for each week (proportion of correctly classified students) is shown in Table 1.

Table 1. Cross-validation accuracy measures by week

W1	W2	W3	W4	W5	W6	W7	W8	W9	W10
0.46429	0.47619	0.51786	0.55357	0.55655	0.60417	0.63691	0.66071	0.67560	0.74107

As expected, the more data about students, the better predictions. Although better results could be expected, the complete results for all the badly-classified students show that most of them have the correct result as 2nd option (by probability) with a very narrow margin (typically < 0.05). Better results are probably hidden by a great amount of variance, coming from feature design. A detailed analysis of these results goes beyond the scope of this paper.

The main idea behind this work is to provide trend information about students through progressive predictions. The system produces evolutive graphs (Fig. 1), showing the estimated probabilities for each student to become great (green/top), normal (blue/center) or underperforming (red/bottom). Probabilities are calculated each week, showing student trends.

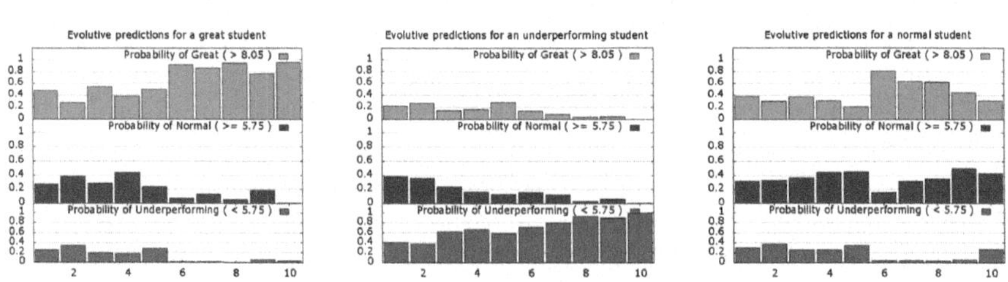

Fig. 1. Evolutive probabilistic graphs for 3 typical students (Color figure online)

The students in Fig. 1 are three typical examples of each class: a great student (left, 9.75 out of 10 points), an underperforming student (center, 1 out of

10 points) and a normal student (right, 6.4 out of 10 points). By analyzing the graphs on the left and in the center, two opposite trends are clear. These two students show very clearly where they are heading around weeks 4 to 6. Student in the center is a nice example of an early detection of a problem, that should trigger a more detailed analysis from the teacher. In contrast, grasping a pattern for student on the right gives a harder time. Up to week 5, student status tends increasingly to normal but, suddenly, it changes to great and then continues deflating to normal again. It is probably due to the student solving a lot of mazes between weeks 5 and 6, and then getting comfortable with the global mark achieved and just stopping doing anything.

This simple analysis represents one of the main goals of this work: it shows how pattern discovery makes teachers able to act upon students at early and middle stages of the learning process, improving their probabilities of success.

5 Conclusions and Further Work

In this paper we have shown how the information produced by our previous learning system, PLMan, can be used to predict student performance. We highlight two main contributions: the design of a progressive prediction system based on a SVM, and an intuitive way to show and exploit this information with trend graphs. These trend patterns enables teachers to early guide students to success. We think this is a solid step towards great improvements of the learning process.

As next steps to this work we plan to design more advanced features and conduct studies to determine which ones are best. We also plan to elaborate predictions of probability of success and development time a student will need to solve a future maze, depending on maze difficulty and student historical data.

References

1. Vila, A.I., Ferrer, J.C., Gallego-Durán, F.J., Largo, F.L.: Predicting student performance in translating foreign languages with a serious game. In: INTED2013 Proceedings, 7th International Technology, Education and Development Conference, pp. 52–59. IATED (2013)
2. Kapp, K.: The Gamification of Learning and Instruction: Game-based Methods and Strategies for Training and Education. Wiley, New York (2012)
3. Kotsiantis, S.B.: Use of machine learning techniques for educational proposes: a decision support system for forecasting students' grades. Artif. Intell. Rev. **37**(4), 331–344 (2012)
4. Villagrá-Arnedo, C., De Haro, M.C., Gallego-Durán, F.J., Puig, C.P., Pérez, P.S., Vaíllo, S.C.: Real-time evaluation. In: EDULEARN09 Proceedings, pp. 3361–3369. IATED, Barcelona (2009)
5. Cortes, C., Vapnik, V.: Support-vector networks. Mach. Learn. **20**(3), 273–297 (1995)
6. Vapnik, V.N.: The Nature of Statistical Learning Theory. Springer-Verlag New York Inc, New York (1995)
7. Vapnik, V.N.: Statistical Learning Theory, 1st edn. Wiley, New York (1998)
8. Wu, T.F., Lin, C.J., Weng, R.C.: Probability estimates for multi-class classification by pairwise coupling. J. Mach. Learn. Res. **5**, 975–1005 (2004)

Creating and Sharing Knowledge Through Experiences: A Case Study with Ach so! in Healthcare Education

Marjo Virnes(✉), Jukka Purma, Merja Bauters, and Teemu Leinonen

Department of Media, Aalto University, Espoo, Finland
{marjo.virnes,jukka.purma,teemu.leinonen}@aalto.fi,
merja.bauters@metropolia.fi

Abstract. This paper reports results from a case study that investigated creating and sharing knowledge arising from experiences with the *Ach so!* mobile app for video annotation in healthcare education. The qualitative content analysis of the interview data indicated that Ach so! enhanced reflection when the students saw their action from videos and thus were able to evaluate their own and group performance as external observers and to create knowledge on their experiences. Ach so! promoted knowledge sharing when the students together reflected their performance and annotated successful and failed incidents. Research outcomes contributed to the design of the Ach so! and workplace practices, and suggested applying Ach so! to dynamic learning contexts and scaling the applicability of Ach so! to informal and non-formal learning contexts at workplaces.

Keywords: Healthcare education · Reflection · Sharing · Video annotation · Mobile learning

1 Introduction

Learning processes can be supported with technological tools that enable learners to create and share knowledge arising from their experiences. Ach so! is a mobile (Android) video annotation tool that was designed to support those learning processes in the contexts of construction and healthcare [1]. With Ach so! users record short videos, make annotations to them and share the annotated videos with their peers, supervisors of work and educators. Ach so! enables reflection and sharing that are highlighted as the key elements of learning to support informal learning processes while and after working [2, 3].

This study investigated the use of Ach so! in healthcare education where students used Ach so! to reflect their learning and performance after a proficiency test that was a typical form of exam in healthcare education. The research tasks were (1) investigating students' learning experiences with videos and video annotations in the pre-defined learning contexts and (2) investigating student's expectations with regard to Ach so! as a learning tool for occupational education and workplaces of their field. Students' experiences and expectations were used for evaluating the potential of Ach so! to enhancing learning processes.

© Springer International Publishing Switzerland 2015
G. Conole et al. (Eds.): EC-TEL 2015, LNCS 9307, pp. 642–645, 2015.
DOI: 10.1007/978-3-319-24258-3_78

2 Ach so! Video Annotation Tool

Ach so![1] is an open source application for video recording, annotating and sharing (Fig. 1). It is implemented as an application for Android platform to be used with tablet computers or smartphones. With Ach so!, the users record short videos and categorize them under four genres.

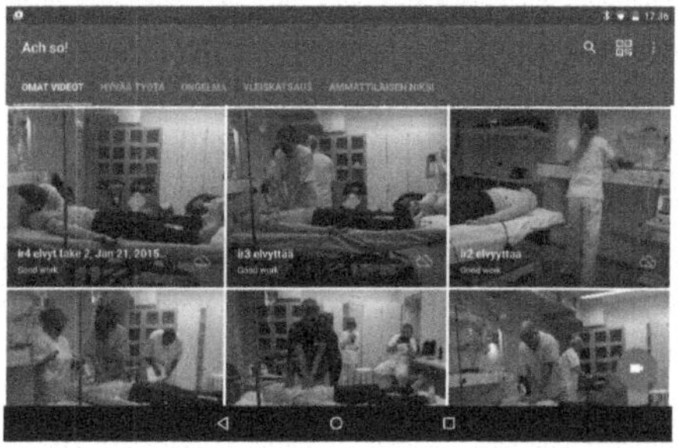

Fig. 1. Ach so! mobile application for shooting, annotating and sharing videos

Ach so! creates MPEG-4 video with serialized semantic annotations. Video descriptions automatically include location, date and creator, and they can be annotated by adding textual annotations, 'points of interest', to specific points on screen and in video timeline. The annotations are placed in the video timeline and have screen coordinates for each, and the playback automatically pauses on each annotation to allow reading the annotation acknowledging the point of interest. The annotated videos can be saved in a cloud or exported from the device with Android's share-intent. The exported videos can be viewed in a browser-based Ach so! Player[2].

3 Research Method and Settings

The research used case study and field trials as methods for investigating the potential of Ach so! to support students' learning processes. Students' learning experiences with the Ach so! were evaluated in healthcare education where 25 third-year students demonstrated their cardiopulmonary resuscitation (CPR) skills in a proficiency test at the premises of the Helsinki Metropolia University of Applied Sciences. Ach so! was used with Android-based Nexus tablet in the groups of four or five students, which emphasized learning not only an individual level but at a group level [4].

The research participants were group-interviewed after their use of Ach so! by using semi-structured interview [5]. Interview questions focused on students' overall experience with Ach so!, their use of videos and annotations and importance that they put on these properties, and their expectancies on the applicability of Ach so! to other learning

[1] Ach so!, http://achso.aalto.fi.

[2] Ach so! Player, http://achso.aalto.fi/player/.

contexts. The transcribed interviews served as the data for the initial qualitative content analysis that used inductive reasoning for revealing students' experiences with Ach so! and categorizing them, and deductive reasoning for evaluating the potential of Ach so!. Ach so! was evaluated by collecting reflections from its users and focusing on the meso level evaluation of Ach so! [6].

4 Students' Learning Experiences with Ach so! and the Potential of Ach so! to Strengthen Learning Processes

In this study, the potential of Ach so! to strengthen learning processes was reported by users in the learning context that required the control of the several simultaneous actions in the group and mastering of extensive knowledge on CPR. The demonstration of CPR required an awareness of one's own individual action and action in relation to the group. In that kind of learning context, the students evaluated to receive benefit from the recording and annotating properties that provided an additional perspective to reflect upon and learn about the multidimensional topic. Based on that, it can be assumed that considerable learning contexts for Ach so! would be a complex and dynamic domains. In the actual situations, the students observed the situation from their individual perspectives, whereas video presented the CPR demonstration from outsiders' perspective and provided the overall picture for evaluation. New perspectives meant that students maybe did not see different things regarding CPR but in different ways. As outsider observers, the students described that they noticed critical points, were able to learn from them and remembered and understood the process better. Videos provided evidences in situations where all of the incidents were not observed by humans during the actual test situation but that were later found important for succeeding in the proficiency test.

Ach so! was used as a tool for teamwork and collaborative learning when the students shared their individual and common experiences and knowledge on CPR. Students observed group's collaboration and performance in the CPR test from the video and indicated successes and failures with annotations for the group and the teacher. In that sense, Ach so! promoted building of shared understanding by creating shared knowledge on CPR from individual experiences and sharing of new knowledge in the group [4]. The analysis indicated that annotations elaborated learning and focused students' attention even more on CPR than watching the plain video. The students highlighted mistakes as they wanted to learn from mistakes and thus improve their skills. They also identified and annotated successful situations and saw them as good exemplars for going through later.

From the learning viewpoint, the students specified in interviews several situations where they gained benefit from the properties of recording, video watching and annotation. Completely new perspectives to reflect their action, general view for understanding the whole CPR situation, and elaborating observations by making annotations were just a few of several exemplars that students gave regarding reflecting, sharing and learning with Ach so!. Reflecting took place by observing either one's own action from video or observing group's action and one's own action in relation to other's action from video. In addition to the process of CPR, students observed their ergonomics, working position and technique, and paid attention to their own irrelevant actions that videos revealed. As Ach so! was developed with above-mentioned purposes in mind, it can be concluded that experiences that student's highlighted met an expected impact of Ach so! on learning processes.

Applicability of Ach so! was seen extensive and valuable in the domains where the documentation of good practices, the demonstrations of skills, and identifying of issues are essential to take into account. The suggested domains were patient cases, extensive simulations, operations such as putting continuous positive airway pressure (CPAP), and laboratory exercises, such as cannulation.

5 Conclusions

The case study addressed that the advantages that the students described were also the majority of objectives that were set for Ach so! as a learning tool. It seems that Ach so! enhanced and complied into students' learning process in the context where the learning topic required group work, applying extensive skills and knowledge in a dynamic environment, and the students to reflect their individual and group performances. Ach so! enabled reflection and was thus experienced as a learning tool that brought new possibilities for creating and sharing knowledge on experiences as well as added value to learning process. The future research will continue the development of Ach so! and will elaborate the potential of Ach so! in new learning contexts, such as construction education and vocational training at construction sites.

Acknowledgement. We acknowledge with thanks the financial support of the Learning Layers project from 7th Framework Programme of European Commission.

References

1. Bauters, M., Purma, J., Leinonen, T.: In-time on-place learning. In: Proceedings of the 10th International Conference on Mobile Learning, pp. 256–260 (2014)
2. Mann, K., Gordon, J., MacLeod, A.: Reflection and reflective practice in health professions education: a systematic review. Adv. Health Sci. Educ. **14**(4), 595–621 (2009)
3. Prilla, M. Degeling, M., Herrmann, T.: Collaborative reflection at work: supporting informal learning at a healthcare workplace. In: Proceedings of the 17th ACM International Conference on Supporting Group Work, pp. 55–64. ACM, New York (2012)
4. Paavola, S., Hakkarainen, K.: From meaning making to joint construction of knowledge practices and artefacts: a trialogical approach to CSCL. In: Proceedings of the 9th International Conference on Computer Supported Collaborative Learning, pp. 83–92. International Society of the Learning Sciences (2009)
5. Hyysalo, S.: Käyttäjä Tuotekehityksessä: Tieto, Tutkimus. Aalto University, Menetelmät (2009)
6. Vavoula, G., Sharples, M.: Meeting the challenges in evaluating mobile learning: A 3-level evaluation framework. Int. J. Mob. Blended Learn. **1**(2), 54–75 (2009)

Author Index